The
Greenwood Encyclopedia
of
World Folklore
and Folklife

Volume 2
Southeast Asia and India,
Central and East Asia,
Middle East

The Greenwood Encyclopedia
of World Folklore and Folklife

VOLUME 1
Topics and Themes, Africa, Australia and Oceania

VOLUME 2
Southeast Asia and India, Central and East Asia, Middle East

VOLUME 3
Europe

VOLUME 4
North and South America

The Greenwood Encyclopedia of World Folklore and Folklife

VOLUME 2
Southeast Asia and India,
Central and East Asia, Middle East

Edited by William M. Clements

Thomas A. Green, Advisory Editor

GREENWOOD PRESS
Westport, Connecticut • London

Library of Congress Cataloging-in-Publication Data

The Greenwood encyclopedia of world folklore and folklife / edited by William
    M. Clements.
      p.   cm.
    Includes bibliographical references and index.
    ISBN 0–313–32847–1 (set : alk. paper)—ISBN 0–313–32848–X
(v. 1 : alk. paper)—ISBN 0–313–32849–8 (v. 2 : alk. paper)—
ISBN 0–313–32850–1 (v. 3 : alk. paper)—ISBN 0–313–32851–X
(v. 4 : alk. paper)
    1. Folklore—Encyclopedias.   2. Manners and customs—Encyclopedias.
I. Clements, William M., 1945– .
GR35.G75   2006
398'.03—dc22   2005019219

British Library Cataloguing in Publication Data is available.

Library of Congress Catalog Card Number: 2005019219
ISBN: 0–313–32847–1 (set)
        0–313–32848–X (vol. 1)
        0–313–32849–8 (vol. 2)
        0–313–32850–1 (vol. 3)
        0–313–32851–X (vol. 4)

First published in 2006

Greenwood Press, 88 Post Road West, Westport, CT 06881
An imprint of Greenwood Publishing Group, Inc.
www.greenwood.com

Printed in the United States of America

The paper used in this book complies with the
Permanent Paper Standard issued by the National
Information Standards Organization (Z39.48–1984).

10 9 8 7 6 5 4 3 2 1

Contents

Foreword

In many ways, *The Greenwood Encyclopedia of World Folklore and Folklife* represents the completion of a two-volume work published in 1997, *Folklore: An Encyclopedia of Beliefs, Customs, Tales, Music, and Art.* As editor of that encyclopedia, I endeavored to bring together a set of general entries on folklore forms, methods, and theories. Attempting to confine such diverse topics within a two-volume work often compelled those of us who took on the task to violate a guiding principle of folkloristics—the consideration of cultural contexts. To paraphrase a disclaimer included in the Preface to *Folklore*: the variety and wealth of the world's traditions demanded a severely abridged treatment of the subjects.

This concern returned to haunt me in the person of my former editor, Gary Kuris, who had changed presses and saw the opportunity to build on our earlier collaboration. Other obligations compelled me to pass along the editorial duties to William Clements, who had played a major role in the original project. Unable to resist involvement in such an ambitious and meaningful enterprise, I accepted the role of advisory editor. Thanks to Bill, this role has allowed me to be associated with what I believe will prove to be an extraordinary research tool, while requiring very little effort on my part.

Thus, almost a decade after the publication of *Folklore*, Greenwood Publishing Group, in this four-volume *Greenwood Encyclopedia of World Folklore and Folklife*, has provided a venue for redressing the omissions of that earlier project. These volumes flesh out the relatively economical treatments of concepts, forms, and theories with specific discussions of folklore in context; comparisons of art forms and lifeways within the various culture areas of the world; and consideration of topics that transcend cultural, social, and disciplinary borders. As such, the vision of folklore as a culturally situated phenomenon, arising from and contributing to the lives of its bearers, becomes fully apparent.

THOMAS A. GREEN
Texas A&M University

Preface

The term "folk-lore" entered the English language in 1846 when William J. Thoms, writing as Ambrose Merton, proposed it as a "good Saxon substitute" for the Latinate "popular antiquities," which British enthusiasts for the beliefs, behaviors, and objects of the "olden time" were using to denominate their interest. Thoms's contribution was a word (one that had been occasionally in use before his coinage); what it referred to already existed. And, in fact, other European languages had already found their own words for what Thoms was calling "folklore." (The hyphen disappeared in the twentieth century.) Germans were already studying *Volkskunde*, for example, by the time "folklore" appeared over the name Ambrose Merton.

The term may be English and of fairly recent coinage, but the kind of cultural material that it has come to encompass exists in every society, and many societies have been taking an interest in their folklore (by whatever name they refer to it) for quite some time. *The Greenwood Encyclopedia of World Folklore and Folklife* is an attempt to assess this cultural material on an international basis and also to provide some idea of what has been done in each of the represented groups by both group members and outsiders to document, analyze, preserve, and revitalize it.

Like language, religion, politics, and economics, folklore is a cultural universal found everywhere in the world. That fact—and the fact that the materials of folklore often show remarkable similarities in different places and at different times—makes a survey of folklore materials on a worldwide basis especially relevant. Moreover, although the foundations of folklore study—at least in Europe—lay in romantic nationalism, a tradition of internationalism also exists. One need only think of such compendiums as Frazer's *The Golden Bough* (1890 and many subsequent editions), which, although driven by a view of culture that few serious folklorists would endorse today, nevertheless brings together a vast amount of folklore material from all over the world. The first edition of Stith Thompson's monumental *Motif-Index of Folk-Literature* (1932–1937; 2nd edition, 1955–1958) catalogued narrative elements from a range of traditional genres from throughout the world. The *Funk and Wagnalls Standard Dictionary of Folklore, Mythology, and Legend* (1949)—famous among folklorists for its twenty-one different definitions of the term "folklore"—has unsystematic worldwide coverage. Beginning in the 1960s, the University of Chicago Press's Folktales of the World series also adopted the globe as its bailiwick. Each of the twenty or so volumes in that series focuses on the narrative traditions of a particular country (for example, Japan, China, Mexico, France, England, Israel, and India). In 1961, Richard M. Dorson edited *Folklore Research around the World*, a collection of essays that assessed the state of folklore scholarship in several different countries. When he inaugurated the *Journal of the Folklore Institute* (now *Journal of Folklore Research*) at Indiana University, he intended that its coverage be international. Of course, these few examples do not exhaust the attempts by folklorists to highlight what Dorson, in an essay entitled "The Techniques of the Folklorist," called "international relations" in folklore. They do, however, suggest the academic tradition out of which the current work emerges. As far as I know, a vision such as that of Thomas Green and the editors of Greenwood Publishing Group has not found expression in any previous work; the purpose of these four volumes is to survey the world's folklore heritages in a way that emphasizes the international nature of folklore in general and of specific folklore materials, while placing folklore within particular cultural milieus.

The aim of this encyclopedia is to examine folklore within the broad contexts of culture areas and the more narrow contexts of specific societies. To that end, the goal was to sample from every continent and subcontinent and to represent as many of the specific societies on those land masses as seemed feasible. The result is a series of substantial essays by specialists in the folklore of particular groups.

Given that both the specific nature of the folklore and the availability of resources on each topic vary from society to society, contributors had considerable latitude in what they felt to be important to represent the folklore of their societies and in how they decided to present it. However, they were given the following template—intended to be more suggestive than prescriptive—with ten areas that they might attend to in their essays:

1. *Geographical Setting.* The topography, climate, and other features of the physical and natural environment that help to shape the society's culture.
2. *Sociocultural Features.* Subsistence activities, political organization, social organization, and other aspects of the culture that will help readers understand how folklore works in the society.
3. *Ethnohistorical Information.* Migration patterns, political developments, watershed events, and interactions with other societies.
4. *Belief System.* Worldview and traditional religion (including medical practices).
5. *Verbal Art.* Myth, legend, folktale, and other oral forms, approached from an indigenous perspective.
6. *Musical Art.* Vocal and instrumental.
7. *Sports and Games.*
8. *Graphic and Plastic Arts.* Arts, crafts, architecture, clothing, and foodways.
9. *Effects of Modernization and Globalization.*
10. *References and Bibliographical Essay.* A brief history of the study of the society's folklore with a list of works from which the entry has drawn and recommendations for additional reading.

Contributors were encouraged to think not just in terms of folklore "texts" but of the processes of storytelling, singing, and performing folklore.

The four-volume *Greenwood Encyclopedia of World Folklore and Folklife* contains 205 entries written by more than 200 folklore scholars from around the world. To facilitate the comparison of geographically related countries and cultures, the volumes are broken down into the following regional subdivisions:

Volume 1: Topics and Themes, Africa, Australia and Oceania

Volume 2: Southeast Asia and India, Central and East Asia, Middle East

Volume 3: Europe

Volume 4: North and South America

Volume 1 opens with an alphabetically arranged collection of thirty-nine short essays on processes, research tools, social and intellectual movements, and concepts important for understanding folklore on an international, intercultural basis. These introductory entries should equip the reader to appreciate the dynamic nature of folklore through time and as it passes across cultural boundaries. Volume 1 then proceeds to a series of entries on the peoples and cultures of Africa, Australia, and Oceania, which, like all the entries in the other three volumes, are listed alphabetically within a series of regional subdivisions (e.g., Southern Africa, Western and Central Africa, Polynesia).

Most entries run between 3,000 and 5,000 words, although those for older and more complex cultures and societies (e.g., China, India) are often longer. Useful subheads (e.g., Geography and History; Myths, Legends, and Folktales; Music and Songs; Challenges of the Modern World) divide the entries into topical sections, allowing readers quickly to find the aspect or genre of a group's folklore that may be of most interest to them. Written in a clear, readable style, the entries are also based on the best and latest scholarship, offering detailed, current information on the folklore and folklife of particular peoples and cultures. The *Encyclopedia* can thus serve a variety of users, from students (both high school and undergraduate) requiring information for projects and papers in a wide variety of subjects and interdisciplinary classes, to general readers or travelers interested in knowing more about a particular culture or custom, to folklore specialists needing to stay current with the latest work on peoples and cultures beyond or related to their own areas of expertise. By promoting cultural diversity and stressing the interconnectedness of peoples and cultures around the globe, the *Encyclopedia* can also help any user who wishes better to understand his or her own cultural heritage and the influences neighboring and even more distant groups have had on its development. Most entries also help readers understand how the emerging global society and economy have and are affecting the customs and beliefs of peoples around the world.

The *Encyclopedia* also contains maps located at the start of the relevant geographical section and numerous photographs of the peoples and artifacts of a culture. Volume 4 contains a number of additional features, including a glossary that briefly defines some of the terms that recur throughout the entries. The purpose of the glossary is to give the reader a point of departure for understanding some of the language of folklore studies and anthropology used by the authors, and most of these terms merit the much more extended treatments they have received elsewhere, in such works as Thomas A. Green's *Folklore: An Encyclopedia of Beliefs, Customs, Tales,*

Music, and Art (1997). Volume 4 also includes a geographical guide of peoples and cultures to help readers put an unfamiliar culture in geographical context, and a highly selective general bibliography that identifies works offering intercultural perspectives on folklore.

Besides concluding with extensive bibliographies of important information resources, the entries are also cross-referenced, with entry names highlighted in **boldface** type when they are first mentioned in the entry or listed in a "See also" line at the end of the text. To make the cross-references useful across the set, each volume contains a listing of the entries found in the other volumes so that users can quickly identify where to find the entry for a highlighted reference. Each volume also contains a volume-specific table of contents and a complete subject index to the set.

Acknowledgments

Obviously, this work is a team effort. Most of the members of that team are named in the Editors and Contributors section in Volume 4 and appear with their contributions throughout the work. I want to call special attention here to individuals whose contributions might otherwise be unclear and underestimated: Thomas A. Green, who had the idea for this encyclopedia; Gary Kuris, vice president, Editorial, and George Butler, senior acquisitions editor, of Greenwood Publishing Group, who contacted me and helped to devise the formal proposal for the project; John Wagner, senior development editor at Greenwood Publishing Group, who has been the principal editor for this project, with whom I have been in almost daily contact for the last several years, and whose influence is felt in every aspect of the work; Charles R. Carr and Clyde A. Milner II, administrators at Arkansas State University, who arranged for me to have help from graduate assistants and other amenities; William Allen, Jennifer Majors, Cliff Stamp, and Diane Unger, who provided technical assistance; and Frances M. Malpezzi, who helped to keep the work focused during the three years that it has been the major professional aspect of my life. I would also like to thank Tom Brennan for preparation of the maps. The production staff at Westchester Book Group also deserves thanks: production editors Rebecca A. Homiski and Carla L. Talmadge; copyeditors Jamie Nan Thaman, Frank Saunders, Carol Lucas, and Krystyna Budd; and Enid Zafran, who prepared the index.

I also believe I was particularly fortunate in my formal folklore education in having instructors whose view of folklore was truly international. These include Richard M. Dorson, who, though an Americanist, never lost sight of the importance of thinking of folklore globally; Warren E. Roberts, whose work in historic-geographic folktale studies and in material folk culture had a strong international flavor; Linda Dégh, who brought a continental perspective to the Indiana University Folklore Institute in the late 1960s; and John C. Messenger, an anthropologist whose fieldwork has taken him to Nigeria and to the west of Ireland. They and others reminded us that folklore cannot be understood only by looking at it within the context of a single culture. I hope that this work will impress that point on its readers.

Comprehensive List of Entries

Southeast Asia and the Indian Subcontinent

India: States and Regions

INDIA OVERVIEW

GEOGRAPHY

The Indian subcontinent is often conceived as a mixing bowl (or rather "curry pot"), shaped by the southern oceans (the Arabian Sea and the Bay of Bengal) and covered with a lid formed by the northern mountain ranges (the Himalayan range, the Karakoram range, and the Hindu Kush). These impressive geographical features have not, however, constituted a barrier to either external influences on India or the influence of Indian tradition on the neighboring regions, but they did allow the people of the subcontinent to catch, retain, and nurture with their own distinctive character a large, diverse, and continuing repository of cultural tradition over the past 5,000 years or more. Over this long period of cultural history India continued reciprocal exchange with an ever-increasing circle of surrounding territories extending from Central, Eastern, and Southeastern Asia to the Middle East and Western Europe.

FACTORS SHAPING INDIAN FOLKLORE

Ethnographically speaking, India is a cultural meeting place where four language and culture "families"—the Dravidian, the Indo-European, the Sino-Tibetan, and the Munda (Austro-Asiatic)—came into contact with one another, mingled and mixed over several millennia, and, to some extent, merged. The Munda lingual/cultural group seems to have been present the longest but appears to have arrived and settled as a set of independent tribal populations, and in that level of social organization they largely remain today in eastern India (**Orissa** and West Bengal). Then, we know from firm archeological evidence that some time around 2500 B.C.E. a level of socioeconomic integration approaching civilization based in urban administrative and rural agricultural production was established along the Indus River system. This set the stage for a folk-urban distinction and many of the sociological features such as the caste system that have played a major role in the development of what distinguishes Indian folk traditions. Although we have no conclusive knowledge as to when or from where Dravidian lingual and cultural groups migrated and settled in southern Asia, many authorities hold that these developments were the product of Dravidian cultural influences. Recently, however, a number of Indian scholars dispute this. Just as the urban-based civilization arose and flourished during a period of about a thousand years from 2500 to 1500 B.C.E., the precursors to Indo-Aryan languages and culture brought with them new worldviews, a pantheon of new gods, and

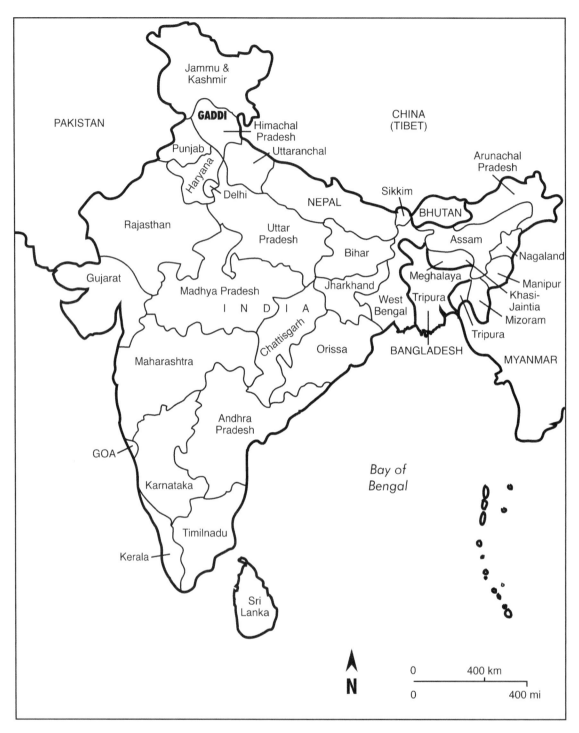

South Asia and the States of India.

a hierarchical mode of social organization which established the preeminence of a priestly class, the Brahmans. These two language and culture families have largely merged with one another over the subsequent millennia. The fourth major body of cultural tradition, beginning perhaps as long ago as 2000 B.C.E., the Sino-Tibetan came from the north and east, bringing what today we see as a welter of different languages and ethnic groups into the present Indian states of **Assam**, **Nagaland**, Manipur, Meghalaya, Arunachal Pradesh, and Himachal Pradesh as well as into the countries bordering India to the north and east: **Nepal**, **Bhutan**, Tibet, Burma, and Thailand.

Unfortunately, our attempts to understand India's ancient ethnohistorical processes have often been misguided, contentious, and hegemonically presumptuous. Earlier, nineteenth-century scholars trying to characterize and understand the diversity of traditions within the subcontinent emphasized the generic layering brought about by successive historical migrations. These older views tended to speak of culture in terms of race under the assumption that physical features compounded with mother tongue formed the basis of behavior and thinking and explained the differences among populations and their culture and folklore. In contrast to these racialist conceptualizations, most scholars today recognize the significance of the blending and mutual borrowing that has taken place between these bodies of tradition over time. One of the first scholars to outline the details of this conceptualization with regard to India as a linguistic area was Murray Emeneau (1980). Making a clear distinction between race and culture, he points out that the languages of India have mutually influenced and borrowed from one another to such an extent and so deeply that they now tend to share more features with one another than they do with other languages of the family that lie outside of India.

There are many factors that combine to shape the folklore profile of a nation, and thus various dimensions could be used to characterize it. One factor, the number and heterogeneity of the populations' ethnicity (languages and cultures within the four "families," as broadly outlined above) suggests that South Asia has one of the richest, most varied populations in the world and has one of its most complex profiles. This is true. But another factor—how a region has been carved up into its present national boundaries—also affects the profile of its national segments. In this regard, because postcolonial contemporary South Asia tended to divide itself along ethnic and religious lines, the national profile of India is somewhat less complex than that of South Asia as a whole.

The homogenizing effect of major religions, with their canonical and linguistic hegemonic tendencies, constitutes a determining factor in another sense too. In this respect, the religions of South Asia differ. On the whole, Hinduism, India's predominant religion, is usually regarded as a relatively tolerant one. It has tended to allow for considerable independent development of its folkloristic potential. Nevertheless, Sanskrit and the values associated with the philosophies of its priestly elite class, called Brahmans, have over the millennia tended to encompass and incorporate considerable local and ethnic variation and relegate it to the relatively lower status of "local," "little," or "folk" practice and belief. The indigenous, Sanskritic term for this distinction is *marga* (path, highway) and *dēsi* (provincial, country, local). The overall effect is sometimes seen as a top-down homogenization process called "Sanskritization" or "Brahmanization."

As a fourth major factor, the nature and size of political units over time shape a region's profile: as sociocultural entities increase their territorial boundaries, incorporating or annihilating neighboring sociocultural units, their cultural hegemony tends to lessen the region's diversity and increase its homogeneity. India has been fairly normal in this regard, but over the millennia the net result has been a few large folkloristic territories, leaving only marginal areas such as mountain ranges and dense jungles where the indigenous cultures retain a high degree of independence. This process, the civilizational process or the "Folk-Urban Continuum," is often summarized by means of social categories associated with different "kinds" of culture: "urban" v. "folk" or village (the agricultural countryside) v. tribal (isolated, remote, unincorporated). While most folklorists now realize folklore exists in all societal categories (urban, village, and tribal populations), folklore was once, in the minds of those who studied it, only found among rural agricultural peasants. Regarding this characterization of India's folklore profile, what we see in an ever-decreasing "tribal" lore, a recently—but rapidly—decreasing "folk" lore, and the rapid rise of popular urban tradition, perpetrated through mass media and having short-term currency among specific urban-based social groups such as political parties, institutions of education, and religious and occupational groups. While Indian (even pan-Indian) urban lore is a vibrant body of tradition, it too will perhaps give way to a Western-dominated global tradition. But in this regard India is not yet ready to relinquish its distinctiveness.

It is perhaps worth noting that defining "folklore" within India's complex milieu of tradition has not been easy. During British rule when folklore studies first became popular, "folklore" was a term most often applied to the cultures of tribes and the lower, less literate castes. In the 1950s when American scholars began to formulate their approach to the study of Indian civilization, they did so with the idea of a folk-urban continuum. Folk culture lay in the middle region of a homogeneity-heterogeneity continuum at one end of which are the so-called tribal cultures occurring widely all over the subcontinent, contrasted at the other end with a pan-Indian culture. At about the same time, Indian folklorists developed new terms in their languages to describe this level of tradition: *janapada* (*jan* meaning "people" or "of the people") or *lōk* (*lōk* meaning "place" or "of a place or region") to distinguish it from the earlier indigenous dichotomy of *marga-dēsi* categories. Although all folklorists working on the region at one time or another have suffered from the limitations these kinds of categories impose on their thinking, on the whole the mix of Western and Indian conceptual paradigms has created a balance, and dialogue at international meetings continues without undue confusion and toward significant mutual benefit.

India's regional sub-units, the states, have a primary (or at most a bipolar) core to their folklore profile. In different states, this core tends to be shaped by one or more of the factors mentioned above. In the case of **Kashmir**, the core is bipolar along religious lines of Hinduism and Islam. In Orissa and Assam, on the other hand, the core entails a distinctive bipolar core of tribal and folk tradition. In other states, such as **Karnataka**, **Uttar Pradesh**, **Haryana**, and **Bihar**, the "folklore" core is centered squarely in a uniform village lifestyle, only now beginning to yield its distinctive character to the increased influence of urban and global culture. The states of Nagaland,

Himachal Pradesh, and Meghalaya are cultural mosaics lying in jungle or steeply mountainous regions, composed of diverse, relatively independent, and distinct tribal groups, speaking different languages often belonging to different linguistic families. In this kind of situation each tribe (linguistically defined) constitutes an independent genre paradigm, with the commonality between them due not to the effects of homogenization but to a family resemblance retained through common cultural ancestry.

Caste

Despite a long history of reform movements and the many modern laws hoping to eliminate it or minimize it as a social force, caste (*jāti* or *kula*) is a reality throughout India. In Indian literary texts another, closely related term, *varṇa*, has been used for centuries as a four-fold categorization of the thousands of *jātis* which can be found throughout India. At base, both terms identify a named, hereditary identity group, with its members largely adhering to a set of practices which include such things as dietary food avoidances (see the later subsection "Food"), manner of dress, specific customs associated with life cycle rituals, and a sense of communal pride embodied in legend and myth. In this sense, a caste is somewhat similar to an ethnic group, and its traditions and customary practices are something like ethnic folklore as may be found in many parts of the world. Besides being a dominant characteristic of folk society, caste pervades the folklore itself as a frequent motif, as a performer worldview which accounts for much of the variation between different versions of a piece, and as a determinant of who may and who may not perform it.

Although it might be an exaggeration to identify it as a system—let alone a pan-Indian caste system (as they may have been codified as *varṇa* in ancient texts)—the castes in a region do tend to see themselves in relation to one another, and many see in those relationships a hierarchy of status (rights and duties), which is actualized in the region's traditional sets of privileges and regulatory rules of conduct and assembly. Many of these sets of privileges and demeaning duties have been outlawed by modern legislation and are becoming irrelevant to life in the cities. Nonetheless, both caste (as a kind of social group) and caste relationships remain infused into all aspects of the folklore of rural villages and towns of every region.

Another dimension of folklore in India is the social specificity of performers and patrons or audiences. Not all forms of folklore are open to all people. Many traditions are carried by performers of a specific caste. For example, the performance of caste origin myths (*kula* or *jāti purāṇa*) are patronized by the members of that caste dispersed throughout the villages of a region. The performers are usually of a different caste, and their profession is to travel to the locations where the patron caste is found and narrate or enact (theatrically perform) the myth. The performers are supported (paid, remunerated, sustained) by the patron caste. The audience for such a performance may be primarily composed of members of the patron caste, but usually villagers of other castes come for the entertainment as well. Many kinds of village life cycle ritual performances such as weddings, name ceremonies, and funerals are of this nature as well.

There is also a large variety of itinerant performers who still travel the countryside performing their tradition door-to-door in villages and on weekly market days in the towns: acrobats, animal trainers, religious mendicants, singers, fortune tellers, and so forth. Most of these professional performers are members of particular castes but are known publicly by the name of their performance. While some regional drama troupes are also of this nature, most are not restricted to caste. Drama and dance performance requires many years of study and appeals to people of a certain personality, but it is generally not a caste profession.

Gender

Although there are a few folk traditions open to both sexes, for the most part participation is segregated by gender, with many kinds of performance being gender specific. Most dance and drama troupes, for example, are composed exclusively of men, some of whom assume female roles. Most professional epic traditions are performed only by men, too. But tale traditions are broadly the dominion of women, especially those associated with ritual and moral duties such as the *vrat katha* (see the "Folktales" subsection) tradition. The Maitili house wall painting tradition was also originally a woman's tradition, practiced by young brides in relation to the duties they are to perform toward their husband and his family and the resultant environment of prosperity they, as wives and mothers, bring to it. Song traditions associated with domestic life cycle ceremonies—particularly birth, weddings, and funerals—are women's traditions too. Generally speaking, public performance is the realm of men; domestic performance is that of women. However, in certain regions of northern India, for several of these life cycle traditions, *Hijras*—transsexuals and transvestites—also hold rights to come and sing.

Hinduism

Hinduism is a term originally applied only by non-Indian commentators for the religious practices, beliefs, and philosophies they found in India. (The label-words "India," "Hindu," "Hindustan," "Hindi," "Sindhi," and "Indus" all derive from the same set perceptions.) Hinduism's comparatively decentralized authority structure allowed for and to some extent acknowledged diversity and the difference between canonical doctrine and local practice, while some of the other religious traditions of India (Jainism, Christianity, and Islam, for example) have been less willing to do so, claiming essentially that folk practice is more or less based in ignorance and misunderstanding and lies outside the purview of orthodox religion. They have thus not accepted folk religious traditions within their community of believers. They are usually relegated to the status of earlier belief and practice followed by the population before it converted to doctrinal social and moral codes and came to regard its previous beliefs as superstition, weakness, or vice. From a folkloristic perspective, however, there is a great deal of obvious and overt syncretization not only between pre-existing local custom and canonical doctrine but also among the different religious communities. It has been somewhat easier to study this phenomenon within the Hindu fold, and indeed the relationship between local and classical Hindu thought and practice pervades most of the work which has been done—to the extent that often the relationship between local Hindu practice and the influence and borrowing that has taken place between it and the other religious traditions (Islam, Christianity, Jainism, and Buddhism) remains ignored and unexplored.

GENRES IN INDIAN FOLKLORE

Dealing with Indian folklore in terms of genre categories has stimulated the discipline of folklore to rethink some aspects of the way we label some kinds of folklore, and it has greatly expanded our knowledge of the way society and performance contexts affect the nature of many genres. While some genres of folklore in the West have virtually disappeared as living traditions and scholars have often had to content themselves with what remains preserved in literary tradition as a survival of oral text, those working in India where these genres continue to exist in vibrant living tradition can include the text's larger context, which often involves costumed dance, song, musical accompaniment, spirit possession, and a variety of highly meaningful ritual acts. This opportunity has enabled folklorists to define folklore in its performance context more fully and to investigate more closely what contextual factors drive the shaping of an oral text. Thus, along with a huge body of new material, new conceptualizations of folk genres and new methodologies have been developed, while old ones have had to be modified or abandoned.

Folktales

Once upon a time folklore scholars thought India was the very source of the folktale as well the home of the vast majority of the tales themselves. It is now understood that this is not exactly the case, but it was in India (or at least the greater South Asia that was "India" at the time) that folktales were first collected, standardized, and aggregated into didactic literature. Some of the largest and most influential tale collections—the *Hitopadesha*, the *Panchatantra*, the *Jataka* tales, and the *Kathasarasagar* among others—were written or committed to memory and were carried along Buddhist monastic and Hindu mercantile trade routes north and east into central, eastern, and southeastern Asia and west to Europe. These literary works provided not only form for the tales themselves but also a literary frame for the aggregation of tale collection and a characterization and reputation of the folktale as a medium for moral education. At least some of the oral narrative performance traditions seem to have been visualized in a variety of distinctive "picture story telling" traditions which then accompanied the spread of tale tradition from India throughout East and Southeast Asia and westward into Europe. Some of these developed into forms of marionette and shadow puppetry, scroll paintings, narrative picture boards, cloth wall-hangings and mural painting, and so forth. In contemporary India this process continues into the mass media from its inception with the introduction of printing presses to the beginnings of India's comic books and children's literature. But folktales also thrive in oral tradition throughout the country as well. Increasingly, however, the oral tradition is being replaced with printed versions learned by educated children at home and in school. Nevertheless, everyone loves to listen to tales, and skilled tellers and their performances are still greatly appreciated and respected.

There are still a variety of occasions at which what we would call a folktale is in India a mandatory part of rituals. Most widespread of these is the *vrat katha* (*vrat* meaning "vow" and *katha* being the most usual term used for "tale" or "story"). Another very widespread, but probably modern ritual form in which a tale (a specific tale) is mandatory is the enormously popular *Satyanārāyaṇa Pūja*. The ritual (*pūja*) may be performed at any auspicious occasion in hopes of general prosperity and well-being. And over most of southern India one can find a popular recitational form called a *harikatha* (god's story). While the larger frame for this performance is an epic-length recitation in song of the life and deeds of a particular deity or hero, the song is interspersed with long commentaries based on accentuating the moral lessons to be learned from the hero's actions; further parallel examples are presented by way of well-known tales and extemporized commentary on contemporary politics and social mores. Aside from such formal occasions, family gatherings and bedtime are typically occasions for storytelling. In fact, in many of India's languages the most familiar term for folktale is *ajji katha* (grandmother tales).

Folk Epics

By most definitions a folk epic is any long, sung narrative performed in the oral tradition. Even today India's two major classical epics the *Mahābhārata* and the *Rāmāyaṇa* fit easily into this definition. And although before 1980, most of the folklorists of the world were only familiar with these two Indian epics, dozens of other epics all around the country have now been collected, published, and are available for study. None are as long as the classical epics—which, with the former consisting of over 100,000 verses and latter slightly less, are the world's two longest epics. But many of the regional folk epics are very long, taking days, not minutes or hours to recite. But it must be kept in mind that in their performance forms, the classical epics too are presented in episodes. Only rarely and only in a few locations is a complete version of the epic presented.

Like other areas around the world, most Indian oral epic traditions are hero-based and center on great battle scenes. The heroes of most Indian epics, though, are gods, either incarnate human forms of deities (*dēva*) or warriors (*vīra*) deified and worshiped by their communities after their heroic deaths. Epic performance traditions are thus often embedded within forms of religious ritual, some of which even include the hero's possession of a professional medium through whom he is able to dance and speak to the audience, receive honorific gifts, and convey his blessings and promise continued protection of the community from his spiritual realm. This is widely the case throughout southern India. The *Kātama Rāju* and *Palnāḍu* epics of Andhra Pradesh, the many *bhūta kōla* and *teyyam* traditions of Karnataka and Kerala, and the *Aṇṇanmār Kathai* of Tamil Nadu are examples of this kind of performance. Another distinctive characteristic of Indian oral epic traditions is the prominent role given to females either as heroine and central figure of the epic, or as providing supernatural protection and assistance to the central male hero. This is as true of the northern *Ālhā* epic of Uttar Pradesh as the *Aṇṇanmār Kathai* of Tamil Nadu.

Not all Indian epic traditions are epics about warrior heroes. Some are more appropriately described as "Romantic" epics. The epic called the *Chandaini*, for example, narrates the tragic love story of Lorik and Chanda, and another, the *holā*, treats the love between Nala and Damyanti. Others deal with saints, or rather deities incarnate as spiritual leaders, and the deeds and miracles they performed to reveal their true identity and power and to effect moral precepts. The *Manteswāmi* and *Male Mādēshwara* epics of Karnataka are some of the most pure forms of this kind of epic, but versions of the *Panch Pīr* and *Rāmdev* epics of Rajastan in northern India also have heroes who are clearly regarded as saintly teachers as well as protectors of the faithful.

One other notable feature of many Indian epic traditions is the props that are used in performances. Often their very presence is essential to the performance, even if they play no other function. In the bow song (*vil pāṭṭu*) tradition of Tamil Nadu, a manuscript version of the story must be present even if it is never read from and the raconteur is illiterate. The bow (*vil*), too, from which the tradition derives its name, a ten-foot-long instrument with bells hung along its string, which jingle loudly when the string is struck with a stick, is also essential for the performance. Several epic traditions in northern India require a cloth on which the story is painted, such as the *pāṛ* which depicts the *Pabuji* and *Devnaryan* epics of Rajastan, or the nine-yard-long scroll paintings accompanying the many caste *purāṇa* recitations of Andhra Pradesh. In some instances at least these painted story cloths are regarded as a sort of portable temple embodying the image of the deity or the patron deity of the hero. Similarly, itinerant singers of epics such as the *Ellamma* epic, carry a "god-box," a portable wooden temple containing an image of the deity with pictures painted on it depicting the god's or goddess's deeds.

Dance

India abounds in local dance traditions. Most of the well-known, named Indian dances depended on local royal and wealthy patronage and were nurtured within an elite class of audiences and thus exist on the boundary between folk and classical. Most of these have in common a strongly narrative quality, enacting through dance a series of pantomime gestural and postural representations of characters of myth and legend (drawing primarily from the classical epics, the *Mahābhārata* and *Rāmāyaṇa*, as well as other religious texts [*purāṇas*]) whose endearing behavior and qualities are familiar to the audience from poetic literature and song. In this sense, they are as much drama as dance and are often identified as "dance-dramas." In some, musical accompaniment is provided only through instrumental means (particularly various kinds of drums), while others emphasize specific forms of semi-classical vocal music. *Yakshagana*, a dance-drama of Karnataka, combines all of these with impromptu spoken lines by the dancers in a form somewhat resembling opera in the West or the Beijing opera of **China**. Some, such as *Kathak*, accentuate complex foot rhythms, while others, such as *Kathakali* of Kerala, utilize highly refined traditions of facial and hand gestures (*mudras*). Yet others (for example, *Rām Līla* performances in some locations) are virtually motionless, conveying the narrative they celebrate through a series of tableaux, centered on a procession involving the audience as well as the actors, or entailing circle dances in which the distinction between actors and audience is further blurred (for example, the many forms of *Rām Līla*).

Many of these semi-folk/semi-classical dance traditions have roots in folk forms. Kathak, for example, now regarded as a semi-classical form open to all who wish to study it, was originally the purview of a caste of dancer-musicians who have been performing and teaching this dance style within their community for hundreds of years. Males of the Kathak caste were professional storytellers who enhanced their recitations with song and dance in order to attract wider audiences as they wandered from town to town. The origins of most of the dance forms still remain obscure, sometimes somewhat purposefully so. Bharatha Natyam, now regarded as almost a national dance form of classical nature, was once performed in south Indian temples and in some places by female dancers who were "gifted" to the temple and whose professional duties included sexual favors to the temple patrons. The association between temple dance and this kind of religious *dēvadāsi* service (so-called "temple prostitution") was once widespread and common in the social category of folk professions. It is still practiced today despite being outlawed.

Although many dance traditions are closely associated with religious narrative, many that are clearly in the folk category are primarily secular in nature too. Some of these are associated with seasonal activities, especially agricultural activities, or life cycle events such as weddings. Large communal dances are quite common in tribal areas. Most notable among these, and not confined to the tribal populations, are the circle dances of Rajasthan and Gujarat. *Rās*, to use a Gujarati example, is a circular dance performed by males who strike small sticks (*dāṇḍiā*) against those of their partners. *Garbā* (also Gujarati) is danced by women clapping their hands. They go around an earthen pot called a *garbo* (meaning literally "womb") that has tiny holes and a lit earthen lamp placed inside it, symbolizing the eternal light of the goddess Amba. During *Navarātri* (the festival of nine nights), the whole of Gujarat echoes with singing and dancing, the beating of the drums, striking of the sticks, and clapping of hands. Similar circle dances are widespread: the Kodavas of Karnataka, for example, have a number of variations on a "lamp dance" (*boḷkoṭ*) which include intricate circle dances by men using sticks and whisks and a dance called *umattāṭa* performed by women around a large oil lamp placed in the center of their circle. Generally men and women do not dance together or with one another, though this is now popular in urban nightclubs.

Songs

Sung narrative—epic, ballad, song cycles, and others—do not easily fit into Western categories. For example, folklorists label the Tuluva *pāḍḍana* and Kerala Torram song traditions variously as epic, ballad, myth, and legend. Like many of the longer sung narrative traditions such as epic and ballad cycles, some of the shorter song traditions are religious songs. Indeed, these often depend on frequent allusions and reference to the epics and to literary works, but their emphasis here is on blending image with song in order to inspire a deeply devotional mood. The genre itself is called *bhakti* music. *Bhajan, kirtan, dahe* (a Muslim song tradition), and the Baul songs of West Bengal are traditions of sung poetry inspired by deeply religious and philosophical insight. On the other hand, there are many secular song traditions as well. Wedding songs, death songs (Tamil laments), birth songs (sung by Hijras), lullabies, popular film songs, and many others at best make only general or coincidental reference to religious themes.

Festivals and Celebrations

Religion pervades almost all Indian folklore genres as a dominant aspect. Likewise, but from a different perspective, we can see that folk religious gatherings and celebrations are times when many genres come together to form a distinctive set.

The most common component of all Hindu religious festivals is a *pūjā*. This is a ritual which anyone can perform at home, usually in a shrine room, to an image (*murthi*) or photo of a deity or saint. It can take as little as a few minutes or as long as an hour or more, depending on the occasion. Daily household *pūjās* are usually done by the man of the house after gathering flowers and food offerings on a metal platter and refilling oil lamps (these activities may be done by other household members) and after bathing and changing into clean clothes. The *pūjā* begins with lighting the oil lamps and "awakening" the deity with a clap of the hand, a song, or just mentally. The image may then be bathed in water or in milk and dressed in clean cloth. An act called *ārati* is performed by encircling the image an auspicious number of times—three being the minimum—with a hand-held oil lamp. The *ārati* may be repeated with a variety of different lamps or with a plate holding incense, camphor, or flowers. Next, pure foods, such as raw fruits (a banana and coconut combination is most common) and sweet mixtures of grains, generally uncooked or mixed with ghee, are offered, usually using the same circular motion of the *ārati*, and "fed" to the deity by opening the fruit and spooning out a small amount of the prepared food. Often, then, a song (*bhajan* or *kirtan*) is offered, not so much as prayer but as sharing the pleasant recollection of those deeds and acts of kindness and protection fondly remembered by his or her followers and devotees. The plate of remaining offerings are brought or passed around to anyone present so that they may share that blessed by the deity's "touch." The short ritual ends with an act of obeisance by the worshipers.

Sacred places abound in the Indian landscape, and whole sets of narrative and ritual tradition aggregate into bodies of sacred geography. Sarnath, where the Buddha gave his first sermon, and other locations are part of an extensive geography of pilgrimage sites held sacred by Buddhists. Ayodhya, the birthplace of Rama, the hero of the *Rāmāyaṇa* epic and incarnation of Lord Vishnu, has skyrocketed in fame as a pilgrimage site in recent times due to its disputed status as a holy site also for Muslims. The Ganges, of course, is a sacred river; and on it lies Banares (Varanasi), which, as the result of the coalescence of many historical and geographical factors, is a sacred place renowned for funerals and as repository for cremated ashes. It is a pilgrimage place that most Hindus wish to visit at some time in their lives. At the confluence of the Ganges, the Yamuna, and the invisible Saraswati rivers lies Allahabad, a medium-size mercantile city most of the time; but it is where once every twelve years some 45 million Hindus gather at a time to bathe. The world famous Taj Mahal has become the site of choice for urban Indians and as a modern day secular pilgrimage site for lovers and honeymooners. Apart from the sacred place itself, the destination of pilgrims, pilgrimage is itself a form of folklore. Replacing the well-known customs and practices associated with traditional pilgrimages are thousands of modern tour bus companies, a huge business providing Indian tourists with highly standardized tours to largely secular locations in the natural landscape (ocean beaches, waterfalls, historical locations) in luxury buses outfitted according to modern, urban Indian expectations (including ultra-loud audio-taped music) and tour guides.

Processions are a widespread and common feature of many kinds of festive celebrations, including Hindu temple festivals, celebrations at a Muslim mosque, saint's day celebrations at Christian churches, funerals, and even political rallies. Processions are customary forms of gatherings, a folk form in themselves, but they also often include other folk forms such as acrobatic performances, costumed dance performances, troupes of musicians, carrying banners and flags, chanting slogans, singing songs, platform speeches, and a variety of folk rituals. In their turn, processions are often a part of yet more complex festival activities and celebrations. In India, processions commonly include placing the image of a deity on a cart (or a wheeled wooden animal such as a horse or a tiger) and pulling the cart through the town, neighborhood, or village, stopping at the houses of patrons to allow the women of the household to offer their worship at the doorstep. The deity's ride is analogous to (or symbolic of) a royal visit through the lord's realm, inspecting the state of affairs, a show of the lord's presence and blessing. It is also an honor to be a part of the team pulling the cart, an act symbolic of and analogous to one's devoted service to the deity. At the famous temple in Puri, Orissa, where a huge cart is pulled in procession of Lord Jaganatha ("Lord of the World," Krishna), it is not unusual that in the rush of people striving to pull the cart, some get crushed by the enormous wheels and die. They are blessed and go straight to the Lord's abode.

Festival days are either auspicious times in the Hindu calendar during which to do a special *pūjā* to honor a particular deity or to celebrate the birthdays of or mythic events associated with particular deities. They are largely held as household or village celebrations. Examples include Holī; Dīpawālī ("festival of light" associated with the goddess Lakshmī, the goddess of prosperity and fruitfulness); Navarātrī ("nine nights" with a group rituals associated with goddesses, especially Durgā) to be performed on different days, concluding with Dasara famously celebrated in the city of Mysore with a grand procession; Krishna Astami ("Krishna's tenth," meaning the tenth day of the lunar month on which his birthday is celebrated); and Ganapati Chaturti (Gaṇapati, the god Gaēsh's fourth). Special foods are associated with each festival.

There is considerable variation in the way festivals are celebrated across the country, and some festival days are more popular in certain locations than in others. There are even differences in the way some castes and some occupations celebrate certain festivals. While in most parts of India women take the leadership roles in the nine-day series of rituals associated with the goddesses Durgā, Saraswatī, and Lakshmī during Navarātri, there is considerable variation in the particular customs and the kinds of gathering that take place. While almost all over India people celebrate Dipawali by honoring the goddess Lakshmī with a display of lamps and lanterns, the farmers in coastal Karnataka celebrate it by constructing a shrine in their fields for Baliyendra, a demon conquered by the Vamana incarnation of Vishnu, and then calling him in the middle of the night. Some have rather dissimilar variations in different parts of the country. In northern India, Holī is associated with burning the demoness Holikā in a huge communal bonfire, role reversals that would be unthinkable at other times of the year, and wild splashing of one another with dye-colored water, but in the south it is associated with Parvati arousing her future husband, Shiva, from his deep state of meditation. And in Kerala women perform a ritual bathing ceremony symbolizing the death of Kāma, the god of love.

Food

A brief discussion of common folk food beliefs and customs and their associations with ethnicity and religion is necessitated by the fact that Indians themselves overtly and readily make these identifications. One of the most widely known "facts" about Indian culture is its practice of vegetarianism. What is not well-known, apparently, is the reality that only a relatively small percentage of the population is vegetarian, and most of those are of a particular caste, Hindu Brahmans. Most other segments of the population eat meat. But here, the situation becomes more complicated: most Hindus will not eat beef. It is regarded as "lowly," not because cattle are lowly or impure—quite the opposite: they are "sacred." It is those who consume beef that are regarded as "low" and "impure." The pig, on the other hand, is regarded by many castes (it is a folk tradition of those castes) as "low" and "impure," and those who consume its flesh are regarded as impure. Muslims believe pork to be impure, but Christians do not. Among Hindus, on the whole, pigs are merely "disgusting" in their habits, and most Hindu castes proscribe its consumption. In parts of India some castes regard chicken as similarly dirty—indeed, almost all animals living among human populations have dirty eating habits—and proscribe eating their flesh but allow eating animals hunted in the wild. The animals preferred by those who permit the consumption of meat are sheep and goats, the latter preferred over the former for matters of taste. Clearly, eating food is a language of meaningful discourse and practice as well as of rivalry, contention, and religious and ethnic identity. And it goes much beyond this deeply into the social interactions of every day life.

Another dimension to food classification and eating is who cooks the food and how. *Pakka* food is that cooked in *ghee* (clarified butter fat, a product of the cow, held sacred by Hindus) and metal vessels (most preferably "higher class" metals: gold, silver, copper, and brass); *kacca* food is that cooked in water and earthenware vessels. *Pakka* food is associated with festivals and celebrations; *kacca* food is everyday, ordinary, home food. *Pakka* food is more widely acceptable than *kacca* food. Somewhat similarly, food cooked by a higher caste person (Brahman being the highest) is more widely acceptable than that cooked by someone of a lower caste. The result is that the vegetarian food cooked in *ghee* and metal vessels by Brahmans is relished by the greatest number of people, making it the food of festivals and large gatherings. These kinds of food classification continue into the realms of vegetables and grains and processed foods. The system is summarized in a three-fold classification of food into *satvika*, *rajas*, and *tamas* foods.

It is also believed that the body, mind, and personality are formed by the foods one eats. Ultimately this theory is sometimes used to explain the personality characteristics of the caste (primarily *varṇa*) system. Another important classification of foods into hot and cold categories is used to explain causes of illness and the practice of medicine and cure. So, as we might expect, diet is carefully watched, and the women, the cooks of the family (mothers, wives, and sisters), watch after and protect their family's health in the foods they prepare. Many of these food preparations embody customary sets of ingredients balanced to contribute to the family members' health and prosperity. A knowledgeable woman, then, is like a goddess (the goddess Lakshmī) to the family.

CHALLENGES OF THE MODERN WORLD

Folklore is never static: it is always changing and adapting itself to new situations and media possibilities. This is nowhere more evident than in India. The explosive growth of cities and the development of new technologies have brought many changes to the nation's folklore profile. Some traditions and even whole genres have waned particularly in rural areas, while others, especially traditions which have found a place in new media or have migrated to more urban environments, have expanded. New forms of transportation, particularly buses, have enlarged even rural forms such as festivals, fairs, and pilgrimages considerably.

Virtually all forms of popular oral traditions, for example, are available on audiocassette and are widely distributed for sale at festivals and shops in cities. Many stories derived from oral tradition have been enormously popular as cinema productions. Some of these even preserve elements of the oral traditional style and manner of performance. Virtually every state and language has made popular movies out of its regional epic traditions and regional mythical stories. In Tamil Nadu, for example, with a film industry production rivaling that of many European nations, the tragic epic story of a brother and sister called Nallatangal and Nallatambi has been one of its longest running hits. Songs written for the film version of a local epic made decades ago in the Tulu-speaking region of Karnataka about warrior brothers Koti and Channayya are still popular today. And the *Rāmāyaṇa* television serial brought the country to a standstill every Sunday for many months during the 1990s. While not directly derived from any of the huge diversity of oral tradition productions, elements of these inescapably were brought into the series both unconsciously and overtly.

In such new media as these, traditional folklore has managed to overcome the forces of Western-based globalization at least temporarily. However, India itself is generating its own global cultural hegemony, and the force of this as an influence on folk oral tradition is both powerful and subtle, with some folksongs sounding more and more like film song productions, for example.

Not long after India's independence, Milton Singer wrote in the preface to *Tradition and Change*, "[M]odern nationalism in India . . . has always shown a strong interest in the recovery or reinterpretation of India's traditional culture," and suggested, "The professional student of culture and civilization may contribute something to this inquiry through an objective study of the variety and changes in cultural traditions." This call generally has been met with enthusiasm by scholars. Many universities all around India now have folklore departments and offer degrees in folklore. Part of this is due to Indian states being established on the basis of language and regional pride, which resulted in folklore becoming a part of departments of literature that included the preservation and promotion of not only written literature, but also non-written arts preserved in oral folk tradition such as dance, drama, material culture, and song.

India's central government and most of the state governments have aided folk performance forms by providing monetary support to particular genre performances (especially dance-drama forms); supporting folk festivals (regionally and nationally, as well as internationally); recognizing, organizing, and listing bodies of state-licensed folk performers; and establishing state cultural boards. Equivalent to America's Smithsonian Institution, the Central Government's Indira Gandhi National Centre for the Arts (IGNCA; see ignca.nic.in/js_body.htm) in Delhi has a division devoted to the collection and analysis of folklore materials throughout all of India. The Central Institute of Indian Languages in Mysore also has a folkore division. More pragmatically, most states have established centers helping folk artists make the transition to new urban contexts and new urban patrons. Central and state folk arts and crafts centers have played a particularly strong role training young artists, providing design advice, and establishing distribution and sales outlets. Ironically, perhaps, these efforts have sometimes produced the undesirable results of a decline in the quality of folk crafts and a dependence by artists on politicians and the government rather than the folk as patrons of their art.

Some support for Indian folklore has also come from abroad. In 1985 the United States held a Festival of India, which brought many folk performers and craftsmen from around India to Washington, D.C. The event, organized at the diplomatic level between the Indo-American Council in Delhi and the Smithsonian Institution, not only demonstrated tremendous world interest in India's folk traditions but also gave a tremendous boost to the legitimacy of India's wealth of diversity in folk forms, a legitimacy which has subsequently served to preserve them from annihilation in the face of widespread globalization. Similar festivals were held in a number of European countries.

STUDIES OF INDIAN FOLKLORE

The Ford Foundation has actively shaped folklore collection and scholarship in India with financial support for developing archival centers and international conferences and training workshops (a Web site listing of these centers may be found at www.archive-india.org/abpitarc_memberlist.html). Some of the most active folklore centers today are the Regional Resource Centre for Folk Performing Arts in Udupi, Karnataka State (see www.udupipages.com/culture/rrc/html), Rupayan Sansthan in Rajasthan, and the Archives and Research Centre for Ethnomusicology (ARCE) established by the American Institute of Indian Studies (www.indiastudies.org/) in New Delhi, which is dedicated to collating, centralizing, and preserving collections made of Indian music and oral traditions scattered all over the world for use by Indian scholars and artists. The National Folklore Support Centre (NFSC; www.indian folklore.org/home.htm) in Chennai, which also received startup funds from the Ford Foundation, is currently coordinating many of the activities of folklore institutes around India. It has collaborated in conducting numerous all-India conferences held in various regional locations and has run numerous public programs educating the urban audience of Chennai.

BIBLIOGRAPHY

Ashton-Sikora, Martha. 2004. Bhūta Kōla. In *South Asian Foklore: An Encyclopedia*, edited by Peter J. Claus, Margaret Mills, and Sarah Diamond. New York: Routledge. 65–66.

Beck, B.E.F. 1982. *The Three Twins: The Telling of a South Indian Folk Epic*. Bloomington: Indiana University Press.

Benfey, Theodor. 1859. *Pantschatantra. Fünf Bücher indischen Fabeln, Märchen und Erzählungen*. 2 volumes. Leipzig: F. A. Brockhaus.

Blackburn, Stuart. 1988. *Singing of Birth and Death: Texts in Performance*. Philadelphia: University of Pennsylvania Press.

Blackburn, Stuart, Peter J. Claus, Joyce B. Flueckiger, and Susan S. Wadley, eds. 1989. *Oral Epics in India*. Berkeley: University of California Press.

Blackburn, Stuart, and Joyce B. Flueckiger. 1989. Introduction. In *Oral Epics of India*, edited by Stuart Blackburn, Peter J. Claus, Joyce B. Flueckiger, and Susan S. Wadley. Berkeley: University of California Press. 1–14.

Blackburn, Stuart H., and A. K. Ramanujan, eds. 1986. *Another Harmony: New Essays on the Folklore of India*. Berkeley: University of California Press.

Claus, Peter J. 1989. Behind the Text: Performance and Ideology in a Tulu Oral Tradition. In *Indian Oral Epics*, edited by Stuart Blackburn, Peter J. Claus, Susan Wadley, and Joyce Flueckiger. 55–74.

———. 1998. Folklore. In *India's Worlds and U.S. Scholars, 1947–1997*, edited by Joseph W. Elder, Edward C. Dimock Jr., and Ainslie T. Embree. New Delhi: Manohar. 211–236.

———. 2004. Kātāmarāju. *South Asian Folklore: An Encyclopedia*, edited by Peter J. Claus, Margaret Mills, and Sarah Diamond. New York: Routledge. 329–330.

Claus, Peter J., Brenda E. F. Beck, J. Handoo, and P. Goswami. 1987. *Folktales of India*. Chicago: University of Chicago Press.

Claus, Peter J., Margaret Mills, and Sarah Diamond, eds. 2004. *South Asian Folklore: An Encyclopedia*. New York: Routledge.

Diamond, Sarah. 1999. Karagattam: Performance and the Politics of Desire in Tamil Nadu, India. Diss., University of Pennsylvania.

Eck, Diana. 1982. *Banaras: City of Light*. New York: Alfred A. Knopf.

Egnor, Margaret. 1986. Internal Iconicity in Paraiyar Crying Songs. In *Another Harmony: New Essays on the Folklore of India*, edited by Stuart Blackburn and A. K. Ramanujan. Berkeley: University of California Press. 294–344.

Emeneau, M. B. 1980. *Language and Linguistic Area: Essays*, edited by Anwar S. Dil. Stanford: Stanford University Press.

Feldhaus, Anne. 1995. *Water and Womanhood: Religious Meanings of Rivers in Maharashtra*. New York: Oxford University Press.

Gentes, M. J. 2004. Pūja. In *South Asian Folklore: An Encyclopedia*, edited by Peter J. Claus, Margaret Mills, and Sarah Diamond. New York: Routledge. 493–495.

Gold, Ann Grozdins. 1992. *A Carnival of Parting: The Tales of King Bhartari and King Gopi Chand, as Sung and Told by Madhu Natisar Nath of Ghatiyali*. Berkeley: University of California Press.

Gold, Ann Grodzins, and Gloria G. Raheja. 1994. *Listen to the Heron's Words: Reimagining Gender and Kinship in North India*. Berkeley: University of California Press.

Mair, Victor. 1988. *Painting and Performance: Chinese Picture Recitation and Its Indian Genesis*. Honolulu: University of Hawaii Press.

Marglin, Frederique Apffel. 1985. *Wives of the God-King: The Rituals of the Devadasis of Puri*. Delhi: Oxford University Press.

Marriot, McKim. 1955. *Village India: Studies in the Little Community*. Chicago: University of Chicago Press.

Ramanujan, A. K. 1997. *A Flowering Tree and Other Oral Tales from India*, edited by Stuart Blackburn and Alan Dundes. Berkeley: University of California Press.

Redfield, Robert. 1956. *Peasant Society and Culture: An Anthropological Approach to Civilization*. Chicago: University of Chicago Press.

Richman, Paula, ed. 1991. *Many Ramayanas: The Diversity of a Narrative Tradition in South Asia*. Berkeley: University of California Press.

Richmond, Farley P., Darius L. Swann, and Phillip Zarrilli, eds. 1990. *Indian Theatre: Traditions of Performance*. Honolulu: University of Hawaii Press.

Roghair, Gene. 1982. *The Epic of Palnāḍú: A Study and Translation of Palnāṭi Vīrula Katha, a Telugu Oral Tradition from Andhra Pradesh*. New York: Oxford University Press.

Schubel, Vernon James. 1993. *Religious Performance in Contemporary Islam: Shi'i Devotional Rituals in South Asia*. Columbia: University of South Carolina Press.

Singer, Milton B. 1959. *Traditional India: Structure and Change*. Philadelphia: American Folklore Society.

———, ed. 1966. *Krishna: Myths, Rites, and Attitudes*. Honolulu: East-West Center Press.

Smith, John D. 1991. *Pābūjī: A Study, Transcription, and Translation*. Cambridge: Cambridge University Press.

Vatsyayan, Kapila. 1976. *Traditions of Indian Folk Dance*. New Delhi: Clarion Press.

Wadley, Susan S. 1994. *Struggling with Destiny in Karimpur, 1925–1984*. Berkeley: University of California Press.

Welbon, Guy R., and Glenn Yocum. 1982. *Religious Festivals in South India and Sri Lanka*. Delhi: Manohar.

Peter J. Claus

ASSAM

GEOGRAPHY

Assam occupies a central position among the seven states of the northeastern region of **India** (often collectively referred to as Northeast India or, simply, the Northeast). The region is strategically located near India's international borders with **China** and **Bhutan** on the north, Myanmar on the east, and **Bangladesh** on the south and west. Since independence, Assam's only link with the rest of India to the west has been through a narrow corridor via North Bengal and **Bihar**. A province under British colonial administration, Assam is now a constituent state of the Indian Union enjoying legislative and executive power as prescribed by the Constitution of India. The state is divided into more than twenty administrative districts with various local governments operating at different levels.

The term "Assam" is the anglicized form of the indigenous name for the land, *Asam* (pronounced *axam*), once earlier interpreted by scholars as being of Sanskrit derivation and meaning "peerless." But academics today associate the term with the original name of the Ahoms, who had ruled over a majority of the area now included in Assam for nearly six hundred years until its annexation by the British early in the nineteenth century.

In ancient and early medieval times Assam was known by such names as Pragijy-otisha, Kamarupa, and Lauhityadesha, and was ruled by successive royal dynasties, including Varman, Salastambha, and Pala. Later ruling powers like the Chutiyas and Kacharis wielded authority over different regions of the land. Then came two mighty royal houses: the Ahoms in the eastern and central portions of Assam and the Koches in the west. Both were instrumental in effecting political cohesion and promoting social and cultural solidarity. Although the Muslim powers from the west had invaded the area several times, they could never overpower the Ahoms, though part of the Koch territory did come under their sway.

The topography of Assam consists of a combination of hills and plains. Stretching from east to west along the course of the Brahmaputra River lies the long and rather narrow Brahmaputra Valley, also known as the Assam Valley. The Barak Valley, named after a river, encompasses the southern portion of the state. In between lie the hill districts of Karbi Anglong and North Cashar nestling on the sub-Himalayan tract that also juts into the plains here and there. Except on the west, where the contiguous areas are the plains of Bangladesh and the state of West Bengal, Assam is surrounded on all sides by the predominantly hilly and mountainous terrains of Bhutan, Arunachal Pradesh, **Nagaland**, Meghalaya, Manipur, and Mizoram. In the fertile valleys frequently inundated by the two major rivers and their tributaries, rice and other crops are grown by settled cultivation, while in the hills tribal communities depend on shifting cultivation known as *jhum*. The climate in the plains is hot and humid during summer and moderately cold and pleasant in winter. The climate in the hills becomes cooler as the altitude increases. Rainfall is copious during the long wet season.

People and Language

Both racially and culturally the population of Assam consists of diverse elements that mingle in a state of juxtaposition and mutual give-and-take. Assam's demographic composition reflects the components that comprise India's population in general: the Austro-Asiatic, the Dravidian, the Indo-Aryan, and the Indo-Mongoloid. The earliest inhabitants were the Austro-Asiatics, followed by the Dravidians. Traces of racial and cultural elements attributed to these groups are still discernible. Since very early times routes of Aryan migration to southeast Asia have passed through Assam, and successive groups of Indo-Aryan people have settled there at different times. But the Indo-Mongoloids, called Kiratas, have been dominant in the population. Waves of people of Mongoloid origin have flowed into Assam ever since Vedic times, and until the recent past and have adapted to the local environment.

In the wake of invasions during the medieval period, Muslims—both soldiers and holy men—settled in Assam, intermarried with local women, and produced offspring who have become part of the state's culture mix. Assamese Muslims constitute a prominent portion of the population, and their contribution to Assam's culture has been substantial. The descendants of a handful of Sikhs, originally mercenaries with the invading armies, similarly remained in Assam to become part of the local population. Christianity has also attracted many adherents among tribal groups, and its influence seems to be increasing.

More recently, other large scale migrations have come into Assam from other parts of the subcontinent: Santals, Gonds, and Mundas from West Bengal, **Orissa**, Jharkhand, Chattisgarh, and Andhra Pradesh were brought in as indentured laborers for the tea gardens; Bengali Hindus entered as seekers of fortune and also as refugees after the partition of India and Pakistan; land-hungry Bengali Muslims came from East Pakistan (now Bangladesh); and other immigrants engaged in various trades and professions. Most have settled permanently in different parts of Assam and have made it their homeland. The unusual influx of migrants has disturbed the social, economic, political, and cultural balance and occasionally has caused ethnic stresses and strains which have manifested themselves in various ways. Meanwhile, a process of adaptation and integration has been ongoing.

Assamese, a Modern Indo-Aryan language with a rich literary tradition, is the primary language of the Brahmaputra Valley. It has incorporated many features from local non-Aryan languages, while influencing those languages to various degrees. While most of the tribal groups retain their indigenous tongues, many have also adopted Assamese as their primary language, and most others speak Assamese with spontaneity and fluency. Assamese, in fact, serves as the lingua franca among various communities, including the newly integrated ones. A dialect of Bengali plays a similar role in the Barak Valley.

Most of the population in the plains consists of Assamese Hindus, among whom Aryan racial features are marked only in the higher castes. The other castes clearly bear signs of non-Aryan strains, particularly of Indo-Mongoloid linkage. The majority of the tribal groups—such as the Bodos, Rabhas, Misings, Sonowal Kacharis, Deoris, Tiwas, Karbis, Dimasas, Kukis, Hmars, Zemi Nagas, and Rengma Nagas—belong to such Indo-Mongoloid stocks as Tibeto-Burman and Siamese-Chinese, including Tai. Apart from the Ahoms, who are descended from a Tai stock but have merged into the Assamese-Hindu caste fold, a few small tribal communities—Khamtis, Phakes, Khamyangs, Aitons, and Turungs—speak Tai and follow the Theravada form of Hinayana Buddhism.

SOCIETY AND RELIGION

The line between tribal and non-tribal has traditionally been rather thin in Assamese Hindu society. Although the caste system and a concept of caste hierarchy date from early times, "non-tribal" Assamese Hindu society betrays many traits that are patently tribal by orthodox Hindu standards. Considerable flexibility exists within the caste framework: castes are not strictly occupation-specific, and caste-based disabilities are limited. The practice of untouchability has been minimal, and atrocities committed on low-caste people have been foreign to the popular ethos. Unlike in other parts of India, the custom in Assam has been for the bride's family to receive considerations. The liberal spirit also extends to Hindu-Muslim relations. Assamese society has been remarkably free of communal conflicts on religious grounds, and an air of mutual understanding and amity has prevailed.

This atmosphere of tolerance and accommodation owes much to the legacy of Sankaradeva (1449–1568), who spearheaded the neo-Vaishnava Bhakti movement in Assam and produced a spiritual as well as social and cultural revival. His influence has been so strong and abiding that its presence can be felt even now throughout

Assamese life, cutting across religious and sectarian divisions. A striking feature of the Assam Vaishnava order is the institution of *satras*, or monasteries, which are not only organizational centers but also repositories of both performing and visual arts. *Nam-ghars* are community prayer halls which also serve as centers for social and cultural activities at the village level.

Before the advent of Sankaradeva the most powerful religious cults in Assam were Saivism and Saktism. At one time Assam was an important center of Tantrik Saktism with the famous shrine of Mother Goddess Kamakhya located there. Siva and Devi (Mother Goddess) enjoy veneration and propitiation even today at both "official" and folk levels. Siva is a widely popular folk god whose shrines dot the plains. Devi is also worshiped in popular and folk forms such as Manasa or Bishohori (Serpent Goddess) and Shitala or Ai (Smallpox Goddess).

Belief in magic and spells is widespread, particularly among the tribal groups. Much of this belief is connected with the success of agricultural pursuits and the curing of certain ailments. Village medicine-men (called *oja* or *bez* in Assamese) often use charms and incantations to propitiate malevolent gods and spirits or to ward off black magic. A rich lore of empirical folk medicine consists of household remedies and preventives to which people resort often alongside modern medicine.

Festivals of the major religions such as Durga Puja, Dīpawālī, Sivaratri, and Janmastami of the Hindus, Id and Muharram of the Muslims, and Christmas of the Christians are observed along prescribed lines, though with some local variations.

Bohag Bihu is the spring festival associated with the vernal equinox. Bihus are the most popular festivals throughout Assam; they are times of much singing and dancing by members of both sexes. (© Lindsay Hebberd/CORBIS)

But it is the folk festivals which bear distinctive local marks. Among them Bihu occupies the pride of place in terms of both importance and colorfulness. Bihu, in fact, stands for a festival complex: there are three of them coming at different seasons of the year and associated with important points in the agricultural cycle. Bohag Bihu, also called Rangali Bihu, is the spring festival held at planting time. It also heralds the Assamese New Year, and its celebration is marked by singing, dancing, and merrymaking. Magh Bihu, also known as Bhogali Bihu, is the winter festival associated with harvesting the major rice crop and is observed with feasts and fire rites. Kati Bihu is a comparatively simple ceremony performed with the lighting of earthen lamps. There are also festivals exclusive to different tribal peoples such as Boisagu and Kherai of the Bodos, Baikho and Pharkanti of the Rabhas, Chomangkan and Hachcha Kekan of the Karbis, Harni Gobra and Busu of the Dimasas, and Sagra-mi-sawa and Wan-sua of the Tiwas. Special holidays of the Assam Vaishnava calendar such as the *tithis* (death anniversaries) of Sankardeva and other venerated figures are also observed. There are a few festivals and ceremonies important in particular regions such as Marai (Manasa), Puja, Bhatheli, Mohoho, Bas Puja, and Kati Puja.

ORAL TRADITION: SONGS, STORIES, PROVERBS, RIDDLES

It is no wonder that this unusually variegated and colorful sociocultural milieu has nurtured a body of verbal folklore massive in volume and rich in variety. It includes songs, ballads, rhymes, and narratives as well as proverbs, riddles, and other genres. The bulk of this lore is in the Assamese language—or rather in dialects of the language spoken in different areas and by different communities. Some verbal material is in the Bengali dialect of the Barak Valley, and the rest is in other languages. Although the written literary tradition is not strong in most of the tribal societies, all have rich oral traditions. Some groups, in fact, excel in particular verbal art forms—such as balladry among the Karbis and Dimasas.

The stock of Assamese folksongs is almost inexhaustible. One might consider the following classification of this vast body of material:

    I. Songs of religious and devotional content
        A. Songs of prayer and supplication
        B. Devotional songs with philosophical overtones
        C. Chants and invocations

   II. Songs of ceremonies and festivals
        A. Songs associated with rituals such as *pujās* and fasts
        B. Songs of seasonal and agricultural ceremonies with religious and
            magical significance
        C. Songs of secular festivals such as Bihu
        D. Songs of ceremonies connected to the life cycle such as marriage

  III. Songs of love and yearning
        A. Love songs in devotional camouflage
        B. Purely lyrical love songs
        C. Songs of pangs of separation

IV. Lullabies, nursery rhymes, and children's game songs

V. Songs and rhymes of humor and jest

VI. Miscellaneous songs.

There are large bodies of narratives that can be categorized analytically as myths, legends, and folktales. It should be noted, however, that storytellers and their audiences do not necessarily identify their narratives using these categories. Moreover, while folklorists think of these as categories of prose narrative, many of them are not presented as prose. While folktales generally are prose, myths and legends often are performed in verse and meant to be sung. Universal **types** and **motifs** and those known throughout India commonly occur in most narratives, but there are also those which betray a local character. Myths and legends are more culture-specific. Hindu mythological tales are current through storytelling, singing, and dramatic presentations. Stories from the two great Indian epics are widely recounted and relished. The *Rāmāyaṇa* has been particularly influential and has percolated to folk and tribal levels. For example, a full Karbi version of the *Rāmāyaṇa* known as *Sabin Alun* is a veritable folk epic. Many myths and legends have developed through the process of Sanskritization of non-Aryan groups. Some of them link particular communities or ruling lines with Hindu gods and goddesses or with important characters of the great epics with the obvious aim of ensuring an exalted status for the community or line concerned.

The vast body of Assamese tales has been grouped into five broad divisions: animal tales, tales of the supernatural, jokes and humorous tales, **trickster** tales, and cumulative tales. Judging from their names and affinities, they have been traced to these sources: (a) early literary sources, (b) local tribal sources, (c) migration from across Assam's borders, and (d) some common fund shared with others within and outside the region.

MUSIC AND DANCE

Assam has its own classically oriented performing art forms comprising the Bargit system of music, the Satriya style of dance, and the Ankiya Bhaona form of drama. But folk art forms are even more abundant. Most of these are integral to the festivals mentioned above. Bihu songs are short lyrical pieces set to catchy melodic and rhythmic patterns and performed in conjunction with lusty dancing to the vigorous beats of the drum (*dhol*)—the whole combination replete with youthful exuberance. Bihu numbers are especially prized in Upper (eastern) Assam, while Lower (western) Assam has others that are particularly popular.

Musically, the songs of most of the tribal communities are generally pentatonic and have a repetitive pattern. Non-tribal Assamese folk music patterns range from the very simple to the quite intricate. A variety of musical instruments, including drums, flutes, pipes, cymbals, and stringed instruments, are used by different communities in different kinds of performances.

As a dramatic performance, the Bhaona form operates at three levels: elite, popular, and folk. Oja-pali, of which there are several varieties, is a semi-dramatic form that combines narrative singing, dancing, and acting. The Dhulyia is a peculiar entertainment vehicle that features an ingenuous mixture of music, acrobatics, and dramatics. Kushan-gan is similar to Oja-pali in some ways, with a leading performer assisted by a number of associates. Bhari-gan is a folk drama in which heavy wooden masks figure prominently. Masks made of various materials are used in several of the performance forms.

ARTS AND CRAFTS

Assam is justly famous for handwoven textiles produced by the women, both tribal and non-tribal, on their traditional looms. Customarily each household has one or more looms, and skill in weaving has been regarded as a desirable feminine accomplishment. The products, for both ordinary and ceremonial use, stand out for their texture, color scheme, and design. Assam also produces three varieties of silk—*eri*, *muga*, and *pat*—the first two being exclusive to the state. Bamboo and cane grow abundantly in Assam, and bamboo is virtually ubiquitous in Assamese material culture. It is the chief material for constructing traditional houses and is also used in fashioning a wide range of items—receptacles, mats, fishing gear, weaving implements, and musical instruments, for example—that represent fine workmanship. The skill and artistry of bamboo craftsmen today cater to modern needs and tastes. Woodcarving and maskmaking are practiced by traditional artisans, a class of whom are called Khanikars. Two potter communities (Kumar and Hira) produce different types of earthenware, including terracotta toys.

Another class of artisans (Mali or Malakar) who work on the pith of a reed locally called *kuhila*, *botla*, or *shola* (*Aschynome asper*) have kept alive a rich folk tradition of toymaking, maskmaking, and painting. While some traditional bell-metal and brass articles made by local artisans are still in demand, items with modified technologies and fresh designs are now flooding the market.

CHALLENGES OF THE MODERN WORLD

Various indigenous ethnic groups had been maintaining their distinctive characters more or less undisturbed until the advent of the British administration and, more or less simultaneously, of the American Baptist missionaries. The introduction of new administrative and economic systems coupled with the opening of new horizons through modern education brought in significant attitudinal changes toward the traditional modes, particularly in those fields in which the impact of external stimuli had been particularly strong. After independence such changes became more pronounced. Traditional social and political institutions were replaced by "modern" democratic ones accompanied by awareness and assertion of rights and privileges. Changes in the landholding pattern together with mass migration from outside threw the traditional economics out of gear, and in the name of development—and later of globalization—a consumer-oriented, capital-intensive, and technology-based economy has emerged with all its outer glitter and inner ruthlessness.

All this has produced a confused state of affairs. On one hand, tradition-bound societies have been plunging headlong into the new "international" modes of living; on the other, the faceless uniformity associated with global culture has led to an identity crisis and search for roots. The indigenous communities, already alarmed by the disturbance of the demographic equation, have become seriously concerned about their survival—political and economic as well as social and cultural. Although the backgrounds are not the same everywhere, the younger generations of the various groups have become restive and demonstrative. In their bid to return to their roots and to sustain a sense of solidarity, they have been turning more and more toward traditional elements in their cultures, including folklore. In fact, selected folklore materials, both verbal and nonverbal, have been adopted as symbols of ethnic identity.

For some time literary and cultural organizations as well as academic institutions have been encouraging and facilitating the collection and documentation of folklore material. Recently government and other public agencies have begun to support and promote the showcasing of folklore in various forms. Meanwhile, the discipline of folklore study has been steadily gaining ground academically. Another striking development is the popularization of folklore. While folklore is displayed through platform performances and public rallies, the mass media—including radio, television, and recordings—have contribution to the proliferation of folklore. Naturally a high degree of professionalization and commercialization has been associated with this process. The materials purveyed and consumed through the media have already become part of popular culture and are being merged into mass culture.

BIBLIOGRAPHY

Barpujari, H. K. 1994–1999. *The Comprehensive History of Assam*, 4 volumes. Guwahati: Assam Publication Board.

Barua, B. K. 1969 (1951). *A Cultural History of Assam*. Guwahati: Lawyer's Book Stall.

Chatterji, S. K. 1974. *Kirqta-jana-Kṛti*. Kolkata: The Asiatic Society.

Datta, Birendranath. 1986. *Folk Toys of Assam*. Guwahati: Assam Directorate of Cultural Affairs.

———. 1990. *Assam, the Emerald Treasureland*. Guwahati: Assam Department of Tourism.

———. 1998. *Folk Painting in Assam*. Tezpur: Tezpur University.

———. 1999. *Folkloric Foragings in India's North-East*. Guwahati: Anundoram Borooah Institute of Language, Art, and Culture.

Datta, Birendranath, and others. 1994. *A Handbook for Folklore Material of North-East India*. Guwahati: Anundoram Borooah Institute of Language, Art, and Culture.

Goswami, P. 1954. *Folk Literature of Assam*. Guwahati: Assam Department of Historical and Antiquarian Studies.

———. 1960. *Ballads and Tales of Assam*. Guwahati: Gauhati University.

———. 1980. *Tales of Assam*. Guwahati: Assam Publication Board.

———. 1982. *Essays on the Culture and Folklore of North East India*. Guwahati: Spectrum Publications.

Birendranath Datta

BIHAR

GEOGRAPHY, LANGUAGE, AND RELIGION

Situated in the northeastern part of **India**, Bihar is bounded by **Nepal** on the north and shares boundaries with three other Indian states: **Uttar Pradesh** on the west, Jharkhand (until recently an integral part of Bihar) to the south, and West Bengal on the east. The city of Patna, whose ancient name was Patliputra, is the capital of Bihar, which was carved out as a separate province in 1936 from the eastern province of British India.

The state has three well-defined seasons: the cool season from November to February, the hot season from March to mid-June, and the rainy season from mid-June to October. The temperatures in December and January fall at times below 5 degrees Celsius, while those in May rise above 40 degrees. The state's mean rainfall is 1,270 millimeters.

About 80 percent of the total population of Bihar is Hindu. At 15 percent, Muslims form the next largest religious group. Other religious groups include Christians, Sikhs, and Jains. The Hindu population comprises the elite up-

Pictured here is a painting of Lord Buddha at Bodhgaya, which Buddhists consider to be the holiest place in the world. (© DPA/SOA/The Image Works)

per castes (Brahman, Bhumihar, Rajput, and Kayastha), the so-called backward castes (Yadav, Kurmi, and Baniya), and the secluded castes (formerly "untouchables": Chamar or Mochi, Dusadhs, and Mushars).

Almost 80 percent of the population of Bihar lives in villages and depends upon agriculture or farming for its livelihood. This makes Bihar one of the least urbanized states in India. The state has a very low literacy rate (below 40 percent). The World Bank Report (2005) states that Bihar is one of the poorest states in India.

Most people in Bihar speak Hindi, Urdu, Bhojpuri, Maithili, or Magahi, though some minority groups also speak Angika or Vajjika. Bhojpuri is spoken in the western part of Bihar, while Magahi-speakers are found in the central and southern part. Maithili is spoken in Mithili (the area of ancient Videha, now Tirhut, where Lord Rama married the local princess Sita). *Chhat* (a three-day-long festival of sun-worship) is a local festival unique to Bihar, though the people also celebrate those festivals found throughout India such as *Holī*, *Dussera*, and *Dīpawālī*.

Sites of religious and cultural interest are found throughout Bihar. Nalanda is the seat of the ancient and celebrated Nalanda Buddhist monastic university. Pawapuri is the place where Lord Mahavira, the founder of modern Jain religion, attained *nirvana* (enlightenment, or freedom from the endless cycle of reincarnation). Gaya is an important place of pilgrimage for Hindus. Buddha Gaya (Bodh Gaya), where Lord Buddha attained enlightenment, is considered by Buddhists to be the holiest place in the world. Rajgir is another holy place for both Hindus and Buddhists. Takhat Shri Harmandirjee Saheb, the birthplace of the last (tenth) Guru of the Sikhs, Guru Gobind Singh, at Patna City is considered a holy place by the Sikhs.

MYTHS, LEGENDS, AND FOLKTALES

The folklore of Bihar encompasses myths, legends, folktales, ballads, riddles, proverbs, superstitions, and play, and Bihar is rich in almost every one of these genres. With a history of more than 2,500 years, Bihar has integrated traditions that represent both the folk and the largely Sanskritic Hindu heritage. The oral traditional materials of Bihar are rich in variety and content. Similarly, the Sanskritic heritage constituting the elite culture is also characterized by its richness. These parallel traditions have co-existed to influence the lives and philosophy of the people for ages. They have become inextricably interwoven in the **worldview** of the people of Bihar. Sanskrit literature—namely, the *Panchatantra* (five stories), the *Hitopdesa* (good advice), the *Vetal-Pancavimshatika* (twenty-five tales of a ghost), the *Shukaspaptati* (the seventy stories of a parrot), and the *Simhasana-dvathmsatika* (thirty-two stories of a royal throne)—are not only very popular but have affected the folk narrative tradition of Bihar.

The ancient kingdom of Magadha played a significant role in the generation, propagation, and preservation of early Indian folktales, especially in the Sanskritic tradition. Pandit Vishnu Sharma wrote the *Panchatantra*, intended originally to impart education to the princes, in Patliputra (now Patna), the kingdom's capital.

Bihar folktales not only provide enjoyment and education but also attempt to explain day-to-day happenings as well as extraordinary events relating to nature and human society. They attempt to answer a range of questions: Why are crows fed during the last rituals of the dead? Why does the water level of the Phlagu River increase suddenly? Why does a particular event happen in a particular way? Why does it not happen in some other way? Behind each query exists a story to satisfy the questioner.

Children would gather around a storyteller as he began to narrate:

A rich property owner was on his deathbed. Gasping for breath, he told his three sons to dig under his bed after he was dead and, while uttering that, breathed his last. Some days later, the sons dug at the spot and unearthed three pots, placed one above the other. The topmost pot contained mud, the middle pot contained dried cow dung, and the lowest pot contained straw. Below the three pots was a silver coin. The brothers were perplexed. "Obviously, Father meant to convey some message to us through the pots and their contents," said the eldest brother, "but what?" They wracked their brains, but none could come up with the explanation.

The storyteller usually stops here so that the children can attempt to solve the problem. They argue with each other and put their heads together to develop a collective response. They use their wit and wisdom and by the next day have come up with different solutions. If they can solve the riddle posed in the story, they will be rewarded or praised. If not, the storyteller will provide the answer to them and make them understand the importance of learning from the old and the wise in the family and society at large. Children thus develop a sense of regard for elderly people of their family and learn to follow their advice. The psyches and feelings of participants are influenced by the psychological and emotional state created by the storytellers.

On some other occasion when a person asks the children to solve a puzzle, they divide themselves into two or three groups and attempt a solution: "You have to take a bundle of grass, a goat, and a tiger across a river. You can take only one item or animal at a time in the boat. If you take the tiger first, the goat will eat the grass, so you cannot do that. You cannot leave the tiger with the goat if you decide to take grass. If you decide to take the goat first, the tiger will not eat the grass, but when you return for a second trip, leaving the goat alone on the other side, what will you take next time? So how will you get the grass, the goat, and the tiger across the river?" Young children first try to avoid solving the riddle saying, "But I do not have any tiger, goat, or grass." Those who know the answer smile at each other and make the children understand that this is only a hypothetical problem. The perplexed children often go to their mothers and fathers for help, making this a family affair and ensuring cohesion through the search for a solution.

Myths are an integral part of folklore. Unlike fairy tales or animal stories, myths are frequently blended with religious sentiments and beliefs. Their forms depend upon their social functions. Hindus believe that Indra, the guardian of the cosmos and the rain god, ensures peace and prosperity on earth. If any individual, sage, or demon dares to throw the cosmos out of balance, Indra and other cosmic entities adopt strategies to divert or destroy the threatening agent. This principle guides many folk narratives. God, *sadhus* (holy men), or even animals come to the rescue of the suffering and punish the wicked. These stories can generate a sense of hope in the life of a poor man. Some stories deal with incidents of human sacrifice. For example, a princess obeying the order of her father enters a tank. The empty tank fills with water, and the princess drowns. Or in order to please a goddess and serve the welfare of the state, a young man beheads himself with a sword. These stories are narrated to instill a sense of sacrifice in young minds. Of course, today human sacrifice is prohibited by law. However, the sacrifice of a goat, pumpkin, or coconut—the latter two symbolizing the human head—is commonly practiced to please the gods.

Myths and folktales related to trees and animals are meant to discourage their destruction by man. Why, one narrative asks, are neema trees but not tamarinds grown near the house? "In ancient times, a woman was anxious that her husband should return home soon when he was preparing to go on a business trip to a faraway place. She sought help from a village medical man. He advised her husband to sleep under a tamarind tree on his way out every night during his travels and to sleep under a neema tree on his return journey. He did so and was soon taken ill owing to the unhealthy acidic vapors emitted by the tamarind. He therefore did not prolong his journey. He had to turn back. He slept under the neema tree on his way back, and by the time he reached home, he was cured."

During smallpox epidemics, festoons of fresh neema leaves are hung at the bedside of the ill as well as at the entrance of Hindu homes. Hindus believe that the neema tree is the abode of the goddess Durga. They do not like to cut it. In some ways, the mythical stories are largely responsible for developing the principles of *satya* (truth), *dharma* (righteous conduct), *shanti* (peace), *prema* (love), and *ahinsa* (non-violence).

BALLADS AND FOLKSONGS

In addition to folktales, Bihar has a rich heritage of ballads and folksongs, which are sung on different occasions to enhance the efficiency of manual labor or to alleviate the tedium. They are also sung to release or reveal emotions. Marriage songs give enthusiasm to the young couple. Songs of ridicule are important as a means of censuring misbehavior. In India, where most families prefer male children, a girl might feel constantly dejected. And in such a situation, the women of Bihar sing during Chhat, one of the most important festivals, *"Runki Jhunki beti mangi la padal pandinva damad oye Chhati mai darshan de hu hamad"* (O Mother Chhat! please give me a daughter and an educated son-in-law), to boost the self-esteem of girls listening. At least once each year, they feel they too are desired. A Bhojpuri folksong related to tattoos, *"Jahu humjanti sasur niharba tu godna; sasur nahi re godaiti appan bahi gadna"* (O father-in-law! If I knew you would stare at my tattoo, I would not have tattooed my arm), shows how a father-in-law stares at his beautiful daughter-in-law on the pretext of watching the tattoo. In Bihar, the father-in-law and daughter-in-law avoid each other in day-to-day life: especially in the traditional family environment. A Mathili folk song, *"Gori kahma godolah godna? Bahiya godauli chhatiya godauli; gorikahma godolah godna"* (O dear fair lady! Where did you tattoo your body? I did it on my arm and on my breast), dramatizes an exchange between a newlywed couple and helps to end inhibition between them. Compilations of folksongs in the Bhojpuri, Magahi, and Maithili dialects are available in print as well as on recordings, which are popular and played during religious or marriage ceremonies.

PROVERBS AND RIDDLES

Proverbs and riddles indicate a rich pool of worldly knowledge. Though the main function of riddles is entertainment, they also serve educational purposes, because answering them requires wit, acumen, and memory. Many riddles are instructive, as they may mention ecological names or contain references to historical events. Certainly, they develop a sense of observation and often contain elaborate and rich linguistic forms—for example, "Nisha is three times as old as Rani. However, in two years time she will be only twice as old as she is. How old are the two girls?" Small children without knowing any algebraic equation would try to answer this mathematical question. Another example is the following: "I am a language spoken in one of the states of India. From beginning to end and end to beginning my name is the same. Tell my name." This starts the children thinking of Indian state names as well as the languages spoken in them. Many stories narrate how solving a puzzle enabled a prince to marry a princess or be rewarded with half of the kingdom or face banishment. Sometimes, an intelligent wife or a wise daughter would help a man in solving the puzzle and save him from embarrassment at the hand of the questioner. These stories can develop family unity.

Proverbs are also very useful. The formal instruction given to young children is often summarized or emphasized using proverbs. In proverbs, children are introduced to general attitudes and principles such as a societal distaste for laziness, rebelliousness, and snobbishness. Proverbs related to agriculture are imbued with some educational notes: *"Gajar, Saljam, aur Murj; tino bowe durj"* (Carrot, radish, and turnip should be sown maintaining distance from each other); *"Pahile Kakri pichhe Dhan, usko kahiye pur kishan"* (A good farmer is one who sows cucumber before sowing rice).

Bihar is famous for folk painting. Madhubani paintings of the state's Mithila region are renowned not only in India but throughout Asia. The Indian government has recently issued a postal stamp showing a Madhubani painting. Wall paintings are used to decorate homes or places of worship in rural Bihar. Following the seasonal cycle, women in rural areas apply a fresh coating of mud and cow dung to the walls of their mud houses. After applying ocher, they decorate the wall with colorful paintings of animals and trees. In urban areas too, it is common to make paintings near the spot of worship during *Dīpawālī* (a festival of light). The wall paintings are meant to evoke emotions and reflect desires in symbolic ways, using patterns from nature. Symbolic descriptions depict their lives and beliefs. With its long leaves and heavy fruit, plantain becomes an emblem of plenty and fertility. Peacock brings rain. Elephant is considered auspicious and indicates royalty. Snake worship is one of the oldest institutions in India and is practiced in Bihar. Sparrows are considered harbingers of harvest. Parrot is the symbol fertility. The story of *Padmavati* shows that another function of the parrot is matchmaking for potential brides and grooms. In Bihar, like elsewhere in India, trees and animals are worshipped. For example, women worship banyan trees for a happy and long married life and the plantain for fertility.

POPULARITY OF BIHAR FOLKLORE

Thus, we find that a range of folk traditions plays an important role in the traditional life of Bihar. It helps in building character, increasing strength of mind, expanding the intellect, and equipping a person to be independent. One can use tales, riddles, and proverbs to educate and discipline young children. Folklore has enough scope and potential for value development. It prepares children to be good human beings so that their potential can be harnessed for social cohesion. It acts as an alternative source of education, which increases children's moral, social, and spiritual value. The various branches of folk tradition which have flourished in Bihar have greatly enhanced the life of the people for many centuries.

The folktales of Bihar are popular not only in Bihar but in other regions also. In ancient times the institution of *kathavachak* (storyteller) involved moving from place to place to disseminate traditional stories and thus encourage understanding and right conduct. Moreover, Bihar hosts *melas* (massive gatherings for religious and trade purposes) which are visited by millions of people. The Hariharchetra *mela* of Sonepur, the Ramnavami *mela* at Sitamarhi, and the Pitripachh *mela* at Gaya are very old institutions where a large number of people periodically gather. The *melas*, which afford a context for storytelling, still attract visitors from Nepal, Tibet, Punjab, Bengal, Uttar Pradesh, Jharkhand, and elsewhere. The geographical position of Bihar has also helped in spreading stories. A marked intermingling of cultures has occurred through the languages of Hindi, Urdu, Mathili, and Bengali. For example, Vidyapati songs and poems are known all over **Assam**, Bengal, and **Orissa**. The Mathili language, in which the renowned fourteenth-century poet Vidyapati wrote, is known by Assamese, Bengalis, and Oriyas.

STUDIES OF BIHAR FOLKLORE

Studies of the folklore of Bihar began with the establishment of the Royal Asiatic Society of Bengal in 1874 by Sir William Jones, but, for the most part, most early work concerned the folklore of what is now Jharkhand. Grierson (1896) was probably the first scholar who recognized the importance of local folksongs and ballads. He published Bhojpuri and other Bihari folksongs with exhaustive notes and English translations in the *Journal of the Royal Asiatic Society* and the *Indian Antiquary*. Christian (1891) collected proverbs and dealt with the Magahi dialect.

During the last century several students conducted research on folklore in different Bihari dialects and published in Hindi. Upadhyay (1979) provides an overview of these studies. Chaudhury (1968) contains folktales of Bihar and Jharkhand in English. Sahay (2000) relates folktales to social customs, and Lourdusamy and Sahay (1996) analyze myths in relationship to rituals.

BIBLIOGRAPHY

Chaudhury, P. C. Roy. 1968. *Folk Tales of Bihar*. New Delhi: Sahitya Akademi.

Christian, J. 1891. *Bihar Properties*. London.

Grierson, G. A. 1896. *Some Bhoj'pūrī Folksongs*. London: Journal of the Royal Asiatic Society.

Lourdusamy, S., and Sarita Sahay. 1996. The Mythological Story of Gayasura and the Performance of Shraddha Yajna in Gaya: Beliefs and Behaviour Patterns of Hindus. In *Studies in Folklore and Popular Religion*, edited by Ulo Valk. Tartu: Department of Estonian and Comparative Folklore, University of Tartu. 197–203.

Sahay, Sarita. 2000. The Folk Tales of Bihar: An Anthropological Approach. *Folklore* 13: 93–102.

Upadhyay, V. S. 1979. Studies on Linguistics and Folklore in Bihar. In *Growth and Development of Anthropology in Bihar*, edited by L. P. Vidyarthi and Makhan Jha. New Delhi: Classical Publications. 105–125.

World Bank. 2005. *Bihar: Towards a Development Strategy*. World Bank Report. www.worldbank .org.in.

Sarita Sahay

GADDI

GEOGRAPHY AND HISTORY

Lying in the western Himalayan region, Himachal Pradesh constitutes one of the hill states of the Republic of **India**. Its territory, which stretches over an area of 55,673 square kilometers, is entirely mountainous with an altitude ranging from 350 meters to 7,000 meters. The physical landscape of the state is marked by four main mountain ranges paralleling each other in an east-west direction. Depending on the altitude, climatic conditions in the state vary from semi-tropical to semi-arctic with the vegetational distribution also corresponding to the elevation. Five main rivers—Satluj, Beas, Ravi, Chenab, and Yamuna—form the watershed of the state and play an important role in the economy and lifestyles of the people. The state has three distinct eco-cultural zones. The upper reaches of the state on the border with Tibet are inhabited by Lahaula and Kinnaura communities, who speak languages belonging to the Tibeto-Burman family and share ethnic affiliation with the people of western Tibet. Their main religion is Buddhism, and they practice pastoralism, horticulture, and animal husbandry. The middle belt of the state is inhabited by groups representing different religious faiths and customs. They belong to diverse ethnic groups such as Kol, Khas, and Kunidas. They speak languages belonging to the Indo-Aryan family and practice terrace cultivation, horticulture, and sheep and goat rearing. The sub-mountainous region is inhabited by immigrants from the plains of India. They follow Hinduism, Islam, Sikhism, Jainism, and other religions. The main economy here is settled agriculture. Wheat, corn, and wet rice are the main crops.

Many tribes populate the region. The Bhot, Kol, Khas, Kinnaura, Lahula, Pangwal, and Gaddi are all concentrated in the middle and higher areas of this mountainous terrain. The Gaddi community inhabiting the northwestern region in the valley of Chamba represents one of the main groups in the region. Scholars have variously described the Gaddis as semi-pastoral, semi-agriculturist, semi-nomadic, semi-sedentary, transhumant, migratory, and mainly agriculturist. Historical accounts

Gaddis herd their sheep along the barren landscape of Spiti en route to green pastures in the lower valleys. (© Lindsay Hebberd/CORBIS)

portray them as a distinct tribe that migrated to the ancient kingdom of Bharmpura in the eleventh century C.E. Other sources treat them as heterogenous groups of people who migrated to the western hills at different times and for different reasons. The present-day Gaddi community organizes itself on caste lines and comprises Brahmans, Rajputs, Khatris, Thakurs, and Ranas (high-ranking castes) and Sippis, Halis, and Reharas (low-ranking castes). The term "Gaddi" is also applied as a caste name under which fall Rajputs, Khatris, Thakur, and Ranas. Some scholars believe the Gaddis to have been present in Bharmour even earlier than seventh century B.C.E. on account of certain references available in Sanskrit texts and link them with groups like Gabdikas and Tristus, who are mentioned in these texts as the original inhabitants of the area.

British archeologists first drew attention to the Gaddis. Fascinated by the old wooden shrines of Chamba, Bharmour, and Lahaul, they surveyed the place, its people, and its architectural heritage. Their reports tried to reconstruct the historical past of the Chamba dynasty and its subject populace on the basis of a critical appraisal of available genealogical records of the Chamba rulers, copper plate and fountain stone inscriptions, and the architectural style and iconography of various shrines. Scholars such as J. Ph. Vogel (1933) and Herman Goetz (1955) tried to explore and explain the sociopolitical and cultural history of the state in light of political trends prevalent in the other parts of Northern India. Goetz did not perceive any direct link between the Gaddis and the Chamba dynasty or its ancestral kingdom Brahmpura. According to this account, Gaddis did not emerge on the scene untill about 1200 C.E. Goetz links them with the Gadhiya tribe of Panjab, who originally came from the Hindu Kush region. They entered Bharmour as mass invaders and established their enclave there at that time.

SHIVA FOLKLORE

Alongside this reconstructed history the Gaddis have a vast repertoire of oral narratives about their origins. Although these narratives do not contest the migration theory, the formation of their identity is seen as a process closely linked with the origin of the community from Bharmour. These narratives revolve around Shiva, the supreme deity of the Gaddis and the lord of the Dhauladhar. This entire terrain is called *shiv-bhumi* (the land of Shiva) and is held to be sacred. The most outstanding and symbolically relevant landmark is Mount Mani Mahesh, situated thirty-six kilometers to the east of Bharmour. It is believed to be the abode of Lord Shiva, who created it after his marriage to the goddess Parvati as the center of the universe. He has dwelt here ever since with his consort in eternal bliss, bestowing a constant benevolent gaze on his chosen devotees, the Gaddis.

According to one of the origin myths, Shiva once created a human being from a speck of dirt taken from his body while he was seated on his royal seat (*gaddi*) at Gadderan (another name for the Gaddi homeland). But this idol of clay was lifeless. Shiva sprinkled water over it and blew air into its nostrils. The idol came to life, and Shiva named him Gaddi. He bestowed upon him his own garb and way of life. Being a nomad and shepherd himself, he gave him a flock of sheep to tend, a woolen coat (*chola*) and belt (*dora*) for protection against chilly winds and snow storms, and a pair of grass shoes (*pulan*) to tread the difficult high passes of this rugged terrain.

The Gaddis believe that their land is situated on the yoni-basin of Shiva or *Jalhairi* (water reservoir) and is immortal. It remains intact during the Great Dissolution, the event that concludes each four-*yuga* cycle in Hindu cosmohistory. This yoni-basin of Shiva has sustained and nurtured the Gaddi ever since their creation and has provided them with a distinct territorial, cultural, and professional identity.

Shiva resides at Mani Mahesh for a period of six months. Then he migrates to *piyalpur* (the nether-world) in the winter months. Following their deity, the Gaddis also migrate during these months to the low-lying valleys of Kangra. Patterned after the life of Shiva, the seasonal migration undertaken by both agriculturists and shepherds demarcates the annual calendar of their activities into two. On *Janamashtami* (a festival celebrated in honor of Lord Krishna), the eighth day of the Hindu month *Bhadon* (August), Shiva hands over the reins of the mortal world to Vishnu, who took birth as Lord Krishna on this day. On *Shivratri* (a festival celebrated in Shiva's honor in the month of January), Shiva returns to Bharmour. The Gaddi shepherd regulates

Shiva and Parvati enthroned on the bull. Eastern Deccan, ca. 1780. (Victoria & Albert Museum, London/Art Resource, NY)

the movement of his flock according to these two dates. From *Janmasthami* onwards he and his flock begin to look toward *jandhar*, the low valley of Kangra, and on Shivratri he starts moving upward to Gadderan. This cyclical movement along a vertical axis finds its reflection in their more sedentary existence as well. In their structure and indoor lifestyle Gaddi houses symbolically replicate this movement.

A traditional Gaddi house is made of pine logs, wooden planks, mud, cowdung, and slate slabs. The house generally consists of three stories. The ground floor is called *obra* and is used for keeping the cattle. A staircase called *manjh* from within the *obra* leads to the first floor, called *mandeh*, which serves as the living room during the winter months. The second floor is called *chchpar* and is used as family quarters in summer. This is the most auspicious space inside the house, and family idols and icons are usually kept here in a cavity called *thola*. The central beam of the roof also rests in this cavity. Following the seasonal migratory pattern of Shiva and Gaddi shepherds, the entire household along with the hearth moves up to the second story in summer and comes down to the first floor during winter. The structure of the Gaddi house and the life within it coincide with a worldview that places the universe on a vertical pole along which are located all the three realms: the celestial, the terrestrial and the nether world. The up-and-down movement on this axis is cyclical and follows the natural rhythm.

PILGRIMAGE TO MANI MAHESH

Before migrating to the lower hills, the Gaddis make a pilgrimage to Mani Mahesh. This pilgrimage in many ways recreates and replicates the first visit by a human being to the holy abode of Shiva. It takes place in the month of August on *Radhaashtami*, which falls on the fifteenth day after *Janamashtami*. The main actors of the event are oracles from Sachuin, who belong to a low-ranking Sippi caste. Their traditional profession is weaving and tailoring. These oracles are called *shiv-chelas* and serve as the human medium of Shiva. A legend associated with their ancestor Trilochan Mahadev serves as the charter of the pilgrimage.

Trilochan was an ordinary Sippi lad who lived in Sachuin. One day when he had gone out to work, Shiva, dressed as an old man, visited his house and asked for two mounds of salt from his mother. The old lady had no salt. However, Shiva insisted that she should go and check her wooden chest. When she opened the chest, it was filled to the brim with salt. Shiva took two sacks full and then inquired if a porter was available. Trilochan soon returned home and agreed to carry the sacks. Following Shiva's steps, Trilochan reached the *dal* lake situated at the foothills of Mani Mahesh. Suddenly he found that the man for whom he was carrying salt had disappeared into the lake. Trilochan jumped into the lake. From here he was led to Shiva's abode, where he became Shiva's tailor. When Trilochan did not return home even after six months, his relatives assumed he was dead and arranged for his funeral feast. On the day of the feast, he returned bringing along with him a boon from Shiva for his kinsmen, who were henceforth to serve as mediums for Shiva. Trilochan later drowned himself at Kharamukh, the meeting point of Ravi and Buddhal. His body was discovered near Dharbala, a village not far from Kharamukh, in the form of a Shiva lingam. This lingam was installed in a temple constructed especially for Trilochan by the Chamba queen. The temple still stands at Dharbala, and a festival, *Trilochan jatar*, occurs here in his honor every year. People who are unable to go to Mani Mahesh come here to take a holy dip and pray at the temple.

The route that Trilochan took to the *dal* serves as the traditional pilgrimage route. This journey is repeated every year during the *Mani Mahesh jatar*. All those places where Trilochan sat with Shiva to rest serve today as stopovers enroute to Mani Mahesh. On a single plane, the legend of Trilochan stresses the unity of the religious, social, and political realms. In earlier times, the king was the main patron of the pilgrimage, and his royal priest at Lakshmi Narayan Temple in Chamba had direct financial control over the *jatar*. Through this pilgrimage the king symbolically mapped the boundaries of his territory. By establishing a link with the Gaddis as their direct descendent, he legitimized his control over the hinterland and its vast natural resources.

For the low-caste Sippi *chelas*, the pilgrimage serves as an empowering event transforming the low-ranking sippi from an ordinary human being into a divine entity.

This transformation is physical, psychological, social, and metaphysical. During the pilgrimage, the Sippi *chela* sheds his everyday clothing to don the traditional Gaddi garb of *chola*, *dora*, and the *chunji topi* (pointed cap)—whose top represents Shiva's Kailash, while the flaps stand for the inner chamber of Parvati, his consort. The belt represents the matted locks of Shiva. The *chola* stands for Shiva's body. Identification of *chela* with Shiva is complete. The *chela* thus dressed symbolically represents *shiv-bhumi*, the Gaddi land, by means of his cap. Through his coat and belt he stands one with the cosmic body of Shiva, and through his speech he represents the god's vital breath. In trance *chela* is said to be bestowed with the air and spirit of Shiva. When he speaks, Shiva speaks through him. Such an empowerment of the low-caste Sippi helps to suspend the social order momentarily. Many other local deities are involved in the Mani Mahesh *jatar*. *Chelas* coming from different areas of the region bring their family and village deities. These deities are given a holy dip in the *dal*, thus rejuvenating and reinvigorating them. This ritual rejuvenation and reinvigoration through the village deities extends to the village boundaries guarded by them. That the deities taking part come from all quarters of the region transfers this ritual reinvigoration to the state boundaries, thus placing the state under divine protection.

THE *SAVEEN* HEALING CHANT

Shiva mythology pervades almost all spheres of the Gaddi community life. The ultimate goal of the human soul is to become one with the cosmic realm of Shiva. After death the soul goes through various ordeals to reach Mani Mahesh. Here Shiva gives her a new body and sends her back to the world. During marriage rituals the Gaddi groom is ritually transformed into Shiva, and the marriage itself is perceived as *shiv-vivah* (the marriage of Shiva). The most important healing chant in Gaddi practices is a *canto* from the Gaddi sacred narrative *Saveen*, in which Shiva holds the first healing séance and reveals the secret powers of magical healing. The musical instrument that accompanies healing chants is believed to have been originally made from different limbs of Parvati's body. The Gaddi homeland repeats the Shiva-Parvati continuum. The *jalhairi*, or the lap of Parvati that constitutes the Gaddi land, has the central axis of its existence in Shiva, who is himself embedded in this *bhumi* (land) in the form of Mani Mahesh. Shiva lore pervades every realm of Gaddi social, ritual, and esthetic experience.

The most vibrant and popular narrative in the Gaddi oral epic repertoire, *Saveen*, is a humanized account of Shiva's life. It comprises several episodes taken from his life that reveal different aspects of the deity: hunter and destroyer of demons, lover and groom, healer and purifier. At another level *Saveen* establishes Shiva as the creator, sustainer, and destroyer of the universe. The most fascinating aspect of *Saveen* is its ability to adapt itself to different contexts and styles of rendering. Three distinct styles of singing *Saveen*, each associated with a specific caste and professional group, context, function, and musical instrument, are evident. One of these styles is called *ainchali*. It is sung mostly by Brahmans during *nuala*, a special worship organized in honor of Shiva, comprising a night vigil, chanting, singing, dancing, trance, sacrifice of a beast, and a communal feast.

The ceremony is held at the time of entering a new house, marriage, and the birth of a male child. The singers of *ainchali* are called *bande*. At the time of *nuala*, it is mandatory to have four performers: one lead and three supporting singers. Two *dholkis* (small percussion drums) and a *dhanthal* (a brass plate put atop a pot containing water that is gently tapped with a stick to produce rhythmic sounds) are the essential musical instruments. The singing is accompanied by a dance called *dandaras*. A group of male dancers moves in a circle turning their bodies halfway with one arm above the head. This dance begins with a single slow beat but can become very vigorous as it progresses. Besides the singers and dancers, the performance requires a *yogi* (ascetic) who witnesses the whole ceremony silently. A group of female singers is also required to provide much needed rest to the bards during their night-long performance. These women singers are ordinary invitees to the ceremony and have no claim to being bards or professional singers. Whenever the bards stop to smoke or drink tea, the female guests begin to sing hymns, called *ainchali*, to Shiva or other deities. The stage for the performance is set by cleaning one of the corners of an east facing wall and plastering it with cowdung. A ritual representation of the earth, a *mandala*, is drawn upon it. The drawing is in the form of a square containing thirty-two smaller squares. In the center of the square is a mound of wheat flour. This represents Shiva's Kailash. Nine woolen threads with flowers are hung down from the ceiling over the mound. These threads represent the nine streams of the celestial river, the Ganga. Roasted wheat cakes (*babru*) and fried doughnuts are placed in the square, and various deities of the Hindu pantheon along with local Gaddi deities are established in these squares. The *mandala* is a consecrated model of the universe. After the ritual sacrifice of a ram, *bandas* take their seat and begin to sing. One of the four *cantos* of *Saveen* is chosen for the night, either by the singer himself or at the request of the guests and the host.

Gardreen, the last *canto* of *Saveen*, is sung during the healing séance called *nalli*. The singers of *gardreen* are called *gardi* and belong to the low-ranking caste of Halis. Their musical instrument (*dhuntaru* or *dopatra*) is a one-string instrument with two gourds and represents Parvati's body. This rendering of the epic is different from that of the *bandas* not only at the level of style but also in the usage to which it is put. The hearing of *gardreen* from a *gardi* on *dopatra* is enough to expel the evil influence of sorcery from somebody. The patient is completely covered and made to sit with hands and feet dipped in water in front of the healer, who intersperses his rendering of *gardreen* with several other healing chants.

Another style of rendering *saveen* is called *musade*. *Saveen* here becomes *shi-katha* (a story in verse and prose). The singers of *shi-katha* are called *ghurai*, and the instruments they use are *rubana* (a stringed instrument) and *khanjari* (a percussion instrument). It is mostly performed at the time of *chaubarkhi*—four years after the death of a person, when he ceases to be a *prêt* (ghost) and becomes *pitr* (ancestor).

FESTIVALS AND FAIRS

Various fairs and festivals, called *jatars*, are held all over Bharmour in honor of Shiva and other village deities. Each village annually celebrates its own *jatar* for its tutelary deity. Hundreds of gods, goddesses, and spirits abound in the Gaddi religious pantheon. Prominent among these are village deities such as the goddesses Bharmani, Baniwali, Shiv-shakti, Lakhna, Chaunda, and Marali; serpent deities like Kelang Digu and Budd Bihari; and numerous deities of high passes and mountain ridges, simply called *jot ki devi* or *devata* (goddess or gods of the high passes). Offerings of songs, dances, and sacrificial beasts are made to these deities during *jatars*. Some of the most famous *jatars* cut across village boundaries and attract people from all parts of the *tehsil*. The Bharmour *jatar* lasts six days and occurs in the famous temple complex of *chaurasi* in the month of August. A big annual market also takes place during the *jatar*, when traders from neighboring states sell their wares. The *jatar* is a moment of heightened religious, social, and commercial activity and is marked by considerable gaiety and fun. At night men and women dressed in traditional costumes and jewelry perform *dandaras* and *dangi* (female dance) in honor of the deity of the day. Chattrari *jatar* is another famous and elaborate *jatar* that lasts three days and is celebrated in Chattrari for the goddess Shiv-shakti, Shiva's consort. This *jatar* is famous for *dandaras* and a masked dance called *khappar buddhe*, which depict the goddess's battle with the evil and sterile forces of nature. These *jatars*, on one level, celebrate the periodic renewal of the cosmos and victory of life over death, and on another they attempt to present Gaddi identity as a cohesive whole, internal conflicts and differentiations notwithstanding. This is achieved through an enactment of Gaddi worldview in a public space, which is presented as all-inclusive. Communal participation generates metaphors and symbols that enable the community to experience itself as a bounded entity, united by common origins, territorial links, cultural behavior, and mythological bonds.

Besides *jatars*, Gaddi celebrate many other festivals such as seasonal and agricultural festivals. The festival of *basoa* celebrates the Gaddi New Year and lasts one whole month, beginning on the first solar day of the Gaddi month *Chaitar* (March) and culminating on 13 April. The festival is marked by eating *pindri* (a special dish prepared with a leafy plant called *kodra* and wheat flour) and singing the *basoa* song by village women and girls every evening. The song poignantly describes the grief of a married daughter who is stopped by her mother-in-law from visiting her parental home during the festival; she commits suicide in the end. *Basoa* also marks the beginning of the Gaddi agricultural cycle and is associated with the sowing of wheat. Another important festival is that of *hairi*. It is celebrated at the end of the Gaddi agricultural cycle in the month of October and is connected to the harvesting of maize. The sickle is put to the maize for harvesting only after the first few cobs have been offered to the village deity and ancestors.

The focus here on folklore associated with Shiva reflects the Gaddis' attempt to use this lore to define their identity at both mundane and cosmic levels. This lore stresses the unity of the physical, religious, social, and political realms. It inscribes itself on the physical landscape and on the human body. It penetrates the realms of music, dance, and musical instruments. It becomes all-pervasive, establishing the interdependence of all realms of existence, borrowing its metaphors from the landscape and movement along its vertical axis.

BIBLIOGRAPHY

Agrawala, V. S. 1968. *India as Known to Panini*. Varanasi: Prithivi Prakashan.

Ahluwalia, M. S. 1988. *History of Himachal Pradesh*. Delhi: Intellectual Publishing House.

Babulkar, M. 1970. *Paschimi Pahari ki Up-Boli ka Lok Sahitya aur Kala*. Allahabad: Bharat Bandhu Prakashan.

Bawa, Seema. 1998. *Religion and Art of the Chamba Valley*. Delhi: Agam Kala Prakashan.

Bhasin, Veena. 1988. *Himalyan Ecology, Transhumance and Social Organization: Gaddis of Himachal Pradesh*. Delhi: Kamla Raj Prakashan.

Charak, S. S. 1979. *History and Culture of the Himalayan State*, Vol. III. New Delhi: Light and Life Publishers.

Dracott, A. E. 1992. *Folktales from the Himalayas*. Gurgoan: Vintage Books.

Goetz, H. 1955. *The Early Wooden Temples of Chamba*. Leiden: E. J. Brill.

Goverdhan Singh, Mian. 1983. *Art and Architecture of Himachal Pradesh*. Delhi: D. K. Publishers.

———. 1992. *Festivals, Fairs and Customs of Himachal Pradesh*. New Delhi: Indus.

Handa, O. 1988. *Pashchami Himalay ki Lok Kalain*. Delhi: Indus.

Jasta, Hariram. 1986. *Himachal Ki Lok-Sanskriti*. Delhi: Sangmarg Prakashan.

Jerath, Ashok. 1995. *The Splendour of Himalayan Art and Cutlure*. New Delhi: Indus.

Kapur, B. L. 2001. *History and Heritage of the Western Himalayas*. Delhi: Agam Kala Prakashan.

Kaushal, Molly. 2001a. Cultural Concepts of Space and Time. In *The Nature of Man and Culture: Alternative Paradigms in Anthropology*, edited by B. N. Saraswati. New Delhi: Indira Gandhi National Centre for the Arts and Aryan Book International. 75–83.

———. 2001b. Diving the Landscape—the Gaddi and His Land. In *The Human Landscape*, edited by Geeti Sen and Ashis Banerjee. New Delhi: Orient Longman, India International Centre. 31–40.

———. 2001c. Saveen-Singers and Performance Context. In *Chanted Narratives: The Living 'Katha-Vachana' Tradition*, edited by Molly Kaushal. New Delhi: Indira Gandhi National Centre for the Arts, D. K. Printworld. 37–41.

———. 2002. The Theatre of the Self: Ritual Performances Among the Gaddis. *Indian Horizons* 49.3–4: 122–140.

———. 2004. From Mythic to Political Identity—Folk Festivals and Cultural Sub-texts. In *Folklore, Public Sphere and Civil Society*, edited by M. D. Muthukumarswamy and Molly Kaushal. Delhi and Chennai: IGNCA and NFSC. 186–196.

Negi, S. S. 1993. *Himachal Pradesh: The Land and People*. Delhi: Indus.

Newell, W. H. 1967. *The Scheduled Castes and Tribes of Bharmour Tehsil of Chamba District*. Simla: Government of India Press.

Ohri, V. C., ed. 1980. *Himachal Art and Archaeology*. Shimla: Department of Languages and Culture.

———. 1989. *A Western Himalayan Kingdom: History and Culture of the Chamba State*. New Delhi: Books and Books.

Parry, Jonathan P. 1979. *Caste and Kinship in Kangra*. London: Routledge and Kegan Paul.

Phillimore, Peter R. 1982. Marriage and Social Organization Among Pastoralists of the "Dholadhar." Diss., University of Durham.

Postel, M., A. Neven, and K. Mankodi.1989. *Antiquities of Himachal Pradesh*. Bombay: Pharmaceuticals Ltd.

Punjab State Gazetters. 1904. Chamba State, 22.A.

Randhawa, M. S. 1970. *Kangra: Kala, Desh aur Geet*. New Delhi: Sahitaya Academy.

Roy, Chaudhury. 1981. *Temples and Legends of Himachal Pradesh*. Bombay: Bhartiya Vidya Bhawan.

Saberwal, Vasant K. 1999. *Pastoral Politics: Shepherds, Bureaucrats and Conservation in Western Himalayas*. Delhi: Oxford University Press.

Shashi, S. S. 1977. *The Gaddi Tribe of Himachal Pradesh*. Delhi: Sterling Publishers.

Singh, K. S., ed. 1996. *Himachal Pradesh: People of India*, Vol. XXIV. Delhi: Anthropological Survey of India, Manohar.

Thakur, M. R. 1981. *Himachal Ke Lok Natya aur Lokaanuranjan*. Delhi: Himachal Pustak Bhandar.

———. 1996. *Pahari Sanskriti Manjusha*. Delhi: Reliance.

———. 1997. *Myth, Ritual and Beliefs in Himachal Pradesh*. New Delhi: Indus.

Thakur, S.S.S. 1971. *Himachal Lok Lehri*. Bilaspur: Lok Madhuri Prakashan.

Vogel, J. Ph., and J. Hatchinson. 1933. *History of the Panjab Hill States*, Vol. I. Lahore: Government Printing Press.

Vyathiti, G. S. 1961. *A Village Survey: Bharmaur, The Census of India, 1961*, Vol. XX, Part VI, No. II. Shimla: Superintendent of Census Operations, Himachal Pradesh.

———. 1991. *Folklore of Himachal Pradesh*. New Delhi: National Book Trust.

Molly Kaushal

HARYANA

GEOGRAPHY AND HISTORY

On 1 November 1966, the modern Indian state of Haryana was carved out of an east Punjab area comprising the hilly tracts now known as Himachal Pradesh. The British had formed an undivided Punjab as a single administrative unit, but prior to that the Haryana area had consisted of a number of principalities ruled by chieftains. A land-locked state, it is surrounded by **Uttar Pradesh** to the east, Delhi and Rajasthan to the southwest and south, Punjab to the north, and Himachal Pradesh to the northeast. Haryana shares its folklore, sociocultural fabric, and **worldview** with its neighbors, owing not only to geographical proximity but also to large-scale migrations from these provinces to Haryana. The state is a vast stretch of flat plains with a climate like that of the north Indian plains: hot summers from April to October, followed by a short winter from November to February, then the spring season in March and the monsoons from June/July to August/September.

The natives are mostly Hindus, but Jains, Muslims, and Sikhs also live in Haryana. Members of all the four Hindu castes (Brahmins, Kshatriyas, Vaishyas, and Shudras) live in relative harmony with other communities. Agriculture is the economic mainstay of Haryana, followed by cattle breeding and dairy products. The well-nourished cattle of Haryana are famous, and the fondness among the natives for milk and milk products is proverbial. They depend upon the ayurvedic system of medicine, based upon herbs, medicinal plants, and concoctions. At times they resort to black magic and tantric medicine for treatment. The villages are controlled by local *panchayats*, a council of five village elders who settle all disputes. The villages are not architecturally distinctive; peasants live in mud huts, while landed gentry have larger brick houses.

Haryana has the largest number of sites pertaining to the *Mahābhārata* epic, including Kurukshetra, where the Pandavas and Kauravas, descendants of its founder Kuru, fought the Great War in 3138 B.C.E. The historical authenticity of the war and its date—"more than 5200 years ago"—are still enshrined in local tradition. Lord

Krishna imparted the timeless message of the *Bhagavadgita* to Arjuna at Jyotisar, one of the numerous sacred ponds in Kurukshetra, where countless pilgrims come to bathe at solar and lunar eclipses. Sacred sites abound around Kurukshetra: Pehowa (Prithudak), Kaithal (Kapisthali), and Kalayat (Kapilmuni), for example. Karnal was the capital of Raja Karna, eldest of the Pandava brothers who fought on the side of the Kauravas. Gurgaon or Gurugram was the site of Dronacharya's hermitage, where he trained the Pandavas and Kauravas in archery and warfare. Pinjaur or Panchpura had also been founded by the five Pandava brothers who, according to the folklore, erected the stepwell near the Bhima Devi temple.

Folklore provides insight into Haryana's ancient history. Sthanvishvar, now Thanesar near Kurukshetra, was the capital city of Harshavardhan (606–647 C.E.), during whose reign the Chinese Buddhist pilgrim Hsuan-tsang visited **India**. Raja Surajpal of the Tomar dynasty (seventh to eleventh century C.E.) built the Surajkund on the outskirts of Delhi. Rulers of this dynasty venerated the sun god and erected the temple whose ruins still stand near the pond. The stepped-stone embankment of the pond collected rain water reputed to possess miraculous healing powers. The three historical battles of Panipat which paved the way for the establishment of Mughal rule were fought here in 1526, 1556, and 1761.

Haryana folklore primarily provides education and recreation for the rural folk of this state. The village well, water pond, or tank is the hub of women's social life. Generally they go to fetch water in groups, singing songs all the way. At the well they meet to gossip, exchange views and news, and share their joys and sorrows. At home the spinning wheel and grinding stone play a pivotal role in their lives, as evidenced by numerous folksongs. Rural men get together in the evenings after a day's toil under a tree or in a large sitting room (*baithak*) in the local guest house (*chaupal*) and discuss matters ranging from their daily lives and problems to local events. The hubbub (*hukka*) symbol of fraternity and togetherness is shared by everyone. If anyone is expelled from the society or group, the popular saying is "*Uska hukka pani band kar diya*"—meaning that he will no longer be allowed to share their *hukka*.

MYTHS, LEGENDS, AND HISTORICAL NARRATIVES

In folklore prose narratives occupy a significant position, for they are easy to transmit in a regional dialect. Popular myths and legends revolve around the prominent deities of the Hindu pantheon, particularly Brahma, Vishnu, Shiva, Durga, and Ganesh. Temples provide the venue for performances of devotional tales and chants. They are also centers for religious festivals. Shivaratri is an important festival in February, celebrated to commemorate the Great God's marriage to Parvati. All Hindu temples are ornately decorated, fasts are observed by all, and at an appointed hour a priest narrates stories to those gathered around. Similarly, on Lord Rama's birthday (*Ramnaumi*) in April and *Krishna Janamashtami* in August, stories from their lives are recounted. On Krishna's birthday, the Raslila troupes arrive from Vrindavan to perform dances. The Navratra festival that is celebrated twice in a year—in April and October—has a dual significance in the worship of Durga in her nine forms as well as in the reenactment of episodes from Lord Rama's life. The celebrations culminate in the burning of the effigies of Ravana by Rama on the Dussehra day. The Shitala Mata temple at Gurgaon is the hub of the Navaratra celebrations. Although a folk deity, Shitala Mata is elevated to Durga's status and worshipped as such. A grand fair is organized around the temple and attended by the devout from throughout Haryana. Singing devotional songs, women throng the temple in all their finery.

Throughout Haryana, Hindus and Muslims venerate the cult of Gugga Chauhan—a Rajput warrior of Bagar in Bikaner (Rajasthan), who fought many battles against the Muslims in the twelfth century. Hindus address him as Gugga Bir (the Brave), but for Muslims, he is Gugga Pir (saint). It may seem strange that Muslims should venerate the warrior who fought against them, but the stories recall that Gugga converted to Islam at the last moment due to Mother Earth's refusal to accept his dead body if he were a Hindu. Both the Hindus and Muslims believe in Gugga's miraculous powers of curing snakebite. His temples are square plinth structures with a vertical slab featuring a snake alongside the equestrian figure of Gugga. The folkloric explanation offered for Gugga's snake form is the curse cast upon him by his mother Bachhal for killing his cousins. *Gugga-naumi* is celebrated each August and features a procession of Muslims carrying standards.

No less popular are the historical narratives of the warriors Alha-Udal, Jaimal Fatta, Bhura Badal, and Vir Jawahar Mal, who laid down their lives for the honor of their beautiful Queen Rani Padmini. Rajasthani puppeteers (*kathputli*) reenact the sagas to the accompaniment of a female singer narrating the story.

Kissas (tales) are an important aspect of regional folklore and range from the historical tales of Raja Risalu and Dhruv to the legends of famous lovers such as Heer-Ranjha, Laila-Majnun, and Dhola-Maru of Rajasthan. Wandering minstrels from Rajasthan sing ballads. Also popular are narratives of the heroic feats of Amar Singh Rathore and others like him as well as a tale narrated on the *Nag-panchami* (snake worship) day about a wife's lament for her husband's death due to snakebite. The *kissa morchhat* or *devrani-jethani* is about the recovery from a disease suffered by two sisters-in-law, the miracle having been performed by a wandering dog. The *kissa tota-maina* (parrot and starling), extremely popular among men all over the state, deals with the sexual weaknesses of immoral women who ensnare men for their own gratification.

Ballad singers with their typical musical instruments.

SONGS, MUSIC, AND DANCE

Folksongs reflect the peasant lifestyle. One can also hear the tinkling of the bells hanging from the neck of the cattle returning home at dusk, visualize green fields aglow with golden wheat and yellow mustard flowers, and react to emotional outbursts of yearnings for love by young married couples separated from one another. Songs record villagers' joys and sorrows, achievements and losses, sociocultural life, hopes and aspirations. All arenas of activity find expression in them.

Folksongs also offer insight into rural women's world: lullabies sung by mothers or grandmothers to their offspring; songs sung on the birth of a son (*holar*); a young girl's romantic longings before marriage, initial inhibitions, usual apprehensions, emotional outbursts, and then the complaints of a young wife overburdened with household chores. Rural women are repositories of folklore, preserved in the form of songs for all occasions, picked up from elderly women in the family, and passed on to the next generation.

Haryana is well known for its *Mewati gharana* (school) of vocal singing, a folk version of the *Jaipur gharana*. The modes of classical singing known as *ragas* are well known and include the *raga malhar*, sung during the rainy season. Instruments to accompany such songs include the *sarangi* (akin to violin), *ektara* (single-stringed instrument), snake-charmer's pipe (*been*) shaped like a coiled serpent, *narasingha* ("S"-shaped instrument for weddings), *bansuri* (flute), *dhol* (drums), cymbals, *daph* (flat drum), and *dholki* (double-sides drum), which is usually played by women.

Dhamal dancers playing a flat drum (*daph*).

The cycle of seasons gives rise to merriment that finds expression in these songs. Although the spring festival (*basant panchami*) takes place in early February—usually on the coldest day of winter season—everyone dresses up in yellow garments, yellow being the color of prosperity, happiness, and fertility.

The spring season, properly speaking, falls in the month of March, when rural folk are free from their harvest toils. This coincides with the festival of colors, *Holi* or *phag*. Nature produces flowers of a wide array of colors. Men and women, young and old, get together to sing and dance, splash colored water on one another, and rejoice. The Ahir community performs the *dhamal* dance on moonlit nights in this month in the villages of Gurgaon, Mahendragarh, and Rohtak districts. In the Bangar tract, young girls perform the *loor* dance at this

Young women performing a *loor* dance.

time of year. The *jhumar* is similar to the *gidda* dance of Punjab, performed only by women. The *jhumar* derives its name from the forehead ornament worn by women. Anyone can perform the *ghumar*, another dance form, at any time, the aim being to rejoice at the slightest opportunity.

FESTIVALS AND CELEBRATIONS

According to the Hindu calendar, the New Year begins on 13 April, the first day of month of Vaishakh, when Hindus bathe in the sacred rivers Yamuna and Ganga and celebrate the Baisakhi festival by singing and dancing. The Navaratra celebrations also fall in this month, and housewives paint the figure of the rural goddess Sanjhi on the mud walls of their homes for worship for nine days.

The Gangaur festival also occurs in April. All single women fast, propitiate the painted clay images of Shiva and Parvati (*Gangaur*) for five days, and pray for an ideal husband. The Gangaur tale is narrated by Brahman women in the homes, and on the last day of the festival, the images are gaily decorated and taken out in a procession for immersion in the local ponds. Women sing songs and dance all the way to this ceremony. This is a simpler version of a festival which is celebrated with great fanfare in its home state Rajasthan.

The month of Savan (*Skt. Shravan*) during the rainy season (July and August) holds pride of place among the seasons. It brings the much-needed relief from the torrid heat of the summer sun. The sky is overcast with dark rumbling clouds, and cool breezes encourage women to leave hearths and homes and enjoy themselves in the outdoors. They join relatives and friends to sing and dance with abandon, perched atop their swings. They dress up in their best clothes and ornaments and paint their hands with henna and their feet with lac dye. For three days, they celebrate the *haritalika teej* festival, singing devotional songs to invoke the blessings of Shiva and Parvati for happy married life. Swings hang from all the trees. Newly married women return to their parental home to celebrate this festival. They deck themselves with white flowers and ornaments, their jingling bangles and anklets providing accompaniment to their merry songs and dances.

In October, the *karva chauth* fast is observed by all married women to encourage their husbands' longevity. The goddess Hoi, Ahoi, or Syahu Mata is propitiated a week before Diwali for the welfare of their offspring. Both occasions offer rural women an opportunity to paint the walls of their mud houses for worship. Symbolic, auspicious designs are drawn with rice, and colored powders at the thresholds of homes welcome Lakshmī, the Hindu goddess of wealth. The goddess's blessings are invoked by singing hymns in her honor. On 13 January, *lohri* is celebrated by lighting bonfires in open spaces or outside homes. Fire gives relief from chilly winters. People sit around the bonfire and chant a folksong based on a historical event that happened in Lahore (now in Pakistan). A young beautiful maiden from a poverty-stricken family was being forcibly sent to the Muslim governor's harem at her uncle's instance, but this was foiled by an intermediary who got her married off to a suitable young man and composed the song on the occasion of their wedding. This festival coincides with *Makar Sankranti*, an important Hindu festival.

Women belonging to the grooms' families compose and sing obscene (*khoria*) songs

A middle-aged couple performing a *svang* or *sang* (folk play) in an open-air theater.

at weddings. After the departure of the marriage party with the groom, women remain at home, for they are not allowed to join in. They make the most of their freedom by singing lascivious songs and enacting different positions for sexual intercourse.

DRAMA

Since antiquity, people in Haryana have entertained themselves with improvisational dramas. The actors (all men) perform in open spaces without props or makeup. The folk dramas are known by such terms as *svang* or *sang*, *nautanki*, and *bhagat*. Initially poetic versions of Hindu myths and legends were enacted in local dialects to the accompaniment of musical instruments. In the nineteenth century non-religious themes, many inspired by day-to-day life, were introduced. Some, for instance, explore the husband-wife relationship, exhorting husbands to practice loyalty and fidelity. The role of *bhats* or *bhands* (minstrels), *behrupiyas* (men assuming diverse disguises to make audiences laugh), acrobats, and eunuchs in preserving traditional folk dramatic forms cannot be overlooked.

Mud-wall painting from a bridal chamber.

ARTS AND CRAFTS

In rural areas, painting the mud walls of homes is common on festive occasions. Before weddings, the bridal chamber (*devghar*) is painted with suggestive, symbolic paintings designed to educate the bride and groom about their new life. Floor decorations are very common. Known as *chowk-poorna*, these auspicious symbols are painted by housewives to ward off evil and usher in prosperity. Wall paintings with religious themes decorate the *chaupals* (village guest houses). No carved stone reliefs or free-standing statues in folk style are seen, not even in terracotta, but potters paint and shape clay toys for sale at rural fairs.

Crafts practiced in the countryside include embroidered *phulkaris* (veils), spinning and weaving, attractively designed *Punja durries* (floor spreads), pottery, stuffed toys, carpentry, iron lamps, silver and gold ornaments, and basketry. The tradition of draping veils is prevalent throughout Haryana, but embroidering black cotton fabrics with patterns drawn from rural life is confined to the women from the Jat community, concentrated in and around Rohtak. Hand-held fans with lacquered wooden handles are decorated with beads and small mirrors. Beads are also used for making *toranas*, decoration pieces hung on the main entrances of homes to welcome the guests.

Women are adept at spinning and weaving fabrics for their personal and family use. They make stuffed toys such as horses, elephants, and birds for sale at fairs. Stuffed birds, tied one on top of another along a string, are hung at the main entrances to dwelling houses to ward off the evil eye. Women distribute sets of colorful paper birds with small bells attached at the main door as wedding decorations.

Women's love for ornaments is proverbial, and a married woman must overload herself with ornaments from head to toe. These can be removed only when her husband dies. Young, unmarried girls are also fond of jewelry, especially bangles, necklaces, earrings, nose-rings, toe-rings, and light anklets (*pazeb*). The jingling sound produced by small bells attached to their ornaments forms the theme of many folksongs.

A variety of material folk culture forms may be glimpsed at local fairs. Though plastic dolls for girls are now available, local potters still make painted clay dolls and doll houses that are intended to train a girl in household chores. With the house come utensils made of clay, metal, or painted wood. Both decorative and practical baskets are available. Their designs tend

A Haryana woman loaded with silver jewelry.

to be simple, unostentatious, geometrical patterns. Despite large-scale electrification, one may find a few blacksmiths still making iron lamps as well as agricultural tools not yet replaced by modern machinery. And though the young often prefer machine-made shoes, many men and women still wear traditionally made leather shoes.

CHALLENGES OF THE MODERN WORLD

In the present age of **globalization**, urbanization, and industrialization, changes are sweeping through the entire state, as everywhere else in the Indian subcontinent. Much of the folk culture is fading amidst the onslaught of Western culture and the pressure by the Indian government to be more competitive in the global market. Though older people in Haryana cling to their lifestyle, the generation growing up now is adopting more and more of the modern ethos, which is evident not only in their preference for cinema and television instead of traditional theater but also in their quest for higher education and greater geographical mobility, a trend threatening to undermine much of local culture. In particular, younger housewives, desiring economic independence, devote little time to traditional arts and crafts. Modern, brick structures are replacing mud houses, while aluminum and plastic utensils are replacing the traditional brass in many homes. However, religious fervor is still very strong. The Raslila performances, Ramlila stage plays and processions, and several traditional festivals—particular Shivaratri, Holī, Ram-navami, Dussehra, and Diwali—are celebrated with traditional respect and enthusiasm, although nowadays one might hear recorded songs emanating from a temple's loudspeakers.

The natives of Haryana, like their counterparts in other Indian provinces, are standing at a crossroads midway between traditional folk culture and modernism. The hold of tradition is still very strong, and the people are unlikely to turn their back on everything traditional. Religious fairs and festivals will continue to be celebrated, and traditional fasts will continue to be observed by women, who will not forget their folk songs and dances. In fact, women have been and will continue to be the custodians of folklore. The latest trend is the formation of the non-governmental organizations (NGOs) that are reviving age-old traditional artistic forms, cultural expressions, and folklore.

STUDIES OF HARYANA FOLKLORE

Two types of books are available on Haryana folklore: one containing texts of folksongs, folktales, and other genres; the other providing commentary on various folk traditions. Included in the first category are volumes by Sharda (1970) and B. Singh (1981) on folksongs and Prabhakar (1984), which covers a range of genres, especially folktales and proverbs. Commentaries on the folklore of Haryana include Yadav (1960), a comprehensive study which suggests directions for future research; Sharma (1983), which treats folk dance; V. Singh (1988), a critical analysis of folk theater; G. Singh (1989), a study of folksongs and their cultural significance; and Sharma (1990), which is about love and devotional poetry by focusing on the contributions of the bard Lakhami Chand.

BIBLIOGRAPHY

Prabhakar, Devi Shankar. 1984. *Haryana: Lok Kathayen tatha Kahavatein*. Delhi: Lakshmi Pustak Sadan.

Sharda, Sadhu Ram. 1970. *Haryana ke Lokgeet*. Panchkula: Haryana Sahitya Academy.

Sharma, Krishna Chander. 1990. *The Luminous Bard of Haryana Lakhami Chand*. New Delhi: Siddharth Publications.

Sharma, Purna Chand. 1983. *Haryana ki Lokdharmi Natya Parampara*. Chandigarh: Haryana Sahitya Academy.

Singh, Bhim. 1981. *Haryana ke Lokgeet*. New Delhi: Arya Book Depot.

Singh, Gunpal. 1989. *Haryana ke Lokgeeton ka Sanskritik Adhyana*. Chandigarh: Haryana Sahitya Academy.

Singh, Vijayendra. 1988. *Haryana ke Saangon mein Saundarya Nirupan*. Chandigarh: Haryana Sahitya Academy.

Yadav, Shankar Lal. 1960. *Haryana Pradesh ka Lok Sahitya*. Allahabad: Deep Prakashan.

Subhasini Aryan

HIMACHAL PRADESH. *See Gaddi*

KARNATAKA

GEOGRAPHY AND HISTORY

One of the southern states of the Republic of **India**, Karnataka, with a population of over 50 million people, is the ninth largest state in the Indian union. Its capital is

Bangalore. Under British rule and even after independence up until 1973, the region was called Mysore. In the context of music, the term "Karnataka" also had been used to denote a major style of classical South Indian music.

In terms of both physical geography and indigenously recognized cultural areas, Karnataka consists of three zones. Furthest west, the narrow coastal belt on the Arabian Sea, green and lush through most of the year, is noted for its paddy fields, coconut and betel nut gardens, and the thick forests along its eastern border at the foot of the Western Ghats. The mountain wall of the Western Ghats that rises steeply from this coastal belt maintains an effective separation between Tulu-speaking culture on the coast and the Kannada-speaking culture to the east. From its 1,800-meter crest, this mountainous area is the second zone, sloping gradually toward the plain forty to fifty miles to the east. At the southern end of the mountainous region lie the high valleys of Coorg, the Kodagu-speaking area. The broad plane between the Western and Eastern Ghats delineates the cultural regions of its major language, Kannada, divided into Northern and Southern parts by the Tungabhadra River. Northern Karnataka had long been ruled by Muslim dynasties and, until India's independence and for a short time afterwards, was included in the independent princely state of the Nizam of Hyderabad. Southern Karnataka, held by Hindu Maharajas, was called Mysore, after its capital city.

Besides physical geography, language and culture are important identifying factors and are nearly synonymous in terms of broadly differentiating Karnataka's folk cultures and sorting out different forms of folk traditions. The state's dominant language, Kannada, covers a much larger territory, has possessed its own script for over a thousand years, and is somewhat more diversified than either of the other two, Tulu and Kodagu. Along the western coastal belt, Tulu language and culture has a number of distinctive forms of public ritual and sung narrative traditions. Kodagu language and culture in the southern Malnad also has distinctive ritual and song traditions, but being a nearly mono-caste region, similar to isolated tribal areas, these traditions could equally be regarded as caste (rather than language) characteristics. Each of the three languages belongs to the Dravidian language family.

Throughout much of its 2,000-year history Karnataka consisted of a shifting mosaic of different indigenous kingdoms and at times experienced considerable influence from the neighboring Tamil-speaking region to the south and the Marathi-speaking region to the north. However, the Kannada language remained a unifying cultural force, supporting a strong classical literary tradition. The region and its arts and language flourished from the fourteenth to the seventeenth centuries as the center of the wealthy and powerful Vijayanagara Empire, which controlled much of southern India. Kannada, the state language, still provides the defining characteristics of the region. Economically and culturally, though, modern Karnataka, like most other states of India, is sharply divided between its rural, traditionally agriculturally based society and its modern urban, commercially based one.

SOCIAL STRUCTURE, RELIGIOUS BELIEFS, AND FOLKLORE

As elsewhere in India, caste dominates especially the rural social structure. Each caste tends to maintain and preserve its traditional identity, relevant traditional practices, and the range and type of relations its members are allowed with other castes, including occupational duties, commensality, and marriage choice. The overall result is that a caste tends somewhat to resemble what is regarded as an ethnic group elsewhere in the world, with many castes maintaining their own folk customs. This results in a variety of folk practices within a shared set of general patterns.

Religion is by far the most important generator of rural folk tradition in India. Historically, Karnataka has experienced the accumulated influences of all of the subcontinent's major religious and intellectual developments: Buddhism and Jainism from at least the second century B.C.E.; Islam from directly from across the Arabian Sea as early as the eighth and ninth centuries and overland from **Persia** after the twelfth century; and Christianity from coastal contacts with the Middle East as early as the fourth century and with European countries from the fifteenth century. Its baseline Hindu culture has been in line with virtually all major developments, even being home to some of its most widespread and most influential movements. Vaishnavite (devotees of the god Vishnu) sects have developed regional variants of drama forms, while Shaivite (devotees of the god Shiva) sects have been particularly prolific in producing epic-length narrative song traditions.

In the Kannada-speaking region a number of the folk religious traditions independently regard their god as an incarnation of the god Shiva. Maleya Mādēśwara, "Lord of the Mountain," is believed by his followers to have been an incarnation of Iśvara (Shiva). An annual pilgrimage to a temple at Mādēśwara Beṭṭa draws devotees from throughout Karnataka and the adjacent areas of Tamil Nadu. The Lord's devotees, called *dēvara guḍḍalu*, come mainly from shepherds (*kuruba*), washermen (*maḍiwāḷa*), hunters (*bēḍa*), and peasants (*vakkaligas*). The narrative song tradition describing his deeds is one of the longest oral epic traditions in the Kannada language. Unlike India's many warrior-hero epics, this one describes the miracles the saint performed as he forced people to become his followers and spread the worship of Shiva.

A martial-cum-ritual dance form, called *kamsāle*, a term derived from the Sanskrit word *kamsatālya*, meaning a bronze cymbal, is also associated with the Maleya Mādēśwara cult. *Kamsāle* is a group dance, similar to stick-dances (*kōlāta*) found in most parts of South Asia. Instead of sticks, the participants hold in one hand a sharp-edged bronze cymbal, called a *gari*, while in the other they hold a smaller, bowl-shaped bronze instrument called a *baṭṭalu*. Attached to the cymbal is a short rope, which is decorated with metal bells. These musical instuments can double as a weapon (the *gari*) and shield (the *baṭṭalu*). During the dance, the instruments are moved around the body of the dancer in a complex series of offensive and defensive maneuvers.

Among the *dēvara guḍḍalu* are mendicants called *kamsāleyavaru*. Parents pledge their eldest or youngest son to the group in hopes of relief in times of family crisis. When the boys are ten to fifteen years old, they are officially initiated into the group, either at the house of a guru or at the shrine on Mādēśwara Beṭṭa, and are thereafter treated as sons of Lord Mādēśwara. Although they are allowed to marry, as members of the group they are expected to go into the streets every Monday as itinerant mendicants and perform the *kamsāle*.

Another folk saint-hero of Southern Karnataka is Manteswāmi, whose devotees have developed a tradition that includes rituals, annual fairs, and an epic tradition. Like Maleya Mādēśwara, Manteswāmi is believed to be an incarnation of Lord Shiva and has a large number of followers among the so-called untouchable castes and Muslims. The epic of Manteswāmi consists of the saint's biography as he tests the integrity and sincerity of potential believers, punishes those who oppose him, and protects those whom he favors.

The mendicant bards of Manteswāmi are called Nīlagāraru or Līlegāraru. They wear a distinctive costume and sing in a group of four—a chorus of three following the lead singer. The chorus uses musical instruments: hollow brass anklets containing metal beads called *gaggara*; a four-stringed musical instrument called a *tambūri*, and a double-headed, hourglass-shaped hand drum with beaded strings called a *ḍamaru*.

Annual fairs of Manteswāmi are held at two monasteries. Everyone offers bananas and coconuts to Manteswāmi, but religious practices such as *maṇḍe sēve* (head shaving) and *uruḷu sēve* (circumambulating the temple in a prostrate position) are offered as fulfillment of individual devotees' vows.

Mailāra, or Mailāralinga, believed to be a form of Shiva incarnated to rid the world of two dreaded demon brothers, Mallāsura and Manikāsura, is the chief deity of an old and important folk religious tradition in many parts of Karnataka as well as other Indian states. A large repertoire of stories and song-cycles recounts the deity's life and deeds. Although they vary from region to region, all include elaborate renditions of killing the two demons, as well as other stories about the god's marriages to two wives, one high born and one from the pastoral castes or forest tribes. The Mailāralinga traditions include both narrative and ritual performances. Dramatizations of the god's myth center on the deity's marriage, the slaying of the demon Mallāsura, and other episodes of the god's legend. During one annual festival there is a form of divination during which a *Gorava* (devotee), in a state of trance and sitting atop a six-meter long bow implanted in the earth, is possessed by the deity and speaks a prophecy in the form of a riddle. Experts interpret the prophecy, and followers use it to predict rainfall and crop yields for the coming year. Although this ritual lasts only a few minutes, hundreds of thousands of people gather annually to witness it.

Devotees identify with the demons conquered by the deity. Goravas and Kanchavīras are two sects of followers of Mailāralinga in Karnataka. While Goravas are mainly minstrels, Kanchavīras perform acts of self-mutilation as religious service to the deity. Piercing their cheeks and hands with iron tridents or passing thick leather thongs through their legs are acts of ritual identification with the deity's legend and meant to appease the demons he killed. Goravas are primarily of the shepherd castes, while Kanchavīras are of so-called untouchable castes. Mendicant Goravas are easily recognized by their costumes, which consist of one of various symbolic representations of the Mailāra legend: a black woolen coat, a bear-fur cap, a turban, a *ḍamaruga* (hand drum), a necklace of cowrie shells, or a *ḍoṇi* (oblong begging bowl representing the defeated demon's skulls). Goravas are classed according to the kind of service (*sēve*) they render to the deity. Chāṭi Goravas lash themselves with whips believing they are horses, the mount of Mailāra. According to legend, Manikāsura, the younger demon brother, after having been vanquished by Mailāra, was blessed by Mailāra to be his *vāhana* (mount) forever. Other Goravas bark and eat like dogs from meal bowls representing skulls or dance like horses and eat roasted rice, bananas, and other foods favored by horses.

Although Junjappa is a cultural hero of the Kāḍugollas, a pastoral tribe of the central Karnataka plain, people of many castes worship him because they believe he can cure snake and scorpion bites. Temples of Junjappa are round, thatched huts, the traditional shape of a Kāḍugolla house. Junjappa Jātres (festivals) are performed annually at traditional centers. Devotees bring *ghī* (clarified butter) and pour it in a lamppost set up for this purpose during the Dīpāvaḷi festival time (October). Devotees who have been cured of snake or scorpion bites also offer figures of snakes and scorpions made of gold, silver, or copper plating as fulfillment of vows (*harake*).

The epic of Junjappa consists of four parts: his supernatural birth (it is believed he was born through his mother's backbone), his adventures, his death, and his post-death adventures causing the destruction of his enemies and performing miraculous cures for his worshipers. Major points of the epic include his battles, with the help of his ferocious bull Baḍamyla, against the local chieftains and his conflicts with his jealous maternal uncles. The length of performance of the Junjappa epic varies from half an hour to fourteen hours, the variability depending on which and how many of the episodes of his life are sung. In men's performances, one person sings the epic, and another person plays a *gaṇe* (flute). Male priests sing portions of the epic and play the *gaṇe* as a prelude to divination activities. Women in groups of two to four or more also sing the Junjappa epic on occasions such as during processions or as a form of prayer when sitting up all night attending a person sick with a serious disease. Women do not accompany their singing with a *gaṇe*, and men and women do not perform together. Men's and women's performances are, in fact, quite different in both text and delivery styles.

Religious beliefs and practices throughout Karnataka often combine folk and classical traditions. Nāgas, serpent gods, are regarded as an ancient and separate class of deities of the forests and mountains. They are worshipped in the form of carved half-human, half-serpent beings or as intertwined cobras, located in sacred groves, near a *pīpal* tree (*Ficus religiosus*) or in pots, small dwellings, or termite mounds. Their worship is directed towards family perpetuity, fertility, and curing children's diseases. Household, lineage, village, and temple worship varies by region, caste, and class, combining variously with the worship of other gods and goddesses. The deity associated with Nāga in the Tulu-speaking area is known as Subramanya, a son of Shiva, but on the eastern side of Karnataka the worship of Nāgas coincides with that of Ellamma.

Ellamma is one of several major village goddesses worshiped in Karnataka and neighboring states. She

Coiled nāga (serpent god), ca. seventh–eighth century. (The Ancient Art & Architecture Collection, Ltd.)

is worshiped in many forms: a stone or mud figure with the trunkless head of a woman, a termite mound, a cobra, or a stone figure of a human female infant lying on the ground face up. Ellamma is one of the Seven Sisters, or *śāpta mātrikā*. Despite her benevolent facial expression, she can cause epidemics and requires animal sacrifice. Her worshipers are predominantly non-Brahmans, particularly the so-called "untouchable" communities who must live outside the village. For many non-Brahmans Ellamma is a household deity. Their households have a mud altar on which a pot signifying Ellamma is placed. Ellamma is also identified with the classical myth of Rēṇuka, wife of a Brahman sage Jamadagni and mother of the sage Paraṣurāma. Her story provides an explanation of why Ellamma is worshiped in different forms. According to all versions of this story, Jamadagni, Rēṇuka/Ellamma's husband, suspected her chastity when he used his supernatural power of vision and saw she empathized with the love-play between a king and his queen when they came to the river where she was fetching water. He asked his sons to behead her as punishment. Only the youngest son, Paraṣurāma, obeyed his father's orders and severed his mother's head with his ax. When his father offered him a reward for his obedience to his father's words, Paraṣurāma asked for the revival of his mother. The sage granted to Paraṣurāma that the head of Rēṇuka would become a goddess, Ellamma, worshiped by the whole world. According to another of the most popular versions of the myth, she was found in the form of a snake by the king and queen. When she revealed herself as a child, they raised and cared for her. Later, out of anger she again took the form of a snake and hid herself in a termite mound. People could entice her to come out of the mound only after offering her foods she was fond of—hence her worship in the form of a snake in a termite mound.

FOLKLORE OF THE TULU-SPEAKING REGION

The coastal Tulu-speaking region is distinctive in many ways. Socially, it differs in that most of its non-Brahman castes are matrilineal. Agriculturally, a system of monsoon-dependent rice cultivation dominates, and the population is dispersed along temporary water courses fed by the heavy run-off. Until recently land in this region was owned in large tracts by powerful landowners who divided it into small, self-contained plots which they rented on a sharecropping basis.

The religious folklore of the Tulu region more closely resembles that of Kerala to the south than it does the regions of Karnataka east of the Ghats. At the core of the religious complex is a form of sung oral poetry called *pāḍdana*, which narrates the lives and incarnations of several classes of spirits called *bhūta* and *siri*. *Bhūta*, a Sanskrit word meaning "ghost," here refers to spirits within the local cosmology which can grant boons as well as cause harm and offer protection and blessings as well as inflict misfortune, illness, and crop failure. The *bhūta* pantheon consists of anthropomorphic heroes representing particular castes and ferocious animals. *Bhūta* are central to all forms of village worship. The *Bhūta* cults link the domains of household, village, and kingdom, reproducing the ideology of the feudal relations, which underlie the social and moral order. At the household level *kuṭumbada bhūta* are regularly worshipped in shrine rooms through rituals meant to protect house and family.

At the village level, *ūruda bhūta* protect local boundaries. The worship of particular *bhūta* depends on one's residence, caste affiliation, and ties to a specific household.

Pāḍḍana (from a Dravidian root *pāḍ-*, "to sing") are sung narratives of several closely related traditions. The individual songs—perhaps over 200 in total—range in length from less than an hour to as many as twenty hours, with most taking about two to four hours to sing. Scholars have variously classified them as epics, myths, ritual songs, or ballads, depending on the context or purpose for which they are sung. Their major subjects are the deeds of the *bhūta*. Some of the songs—particularly those sung by professional bardic castes at rituals—are little more than catalogs of the deities' activities, while those women sing during the planting season treat the lives and tragic deaths of devotees, are more lengthy, and have strong narrative development.

Annual *bhūta* rituals (*kōla*) include spirit possession, giving devotees an opportunity to interact with the *bhūta* and a sacred court for hearing disputes judged by possessed spirit mediums. During a ceremony both a dancer (*nalke*) and a priest (*pātri*) become possessed by the *bhūta* in a set sequence. Typically, the *kōla* begins with chanting the *bhūta*'s story (*pāḍḍana*) by a member of the dancer's family while the dancer applies elaborate make up. Once costumed, the possessed dancer holds fire torches to his chest or walks on glowing coals to demonstrate the validity of his possession. He dances for several hours to mesmerizing music. Later in the ceremony, the spirit enters and speaks through him.

Siri and the *siri* deities are worshipped in connection with regionally organized annual rituals (*jātras*), at which the *siri* spirits possess the mass of participants. Siri is a goddess worshipped throughout the Tulu-speaking region, where the same term (*siri*) can also refer to a class of deities. Women who participate in the cult are also sometimes called *siris*. The *Siri Pāḍḍana*, an oral narrative—mythic in quality, epic in length—tells the lives of the *siri* spirits, beginning with the miraculous birth of Siri, her disastrous marriage to an unfaithful husband, and her subsequent remarriage. By her first husband, Siri has a son, Kumar, and by her second, a daughter, Sonne. The myth continues into subsequent generations of this matrilineal family. Sonne gives birth to twin daughters, Abbaga and Daraga, who die tragically, playing a game of *cenne*, one killing the other in a fit of jealousy and then taking her own life.

The annual ceremonies take place at fifteen to twenty locations, called *āluḍe* (most likely from *āl-*, "to rule" and *-aḍe*, "place"), or *mūlasthāna* (*mūla*, "root, origin," and *sthāna*, "place"). At some locations a dramatization of the myth precedes the rituals. During the rituals spirits possess up to a thousand or more women and men, gathered into groups of twenty to thirty. The participants are not regarded as professionals and come from different villages, castes, and backgrounds and usually have little contact with one another during the rest of the year.

Most of the ritual at the annual ceremonies consists of cases of spirit investigation. Novices (first-time participants), mostly young women, come to the Siri festival because they have been experiencing spirit possession in their homes, which can be embarrassing and disruptive and is regarded as undesirable. During the rituals such cases are dealt with one at a time through an investigation with the young woman and her family. Investigations are led by Kumar with the assistance of the *siris*. The process normally involves getting the young woman into a state of possession and then inquiring into the identity of the Siri spirit and why it is troubling the girl. At the end of each "case" the spirit in the young woman must identify itself and clarify why it has been intruding on the lives of the family. The family promises to meet whatever demands the spirit might make. Although her home life usually stabilizes and she subsequently behaves according to social norms, the young woman must return to the Siri festival annually. She becomes a medium for the spirit and joins the ranks of the other women as an adept. All of this occurs in a sing-song speech style characteristic of Siri rituals. Some of Kumar's discourse uses fragments of the *Siri Pāddana*, but most of it is impromptu sung speech. Meanwhile, women possessed by a Siri spirit may be reciting episodes from the *Siri Pāddana* either alone or with another woman.

The distinctive folk traditions of the Kodagus stem mostly from a form of circle-dance singing, which has male and female variants. Men perform varieties of dance which include songs (*pāṭü*) accompanied by a drum (*duḍi*). The basic form is the *boḷakāṭ* or "lamp dance." Variant song traditions are known either by the occasion on which they are sung (such as the *pūttari pāṭü* at the new rice ceremony) or by the implements involved (a stick-dance using two three-foot long sticks, a sword-dance, a whisk-dance, or a dance during which deer antlers are carried, for example). Other songs are sung in the worship of particular local deities and named after the deity— for instance, the *Mandakkana pāṭü* to the goddess Mandakka. Women also perform circular dances around a lamp, the most famous being the *umattāṭa* dance, which may be performed for any festivity (such as Ṣaṣti, Dīpāali, Ugādi, and Sankrānti and throughout the harvest months of Suggi and Wasanta) in which the women dance around a special lamp (*dīpa*). The women's dance perhaps has its origin in *tummattāṭa*, performed at a girl's first menstruation.

DRAMA AND FOLK PERFORMANCE

The classical Sanskrit epics, *Mahābhārata* and *Rāmāyaṇa*, related to the Krishna and Rāma incarnations of Vishnu, have generated several important folk performance forms in Karnataka. These are generally patronized by the more urban and literate classes than are the Shaivaite traditions. Chief among these is a set of regionally distinctive dance-drama-music forms called *yakṣagāna*, which refers to an old style of South Indian music. Drama forms using this style are performed widely in Karnataka. The style of the *yakṣagāna* in Karnataka's coastal districts, however, is the most well-known and best documented. In that area, the troupes' elaborate costumes include intricately carved and decorated crowns and neck, shoulder, chest, wrist, and waist ornaments. Historically, it seems likely that during the Vijayanagara period (fourteenth through sixteenth centuries) *yakṣagāna* was used to propagate wider Hindu values and practices. Although the story lines (*prasanga*) draw from the classical epics, some dramas are more immediately based in myths (*sthala purāṇa*) and legends (*mahime*) associated with local temples. Recently several *pāddanas* of local *bhūta* heroes and the heroine Siri from the Tulu language have become highly successful *yakṣagāna* dramas.

The traditional site for a *yakṣagāna* performance is a harvested rice field. An area of about twenty-by-twenty feet is marked at each corner with bamboo poles, which are joined at the top with strings of mango leaves, flowers, and sometimes fruits and areca nuts. Nearby is the dressing room made of palm-frond matted floors and walls where actors apply makeup and don costumes. Originally both areas were lighted only by fire torch and oil lamps. Sponsored by a wealthy landlord, *yakṣagāna* was free for everyone to see. Over time, additional types of staging and lighting have emerged. First, kerosene lanterns were added to supplement traditional firelight. Then came a raised mud platform stage. Next, a large tent covered the stage and audience area, and admission was charged. Then an indoor theater with proscenium stage was introduced along with electric lighting, sound system, and admission fees. Today, *yakṣagāna* is performed in combinations of all of the above. The performance consists of vocal and instrumental music, dance, costumes and makeup, and extemporaneous dialogue. The vocal music includes the literary text and folksongs. Instrumental music is performed on two drums—the *maddale* and the *caṇde*—and either small metal cymbals or a gong. Hand gestures are mainly those used in everyday conversation, and facial expressions are more realistic than stylized.

Other forms of drama related to *yakṣagāna* are *doḍḍāṭa*, a distinctive Northern Karnataka variety of *yakṣagāna*, and *pārijāta āṭa*. While the former utilizes stories from the *Mahābhārata* and *Rāmāyaṇa*, the latter is confined to a story concerning the mythological origin of the *pārijāta* tree, which blooms during the night and then loses its beautifully scented flowers the next morning. According to tradition, the tree was stolen from the god Brahma's heaven by Lord Krishna for one of his wives, Satyabhama. This engendered the jealousy of his other wife, Rukmini. Only Krishna himself could settle their disputes. The story derives from a few lines in an early Sanskrit text, expanded in the *Mahābhārata*, and later elaborated in devotional literature. In the theater form, much of the action derives from additional sources focusing on intra- and inter-gender rivalries.

Other distinctive folk performances in Kannada-speaking regions include *vīragāse*, a dance peformance by devotees of Shiva accompanied by singing the *Dakṣayajña* (the sacrifice of Daka) and piercing the cheeks with iron spears; Kalgi and Tura songs (*lāvaṇi*), frequently competitive women's songs; and Gondaligāra *āṭa*, a ritual performed by mainly Marathi immigrant communities for appeasing *gaṇas* (retinue of spirits) of Shiva and Ammanavaru, a form of the mother goddess. In southern Karnataka many villages worship local spirits with *soma kunita*, rituals by dancers wearing huge, colorful masks. The term *soma* refers to warriors who, after death, become guardians of local goddesses. The color of the masks depicts the nature of the spirit: red represents a benevolent spirit, while yellow and black are malevolent.

Leather and wooden string puppets are also used for village drama performances. Performances are generally—especially those of string puppets—influenced by *yakṣagāna* and like them draw from the classical Sanskrit epics for their themes. The craft of making the puppets, worthy of appreciation in itself, belongs to the several communities of puppeteers.

GAMES AND RECREATION

Of the few folk performance traditions not overtly religious in tenor, dancing bears, snake charmers, fortune-telling parrots, and thieving monkeys are among the animal acts one can see in towns. Members of the Gangettinavaru community lead trained bulls—invariably named Rāma and Sīta and which appear to be able to count and do simple mathematics—door to door around the countryside. Other forms of street performance include acrobats (ḍombarāṭa) and magic shows. Secular drama resembling vaudeville produced and acted by urban troupes, but popular in villages thirty years ago, has become rare now due to the availability of television.

Cock-fighting, called kōḷikaṭṭa in Kannada and kōrikaṭṭa in Tulu, is an especially popular sport in the coastal region. It is customarily held on days following festivals and public ceremonies such as jātras and bhūta kōlas. It starts in the late afternoons and lasts until late into the night. A post-harvest paddy field or any level ground serves as the arena. The number of spectators, who hear of the event by word of mouth, may vary between fifty and five thousand. Fighting cocks receive special care and attention. If the owner of a cock is rich and powerful, a large retinue of followers will accompany him as he takes it to the arena. Many of them are in charge of a particular task related to the competition: feeding the cock, supplying it with water, tying the blades, releasing the cock into battle, fanning it when it is wounded, and treating its wounds. Before the cocks are set against each other, members of the audiences bet sometimes as much as Rs.500,000 ($10,000). Two cocks are matched for a contest on the basis of their height, an intricate classification scheme based on their color, and other factors. In Tulu, for example, the following are some of the common distinctive terms used in this color scheme: boḷḷe (white), karboḷḷe (black and white), kempe (red), manjale (yellow, turmeric), kakke (crow-colored, black), nīle (blue), kuppule (crow pheasant color, deep brown), gāruḍa būdi (eagle and ash, gray), karinīle (dark blue), kemmaire (dark red), and giḍiye (hawk-colored). Large cocks are called paika; small ones, jīka. A traditional Kōrita Pañcāṅga (cock almanac) gives details about the birth, growth, adulthood, old age, death, and other aspects of the lives of cocks. It also prescribes which colors of cocks should fight each other, mentioning the probable color of the winning cock on a particular day of the week or in a particular week of the month.

Buffalo racing is also a well-organized sport peculiar to the Tulu-speaking region. The race is held in a specially prepared, flooded paddy field. Buffalo not only race one another in time and speed trials, but also their handlers compete in achieving various feats such as splashing the muddy water produced in the wake of a harrow on which they stand behind the speeding animals. Special breeds of buffalo are raised for racing, and prized animals sell for enormous sums of money. The sport draws thousands of spectators and, like a fair, is accompanied by other forms of entertainment. It also has ritual overtones associated with feudalism, fertility, and prosperity.

Dozens of folk games, mostly children's games, are played at the village level. Adult gambling games played with coconuts, stones, sticks, cowrie shells, and other local materials are also popular. At many temple and festival locations competitive ball games and even combatant games using firebrands and weapons are played in a ritualistic fashion. Folk board games are often carved into the stone verandah of temples, drawn on cloth for portability, or scratched in the earth. The most popular include pachisi (parchesi), snakes and ladders, marbles, hopscotch, and various stick games. The game *cenne* is a version of *mancala*, an Arabic term used by game scholars to designate varieties of a game played throughout a region from Africa to the Philippines. In Karnataka the *cenne* board is usually twelve to twenty-four inches long, with two rows of cup-shaped "pits" and two larger cavities at either end for storing captured pieces. Ordinary boards are usually made of wood, sometimes painted an auspicious yellow and decorated with designs. The games are played by taking the pieces from one pit and distributing them in a given direction. Various games, each with a distinctive name, can be played on the board. The number of players is generally two, but there are also solitaire forms and forms for three or more players. All are highly competitive games of skill, associated especially with women. Frequently there are restrictions on the play of the game: in the Tulu-speaking area, for example, the game cannot be played when seed beds have been planted, and sisters should never play this game together. Gambling, a common dimension of the game elsewhere, is generally proscribed in Karnataka except when played by men.

ARCHITECTURE

Rural house architecture varies considerably from region to region, depending on available materials and climatic conditions. In many parts of the region, village layout and house construction took into consideration the need for defense and security, but today wealth, class, and occupation usually determine house size, style, and location. While traditionally village houses were built of mud and stone walls with wooden beams and thatch used for a roof, these materials have widely given way to cement walls and tiled roofs. In many areas livestock is still kept in an attached entranceway to the house. In the past, some of the more itinerant castes such as cow herds (*Golla*) and hunters (*Bēḍa*) traditionally built circular houses entirely of thatch, but almost all have now shifted to a rectangular design of either mud or cement walls.

Vernacular temples and small shrines—that is, those not built under royal patronage and served by canonical priests—abound. Some are reconstructions from the fallen and even scattered remains of ruins that had once been larger and in a more classical style. Many are of relatively recent construction: smaller ones consisting of a single square shrine room (but more often two or more joined shrine rooms) with a stone slab verandah (*cāwaḍi*) in front where worshippers gather and villagers sit and discuss village matters. Construction is usually of local stone covered with mud and whitewashed. In Gollas settlements one still sees traditional round structures covered with thatched roofs. *Nāgas* (serpent deities) are often worshipped on an elaborate circular design (*maṇḍala*) of colored sands drawn on the floor.

Carved wooden statues, life size and larger, and other representations of deities are found in many regions. While most of these are anthropomorphic, wooden horses and other animal figures representing the vehicles (*vāhana*)—and by extension, perhaps the devotees too—of the deity are also found. In Mailāra temples gigantic leather sandals (*chappals*) and carved wooden horse figures are given as offerings.

CHALLENGES OF THE MODERN WORLD

Most of these traditions have incorporated modern systems of transportation and communication and utilize a wide array of current technology. Virtually all forms of popular oral traditions, for example, are available on audiocassettes, which are distributed for sale at festivals along with "God photos," lithographed paintings of the statuary images used in temple rituals. Commercial films have been made of many popular mythical stories and are available on videocassette. Drama forms such as *Yakṣagāna* are extensively covered in the news media; even buffalo races are announced. Festivals are covered on television. Government and private bus companies provide fleets of vehicles to transport devotees to popular pilgrimage centers.

Itinerant performance traditions, though, especially secular ones and ones that depend on the patronage of a particular caste (genealogy-keeping and caste myth performance traditions), have generally not fared as well in the face of modern employment opportunities. Many communities which maintained themselves by these traditions have been placed on preference lists for government employment and educational opportunities, and villagers now have lucrative alternatives available to them. In other cases, their patron castes no longer wish to have their status associated with the deeds of their ancestors and are unwilling to support those who remember their history. The folk arts have not so much declined as the social values have changed and modernized.

Although the folklore of Karnataka remains a vital part of the state's culture in the face of Western-defined modernism and **globalization**, Karnataka regional folk traditions' relationship with pan-Indian and more quasi-classical cultural forms is perhaps more problematical. Many local traditions are in danger of extinction due to competition from Hindi films and film songs, classical dance classes, government disseminated and media advertised medical and health products and practices, and social customs related to an Indian urban lifestyle (weddings, ritual practices), craft styles (carving, painting, cloth design) generated by government craft training centers, and pan-Indian cuisine.

STUDIES OF KARNATAKA FOLKLORE

Folklore has been actively researched in Karnataka for nearly two centuries. During colonial rule and even before, Western missionaries and administrators had written extensively on the customs and practices of the region and collected **repertoires** of proverbs, tales, legends, and ballads. The early collection of Tulu *pāḍḍanas* by several members of the Basel Mission, published in 1886 in Tulu using a modified Kannada script and in both transliteration and English translation in *Indian Antiquary* between 1894 to 1898, is particularly valuable.

After independence, Karnataka folklorists began to make significant strides collecting and analyzing the state's wealth of local material. Mysore University led the development of modern folklore studies, creating a department of folklore and developing a museum of folklore in the 1960s. Folklore is now taught in the curriculum, often in departments of literature, in all of the state's universities. As a result, virtually all genres of folklore have been collected and studied in all parts of the state, and there is now a wealth of publication on this topic, most of which is in the Kannada language. Folklore is also a popular subject in the mass media. Newspapers carry illustrated articles on folklore topics in their Sunday editions, and weekly and monthly magazines almost always carry articles on folklore.

Western scholars have recently taken a strong interest in the region's folklore. In the 1980s the Ford Foundation funded an important archival center, the Regional Resource Centre for Folk Performing Arts, M.G.M. College, Udupi, and through it organized a series of international folklore workshops meant to open the study of Karnataka's folklore to a wider scholarly audience and to integrate Indian and Western research. Today the archive houses an impressive collection of audio- and videotapes and photographs documenting many genres and all regions of the state. Several team projects by Indian and international scholars have been undertaken in recent decades. A wealth of information on the folklore of Karnataka has been published in books and articles. One can also consult the Web site www.udupipages.com/culture/folk.html.

BIBLIOGRAPHY

Anata Krishna Iyer, L. K., and H. V. Nanjundaiah. 1926–1935. *Mysore Tribes and Castes.* 4 volumes. Bangalore: Mysore Government Press.

Blackburn, Stuart H., and A. K. Ramanujan, eds. 1986. *Another Harmony: New Essays on the Folklore of India.* Berkeley: University of California Press.

Claus, Peter J. 1986. Playing *Cenne:* The Meanings of a Folk Game. In *Another Harmony: New Essays on the Folklore of India,* edited by Stuart Blackburn and A. K. Ramanujan. Berkeley: University of California Press. 265–293.

Claus, Peter J., Margaret Mills, and Sarah Diamond, eds. 2004. *South Asian Folklore: An Encyclopedia.* New York: Routledge.

Dubois, J. A., and Henry Beauchamp. 1906. *Hindu Manners Customs and Ceremonies,* translated by H. K. Beauchamp. Oxford: Oxford University Press.

Hanur, Krishnamurthy, ed. 1991. *Encyclopedia of Karnataka Folk Culture.* 6 volumes. Madras: Institute of Asian Studies.

Ramanujan, A. K. 1973. *Speaking of Siva.* Harmondsworth: Penguin.

———. 1997. *A Flowering Tree and Other Oral Tales from India,* edited by Stuart Blackburn and Alan Dundes. Berkeley: University of California Press.

Ramchandran, C. N., and L. N. Bhat, trans. 2001. *Male Madeshwara: A Kannada Oral Epic.* New Delhi: Sahitya Akademi.

Shankaranarayana, T. N. 1991. Three Folk Epics. In *Encyclopedia of Karnataka Folk Culture,* edited by Krishnamurthy Hanur. 6 volumes. Madras: Institute of Asian Studies. 314–330.

Thurston, Edgar. 1907. *Ethnographic Notes in Southern India.* 2 volumes. Madras: Government Press.

———. 1909. *Castes and Tribes of Southern India.* 7 volumes. Madras: Government Press.

Peter J. Claus and S. A. Krishnaiah

KASHMIR

GEOGRAPHY AND HISTORY

The northernmost state of the Indian Republic, usually referred to as Kashmir, covers an area of approximately 86,024 square miles, including the valley of Kashmir and the areas of Jammu, Ladakh, Baltistan, Gilgat, Hunza, and Nagar. Both culturally and geographically, Jammu, Kashmir, and the Ladakh regions have been distinctly separate entities. With the Kashmir valley securely nestled among the Himalaya Mountains, the hilly tract extending to the plains of Punjab on the south is the Jammu region, inhabited by a hardy people known as Dogras. Cultural contacts between the people of Kashmir valley and the Dogras have been very ancient. Although influenced by the Kashmiri language and culture, their ceremonies and festivals have more affinity with the plains people of **India**. In the northeast of the valley is the "magic land" of Ladakh. Ladakhis are a Tibeto-Burman race, speak languages belonging to the Tibeto-Burman group of languages, and have a distinct culture of their own.

The inhabitants of Kashmir call their language "Këëshur" and the land "Këshiir." Outsiders use the term Kashmiri for both the inhabitants of the valley as well as the language they speak. The people of Kashmir belong to a branch of the Aryan race who are believed to have migrated to northern parts of India and brought with them the languages of the Indo-Aryans. The Kashmiri language is affiliated with the Dardic group of the Indo-Iranian language family.

The valley of Kashmir occupies a strategically important position with its borders touching the plains of mainland India in the south, Pakistan in the west, and **Russia** and **China** in the north and northwest. Located on the old Central Asian trade route, it became the focal point for important cultural links between the Indian subcontinent and Central Asia. Kashmir in its historical past came into contact with the great civilizations of the world. Surveying the valley of Kashmir and its surrounding areas in historical retrospect, one is apt to notice the checkered nature of Kashmir's past—the history of war and conquest, oppression, subjugation, and conversions—that has influenced other aspects of social life in the valley. As a result of this constant contact with the different cultures, the processes of acculturation and identification have played their roles in shaping the present culture of Kashmir and its people. Such processes of cultural pluralism and synthesis are very clearly reflected in the folklore traditions of Kashmir: its material culture, oral narratives, belief systems, performing arts, arts and crafts, and more.

The Kashmiri language is spoken in the Kashmir province and some surrounding areas of the state of Jammu and Kashmir. It is also spoken in a small area in West Pakistan.

Children playing hopscotch in Kashmir, India (1903). (Courtesy Library of Congress)

The Kashmiri population consists of Hindus, Muslims, Sikhs, and others. Hindus, popularly known as Pandits and considered the purest specimens of the ancient Aryan settlers in the valley, form a distinct class of their own. One of the typical features of the present Pandit community is the absence of the caste system prevalent in other Hindu communities of India. All Kashmiri Pandits are Brahmans. It is believed that before the advent of Islam in the early thirteenth century, the population of Kashmir was not entirely Brahmans. However, during numerous political vicissitudes experienced by the people of the Kashmir valley, all other sects were converted to other religions, leaving only one Hindu class of Brahmans—the Pandits. In terms of numbers, Kashmiri Hindus or Pandits constitute a very small but highly educated community that has produced a galaxy of philosophers, scholars, administrators, and politicians; Pandit names such as Abhinavagupta, Kalhana, Bilahana, Somadeva, Mamatacharya, Kshemendra, and Gunaddhya are of pan-Indian fame.

Muslims are a majority community in the valley. While apparently only a few adventurers and their families came from outside, Islam became the dominant religion as a result of mass conversions. Many historical legends still extant tell the stories of these conversions and the eventual domination of Islam, offering pictures of religious bigotry, mass conversions, killings, compulsions, persuasions, and opportunism. Numerous Muslim saints and dervishes propagated their religion through preaching the purest and truest doctrines of Islam, which considerably influenced the religious and the philosophical thoughts of Kashmiris. Persian language and literature with its Islamic background enriched the cultural treasure of Kashmir, particularly folklore. One finds a variety of Islamic themes or motifs either independently knitted into some items of folklore or implanted very artistically into the already existing folklore of the original settlers. A variety of Hindu surnames such as Dar, Bhatt, Handoo, Kachru, Kichlu, Matto, and Pandit persist in Muslim families. Presumably these Muslims might have retained some Hindu customs and ceremonies after conversion to Islam, but few traces of such customs remain. As elsewhere the Muslim population of Kashmir is divided into Sunni and Shi'a sects, the former being in majority.

WRITTEN FOLK NARRATIVES

Kashmir has a rich tradition of folk narratives such as myths, legends, tales, songs, proverbs and riddles, folk music, performing arts, customs, and beliefs. Kashmir became the fountainhead of Asian and later European tale traditions. The famous *Panchatantra*, a collection of fables, was supposed to have been composed in Kashmir. Originally written in Sanskrit, a handful of already available oral animal tales may have been selected, retold, and written to train the princes of Kashmir in the art of politics and royalty. Some structural changes are apparent when one looks into the plot structure of these tales. Of equal importance in this written oral tradition is *Kathasaritasagara* (The Ocean of Story) of Somadeva. This work, composed and written for Queen Suryamati, wife of King Ananta of Kashmir (1028–1063), is supposed to be based on the Gunaddhya's famous collection of stories, *Brihatkatha*, which is no longer extant. Gunaddhya is believed to have written down the current oral tales of Kashmir in the Paisachi language in seven volumes, which he later burned after being ridiculed by King Satavahana of Kashmir for writing in a non-elite language spoken by the tribes of the area. Extremely dejected by the insult, he lit a fire and, after reading each volume to his disciples, consigned it to flames, burning six of them. When news reached the king, he rushed to save the seventh volume and sought pardon. There are a number of versions of this story of *Brihatkatha* available in Kashmir and elsewhere, sharing more or less the same structure. A Brahman priest in Srinagar possesses a rare manuscript having some structural-contextual relationship with the original *Brihatkatha* and the same title. This manuscript is treated as sacred, having a ritualistic function for some people, particularly the Hindu community of Kashmir. This written tradition of materials being lost due to some cruel king's deceit or for reasons of prestige is an inseparable part of Kashmiri metafolklore as it is in Indian narrative lore and Persian folklore and literature.

ORAL FOLK NARRATIVES

In addition to this written tradition, the oral narrative tradition in Kashmir still flourishes and is equally significant, including a variety of tales, myths, legends, jokes, and anecdotes. Myths of the origin of the valley and other etiological myths share several features with the pan-Indian myths as well as the biblical myth of Noah's ark. The diffusion of mythic elements, characters, and motifs from Sanskrit Hindu tradition and Islamic or Persio-Arabic sources, blended with the native traditions, has synthesized over time, and from this emerged a combination of new blends of characters, objects, and motifs that characterize Kashmiri folklore. Thus one notices the characters of *sadhu, gosony, fakir, pari gin,* and *bombur-yamberzal,* and objects such as *koh-I-kaf, harmokh,* and *sang-I-faras* side by side in folktales and other oral narratives, making it hard to separate these despite their origins in different sources.

The distinct position of the folktale among Kashmiris can be treated as a culture-specific characteristic, though this does not mean that the other narrative forms are absent. They are very much present and function actively in the communication system of the culture. But the folktale seems to have formed an essential part of communicative behavior in this culture. This is clear from the different meanings of the term *kath* (story) in Kashmiri. In the Kashmiri language, *kath* (a form of Sanskrit *katha*) means talk, speech, saying or proverb, and language itself in addition to story and myth.

SONGS

Folksongs of Kashmir preserve myths, epics, ballads, legends, customs, and traditions. These present considerable variety of themes, content, and form. They can broadly be classified as ceremonial and non-ceremonial. Ceremonial songs are mainly associated with rituals and religious festivals. Their form and content remain specific to particular religions, deriving from Hindu-Sanskrit and Persio-Arabic Islamic sources. Ceremonial songs include life cycle events such as birth, initiation, marriage, and death. Non-ceremonial songs are secular in content and are associated with the activities of daily life. They encompass pastoral songs, worksongs, romantic ballads, songs sung during different seasons and secular festivals for entertainment, lullabies, and operas. Love, romance, poverty, floods, famines, scenic beauty of the valley, joys and sorrows of life, and social and domestic strife are the predominant themes of these songs, and these are shared by both communities in the valley. The case is similar for *ladishah*, a series of satirical verses with sociopolitical themes. These are popular among all the religious communities. *Ladishah* or *larishah* are the terms used for both the singer and the songs he sings, which besides describing natural calamities such as earthquakes, famines, and floods, target corrupt politicians and officials, religious exploiters, and economic offenders.

Kashmiri folksongs have been collected extensively. Besides some individual collections, the Jammu and Kashmir Academy of Arts, Culture, and Languages issued a seven-volume collection of Kashmiri folksongs in the Kashmiri language. A descriptive classification and study of Kashmiri folksongs is presented in *Kashmiri aur Hindi ke lokgeet: ek tulnatmak adhyayan* (A Comparative Study of Kashmiri and Hindi Folksongs) by J. Handoo. Kashmiri has a very limited number of folk epics. While *Rāmāyaṇa* and *Mahābhārata*, the two Indian epics, are popular with the Hindu population, *Akanandun*, a religious folktale versified as a small epic, remains a very popular native epic among the folk, cutting across religious barriers. Other folk epics such as *Gul-Snober*, *Gulrez*, *Hatim-Tai*, *Laila-Majnu*, and *Yusuf-Zulekha* are more or less translations or adaptations of Persio-Arabic epics.

DANCE

As in the rest of India, classical dancing in Kashmir appears to have had a religious background. One of the last Hindu kings of Kashmir, Harsha (1089–1101 C.E.), was a lover of music and arts and patronized dance and drama. King Kalasa (1063–1089 C.E.) is believed to have introduced ballet dancing and choral music. The synthesizing cult of Sufism favored dance and music, and like other genres of folklore the classical dance forms prevalent in Kashmir have absorbed influences from the dance techniques of **Persia** and Central Asia. A peculiarity of Kashmiri folk dance forms is that most are exclusively all-male or all-female performances. Intermingling of the sexes in performance is not often permitted. *Rouf* is the most popular dance in the Kashmir valley. Performed by women on various celebratory occasions—weddings, local festivals, and harvest celebrations—it is a staple of the month of Ramazan when every street and corner in Kashmir resounds with *Rouf* songs and dance.

Dameëly is another well-known dance form, devotional in nature and performed by men on ceremonial occasions such as the *urs* or anniversaries of the Sufi saints. Performed by a group of ten to fifteen men known as *damaali faqir* or *damaali maty*, who dress in their traditional finery, it demonstrates martial capabilities to the tune of *dhol* (drum) and *manjeera*. The flag bearer leads the dancing party in the procession. The *alam* (flag), believed to be the symbol of fertility and perpetuity, is fixed in the ground, and the dancers form a circle around it. Unlike *bhands*, the *damaaly* performers are held in high esteem and warmly welcomed since they are believed to be invoking the blessings of the gods.

Bachi nagama, a popular folk dance form said to have gained momentum during

Afghan rule of Kashmir, is a version of the Hafiz-Nagma, a dance performed by Kashmiri women to the accompaniment of *sufiana kalaam* and meant for a sophisticated and initiated audience. Today a young male dressed like a woman replaces the Hafiza-a female dancer and sings and dances to the accompaniment of musical instruments. Generally performed at night, *Bachi nagama* is a part of any jubilatory celebration. *HikkaT* is a playful dance of young boys and girls in Kashmir. They form couples, and the partners, interlocking their arms, hold each other's hands. Putting their feet close together, they bend their bodies and heads backwards. Facing each other, they go round and round with perfect precision in a fast dizzying spin. This sometimes is accompanied by singing. However, no musical instruments are used during the performance. Though less well known, the most ancient dance forms of Kashmiri Pandit women, *arnirouv* and *viigis natsun*, are ritual dances associated with weddings and *yegnyopavit*, or initiation ceremonies. These have changed very little. In both dances the women relations of the groom or the boy who is getting married or initiated into adulthood dance to the tunes of songs propitiating God and seeking his blessings for the entire family.

Bhand Pëëther and *bhand jeshin*, two major folk theatrical forms also known as dance dramas, are very popular with commoners because they have remained their sole patrons. *Pëëther* in Kashmiri means a drama, while *Bhand* is the performer or actor. The *bhands* normally do not have a ready-made theme. The performers show their ingenuity by improvising according to the situation and the material available. These *bhands* perform folk plays known as *luki pëëther*, which mock rulers and dogmatic religious and social leaders such as Pirs, Khwajas, and Hindu priests. The *bhand jeshin* (festival of clowns), a 300- to 400-year-old genre of Kashmiri folk theater, is performed by a group of artists in their traditional style accompanied by light music satirizing social situations and political institutions The musical instruments used in *Jeshin* are *surnai*, big *dhol* (drum), and *nagara* (trumpet). Kashmiri folk theater is a male domain; males dressed as females perform the female roles.

DRAMA

Kashmir has its own genre of theatrical performances, formed primarily from an amalgm of different genres. Dance, drama, music, and the fine arts date back to antiquity in the state. King and commoner alike cultivated music as a fine art in ancient Kashmir. Music was apparently played in Buddhist Viharas during the reign of Jalauka. Music was requisite at religious ceremonies, particularly those connected with tantric worship. Like other genres of folklore, Kashmiri music is highly influenced by other cultures with which it came in contact, mainly Sanskrit and Persian traditions. A distinct feature of Kashmiri folk music is that it is usually sung by a chorus; solo music is very rare. In the villages music is not just a form of entertainment but an essential element in many of the activities of daily life. It plays a prominent part in most rituals. These songs are usually sung by all of the people participating in the activity.

Highly influenced by Sufi thought and music, Kashmiri music developed affinities with both Indian and Persian prototypes and evolved musical forms with elements from both cultures. Now a classical form of Kashmiri music, Sufiyana Kalaam seems to have spread with Sufism in the form of religious folk music. However, in spite of these influences traditional folk music, mainly ritualistic and associated with religious ceremonies, seems to have retained its basic features and function. Kashmiri ceremonial music (known as *vanavun, vanvavan hur,* and *vatsun*) has not been altered in the least. Kashmiri Hindus claim that *vanavun* is an adaptation of the Vedic chants of Samveda, retaining its original tune. The *vanavun* of the Muslim community has not changed either. *Väkh* is another folk form which has become a respectable literary form of poetry and has acquired distinctive generic qualities. Other popular forms of Kashmiri folk music that have not undergone much change are *Ladishah, Chhakar,* and *Leela. Löl* (love lore), an equally ancient form of folk music, seems to be less resistant to change. *Chhakar* is the most popular form of folksinging in Kashmir. It occurs on all festive occasions, ceremonial and secular. It can be traced back to the twelfth century C.E. In *Chhakkar* musical instruments such as *Rabab, Not* (an earthen pitcher), *Gaagar, Thälija Tumbakhnëër,* and *Sarangi* are played as accompaniment for a chorus. In modern times, however, the harmonium is also played in *Chhakar.* Depending on the availability, location, and occasion, one or more of these instruments may be omitted or replaced. *Sarangi, Rabab, Santoor, Yaktar* (one-stringed), *Sitar, Surna,* and *Tumbaknëër* are the major musical instruments of Kashmir. *Surna* or *surnai* is a trumpet-like instrument resembling the Indian *Shehanai. Tumbakanëër,* a *surahi*-shaped earthen instrument, is used for every singing occasion in Kashmir.

FESTIVALS AND CELEBRATIONS

Kashmiris celebrate various fairs and festivals, religious and secular. Kashmir has been a very important seat of Shaivism, which remains the most important form of religion among the Pandits of the valley. However, in time Vaishnava philosophy penetrated the valley and influenced its inhabitants. This dichotomy of Shaivite and Vaishnavite philosophy on one hand and that of Hinduism and Islam on the other has gone much deeper into the religious and cultural psyche of the Kashmiris in shaping their religious thought and worldview. This is also evident in temples and religious places being marked as vegetarian and non-vegetarian based on the offerings made therein. Often we find Hindu and Muslim religious places located side by side or even in the same compound. This synthesis is reflected in the fairs and festivals as well. The major Hindu festivals of Kashmir are *herath* (*Shivaratri*), *navreh* (New Year), *khetsimaavas, gaadabatI, zaramIsatam* (*Janamashtami*), *Ramanavam* (*Ramanavami*), and *shraavana punima.* Those celebrated by

Kashmiris celebrate various fairs and festivals, religious and secular. Pictured here is the festival of Hemis Temple. (© Tatsuo Kume/HAGA/The Image Works)

Muslims are *Idd, Milaad-u-Nabi, Id-ul-Fitr, Id-ul-Zuha, Shab-e Qadar*, and *navaroz*. Besides these annual events, *urs* are held at the shrines of famous and revered local Rishis and Sufi saints.

STUDIES OF KASHMIR FOLKLORE

Lawrence's work (1895) remains the only detailed work on Kashmiri material culture and folklife. The Jammu and Kashmir Academy is involved in collecting material, but no attempt to study these materials analytically from sociocultural or psychological perspectives has yet been made except for some work by individual scholars.

BIBLIOGRAPHY

Bamzai, P.N.K. 1962. *A History of Kashmir*. Delhi: Metropolitan.

Faroq, Fayaz. 2001. *Folklore and History of Kashmir*. Srinagar: Nunaposh.

Handoo, J., and others. 1987. *Folktales of India*. Chicago: University of Chicago Press.

Handoo, Lalita. 1994. *Structural Analysis of Kashmiri Tales*. Mysore: CIIL.

Kalhan, Pandit. 1961. *Rajatarangini*, translated by Aurel Stein. 2 volumes. Delhi: Motilal Banarasidass.

Kashkari, Sudershan. 1953. *Keys to Kashmir*. Srinagar: Lalla Rukh.

———. 1962. *The Wit of Kashmir*. Srinagar: Research and Publication Department, Jammu and Kashmir Government.

Knowles, J. H. 1885. *A Dictionary of Proverbs and Sayings*. London: Kegan Paul Trubner.

———. 1893. *Folk-Tales of Kashmir*. London: Kegan Paul Trubner.

Lawrence, Walter. 1895. *The Valley of Kashmir*. London: Henry Frowde.

Madan, T. N. 1965. *Family and Kinship: A Study of the Pandits of Rural Kashmir*. Bombay: Asia Publishing House.

Majid, Gulshan, ed. 1997. *Aspects of Folklore, with Special Reference to Kashmir*. Srinagar: University of Kashmir.

Ryder, A.W., trans. 1949. *The Panchatantra*. Bombay: Jaico.

Stein, Aurel, and George Greirson. 1937. *Hatim's Tales: Kashmir Stories and Songs*. London: John Murray.

Lalita Handoo

KHASI-JAINTIA

GEOGRAPHY AND HISTORY

The Khasi-Jaintia inhabit the Khasi and Jaintia Hills of Meghalaya, a state in northeastern India. Two of the five major groups who were earlier known by the generic term Khasi, they came from the same stock of people. Although the migration routes cannot be firmly established, scholars have traced a relationship between them, the Mons of Myanmar, and the Khmers of Kampuchia. A linguistic and cultural connection has also been sought between them and Austric groups such as the Ho-Mundas of central India. The Khasi-Jaintias, hence, are identified as a Paleo-Mongoloid group, speaking a language of the Mon-Khmer branch of the Austric family.

With a land area of 14,375 square kilometers, the Khasi-Jaintia territory is a landscape of hills, plateaus, ravines, brooks, rivulets, lakes, and waterfalls. The Khasis live mainly in the central plain between 1,500 and 2,000 meters above sea level. The Jaintias live in the Jaintia Hills and the lower country bordering the Barak Valley of the Indian state of **Assam** and the Surma Valley of **Bangladesh**. The region experiences a tropical monsoon climate with summer temperatures reaching as high as 25 degrees Celsius and winter temperatures falling as low as 5 degrees with occasional dips to near the freezing point at night and early morning frost at higher elevations. Cherrapunji and Mawsynram in the Khasi Hills record the highest average rainfall in the world. Based on rainfall, terrain, and soil characteristics, the area can be broadly classified into three zones: temperate, subtropical hill, and subtropical plain.

Cultivation of rice forms the primary subsistence base. Ricegrowers use both shifting and settled methods depending on the nature of the land. Wet-rice cultivation is practiced in river valleys and flatlands. Particularly in the Jaintia Hills, farmers use cattle for plowing. Horticulture was once a major basis for trade, and oranges and pineapples are still grown extensively.

SOCIAL STRUCTURE AND RELIGIOUS BELIEF

Social organization focuses on the institution of matriliny. Descent is matrilineal (through the mother), and residence is matrilocal (with the wife's family). Mother controls household property and religious rites. She is succeeded by her youngest daughter. The eldest son enjoys authority in making decisions in the family council (*durbar iing*) and plays a dominant role in the clan council (*durbar kur*). A man may join his wife's family or, particularly in the Jaintia Hills, retains residence in his mother's household and visits his wife.

The matrilineal principle is also evident in the clan-centered religion, which revolves around a triad: the progenitress (*Ka Iawbei*), the progenitor (*U Thawlang*), and the eldest son of the progenitress (*U Suidnia*). A basic tenet stresses the consciousness of kinship principles. Thus religion is essentially a shared experience with predominantly female principles being ritually propitiated. Female deities relate to general welfare, production of wealth, and protection from diseases and other calamities, while male deities' duties include defense of state, village territories, and markets.

Colonization and the advent of Christian missionaries resulted in the majority of people converting to Christianity, and at present more than half of the Khasi-Jaintia population are Christians. The missionaries also introduced Roman script to transliterate the indigenous language, which until then remained unwritten. This contributed to the codification of religious tenets with an emphasis on monotheism through the efforts of a group of educated youth who formed an association called *Seng Khasi* in 1899. Motivated by a concern for the future of their society whose faith and cohesion was perceived as being threatened by the activities of missionaries with the backing of colonial administrators, this group developed the Khasi religion, *Ka Niam Khasi*, originally structured by shared rituals, into a monotheistic ethical faith. The three commandments—*Kamai ia ka hok* (Earn righteousness); *Tip Briew, Tip Blei*

(Mankind conscious, God conscious); and *Tip Kur Tip Kha* (Know maternal and paternal kin)—represent theological constructs based on moral, religious, and kinship concerns. Ethnic identity and religious identity have become juxtaposed. The central idea focuses on mankind's reconciliation with God, the supreme being. *Ka Niam Khasi* has now emerged as a distinct faith with an ethical system appropriate to both the age-old ritual system and the matrilineal social order.

The importance of clan extends to politics. The clans that settled an area first—acknowledged as aristocrats (*bakhraw*)—received the privilege of sharing arable lands with family ownership rights (*ri kynti*) and of forming the ruling council (*durbar*) of the pre-state political formation (*hima*). Designated as ministers (*myntry*), clan members retain the right to choose the chief of the *hima* (called *syiem*) from among persons not belonging to the clans and guiding him in the state council (*durbar hima*). Ultimately, though the clan of the appointed *syiem* joined the clans of the *bakhraw*. The principle of succession to the position of *syiem* became limited to the son of sisters of their deceased predecessor. These procedures existed before the formation of the state and continued even when, between the twelfth and fourteenth centuries, a kingdom was established in the Jaintia Hills and extending into the foothills and plains now in Bangladesh. The kings adopted Hinduism, though the hillfolk retained their indigenous religion.

MYTH AND LEGEND

The folklore of the Khasi-Jaintia has largely been an expression of clan, ethnic, and religious identities and of the sanctity of the matrilineal order, social organization, and political system. Beginning with the origin myth, many narratives—as well as rituals and festivals—emphasized the approved social norms. The origin myth explains why people should be recognized as the children of seven mothers.

According to the myth, in the beginning God created sixteen families and made them stay with him in heaven. A tree, called *U Lum Sohpetbneng*, stood atop a hill at the center of the earth and served as a ladder for the sixteen families to commute between earth and heaven. One day when only seven women were on earth, an evil spirit chopped down the tree, forcing the women to remain there. These seven women mothered mankind. Children of these seven women, known as *Ki Hynniew Trep*, could not travel between heaven and earth, nor could they converse directly with God. When God allowed the seven families to remain on earth, he gave them commandments to follow which would enable

Ritual lifting of three logs representing three of the *saw kpoh* during *Behdienkhlam*.

A traditional Jaintia house decorated with tree branches during *Behdienkhlam*.

Musicians performing during *Nongkrem*.

them to join the nine families (*Ki Khyndai Ha Jrong*), who stay with him in heaven, when their term on earth ended. In one version of this myth collected in the Jaintia Hills, the children of *Ki Hynniew Trep* received these commandments through their chief (*syiem*) U Lakriah when he encountered God somewhere in the hills.

The Jaintia version of the myth is ritually chanted during a festival, *Behdienkhlam*, held annually in Jowai, the principal town in the Jaintia Hills, along with another myth dealing with four (*saw*) mothers (*kpoh*—that is, "womb") who are believed to be the progenitresses of the clans that settled in Jowai.

FESTIVALS AND CELEBRATIONS

The *Behdienkhlam* festival has two purposes: protection of crops after sowing and veneration of the ancestress. Chanting the myth of *Saw Kpoh* and cleaning the clan cemetery promote clan solidarity during the festival, which is held in July. The Khasi-Jaintia equivalent for July is *Naitung*, which means "ill-smelling month" because of decaying vegetation. Folk belief holds that plague and pestilence are caused by a female demon called *khlam*, who must be driven away (*beh*) by using a tree (*dien*)—hence the festival's name. A tree trunk (*khnong*) is brought from the forest a month before the final days of the festival for ritual propitiation. Every house in Jowai places a small tree branch at the entrance. Tree trunks also come from the forests on the first day of the final three days of the festival, and people dance around them to drum accompaniment. The propitiation of the *khnong* occurs in an area called *Shilliangraj*, supposed to be the habitat of the clan which traces its origin to the youngest of the four mythological mothers. Her three sisters receive veneration on the morning of the last day of the festival in the courtyard of the house of the priest (*lyngdoh*) when three logs are lifted as a narrator consecrated by the chief (*daloi*) chants the myth of the four mothers. The bones of people who have died during the year are placed in ossuaries in the cemeteries, which are cleaned before the festival. The final scene of the festival occurs in a sacred pool (*aitnar*), where dancing celebrants immerse the *khnong* and decorated chariots (*rot*).

A Khasi festival called *Nongkrem* for the headquarters of the *hima* where it is held is organized annually by the chief (*syiem*) and ministerial council (*durbar*). Also known for its ritual sacrifice of goats, *pomblang* (from *pom*, meaning severing or cutting, and *blang*, meaning goat) is associated furthermore with the syiemship of Hima Khyrim and is sometimes identified as *Pom blang U Syiem Nongkrem*. The *durbar hima* (political council) and the *syiem* fix the festival's dates—usually in November, though once it was held in May, June, and July. The only public ritual in this festival is the sacrificing of goats, which occurs in full public view in the courtyard of the *syiem*'s residence on the evening of the festival's last day after a divination process using a fowl (hepatoscopy). The other rituals are performed in the residence of the *syiem* in the presence of the members of his family and of members of his council under the direction of his eldest sister (*Ka Syiem Sad*), who is recognized as chief priestess. With libations of rice beer, these rituals invoke the blessings of *U Blei Shillong*, the founding deity of the *hima*; *Lei Long syiem*, ancestress of the *syiem* clan; and *U Suidnia*, the first maternal uncle. They are performed before a sacred oak pillar (*Rishot Blei*) placed in the central hall of the *syiem*'s residence (*iing sad*) after the founding of the *hima*. Among the various dances performed is *shad tyngkoh*, danced by pairs beginning with the chief priest

The *iing-sad*, where rites for *Nongkrem* are performed.

and a drummer, then governors (*sirdars*) of the units (*elaka*) of the *hima*. The sixth pair consists of the *syiem* and a minister (*myntri*), and pairs from the general public follow them. Members of the family of the *syiem* perform another dance, *noh kjat*.

DANCE

The festival's most significant dance occurs on the fourth day. This dance of the virgins (*shad kynthei*), a thanksgiving dance, is paralleled by a dance by males, *shad mastieh*. *Shad kynthei* is structured simply: girls, dressed colorfully in traditional attire known as *jainsem*, ornamented heavily, and crowned with gold or silver tiaras, dance either alone or in groups of two or three. Their eyes fixed on the ground with faces inclined downward, they make only elliptical movements in very slow motion as if they are focused only on their footwork. They do not move the upper parts of their bodies. The dancers rotate backward and forward in the courtyard in time to slow drumbeats. The rhythm vibrates through their whole bodies to communicate

The virgin dance (*shad kynthei*) during *Nongkrem*.

Male dancers ready for *shad mastieh* during *Nongkrem*.

through both time and space. A pervasive ritualistic charge suggests that the dance does not take place for its own sake or for viewers, the general public who understand the ritualized dance's symbols and message; the dance's function serves to restrain change. In *shad mastieh* a group of young men, armed and holding whisks made from the tails of yaks, dance at the outer ring of the courtyard. Their movements are as slow as those of their female counterparts, but their bodies and hands move to suggest an attempt to drive away evil—thus conveying a message of protection.

Although a few other dances—such as *laho* and *longhai*, basically harvest dances—have traditionally occurred in the Jaintia Hills, *shad kynthei* and *shad mastieh* have come to epitomize typical Khasi dance forms. Even an improvised festival, *shad suk mynsiem*, which was introduced early in the twentieth century by Seng Khasi includes dances patterned after these. *Laho* and *longhai*, though, differ from these patterns. *Laho* involves two boys and one girl dancing hand-in-hand to a faster drumbeat than that used in the dances from the *Nongkrem* festival. *Longhai* has men and women dancers facing one another, each holding a hoe (reflecting the Khasi-Jaintia economic identity as shifting cultivators). The dancers place their hoes on the ground with one hand and lift them with the other, rhythmically following the music and drumming.

A couple of narratives explain how these dance patterns, especially *shad kynthei*, *shad mastieh*, and *laho*, became part of local ceremonies. These have been linked with social and religious norms and taboos. Syiem U Lakriah, who is God's emissary on earth, is supposed to have introduced *laho* after ascertaining the godly will through divination. The virgin's dance, *shad kynthei*, came about through the taboo prohibiting relationships between girls and boys of the same clan.

TALES, PROVERBS, AND POETRY

Khasi-Jaintia narratives are mostly etiological and prescriptive. While explaining the interplay of the forces of nature, mankind's relationship with the ecological order and animal world, and other such lofty topics, the stories encourage conformity with kinship norms, sociopolitical customs, and religious-moral codes. Hence a major genre in the Khasi-Jaintia narrative repertoire is the fable, which is simple and straightforward in structure. Fairy tales are more limited in number.

The concern for social control and prescriptive norms has often blurred the distinction between proverbs and aphorisms. Analyses of both narrative texts and proverbs show that they are designed very often to justify a system or a political order. The strategies involved include manipulation of codes, both social and political, in order to effect control. Not much scope for varying interpretations is allowed. While one proverb, *Long jaid na ka kynthei* (From the woman springs the kin), assigns women respectful status as mothers in the matrilineal order and as keepers of the domestic group (*ka nongri iing*), others justify denying women any role in the sociopolitical domain. Examples include *Adur lanot, wei ba la kynih ka'iar kynthei* (Woe the day when the hen begins to crow) and *Ka akor khasi ka khang bah kynih ka iar kynthei ne said thma ha dorbar*, which forbids women from wearing masculine attire and speaking before the *durbar* (council). A woman is like a queen bee, the keeper of the domestic group: *ka Nongri iing* (like a goddess) *ka kynthei ka long kum ka lykhimai* (who becomes fragrant by listening and who loses her honor if she crows like a cock). Such aphorisms keep women "in their place."

Phawar is a distinctive form of oral poetry with a musical quality between chant and song. It consists of a rhyming couplet, which may be sung or chanted to pipe, stringed instruments, or percussion on occasions ranging from rituals to sports competitions. Different categories of *phawar* reflect these different performance situations: at socioreligious occasions such as births, marriages, and funerals; at celebrations of military victories or of successful hunts; during archery competitions; at the erection of megaliths; and during festivals. Whatever the occasion, the *phawar* carries a social or moral message. Each line of the couplet is usually divided into two parts. Both parts of the first line are sung by a "rhyme setter" with a chorus taking up the second line. The first line seems to be a meaningless string of words with the second line presenting the couplet's message—for example, *U kyndeh ka jalyngkhan, u sohbrap ho ia ka skei. / Wat leit leh kam bymman, io timpap ka blei* (He pants for curry leaf, for the passion fruit, ho! For the deer. / Never do what is evil, or the goddess will curse). Another example illustrates this song form:

Wat shaniah jindei tang ha la ka mon,	Do not put too much trust on your own self-will. It is ungrateful.
Haramjat, kum ka mon laitluid ym ju don	Such unbridled freedom [willfulness] has no regard for taboos.
Ka mon khlem nia kam ju niew ia ka sang,	It transgresses limits set by the ancients.
Wat i'u pud ki barim ka nud ryngkang;	Be wise; live according to the rules. Stand on truth in death and life.
Hei khun pyrsa ha mon laitluid aili	Oh children, do not give in to self-will and unbridled freedom.
Suitnia, Iawbei, Thawlang ruh kin diangti.	Only then will you be able to please your ancestors, the family triad.

Ki sur phawar, the musical setting for these couplets, itself has socioreligious associations. The people of Khasi-Jaintia recognize two kinds of music: *ka tem hima* (the beat of the state) and *ka tem shnong* (the local beat). The former is played at state festivals strictly according to traditionally prescribed rhythm, while the latter is associated with local ceremonies connected with naming a child, marriages, funerals, and similar occasions. The performers of *ka tem hima* come from clans believed to be carriers of musical arrangements created by the ancestors, *kumba ialam u longshuwa manshuwa*. Musical arrangements that follow religious prescriptions (*ka niam ka rukom*) are more rigid than those of *ka rong ka taw* ("delightful" celebrations). The former is basically rhythmic, because dancing figures into most religious events. Generally, though, Khasi-Jaintia music is more melodic and rhythmic than harmonic. The most common instruments are a bamboo flute (*tangmuri*), which is much like a clarinet, a large drum (*nakra*), a reed flute (*ka sharati*), and a harp (*duitara*). *Tangmuri* and *nakara* are often used in religious and festive situations, and the music they produce is primarily rhythmic. *Ka sharati* is mostly used to produce melodious tones with romantic overtones as well as in music invoking the spirits of the dead. *Duitara* seldom is used in religious music; instead minstrels accompany themselves with it as they sing "story songs" (*ka sur parom ka maryngthing, duitara bad maryngod*), which are similar to ballads.

A *phawar* sung at an archery competition goes, *Tik ho lih baiong. / Ia i mem shi-liang ly-bong* (Shake, you black arrow. / Hit the one-legged white woman). Usually one archer would lead the *phawar* while others would follow with the cry, *hoi kiw*. But who is this "one-legged white woman"? It is the target (*u skum*) made of small bundles of grass measuring about a foot long and four inches in diameter. The Khasi name for a bow is *ka ryntieh*, and the arrows are called *ki khnam*. The bow is usually about five feet tall. There are two kinds of arrows: *ki pliang*, which have barbs, and *sop*, the plain-headed. The first is meant for hunting while the second is used in archery competitions. Before a competition between teams from two villages begins, incantations occur. *Phawar* also enters into the competition. Other favorite sports in Khasi-Jaintia are hunting, bird-catching, and fishing. Archery, however, occupies a place of pride as the national sport and is believed to be of mythological origin: the first mother, *ka mei-kha*, taught it to her sons.

Ancestor Cult

Frequently Khasi-Jaintia folklore seeks a mythological and legendary connection for every ritual, performance, and sport. In most cases, those connections involve ancestors or ancestresses. Consequently an elaborate ancestor cult has developed with the erection of megaliths as a prominent activity. The people of Khasi-Jaintia believe that dead ancestors once freed from earthly bondage (*ka ruh shong bynda*) are elevated to a higher supernatural status making them capable of aiding mortals in times of crisis. This belief definitely affects the erection of megaliths. All funeral rites involve setting up stones. After cremation, bonechips are collected in a piece of cloth and taken to a small stone chamber called *mawshieng*. The chips are transferred to a clay pot and placed inside the chamber. Later the bundle is taken to the clan ossuary (*mawbah*). Three pairs of monoliths form a line behind two dolmens (*mawkjat*), one for the male and the other for the female relatives. The monoliths (*mawbynnna*) are divided into two major categories: *mawniam*, religious stones, and *mawnam*, memorial stones. Generally erection of *mawniam* follows a pattern: three vertical stones and one horizontal. The middle of the three vertical stones is called the stone of the maternal uncle (*mawknie*), the other two are the maternal nephews (*mawpyrsa*), and the horizontal stone becomes the ancestress stone (*mawkiaw*).

CHALLENGES OF THE MODERN WORLD

Although the social structure, kinship system, family practices, and broad cultural patterns remain traditional, obvious changes have occurred in Khasi-Jaintia folklore during the last century and a half. **Colonialism**, the advent of Christianity, the spread of modern education, modernization, sharing of political power in independent India, occupational mobility from primary to tertiary sectors, and the emergence of a professional middle class with active political leadership have affected most religious behavior, residence patterns (which have shifted from matrilocal to neolocal), and traditional economic pursuits especially in arts and crafts. For instance, the practice of erecting megaliths has mostly stopped due to the preference of burial instead of traditional cremation. Weaving is a lost art in Khasi-Jaintia. Other crafts such as basketry using cane and bamboo—once a prime activity—is also waning. Once fourteen varieties of baskets, mostly conical, characterized this art form.

While changes have occurred since colonization and are happening quickly in all aspects of life, the people of Khasi-Jaintia remain highly conscious of their distinct cultural identity and use oral tradition, particularly myths, to assert their identity in the modern world.

Important sources on Khasi-Jaintia folklore include Bareh (1967); Chowdhury (1978); Gurdon (1975 [1907]); Mawrie (1980); Roy (1979); Sen (1985, 1988, 1992, 2004).

BIBLIOGRAPHY

Bareh, H. 1967. *The History and Culture of the Khasi People*. Shillong: Self-published.

Chowdhury, J. N. 1978. *The Khasi Canvas*. Shillong: Chapala.

Gurdon, P.R.T. 1975 (1907). *The Khasis*. New Delhi: Cosmo.

Mawrie, O. H. 1980. *The Khasi Milieu*. New Delhi: Vikas.

Roy, H., ed. 1979. *Khasi Heritage*. Shillong: Seng Khasi.

Sen, Soumen. 1985. *Social and State Formation in Khasi-Jaintia Hills: A Study of Folklore*. New Delhi: B. R. Publishing.

———. 1988. *Between Tradition and Change: A Perspective of Meghalaya*. New Delhi: B. R. Publishing.

———. 1992. *Women in Meghalaya*. New Delhi: Daya.

———. 2004. *Khasi-Jaintia Folklore: Context, Discourse, and History*. Chennai: National Folklore Support Centre.

Soumen Sen

MEGHALAYA. *See* Khasi-Jaintia

NAGALAND

GEOGRAPHY AND LANGUAGE

Situated in the extreme northeast of **India**, Nagaland is home to a number of tribes collectively identified as the Nagas. Before it attained statehood on 1 December 1963, the areas occupied by these tribes were known as the Naga Hills and the Tuensang Area of the then undivided state of **Assam**. Nagaland has an area of 16,579

Traditional house of an *angh*, a Konyak Naga chief. (Photograph by Temsula Ao)

square kilometers and is bordered by Myanmar on the east, Assam on the west, Arunachal Pradesh on the north, and Manipur on the south. The major tribes of Nagaland are Angami, Ao, Chakesang, Chang, Khiamungan, Konyak, Kuki, Lotha, Phom, Pochury, Rengma, Sangtam, Sema, Yimchunger, and Zeliang. Besides these, a number of sub-tribes are yet to be officially recognized by the government. All these tribes speak different languages mutually unintelligible to each other, and within each language exist innumerable dialects. Thus, while no common Naga language exists, there are as many Naga languages as there are tribes. Naga languages belong to the Indo-Tibetan family, and the Naga **race** is classified as Mongoloid.

Despite the linguistic diversity, the Nagas share many cultural traits as they have lived in contiguous territories for centuries. This factor has therefore facilitated the description of the Nagas as a culturally homogenous group of people. The Nagas live in well-defined territories. They are permanent land dwellers and live in compact villages. The number of villages within a linguistic group varies from tribe to tribe. Each Naga village is an autonomous unit with its own council of clan representatives, which constitutes the authority governing all aspects of village life. The clan distinctions among the Nagas are perhaps the most important institutions that have defined and governed Naga society, which is basically egalitarian and patrilineal and practices exogamous marriage.

In spite of the many shared cultural affinities, linguistic diversity poses a difficult problem for anyone trying to treat Naga life in a comprehensive manner. Therefore, to speak of the folklore of Nagaland, one would obviously be referring to particular tribal lore only. Most of the references would be to the oral forms as there are not many written records. The bulk of the recorded literature of the major tribes is comprised of the accounts left by foreign anthropologists, missionaries, and British administrators written in English. The few indigenous writings are in the different Naga languages, though a few books have now been written in English by Naga writers. However, these books also pertain to specific tribal lore.

MYTHS, LEGENDS, AND FOLKTALES

Most of the written accounts contain myths, legends, and folktales of different kinds as well as various types of folksongs. The recurring themes in the myths and songs concern the origin of the different tribes and their subsequent migration from the places of origin to the present areas of settlement. The tribal folklores also contain proverbs, idiomatic expressions, superstitions, and dreamlore. Stories about nature, animals, and supernatural beings, though not believed to be "true," are, however, integral components of Naga folklore.

Most Naga myths relate to the origin of the tribes and clans, and these are believed to be true. For example, the Aos believe that the first people of the tribe, three males and three females, emerged from six stones at a place called Lungterok, which literally means "six stones." The myth also specifies that these people belonged to the three main clans of the Aos—Pongener, Longkumer, and Jamir—and that the first exogamous marriages took place among the three men and three women of these clans. The exogamous marriages thus recorded in the myth have been practiced by generations of Aos down to the present. Some other Naga tribes such as the Changs and Angamis have similar origin myths. But the origin myth of the Angami holds that their forefathers came out of the earth somewhere south of present-day Angami country. The Chang myth says that all living creatures, humans, animals, and birds emerged from a big hole in the earth. A big door on the "wall of the earth," from which all these creatures emerged, is supposed to have been opened. But the opening was only for a short duration. Soon thereafter it was closed forever. It is also said that all these creatures lived together, spoke the same language, and ate the same food because there was no distinction between people, animals, and birds at this stage. The Changs call this the "senseless stage" or *Mungyangyangabu Mutdhen*. The Lothas and Semas have similar origin myths. These myths therefore can be considered as the bases of the tribes' history from which follow all related lore of the different tribes. Some creation myths also credit a "super" being or power with the creation of human beings and other animals. The Aos believe that *Lijaba* is the creator of all life on earth. For the Rengmas, it is a powerful being called *Songinyu* or *Aniza*; the Semas call him *Alhou* or *Timilhou*; and the Angamis believe that *Ukepenopfu* is the creator of all living beings.

A Konyak *angh*'s wife. (Photograph by Temsula Ao)

Legends too are considered to be true, as they pertain to tribal migrations and exploits of tribal heroes. But they are less sacrosanct than myths because they are about human beings rather than some supernatural phenomena which resulted in the very "being" of the tribes. Within a tribe, it has sometimes been observed that the authenticity of certain legends is challenged when, for example, the seniority of a clan over another is disputed. But in any Naga tribe, to raise doubts about the origin myth is an unpardonable crime because by doing so the very existence of the tribe is being questioned.

Folktales belong to that category of narratives that, though not believed to be true, nevertheless are found among all the Naga tribes and cover a variety of subjects, including nature, animals, and human beings as well as the supernatural. For example, an Angami tale depicts the sun as male and the moon as a female upon which grow nettles and a cotton tree perhaps to explain dark spots on the moon. The Ao story about the moon says that the moon's dark spots are cow dung and ashes thrown at it by mischievous children who chased it far from the earth. In almost all the Naga tales about animals, the interesting feature is their ability to use human language. J. H. Hutton (1968a) records a Kacha Naga story entitled "The Wild Dog," which features a dog and his master speaking to each other, and many such stories occur among other Naga tribes. The supernatural tales often depict a romantic union between a human being and a supernatural. Among the Semas are two different stories entitled "A Fairy Wife" and "A Fairy Husband" which speak of such a union. An Ao Naga story tells of a girl who was loved by a tree-spirit.

Certain distinctive tales seem to be confined to only a few of the Naga tribes. One such story entitled "Amazons" is about a village only of women, who drive away male intruders with war bows. When a man goes there, they are so eager to possess him that they tear him to pieces. This story can be found in Angami and Sema folklore—the latter even placing the Amazons in a village east of the Patkoi-Barail range. Another Ao story, recorded by J. P. Mills (1973 [1926]), treats a group of cannibals with long ears and upside-down noses. Mills adds that this story is an ancient one traceable to the Roman author Pliny and also that the Bila-an of the Philippines say that the first men created had upside-down noses and were greatly inconvenienced by the rain falling into them. Stories about the diversity of Naga languages are also found in Angami, Chang, and Rengma folklore. Hutton calls the Angami tale "The Tower of Babel," while Mills calls a similar Rengma story "Confusion of Tongues." The Changs have a story about a great flood in which a beautiful girl called Momola is loved by a river deity. Because the girl's mother reneged on her promise to let the river deity marry her daughter in return for a plentiful harvest, the river deity caused a great flood that threatened to sweep the entire village away. It was only after Momola was given to him that the flood subsided. Many Naga tales also speak of transformations: of humans becoming birds, monkeys, fish, and other creatures and also of the forms of animals undergoing drastic changes from their original shapes and sizes. Hutton has remarked about the ending of the recorded stories, "The 'lived happily ever' ending is conspicuous by its absence in Naga stories."

Funerary offerings at the gravesite of an *angh*. (Photograph by Temsula Ao)

Yet another type of tale in the folklore of some tribes presents a mischievous character which may be characterized as a **trickster**. In Angami stories this character is called *Mache*, while the Semas call him *Iki*, the Lothas *Apfuho*, and the Rengmas *Che*. Conversely, in Ao folklore a character called *Alokba* is portrayed as the proverbial numbskull or blockhead.

SONGS

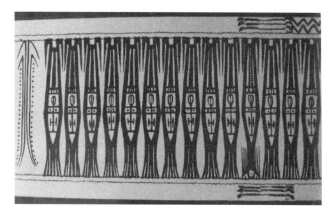

Paintings using *Teri Phiketsu* on the center strip of a Rengma Naga warrior shawl. (Photograph by Temsula Ao)

The performance of various types of songs has been an integral part of Naga community life. Whether at home or in the fields, during festivals or funerals, at happy or sad occasions, songs were composed and sung to suit the situation. The contents of Naga folksongs range from myths, legends, hymns to various gods, and dirges to love songs and lullabies. Among the Nagas, singing various types of songs is subject to certain conditions. For example, in Ao society, there are songs which can be sung by men only and others which only women sing. The former category includes origin songs, war songs, hunting and fishing songs, and group songs sung during the Moatsu festival when groups of men visit households and drink newly brewed rice wine. The women's songs include dirges or funeral songs, love songs, and lullabies. Songs which are sung in the fields while working are not generally sung elsewhere. In the same way, hunting and fishing songs can be sung only in the appropriate contexts.

Another significant role played by songs in the collective life of the Nagas is as interlocutors in prose narratives and authenticators of historical facts. In narratives where the contents relate to important aspects of life such as the origin and migration or the first founding of particular villages, the punch line is always delivered in the form of a song.

Paintings using *Tsungkotepsu* pattern on the center strip of an Ao Nago warrior shawl. (Photograph by Temsula Ao)

ARTS AND CRAFTS

Among the material forms of folklore, textiles have played a significant role in Naga society by documenting and preserving tribal and individual distinctions among the people. Moreover, the history represented on textiles is closely linked to the evolution of Naga culture. Each Naga tribe has distinctive designs and color combinations which serve as tribal identity markers. Using these designs and colors, Naga women have effected innovations, but certain textiles are recognized as "traditional" and are not supposed to be altered or added to. Also, gender distinctions regarding textiles are strictly followed. For example, the Ao warrior or headhunter's shawl known as the *Tsungkotepsu* or *Mangkotepsu* cannot be worn by a woman. Similarly, men would never wear a woman's skirt or shawl, for that would symbolize loss of manhood. Within particular tribes, different clans have evolved specific designs, mainly in women's wear, which identify the wearer's clan. In addition, each tribe has its class markers. Tradition has designated certain textiles as "exclusive." In the past if "undeserving" people wore them, they were fined according to customary laws for violating norms. These exclusive garments, commonly called "rich man's" or "rich woman's" wear,

Tattoos on the face and body of an *angh*. Note the turquoise bead knee circlet (royal marker) and necklace of human head replicas and boar's teeth. (Photograph by Temsula Ao)

could be worn by people who had taken heads in warfare as well as those who had given feasts of merit. Their wives could add extra ornamentations such as tassels of goats' hair or silver bells to their garments. The Ao warrior shawl mentioned above belongs to this "exclusive" category of textiles.

Among the Aos, the right to wear certain ornaments—such as ivory armlets by men and brass rings as head decorations by women—is steeped in ancient lore. For example, men of the Jamir clan among the Aos can wear only one such armlet, whereas men from the senior Pongener clan can wear armlets on both arms.

Among the Konyaks, only the traditional and hereditary chiefs called *Anghs* have the right to wear particular beads, turquoise in color, around their necks and knees. This bead is thus identified with royalty in this tribe. Again, only royal persons among the Konyaks can wear tattoos of a special design. Tattooing as body ornamentation exists among some other tribes too, but the significance differs from that of the Konyaks. Among the Aos, tattoos are done on women only to signify a girl's coming of age. Also, the designs differ from clan to clan.

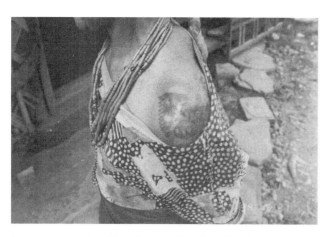

A tattoo on the shoulder of a Konyak *angh*'s wife. (Photograph by Temsula Ao)

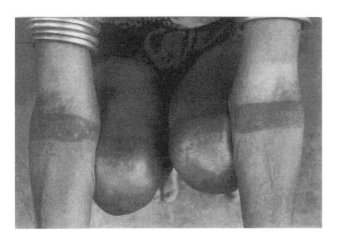

Tatoos on the knees and forearms of a Konyak *angh*'s wife. (Photograph by Temsula Ao)

NAMES, SYMBOLS, AND MEANINGS

The significance attached to names embodies much lore about the evolution and history of tribes as well as of different clans. J. H. Hutton (1968a) says that some Angami names have abstract meanings, which indicate good qualities or good fortune: Kevise suggests "arriving at a good time," and Viyale means "let your share be good," for example. On the other hand, J. P. Mills (1982) remarks that Rengma names have few remembered meanings. Giving a second name has been observed among the Angamis, Rengmas, Semas, and others. Among the former, if a child is born under conditions of unusual distress or affliction, the mother gives a suitable second name of precisely an opposite nature to that of the ones mentioned above. The Aos and Rengmas follow a slightly different custom of changing a child's name, which amounts to giving a second name. If after naming, a child cries continually or is ill all the time, it is believed that the aura of the lore in the name is too awesome for the child, and a more suitable name is given. Names of ancestors and other relatives but never that of a living person are also chosen for the new arrivals. If a living person's name is given, the Semas believe that the elder one will die because it would be like burdening one soul with two physical bodies, one of which, being useless, would die. This concern may relate to the belief that a person's soul responds to the name as well to the body. According to Ao custom, no duplication of names can occur within a clan. If inadvertently a child has been given a name which a clansperson already has, the younger one must relinquish the name, and the parents have to find another for the child. Renewing ancestral names ensures the continuity of clan lore. Taboos are attached to names of persons who have died unnatural deaths like drowning or falling from trees or cliffs, whose heads were taken by enemies, who were killed by wild animals, and who committed suicide; such names are not renewed. Also, if the holders of a name die childless for three successive generations, the clan abandons that name. Taking the names of parents, of elders, and of husbands by wives is taboo among the Nagas because this amounts to showing disrespect to elders.

This outline of Naga folklore indicates how pervasive it has been in helping people to articulate their views about themselves and the world around them. Through the various narratives and songs, the Nagas have expressed their attitudes to perceived and experienced reality while reflecting upon the possibilities of magic reality in their existence. The animal tales where humans and animals are shown speaking the same language reveal the close kinship that existed between humans and animals. In the various supernatural tales, we can see elements of animism, the traditional religion of the Nagas. The symbolism attached to textiles, ornaments, names, and other artifacts encapsulates much of the people's lore. Folklore for the Nagas has been and still is the storehouse of racial history, regulator of social behavior, and encoder of the fundamental principles according to which the traditional Naga society has evolved and survived.

A wooden receptacle with relief carvings of human heads and *mithun* (bison) horns. (Photograph by Temsula Ao)

BIBLIOGRAPHY

Ao, Temsula. 2001. *The Ao-Naga Oral Tradition*. Baroda: Bhasha Publications.

Hutton, J. H. 1968a. *The Angami Nagas*. Bombay: Oxford University Press.

———. 1968b. *The Sema Nagas*. London: Oxford University Press.

Mills, J. P. 1982. *The Rengma Nagas*. Calcutta: Directorate of Art and Culture, Government of Nagaland.

———. 1973 (1926). *The Ao Nagas*. London: Macmillan.

Temsula Ao

ORISSA

GEOGRAPHY AND HISTORY

Situated on the eastern coast of **India** between Kolkatta and Chennai, the state of Orissa is like a bridge between northern and southern regions of the Indian subcontinent and represents a cultural synthesis between different ethnic and religious groups. Its population of over 37 million spreads over a landmass of 1,550,707 square kilometers, a third of which is covered by dense forests. Forty percent of the population is of tribal origin and includes sixty-two ethnic groups. The native language is Oriya, one of the regional languages of India, which has a distinctive alphabet and literature. Though endowed with mineral resources, Orissa is primarily an agrarian state with rich varieties of maritime activities developed along a coastal belt that runs for over 480 kilometers along the Bay of Bengal.

Historically Orissa has been the theater for upheavals, frequent reversals, and dominations which have shaped the state's cultural and religious identity. Orissa emerged into history during the third century B.C.E. when the emperor Ashoka conquered a part of the region, then called Kalinga. He left evidence of his conquest, his administration, and his conversion to Buddhism in rock inscriptions which are spread throughout the state. Similar inscriptions commemorate the reign of the emperor Kahravela in the second century B.C.E. They illuminate Jainism, the faith he adopted, and his type of administration and governance.

During the first centuries of the common era the prevalent religion blended Tantrism and Buddhism. This paved the way for two main streams of Hinduism: the Shiva cult, practiced since the sixth century by the rulers of the Kesari dynasty who were responsible for constructing the major Shaivaite temples at Bhubaneswar, the present capital of Orissa; and the Vishnu cult, which become predominant under the Ganga dynasty from the eleventh century onwards. Many consider this the golden period in Orissa's history, when major works of architecture, art, and literature were produced. Orissa lost its independence in 1568, when the Afghans of Bengal came to power. A series of foreign dominations followed: Muslims until the beginning of the eighteenth century, then the Maratha domination which lasted until the British conquered Orissa in 1805. British rule continued until 1947 when the new constitution of India made the region a part of a newly independent nation.

MYTHS OF LORD JAGANNATH

In addition to its strong military situation, Orissa based its identity in spite of its turbulent history on beliefs associated with Lord Jagannath ("Lord of the Universe"), the protector deity of the population. Although different cities have served as administrative capital through the years, the real soul of Orissa lies in the city of Puri, also called Purushottama Kshetra, where the temple of Lord Jagannath is located. This deity and his cult have provided the people of Orissa with a sense of cultural unity.

The myth of origin associated with the cult of Lord Jagannath blends mythological motifs with philosophy and social study. Lord Jagannath has inspired many legends, folktales, literary works, and philosophical studies. His origin myth links different layers of belief and social strata.

The first link connects two mythological ages through the theory of reincarnation of the same god: the pastoral deity Krishna of the age of Dwaraka becomes the tribal god Nilamadhava in the age of Kali. In this incarnation he is associated with tree-worship and abides in a secret spot in the middle of a dense forest. He is known only to the Sabara tribes and is looked after by their chief Viswabasu. The legendary king Indradyumna helped by his Brahman priest Vidyapati is able to find the idol, but his wish to retrieve it and build a proper place for its worship is postponed because Nilamadhava suddenly disappears. At this point comes the second link in the narrative: the passage from the aboriginal aspect of Jagannath to his iconographic form. The king gets information in a dream that the log (*dharu*) containing the sacred remains of Lord Krishna will appear on the seashore and that he should build a temple and call Lord Brahma from heaven for its consecration. Indradyumna has to stay in heaven waiting for Brahma to awaken from his meditation. Meanwhile, many things change on earth, and the temple he constructed is submerged by sand. A new generation of rulers have now come to power, and one day King Galamadhava's horse strikes something hidden in the sand. The king discovers the temple and claims it as his own construction. Eventually Indradyumna returns from heaven to regain control over the situation, and Galamadhava is exposed as an impostor and condemned to remain unworshipped outside the temple premises.

Now comes the time to retrieve the log that the sea has brought ashore and to construct an idol from it. Nobody can draw the heavy log from the waters, and the god again appears in a dream to Indradyumna and advises him to send the two devotees Viswabasu and Vidyapati to retrieve it. Building an idol from the log also poses difficulties. None of the artisans engaged in the job can make any progress. Finally an old man appears and asks to be locked in a room with the log and not to be disturbed. After fourteen days the king, prompted by the queen, Gundicha, breaks the seal to find an unfinished idol and no trace of the old man. Lord Jagannath is born without hands and feet and with a body that retains traces of his previous manifestation linked to tree worship.

Lord Jagannath's story connects the aboriginal tribal population of the land to the brahmanical Aryan civilization. This creates a syncretistic worldview that is also reflected in rituals associated with his cult. He is attended by two categories of temple servants: the *pandas*, who represent the Brahmans, and the *daitas*, who resesent the aboriginal Sabara who first discovered the god. Although the two categories of servants have clearly distinct duties and do not interfere with each other, that both contribute to the worship of Lord Jagannath represents Orissa's cultural synthesis and tolerance. The present temple of Lord Jagannath at Puri is attributed to King Chocagangadeva, who ruled Orissa in the first half of the twelfth century. But prior to this, legend testifies to the existence of an earlier shrine.

MYTHS OF THE KONARK TEMPLE

Another king of the Ganga dynasty, who left behind a lasting monument of fame, is Narasinha Deva, who reigned from 1238 to 1264. He built the famous Konark temple, which, in the shape of a huge chariot, is homage to the Sun god. Temple construction began at the end of a victorious military expedition against the Muslim invaders and was intended to celebrate the victory of the Sun over the forces of darkness. A number of myths and legends are associated with the construction and subsequent fall of this monument of faith. The place where the present temple stands used to be the mouth of the Chandrabaga River, associated mythologically with Samba, son of Lord Krishna, who, afflicted with leprosy and banished from his father's court for accidently looking upon the nymphs of the palace while they bathed naked, was cured at this spot by the Sun, of whom he became a dedicated devotee.

The Sun Temple at Konark, also called the Black Pagoda, has become the most legendary of all the temples in Orissa as well as subject of ballads, poems, plays, and dance dramas. According the legend, twelve hundred craftsmen were engaged by the king for twelve years to build the temple at a cost of twelve years of the kingdom's revenue. The king ordered the masons not to leave the site before the completion of the temple. The twelve years had almost elapsed, and still the temple could not be completed because the huge top-stone (*kalasa*) could not be fixed on the neck of the temple. Annoyed, the king had ordered that if this was not done by a particular date, all the craftsmen would lose their heads. Eventually the chief architect's son, a twelve-year-old boy, solved the riddle. He had come to the construction site to see his father, whom he had never seen before. The story ends with this talented boy throwing himself from the top of the temple into the Chandrabaga River to save the lives of the 1,200 masons, who feared that the king—upon hearing that a boy rather than they had solved the riddle of the top-stone—would decapitate them. Local people still say that this sacrilege prevents the temple-chariot from being able to rise into the sky with the Sun aboard.

DANCE

The cult of Lord Jagannath also nurtured *odissi*, the region's classical dance form, which is accompanied by a style of singing by the same name. Although we have evidence of this dance form in some of the bas-reliefs found in the Jain caves of Emperor Karavela, it is as a daily service to Lord Jagannath performed by a class of female temple servants called *devadasi* that the dance flourished and developed. Interference by invaders from the fifteenth century onwards almost caused the dance to have disappeared by the beginning of the twentieth century, but intellectuals, scholars, traditional masters, and *devadasi* revived it after independence and gave it a secular form. A class of boy dancers called *gotipua* has also played a role in preserving this dance form. Their style of dancing is more vigorous and rhythmic than that performed by the *devadasi*, and it is characterized by intricate acrobatics and footwork. The *gotipua* survive in a few villages near Puri, and they learn the dance in the traditional *guru-shishya parampara* system.

The military structure of the Orissa has joined religion in shaping its population's social and cultural identity. The feudal system, which existed from the eighth century until British hegemony, demanded that vassal states, located on the **frontiers** would receive some autonomy in exchange for protecting the region from foreign invasions, supplying troops, and paying a nominal tribute. To fulfill military obligations as well as to ensure their own safety, hill chiefs maintained their own militias. During war, contingents of footsoldiers or *paiks* constituted the bulk of the imperial army, while during peacetime they kept themselves in condition through exercises and training conducted in the gymnasium or *akhada*. The style of dance called *chhau* (from *chhauni*, meaning military camp) derives from these exercises and from the tribal dances prevalent in the Mayurbhanji district of Orissa, where the dance flourished under royal patronage. Performed mostly by men, the *chhau* is very vigorous and is accompanied by different types of drums (*dhol, dhumsa,* and *chadchadi*) and a pipe called *mahuri*.

Another dance which requires martial attire is the *naga* dance performed in the streets of Puri at the time of *Rama novami*, celebrated on the ninth day of the full moon of *Chaitra* (March–April). Dancers come out of the streets dressed in a costume of tiger skin and peacock feathers, holding sword, shield, and bow and arrows. They dance with forceful steps and a ferocious look in their eyes. Local opinion holds that the *naga* are religious men who came down long ago from the Himalayas to visit Lord Jagannath and that they have developed their ferocious, barbaric personas due to the long journey and all the battles they fought along the way.

Every tribe in Orissa has its own form of dance, performed for marriages, death anniversaries, birth celebrations, and seasonal occasions. Tribal women perform their dances mostly in circular patterns, forming a chain by connecting arms. At one end of the chain is the leading dancer who usually holds a peacock feather or handkerchief in her free hand and gives the signal for changing the stages. The other end is kept open so that women may join the dance at any time. The steps are relatively simple but are generally performed with extreme grace and synchronization. Men usually provide musical accompaniment by dancing and playing percussion instruments. They place themselves either in the center or on the outer ring of the chain. An important element in tribal dances is the dialogue between males and females in the form of witty, humorous, often improvised songs.

Though performed traditionally at certain seasonal events in western Orissa, the dance form known as *dalkhai* is often presented nowadays at major dance events and cultural functions throughout the state. The dancers wear colorful Sambalpuri saris woven by local artisans and hold both ends of a scarf worn over the shoulders while dancing. They perform their steps, accompanied by the rhythm of several drums, by placing the legs close together, bending their knees, and moving back and forth in a half-seated position.

FOLK THEATER

Folk plays have been associated with rituals and festivals in honor of various deities. These forms of popular entertainment involve dance, music, and singing as well as acting and dialogue. Male actors take the roles even of female characters. Called *pala*, *swanga*, *leela*, *nata*, *nataka*, and *yatra*, the plays share a high degree of dramatization and melodic content. They represent a storehouse of folk stories, ballads, myths, popular characters, and folk beliefs as well as classical and folk melodies. Some of the *leela* bear the names of the gods and goddesses whose stories they enact. For example, *Krishna leela*, *Radha-prema leela*, and *ras leela* depict episodes from the story of Krishna, his sports with cowherds in the forest Vrindavan, and his amorous play with his favorite companion Radha. From the sixteenth century Orissa has been influenced by Sri Chaitanya, a Vaishnava saint whose religious teachings of erotic mysticism inspired a number of poets to write songs of devotion pertaining to Radha and Krishna. They added music to their songs and prescribed *raga* (melodic patterns) and *tala* (rhythmic patterns) for them. A libretto for a *ras leela* or *Krishna leela* would be formed from these songs, to which a few lines of dialogue would be added. While *leela* are mostly religious or epic in character, other folk plays such as *pala* and *swanga* are more secular and include topics and characters from history and everyday social life.

Danda nata is an interesting mixture of austerity practices, religious fervor, and histrionics. *Danda* means "pole," and *nata* means "play." This performance occurs during the thirteen days preceding *pana sankranti* (March–April) in honor of the god Shiva, whom the phallic pole represents, and the goddess Shakti, the feminine aspect of Shiva represented by two cane sticks covered with red bangles, strips of black cloth, and a sari. *Danda nata* includes dance, song, dialogue, and physical action. The performers, who are usually lower-caste Hindus, must adhere to a vow to fast rigorously during the entire festival period. During the days they engage in activities such as *dhuli danda* (which depict agricultural operations performed on hot sand), *pani danda* (water acrobatics), and *agni danda* (walking on hot coals and other rituals involving fire). In the evenings, the performers act out *swanga* (plays) before the houses of the people who have sponsored the festvial.

In the *danda nata* the themes of the plays often come from ordinary life and the relations of tribal peoples. The most popular characters include bird-hunters, hermits, mendicants, nomads, and a tribal married couple. The steps of the dances are vigorous and performed at a fast tempo. Dialogues among the main players alternate with songs directed to the audience and dancing. The accompanying orchestra includes percussive instruments (*packawaj*, *dholak*, and *jodinagar*), *jhumuka* (metal balls with pieces of iron inside), harmonium, *gini* (cymbals), and wind instruments (*mohuri* and *kahali*).

The latest form of literary folk play, which came to Orissa from West Bengal in the early nineteenth century, is *yatra*, a dramatic performance which gained immediate popularity because of its rich variety of instrumentation and decoration when compared to the local *swanga*. Orissa *yatra* came to be known as "opera" and developed from relatively small-budget entertainments presented in the courtyard of a *raja-zamindar* (local landlord) into a major extravaganza that operates on a three-level stage. While once the proprietor of the party was also playwright, director, and musical composer, nowadays a *yatra* party consists of more than two hundred people, including actors and actresses, dancers, musicians, and technicians. These are supervised by a full-time manager who along with choreographers and composers are hired on a contract basis. Although the acting style has retained its theatrical, almost melodramatic flavor, costumes, set and light designs, music, and dancing style reflect current trends in Hindi films.

ARTS AND CRAFTS

The temples and their associated festivals and rituals provide a basis for Orissan handicrafts. The exquisite stone carvings which adorn the outer walls of the temples best exemplify Oriya traditional stonework. Huge crowds of pilgrims who visit temples during festivals provide a steady income for artisans. Customarily, all pilgrims to Puri should return home with five sticks of cane, five necklaces made from *tulsi* seeds (a sacred plant similar to basil), five small baskets of *mahaprasad* (food cooked in the temple kitchens), and five *patta-chitra* (traditional paintings on canvas). The work of *chitra-kara*, painters who live in Puri and surrounding villages, these paintings and many other articles—such as papier-maché masks and toys, *tala-patra* (paintings on palm leaves), *matta-chitra* (paintings on raw silk), *noria-chitra* (paintings of coconuts), and Jagannath idols—are on sale alongside the main road into the community. The *chitra-kura* still paint in the traditional style, using five basic colors (red, yellow, indigo, black, and white) obtained from natural ingredients. They prepare their canvases using old cloths stiffened with tamarind glue and chalk powder.

While *patta-chitra* illustrate stories of gods and goddesses, symbolic and or-namental motifs characterize the wall and floor paintings done by women as part of domestic rituals. These paintings are produced to fulfill desires and to protect family members, and the images may invoke specific deities for each day and each month. *Jhoti* (designs made on the ground or walls by dipping the fingers of the right hand into rice paste), *muruja* (drawings created on the floor with a white powder made from ground stones), and floral decorations made from colorful grains are part of the indigenous art produced by genera-tions of women in Orissa.

A *patta-chitra* painting. (Photograph by Ileana Citaristi)

The tribal population living mostly on hilltops and in forested areas of western and southern Orissa build their houses using vernacular technology and local mate-rials. They decorate these residences with paintings and artifacts which reflect their way of life. For example, the highly figurative wall paintings (*ittal*) of the Lanja Saura, who live mostly in the Ganjam and Koraput districts of southern Orissa, re-flect the cult of the dead, while the Juanga dormitory, where young boys and girls meet for the first time, also serves as a gallery of wood carvings and mud wall reliefs. The Santals of northern Orissa paint their mud houses with beautiful decorative tones of black and red clay, while the Kondhs paint their walls with dream-inspired motifs.

The Sithulia, nomadic tribes of Ganjam, produce metalware items (boxes, lamps, and figures of deities) that are meticulously cast in brass using a lost-wax process. They are intricately decorated with a wire work finish. Utensils and decorative ob-jects made of bell metal, brass, horn, silver filigree, papier-maché, lacquer, and wood along with handloomed silk and cotton fabrics colored with the tie-and-dye process are part of the region's rich handicraft heritage. Display of these items at interna-tional fairs and exhibitions and an increasing export demand have reoriented forms and designs without compromising traditional methods and values. The appliqué worker in Pipli no longer produces only canopies and traditional umbrellas for the car festival of Lord Jagannath, but beach and garden umbrellas with fittings for steel frames to be sold in Paris and New York. The silver filigree of Cuttack has been re-oriented for candle stands, cigarette holders, tiepins, and tableware as well as cos-tume jewelry. An alarming trend is the increasing number of plastic objects and synthetic fabrics which one finds in stalls at local markets and fairs. It seems that while artisans' work is gaining appreciation in faraway lands, it is losing ground among traditional consumers.

FESTIVALS AND CELEBRATIONS

A number of religious festivals (known as *yatra*, *utsava*, and *parva*) associated with Lord Jagannath occur not only in Puri but in every household and shrine throughout Orissa. The proverb that says, "There are twelve months in a year, but in Puri thirteen festi-vals are celebrated," indicates the proliferation of such occasions. Although they hap-pen throughout the year, October through April witness most festivals related to agricultural procedures, such as planting and harvesting and to the change of seasons, join those associated with gods and goddesses. If one adds the distinctive festivals celebrated by tribal populations, the number of celebrations becomes staggering.

One of the most important festivals associated with Lord Jagannath, his elder brother Balabhadra, and his younger sister Subhadra is the Ratha Yatra, performed during the lunar month *Asadha* (June–July) for nine days starting from the second day of the full moon. On the first day of the festival, the three deities are placed on decorated chariots and pulled by devotees toward the abode of their aunt Gundicha, from where they will return after seven days. The importance of the *yatra* lies in its allowing all people, regardless of caste, creed, or religion, access to the deities, whom they can see, touch, and worship without restriction. This is the only occasion during the year when the deities emerge from the temple in their original form. During other festivals performed outside temple precincts, only their representatives are brought out.

The construction of the chariots for the three deities begins on the day called *akshaya trutya*, which falls on the third day of the full moon of the lunar month *Vaishakha* (April–May). This day is therefore considered auspicious for starting any kind of building activity and is particularly celebrated by farmers as the first day of ceremonial sowing of rice.

During the preceding month, *Chaitra* (March–April), a number of festivals occur in different parts of Orissa, especially coastal areas, to propitiate the gods in anticipation of the beginning of the agricultural year. People make vows (*brata*) and penances to appease the gods, hoping for a good rainy season and consequent crops. On the last three days of the month, which precede the beginning of the new solar year (*pana sankranti*), devotees (*bhakta*) perform physical feats of endurance such as walking on burning coals or rolling on sharp, thorny branches for the benefit of the entire community.

Fishing communities celebrate the passage between *Chaitra* and *Vaishaka* with a festival called *Chaitighoda-nata*, during which they worship the horse-headed Basuli, goddess of wealth, who is their patron deity. They celebrate the goddess by dancing and singing around a horse made of wood and bamboo, decorated with garlands of red flowers, and moved about by a man who appears to be riding it. Local belief holds that this festival originated during the first century C.E., when Tantrism began to gain ground in Orissa. The horse-headed goddess wears a blood-red cloth over her body and is worshipped by devotees each Saturday and Tuesday throughout the year.

Two popular festivals focus on unmarried girls: *kumar purnima*, celebrated on the night of the full moon of *Ashwina* (October–November), and *raja sankranti*, which starts on the first day of *Asara* (June–July) and continues for three days. During *kumar purnima* young girls wishing for a handsome husband fast and make special offerings of food to the god Kumar, the son of Shiva. They offer special prayers to the Sun early in the morning and fast during the day. In the evening when the moon rises, they dance, sing, and play a game called *puchi*, which involves jumping and other movements. *Raja sankranti* is a fertility festival celebrated at the onset of the monsoon season. It is believed to coincide with the menstruation of Mother Earth. Because the earth is supposed to be resting, all agricultural operations cease, and young unmarried girls are not supposed to walk barefoot, scratch the earth, grind, or tear anything apart. Dressed up and decorated, they swing joyfully on improvised swings, sing special songs, and eat *poda pitha*, a cake prepared from rice powder, molasses, coconut, and *ghi*, instead of rice.

Kartika (October–November) is considered to be the most sacred month of the year. During the last five days (*panchaka*) ending with the night of the full moon (*kartika purnima*) devotees take early-morning baths and fast all day. *Kartika* is supposed to be propitious for commemorating the dead ancestors, and widows especially fast and take ritual baths throughout the month. On the full moon day, another festival occurs which recalls maritime expeditions from Orissa toward **Bali**, Java, and Sumatra, which used to commence every year on this day. People assemble early in the morning near a river or sacred tank to float tiny boats made from banana stems or colored paper, which carry lamps and small presents of betel leaves or betel nuts. On this day in Cuttack, an ancient town on the Mahanadi River that was Orissa's capital for centuries before being replaced by Bhubaneswar after independence, a big fair called *bali jatra* starts. Thousands of people gather at the fairgrounds where they may buy and sell a variety of goods.

STUDIES OF ORISSA FOLKLORE

Important general sources on Orissa include Chatterjee (1966); Hunter and Stirling (1980); and Ramsay (1982). Overviews of art and folklore include Das (1991); Das and Mohapatra (1979); and Fabri (1974). More specific sources deal with tales and songs (Mahapatra 1988, 1991), folk theater (Das, Kar, and Kar 2000 and Pattanaik 1998), and religion and festival (Citaristi 2004; Dehejia 1979; Mishra 1984; Mulk 1968; and Pattanaik 1982). Periodical articles dealing with material folk culture include Citaristi (1995) and Sandal (1995). Additional sources of various of aspect of Orissan folklore are articles appearing in souvenir booklets accompanying festivals, exhibitions, and other events.

BIBLIOGRAPHY

Chatterjee, S. K. 1966. *The People, Language, and Culture of Orissa*, Artavallabha Mohanti Memorial Lectures. Bhubaneswar: Orissa Sahitya Academi.

Citaristi, Ileana. 1995. An Artists' Village: Raghurajpur. *Know India*, May: 6–7.

———. 2004. Celebrating Spring. *Discover India*, May: 50–53.

Das, H. C., I. B. Kar, and B. B. Kar. 2000. *Tradition of Folk Theatres*. Bhubaneswar: Advanced Center for Indological Studies.

Das, K. B. 1991. *Folklore of Orissa*. Bhubaneswar: Orissa Sahitya Academi.

Das, K. B., and L. K. Mohapatra. 1979. *Folklore of Orissa*. Bhubaneswar: Orissa Sahitya Academi.

Dehejia, Vidya. 1979. *Early Stone Temples of Orissa*. New Delhi: Vikash Publishing House.

Fabri, Charles Louis. 1974. *History of the Art of Orissa*. Bombay: Orient Longman.

Hunter, W. W., and Andrew Stirling. 1980. *A History of Orissa*. New Delhi: Bharatiya Publishing House.

Mahapatra, Sitakant. 1988. *The Tangled Web: Tribal Life and Culture of Orissa*. Bhubaneswar: Orissa Sahitya Academi.

———. 1991. *The Endless Wave: Tribal Songs and Tales of Orissa*. Bhubaneswar: Orissa Sahitya Academi.

Mishra, K. C. 1984. *The Cult of Jagannath.* Calcutta: Firma KLM.

Mulk, Raj Anand. 1968. *Konark.* Bombay: Marg Publications.

Pattanaik, D. N. 1982. *Festivals of Orissa.* Bhubaneswar: Orissa Sahitya Academi.

———. 1998. *Folk Theatre of Orissa.* Bhubaneswar: Orissa Sangeet Natak Academi.

Ramsay, L.E.B. Cobden. 1982. *Feudatory States of Orissa.* Calcutta: Firma KLM.

Sandal, Venu. 1995. The Crafts of Orissa. *Discover India,* February: 40–43.

Ileana Citaristi

UTTAR PRADESH

GEOGRAPHY AND HISTORY

India's largest state and home to some 170 million people, Uttar Pradesh is the site of the holy city of Varanasi, the most sacred of Hinduism's cities and the goal of some 70,000 persons a day who visit its more than 1,500 temples. It is also home to the Kumbh Mela at Allahabad, where the three sacred rivers, the Ganges, the Yamuna, and the invisible Saraswati, merge. Here some 45 million people gather every twelve years to purify their bodies and souls so that they may leave the cycle of birth and rebirth. While the population today is predominantly Hindu, for more than 400 years much of what is now Uttar Pradesh was ruled by Muslims, and the Muslim influence is seen in the content of oral traditions, in architecture, and in language, with many Arabic and Persian terms entering the dialects of the region. On the western fringe of the state in the city of Agra is the Taj Mahal, built in the 1630s by the Mughal ruler Shah Jahan as a tomb for his beloved wife Mumtaz. To further complicate the religious picture of the state, just outside of Varanasi is Sarnath, the site of the Buddha's first sermon.

Interior view of the monkey temple at Varanasi, India, showing elaborately carved columns and doorways. (Courtesy Library of Congress)

Uttar Pradesh spans central north India from the lower reaches of the Himalayas south across the Gangetic plain. Almost 80 percent of its population lives in rural areas. Literacy remains low, with a mere 43 percent of the female population literate, while 70 percent of men are literate. The language of schools and government is standard Hindi, but those with little access to schooling and urban areas continue to speak one of the many Hindi dialects used throughout the area, many not intelligible to a standard Hindi speaker.

Whether one lives in cities or rural areas, the seasons dramatically affect one's life. While night-time temperatures during the months of December and January may dip to almost freezing (and lower in the Himalayan foothills), temperatures in the hot dry months of May and June often reach 120 degrees Fahrenheit. With the onset of the monsoon sometime in late June or July, temperatures drop to the nineties while the humidity increases. Farmers plant rice and corn in the rainy season, with a second crop of wheat in the cooler fall and winter. Most fields lie fallow from April to June. The agricultural seasons are reflected in folk rituals, with harvest festivals in October–November and again in March–April. Given the heavy work load of farmers, most weddings traditionally took place in the off-season months of May–June, though there is a burgeoning second marriage season in December–January, especially for urbanites.

The Taj Mahal. (Courtesy Library of Congress)

Rural people reside in nucleated villages surrounded by fields. While many still live behind the mud walls of traditional houses, houses of baked brick are becoming prevalent. Moving through the narrow unpaved lanes, one makes one's way around the ever-present water buffalo and approaches a typical house by greeting the men sitting on string cots on the front verandah. Behind them is a room used for sleeping in the rains or cold or even for housing the necessary cow or water buffalo. Behind the front room is a large open courtyard with a walled area for cooking on a small clay hearth: this is the space used by women, and men announce their entrance to this space with a cough or shout so that the younger wives can cover their faces and maintain *purdah*. Another room off the courtyard provides sleeping space for the women and children as well as storage areas.

Women are expected to maintain *purdah*: here Hindu women cover their faces before men of their husband's village older than he. Muslim women regularly cover their faces when in public spaces. Village exogamy demands that a woman marry into a village different from her natal one, a theme that runs through women's marriage songs, which speak of the "bird that must fly away" and leave her natal home. Out of respect, women also cover their faces before female relatives on ritual occasions. While these practices are vastly diminished in urban areas, more traditional families maintain them, especially for younger wives. *Purdah* also varies by class, as poor families whose women must work out of the home cannot provide the resources needed to maintain a secluded courtyard for their women. Various services such as water carrying, washing clothes, and delivery of various goods are needed if women are to remain in strict seclusion. Women belonging to lower-class families often provide these services.

Caste remains a feature of both rural and urban life, with any one village having as many as twenty to thirty castes resident in it. A caste is a hereditary grouping associated with levels of ritual purity, with occupation, and with wealth: each caste has its own caste culture that influences such factors as literacy and fertility rates. Nowadays castes are important in Indian politics, with national and regional political parties focusing on the allegiance of particular caste groupings. Even today marriages are expected to be within one's caste. These various castes have different folk traditions that emphasize such things as particular epic traditions, drumming patterns, or women's folksongs.

Given its large size, its rural and poorly educated population, its strong gender segregation, its many dialects, its numerous religious traditions, and its multitude of caste groups, the folklore of Uttar Pradesh is highly variable and barely investigated. The following sketches the outlines of what is known.

FOLK BELIEFS AND MEDICAL PRACTICES

Beliefs and practices associated with Hinduism and Islam provide the backdrop for much folklore in Uttar Pradesh, whether women's songs, men's epics, yearly ritual cycles, or medical practices. Both religions share a belief in fate, though in Hinduism it is clearly linked to concepts of rebirth through the idea of *karma*, or reaping the fruits of one's actions. However, unlike some classical Hindu traditions, folk Hinduism clearly states that one receives the benefits of *punya* (merit) and *pap* (sin) in this life as well as the next one. Folk stories told as part of ritual exegesis, known as *vrat katha*, often tell of the merits of the ritual and the benefits that worshipping the given deity will bring in this lifetime, as hearing the story "will remove sorrows and bring happiness."

The two dominant traditional medicine systems of the area are *ayurvedic*, a Hindu system based on three humors that has existed for thousands of years, and *unani*, a Muslim system that has its origins in Greek systems of medicine, based on four humors. In both, the goal is a bodily balance that is closely related to the gender, caste, and age of the person as well as the season in which he or she falls ill. Beliefs about foods are closely related: *gur*, unrefined raw sugar, is "hot" and eaten in cold weather; refined white sugar is "cold" and eaten in hot weather. Similarly, peanuts are hot and eaten only in the winter, while yoghurt is cooling and eaten especially in the summer. If a patient runs a fever for days, the leaves of the neem tree, believed to be cooling, will be placed on his or her body. Many practices exist to ward off evil eye, *nazur lagana*, such as making lampblack (*kajal*) and putting it on a baby's eyes or dabbing the herb asafoetida (*hing*) on its soles and palms.

In the Hindu tradition, various deities are known to possess the body of a devotee or victim. In western Uttar Pradesh, the snake king, Vasuki, is believed to take over the body of a person bitten by a snake, and a ritual called *dank* involving song, drums, and powerful ritual sayings is performed to rid the victim of the invading deity. On other occasions, a healer will become possessed by a deity to whom she or he is devoted in order to learn from the gods what will cure someone who is ill. All of these practices are challenged in folk stories that question the validity of the possession, though the possession rituals continue to be enacted.

Omens are also firmly believed in, and nowadays the overloaded trucks plying India's poor highways are covered with auspicious symbols to help ward off accidents. A cow and calf are especially auspicious as are a milkmaid with a pot of milk.

STORIES AND EPICS

Various forms of story exist. Most popular are *kissa*, often lengthy stories of kings and queens having fantastic adventures. These stories are believed to be true, and the teller begins with a frame that announces the truthfulness of his ensuing story. (These are related in idea if not always in content to *qissa*, found in the folklore of

Persia.) *Kahani* are shorter stories and usually treat stereotypical characters such as members of a particular caste. *Vrat katha* are the religious stories told as part of Hindu rituals. All of these exist orally, but many can also now be found in cheap pamphlet form in the markets outside temples or at other spots where crowds gather.

Several oral epics are found in Uttar Pradesh, though these vary by region. These are all sung, often to melodies associated with the particular epic. They take many nights to sing, though most are not sung as a continuous story so that only the most popular episodes are presented by their often lower-caste male singers. Most popular in the Braj region in the west is *Dhola*, a tale of the Raja Nal, his wife Dumenti, and the goddess who continually comes to their aid. Raja Nal, whose story is also found in the *Mahābhārata*, here becomes a king in search of recognition, and his story is loosely related to the history of the region. *Alha*, an epic of Muslim and Hindu wars that celebrates Raja Prithvi, is very popular in western and southern Uttar Pradesh, where yearly singing contests are still held. In eastern Uttar Pradesh, we find *Lorik-Chanda*, a story of the love of the princess Chanda, whose husband is impotent, for Lorik, a married man. The two elope, have many adventures, have a son, and ultimately return to their village.

Songs and Music

Many genres of folksong are found—some associated with life cycle events, others with seasons, and yet others with particular rituals. For women, the songs of marriage and childbirth are undoubtedly the most important, even for those in urban areas. Women gather in both the bride's house and the groom's house to celebrate with songs called *varni* (bride) and *varna* (groom). Women's song fests always take place inside, usually in the open courtyard, and men are not allowed to be present. Some songs are associated with special events in the marriage such as the *mehendi*, the making of henna designs on the bride's hands and feet. When the groom's procession reaches the bride's house, her female kin sing *gali*, obscene songs that challenge the birthright of the groom and his kin. The birth of a son is celebrated with songs called *jacca*. (Rarely is a girl's birth celebrated.) One very popular women's genre is *malhar*, the songs of the rainy season when a married woman is expected to visit her parents' house. These songs affirm the importance of her natal kin, especially her brother, who is her main link to her natal family. Any ritual occasion provides the opportunity for women to sing *bhajans* and *kirtans*, songs that show devotion to the gods. Women sing on those days when they travel to the temple to worship the goddess. Men also sing *bhajans* and *kirtans*, though their performances usually take place on the outer verandahs and are more public and often competitive, troupes of singers from different communities vying with each other. One especially competitive genre is *jhikri*, riddle songs that the opposing side must properly complete to win. During the spring festival of Holī, troupes of men sing *phag*, overtly erotic songs that tell of the god Krishna and his lovers. Also at Holī, men of a particular caste go to every house in the community where a death has occurred that year and sing *anaraya*, songs to release the family from their sorrow so that they can join the festivities.

A third group of singers are the Hijras, the transvestite community of India, made up mostly of hermaphrodites or eunuchs. The Hijras work especially throughout urban areas where they parcel out the community and lay claim to being present at auspicious events, where their curse is feared, their obscene songs tolerated, and their tips awarded.

The most common musical instrument in the area is the *dholak*, the two-headed folk drum. In addition, various kinds of cymbals are common as well as a pair of long steel tongs called *cimta*. String instruments are rare, though epic singers use various kinds of folk *sarangi*. In the urban areas and among upper-caste men, the harmonium is popular.

FOLK THEATER

Popular too are various forms of folk theater, with the *Ram Lila*, the theatrical rendition of the Hindu epic the *Rāmāyaṇa*, being the most popular. In Varanasi, the Maharaja of Banaras sponsors a thirty-day performance, while many urban neighborhoods and villages throughout Uttar Pradesh put on their own *Ram Lila* performances, usually for ten days during the month of October at the time of the festival of Dassehra. These all-male *Ram Lila* performances involve the reading of some esteemed version of the *Rāmāyaṇa*, usually those by the poet Tulsi Das, though each community has its own traditions such as the use of the potter's mule to bring the demon Ravana to the play or the singing of a particular love song as Sita weds Ram. Further, each town's performance involves burning an effigy of the demon Ravana when he is killed by the god-hero Ram. Nowadays, more stylized and brief two- to three-hour renditions of the *Ram Lila* are performed by dance troupes in cities like Delhi.

Localized to the area of Mathura and Vrindavan, where the god Krishna is believed to have been born and raised, troupes perform the *Krishna Lila* at the time of Krishna's birth in the month of August. Krishna reappears in a ritual after Divali, the autumn festival of lights meant to guide Lakshmī, the goddess of prosperity, to one's house. It is celebrated by lighting lamps or candles and placing them around rooftops, in windows, and in auspicious places. Fireworks aid in summoning the goddess. The next day families in western Uttar Pradesh in and near the region of Krishna's birthplace gather to celebrate Govardhan, literally "cow dung wealth." Govardhan is the mountain near Krishna's home that he held up on his finger when the god Indra sent a deluge to destroy his community. Using the mountain as an umbrella, Krishna protected all those beneath it. This story is enacted when women make cow dung figures of all the animals and humans in their house and surround them with mountains of dung and the face and arms of Krishna. When worshipping, women invoke Krishna's protection for their families as he has protected the residents of his childhood home. While still celebrated in the villages and small towns, Govardhan appears to be disappearing in urban areas where the requisite cow dung is not available and where the idea of agricultural wealth is not dominant. Further, the educated teenage girls in the village are rebelling against the continual use of cow dung as an auspicious substance that must be used to purify courtyards and verandahs before any major ritual; to these modern girls, cow dung is not purifying but filthy.

Muslim women sing life cycle songs comparable to those of their Hindu neighbors, and Muslim men participate in oral poetic events known as *mushira*. Sometimes held as small events for friends and neighbors, but frequently attracting audiences of over 10,000, the *mushira* presents men reciting poems of their own composition to the acclaim or disdain of the audience.

Other forms of folk theater are in decline, though the government still uses *nautanki* troupes to pass on messages regarding education and health. Cinema halls have now replaced the tents with folk theatrical troupes at district fairs. The epic *Dhola* was performed as a folk opera at district fairs through the 1970s, but the troupes who gave these performances no longer exist.

SPORTS AND RECREATION

The most popular sport for men is undoubtedly wrestling, which has recently become attached to militant Hinduism. Villages set up matches against one another, and pride in one's *Palwan* (great wrestler) is enormous. Urban areas have *akhara*, or wrestling pits, where boys and men train together.

Rural girls focus their play around rituals that bring them good husbands and prosperity. One fall ritual is *samara-simaraya*, in which a bride and groom are made out of clay, worshipped for ten days, and then married. The girls make clay items for the bride's dowry and processional figures for the groom's procession. This ritual is a light-hearted approach to a wedding, in contrast to the very serious and contentious quality of real weddings.

Students watch a wrestler swing metal clubs around his torso, an exercise at a wrestling school that teaches an ancient Indian form of the sport. (© Lindsay Hebberd/CORBIS)

ARTS AND CRAFTS

The most common folk art forms are those attached to rituals, such as the clay elephant that the potter makes for women to worship in the annual ritual. In eastern Uttar Pradesh the potter community near the town of Gorakhpur began to develop a more artistic form of ritual gods and goddesses that eventually came to be sold in the urban art markets. Likewise, women themselves make wall drawings for ritual such as *karva cauth*, "Pitcher Fourth," that honors their husbands or Krishna Jamanastami, Krishna's birth. But nowadays it is easier to buy a paper version in the market than to create one's own design on one's wall.

CHALLENGES OF THE MODERN WORLD

Undoubtedly the folk traditions of Uttar Pradesh are changing with some dying and others gaining new vigor. The addition of printed folk materials allows for the spread and retention of some folk stories in this new form. Audio cassettes and the possibility of making cheap short runs of cassettes have led to some local traditions making it to the market. The electronics market at Red Fort in New Delhi has close to one hundred stalls where local producers from the outlying regions sell cassettes to buyers for markets in urban areas and in rural areas where male workers have migrated. The Hindu nationalist movement has given new life to *Ram Lila* performances, while for a few potters and other skilled craftsmen the urban art mart has led to new customers and new art forms. In the cities, one can hire a troupe of women to perform at marriages instead of relying on one's memory and neighbors. Yet as old forms of storytelling and singing fade, new ones emerge. Nowadays a popular game with teenagers borrowed from television involves singing songs whose first line begins with the last letter of the previous singer's line. While the songs are more likely to be film songs than the songs of their grandmothers, singing remains popular.

BIBLIOGRAPHY

Blackburn, Stuart, Peter Claus, J. Flueckiger, and Susan Wadley, eds. 1989. *Oral Epics in India*. Berkeley: University of California Press.

Manuel, Peter L. 1993. *Cassette Culture: Popular Music and Technology in North India*. Chicago: University of Chicago Press.

Wade, Bonnie, ed. 1992. *Texts, Tunes and Tone Parameters of Music in Multicultural Perspective*. New Delhi: Oxford and IBH Publishing.

Wadley, Susan S. 1975. *Shakti: Power in the Conceptual Structure of Karimpur Religion*. University of Chicago Studies in Anthropology Series in Social, Cultural, and Linguistic Anthropology No. 2.

———. 2005. *Raja Nal and the Goddess in the North Indian Oral Epic Dhola*. Bloomington: Indiana University Press.

Susan S. Wadley

South Asia

BANGLADESH

GEOGRAPHY AND HISTORY

Linguistic homogeneity—and the cultural commonality that proceeds from such homogeneity—characterize Bangladesh. Irrespective of religious divisions, more than 90 percent of its population speaks Bengali. In fact, Bengali nationalism was the main factor in the country's struggle for freedom from Pakistan, of which it was the eastern province before independence. The culture of the country evolved under the greater Bengali umbrella, which also envelops the West Bengali culture. In fact, before **India** gained independence and Bangladesh became East Pakistan, it formed the eastern region of the Bengal province of the British Raj. This historical connection therefore makes it impossible to deal with folklore studies in Bangladesh without reference to Bengali folklore studies in India, just as it is not possible to talk of Bengali culture in its totality without considering the culture of the erstwhile East Bengal.

Casual curiosity, missionary motives, and political necessity motivated colonizers to begin to study the culture and way of life of the colonized Indians, among them the Bengalis. The Asiatic Society of Bengal was set up in 1784 to study the annals and traditions of Bengal. After the 1857 Sepoy Mutiny in India, the colonizers modified their policy of indifference and decided to take official note of their colonized "subjects" as human beings with a culture of their own. The result was a few ethnographic surveys, which, though primarily aimed at facilitating administration, are nonetheless invaluable for folklore research. The initiative of the Christian missionaries also produced translations of religious and mythological texts.

Scientific and systematic enquiry into the folklore of Bengal really began in the last part of the nineteenth century. The Folk-Lore Society was founded, and its journal became the hub of folklore scholarship. By the 1930s a sizeable amount of scholarly work had been done by Indologists such as Max Müller, Theodor Benfey, Charles Henry Tawney, and E. B. Cowell.

With the rise of Indian **nationalism**, many Bengali scholars came to the fore of folklore studies. Among them were Dinesh Chandra Sen and Sarat Chandra Mitra. Also, Rabindranath Tagore's fascination with Bengali folklore and his usage of folk elements in his literary creations are quite well known. Following the Language Movement of 1952, which began as a reaction against the domination of West Pakistan, the Bangla Academy was set up at Dhaka in 1955 as a national institute for developing language, culture, and literature. Since then, considerable advance has been made in the field of folklore studies in Bangladesh.

Geographically, Bangladesh is situated in southern Asia, bordered by the Bay of Bengal. India and Burma are its nearest neighbors, and migration of population to and from these countries has given Bangladesh a richly diverse demographic profile. Other than the Bengali Muslims who expatriated from West Bengal after the partition of India, another major group of people, Urdu-speaking, non-Bengali, Muslim refugees from **Bihar**, originally came from India. Various other tribal peoples in

Bangladesh—mainly Chakmas, Marmas (or Maghs), Tipperas (or Tipras), and Mros (or Moorangs)—are of Sino-Tibetan origin and share a close kinship with the tribes of India and Burma. These tribes differ from the rest of the country's population in their social organization, marriage customs, birth and death rites, food, and religion—practicing various forms of Hinduism, Buddhism, Christianity, and animism.

Islam, the main religion in Bangladesh, is distinctive in that it evolved independent of the dominant Islamic trends in India under the influence of pre-Islamic Hindu and Buddhist cultures. The influence of the Hindu festival of lights, Dīwalī, can be seen in the lighting of lamps during Shab-e-barat; exorcism of evil spirits by those who believe in *jinnis*, is performed through rituals that show marked Hindu influence; and often, especially in rural areas, the distinction between Hindu and Muslim shrines is lost. People from either community, for instance, might go to the *satyapirs*, shrines to the goddess Olabibi who should be propitiated to cure cholera.

A low-lying country, Bangladesh consists mostly of flat alluvial plains, with some hills towards the southeast. The climate is tropical, with mild winters, hot humid summers, and very wet monsoons. Bangladesh's riverine topography explains why it is predominantly an agrarian country with vast reserves of arable land, but also at the same time a poor country staggering on its way to economic development. The country is situated on the deltas of major rivers like the Ganga and the Jamuna (the Brahmaputra in India), joined by the Meghna that ultimately flows into the Bay of Bengal. Rivers may be the providers of food, but they also bring floods. Almost one-third of Bangladesh is flood-prone. Where it is not flooded, the country is drought-prone, and because most of the population is agrarian, land that is cultivable throughout the year is scarce.

The new political entity that is Bangladesh came into existence in 1971. After the partition of India in 1947, East Bengal was annexed to Pakistan on the basis of religious similarities and in the process divided from West Bengal, with which it shared cultural and linguistic affinities. But when it became evident that Pakistan would always treat its eastern region, so far removed from its center, with contempt and discrimination, Bengali nationalism—always a strong element in the Bangladeshi makeup—started to reassert itself. The result was a war of liberation and the formation of the country. The red sun at almost the center of the green flag of the new nation signifies the blood shed in the fight for freedom, while the green background stands not only for the greenery of the countryside but also represents the Islamic tradition.

MUSIC AND SONGS

The *bayatis* (bards) of Bangladesh still sing about the gore, the glory, and the agony of the Liberation War. *Gambhira*, especially, is one performative folk narrative that has assimilated the episodes of struggle for independence into its **repertoire**. *Gambhira*, one of the oldest Bengali art forms, was originally a religious performance consisting of dances and songs in praise of the Hindu god Shiva. With the passage of time however, it took on a secular nature and metamorphosed—especially following the Liberation War—into a sociocomic form. Due to its ability to integrate elements of contemporary culture, *Gambhira* satirizes a range of social, political, and economic failures and problems, presenting them with wit, humor, and drama.

Various other forms of verbal art in Bangladesh can be divided for the sake of convenience into religious/spiritual, secular/functional, and romantic types. Among the spiritual or mystic singers of Bangladesh, the most well known and well loved are the *bauls*. The *baul* songs cut across religious boundaries, showing Sufi influence as well as that of Vaishnava and Bhakti literature. Either the one-stringed musical instrument called the *ektara* or the two-stringed *dotara* accompanies the *baul*'s compositions. The *baul* singers are wandering minstrels, *faqirs*, and *yogis* who praise the most high and sing of the transience of this world and the desirability of the next. Lalon Shah, for instance, sings:

> Touched by the ill wind
> the bird may fly away from the cage any day.
> The cross bar in the cage
> may break down;
> What will the bird stand upon then?
> As I thought about it,
> I felt all over my body
> a sudden feverish heat.
> Whose is this cage?
> Who is this bird?
> For whom do I weep?
> Living in this cage,
> Who is it that wants to bewitch me?
> If I knew before the wild one could never be tamed,
> I wouldn't have fallen in love with him ever,
> says Lalon with tears in his eyes.

Other mystical musical forms include the *marfati*, *murshidi*, and *bisched* songs. The *marfati* and *murshidi* are types of *baul* songs—the latter sung in praise of the *murshid*, or the spiritual guide of all moral beings swimming in the ocean of love. *Bisched* songs are similar in their mystical longing, but they use the symbolism of Radha and Krishna and the sorrow of their separation to reflect the sorrow of the human soul in its distance from the spiritual.

Among the religious folk music of Bangladesh are the *kavi* and *jari* songs. The *jari* songs are a kind of dirge sung in memory of the deaths of Hazrat Imam Hassan and Hussein. They are sung during the Muharram celebrations, especially by the Shia Muslim community. The *kavi* songs also began as religious songs but like so many folk forms have taken on a secular character. Today, *kavi* songs are performed for popular entertainment. They are extempore and resemble a dialogue in verse between two contesting poets.

Other folksongs that use religious characters and symbols are essentially romantic and secular. In their lilting *jhumur* songs, the Santhal tribesmen, for instance, use the love of Radha and Krishna to depict earthly fervor, as also do the *Ghatus*. The *Ghatus* are riverside people, and their songs are sung in autumn and during the rainy season on boats at the riverbanks, or *ghats*—hence their name. The most remarkable feature of the *Ghatu* song, however, is that it is led by a teenaged boy dressed as a young girl. When the leader stops, the chorus picks up the song, and the leader performs a sort of a ballet.

The river folk have another very popular form of music called *bhatiyali*, usually sung by the boatmen. Depicting the soul's urge to meet the creator, *bhatiyali* songs are characterized by nostalgia, represented in real terms by the boatman's longing for the shore and home. *Sari* is a kind of song performed in chorus during boat races. Unlike the *bhatiyali*, these songs concern licentious love and adultery.

The northern districts boast of other folk musical forms like *gambhira*, *bhawaya*, and *jag*. *Bhawayas* are love songs; *bhawaya* songs of forbidden love are called *chatka*. *Jag* songs are narrative songs of heroism as well as local history and miracles performed by *pirs* (Muslim holy men) and saints. On occasions, these songs also narrate legends of Krishna and Shree Chaitanya.

Bangladeshi folk culture features a number of functional songs such as boatmen's songs as well as those performed during harvesting, sowing, snake-charming, cowherding, and fishing. Peoples engaged in different functions or jobs sing these songs to relieve the monotony of their jobs and fight fatigue. One such type of song is called the *chhad-peta gaan*, sung by day laborers while building the roofs of houses. Besides providing insight into the minds of people engaged in different occupations, these songs also give a vivid picture of social stratification and functional division.

SOCIAL STRUCTURE

Bangladeshi society is predominantly patriarchal, though nowadays more and more women are seeking economic independence as well as freedom from male dominance. In Bangladeshi society, the family forms the nucleus. It is traditionally a joint family, though like most traditions this custom is dying out. After marriage, the bride and groom usually come to live with the groom's parent's family, and it is not unusual to find three to four generations living under one roof so long as it is economically viable and amicable.

Though polygamy was common in earlier days—and not just among the Muslims—it is now dying out. The main rationale for a polygamous family was economic: more wives would mean more children who would provide more hands to work on the farm or family business. However, big families are no longer economically viable. Western education and exposure to Western social systems also have much to do with the trend toward monogamy. In the polygamous family of yore, the eldest wife enjoyed greater economic rights and was obligated to take up more family responsibilities. This was perhaps a compensation for the love and attention that was likely to be showered by the husband on the youngest, or latest, wife. Usually the many wives co-existed in relative harmony and contributed to running the family each in her own way, but folktales about jealous co-wives abound. In one such tale of the *Seven Champa Brothers*—belonging to the "wicked stepmother" type—the elder wife of a king buries the younger queen and her seven sons and daughter in the backyard. The sons grow into champa trees, and the girl into a creeper. The champa trees refuse to let anybody pluck their flowers until the king comes in person and is told the tale of betrayal, at which point all regain their human forms.

MYTHS AND FOLKTALES

Folktales of Bangladesh include *rupkatha* or *parikahini* (that is, fairy tales)—the märchen type of German tales—complete with handsome princes, beautiful princesses, heroic deeds, supernatural aid, and magical powers. Legends built around historical characters also abound and are known as *romancha-katha*. Tales of King Vikramaditya from the *Vetalapanchavingshati* are often recounted to Bangladeshi children. *Birkathas* (tales of heroism) also sometimes fall into this category. Fables or *nitikatha* are also often told to Bangladeshi children, as are numbskull stories or *rang-akatha*. Local legends like that of *Kamalasundari* or *Chaudhurir Ladai*; creation myths or *sristikatha* that try to explain how the world came into being or why the tiger is striped or why a river is so called; traditional tall tales (*ganjakhuri galpa*); tales for testing intelligence that have riddles woven into them (*dhandhamulak galpa*); and cumulative tales in which characters and plots keep building on top of each other (*shikli galpa*) are other common types of folktales in Bangladesh.

DANCE AND DRAMA

Another major form of folk entertainment is folk dances. Among the folk dances of Bangladesh are the following, as categorized by Mazharul Islam: religious—*jarinach, jakirnach,* and *kirtannach,* for example; social, including *gambhiranach, dhalinach, lathinach,* and *roybenshenach*; ceremonial, such as *ghatunah, khemtanach, sarinach,* and *bolinach*; and purely musical, a category that includes *baulnach, jarinach,* and *gambhir-anach*. Of these, religious performances such as *kirtan* recitation, *baul* and *faqir* rites, and *jari* singing have given the accompanying dances their names; *dhali, roybenshe,* and *lathi* dances are forms of martial arts; the *gambhira* dance is sometimes masked and accompanies *gambhira* songs; and the *khemta* dance is performed by women or eunuchs on ceremonial occasions.

Jatra performances are also held occasionally. *Jatra* is a folk drama form, combining acting, singing, and dancing and characterized by exaggerated delivery and stylized oration. Traditionally it drew on mythological and religious subject matters, but it has incorporated more and more social satire into its oeuvre. Performed traditionally by men attired as women, this drama form has evolved through the ages and can be seen in certain pockets even today, though with marked changes in tone, performance, and characterizations.

FESTIVALS AND MARKETS

The folk forms discussed above are basic to Bangladeshi life and are especially prominent during festivals. Most of these festivals are agrarian and aim to propitiate the gods so that they give good harvest. *Byanbiye, badnabiye, megharani,* and *hudumadeo* rites and *punyipukur brata* and *basudhara brata* are some of the folk rituals associated with agriculture. Other festivals include *ambubachi,* which observes the union of the earth and the sky in the Bengali month of *Asadh*; *berabhasan,* a raft festival observed during the Bengali month of *Bhadra* in honor of *Khowaj-khizir* (who in his Hindu avatar is the water god Varuna); *gasbi,* an autumn festival observed to ensure a better harvest; *pausparvan/posla,* a crop festival; and *pahela baisakh* or Bengali New Year's Day. Among the tribal festivals are *karam puja* of the Oraon tribe, dedicated to worshipping the karam tree, and *sagrai*, the New Year festival of the tribes of the Chittagong Hill.

In addition to the observance of common festivals, the feeling of community and belonging is also kept alive by a very important social institution of Bangladesh called the *haat*. The *haat* is a market—its presence more marked in rural areas—where agricultural and livestock products, handicrafts, local medicines, and other products are bought and sold once or twice a week. Buyer and seller negotiate the price. Much of the folklore of Bangladesh thrives through and in these *haats*. Here is where the local wit poses his riddles and does his act, the village bard sings his songs and plays his tunes, the *jatra* actors perform their plays, the elders recount myths and legends, and people who come to purchase goods enjoy it all.

ARTS AND CRAFTS

Handicraft goods form a major trade commodity in the *haats*. Of these, perhaps pottery is the most prominent. Pottery is traditionally the preserve of people called the *kumars*. They engage in both religious and secular work. The former includes terracotta tiles in mosques and temples depicting mythological and religious scenes. Also common are figurines of Hindu goddesses such as the bird goddess Subachani of Mymensingh, the snake goddess Manasha, and the goddess of health Sitala. The eminence of the goddess Manasha in Bangladeshi folklife can be seen in the various cobra-shaped artifacts the *kumars* make out of clay. Secular pottery includes construction of articles for day-to-day use such as pots and pans that are still employed in many households for storing water, making curd, and other uses as well as toys and figurines.

Some *kumars* hand paint and decorate their creations. For instance, the goddess of wealth Lakshmī is frequently painted on earthen tablets or plates with her attendant owls. Pots, or *ghots*, often come painted, especially for auspicious occasions. The *sakher hari* is one such earthen pot painted with various flora and fauna and other symbols such as combs or creepers that denote fertility. They are used to carry sweets in marriage ceremonies. These **motifs** and symbols are repeated because of their particular significance and prominence in folklife and may appear in the crafts of the *sutradhars*, who make animal figures; *patuas*, who create linear paintings; or *malakars*, who are adept at *shola* or spongewood decorations.

Most of these motifs probably originated in *alpanas*, or floor paintings. Done by women on auspicious occasions with colored rice powder (traditionally produced by mixing the ground rice with brick powder, ash, cow dung, vermilion, or turmeric, though artificial colors are more common today), these *alpanas* depict not just the motifs discussed above but also cosmic symbols of the sun and the moon, geometric designs, and the very common Bengali motifs of the lotus and the conch shell (*shonkho*). Other common motifs—mainly depicted in abstraction—include elephant, horse, peacock, swastika, circle, waves, temple, and mosque. *Alpanas* are not merely drawn in Hindu households but during Muslim festivals and weddings as well. It is only the motifs that vary. Symbolically, each *alpana* motif has a different significance. The fish represents fertility, the sheaf of rice prosperity, the lotus purity, and the swastika good fortune. The main colors used in *alpana*-drawing as in other folk paintings derived from it are the basic reds, yellows, greens, and blues.

Body painting is also known in Bangladesh. Tattooing, or *ulki*, is a common form of body art done using permanent pigments. Various religious significances are associated with most tattooing. Temporary tattooing in the form of *mehendi* or henna designs is especially popular during weddings and certain religious festivals. In all such tattooing, the motifs are intricate and mostly of the same folk origin as other types of painting in Bangladeshi folk culture.

Sweets are an integral part of Bangladeshi cuisine. These sweets are transformed into art through shaping and carving. Bangladeshi women often mold *sondesh* and *amsath*—different kinds of sweets—into the shape of conch shells and *kalkas* or decorate them with floral motifs. Decorative cakes called *nakshi pitha* are also made by shaping dough of rice powder into different shapes and designs. Traditional motifs for *nakshi pithas* include geometric patterns, wheels, betel leaf, flowers, fish, and birds. More popular in Dhaka and Mymensingh, these *pithas* are used at various social and religious occasions such as weddings, Eid, Shab-e-barat, and Annaprashan.

Embroidery, another favorite occupation of Bangladeshi women, is also done in these designs. The embroidered quilt, or *nakshi katha*, for instance, is made out of old saris stitched together in layers where folk motifs are embroidered in red, blue, yellow, and green. Around these motifs, fine white stitches bind the layers together and give a ripple-like effect to the fabric. Though the style varies from region to region, the motifs are all part of the Bangladeshi woman's folk repertoire, and each tells a different story. *Kathas* were originally stitched by the Bangladeshi mother as a wedding gift for her daughter, but they can also be used as a seat for the priest or bridegroom, as a bedcover (*leph* or *sujni*), to wrap food or toiletries, to make bags or *tholis*, or as a cover for the Qur'an Sharif.

The weaving styles and woven patterns of Bangladesh are equally varied and intricate. Assimilating the influences imparted by Hindu, Muslim, Indian, and Persian styles, the Bangladeshi *tanti* or weaver creates magic out of a variety of materials. Different schools of weaving are based on fabrics or patterns used.

Until the nineteenth century Bangladeshi fabric and weaving were much in demand in Europe and elsewhere. But due to decreasing numbers of *tantis* who hereditarily learn the

Bangladeshi women embroider clothes for sale in the village of Savar near the capital, Dhaka, 28 July 2003. (© Reuters/CORBIS)

trade of their ancestors, these crafts are on the decline. One main reason for people abandoning weaving is that it is very labor intensive, taking days and months, but the returns are very low, the market too restricted, and the craft very little in demand except on special occasions like weddings. Western clothing and machine-made fabrics have brought the handloom industry almost to the brink of extinction.

Similar is the case with tribal weaving. The tribes of Bangladesh use the bain or backstrap loom and have their own set of intricate designs, which, for the Chakma girl for instance, is catalogued as the *alam*. The *alam* then becomes her reference for weaving designs into the borders of her sarong, known in her language as the *tongc-hongya*. The breast cloth sometimes has beadwork woven into it.

The tribal population of Bangladesh is also adept at a variety of other crafts. They make beautiful baskets out of cane and bamboo that are put to various uses and come in different shapes and sizes typical of certain areas. River rushes, reeds, and grasses are used to weave utilitarian and ornamental items such as fish traps, chicken coops, baskets, and sieves. The Bangladeshi craftsperson can also weaves mats known as *sitalpatis* out of reeds and grasses. Bamboo is also the raw material for making common folk musical instruments such the flute and the *ektara*, a one-stringed instrument commonly played by *bayatis* (folksingers), *bauls*, and *faqirs*.

ARCHITECTURE

The architecture of any place depends mainly upon three factors: climate, available materials, and politicocultural influences. Cane, bamboo, and thatch are materials that grow in plenty in Bangladesh. Therefore, the people of rural Bangladesh use these materials and mud to build their houses. Bangladesh is prone to heavy monsoons, and so the houses are usually built with roofs that are markedly curved to facilitate the drainage of rainwater. This curvilinear form is easily made by using bamboo, which is quite flexible and given to curvature. Thatch covers the frame of the roof, and mud covers the walls made of bamboo. For the poverty-stricken people of Bangladesh these mud and thatch houses are convenient not only because the raw material is ready and often freely available but also because in case of natural calamities they can easily rebuild. Of course, this curvilinear structure has not remained confined to the rural dwellings alone and is to be seen even in wooden houses and modern-day brick and mortar houses.

The discriminating feature in the curvilinear roofs is the number of segments—from two to twelve—into which these roofs are divided. The two-segmented roof is the most basic. It consists of sloping sides that form a ridge at the top and with gable ends on the north and south. Various Hindu and Islamic monuments have borrowed this type of bungalow roof structure. Among them are the gateway to the mosque of Shah Mohammad and the temple of Khalia at Faridpur, both built in the seventeenth century.

FOLK MEDICINE

Belief in folk medicine is still rife in rural areas. Folk doctors prescribe cures—be they herbs, incantations, rituals, or charms—for every ailment. Village people have their own terminology for different illnesses and attribute them all to one or another cause, which determines the kind of treatment or healer they would approach. Erratic behavior, for example, was attributed to the ailing person's having been touched by an ill wind or possessed by a disembodied spirit, called *batash laga* or *alga batash*. And the *bede* or *ozha* was called in to cure such a patient. The *ozha* traditionally acted as a bridge between this and the other world for people who consulted her. She could cure possession through dialogue with the spirits; some diseases she could suck out of the patient; and for some other diseases, she performed religious rites and sacrifices.

Holy men or mystics such as the *pir* or *maulvi* were approached in case of most illnesses, and their prescriptions usually consisted of *pani pada* (water incantation), *jhad phook* (oral incantation), *tabij* (sacred amulet), and *tel pada* (oil incantation). A *kabiraj* was one who prescribed herbal medicine he himself manufactured.

The folk healer was often also called upon to perform religiomagical miracles such as tracking a common thief or petty offender, which she did by using tricks and techniques such as *ayna pada* (sanctified mirror), *bati chala* (throwing an enchanted bowl), or *lathi chala* (sanctified stick). Many of these practices are animistic survivals that have been incorporated into the major religions of Hinduism and Islam.

RELIGIOUS BELIEFS AND CUSTOMS

A number of folk sects emerged out of this synthesis of religions. These sects or communities aligned themselves with different folk religious beliefs, and though not cut off from the major religious streams, they profess independent views about life and culture. Among them are the Balahadis, Bauls, Kartabhajas, Jagomohanis, Matuyas, Nyadas, and Sahebdhanis. The Balahadis believe in a deity called *Hadirama* by the Hindus and *Hadi-Allah* by the Muslims, and emphasize living life above avarice and sensuality. The Bauls combine the spirituality of Sufism and the Bhakti cult, and wander around singing songs in search of the *maner manus*—the ideal being. The Kartabhajas follow the spiritual teachings of Awul Chand. The Jagomohanis believe in the Vedas and lead ascetic lives. The Matuyas are completely engrossed in loving and serving God's creations. The Nyadas live on alms and profess similar beliefs as the Bauls and the Vaishnavas. The Sahebdhanis are iconoclasts who believe in congregations and engage in certain esoteric sexual practices.

A number of taboos and superstitions relate to religious practice in Bangladesh. The wife keeps fasts and performs various *pūjas* for the well-being of her husband. The verses of the Qur'an are hung in many Muslim homes to keep evil at bay. Fear of spirits and ghosts haunts rural Bangladesh. *Yakshas* are said to be hiding in tanks guarding hidden treasure, and *Nishi* or the night demon is supposed to walk the streets at night and lure unsuspecting travelers into the forest to kill them. *Shankchunni*, *Chorachunni*, *Penchapechi*, and *Mamdo Bhut* cause different diseases. Anyone can cast an evil eye with malice. The Brahman priest or the Muslim *dervish* or *pir* can ward it off.

Varied preventative means can counter superstitious fears. Causality binds every step of life of the Bangladeshi folk, be it birth or death, love or marriage. Pregnancy, for instance, is circumscribed by various taboos that prevail irrespective of religious and social backgrounds, though Westernization among some has reduced blind adherence to them. For example, a pregnant woman should not eat from an earthen pot or plate, or she risks delivering a pot-bellied child. Nor should she cut anything during an eclipse, or her child will be born with physical imperfection.

From birth through puberty and marriage to death, every major incident in a person's life is marked by folk beliefs and ceremonies. Food taboos exist for pregnant women until about the seventh month of pregnancy. But during the fifth or sixth month of the first pregnancy, the woman's family makes a social occasion out of sending a big fish with scales symbolizing fertility to the woman's husband's house, and the woman is allowed to partake of any dish she wishes. Her *sadh*, or desire, is thus indulged, she is dressed in new clothes, and children are made to cling to her to ensure she has as many children of her own. A feast, called *bavar* in certain parts of Bangladesh, is usually held to mark the occasion.

After the birth of the child, ceremonies mark its naming, its first solid food intake, and other milestones. A social occasion, the scale of which is determined by the social and economic status of the family, occurs with each. As the child grows and reaches puberty, ceremonies mark her coming of age as well. The girl's first menstrual period is marked by a social feast, as is the Muslim boy's circumcision or the upper-caste Hindu boy's sacred thread-taking ceremony.

Marriage in Bangladeshi society is still very much an arranged affair, the arrangement being made by the parents and relatives through professional mediators. Though self-arranged weddings are on the rise now, parental blessings are still sought to avoid unpleasantness. Weddings are huge community affairs marked by numerous social customs before, during, and after the actual event. The dowry system has marred many marriages. Originally intended as a gift by the girl's family to the newlywed couple so that they may begin their married life without any material discomfort, the dowry gradually became a matter of prestige for the bride's family and later cause for avaricious demands made by the groom's side. Today it has become almost a price for purchasing the groom. Insatiable demands are made by the groom's family, and the bride's parents—who already consider having a daughter a cause of great responsibility—find themselves wishing they had no daughter. Inability to fulfill dowry demands has led to the torture, both mental and physical, and even murder of many brides. Tradition therefore is being turned to trade.

To end on such a gloomy note would not be fair, though, to the vibrant traditional folklife of Bangladesh. Tradition, after all, shapes the way it is shaped. If in some ways it is being abused, it is also being reproduced and revived to give the people of the country a sense of pride in their heritage. Where the intangible elements of Bangladeshi folk culture are being recalled—through, for example, fusion in music in form such as *baul grunge*—and given a new lease on life along with a new attitude in keeping with changing times, the material culture is also being restored to currency and given international exposure. With the emergence of concepts such as ethnic chic, more and more people are turning toward handmade *kathas*, woven *jamdanis*, and traditional silks. Folk motifs are being introduced into articles of use, which are in themselves not of traditional or folk origin. Folk culture, after all, never dies; it merely reinvents itself.

BIBLIOGRAPHY

Ahmad, Wakil. 1973. *Banglar Loka Sanskriti* (Folk Culture of Bengal). Dhaka: Bangla Academy.

Banglapedia: National Encyclopedia of Bangladesh. www.banglapedia.search.com.bd/index.html.

Chowdhury, Kabir, Serajul Islam Chowdhury, and Khondakar Ashraf Hossain, trans. 1985. *Folk Poems from Bangladesh*. Dhaka: Bangla Academy.

Hafiz, Abdul. 1985. *Folktales of Bangladesh*. Dhaka: Bangla Academy.

Haque, Zulekha. 1984. *Gahana* (Jewelery). Motijheel: Bangladesh Small and Cottage Industries Corporation.

Huda, Muhammad Nurul. 1986. *Flaming Flowers: Poet's Response to the Emergence of Bangladesh*. Dhaka: Bangla Academy.

Islam, Mazharul. 1970. *A History of Folktale Collection in India and Pakistan*. Dhaka: Bangla Academy.

Khan, Shamsuzzaman. 1987. *Folklore of Bangladesh*. Dhaka: Bangla Academy.

Khan, Shamsuzzaman, and Momen Choudhury. 1987. *Bibliography on Folklore of Bangladesh*. Dhaka: Bangla Academy.

Loka Sahitya Sankolan (Anthology of Folk Literature). 1963–1986. Vols. 1–48. Dhaka: Bangla Academy.

Qureshi, Mahmud Shah, ed. 1984. *Tribal Culture in Bangladesh*. Rajshahi: Institute of Bangladesh Studies.

Rushd, Abu, trans. 1965. *Songs of Lalan Shah*. Dhaka: Bangla Academy.

Shahidullah, Muhammad, and Muhammad Abdul Hai. 1963. *Traditional Culture in East Pakistan, A UNESCO Survey*. Dhaka: Dhaka University.

Siddiqui, Ashraf. 1976. *Folkloric Bangladesh*. Dhaka: Bangla Academy.

———. 1983. *Loka Sahitya* (Folk Literature). Dhaka: The Student Ways.

Zaman, Niaz. 1981. *The Art of Kantha Embroidery*. Dhaka: Shilpakala Academy.

Uddipana Goswami

BHUTAN

GEOGRAPHY AND HISTORY

Historically known as *Lho Men* (the southern land), *Lho Tsendenjong* (the southern land of cypress), *Lhomen Khazhi* (the southern land of four approaches), and many other names, the outside world calls the country "Bhutan"—the meaning of which is shrouded in myth and mystery. The people call themselves Drukpa and their country Drukyul (the land of thunder dragon), or simply Druk (dragon), the creature which adorns the national flag. Tsangpa Gyare Yeshey Dorji, the founder of Drukpa Kagyud School of Buddhism, once saw a valley hallowed with rainbow and light. He considered the sight auspicious for constructing a monastery. At that moment the sound of a dragon resonated thrice in the sky. Tsangpa Gyare then predicted that his teachings would flourish as far as the thunder was heard. He built a monastery in 1189 C.E. on that site, naming it Druk Ralung. His teachings and the school known as Drukpa Kagyu later spread to Bhutan. Hence the name Druk for the country.

Located on the southern slopes of the eastern Himalayas, Bhutan is landlocked between the two great Asian civilizations: Tibet (now part of **China**) to the north and **India** to the south. The land rises from 200 to 7,000 meters and consists mostly of high rugged mountains crisscrossed by a network of swift rivers that form deep valleys before draining into the Indian plains. The climate varies from the southern

The dragon is the principal symbol on the national flag of Bhutan.

foothills, with their dense subtropical forests, to the northern alpine slopes, which are very cold and experience little rainfall. Human settlement is confined mostly to central river valleys and a swath of southern plains bordering India, though nomads and other tribes live in the north, raising sheep, cattle, and yaks. The geographical divisions of the country have allowed different regions to evolve distinctive cultures and institutions, especially since the first motor car was introduced only in 1961. About two-thirds of Bhutanese live in rural villages and pursue subsistence agriculture.

Before 1616, Bhutan consisted of many small autonomous principalities and valley kingdoms, and the various kings waged war for more territory and influence. Around 1650, Zhabdrung Ngawang Namgyal unified the country and codified the customary laws based on Buddha's teachings. He formed a government, defining and separating spiritual and civil matters of governance. The political system he created still exists in some forms, though monarchy was established in 1907.

Society was traditionally divided into the *zhung* (monarchy), *dratshang* (religious community), and *misey* (people) without a caste system. During the medieval period, when a loose form of feudalism prevailed, people working for the kings and lords in different *dzongs* (forts) were categorized by their professions. The division was not rigid because anyone could rise to the highest position; all people were taxpayers.

There are four main ethnic groups. *Sharchop* largely live in eastern Bhutan, the *Khengpa* of central Bhutan are believed to be the earliest inhabitants, while the *Ngalop* of western Bhutan were people of Tibetan descent who immigrated as early as the seventh century. People of Nepalese origin (see **Nepal**) settled in the south of the country toward the end of the nineteenth century. However, the ethnic division is becoming blurred with increasing intermarriage, migration, and settlements. Bhutanese speak as many as nineteen dialects besides Dzongkha, the national language and lingua franca. English is the official language.

Two watershed historical events are the visits in the eighth century by Guru Padmasambhava, a great Indian saint who introduced tantric Buddhism, and the arrival of Zhabdrung Ngawang Namgyal in 1616 from Tibet. However, the establishment of monarchy in 1907 is the most important event in modern history. The third king, His Majesty Jigme Dorji Wangchuck (who reigned from 1952 until 1972), reformed the old feudal systems by abolishing serfdom, redistributing land, and reforming taxation. He also introduced many executive, legislative, and judiciary reforms. The fourth and present king, His Majesty Jigme Singye Wangchuck, took decentralization to the next level, reallocating all executive powers to a council of ministers elected by the people in 1998. He also introduced a system of voting no confidence in the king, thus empowering the parliament to remove the monarch. Recently, the country has drafted its first constitution.

RELIGIOUS BELIEFS

Buddhism plays a central role in people's life and culture. People are deeply religious, and their lifestyles and culture are rooted in Buddhist philosophy. Buddhism accords respect to all forms of life and teaches interdependence among all life forms. The mountains, rivers, lakes, cliffs, rocks, and soil are considered to be the domains of different spirits, and any pollution or disturbance of these habitats brings death, disease, and destruction.

Before Buddhism was introduced in the eighth century, people practiced shamanism alongside a pre-Buddhist faith called Bon. The last vestige of Bon is still being practiced in rural areas, not as a faith but more as a community culture and celebration. Bon priests known as *bonpo* command as much reverence as Buddhist monks, and at times of sickness, people first consult a *bonpo* or Buddhist astrologer. Guru Padmasambhava introduced Buddhism in Bhutan in the eighth century. In the centuries that followed, Bhutan was home to many sages and saints, including the great saints-scholars, Kuenkhen Longchen Rabjam (1308–1363) and Pema Lingpa (1450–1521). Various schools of Buddhism assimilated other earlier practices and beliefs. The aspiration for enlightenment is widely shared among schools. Although Mahayana Buddhism is the popular faith, Hinduism is practiced in Southern Bhutan. The Hindu religion shares many saints and divinities with Mahayana Buddhism.

The importance of religious institutions, signified by the number of monks who total over 4,000 in *Dratshangs* or *Rabdeys* (state-supported monastic establishments), continues in present-day Bhutan. *Rabdeys* are based mainly in *dzongs* (fort-monasteries). Each *Rabdey* is headed by a *Lam Neten* who is appointed by His Holiness the *Je Khenpo*, the Supreme Head of the Central Monk Body, who is also elected. Monks continue to play an important role in the daily lives of the people. By promoting religious ceremonies and preserving scholarship, they have remained relevant in changing times.

FOLK MEDICINE

Bhutan has a tradition of indigenous medicine. Though largely derived from Tibetan medicine, this indigenous medicine, *sowai rigpa*, has well-developed methods of diagnosis: feeling the pulse, examination of urine, eyes, and tongue, and interviewing patients. Therapeutically, it relies on herbal combinations, acupuncture therapy, golden needle, heat applications, and minor surgery performed in the context of Buddhist rituals. In Bhutan traditional medicine has been incorporated into the modern healthcare system, and there are traditional medicine units and outlets in major hospitals, manned by a *dungtsho* and a *menpa* (indigenous health worker) complementing the modern medical services. The National Institute for Traditional Medicine trains *drungtsho* and *menpa*.

FOLKTALES

Myths, legends, folktales, folksongs, and other examples of folklore flourish, particularly in rural areas. Folktales are by far the most important, each village or community abounding with different tales. Before modern education, folktales were the main educational tool and entertainment. They were key instruments in preserving the country's tradition and culture. Some fundamental beliefs and values are embedded in the tales, and it was only through this folk literary genre that culture and values were passed down from one generation to the next. Like those elsewhere in the world, Bhutanese folktales feature a range of characters from kings and queens to gods and demons as well as various animals. In most stories, humble characters such as farmers, the poor, women, and children are portrayed in a good light in opposition to characters like kings, rich people, and beasts. In tales, at least, the social system gets overturned. Storytelling is not entertainment alone but serves a variety of purposes: to warn of the danger of wild animals; to cultivate universal values such as compassion, while promoting disapproval of such attributes as greed and dishonesty; and to assure that good will defeat evil in the end. Some Bhutanese folktales are similar to those in neighboring societies, especially Tibet, India, and Nepal. Some definite influences came from the Jataka tales—fables depicting the activities of various incarnations of Lord Buddha—and from Tibet through Buddhist texts, travelers, and pilgrims.

As in other Himalayan regions, tales of yeti—the "abominable snowman"—are common in every community. Usually, cattle herders or travelers are said to encounter the yeti unexpectedly during bad weather in high altitudes. In Bhutan, the yeti is known as *migoi* or *gredpo* and is described as being of either a reddish-brown or grayish-black color, with an ape-like body and hairless face.

LOZEY AND TSANGMO

Another folk literary genre is the *lozey*. *Lozey* can be literally translated as an "ornament of speech." It resembles the Western ballad. *Lozey* is a rich source of information on Bhutanese culture, customs, dress habits, and literature, which vary from place to place. Unlike other traditional literary genres, *lozey* is composed and recited in colloquial language. In fact, *lozey* is recited in competitions between ordinary folks in the villages. Despite the usage of ordinary language, it achieves poetic height. It is never direct; meanings are conveyed through similes, metaphors, and symbols. There are two types of *lozey*. The first is a usually short exchange of feelings either of love or of difference of opinion. The second narrates a story, often of epic dimension, in a very musical fashion. During gatherings people who can neither write nor read conpete either individually or in groups in exchanging *lozey*. Competition is mostly held between men and women.

Tsangmo is probably the most popular folk literary genre in Bhutan. Every Bhutanese is familiar with at least a few *tsangmo*. Consisting of four lines or a quatrain with two couplets, it is a well-structured piece of poetry. Each couplet is a self-contained entity. The first couplet usually makes a statement or describes a situation. The second couplet concludes or summarizes the points made by the first. The *tsangmo* is not recited but sung to a particular tune. It must engage an opponent. The subject is either of love or hate, abuse or ridicule, as in the following (translated by Kuenzang Dechen):

> Though the leaves are lovely,
> The size of the radish cannot be known.
> Though the girl is beautiful;
> Her character cannot be known.

As with *lozey*, *tsangmo* competitions are held between male and female groups. First, a person will sing a particular *tsangmo*, and, depending on its meaning, the opponent will respond. It contains a veiled message, the meaning of which depends on who is singing it to whom.

SONGS

An integral part of Bhutanese culture, folksong is a highly refined art that reflects social values and standards. Bhutanese folksongs can be classified into two broad categories: *zhungdra* (literally, "the melody of the center"), songs that originated in the *dzongs* and later spread elsewhere; and *boedra*, popularized by medieval court servants known as *boed garps*. Other minor categories include *zhey*, *yuedra*, *zheym*, *tsangmo*, *alo*, *khorey*, and *ausa*. Some songs are dance-oriented, while others are voice-oriented. Little is known about the lyricists of songs. The few who are known were mostly lamas, monks, and scholars. Therefore, religious themes permeate most traditional songs. Folksongs contain historical and social information, for they narrate legends, stories of human dilemmas and relationships, and travelogues. Some are commentaries on *dzongs*, monasteries, *lhakhangs*, and sites of pilgrimages and ordinary houses. They are both repositories and vehicles for transmitting social values.

Transmission of songs through memory and oral recitation is still an important part of the learning process in Bhutan's largely oral society. Folksongs and music play a pervasive role in the lives of the common people. Besides being a primary medium of entertainment and celebration, folksongs also act as vehicle for moral and spiritual instructions for people who lead hard and uneventful lives. Some songs are not intended for social entertainment but for prayer and rituals and are thus meant to invoke religious faith in the audience. Singing is supposed to accumulate merit at two different levels.

MUSIC

Folk musical instruments differ from those used in religious ceremonies in that the former are usually stringed. Religious chanting and sacred tantric dances are accompanied by a *dungchen* (long trumpet), *jaling* (double-reed oboes), *nga* (handled drum), *dungkar* (conch shell), *damaru* (waist-drum), *kangdung* (thigh-bone trumpet), *relmong* (cymbals), or *drilbu* (brass bell). The most popular Bhutanese folk instrument is the *dra-nyen*, a seven-stringed lute that accompanies most folksongs. The *pchiwang*, which usually accompanies *boedra*, is a two-stringed instrument featuring an unfretted fingerboard attached to a hollow resonating drum. Tradition holds that the sound of a *pchiwang* symbolizes the horse, and indeed one of the strings is made of horsehair. The *lingm* is a six-holed flute usually made from bamboo. There are two types: the front-blown (*dong-lingm*) and the side-blown (*zur-lingm*). The *yangchen* (hammered dulcimer) became popular in the early 1960s when Tibetan refugees brought it to Bhutan. The Chinese word *yang chen* means "foreign zither." The Chinese and Tibetans seem to have obtained it from early European visitors. Bhutanese *yangchen* differ from the zither used by folk musicians in **England** and the United States. Other common instruments include the *tangtang namborong*, a four-holed bamboo bass flute popular in eastern Bhutan; the *paywang*, another kind of bamboo flute usually used as a learning instrument; the *kongtha*, a simple bamboo mouth harp; and the *gombu*, a horn made from the horns of bulls and buffalo, usually blown to call the animals home for the evening.

FOLK THEATER AND DANCE

Traditional Bhutanese theater differs from its Western counterpart. Here, theatrical performance is conducted through religious masked dances or *cham* performed in the open courtyards of *dzongs* and monasteries. They also differ from secular theater in both form and content. The monastic community developed a rich corpus of liturgical melodies for many rituals. These melodies are tonally very different from secular music. Dancers wear masks of animals and other mythical creatures and don long flowing robes. They perform to the music played by an orchestra positioned at the other end of the courtyard. The choreography of the dance differs among dances. *Cham* is one of the grandest spectacles in Bhutanese performing tradition. It is a meditation in movement, the dancer conceiving himself as the deity he is representing, with every gesture not only symbolic but imbued with power. The dance is accompanied by Buddhist chants, music, and customs. The dancer views his art as an offering to the deities; people believe that gods are pleased by dramatic representations of themselves.

Some dances are re-enactments of episodes from *namthars*, spiritual biographies of holy people. For example, the dance of *Dramitse Nga Cham* dramatizes what the nun Choeten Zangmo, daughter of Pema Lingpa, saw in the realm of the Buddhas. In the fifteenth century, Choeten Zangmo was meditating in a cave in Dramitse in eastern Bhutan. One night, she was transported to the Buddha realm, where she witnessed the attendants of Guru Rimpoche performing a dance in a hundred peaceful and a hundred terrifying forms. With drums in their left hands and drumsticks in their right hands, they were performing the majestic dance. She later introduced it in Dramitse.

The religious masked dance was introduced in the eighth century by Guru Padmasambhava, who subdued the deities through a miraculous dance performance. Similarly, Terton Pema Lingpa and Zhabdrung Ngawang Namgyal introduced many dances, which are still performed. Masked dances are primarily performed in the courtyard of *dzongs* and monasteries, mostly during religious festivals. They dramatize the life and works of enlightened saints and sages.

For people living in the rugged mountains, *cham* is an important occasion when friends and relatives meet and socialize. Dance entertains and reaffirms the devotion and commitment of the people to live religious lives. At a higher level, it serves the causes of liberation and enlightenment. By merely watching the dance, sentient beings are liberated. Watching a dance is one of six ways to become liberated. The *mudras* and gestures symbolizing nine skills of dancing and eight divine manifestations of peaceful and wrathful deities remind people of their spiritual duties and obligations. Masked dancers are believed to be the manifestation of the Lord of Death. A masked dance acquaints people with features of the afterlife one is believed to encounter during the transition of consciousness. Depending upon a person's virtues or vices, the dancers are visualized in either their peaceful or wrathful forms.

SPORTS AND RECREATION

By far the most popular Bhutanese sport is archery. Traditional archery, though a national sport, has indigenous roots. Come the New Year, national holidays, or community observances, the different valley communities bustle with archery games. Archery has evolved from its origins in warfare to become a national sport, and the houses of protector-deities of different communities are decorated with bows and arrows. The appeal of the game has endured for a long time because the material for making archery sets is readily abundant: for example, reeds, bamboo, pheasant feathers, stinging nettles, and iron ore for arrowheads. An important characteristic of Bhutanese archery is its emphasis on psychology and spirituality rather than only skill. Invocation of deities and prayer play a big part in game.

ARTS AND CRAFTS

Bhutanese art does not exist for its own sake. More important than their esthetic quality, which is valued though antithetical to Buddhist values of non-attachment, paintings of Bodhisattvas and the like exist for instructional purposes. Art is mostly a religious obligation, the anonymous creators of such works blending indigenous and Tibetan Buddhist traditions. These highly decorative and ornamental paintings are most often seen in *dzongs*, monasteries, *lhakhangs*, and household shrines.

Bhutanese art, craft, and architecture are popularly known as *zorig chusum*—thirteen traditional crafts. *Zo* refers to the ability to make something, *rig* is the art or craft, and *chusum* is thirteen. Artists' skills and knowledge are passed on through successive generations within their own family or to selected apprentices.

Shingzo is woodworking used in the construction of *dzongs*, monasteries, palaces, and houses, as well as the manufacture of farm tools and other implements. Stoneworking is called *dozo* and includes stone pots and tools, millstones, and *tsigzo*—the building of stone walls. The carving of wood, slate, and stone is known as *parzo*. *Lhazo* includes all types of painting such as *thangkas*, mandalas, murals, wall-painting, and house decoration. The craft of making statues, pottery, and rammed-earth construction falls under *jinzo* (clay arts). *Lugzo* is the casting of statues, ritual tools, musical instruments, farm tools, kitchen utensils, and jewelery. *Shagzo* is wood-turning to produce bowls, plates, buckets, ladles, and small hand drums. *Garzo* is blacksmithing. *Tröko* is the making of metal ornaments, including those made from gold, silver, or copper. It also refers to the manufacture of elaborately decorated containers. *Tshazo* are products of cane and bamboo such as containers, mats, hats, and bows and arrows. The art of traditional papermaking is *dezo*. *Tshemzo* encompasses sewing and embroidery, including appliqué work and patchwork as well as hat- and boot-making. The thirteenth art, *thagzo*, refers to weaving, including the dyeing of yarn.

ARCHITECTURE

The most distinctive Bhutanese architectural landmarks are the monumental *dzongs*. Usually of towering height, size, and shape, most are built on strategic sites such as mounds, hills, or ridges. Overlooking entire valleys, *dzongs* controlled important land routes. During the unification of Bhutan and subsequent invasions from Tibetan and

Mongol forces, many *dzongs* were built as a chain of defensive fortresses with watch-towers and observation posts. Later they served as administrative and religious centers to fulfill emerging sociopolitical needs. They are mostly built from clay bricks, stones, and wood, not a single iron beam or nail being used.

CHALLENGES OF THE MODERN WORLD

When there was no modern education, and monastic education was accessible only to a very few privileged male children, Bhutanese children grew up hearing folktales from their grandparents or parents. This rich oral tradition was instrumental in children's education and the transmission of values, beliefs, customs, and history. But Bhutan has come a long way from being an idyllic, medieval country. The physical and spiritual contours of Bhutan are slowly being changed by modern development. The **modernization** process of the early 1960s brought roads, which were followed by an English education system and other developments. This had considerable impact on different aspects of society, oral literature being the most negatively affected. As mass media and modern education supplement the function of oral tradition, much folklore is fast disappearing. Urban-bred children show little interest in the folklore of their parents. Even in remote villages, one comes across only a handful of people who know folktales, and even fewer people who are willing to narrate one. The older people—a rich repository of age-old values and rich traditional culture and heritage—are losing their status, a development detrimental to Bhutan's long and rich folk literary traditions. Bhutan now has the Internet, television, and print media. The young Bhutanese (53 percent of the population) who grow up away from their cultural roots seem to take the least interest in their traditions. Unless it is promoted and cultivated vigorously, folklore could be lost in one generation. Efforts are being made to preserve these rich traditions through the recording and translation of biographies, songs, tales, proverbs, and more. The quest to document these traditions has been joined by even some private individuals. With a growing number of children uninterested in their heritage, the preservation of it relies increasingly upon documentation.

BIBLIOGRAPHY

Acharya, Gopilal. 2004. *Bhutanese Folk Tales (From the East and the South)*. Thimphu: Pe khang Publications.

Choden, Kunzang. 1997. *Bhutanese Tales of the Yeti*. Bangkok: White Lotus Press.

Dorji, Tandin. 2002. Folklore Narration: A Retreating Tradition. *Journal of Bhutan Studies* 6: 5–23.

Hasrat, Bikrama Jit. 1980. *History of the Peaceful Dragon*. Thimphu: Education Department.

Kinga, Sonam. 2001. The Attributes and Values of Folk and Popular Songs. *Journal of Bhutan Studies* 3.1: 134–175.

———. 2003. *Impact of Reforms on Bhutanese Social Organization*. Thimphu: The Centre for Bhutan Studies.

Norbu, Jamyang. 1986. *Zlos-gar*. New Delhi: Library of Tibetan Works and Archives.

Penjore, Dorji, and Sonam Kinga. 2002. *The Origin and Description of the National Flag and National Anthem of the Kingdom of Bhutan*. Thimphu: The Centre for Bhutan Studies.

Ura, Karma. 2004. *Deities, Archers, and Planners in the Era of Decentralization*. Thimphu: Karma Ura.

Dorji Penjore

NEPAL

GEOGRAPHY AND HISTORY

The Kingdom of Nepal is a small landlocked country in South Asia, bordered on the north by the Tibetan Autonomous Region of **China** and on its other three sides by **India**. Located between latitudes 26 degrees to 28 degrees north and longitudes 80 degrees to 88 degrees east, Nepal has a roughly rectangular shape extending approximately 850 kilometers from southeast to northwest with an average width ranging from 140 to 240 kilometers from north to south and enclosing 147,000 square kilometers.

Geographically, Nepal is divisible into three regions: the Great Himalayan Mountains running across the north of the country, a central hilly region covering two-thirds of the country, and the lowlands of the Gangetic plain, known as the Tarai, along the southern border. Nepal's mountainous north includes eight of the world's ten highest mountains, including the highest, Mount Everest, at 8,848 meters above sea level. Suggestive of Nepal's ecological diversity, the lowest point in the country in the eastern Tarai is only seventy meters above sea level. The climate of Nepal ranges from subtropical monsoon conditions in the Tarai to alpine conditions in the Himalayas. Less than 20 percent of Nepal is arable land. The Tarai is flat and fertile but was dangerously malarial until well into middle of the twentieth century and so remains relatively underpopulated. Most of Nepal's 26 million inhabitants live in the rugged middle hills, a complex system of ridges and river valleys varying between 700 and 4,300 meters in elevation. These ranges enclose the Kathmandu Valley (1,300 meters above sea level), home to Nepal's capital, which is the most densely populated area of the country. Some estimates suggest that nearly a million people may now live there.

As a result of its geographical inaccessibility and a historically repressive political system sustained by inequitable land distribution and exploitative methods of agricultural taxation, Nepal is one of the least developed countries of the world, with an extremely low standard of living. Nepal's per capita annual income remains less than U.S. $200 with more than half of the population living below the absolute poverty level. Average life expectancy is fifty-five for both males and females, and overall infant mortality is 10 percent. Approximately 40 percent of males and 15 percent of females are literate. Subsistence agriculture and pastoralism are the most common economic activities, employing most of the work force in non-mechanized, labor-intensive farming with one of the world's highest ratios of laborers per hectare. Productivity is low, leading to chronic food shortages and periodic famines. Rice is the leading staple but is a luxury in the more remote parts of the country, where corn (maize), wheat, and millet are the staple crops. Most houses are small, two-story buildings made of mud bricks without electricity or running water. Wood and dried dung are the standard fuels for cooking. Despite a slowly developing road system, most villages in Nepal remain connected only by footpaths. Nepal's precarious economy is sustained by foreign aid and tourism; India dominates trade.

Despite high mortality rates and out-migration to India, Nepal's population continues to grow rapidly, with 40 percent of the people younger than fifteen years of age. Except for the urban concentration of the capital, Kathmandu, and a scattering of provincial towns, nearly all the population remains in small rural villages. Complicating its economy as well as its foreign policy, Nepal provides refuge to nearly 100,000 recent refugees from **Bhutan** as well as to more settled communities of Tibetan refugees, who began arriving after the Dalai Lama fled Tibet in 1959.

Siddhartha Gautama, who became known as the Buddha, was born in Lumbini, territory now part of Nepal, 2,500 years ago, as commemorated by a pillar erected on the site by Emperor Asoka (third century B.C.E.), who is also credited in legend with founding the city of Patan in the Kathmandu Valley. By the fourth century C.E., Nepal emerged as a nation, as documented by the earliest surviving inscriptions, but it originally consisted only of the Kathmandu Valley and varying small amounts of nearby territory. The modern state of Nepal emerged in the late eighteenth century when the king of a hill principality called Gorkha, began a successful campaign of military expansion, conquering the sophisticated Newari city-states of the Kathmandu Valley in 1769. That king, Prithvi Narayan Shah, founder of the present dynasty, described his kingdom as "a flower garden of four castes and thirty-six subcastes," a phrase figuratively conveying Nepal's numerous ethnic distinctions and its vibrant cultural diversity. Military interventions by the British in the early nineteenth century established the present borders of the kingdom but allowed Nepal nominal independence, an autonomy that was strengthened by Nepal's strong support of the British during the Indian sepoy mutiny of 1857. Democratic government was introduced in 1991 after years of absolute monarchy, but the contemporary political system remains extremely factionalized. Since 1996, an increasingly violent Maoist insurgency has spread throughout the country, claiming more than 11,000 lives in the past eight years. In June 2001, King Birendra and Queen Aishwarya were assassinated along with their younger son, their daughter and her children, the king's younger brother, his three sisters, and other relatives. In the official report, regarded as the equivalent of a folktale by many Nepalis, it was concluded that Crown Prince Dipendra committed regicide, patricide, matricide, and fratricide before fatally shooting himself. He is reported to have shot his father the king from different directions using several different weapons, then killing his mother and brother elsewhere in the palace before shooting himself unobserved in the gardens outside. Eleven months later, the new king, Gyanendra, suspended parliament and in October 2002 dismissed the prime minister to rule by royal decree.

Never having been colonized, having rigorously outlawed all missionary proselytizing, whether by Christians or Muslims, and isolated by difficult geography and xenophobic rulers, Nepal preserved many of its diverse cultural traditions, although they are currently threatened by the continuing Maoist revolt and, more devastatingly, by the homogenizing forces of **globalization** and **modernization**. In keeping with Nepal's self-proclaimed identity as "the world's only Hindu state," more than nine-tenths of the population are classified "Hindu," a designation that officially includes Buddhists as well as many local variations of ritual practice—as long as the ethnic group involved observes in some way the Hindu caste system, which was codified in Nepal's first legal code, the *Muluki Ain* of 1853/1854. There are a very small group of Muslims in Nepal and an even smaller scattering of Christians, mostly repatriates from elsewhere in South Asia, though conversion numbers have increased since the liberalization of the constitution in 1990.

Well known ethnic groups of Nepal include Newar, Sherpa, Rai, Limbu, Sunuwar, Dhimal, Santal, Yolmo, Tamang, Gurung, Thakali, Raji, Chantel, Magar, Chepang, Tharu, and Raute, besides the geographically widespread "Brāhman-Chetris," as Nepali-speaking castes throughout the kingdom are euphemistically called. This synecdoche conveniently ignores the majority of Nepali speakers, who belong to castes regarded as ritually impure. Other groups, particularly those along the Tibetan border, are identified by their area of residence—for example, residents of Dolpa, Mustang, Manang, Mugu, and Humla—while groups along the Indian border tend to be identified by their primary language, including those who speak Maithili, Rajbangsi, or Bhojpuri. Lowland languages belong, for the most part, to the Indo-Aryan family, while languages of the hills are usually Tibeto-Burman, a distinction that roughly corresponds to Hindu or Buddhist religious practices, though clear distinctions between the two are often blurred, as are most ethnic boundaries. Nepal's significant cultural and linguistic diversity is exemplified by the 120 distinct languages that have been recorded in the country, of which at least forty are still used as the primary language of a local community. Most inhabitants understand the national language, Nepali, an Indo-Aryan language derived from Prakrit that resembles Bengali and Gujarati, with an ever-increasing number of loan words via Hindi of Persian or Arabic origin.

SOCIAL AND FAMILY STRUCTURE

Despite many songs valuing romantic love, family structure in Nepal remains very traditional. Most marriages are arranged and are caste-endogamous but frequently village-exogamous. Girls tend to be married by age sixteen, boys slightly older. For many groups, marriages are arranged by parents following the advice of astrologers. In some groups, such as the Newars of the Kathmandu Valley, both men and women tend to be married at later ages. Newari girls are ritually married between the ages of seven and nine to the god Narayan (Vishnu), symbolized by a *bel* fruit (*Aegle marmelos*)— a ceremony that de-emphasizes the urgency and the solemnity of later marriages and allows widows to re-marry. Most Brāhman girls, in contrast, are married by age ten, because Brāhmans obtain religious merit by giving away very young daughters. According to tradition, the preferred age for a Brāhman girl to marry is six, although urban families are less likely to follow this custom. In groups whose cultures evince Sanskrit influence, girls are expected to be virgins at marriage, but this stricture is weakly observed in Tibeto-Burman communities. The status of Hindu wives is graphically depicted by a rite within the marriage ceremony during which the bride washes her husband's feet (considered the most impure part of the human body) and sips the water. In very traditional families, a wife always greets her husband by touching his feet, often with her forehead. It is common for a husband to take his meals before his wife does and for her then to eat what he leaves on his plate.

Pregnancy is socially recognized by the fifth or sixth month, when it is held that the life-breath has entered the embryo. From this point, the woman, regarded as being two individuals, may not participate in religious ceremonies. The umbilical cord is usually cut on the same day that birth takes place, but it may be tied and the cutting postponed to avoid astrologically determined complications or to allow a scheduled wedding or ritual to take place, as these must otherwise be postponed for eleven days for all in the immediate family. Symbolic of patrilocality, the placenta of a male child is buried under the kitchen floor near the hearth and that of a female child outside the home. A section of the umbilical cord may be dried to treat colic.

After a child is born, parents consult an astrologer to calculate the child's future and to choose an auspicious name, which will be based on the time of birth. Astrologers check carefully for the serious astrological disturbance known as *mūl pāryo*. This occurs when certain planets of the child and either of its parents occupy the *mūl nakṣatra*, one of twenty-seven subdivisions of the lunar elliptic. The parent who shares the configuration is fated to die quickly if he or she sees the child within *mūl*'s duration, so a child designated a *mūl* birth may be placed outside of the family to be raised as an orphan. In many communities, only after an astrologer has been consulted does the baby's father see the child. On the sixth night after birth, Bhabi, goddess of fortune, comes to write a child's fate on its forehead. Parents traditionally leave a light burning all night in the room with the baby so that the goddess makes no mistakes, sometimes supplying a pen and inkpot. Families who have suffered the loss of several children may try to trick fate by giving their child a name ordinarily used only by a lower caste.

For high caste, "twice-born" males, the most important childhood ceremony is to receive the sacred thread. Brāhman boys usually receive this at age seven or nine, while Chetris may wait until their teens. Once invested with a thread, a boy has many new ritual responsibilities and privileges such as now being allowed to eat in the company of adult males. There is no parallel ceremony for girls. First menstruation marks the beginning of adulthood for women. No special ceremonies are performed, but in some communities the girl is secluded for fifteen days, during which time she may not be seen by males. Menstruation is regarded as ritually unclean, and a menstruating woman must follow many rules. She is treated as an untouchable, even by other women, and should maintain physical isolation for the first four days of her period, must not cook or fetch water, and may not perform any religious rites.

A coin is placed under the tongue of a dying person. If it is not spat out, death is considered imminent. A drop of water purified by having had gold dipped into it is poured through the dying person's lips. After death, the body must be handled properly, touched only by persons of equal or higher caste; otherwise the deceased may later haunt his family. Immediately following the last breath, a body is wrapped in a white or saffron shroud and tied to two bamboo poles to be carried to the cremation or burial site. Cremation on a riverbank is the preferred method for funerals, though both earth and "sky" burials are practiced in some communities—the latter found in some Tibeto-Burman communities who expose the body on an elevated platform to be consumed by vultures, graphically "paying back" to nature the debts incurred in a lifetime of dependence on the world. Children who die before puberty are usually buried as are Christians and Muslims.

Mourning by the immediate family is marked by fasting, including abstinence from salt, oil, and meat for thirteen days. More distant relatives observe one day of fasting. Males have their head shaved as a sign of mourning, while women dress in white, leave off their jewelry, and leave their hair uncombed and unbound. The death of progenitors is commemorated by annual *sraddha* rituals, in which the ancestors are offered balls of rice by all male descendants. This rite reinforces patrilineal kinship networks. Some families place a lighted lamp next to a dish of uncooked rice grains in the main doorway the night before ancestors are worshipped, hoping to record a footprint indicating the ancestor's current incarnation.

In Nepal, the Hindu custom of *sati*, the immolation of widows with her husband's body, was never common except among royalty. It was abolished in 1920, at which time it became punishable as homicide. The *sati* gate of Pashupati temple, the holiest site in Nepal, through which widows had been taken to their husband's pyres, was bricked shut at that time.

FOLKTALES AND BELIEFS

For Nepal as a whole, folk speech is an area where considerable collected material is available, even if little systematic analysis has been done to anchor it in its social contexts. Even without contextual studies or thorough inventories, folklore can contribute much to a deeper understanding of Nepalese culture and society. For example, the prevailing practice among Nepali speakers of a woman never uttering any man's name, not even her husband's, is illustrated in the common proverb: "When co-wives are angry, they use their husband's name." This confirms the subservient position of wives as well as documenting the practice of polygyny, as does the more pointed variant, "A co-wife when angry will pee in her husband's lap." **Gender** imbalances and family tensions are also revealed by common proverbs such as "If you have no other work, daughter-in-law, go scratch the calf" or "The father and mother-in-law order the daughter-in-law, the daughter-in-law orders the dog, the dog wags its tail." (These examples come from the Jajarkot, Jumla, Rukum, and Baglung Districts in western Nepal.)

Common sayings such as that to sneeze while eating indicates that you've been touched by an untouchable (so that someone should immediately sprinkle you with water before you resume the meal) reveal embedded caste prejudices. Caste stereotypes—that Brāhmans (priests) are greedy, Magars filthy, and Newars untrustworthy—are also topics represented in Nepali proverbs, including these:

If bananas are supplied, a Brāhman is big-eyed.

Yogurt, where? A Brāhman, there!

In a pig's stomach, the Magar's stool; in a Magar's stomach, the pig.

Never a father offend or a Newar befriend.

Other common proverbs comment more universally on life, as shown by a few examples:

A friend when hungry, a stranger when fed.

A guest leaves a house as a dog leaves a bone.

A rock is harder than all else, but poverty is harder than a rock.

Save your body in a fight; save your seeds in a famine.

If you need to awaken the guru, what kind of blessing can he give?

In the mouth a prayer, in the pocket a knife.

Some folk beliefs, such as the idea that you must never hand a chili pepper to another person or a dispute will result or that to see one crow feeding another indicates a guest is coming, reveal basic notions of mimesis between the natural and social worlds. Other beliefs not anchored in religious traditions—such as insisting that if you either eat out of the cooking pot or lick the stirring stick as a child, it will inauspiciously rain on your wedding day, or that if you always finish every course at a meal, you will have only daughters—may conceal basic concepts of proper manners and hygiene. Some omens, such as that hiccups are a sign that someone far away is thinking of you or that a woman's hair braid twisting at the back of her neck and refusing to sit flat means that her husband plans to take another wife, seem to have lost whatever relevance that they may once have had to wider social issues.

The interpretation of dreams reveals hypothetical connections between daily accidents and wider states of uneasiness, indicated in the lines of a shamanic recital to treat nightmares:

> In your house, dreams may be broken, visions may be broken.
> From the dream, a ladle breaks, a stirring stick breaks,
> the drying rack falls, a wall sags, it dries up,
> a rockslide falls, a landslide falls.

Without recourse to a shaman, one may simply throw a handful of ashes toward the rising sun or toward the mountains to ask that a dream not come true. If you have a good dream, you should stay awake the rest of the night, praying that it does come true. You should not reveal its contents to anyone.

MUSIC

Nepal has few indigenous traditional musical instruments, but three of note, played throughout the country, are the bamboo flute, *bãsuri*; the double-headed wooden drum, *mãdal*, played horizontally with two hands; and a wooden violin-like four-stringed instrument, the *sãrangi*. *Sãrangi* are most often played by members of the Gandarva caste, whose traditions of ballad composition are now eclipsed by competition from Nepali radio and other electronic music sources. Of considerable ethnographic interest are the one-sided shaman drums with crossed inner handles played by *Kãmī* (blacksmiths), Magar, and Chepang shamans in western and central Nepal. These contrast with the double-sided drums with an external handle played by *lamas* in those communities that have been more influenced by Tibetan traditions. Throughout much of Nepal, a traditional caste of professional musicians, whose caste name, Damãi, comes from a large kettledrum, play an assortment of wind instruments, drums, and cymbals for auspicious occasions such as weddings, festival processions, and other rituals. The composition of the ensemble apparently dates from the fourteenth century and was probably introduced to Nepal by Hindus from northern India fleeing the Muslim conquests.

DANCE AND GAMES

Every ethnic group in Nepal has a tradition of folk dancing, much of which is devotional in character. Best known are the masked Tantric dances of Newars in the Kathmandu Valley and those of Sherpa monks, whose masks, carved from wood or sculpted in clay, depict deities, demons, heroes, and comic characters of Buddhist and Hindu tradition. Although the overall prognosis is poor for the preservation of genuine folk traditions that have not been debased into "culture shows" for the entertainment of tourists, one apparent success is with the revival of the Tharu "*barka*" dance, a village version of the *Mahābhārata* that had not been performed since 1963 but has recently been revived with foreign assistance.

Nepal's position between India and Tibet accurately predicts that many of its folk traditions overlap with those from these culture areas. However, as a result of their long isolation from the wider world as well as from each other, each culture within Nepal maintains distinct and extensive folklore traditions. Unfortunately, no published documentation exists for many key folklore domains, including children's games, riddles, nursery rhymes, insults, jokes, gambling methods, and the social satires performed for the festival of Gai Jatra. Most published studies are in local languages. Collections that have appeared in European languages, like those published in indigenous languages, tend to present material separated from its social context with little regard for the caste, ethnicity, gender, or status of the sources and "polished" into elegant literary texts that conceal their oral origins. Without information on informants and their social situations, much of this material is reduced to curious tales and fragments of seemingly bizarre knowledge, curiosities that contribute little to our understanding of Nepal's peoples or their cultures. Meaningful social worlds are created and maintained through minute details. Conversely, such details must be understood within that context if their meaningfulness is to be preserved.

ARTS, CRAFTS, AND ARCHITECTURE

Nepal's art and architecture reached its highest point of development during the Newari Malla dynasties of the seventeenth century, before the kingdoms of the Kathmandu Valley were conquered by the Gorkhalis. Within the Valley's 250 square kilometers are over 2,000 major temples, many of which are constructed in the multistoried "Pagoda" style, a design that originated in Nepal before the seventh century and spread via Tibet throughout east Asia as far as **Korea** and **Japan**. A more recent architectural feature of the Kathmandu Valley, where urbanization has destroyed much of the old cityscape, are ostentatious neoclassical palaces built by members of the Rana family, hereditary prime ministers, during the late nineteenth and early twentieth centuries. Many of these have been recently converted to hotels or government ministries. Nepal's two most impressive monuments are the ancient stupas of Swayambunath and Boudhanath. Stupas are large hemispherical mounds constructed as three-dimensional mandalas. They symbolize the five elements as they should be properly ordered in an enlightened mind: the cubical base of the stupa signifies earth; the spherical dome, water; the spire, fire; the prongs above the spire, air; and the gold sphere at the pinnacle represents purified consciousness.

The Swayambunath stupa in Kathmandu. (© Alison Wright/The Image Works)

Children playing on the image of the god Bhairab during the Indra Jatra Festival, which honors the god of rain and king of heaven, in Kathmandu. (© Topham/The Image Works)

A well-developed tradition of wood carving flourished in the medieval Newari kingdoms, as did a sophisticated technique of lost-wax bronze casting of sacred images. Both traditions have been in decline for nearly three centuries, a decline accelerated in the past fifty years as religious crafts have been commodified for the tourist trade. Meanwhile, much of Nepal's ancient art continues to be stolen for foreign collections. Throughout the country as recently as thirty years ago, many decorative traditions in metal and wood for common domestic items flourished, including milk jugs, water containers, and other kitchen utensils, but most of these have been replaced by mass production and plastic. It has become nearly impossible to find even a well-made traditional kite as the last generation of traditional kite-makers is dying out. Some genuine *khukuri* knives, symbolic of the fierceness of Nepali soldiers, are still forged for the military, though they too are swamped by cheap imitations. One surviving folk tradition in the Tarai is the vibrantly colored wall murals painted by Maitali and Tharu women, though many now paint on paper for an international market. Another form of folk art still practiced, though borrowed from **India**, is the colorful painting of bicycle rickshaws, trucks, and buses, adding color to both the increasingly congested city streets and the precipitous mountain highways.

FESTIVALS AND CELEBRATIONS

Nepal has several different calendars. In official use is the Hindu Vikram Sambat system, which had reached the year 2056 when much of the world was celebrating a new millennium according to the Gregorian calendar. However, by the Newari calendar, 2000 C.E. was only the year 1120 N.S., and by the Sakya calendar introduced by the Licchavi dynasty it was already 2126, as it was Earth-Hare year 2126 for Tibetans. Meanwhile, for Muslims it was the middle of Ramadan, Islamic Hijri 1420. Other than the various celebrations of the New Year, most festivals, however, are fixed not by any of these calendars, but by lunar calculations. While every community has its own festival cycles, two of the most important major national holidays are Dasaĩ and Tihār. Occurring in the fall, Dasaĩ lasts a lunar fortnight. Its ninth day is marked by thousands of animal sacrifices to the goddess Durga Bhawani, and the festival culminates with family members exchanging blessings symbolized by forehead dots (Nepali: *ṭikā*) and fresh barley shoots. The lunar month following Dasaĩ includes the five-day festival of Tihār, each day of which is marked by a different focus of worship: crow and dog, both connected to Yama, the Lord of Death; then the cow and Laxmi, Goddess of Prosperity (the evening of her day characterized by rows of tiny lamps lit on every house); and on the final day the blessing of brothers by their sisters, who receive gifts in return.

SONGS

Elements of ethnopsychology begin to emerge from the emotions revealed in many folk lyrics. The Khas Chetri of Western Nepal have a tradition of song competitions between young men and women, in which the first lines come from a standard repertoire while the second lines are improvised. From such songs, we discover the value of romantic and illicit love in a society often represented as lacking it and a more flirtatious orientation than the doctrines of arranged marriage would suggest:

> Where can the dregs of wealth go,
> except along with the wealth?
> Where can the dregs of life go,
> except along with one's love?
>
> The house is built with pine rafters
> and chestnut beams.
> My mind is criss-crossed with feverish memories
> and useless dreams.

CHALLENGES OF THE MODERN WORLD

During the past three decades, Nepal has experienced more social change than it had throughout its entire previous history. These changes have left large segments of the population increasingly marginalized economically and politically. Buffeted by rapid change, Nepalis tend to be very fatalistic. All concepts of life, death, and suffering are permeated by the theory of Karma, with its cycles of rebirth that connect morality with retribution and reward. One's caste and gender, for example, are recognized as reaping what was sown in previous lives. Nepalis observe that this is the Age of Darkness (*Kali Yuga*), when even the gods lie and cheat, and they find confirmation daily in the inevitable deterioration of the world at personal, social, and cosmic levels.

STUDIES OF NEPALESE FOLKLORE

Various anthropological and religious studies reveal elements of Nepalese folklore. For any particular community, the ethnographic literature offers the best starting point for additional folklore studies. Important sources include the works of von

Fürer-Haimendorf (1964) and Ortner (1978) on Sherpas; March (2002) on Tamangs; Pignède (1966) on Gurungs; Oppitz (1991) and Lecomte-Tilouine (1993) on Magars; Toffin (1984) on Newars; and Bennett (1983) on "Brāhman-Chetris." Of particular note are the exemplary works of John Locke (1980, 1985), with their thorough and accurate presentation of detail documenting traditional monastic organization and religious observances of Kathmandu Valley Newars. Studies of traditional medical practitioners, a diverse group including shamans, oracles, spirit mediums, Buddhist lamas, Tantrics, astrologers, wandering ascetics, and herbal healers, and the related areas of ethnomedicine and ritual texts also contain considerable folklore. Significant works in these areas include those of Subedi (2001), Höfer (1981, 1994, 1997), Gaenszle (2002), Maskarinec (1995, 1998), and Desjarlais (1992, 2003). These works demonstrate the close connections between language, belief, and sociocultural practices. For example, shaman mantras (spells) against witches are a source of considerable lore such as this categorization of types of witches from Maskarinec (1998):

> Water-born witches, water-born witches,
> air-born witches, earth-born serpent witches,
> awakened dead-witches of the four directions,
> the east's Nine Little Sisters all-skillful,
> killing the glances of the Four Dead-witches,
> I stomp you through seven underworlds!

BIBLIOGRAPHY

Anderson, Mary M. 1971. *The Festivals of Nepal.* London: Allen and Unwin.

Bangdel, Lain Singh. 1989. *Stolen Images of Nepal.* Kathmandu: Royal Nepal Academy. (Updated at The Huntington Photographic Archive of Buddhist and Related Art: Lost and Stolen Images: Nepal at kaladarshan.arts.ohio-state.edu/loststolen/lsnepal.html.)

Bennett, Lynn. 1983. *Dangerous Wives and Sacred Sisters: Social and Symbolic Roles of High Caste Women in Nepal.* New York: Columbia University Press.

Desjarlais, Robert R. 1992. *Body and Emotion. The Aesthetics of Illness and Healing in the Nepal Himalayas.* Philadelphia: University of Pennsylvania Press.

———. 2003. *Sensory Biographies: Lives and Deaths among Nepal's Yolmo Buddhists.* Berkeley: University of California Press.

Diwas, Tulsi, ed. 1975–1976 (V.S. 2032). *Nepālī Lokakathā* (The Folk Tales of Nepal) [in Nepali]. Kathmandu: Royal Nepal Academy.

Fürer-Haimendorf, C. 1964. *The Sherpas of Nepal: Buddhist Highlanders.* London: John Murray.

Gaenszle, Martin. 2002. *Ancestral Voices: Oral Ritual Texts and Their Social Contexts among the Mewahang Rai of East Nepal.* Piscataway, NJ: Transaction.

Höfer, András. 1981. *Tamang Ritual Texts I. Preliminary Studies in the Folk Religion of an Ethnic Minority in Nepal.* Wiesbaden: Franz Steiner Verlag.

———. 1994. *A Recitation of the Tamang Shaman.* Bonn: Wissenschaftsverlag.

———. 1997. *Tamang Ritual Texts II. Ethnographic Studies in the Oral Tradition and Folk-Religion of an Ethnic Minority in Nepal.* Wiesbaden: Franz Steiner Verlag.

Hutt, Michael, ed. 1995. *Nepal. A Guide to the Art and Architecture of the Kathmandu Valley.* Boston: Shambala.

Josi, Satyamohan. 1957–1958 (V.S. 2018). *Chunākh (ukhānko)* [in Nepali]. Kantipur. Saraswati Press.

Krauskopff, Gisèle, and Marie Lecomte-Tilouine, eds. 1996. *Célibrer le pouvoir. Dasai, une fête royale au Népal.* Paris: CNRS Editions.

Lal, Kesar. 1991. *Gods and Mountains: The Folk Culture of a Himalayan Kingdom, Nepal.* Jaipur: Nirala Publications.

Lecomte-Tilouine, Marie. 1993. *Les Dieux du pouvoir: Les Magar et l'hindouisme au Népal Central.* Paris: CNRS Ethnologie.

Locke, John K. 1980. *Karunamaya: The Cult of Avalokitesvara-Matsyendranth in the Valley of Nepal.* Kathmandu: Sahayogi Prakashan.

———. 1985. *Buddhist Monestaries of Nepal.* Kathmandu: Sahayogi Prakashan.

March, Kathryn S. 2002. *If Each Comes Halfway: Meeting Tamang Women in Nepal.* Ithaca: Cornell University Press.

Maskarinec, Gregory G. 1995. *The Rulings of the Night. An Ethnographic Study of Nepalese Shaman Oral Texts.* Madison: University of Wisconsin Press.

———. 1998. *Nepalese Shaman Oral Texts.* Cambridge: Harvard University Press.

Meyer, Kurt, and Pamela Deuel. 1998. *Mahābhārata. The Tharu Barka Nāc.* Lalitpur: Himal Books.

Nepal, Purnaprakash "Yatri." 1994–1995 (V.S. 2051). *Bherī Lokasāhitya* [in Nepali]. Kathmandu: Nepal Royal Academy.

Oppitz, Michael. 1991. *Onkels Tochter, keine sonst.* Frankfurt am Main: Suhrkamp.

Ortner, Sherry B. 1978. *Sherpas Through Their Rituals.* Cambridge: Cambridge University Press.

Pal, Pratapaditya. 1985. *Art of Nepal.* Berkeley: University of California Press.

Pant, Jayaraj. 1998–1999 (V.S. 2055). *Anjulībhari sagun polṭābhari phāg* [in Nepali]. Kathmandu: Nepal Royal Academy.

Pignède, Bernard. 1966. *Les Gurungs: une population himalayenne du Népal.* Paris and The Hague: Mouton.

Sakya, Karna, and Linda Griffith. 1992. *Tales of Kathmandu. Folktales from the Himalayan Kingdom of Nepal.* Kathmandu: Mandala Book Point.

Shrestha, Hari, ed. 1974–1975 (V.S. 2031). *Nepāli lokā gīt* [in Nepali]. Kathmandu: Royal Nepal Academy.

Slusser, Mary Sheperd. 1982. *Nepal Mandala: A Cultural History of the Kathmandu Valley.* Princeton: Princeton University Press.

Subedi, Madhusudan Sharma. 2001. *Medical Anthropology of Nepal.* Kathmandu: Udaya Press.

Tingey, Carol. 1994. *Auspicious Music in a Changing Society. The Damāi Musicians of Nepal.* London: School of Oriental and African Studies.

Toffin, Gérard. 1984. *Société et religion chez les Néwar du Népal.* Paris: Editions du Centre National de la Recherche Scientifique.

Gregory G. Maskarinec

SRI LANKA

GEOGRAPHY AND HISTORY

An island with an area of 25,000 square miles, Sri Lanka is located off the southeast coast of **India** in the Indian Ocean a few degrees north of the equator. A central highland core divides the country into two main climatic areas: a wet zone in the southwest which receives rain all year, especially between May and July from the southwest monsoon; and a dry zone which gets its rainfall mainly between November and January from the northeast monsoon. The southwest region is thus very wet and was once thickly forested. As a result, the earliest Sri Lankan civilizations, which date from the third century B.C.E., flourished in the dry zone. Highly elaborate irrigation systems were developed with complex networks of reservoirs, dams, and channels that conserved and distributed rainwater for extensive rice cultivation, which provided the foundation for a flourishing society.

South Indian incursions during the tenth to the twelfth century C.E. and the destruction of the irrigation networks resulted in a shift of the kingdoms and populations to the south and west. The subsequent development of maritime trade with Europe further accelerated this westward movement, and the once-flourishing cities in the dry zone were abandoned. By the fifteenth century several semi-independent Sinhala kingdoms had been established in the south and west as well as a Tamil kingdom in the Jaffna peninsula in the very north. Between the sixteenth and eighteenth centuries European colonial conquest of the coastal regions successively by the Portuguese, Dutch, and British destroyed these Sinhala and Tamil kingdoms. Only one indigenous kingdom survived in the central highlands—the Kingdom of Kandy—but the British annexed that also in 1815, and Sri Lanka (then called Ceylon) became a colony of the British Empire. It regained its independence in 1946.

The population shift to the southwest resulted in the large land area of the dry zone remaining underpopulated, impoverished, and basically rural. It has remained so to this day. It is in this area and in the rural villages of the former Kandyan Kingdom that traditional cultural practices, rituals, and folkways still exist. The southwestern area under colonial domination developed a more diverse economy, based on plantation agriculture, trade, and modern commerce. It is today the more urban and developed sector of the island.

ETHNIC GROUPS AND RELIGIONS

Sri Lanka has two ethnic communities: the Sinhala, who comprise 70 percent of the total population, and the Tamil, who make up 17 percent. The distinction between the two groups is one of language rather than race as both the Sinhala and Tamil communities were probably peoples who migrated to the island from the south Indian Deccan peninsula at different times during the pre- and proto-historic periods. Their origin myths are, however, distinctly different. The Sinhala people claim to be originally from north India as their language has Indo-European roots, while the Tamils claim south Indian ancestry and speak a Dravidian language. The Sinhala are mainly Buddhist in religion and the Tamils largely Hindu. Over the centuries, however, religious distinctions between Buddhist and Hindu have become blurred as Buddhists have incorporated Hindu gods into their own pantheon.

A small remnant of the very early settlers remained non-Buddhist and continued to practice hunting. They are known as Veddas (hunters, from *vid*, meaning "to shoot"). While there were periods when some Veddas operated within Sinhala society and were often assimilated into it, other groups remained forest dwellers and hunters. Nineteenth-century scholars categorized the Veddas as aborigines and primitives. Today, these small groups have forged a fiercely distinctive "primitive" identity and call themselves *Vanniye aththo* (forest dwellers).

A small but fast-growing Islamic community comprising about seven percent of the total population has also carved out a distinctive identity. Some of them are descended from early Arab traders while others are of later migrant groups from parts of India and Malaysia. Here religion and not language is the defining difference. Muslims speak either Tamil or Sinhala depending on where they reside.

There is also a small Catholic community dating from Portuguese times and a Protestant Christian community, a carryover from Dutch and British colonial rule. These religious groups cut across ethnic and linguistic lines as they are drawn from both the Sinhala and Tamil communities. Like the Muslims they speak either Tamil or Sinhala depending on where they happen to live. While ethnic and linguistic distinctions are blurred, the Buddhists are sharply defined.

This complicated interweaving of ethnic, linguistic, and religious identities has religious distinction between them and the Hindus and resulted in a complex cultural mix among the different communities. Thus, many aspects of Hindu ritual have seeped into Buddhism, Sinhala traditional practices have been absorbed into Christian rituals, and almost all communities worship (each in their own fashion) at some of the same sacred shrines such as those at Siripada, Kataragama, and Munneswaram.

Three Sinhalese girls, 1905. (Courtesy Library of Congress)

The Buddha does not claim to be a deity or to control the fate of humans. He is the supreme teacher who shows people the path to salvation. Buddhists therefore have incorporated into their pantheon gods from Hinduism who can grant favors and intervene in human affairs. Four such major deities are Vishnu, Skanda, Pattini, and Kali. Their shrines are often located around or attached to a temple of the Buddha. There are also many other lesser deities such as the *kiri ammavaru* (mother goddesses), the *bandara deviyo* (local heroes who have been deified), various demons (*yakku*), and *prethas* (restless ghosts of dead ancestors) who are all propitiated with their special rituals. Thus the Buddhism practiced today by many Sri Lankans combines canonical teachings with worship of Hindu and folk deities incorporated into a single belief system.

Rituals to the Buddha were traditionally minimalist and individualistic such as the offering of flowers, lights, and food and chanting. One ritual of a more communal nature with roots in Buddhist history is the *pirit* ceremony. Buddhist monks, seated within a ritually sanctified space, chant the *suttas* (stanzas from the canon) to bring blessings on the listeners. Another more recently developed communal ritual is the *Bodhi puja* (offerings to the Bodhi tree or *Ficus religiosa*). Individuals or groups light hundreds of lamps around a Bodhi tree and chant religious verses as a safeguard in times of trouble.

Belief in malevolent forces produced by demons, *prethas*, magical charms, and negative planetary influences is widespread. Ritual specialists perform elaborate exorcist ceremonies called *thovil*, *bali*, and *kankari* with drums, masks, dance, songs, and comic dramatic interludes. Less elaborate performances such as *shanti karma* (acts of peace), *dehi kapima* (cutting of limes), and *huniyam kapima* (cutting of magical charms) occur on a smaller scale and at a more local level.

Some Christians also perform rituals to exorcise evil spirits, somewhat different from those performed by Buddhists, and Muslims may perform rituals to ward off the effect of evil charms at the mosque at Kahatapitiya.

Pilgrimages to ancient Buddhist sites as a meritorious act have long been part of traditional culture. The sacred geography of the Buddhists marks eight, twelve, or sixteen sites located around the island. Today these pilgrimage sites are still visited but as a combination of a sightseeing holiday and an act of religiosity. Shrines of certain major deities have a further function. Here offerings are made, favors invoked, vows made, and penance (sometimes extreme such as fire walking, hook hanging, or rolling in the sand) performed by devotees. Such acts of intense devotion performed at shrines such as Kataragama have also become tourist attractions because of their bizarre nature.

Catholics make annual pilgrimages to their important shrines at Madhu and Wahacotte, where festivities with a carnival atmosphere prevail. Muslims who can afford it make the pilgrimage to Mecca, but while local mosques are heavily patronized for regular worship, no places of specific national significance have developed. Some do visit shrines like Siripada, Munneswaram, and Kataragama, now frequented by all religious groups.

FOLK RITUALS

Ritual games such as *an adilla* (pulling of horns), *pol keliya* (coconut game), and *dodam keliya* (game of oranges) are occasionally still performed as part of the rituals for the goddess Pattini. Folk games associated with the secular New Year festivities such as climbing a greased pole, tug of war, and *chak gudu* are played in villages, though now more as a self-conscious attempt at revivalism. Volleyball can be considered a new "folk sport" popular in villages because any number can participate and the equipment needed is minimal. Cricket, however, can be termed the most popular folk game today. Children in almost every village can be seen playing cricket, sometimes with makeshift bats made from a coconut branch and a piece of tin or sticks serving as a wicket. It is played in its more sophisticated form by adults in urban centers.

Many folk rituals and practices associated with rice cultivation have survived for many generations perhaps because of the positive role they play in agricultural production and in fostering village solidarity. The *Vap magula* (Festival of the Plow) is collectively performed at the beginning of the cultivation season. On an auspicious day at a time determined by the local astrologer, farmers gather with their buffalo, and the village chief or head leads his team to plow the first furrow. He is followed by other teams. At noon, farmers partake of a festival meal prepared collectively by the village, and the animals are fed and rested. The plowing continues for several days until all the village fields are plowed. Another ritual termed *attam kayya* (labor exchange) provides cooperation for activities that need several hands, while *pin kayya* (merit exchange) occurs when labor is performed as a simple act of charity to help a sick or disabled fellow villager. Other village rituals known as *kem* or charms are magical practices to counter problems of pests and disease in the rice fields.

WRITTEN AND ORAL FOLK TALES

With the coming of Buddhism in the third century B.C.E., a tradition of writing quickly developed. Thus folk literature in such forms as legends, stories of historical events, poems, songs, and dramatic performances began to circulate very early, both in oral and written form, each influencing the other. For example, the Jataka Tales (Birth Stories of the Bodhisattva) from the Pali textual tradition were related by monks in sermons to villagers and then took on a life as orally circulating folk stories. Similarly oral legends of mythical ancestors such as the stories of Vijaya and Kuveni were embedded in historical chronicles written by monks and became part of the island's history. These early "chronicles"—the *Dipavamsa* (fourth century) and the *Mahavamsa* (sixth century)—blend actual historical events with oral myths and stories as in epics. Incidents from these chronicles flow back into the oral culture.

By the seventeenth and eighteenth centuries this interaction between the oral and written traditions was pervasive. Many ritual performances, whether directed toward deities or demons—such as the *Pattini halle* (Story of Pattini), the *Kohomba kankariya* (performance to the Kohomba gods), or the *Sanni yakuma* (rituals to the Demons of Disease)—had both an oral and a written text. Songs were sung and handed down orally but were also written in palm leaf manuscripts and carefully preserved by the families of ritual specialists. This was true of many kinds of folk compositions such as the poems about events (*vitti kavi*), battle poems (*hatan kavi*), or narrative poems such as the *Yasodaravata* (story of Yasodara) or the *Vessantara kathava* (Story of Vessantara). Folksongs of four-line verses composed individually or communally by peasants during their agricultural and other activities were popular and pervasive. When printing became accessible in the late nineteenth century, many such folk poems, tales, and songs moved from palm leaf manuscripts into print. They were sold in the marketplaces and at fairs by vendors who sang the familiar verses aloud to attract customers.

The conventional distinction between the oral, categorized as "folklore," and what was written as part of a textual scholarly tradition thus did not apply in the Sri Lankan situation. This was partly because literacy was fairly widespread and the ability to read and write was not uncommon even in villages. The tradition of composing poetry and writing it down finds its earliest expression in the graffiti poems scribbled on the rock wall of the fortress at Sigiriya between the seventh and ninth centuries C.E. They were the work of ordinary folk, "tourists" spontaneously exclaiming in poetry about the wonders of what they saw and scribbling their verses on the rock wall. Sri Lanka has thus a tradition of folk literature, stories, poems, songs, puns, aphorisms, riddles, ritual performances, and secular dramas both in oral and written form.

Today the oral forms are dying out even in the villages, as the activities associated with them and which helped to perpetuate them are disappearing. The demise of bullock cart transportation has spelled the end of carters' songs (*caratta kavi*) sung by individuals as they traversed slowly along lonely roads. The songs of ferrymen have died out with the disappearance of small-scale ferry crossings, and *pal kavi* (sung in watch huts to drive away marauding animals) are now seldom heard. What has remained are some folksongs associated with rice cultivation such as *nelum kavi* (weeding songs), *kamath kavi* (threshing floor songs), and fishermen's songs as they haul their nets.

Baila and *kaffiringa* are popular forms of song and dance derived from Portuguese tunes with a regular beat that permits easy extemporaneous compositions. They are now part of folk culture, widespread among urban youth, and sung at parties, at picnics, or in chartered buses when traveling for specific events.

In the fast-changing context of modern Sri Lanka with the media and communications explosion of recent years and the rapid inroads of globalization, "folk culture" among urban youth has taken the form of a "popular culture" of pop music, film songs, and "Bollywood" dance forms adapted from the Indian film industry. Only in the more rural peasant communities still dependent on rice cultivation are traditional folk practices still found.

FOLK THEATER

Sri Lanka has no record of a classical dramatic tradition, but it does have a rich folk performance tradition associated with village rituals for deities and demons. Such propitiatory rituals perhaps pre-dated the introduction of Buddhism, but they have continued to influence the manner in which Buddhism is perceived and practiced by villagers. Twentieth-century social scientists have done exhaustive surveys of these rituals. The comic interludes that were a part of these ritual performances later took on a life of their own and gave rise to secular dramas such as *Kolam* (comic impersonations with masks), *Nadagam* (a form of folk opera), and *Sokari* (a satiric counterpoint to the Pattini story). The satiric, often obscene comic interpolations in ritual performances, intended perhaps to wake a sleepy audience, also provided a critique of local authority figures. The extemporaneous dialogue was only tangentially related to the main performance. However, the ritual arena became a "permitted space" in which political and social criticism received public expression through satire, comedy, lampooning, and banter. This satiric tradition has continued into the modern Sinhala theater, where biting political satire is both popular and permitted.

A folk play popular in the Catholic community is the Passion Play or *Pasu* performed annually during Holy Week at Duwa (an island off the west coast). Statues as well as actors are used in the cast. A stage is constructed but much of the action takes place in the open amid crowds who actively participate. Puppet plays performed at carnivals and on festive occasions by skilled puppeteers, who both create their wooden puppets and operate them, were another form of folk entertainment.

ARTS, CRAFTS, AND ARCHITECTURE

Painting frescoes on temple walls was very much a folk tradition that probably had its roots in early Buddhism. It continues today, though the recent work seems sadly lacking in the esthetic sense of its predecessors. Striking examples of secular art are the Sigirya frescoes from around the sixth century C.E. Sculpting the Buddha image was yet another "folk" art, though sponsored no doubt by kings and noblemen. Before the eyes are painted on, special rituals are performed as an act of consecration. Some of the greatest works of Buddhist sculpture are to be seen among the ruins of the ancient cities.

Sri Lankan architecture has been open to influences from Tamil Nadu, Kerala, Portugal, **The Netherlands**, and Victorian **England**. Examples of these different influences through time can be seen around the country, designed and constructed by anonymous builders. Perhaps one architectural structure that is uniquely Sri Lankan in its classical simplicity of form and massive size, replicated in different parts of the island, is the *stupa* (Buddhist reliquary).

Some of the greatest works of Buddhist sculpture are to be seen among the ruins of the ancient cities, such as this Reclining Buddha, Gal Vihare, Sri Lanka. (Ann Ronan Picture Library/HIP/The Image Works)

Pottery, wood, brass, ivory carving, silver and gold jewelry making, and gem cutting can all be considered part of folk activity, though often sponsored by kings and noblemen. Good examples of these skills can be found even today, but commercialization is making such rapid inroads that the quality of the work produced is deteriorating.

BIBLIOGRAPHY

De Silva, K. M. 1981. *A History of Sri Lanka*. Delhi: Oxford University Press.

Dharmadasa, K.N.O. 1990. *The Vanishing Aborigines: Sri Lanka's Veddas in Transition*. Colombo: ICES.

Kapferer, Bruce. 1977. First Class to Maradana: Secular Drama in Sinhala Healing Rites. In *Secular Ritual*, edited by Sally Moore and Barbara Myerhoff. Amsterdam: Royal Van Gorcum. 91–123.

————. 1991. A *Celebration of Demons: Exorcism and the Aesthetics of Healing in Sri Lanka*. 2nd edition. Providence, RI: Berg.

Keyt, George. 1954. *Sinhala Folk Poetry*. Colombo.

Mills, Margaret, Peter J. Claus, and Sarah Diamond, eds. 2002. *South Asian Folklore: An Encyclopedia*. New York: Routledge.

Obeyesekere, Gananath. 1984. *The Cult of the Goddess Pattini*. Chicago: University of Chicago Press.

————. 1990. *Medusa's Hair: An Essay on Personal Symbols and Religious Experience*. Chicago: University of Chicago Press.

Obeyesekere, Ranjini. 1990. The Significance of Performance for Its Audience: An Analysis of Three Sri Lankan Rituals. In *By Means of Performance*, edited by Richard Schechner. Cambridge: Cambridge University Press. 118–130.

Obeyesekere, Ranjini, and Gananath Obeyesekere. 1976. Psychological Release: Comic Ritual Dramas in Sri Lanka. *Drama Review* 20: 5–19.

Parker, Henry. 1910. *Village Folk Tales of Ceylon*. London: Luzac.

Raghavan, M. D. 1967. *Sinhala Natum: Dances of the Sinhalese*. Colombo: M. D. Gunasena.

Sarachchandra, Ediriweera. 1966. *The Folk Drama of Ceylon*. Colombo: Department of Cultural Affairs.

Seligman, G. C., and B. Z. Seligman. 1911. *The Veddahs*. Cambridge: University Press.

Ranjini Obeyesekere

Southeast Asia

ISAAN

GEOGRAPHY

The northeastern region of Thailand, whose 66,250 square mile area holds one third of the country's population, is the Isaan culture area. A series of mountain ranges divide it from the rest of Thailand, while the Mekong River marks the border with Laos. Isaan may not be the richest or most fertile land, but it is well known for its long history of civilization, containing more than 500 archeological sites. Because of these discoveries Isaan is recognized as an important region of Thailand, and many studies of folklore have been carried out there.

RELIGIOUS BELIEFS AND RITUALS

Isaan people believe that a *khwan* or spirit resides within each person from the day he or she is born. When this *khwan* stays in the body, the person enjoys a good and healthy life. If it leaves the body, the person may fall ill or may experience some other misfortunes. The *khwan* may be frightened away from the body when a person is entering a new stage of life—for example, when about to leave home or enter a new community, at marriage, or when recovering from a serious illness. If that happens, a ritual called *suu khwan* (or *suut khwan*) will be held. *Suu* means "to go to" or "to visit"; the word comes from Pali *sutta* or from Vedic *sutra*, which means to recite incantatory words. *Suu khwan* could be considered a blessing ceremony.

This ritual involves preparation of a tray called *phaa khwan* on which is placed a decorative banana leaf cone that can be arranged in three, five, or seven tiers depending on the status of the person for whom the ritual is arranged. (There are a variety of rituals depending upon the position of the person in the community as well as some rituals for animals, plants, and inanimate objects such as rice granaries.) The ceremonial leader—*mo khwan* or *mo phram* (the Brahman)—sits on one side of the tray, and the supplicant faces the Brahman, touching the tray with the right hand while the Brahman recites an incantation to call back the *khwan* and to bless the *khwan*. Everybody else sits around the tray on the outside row, sending their energy to the *khwan* to aid in its return to the body.

Isaan in Thailand.

Suu khwan ceremony with large, five-tier *phaa khwan*. The Brahman ceremony leader is in the white coat, holding the cotton string connected to the *phaa khwan*. This string will be tied around the wrists of the guests after it has been blessed. (Photograph by Leedom Lefferts, 1981)

After the incantation the Brahman will tie the blessed cotton string around the person's wrist. The other guests will then do the same. After that the host will provide food to all. Though the origin of the ceremony lies in Brahmanism, the prevalence of Buddhism among the Isaan has brought changes so that Buddhist monks may sometimes conduct the ritual chanting.

The Isaan people also believe in a variety of supernatural powers, particularly the rain god, Phya Thaen—which is to be expected because Isaan is the driest region of Thailand. An ancient myth describes the conflict between the rain god and a human king known as Phya Khankhaak ("the Toad King") on account of his appearance. Phya Khankhaak had to lead an army of humans, animals, and celestial beings to fight Phya Thaen and extract from him the promise to send down rain on a yearly basis. To this day, the Isaan hold a yearly ritual, *Bun Bagfai*, usually in the sixth lunar month, as a commemoration of that promise. Each community makes a homemade rocket with gunpowder and bamboo pipes, which are decorated and carried in procession to a special place before being fired off into the sky in order to remind Phya Thaen of his duty. With bamboo hard to find nowadays, some people use plastic pipes. Chanting—often of an explicitly sexual nature— is common throughout the ritual, and during the parade, wooden constructs of the phallus and vagina are prominently displayed as befits a fertility rite. The need for rain being so great in Isaan, the people there have a number of other elaborate rituals, one involving a procession in which cats are splashed with water, the belief being that their cries will bring about rain because they hate being wet—a reversal of cause and effect.

The Isaan people also believe in the presence of their ancestral spirits called *phii puu taa*. *Phii* means ghosts or spirits, *puu* refers to the grandparents on the paternal side, and *taa* refers to the grandparents on the maternal side. In reverence toward their ancestors, the Isaan set aside a large piece of land with a spirit house for them, called *don puu taa* or the forest of the ancestors. No one can go to this place without

Decorated *Bun Bagfai* festival rocket on a pickup truck float. (Photograph by Leedom Lefferts, 1992)

showing respect. No tree is to be cut, nor any animal hunted. Anyone who violates this rule may become sick or meet with disasters. When that happens, the village shaman is called to hold a ritual to beg for forgiveness from the ancestors. Every year in the seventh lunar month, the people hold a ritual to pay respect to the ancestors in this area of the forest. After the ritual, the people share food and fellowship. Nowadays industry has deforested much of the land, and one can find the ancestors' forest only in very remote villages in Isaan. However, a network of villagers in Mahasarakham, Roi-et, Kalasin, and a few other provinces in Isaan have formed movements to preserve this land. They have changed its name to *paa chumchon*, or the community forest, which people guard against forest fire and theft. The members can go there to gather forest foods and herbs, but not to cut down trees.

Shrines to *phii puu taa* in village forest land. (Photograph by Leedom Lefferts, 1981)

The Isaan believe in three major concepts of Buddhism: cosmology, reincarnation, and merit accumulation. Buddhist cosmology recognizes thirty-one realms within the three worlds: the world of desire, the world with only a remnant of Material Factors, and the world without Material Factors. Yet most Isaan people choose to believe in eight different realms, a belief found in the folk epic *Phadaeng Nang Ai*. The human realm refers to villages, towns, and cities where the people are living presently; only in this realm can people do good deeds and earn *bun* or merit. The animal realm exists in the forest; people who have committed certain types of bad deeds are reborn in this realm after they die. In addition, there are the realm of wandering and suffering ghosts, the world of the *naga* (a mythical serpent), a hell for sinful people, and the realms of the gods. Finally, the ultimate goal of all Buddhists is to achieve the realm of *nirvana*, where people who have been able to get rid of all worldly attachment go. In this realm, they will suffer no more birth, aging, illness, and death. Most people cannot begin to hope for this realm, as they would have to be born and reborn on earth so many times to accumulate sufficient merit. So far only the Buddha and a few of his disciples have reached this state.

The Twelve Monthly Rituals (or *Heet Sipsong*) are common in all parts of Thailand and Laos. Many of these rituals in Isaan are similar to those in other regions of Thailand, as they have

Phadaeng Nang Ai actors sitting on a white horse carried by a pickup truck during *Bun Bangfai*. (Photograph by Leedom Lefferts, 1992)

gradually been influenced by Buddhist beliefs. However, those in Isaan and Laos especially resemble each other because of similar geography and history. Many of the twelve monthly rituals are presumed to be of pre-Buddhist origin. The Buddhist rituals were apparently added much later in the time of Phra Ubali-kunuupamajan (1856–1932) during the reign of King Rama V or King Chulalongkorn (1868–1910).

The Twelve Monthly Rituals usually begin with the Thai/Lao New Year called *kud songkaan* or *Songkran* in Thai. The celebration falls on the fifth lunar month, which is usually in the middle of April. In this ceremony, people splash water on each other, have a *Songkran* procession, clean, wash, and pay homage to the Buddha images, pour lustral water on respected persons, and build sand stupas on the temple grounds. Following the New Year, in the sixth lunar month occur the *Bun Bangfai* as well as the feast of *phi taa haeg*, a ceremony designed to propitiate the rice-planting spirit, and the Buddhist *Wisakhabucha* Day, the anniversary of the Buddha's birth, enlightenment, and entry into *nirvana*. On this day, people mark the beginning of the rice-planting season and construct houses for newly married couples.

Several more predominantly Buddhist rituals follow. In the seventh lunar month, people observe the celebration of the city spirit and *siva linga* of the town or city; *Bun Chamra* (the cleansing ceremony and the preparation of rice-planting tools such as plows, rice forks, and spades); and *phii puu taa*. *Asanhabucha* Day dominates the eighth lunar month. Held on the full moon, it marks the anniversary of the Buddha's First Sermon to his first 12,050 disciples at Deer Park in Benares. Buddhist Lent, during which many will visit holy places and study the Buddhist scriptures, begins the next day. *Bun Khao Pradab Din* follows in the ninth lunar month and requires that people prepare and set on the ground four sets of rice and food in small banana-leaf packets, the first being for monks, the second for family members, the third for other relatives, and the last for the dead. *Bun Khoa saak* occurs in the tenth lunar month and involves monks drawing the names of local individuals to determine who will donate food to them. The Buddhist Lent ends the next month and includes yet more offerings to monks as well as a boat race to celebrate the Naga Kings' well-being. Likewise, *Thod Kathin* in the twelfth lunar month centers upon offerings of new robes to the monks.

The Isaan hold a celebration in the first lunar month called *Bun Duen Aay*, during which the people prepare the rice-threshing ground and begin harvesting as well as holding drum contests and participating in *Bun Khao Kam*, a ceremony in which monks take a vow of penance for any sins, conscious or unconscious. During the next month, they hold *Bun Khoonlaan*, the ceremony of putting the rice on the threshing ground. *Bun Khaoci* in the third lunar month centers on chants of praise to the rice spirit and offering roasted glutinous rice to the monks. People will attempt to do good deeds particularly on *Makhabucha* Day, an anniversary of another of the Buddha's important sermons. Another Buddhist ceremony, *Bun Phra Wate* or *Bun Mahachaat* (Festival of the Great Birth), dominates the fourth lunar month and includes many processions and sermons. At one time, it entailed the departure of caravans, buffalo, and oxcarts for sale and trade in distant lands, but modern transportation has effectively ended that.

MYTHS AND LEGENDS

Issan narratives include myths, historical chronicles called *phongsawadaan*, sacred texts about the Buddha's *Jataka* tales and teachings, *sutra* or *mantra* or words of chants and incantations, folk law, folk medicine and remedies, and didactic texts.

Usually regarded as sacred texts, Issan myths cover such topics as the origin of human beings, the relationship between humans and gods, and the origin of the Mekong River. According to one story, the narrator of which was said to be the historical Buddha, the first people were created by the first Buddha, Phra Pathomma, who meditated so strongly that he perspired. Mixing the sweat with water and soil, he fashioned a human couple known as Puu Sanggasa and Yaa Sanggasi, who were without hunger or lust. After discovering and eating rice, however, they were endowed with physical needs and had to be instructed by the Buddha in what to do to achieve enlightenment.

The myth of the origin of the Mekong River recounts that a misunderstanding occurred between two *naga* kings, Suwan and Suttho, who lived in the Nongsae River. They began fighting with such intensity that it laid waste to much of the region, killed many living beings, and forced some of the gods to move away. The king of the gods interceded and ordered them to make two rivers to compensate for their deeds—the Mekong and the Nan.

Though Issan folklore contains a variety of legends, trickster tales, animal stories, and other narratives, what stands out most are the *Jataka* tales relating the past lives of the Buddha. These stories were believed to be told by the Buddha himself in certain situations such as when he wanted to clarify his teachings. Later, the Buddha's disciples retold these stories in their sermons or teachings. Thus, the *Jataka* tales have been closely related to storytelling in various forms. As time goes by, more stories may be added to the original *Jataka* collection; some may come from the *Panchatantra*, a collection of Buddhist animal fables in Sanskrit dating from before 500 C.E. In Lao folktales, the stories within the *Panchatantra*, often overlap with those in the Buddhist *Jataka* tales. No matter from which collections these tales come, they share a similar purpose: to teach some moral points. Thus, we might dub these tales moral tales as well.

PROVERBS AND RIDDLES

Proverbs and sayings are called *phayaa* or *phanyaa*, which means wisdom or knowledge. Most of the proverbs and sayings use simple forms of poetry to deliver messages. These proverbs and sayings could be divided into several categories, ranging from practical advice to religious beliefs and moral conduct, and may be used in rituals of courting and during the task of transplanting rice as well as in teaching. *Phayaa* also reflect and preserve people's ways of life, cultural practices and beliefs, and social values. Examples include *Gin mam mam bo khlam boeng thong* (The eyes are bigger than the stomach); *Maen si mee khwam huu tem phung phiang paak kataamthon* (He is full of knowledge like a being full from food up to the stomach and mouth); and *Khan maen son to eng bo dai phai si yong wa dee* (If he cannot teach, he fails to teach himself; he is not well respected).

Riddles are a game by which children hone their wit and intelligence. Isaan riddles are usually divided into general and Buddhist riddles and cover such subjects as nature, tools, utensils, and more. General riddles include those based upon the observation of nature: *Suk tem din keb kin bo dai?* (What is ripe on the ground but we cannot pick it?—Sunlight); *Lek daeng daeng thaeng din khue an yang?* (What is the red iron rod that stabs through the ground?—Sweet red yam). Examples of riddles about animals include *Yuen tam nang suung?* (What is short when standing and tall when sitting?—A dog); *Sii tiin yaang maa langkha mung kabueng?* (What walks on four with a tile roof?—A turtle); and *Maak lumphuk tok puk kaang nong khii ngua thong ook pai ao ka bo dai* (When a shining fruit falls in the middle of the swamp or river, we can never ride a golden ox to fish it out of the water.—The shadow of the sun in a lake).

Buddhist riddles are quite complicated and need considerable explanation. Usually monks or learned persons ask these questions to provide an opportunity for instructing people. Here are some examples from Phra Inta Kaweewong's unpublished versions of these Buddhist riddles: *Taai bo nao kao bo pen* (When it's dead but does not disintegrate, it is long lived without being old.—A good deed); *Baan kai khang yom khang bo daeng yaam mue laeng fing daed bo oun suad jum bum mue um bo thoeng* (The house near the beeswax cannot dye anything red, one cannot get the heat from the evening sunshine, and although it looks so obviously big, we cannot grasp it with our hands.—When one's house is near the temple but one never goes to listen to Buddha's teachings, it is impossible to see the truth even when it is so obvious); *Yaang yong yong huo taeb khi din mob mob khao huo thao ngaa yaang* (Walking tall, you may fall on the ground; walking low, you may grow tall like a rubber tree.—When one is arrogant one tends to fall; when one is humble and modest, one tends to grow tall.).

SONGS

Folksongs in Isaan can be categories based on the purposes the songs serve. One type is called *lam*. The word *lam* refers to the singing, the dance, and the *khaen* musical instrument accompanying the singing. The singer of the *lam* is called *mo lam* (specialist in singing *lam*). The purposes of this kind of singing are varied. The *lam soeng* or *lam phii faa* could be used for healing. Songs for entertainment include *lam thaang san* (fast-paced singing), *lam thaang yao* (slow and lingering singing), *lam toey* (singing using a mixture of foreign words and tunes), *lam phuen* or *lam klon* (story songs, relating mostly folktales), and *lam muu* (a theatrical style of singing with a group of performers and musicians). Other types of Isaan folksong exhibit styles that depend upon their usage, be they for rituals, teaching, or children's games.

WAIKHUU CHANT

The following verse is a *waikhuu* chant (*wai* means to join hands in a prayer gesture; *khruu* mean teachers) to pay respect to all teachers—religious teachers, parents, teachers in schools, and others:

Mala duang dok mai	Garlands and flowers
Mala duang dok mai	Garlands and flowers
Ao tang wai phua bucha	We place for worship.
Kho bucha khun phraphut	We bow to Buddha,
Kho bucha khun phraphut	We bow to Buddha,
Phu dai trat sa ru ma	Who attained enlightenment.
Kho bucha khun phratham	We bow to *Dhamma*,
Kho bucha khun phratham	We bow to *Dhamma*,
Thi dai nam sang son ma	Which brings contentment.
Kho bucha khun phrasong	We bow to *Sanga*,
Kho bucha khun phrasong	We bow to *Sanga*,
Phu dai thong phra winai	Who maintain disciplines.
Duay jit an nob nom	We bow with humble mind,
Duay jit an nob nom	We bow with humble mind,
Phrom duay kai lae waja	Our refined actions and speech.

Usually chanted before undertaking a difficult task, the *waikhuu* is indicative of the humility needed to be successful in any endeavor. Apart from humility, the Issan belief system includes at least three major factors: the belief in certain supernatural powers or spirits known as *khwan*; the performance of rituals to achieve certain, tangible ends; and the influence of Buddhism.

MUSIC

The Isaan people's love of music is well known. They can make music from many kinds of natural materials. Six major Isaan musical instruments are still seen in Isaan folk music groups: *woad*, *pong laang*, *huen*, *sanuu*, *khaen*, and *kapkaep*. All of these musical instruments can be played alone or in an ensemble.

The *woad* was originally made of fresh rice straws. Later this musical instrument was made from small bamboo pipes tied together around a core made of a bigger bamboo pipe with beeswax welding them together. Players usually blow into the pipes or may even throw it into the air in such a way as to make music with the wind. Originally the *pong laang* was a cow or buffalo bell and a piece of hardwood used to toll the hour in villages. Later, people put these pieces together like xylophones, hitting them with wooden mallets to make music. The *huen* was a musical instrument first made from a leaf. To make music one blows on the leaf. Later, it was developed into a more permanent instrument by using bamboo pieces with a reed in the middle. To play the instrument, one holds the bamboo near the open mouth and with the other hand picks the reed.

The *sanuu* is made of the shredded palm leaves tied at the two ends of a bow-like instrument. The player can swing the bow, producing music through the vibration. People also tie this instrument at the head of a kite to produce a melody in the air. The *khaen* is a woodwind instrument made of a special kind of bamboo pipe with a silver reed inside. The instrument comes in different sizes: it can be made of six, fourteen,

Soeng row dancing during *Bun Bangfai*. Young girls on the right are dressed in traditional Isaan women's dress, older women on the left are in men's costumes, both with ceremonial hats. (Photograph by Leedom Lefferts, 1992)

sixteen, or eighteen pipes. The pipes are stuck to a mouthpiece made of a hard wood. Beeswax holds the pipes together. The *kapkaep* is a simple percussion instrument made of two small pieces of hard wood. Each piece could be about five to ten centimeters long and one centimeter thick. The player will hold two pieces of the *kapkaep* in each hand and bring them together to produce a sound.

DANCE

A few major Isaan dances are still performed nowadays: *soeng* dance; *phutai* dance; and *kranoptingtong*, *ruem-an-re*, *jaruang*, and *kantruem* of the Thai near the Cambodian border. Isaan dancing is distinguished by the way the dancers hold their fingers and their hands. Most Isaan dancing is fast-paced. *Soeng* dancing is performed during the *Bun Bangfai* fertility rite. Dancing patterns are adapted from the actions of rice cultivation. The entire music ensemble is used to accompany the dance, but if there are not enough instruments or musicians, the instruments could be reduced to just a *khaen*, drums, gong, and cymbals. The costumes are simple tube skirts with local Isaan designs and a blouse with a shoulder cloth.

Phutai dancing is the dance unique to the *Phutai* ethnic group in five provinces in Isaan: Renunakhon, Nakhonphanom, Sakonnakhon, Kalasin, and Mukdahan. The dancers wear their *phutai* costumes, which are plain blue or black tube skirts with red stripes on the bottom edge, at the end of the sleeves, and around the collar. Dancers usually wear ornaments such as rings, necklaces, bracelets, and silver earrings. Some groups of *phutai* also wear long fingernails made of silver or gold paper. The dance originally was meant to pay homage to the Buddhist stupas in Sakonnakhon and Nakhonphanom. Nowadays the dance is performed when honored guests visit the village.

The performances of the Isaan people living near the Cambodian border bear some similarity to the dances and music of their neighbors. One example, *kranoptingtong*, is a dance of the grasshoppers. The dance portrays the male and female grasshoppers teasing each other lovingly. The costumes imitate the appearance of grasshoppers. Dancers wear green clothes with wings. The musical accompaniment is flute, small cymbals, and two-faced drums.

SPORTS AND GAMES

Isaan people, like most Thai and Lao people, are fun loving. They are ready to participate when situations for games and traditional play arise. However, children in big cities, preoccupied with television, may be ignorant of some of these pastimes.

Attempts have been made to revive games and plays during festivals. For the Songkran festival, people may play two kinds of tug-of-war: by using a cowhide rope, or by using a rope tied to a wooden mortar and pestle. There will also be a drum contest and a game of *sabaa*. The latter refers to a large seed of vines grown along the bank of the Mekong, which would float in the river in the rainy season. People would collect and save them for the game. In this game, two sides compete—one side setting their *sabaa* and watching the other side roll the *sabaa* from the starting line. When the *sabaa* stops, the roller will squat, put the *sabaa* on his knees, and shoot at the sitting *sabaa*. If he hits the sitting *sabaa*, he has another turn. But if he misses, the other side will roll the *sabaa* while the opponents look on.

During a wake, people may play a game called *Putta Kin Kai* (Grandpa Eats Chicken). Each player has a piece of paper that represents Grandpa, chicken, and termites. The players are divided into two sides. At the count of three, the players on one side will hold a piece of paper out. Each pair will open their hands at the same time. If Grandpa is opposite to the termite, Grandpa loses because the termite will eat Grandpa's house. If Grandpa is opposite the chicken, Grandpa wins because Grandpa can eat the chicken. The chicken will eat the termite.

The performance of *lam* in story-theater style with an ensemble of Isaan folk musicians to accompany the dancing and singing was quite popular. This kind of folk drama is call *lam muu*. A troupe would be hired during a village festival, at a wake, or at other festive occasions. This kind of performance could go on all night. The actors and actresses performed in glittering costumes. The introduction of television and movies has essentially caused traditional *lam muu* to become extinct as performers now adopt Western music, dancing, and costumes in a style dubbed *lam cing* (the word "*cing*" may come from the word *racing*).

CHALLENGES OF THE MODERN WORLD

Globalization has done away with much traditional folklore, including storytelling, which used to be ubiquitous among the Isaan as a part of many communal celebrations. However, in remote villages the impact of globalization is not that strong. One can still find much of the old folklore. Some attempts are also being made to revive some traditional beliefs and practices. Hopefully, these movements will be successful so that the younger generations will be able to experience the traditional life a little longer.

BIBLIOGRAPHY

Anuman Rajadhon, Phya. 1972. *Muangsawan lae Phisang Thewada* (Heaven and Ghost and Devata). Bangkok: Bannakan.

Archeology Project of Northeast Thailand. 1979. Report on the Study of Ancient Cities in Northeast Thailand.

Ariyanuwat Khemajari, Phra. 1982. *Nang sue praphenii boran isaan bang ruang* (Book on Some Ancient Customs). Mahasarakham: Mahasarakham Cultural Center.

———. 1985. *Luepppasun* (Extinguishing the Light of the Sun). Mahasarakham: Wat Mahachai's Center for the Preservation of Northeast Folk Literature.

———. 1990. *Thao Siew Swaat*. Mahasarakham: Aphicat Printing Press.

Inta Kaweewong, Phra. 1998. *Thao Siew Swaat*. Khonkaen: Klang Nanatham.

———. N.d. *Kham Klon Son Lok* (World Teaching Verses). Mahasarakham: Wat Mahachai's Center for the Preservation of Northeast Folk Literature.

Jaruwan Thammawat. 1979a. *Wikhro nithan chaoban isaan jaak saam muu ban* (Analysis of Folktales from Three Villages). Kalasin: Jintaphan.

———. 1979b. *Wikhro Phleng Dek Isaan* (Analysis of Isaan Children's Songs). Kalasin: Jintaphan.

———. 1983. *Phayaa Botkawee khong chao ban* (Proverbs and Sayings, the Poetry of the Folk). Kalasin: Jintaphin.

———. 1988. *Cheewit lae phon ngan Phra Ubali-khunuupamajan; phalang haeng kan patiruup hou muang isaan* (Life and Works of Phra Ubali-khunuupamajan: The Power of Reforms in Isaan Cities). In *Phumpanya haeng Isaan* (Wisdom of Isaan): *A Collection of Papers on Isaan Studies*. Mahasarakham: Thai and Eastern Languages Department, Mahasarakham University.

———. 1997. *Katichaoban Isaan* (Isaan Folklore). Bangkok: Aksonwatthana.

———. 1998. *Legends and Folktales of Isaan*. In *The Laos Perspective in Communities on Both Sides of the Mekhong Basin*, edited by Jaruwan Thammawat. Ubonratchathani: Siritham.

———. 1999. *Orphan Tales: Reflections of People's Lives with Restricted Opportunities and Ethnic Relationships in the Middle Southeast Region: A Research Report*. Ubonratchathani: Siritham.

Kingkaew Attathakora. 1977. *Folklore*. Series of Educational Supervision Paper No. 184. Bangkok: Fine Arts Department, Ministry of Education.

Koret, Peter. 2002. Leup Phasun (Extinguishing the Light of the Sun): Romance, Religion, and Politics in the Interpretation of a Traditional Lao Poem. In *Proceedings on the Theme on Thailand and Laos, the Eighth International Conference on Thai Studies, January 9–12, 2002*. Nakhonphanom: Ramkhamhaeng University. 84–106.

Lithai, Phya. 1982. *Three Worlds According to King Ruang*, translated by Frank E. and Mani B. Reynolds. Berkeley: University of California Press.

MacDonald, Margaret Read, and Wajuppa Tossa. 2004. *Folktales and Storytelling*. Mahasarakham: Aphichat Kanphim.

Maha Sila Viravong. 1974. *Hiit sip soong*. Vientiane: Kom Wannakhadii (Literature Department).

Niyaphan Wannasiri. 1984. *Lakkan, thitsadee, lae withikansuksa wannakam phuenban* (Principles, Theories, and Methods of Folk Literature). *Sangkhomsaat* March: 170–189.

Nou Xayasithivong, and others. 2002. *San Lupphasun* (Letters on Extinguishing the Light of the Sun). Vientiane: Education Printing Enterprise.

Phongsawadan huo muang monthon isaan (The Chronicles of Cities in Isaan). 1963. Bangkok: Khurusapha.

Prasong Saihong. 2003. Storytellers in Northeast Thailand. Thesis, Northern Illinois University.

Preecha Phinthong, Phra Maha. 1982. *Prapheni boran isaan*. Ubonratchathani: Siritham.

Raendchen, Oliver. 1988. *Thai Customs and Beliefs*. Bangkok: Office of the National Culture Commission, Ministry of Education.

———. 1994. Laos. In *Traveller's Literary Companion to South-east Asia*, edited by Alastair Dingwell. Brighton, UK: Print Publishing. 120–153.

———. 2001. The *Hiit-khong* Codes of the Lao. *Tai Culture* 6.1–2: 182–199.

———. 2002. *Sun khwan*: Ritual Texts and Ceremony in Laos and Northeast Thailand. *Tai Culture* 7.1: 155–175.

Sawing Bunjoem. 1994. *Phaya* (Wisdom). Ubonratchathani: Moradok.

———. 1996. *Tamra moradok isaan* (Textbook of Isaan Heritage). Ubonratchathani: Moradok.

———. 1999. *Khwam soi khwom thuay* (Witty Additional Words and Riddles). Ubonratchathani: Moradok Isaan.

Sinam Janphen. 1997. *Nangsue moonmang isaan* (Book of Isaan Heritage). Kalasin: Prasankanphim.

Srisak Walliphodom. 1988. *Tamnan urangkhathat* (The Legend of Thatphanom Stupa) and *Phongsawadan huo muang monthon isaan* (The Chronicles of Cities in Isaan). Bangkok: Ruangkaew.

Suphon Somjitsipanya. 1986. *Puu sanggasa yaa sanggasi jaak nangsue kom* (Grandfather Sanggaa and Grandmother Sanggasi from the Small Palm Leaf Texts). Mahasarakham: Arts and Culture Center of the Rajaphat Institute.

Tossa, Wajuppa. 1990. *Phadaeng Nang Ai: A Translation of a Thai/Isan Folk Epic in Verse.* Lewisburg, PA: Bucknell University Press.

———. 1996. *Phya Khankhaak, the Toad King: A Translation of an Isan Fertility Myth into English Verse.* Lewisburg, PA: Bucknell University Press.

Wajuppa Tossa

MALAY

GEOGRAPHY AND HISTORY

Malay, or *Melayu*, is the primary racial group inhabiting the Malay Peninsula, Singapore, the southern tip of Thailand, the southern islands of the Philippines, the eastern coast of Sumatra, the coastal area of Borneo, and the surrounding islands of the Malay Archipelago. The language is also called Malay, a member of the Malay-Polynesian group, and the most prevalent religion is Islam.

The ancestral home of the Malays is believed to be in the southern part of **China**, from which they migrated southward until about 1500 B.C.E., when they started to settle in the regions of the Malay Archipelago and the southern Pacific. The Malays were seafaring people and usually settled along coastal areas where they formed small communities that later became institutionalized into city-states. The earliest of the Malay states was Srivijaya (seventh to twelfth centuries C.E.), located in the southern part of Sumatra. Srivijaya was a Malay Hindu kingdom whose empire encompassed the entire coastal region of the Straits of Melaka as well as the Malay Peninsula. The next great Malay kingdom was Melaka (fourteenth to sixteenth century), a prosperous seaport

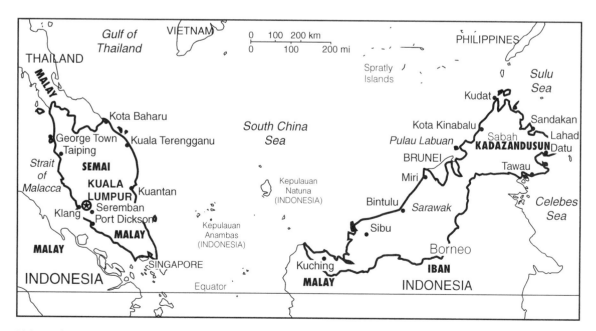

Malay and Semai in Malaysia and Indonesia.

A group of wealthy Malays. (Courtesy Library of Congress)

city-state that controlled not only the trade route between the east and west but also the hinterlands of the Malay Peninsula. Melaka was a Muslim state, and during its heyday Islam began to establish a strong foothold in the Malay Peninsula.

During the period of the two major kingdoms, Malays had experienced at least two major cultural revolutions, the first centering upon Javanese-influenced Hinduism and the second upon Islam, which came by way of Arabs and Persians. Malay culture still manifests this mixture of Hindu and Islamic influences. But more importantly, these two cultures helped to shape the traditional arts and literature (both folk art and "high" art) of the Malays (as now Western influence, beginning at the turn of the nineteenth century, is also doing). The intense contact with both traditions gave rise to genuinely distinctive Malay literatures that synthesized elements into the framework of the indigenous prototypes. These literatures of synthesis form the bulk of traditional Malay literature of the Hindu-Islamic period.

The common sociocultural experience of the Malays throughout Southeast Asia and the Indies had created a similar cultural heritage, as witnessed in its material and literary traditions. Discussions of folklore only on the Malay Peninsula can represent Malay folklore in general.

MYTHS, LEGENDS, AND FOLKTALES

The Malays possess an extensive corpus of oral lore, ranging from folktales, legends, and myths to various poetic forms, riddles, and proverbs. Magical tales (*märchen* or fairy tales whose morphological structure resembles that identified for Russian tales by folklorist Vladimir Propp) exploit the secondary world of high fantasy peopled by ordinary and supernatural beings (in Malay these are called *peri*, *jin*, *dewa*, and *dewi*). Narratives of marvelous adventures and courtly romance, these tales are popular among wandering bards (singers of tales called *Awang Belanga* and *Tarik Selampit*). Also known as folk romances, these magical tales appear under the Arabic title "*hikayat*" (for example, *Hikayat si Miskin*), though they are mostly of Indian origin. The Malay folktale **repertoire** also includes cycles of beast fables, especially the trickster type (the *Cerita Sang Kancil*), farcical tales about fools such as *Pak Pandir* and *Pak Kaduk*, and stories about luckless people such as *Lebai Malang*.

Besides these lighthearted tales, more serious and sacred narratives such as myths and legends occur in Malay folklore. Myths of origin, founding myths, and dynastic myths are some of the more well-known Malay tribal or primeval myths. They manifest an indigenous animistic worldview even though most of the motifs are derived from the Hindu-Buddhist complex of myths. One of the most popular myths is the *Saguntang* myth, which accounts for the origin of the Malay rulers. Various types and subtypes of legends form the largest corpus of oral narratives. Among the most popular are legends about patron saints (*keramat*) and Malay heroes. One example is the sacred *Mahsuri* legend set on the island of Langkawi. Mahsuri was believed to have put her curse on Langkawi so that for seven generations the island would remain impoverished. Now people believe the seven generations have lapsed, and Langkawi is freed from the curse. Perhaps this explains why Langkawi has become one of the most popular and prosperous tourist destinations in Malaysia. Unlike other folk narratives, legends are continually being created orally, and the most popular contemporary legend concerns sinners. The prototypical character of this legend is *Si Tenggang*, a treacherous son who was turned into stone. These are urban legends that have deep Islamic moral tones and probably serve as social deterrent against vices and unethical conduct.

POETRY AND FOLK THEATER

Various oral poetic verse forms are abundant as well: the four-line, witty *pantun* with its beautiful imagery and depth of meaning; the short, rhythmic, formulaic *talibun*, in which verse is interspersed with the prose of oral narration; the cynical and satirical *seloka*, loose in structure; and the longer free-verse *teromba*, which enumerates the customary laws of the ethnic Minangkabau Malays. The *mantera*, another poetic form, functions as a magical incantation. These magical words are used in rituals and shamanic practices. Also abundant are folk maxims and proverbs and short, witty riddles.

Folk performance forms a rich cultural heritage for the Malay world, as well as throughout Southeast Asia. The *wayang kulit* (shadow play), of both Thai and Javanese origins, is popular in folk and court performances. *Wayang kulit* involves leather puppets whose shadows are projected upon a white screen. The *Menora* and *Mak Yong* are stylized forms of dance theater that incorporate song and dialogue and are very popular in the northern region of the Malay peninsula. They demonstrate a synthesis of Malay and Thai culture. Both are court performances and display elaborate and refined costumes appropriate for the courtly culture they represent. More localized performance genres have lost some of their popularity. Most Malay folk performances are highly ritualized and usually preceded by incantations or *manteras* as well as offerings to pacify the guardian spirits of the performance venue. The performing arts are usually accompanied by folk musical instruments, the most popular being the *rebab* (a stringed instrument), the *serunai* (flute), and the *gendang* (drum).

ARTS AND CRAFTS

Malays can also be proud of their folk art. The *Wayang* puppets themselves are very ornate figures with intricate designs made from colored leather. Another spectacular Malay craft is woodcarving. Examples adorn ancient Malay palaces, houses, and furniture. The basic design in Malay woodcarving is the *awan larat* (extending clouds), and other frequently used motifs are bean tendrils, leaves, and flowers. Today these beautiful carvings are found as wood panels decorating modern buildings such as mosques, hotels, and business and administrative centers.

The basic Malay art motifs are also found on *batik* cloths (the Malay traditional

An ethnic Malay woman in traditional clothing with covered head. (© James Marshall/The Image Works)

sarong). Patterns using these traditional motifs are usually painted by hand. But today batik craft is highly commercialized, and new patterns with modern motifs are more in vogue. *Songket*, a traditional Malay fabric, woven by hand in gold and silver threads, is another famous Malay craft. Like *batik*, *songket* is patterned after the local flora and fauna, but *songket* is not for daily use. Traditionally it was worn only by the palace elites. Today *songket* makes up the customary costumes worn for important occasions such as weddings and formal gatherings.

Malays would pass their nights either hearing wondrous narratives from storytellers or watching theatrical performances, either of which could last up to several nights. During the day, especially after harvesting time, leisure hours would be occupied with making kites and *gasings* (tops), two very popular folk toys. Malay kites are colorfully designed using local motifs, usually fish or birds. In Malay, kite is called *wau*, named for the echoing sound it produces as it flies in the air. *Main gasing* (spinning tops) is another popular folk game. The *gasing* is a huge circular disk of wood with an iron rod implanted in the middle. Spinning these huge tops requires considerable skill and talent. Both kite flying and spinning tops are usually competitive, and the competition offers an opportunity for people from several communities to socialize. Folk games remain popular especially among the people of the eastern coast of the Malay Peninsula.

CHALLENGES OF THE MODERN WORLD

Like many traditional heritages most types of Malay folklore are fast becoming things of the past. With its emphasis on electronic entertainment, **modernization** has almost put an end to storytelling and theatrical performance. To survive or remain sustainable, both these arts need audiences and patronage, both of which now are quite rare. The traditional artists themselves are mostly aged. Those who have died may leave no successors. Fortunately, though, efforts are being undertaken to record these arts on videos so that they can be preserved for future generations. Universities and the Ministry of Culture are researching and reviving traditions, so now they have found new platforms in urban areas, in media, and in tourist packages. Although these environments are not natural for these performances, at least the traditions are being preserved. With newly emerging interests in traditional heritage among postmodern societies, there is a future for these dying arts.

STUDIES OF MALAY FOLKLORE

Western historians including Moorhead (1959) and Hall (1964) provide useful background information for the study of Malay folklore, as does *Ensiklopedia Sejarah dan Kebudayaan Melayu* (Encyclopedia of a Malay History and Culture; 1999). Many non-Malay researchers have collected and published Malay myths, legends, and folktales: Winstedt (1972), Knappert (1980), and Skeat (1984), for example. Local researchers such as Mustapha Mohd Isa and Siti Aishah Ali have also collected Malay folktales.

BIBLIOGRAPHY

Ensiklopedia Sejarah dan Kebudayaan Melayu. Jilud 2. 1999. Kuala Lumpur: Dewan Bahasa dan Pustaka.

Hall, D.G.E. 1964. *A History of South East Asia*. London: Macmillan.

Knappert, Jan. 1980. *Malay Myths and Legends*. Kuala Lumpur: Heinemann Educational Books.

Moorhead, F. J. 1959. *A History of Malaya and Her Neighbours*. London: Longmans.

Mustapha Mohd, Isa. N.d. Awang Belanga: Penglipur Lara dar Perlis. Thesis, University of Science of Malaysia.

Siti Aishah Mat Ali. 1974. Satu Kumpulan Cerita Rakyat dari Kampung Mertuan, Kelantan—Klasifikasi Motif dan Taip-Cerita. Thesis, University of Malaya.

———. 1976. *Cerita-Cerita Rakyat*. Kota Bharu: Al-Ahliyah.

Skeat, Walter William. 1984. *Malay Magic: Being an Introduction to the Folklore and Popular Religion of the Malay Peninsula*. Singapore: Oxford University Press.

Winstedt, R. O. 1972. *A History of Classical Malay Literature*. Singapore: Oxford University Press.

Noriah Taslim and Low Kok On

SEMAI

GEOGRAPHY AND HISTORY

The largest linguistic group of Orang Asli, the indigenous people of the peninsula of west Malaysia, is the Semai. Counting people in towns, there are about 100,000 Asli, divided into over a dozen language groups, each with its distinctive way of life. Their languages are related to the languages of Cambodia's Khmer but are unrelated to the languages of the later-arriving immigrant **Malay**, now the dominant people of the peninsula. Like most indigenous groups the Semai call themselves simply "People" (*Senoi*). There were about 30,000 Semai in 2004.

Semai were traditionally agroforesters. They cleared and burned their fields in the heart of the rainforest, usually targeting areas where trees were still small enough to cut down and burn easily. It takes two men with traditional tools a day to cut down a rainforest giant. For that reason, they usually cleared fields in the secondary forest that grew up where they had cleared fields before. They spared trees that produced valuable products such as fruits or blowpipe dart poisons. They also planted or tended these trees in their fields or in the forest. The result was a forest rich in valuable species of trees with a greater variety of plants and animals than untouched forest could sustain. This adaptation lasted for thousands of years.

Malaysia lies close to the equator. The monsoons, two a year, create a recurrent pattern of wet and dry seasons. Human activities such as farming and agroforestry

Semai children, 1992. (Photograph by Robert Knox Dentan)

mesh with this pattern. The story of the androgynous Elder Cuckoo, representing a migratory bird whose distinctive call marks planting season, explains how the people learned the seasonal discipline of time and the hard work of farming. It seems to be a modified version of an older story, in which another bird, a ground dove, introduces agroforestry.

Besides being regular, the biennial monsoons generate terrifyingly violent thundersqualls, sometimes of hurricane force. The skies turn chilly and black. The rain is blinding, its sound like assault rifles. The huge forest giants creak and snap and break, crashing down and dragging smaller trees with them. Rivers crashing down the steep limestone mountains rise visibly, inches in an hour. The soaked rainforest soils may collapse in huge mud landslips, and the limestone beneath the earth, rotten from centuries of erosion, may collapse into giant sinkholes. The experience of this terror makes a natural metaphor for the experience of the slaver terrorism discussed next. Semai religion can be partially understood as a way of dealing with human and natural horrors.

For centuries, until about 1920, Semai suffered from a particularly brutal form of slaving by their powerful neighbors, the Malays. The experience of having their children stolen to be abused for the entertainment of rich Malays seems to have affected their folklore and led to the peaceable lifestyle for which they are famous. Early European and Malay observers described Semai as timid and wild. Although there were trade ties between the powerful Malays and the relatively powerless Semai, Malay patrons often exploited their Semai clients. Semai timidity was a reasonable response to their political environment, which, especially as the colonial government sought to develop the country after 1874, involved increasing displacement and enslavement by Indonesian immigrants who had no ties with Semai and who exterminated other groups of Orang Asli. The slavers particularly targeted children, because they were easy to steal and domesticate as slaves for rich people to abuse physically and sexually. Semai became deeply distrustful of outsiders and still teach their children to fear and flee from strangers.

Religious and Folk Beliefs—Semai Peaceability

Traditional Semai "blood sacrifice" enacts the violence of slavers and their state, making it meaningful. The fear is obvious in a 1979 description in the *American Ethnologist* by Clayton A. Robarchek, who has written extensively about Semai peaceability:

A storm comes up very fast; heavy rain, hard wind, much thunder and lightning. . . . [Men] are out in the rain, pounding the ground with heavy pieces of firewood and shouting "go down, go down!" The headman shouts to the others "hit, hit, hit!" (They are trying to keep [the Lord God's] wife . . . an enormous horned dragon, from bursting up out of the ground bringing with her a torrent of mud and water that would sweep away the hamlet. . . .) The headman comes into the house shouting "burn [incense]; someone answers that there is none. Headman shouts "We are all going to die because we don't have any incense!" Bah Bidn runs into the house bringing some incense. Headman puts it with some coals on a piece of firewood and goes outside and burns it, chanting to [Thunder] to go away. He shouts at kids to cut their hair. Runs back outside, pounds the ground shouting "Go down." Bedlam; people running in and out of the house screaming at each other above the storm. Many people outside pounding the ground. . . . Wind increases; houses shaking. . . . Kning Ledn throws salt on the fire, it crackles and smokes. Shouting and screaming all around. Loud clap of thunder, more shouts:

["Stop, Lord"!] . . . Raining a torrent. Front flap has blown loose on Bah Les's house and rain is streaming in. Headman tells everyone to get out of the house; some do, and go underneath. . . . Wind abates slightly; headman still chanting . . . "we're not guilty; we're just poor miserable people," throws salt on the fire. Kning Ledn pounds some lemongrass with a [bush knife], throws it on the fire. Headman tells her to cut hair from all the kids and burn it. She does; pounds the hair against a log with a [bush knife], throws it into the fire. . . . Headman tells the Lord to take the storm to the lowlands, to the Malays: "if you keep it up, we'll die. Maybe we're a little guilty, but not much; this is no way for you to treat your grandchildren; we're just poor, ignorant people. Go down to the Malays!

The Lord of Thundersqualls is a ludicrously stupid, chilly, sex-crazed, violent, black-and-scarlet (or bone-white) monster. Because of His stupidity, maleness, and chilliness, women can drive him off by slashing their shins with a bamboo knife and throwing the hot blood into the cold storm, crying "Ow, ow, ow," as if they were being seriously hurt. Or people shout reminders of his stupidity at him, to embarrass him. This deity resembles the old Vedic god-demon Rudra, who gradually evolved into Shiva the Destroyer. The Lord punishes acts that violate Semai notions of reasonableness, mutual respect, and maturity: excessive laughter, incest, and the like. Because children often misbehave, adults constantly warn them that being boisterous will bring on a squall and, during a squall, pretend to punish the kids by pounding or burning locks of their hair. The Lord's folly is the folly of the powerful, rejecting the limits whose violation he punishes but easily fooled by symbolic sacrifices. When people laugh at him, they laugh at themselves, at their own inadmissable lusts, and at the hypocritical excesses of slaver state power.

The Lord is also the Lord of Beasts and therefore Lord of the Dance. The relationship works this way, say the Semai. Animals are people, though not human people. The souls of animals are "demons." They are opposite to humans in all ways. In fact, people looking at photographic negatives immediately recognize them as demons. As humans kill and eat animals, the animals' demonic souls, minions of the Lord, devour and kill humans' souls. The only cure for this cycle of terror and killing, Semai say, is love and fostering.

The Lord and his demons brought sickness into the world, so they can cure it. Long ago, Semai say, they tricked the Lord into sharing his "cool" demonic power. Since then, adept humans may get demonic "lovers." In certain dreams, these lovers give their chosen adepts a melody. Singing the melody will draw these yearning demonic lovers to the yearning singers. When a settlement needs spiritual refreshment or several people are pregnant or sick, Semai set up spirit meeting houses ornamented with beautiful flowers and fragrant leaves. That night they gather for a seance, during which adepts sing down their demon lovers.

The music and costumes are like those used in traditional Cambodian court rituals. Customarily, a group of women beat out a complex, gradually accelerating rhythm with bamboo-tube stampers, one ("male") long and one ("female") short: tuk tuk TOK. In some areas everyone dances; in some just the adepts. Taking turns, adepts chant their melodies. In some places a chorus reprises each stanza in simpler form. Finally, the celebrants put out all the fires, leaving the house in the darkness that is light to demons. Seduced by the fragrant darkness and by the succulent human bodies, the demons fly in and possess their lovers. During these séances, the adepts can cajole their demon lovers to help diagnose and cure individual patients or the community. Patients and shamans may get ritual baths, and in some areas, successful Semai hunters go through a ritual bath to thank and placate their "hunting wives." Midwives, the usually but not always female equivalent of the usually but not always male adepts, either have spirit guides of their own or appeal to the seven "Original Midwives."

Domesticating horror this way makes it tolerable. However, for Semai, the demonic trance connects intimately with violence. Most noticeably, people equate "blood intoxication" with possession by demon lovers. The sight of blood, especially human blood, may make Semai dizzy, nauseated, and disoriented. These are also stages of Semai trancing. "Blood-intoxicated" Semai can then become obsessively violent. For instance, when Chinese terrorists attacked a Semai settlement, killing two people, some Semai men became blood-intoxicated and massacred innocents in a Chinese village. Also, although they could not defend themselves against Malay slave raiders, they could repel invaders who sought to wage genocidal war against them to take their lands, a tale they recount in the "Sangkiil War" epic.

The Lord is most salient in the remote eastern part of Semai country. In the west, another deity, "Ancestor," is more important. Like the cuckoo god, Ancestor has no gender, though its name seems to come from a word for "grandmother." It manifests and nurtures the primeval and eternal nature of all living beings. Therefore, Semai think that people need to respect the essence of all creatures. Every creature deserves to live as itself, free from coercive change. Mocking animals by treating them as if they were human—for example, laughing at them—will bring down the wrath of the Lord rather than of Ancestor, which does not intervene in the world.

Because the cosmos was so fearsome, Semai turned inward, developing an ideology in which loving one's friends and neighbors became a matter of survival, and quarreling was a threat to one's life. A number of ways emerged to minimize violence within the society. Traditional Semai say that, most of the time, violence is ludicrous and stupid. Although Semai are capable of violence when it's safe and necessary or appropriate, they prefer peace. They are one of the least violent people known to anthropology. But Semai do not much enjoy having that reputation. They know that most other Malaysians associate Semai peaceability with cowardice and do not see it as an extraordinary human achievement.

SOCIAL STRUCTURE AND SEMAI DEMOCRACY

Before coming into close contact with Malays and Europeans, Semai were egalitarians. They knew, however, that as people grow older, they accumulate experience and, to that extent, become wiser. The age-grade system distinguishes between children, adolescents, mature people, and old people. Any grown-up who is especially knowledgeable about a particular activity—hunting or fish-poisoning, say—and who convinces other people of his skill is a leader as long as the activity continues. When the activity stops, however, the person stops being a leader. People are suspicious of anyone who is glib or ambitious for fear that person will exercise undue influence. No one has a right to coerce anyone else. When a child refuses to follow a parent's order, the matter is closed. Trying to coerce children would spiritually damage and perhaps kill them.

Outsiders found (and continue to find) this total democracy frustrating. No Semai speaks for anyone else, and no one listens to anyone they do not want to hear. The outsiders' solution was to recognize someone—a man brave or greedy enough not to flee from outsiders—as "headman." They then rewarded this man by giving him some power in their scheme of things, although usually his power within the community went away as soon as they did. Failure to respect intercultural differences in political organization has led to many misunderstandings.

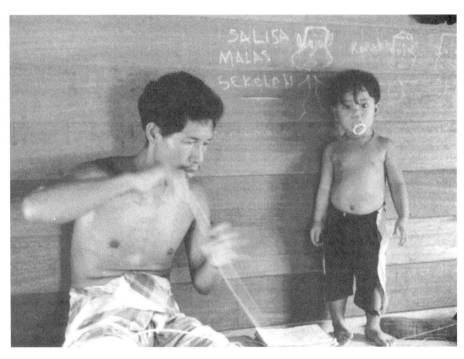

Observed by his child, a Semai man works on a fish trap, 1992. (Photograph by Robert Knox Dentan)

CHALLENGES OF THE MODERN WORLD

When the possibility of joining the Malaysian mainstream economy emerged, Semai responded by adapting their traditional agroforestry. They began to grow trees as cash crops. But, as time went on, Malaysian governments regrouped most Semai into densely populated villages and turned their orchards and forests over to loggers and developers.

Semai boys playing, 1992. (Photograph by Robert Knox Dentan)

The shift of political control from British colonialism to domination by Malays, who now control the government, has brought few beneficial changes. Increasingly nowadays Semai are becoming small-scale commodity producers and unskilled occasional laborers. Like Orang Asli in general, they are worse off than ever—by almost any measure, the poorest people in Malaysia. The government pays lip service to the idea of Semai autonomy. But the entanglement of Semai folklore with the traditional non-Islamic religion makes it worrisome to Malays. They would prefer to incorporate Semai into their own Islamic culture and see destroying Semai traditions as a price worth paying. Serious séances have become rare and secretive as people seek to avoid offending their Muslim neighbors. To placate their rulers and make a little money, Semai still sometimes perform sanitized versions of their ceremonies in the daytime (when demon lovers would be afraid to come) for tourists and government officials—with the women dressed in bras and shorts so as not to excite the prurient moralism of tourists and Malay onlookers. But government officials sneer at Semai folklore as "mumbo jumbo stuff" and actively seek to convert the people to what they regard as a progressive and civilizing religion—that is, Islam.

The government also "regroups" Semai into special areas ostensibly to provide services for them—religious education, for example—freeing up their traditional territories for exploitation by non-Semai. Regrouping and dispossession have led to alcoholism, among other things, and have undermined traditional Semai values so that squabbling now leads oftener to fights and violence. Some Semai find conversion to Islam a useful tactic to placate bureaucrats and prevent alcoholism. Others are beginning to investigate their traditional beliefs, giving them a more authoritative form than the vague nonhierachical consensus of olden times.

STUDIES OF SEMAI FOLKLORE

For general background on Semai, one might try Dentan's nontechnical ethnography (1979) or, for today's Orang Asli in general, the slightly more technical by Dentan and others (1997), a multinational collaboration. Both are now out of print, however, and Nicholas (2000) is a good replacement. Nicholas, Chopil, and Sabak (2003)—the latter two authors are Semai women activists—covers traditional and modern Semai. For more on Semai religious practices, see Dentan (2002, 2003). For shamanism and gender, Dentan (1988) can be consulted. For regionally different stories about how about the Bird God brought farming to Semai, see Dentan (1995, forthcoming). For Semai nonviolence, see Dentan (2004), and for "blood intoxication," Dentan (1995) is a good source.

BIBLIOGRAPHY

Benjamin, Geoffrey, and Cynthia Lau. 2003. *Tribal Communities in the Malay World: Historical, Cultural, and Social Perspectives*. Singapore: Institute for Southeast Asian Studies.

Dentan, Robert Knox. 1979. *The Semai: A Nonviolent People of Malaya*. New York: Harcourt Brace.

———. 1988. Lucidity, Sex, and Horror in Senois Dreamwork. In *Conscious Mind, Sleeping Brain: Perspectives on Lucid Dreaming*, edited by Jayne L. Gackenbach and Stephen LaBerge. New York: Plenum. 37–63.

———. 1995. Bad Day at Bukit Pekan. *American Anthropologist* 97: 225–231.

———. 2002. "Disreputable Magicians," the Dark Destroyer, and the Trickster Lord: Reflections on Semai Religion and a Possible Common Religious Base in South and Southeast Asia. *Asian Anthropology* 1: 153–194.

———. 2004. Cautious, Alert, Polite, and Elusive: The Semai of Central Peninsular Malaysia. In *Keeping the Peace: Conflict Resolution and Peaceful Societies Around the World*, edited by Graham Kemp and Douglas Fry. New York: Routledge. 167–184.

———. Forthcoming. How the Androgynous Bird God Brought Agriculture to Semai of West Malaysia: Discipline, Hard Work, and Subordination to the Cycle of Time. In *Les Messagers Divins: Aspects Esthetiques et Symboliques des Oiseaux en Asie du Sud-Est*, edited by Pierre Le Roux and others. Paris: Editions Seven Orients.

Dentan, Robert Knox, and Ong Hean Chooi. 1995. Stewards of the Green and Beautiful World: A Preliminary Report on Semai Aboriculture and Its Policy Implications. In *Dimensions of Traditions and Development in Malaysia*, edited by Rokiah Talib and Tan Chee Beng. Peteling Jaya, Malaysia: Pelanduk. 53–124.

Dentan, Robert Knox, and others. 1997. *Malaysia and the "Original People": A Case Study of the Impact of Development on Indigenous Peoples*. Boston: Allyn and Bacon.

Nicholas, Colin. 2000. *The Orang Asli and the Contest for Resources: Indigenous Politics, Development, and Identity in Peninsular Malaysia*. Copenhagen: IWGIA.

Nicholas, Colin, Tijah Yok Chopil, and Tiah Sabak. 2003. *Orang Asli Women and the Forest*. Subang Jaya, Malaysia: Center for Orang Asli Concerns.

Robert Knox Dentan

East Indies

BALI

GEOGRAPHY AND HISTORY

The island of Bali lies approximately six degrees south of the equator near the middle of the southern arc of islands that make up the Indonesian Republic. Its total surface is 5,632 square kilometers. A chain of active volcanoes runs across the island from east to west, dominating the landscape. The mountains slope steeply to the sea on the north side and gently toward the Indian Ocean on the south. At the beginning of the twenty-first century, the total number of inhabitants of Bali was more than 3,357,000. The island is densely populated, and until quite recently, most Balinese engaged in wet-rice agriculture, concentrated along the rivers that flow south from the volcanoes to the sea. Like the population on most islands in the Indonesian archipelago, the original inhabitants of Bali were of Austronesian descent. During the first millennium C.E. traders and travelers from other Asian countries such as **China** and **India** visited the westernmost islands: Sumatra, Java, Kalimantan, and Bali. They brought their culture, their religion, and also, in the case of the Indian visitors, a writing system and a literary language, Sanskrit. These travelers en route to and from India introduced the inhabitants of the bigger islands to the famous Indic texts such as the *Mahābhārata* and *Rāmāyaṇa*, related and unrelated commentaries, and other Hindu and Buddhist works. The content of these works was fully integrated into the local animistic beliefs as can be seen in Balinese religion and culture today, which are extremely rich and varied.

Peoples and Islands of Indonesia.

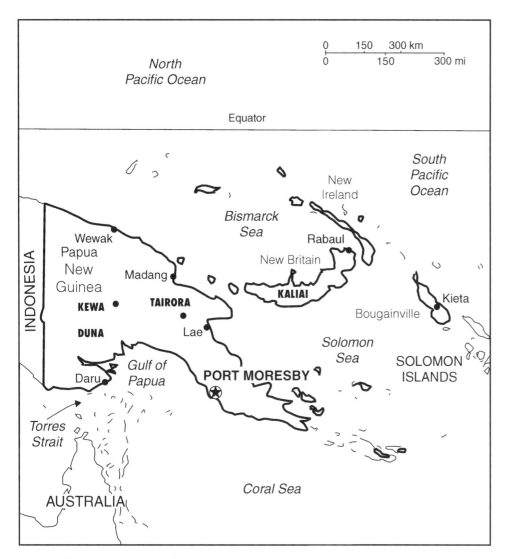

Peoples of Papua New Guinea and New Britain.

The Balinese have a coherent and cohesive worldview and way of living, which means that what in the West would be called "folk" tradition is equally shared among Balinese high and low and even among those who have had long exposure to Western education and lifestyle. In other words, even though there are substantial differences between "high" and "low" Balinese people, we cannot speak of a marked difference among the Balinese between belief systems such as exist in the West or in other countries where a religious or political system has been super-imposed on an existing culture and absorbed in different degrees among the various layers of the population. For example, every year a calendar appears in print, announcing auspicious and inauspicious days for certain activities. It also announces which temples will have festivals called *odalans* (anniversaries), when, and so on. This calendar is sold all over Bali and can be found in most households. It tells on which days, for instance, it is proper to cut trees—after requesting permission of the spirit of the tree, of course. And even though a noble or highly educated Balinese would not cut his own tree, if his gardener informed him that the tree cannot be cut today because it is not a good day, this explanation would be accepted and respected. If the job cannot be finished in one day and the next day turns out to be inauspicious, the tree just lies there until another good day turns up.

Like Balinese culture, the Balinese language reveals its multiple sources: old Javanese, old Balinese, Middle Javanese, Malay, and some Sanskrit forms have all influenced the spoken and written language, and a particularly rich mix, *Kawi*, is used for some religious ceremonies and for theatrical performances. The first inscriptions using an Indic script in Bali date from the late ninth century. They are in several languages, which suggests that different groups of people identified with these languages: an upper class that used more Sanskritized forms and a lower class which used Balinese. Even today, this division persists. In performances, characters will use the language style (or *register*) that corresponds to the status and caste of the person addressed. Such a rich linguistic tradition allows for endless wordplay, etymologizing, punning, and philosophical explanations for religious concepts and ritual based on vocabulary. In improvised performances most jokes depend on pseudo-misunderstandings and the misuse of the correct register or style by the main characters.

The prosperous and fertile bigger Indonesian islands such as Java and Sumatra converted to Islam during the late fifteenth and early sixteenth centuries; the smaller islands further east tended to keep their animistic (or, in the case of Bali, Hindu-Buddhist) beliefs. During the sixteenth and seventeenth centuries many islands in the archipelago were taken over by the Portuguese, British, and Dutch colonial powers. These last remained in control of "the East Indies" until 1949, with an interruption of several years due to the occupation by the Japanese during World War II. Bali, however, escaped both Islamic and Dutch conquerors for a long time. The Dutch fully conquered the island only in 1908 but allowed most surviving rulers to continue in name as long as they obeyed the new colonial rule. Although the material remains of Hindu-Buddhist culture that existed on the larger islands of the Indonesian archipelago remain visible, Bali is the only island where the culture itself survived. There are also small pockets of Hindu-Buddhist believers in West Java and on Lombok, an even smaller island to the east of Bali that was used by the Balinese kings to exile unruly subjects or relatives.

The late conquest by the Dutch had certain advantages for the Balinese, if a conquest can be said to hold advantages. By the beginning of the twentieth century, Western sensibilities had further developed and the uniqueness of the Balinese culture encouraged scholars and administrators alike to find parallels with India, Sanskrit literature, and other ancient traditions. The fact that Bali had "escaped" the Islamic conquest also worked in its favor, given that Islam was blamed for having obliterated the great culture of Java, forcing the Hindu-Buddhist culture mostly into a mishmash of folk beliefs whose *raison d'être* was no longer understood. It was believed that the intense study of Balinese high culture would allow a reconstruction of the pre-Islamic culture of the archipelago. As a result of this focus on high culture, much Balinese folk belief may have been neglected or dismissed. However, the colonial administrators were extremely thorough in the reports they sent home to the Netherlands, and much information on local customs can be found scattered in their accounts and in the colonial newspapers of the time.

Bali avoided much of the destruction of local culture caused by colonial regimes elsewhere such as conversion of the local landscape into tea, sugar, or coffee plantations. At the time of the Dutch conquest most Balinese lived off the land, and the island was self-sufficient. As wet rice farmers, they directed much of their lore and beliefs toward procuring harvests and ensuring that no harm befell growing crops. All personal, family, and village festivals and rituals involve rice in some form in their offerings, and the festivals that are concerned with the harvest and harvesting in particular are the most complex and require much knowledge from the organizers. Farmers may go to ritual specialists who know exactly what is required. Variation in requirements may exist from community to community. But here as in other cases, this knowledge is not seen as a survival of ancient beliefs among backward farmers. On the contrary, it is considered as useful and necessary as having the latest version of important software in commercial or academic circles.

SOCIAL AND FAMILY STRUCTURE

Balinese life centers on the family compound, surrounded by a wall. Rules govern how it should be laid out, where the family shrine, pigpen, and trash heap should be. These rules control the proportion of the measurements and align the microcosmos with the macrocosmos. Some compounds, like some temples, have a wall inside, placed perpendicular to the entrance, so that one has to move either left or right in order to enter. This, it is explained, is done so that bad spirits, which tend to move in straight lines, cannot enter. But more and more this construction is abandoned as the younger generations find it impossible to maneuver their motorbikes in and out of the compound because motorbikes, too, tend to want to move in straight lines.

A festival dancer. (Photograph by Thérèse de Vet, 2004)

Within the compound separate dwellings house each nuclear family, made up of brothers and their wives and children. Several generations live closely together, work together, and share resources. All worship the ancestors of the male line at the family shrine, including the wives who, once they are married, have given up worshipping their own ancestors. Although the type of worship required at the ancestral shrine is standard, that the women have come in from outside and may have loyalties elsewhere is a great source of stress. Thus, women must work hard to avoid accusations of witchcraft, envy, or other evil influence. If, for instance, a sister-in-law is not conceiving, this may be because a new bride—or a brother's wife already there—put a spell on her so her own children may be privileged. Cooperation and trust among the women in the compound can hardly blossom under such circumstances.

RELIGIOUS AND FOLK BELIEFS

One core Balinese belief centers on reincarnation, though in a different fashion from typical Indian beliefs. Most Balinese believe that one gets reincarnated into the same family, so when a new baby is born, the question arises of who this might be. To identify the new baby, consultations with trance mediums (*balians*) are required. These same individuals are also consulted when there are suspicions of witchcraft, when there is illness, or when a series of unfortunate events seems to befall the family out of nowhere. Usually, a jealous human or offended divinity, spirit, or ancestor can be identified, and advice on the appropriate offerings and prayers can be obtained for an additional sum. The evildoer cannot be confronted, however, for fear of provoking more evil!

Pregnant women, babies, and small children are considered very vulnerable. Pregnant women should not be startled for fear the fetus may be affected; their husbands should not cut their hair during their wife's pregnancy; women should not eat

A man and his wedding chicken. (Photograph by Thérèse de Vet, 2002)

leftovers, be suddenly awakened, listen to crude language, or allow someone to be physically above them (because a pregnancy is considered divine, and no one can be above divinities). After birth, a baby is not allowed to touch the ground for six Balinese months, or 210 days, the length of the Balinese calendar year. The afterbirth, considered one of four divine siblings, is buried within the compound and covered with a heavy rock so witches cannot get hold of it and use it for evil purposes.

Ceremonies mark the passing of dangerous periods in the child's first year. At any point between ages eight to eighteen, most Balinese undergo a very expensive and special ceremony, which involves the filing down of their canine teeth. The canine teeth are identified with the base or animal nature present in all humans, and filing off the teeth and bringing them into a straight line with the incisors and molars is intended to prevent its expression. This event defines one as human (and as Balinese). Masked characters in plays, or puppets in a *wayang* (shadow play) performance, can easily be identified as evil or good by the size and pointiness of their teeth. Balinese high and low, "modern" or traditional, submit to this tooth-filing ceremony. Again, the division between folk beliefs and accepted dogma is non-existent.

With the woman entering a new family and compound, marriage is a major event and begins a period of adjustment not only for the new couple but also for all others in the compound. It is understandable, therefore, that much commotion is associated with the wedding event itself. During the ceremony in some mountain villages, a chicken might be placed on the heads of the young couple to be married in order to absorb all evil that may exist in their minds (and by extension, in the minds of the families to be joined). Just to be safe, a man will generally marry a woman whose family he has known for a long time so he can be sure that she is not a witch. Many plays tell the story of men marrying (or wanting to marry) a lovely princess from far away (for example, the *Calonarong*) who in the end turns out to be the daughter of the Queen of the Witches, Rangda (or Durga)—also the goddess of Death. Sometimes, a man can be a witch. The play *Basur* tells the story of a man who uses his witchcraft to become rich. He wants to marry his son off to the beautiful daughter of a poor man. Another suitor had already been accepted for her, so Basur uses his witchcraft to try and kill her. When someone becomes more prosperous than his neighbors, people often suspect him of witchcraft.

Economically, the Balinese family depended on rice farming, some fruit and coconut trees, and keeping some cows or water buffaloes, pigs, and chickens. Much has changed, of course, with the advent of tourism and arts-and-crafts markets. But even those earning their livings carving frogs and cats and large giraffes or creating antiqued furniture for worldwide export participate in the cult of the rice goddess and the required ceremonies and other religious events. Their wealth and "daily rice," it is thought, still come from the goodwill of the gods, so participation in the regional cycles related to rice farming continues. Even the governor, who occupies a secular and political position, attends the largest of these festivals, bringing the heads of all departments under him.

RULES, RITUALS, AND CUSTOMS

The rituals related to the worship of rice have much in common with the life or the phases of human life: birth, pregnancy, periods of rest, and so on. When the rice is "pregnant"—that is, when the seed first begins to set—the rice field requires quiet: menstruating women may not visit the rice field, and the presence of dead animals (or humans) requires purification rites. The different stages of the life of the rice in the field each require an appropriate offering and noting of the event by prayers by members of the family that planted the fields. Sometimes the fields may need protection from pests. That too, can be attempted with the help of priests who provide holy water at the major temples, ceremonies at the little shrine present in each *sawah* (rice field), and prayer. Very religious villages may undertake a joint effort and organize processions or small groups of people to walk around the perimeter of the fields to ensure magical protection. Such excursions require special offerings, special prayers, and special magic. Different villages, even those that are geographically close, may have different methods for averting evil.

Once the rice is ready to harvest, more prayers must be said, permission to proceed needs to be asked from the rice goddess, Dewi Sri, and the first few ears must be cut with a special knife. (The knife must be half-hidden in the palm of the harvester's hand so the rice is not frightened.) The first few "bouquets" are used to create female and male dolls, which can be of different sizes according to local custom and are taken to the special rice barn present in each compound. Indigenous Balinese rice was typically slow growing (it takes about 210 days from the preparation of the field until the harvest, the length of the traditional Balinese year), so only one harvest per solar year was possible. During the dry season vegetables and other crops could be grown in the now-dry fields, or they could be left fallow. No big ceremonies or offerings accompanied that kind of farming, and no taboos affected the fields. Nowadays newer and faster growing rice types have been brought to Bali, and multiple harvests are possible as long as there is enough irrigation water to flood the fields. However, the old rice is the most valued, even though these days it is grown only by a few: unlike the new rice, it is said, the old had a soul. When the new rice is planted or harvested, not so many precautions need to be taken. Perhaps a hundred years from now the ritual related to the old rice will be seen as folklore. At the moment, it is still considered highly relevant, useful, and essential to the well-being of the entire society.

Many more rules and regulations pertain to the growing of rice. Each village had its own set of rules and fines to be imposed on those not obeying the agreed-upon arrangements. These rules were often written down on *lontars*, the stems of dried palm leaves tied together in tight bundles, even in the past when not many knew how to write. Brahmans or officials kept these *lontars* at a central location. Many rules only exist in the memory of the farmers concerned, but on the whole, when groups meet, there are ways to mediate and impose fines. Coming late to the meeting on water sharing or on planting may cost the offender just a little. Graver offenses are the stealing of water at night, diverting water, or planting on days that the calendar has identified as bad days, because such an offense pollutes the entire community. These agricultural laws form part of a larger body of highly variable *adat*—customary or oral law and practices—rules that were recorded by the Dutch administrators, who tried to organize the *adat* rules into a coherent system, valid all over the island. They also intended to incorporate the *adat* rules into the larger, Western system of law introduced to administer the country. *Adat* still is powerful today: thus, when entering a temple for a festival, a worshipper must wear *pakaian adat*, clothes that conform to temple custom. *Adat* also prevents a menstruating woman from entering the inner sanctum or from wearing gold jewelry to the village temple of the dead. *Adat*, then, covers a large area of human activity and may vary from village to village. However, no Balinese would dismiss or identify the *adat* of others as folklore or as superstition. The rules of *adat* apply to everyone.

Adat also extends to the rules that govern the elaborate offerings to festivals or the making of almost daily offerings around the household shrine, the compound, the fields, and, if applicable, the office or shop. *Adat* prescribes which offerings and what kind have to be made, when, and where. The women and girls of the household create elaborate ephemeral baskets and trays out of young bendable palm leaf shoots and fill them with colorful flowers—red, white, red and some green (the colors of the Hindu trinity)—rice, sticks of incense, and coins. Blue hydrangeas and marigolds also figure prominently. Sometimes rice cakes or cookies are baked in brilliant colors and put up in the temples for festivals. Some can be eight or nine feet high and symbolically depict the universe. Personal offerings may include fruit, flattened fried chicken, and ducks. They are carried on the head in colorful processions. The demons or evil spirits (*Butha Kala*) also require offerings. By contrast, theirs are ugly and brown and consist of charred coconut shell, pork fat and tripe, and other dark ingredients. They are put on the ground in front of the house or in the middle of crossroads in contrast to the offerings to the good spirits and gods, which are placed on top of the tall, seat-like constructions present in each compound temple. Such thrones to receive the gods when they visit are also present in larger numbers and larger sizes in each main temple.

The low-high opposition concerning where to place the offerings to the bad spirits as opposed to the good spirits forms part of the Balinese **worldview**. High is

Offerings for the gods are carried on the head. (Photograph by Thérèse de Vet, 2004)

pure, low is impure: thus, upstream is better than downstream, the mountain lakes are pure while the sea is polluted, the head of a person is holier than the feet (which is why you do not pat a baby or child on the head or sit with your feet sticking out in front of you). Humans inhabit the middle world between "high" and "low," and their duty is to keep the world in balance and harmony to ensure that evil does not overpower good. The human world is visible (*sekala*), whereas the world of the gods, spirits, and daemons is invisible (*niskala*). Worship and magic appease the invisible elements all around us. There are other oppositions: the East is associated with life, the West with death and decay; the right hand is good, and the left hand is impure and associated with all kinds of bad things. Thus, no Balinese will ever offer anything to another with the left hand unless the intention is to insult. Bodily functions are considered crude and not to be observed. A culture of convivial eating, for instance, did not develop in Bali. During large festivals, when vast numbers of pilgrims need to be served food at the temples, people may sit together, but eating takes place in silence with eyes downcast and is done at great speed. Little children often have absorbed this custom already and can be seen standing by themselves somewhere in the compound, shoveling some rice into their mouths with their hands. While considerable care is taken to make the offerings to the gods look attractive and beautiful, the presentation of food for human consumption is uninspired. Bathing, by contrast, is related to purification. No stigma or secrecy is attached to that part of daily life, and communal bathing places exist (or did exist) in all Balinese villages. Light and darkness form another pair of opposites. Graveyards, as temporary resting places for the dead before the money for cremation can be gathered, are favorite dwelling places for spirits, witches in search of body parts, dissatisfied ancestors, and dogs. Cemeteries are the most negatively charged areas in all Bali, especially at night. The mentioning of death and dying is avoided: when someone has died in a household, the polite way to ask is to say, "Has a flower withered in your home?"

SPIRITS

The belief that tools and instruments have a spirit which must be kept happy is prevalent also in other trades. Metals, for instance, have great magic. A *kris*, or sacred knife, is a very important and expensive part of a Balinese nobleman's possessions. *Krises* are frequently given names as if they were persons. All performers and male dancers carry a *kris* in a special holster on their backs. They pull the sacred knife out to kill Evil when it makes its way onto the scene. Some *krises* are so powerful that they can kill from a distance. Once a year all metal tools, visible and invisible, must be worshipped as well. This is when Balinese cars and motorbikes get decorated with palm leaf offerings and flowers, and families can be seen praying in front of their medium of transportation. Following the same principle, books, other reading materials such as *lontars* (palm-leaf books), and even computers, also are worshipped once a year, and must be left unopened with proper offerings made. This holiday is popular with schoolchildren.

Belief in spirits for every object in the universe betrays the earlier, animistic roots of Balinese religion. But old and newer beliefs have syncretized so well that one cannot speak of survivals. What especially marks Balinese religion is the belief that evil forces can never be entirely conquered but must be constantly held in check by human actions. Evil not only manifests itself in spirits; it can also exist in humans. Those humans can change themselves into monsters with the use of black magic, which they acquire from *lontars* or from family connections (it is, one could almost say, "genetic" and inherited through the female line). These *leyaks* (black witches) often visit graveyards at night to feast on human blood and remains. If successful, they may become invisible or turn into wild animals or giant birds, but bad smells can tip one off to their proximity. Most Balinese have seen *leyaks* in the process of transforming themselves, when they are still partially visible. Many have suffered by their hands. Strong exorcisms are necessary. The *Barong* and *Rangda*—the ultimate queen of *Leyaks*—are used in villagewide exorcisms, preventive and otherwise. Rangda, whose name means "widow," is the most dangerous female around. Because her husband died, she no longer has male protection but must survive on her wits and witchcraft. Rangda appears in many performances, especially late-night ones. She is truly terrifying: long white hair almost to her feet, pendulous breasts, ten-inch-long fingernails, and a mask with huge fangs. She is brought in sometimes to challenge the local *leyaks*—to remind them who is the queen and exhort them to cease their evil activities—and thus the actor

Offerings to the *Butha Kala* during a big temple festival. Note the pig's head, the little umbrellas made of intestines, and the decorations at the top made from pigskin and fat. The whole construction is several feet high. (Photograph by Thérèse de Vet, 2004)

may attract their ill will. He must undergo special purification before the performance, and he must be very sure of his *sakti* (divine strength) so he will not get killed accidentally by the *kris* of the (actor) prince or any audience members sent to kill the witch. Every Balinese knows of at least some cases where the *sakti* was not strong enough to protect the actor, and injury or death ensued.

The *Butha Kala* (evil spirits) are attracted to blood and death and must be kept at bay by special offerings. One day a year, all activity must cease, no fire may be made, and everyone stays home. Even the International Airport is closed, and airplanes are not supposed to fly over Bali. On that day the *Butha Kala* are flying around, and noise or cooking smells would attract their attention. If they do not hear or smell anything, they continue on and go elsewhere. The *Butha Kala* also enjoy cockfights because blood is spilled. Those fights are held for religious purposes and form part of regional festivals. Gambling is part of this ritual, and fortunes are lost and made during the few days the Indonesian government allows cockfights to take place in select locations. Of course, gambling is not allowed, and officially it does not happen. When the police have tried to close down cockfights for those very reasons, bad things have befallen the communities and the officers trying to enforce the government rulings. In one village, a man went into trance and attacked himself with a knife, shedding blood. In others, the police officers suffered strokes, accidents, and other misfortunes. Fortunately, making offerings and apologizing have helped in their recovery.

Music

All performances, festivals, and parades, small or large, require the participation of the local *gamelan* group, which will play seated behind or beside the performer, sitting in the temple, or while marching along behind the procession. Even entire orchestras, loaded on the back of a truck en route to a festival, will play non-stop. Several orchestras can play at the same time during large festivals. Most musicians are not professionals but have day jobs: rice farming, carving, or working in the tourist industry. To perform in the *gamelan* fulfills religious duties.

The masks, the puppets, the musical instruments, and the creation of all these things involve much prayer, asking of blessings from spirits. Performers, musicians, and mask makers must refrain once a year from using them or the tools employed to create them. On such days—identified on the calendar—offerings are made and blessings are asked. In essence, they represent the tools of the performers' and craftsmen's trade and require respect and care.

Folk Theater

The good-evil contrast is most clearly expressed in the dramatic performances common at any festival or other religious event.

A procession takes off from a temple. (Photograph by Thérèse de Vet, 2004)

161

A *barong* receives offerings in the temple. (Photograph by Thérèse de Vet, 2002)

Because the Balinese view the world as being in precarious balance with evil constantly trying to overcome good, humans have to be ever vigilant to ensure that evil does not get the upper hand. Most villages have a protective *barong*, a large creature consisting of a mask half covering the body of one person and a body carried by a second person close behind, which covers both men entirely. Although the *barong* looks terrifying with a huge mouth that snaps with loud clacking sounds, it really is inhabited by a good spirit. It is taken around the village and dances in the streets, making fake sallies at some in jest. It is the opponent of Rangda or Durga, the goddess of death and destruction, whose mask and costume also exist in most villages and who comes out to challenge the *barong* at the end of his procession. Frequently, the dancers become possessed—go into a trance—and must be quickly replaced by others so the dance can continue. Rangda is never quite defeated. The masks and costumes are considered to have powers that can be activated when brought out. The bringing-out of the costumes is an invitation to the invisible spirits to make themselves visible. *Barongs* exist everywhere. It is just as common to find traffic stopped for a *barong* procession on a country road as it is in downtown Denpasar, the capital of Bali.

Dramatic performances occur in many shapes and forms in connection with festivals or other occasions. Most common are *topeng* performances, which use historical or mythological events recorded in the ancient *lontars* to explain the present. To do so, the narrated events switch back and forth between past and present, between high and low Balinese, between mythical events and contemporary political reality. *Topeng* requires masks. In fact, the meaning of the word *topeng* is "cover" or "mask." These masks also have their spirits, just like the *barong*. The players wear stereotypical costumes and rely on a number of stock characters and situations. The process of improvisation ensures that the plays maintain a connection to the present and to the place of performance. Some performances, notably those involving descriptions of witchcraft, must take place outside the temple. Others, for instance those relating the divine foundation of a temple, can take place in the inner sanctum. *Wayang* (or puppet) performances also occur during festivals.

A *topeng* performer at a festival. (Photograph by Thérèse de Vet, 2004)

Their plots usually come from the Indic poems *Rāmāyaṇa* and *Mahābhārata*, brought to Bali many centuries ago and recomposed for Indonesian use. They must be performed in *Kawi*, the poetic language. Not many modern Balinese understand the performance languages, which are so old and artificial that only other performers can understand and learn them. But because it is important for audiences to understand what is going on, some special characters provide rough translations. They are often called "clowns," though their role is more complex; "jester" would be more correct. During these translations they provide common sense and a running critique of the action, somewhat like the chorus in ancient Greek tragedy, except that their words are not scripted. Their comments are often full of sexual innuendo and obscenities.

Because the gods can see the invisible world, they do not require the screen to enjoy the *wayang* performance at a festival. The puppeteer is holding one of the clown, or jester, figures. (Photograph by Thérèse de Vet, 2004)

CHALLENGES OF THE MODERN WORLD

Much changed—yet much stayed the same—after the international airport was opened in 1969 and increasing numbers of tourists began to visit the island. (Recent numbers indicate an average of about 100,000 visitors per month since 1994.) This influx of large numbers of Westerners and, most recently, Japanese and Chinese tourists, has given rise to a kind of "tourist" folklore—that is, stories about Balinese culture that were created either by Balinese or by foreign advisers for the purpose of increasing and encouraging **tourism**. Many of those stories, anecdotes, and performances influence Balinese beliefs and customs in their turn. For instance, the famous *kecak* or monkey dance, performed by men sitting in a large circle around a burning lamp, was created by a Balinese dancer during the 1930s at the instigation of Western visitors, who felt that his talents were not sufficiently showcased in the much shorter trance dance from which *kecak* derives. This dance has become a staple for the tourist market, but it occasionally gets performed at ceremonies for the Balinese themselves. The visual arts also underwent Western influence. A German painter and musician, Walter Spies, and some Dutch colleagues introduced naturalistic painting to Bali at about the same time, and the many "typically traditional" Balinese paintings of idyllic village scenes for sale everywhere are all inspired by this originally Western and idealized depiction of Balinese culture. In the twenty-first century, with more Western people searching for the meaning of life, a New Age-inspired Balinese spirituality movement has come into existence, promising to teach the knowledge of plants and fragrant oils, Balinese nature spirits, and white magic to visiting foreigners, usually in an expensive spa setting. Here indeed, Balinese beliefs are represented as folklore, a status they do not occupy among the inhabitants.

STUDIES OF BALINESE FOLKLORE

The literature on Bali, the Balinese, and things Balinese is vast. One Balinese was heard to observe jokingly that each Balinese village must have an anthropologist to maintain the sacred balance. Much of the early literature (pre-1908 and for a few decades thereafter) is in Dutch. The archives of the KITLV (Koninklijk Instituut voor Taal- Land- en Volkenkunde) in the Netherlands inherited the records of most scholars and administrators who work on Bali during those decades and later. Anthropologists such as Margaret Mead and Gregory Bateson started to visit in the mid-1930s. After World War II Indonesia was closed for many decades to Dutch scholars, who nevertheless continued to publish from archival material, though some had been in Indonesia for so long that they were invited to remain. Clifford Geertz's publications are among the best known anthropological works. His essay on the cockfight (1972) attempts to peel apart the many and varied layers of meaning and will perhaps provide support for the complexity of Balinese culture and the need to understand it on multiple levels. Word play, sayings, proverbs, songs, melodies, stories, and metaphors are so entwined with the culture and beliefs, historical knowledge, and myth that they are virtually impossible to translate or have their meaning conveyed in one sentence. Performances and music are most charmingly described by McPhee (2002 [1944]), an American composer who lived in Bali during the 1930s. His interest in music took him to many village performances as well as official functions staged for the Dutch administrators. His observations are acute and often humorous. Covarrubias (1999 [1937]), a Mexican painter who also visiting during the 1930s, wrote on Bali, and his book continues to be relevant and highly readable. The observations of Eiseman and others (1989) are of a similar nature: short, highly readable essays. Lansing (1995) gives a general introduction to life in Bali. Masks, carving, and related ritual are described and superbly illustrated in Slattum and Schraub (2003). The history of Bali is capably described by Anak Agung (1991), a member of the local nobility who was educated in **The Netherlands**. A fascinating autobiography of another Balinese nobleman, A.A.M. Djelantik (1997), describes in detail the old Bali of the 1920s and the metamorphosis of the author into an internationally known physician and expert on Balinese art. Today the Balinese are keenly interested in preserving and reviving local culture, and the language and writing system are again taught in schools. Many children's stories are now written down instead of just being told orally. Many have even been translated into English, but they are usually "retold" by a Westerner and therefore omit much of what makes Balinese culture so "Balinese."

BIBLIOGRAPHY

Anak Agung, I. 1991. *Bali in the Nineteenth Century*. Jakarta: Yayasan Obor.

Bateson, Gregory. 1970 (1937). An Old Temple and a New Myth. In *Traditional Balinese Culture*, edited by J. Belo. New York: Columbia University Press. 111–136.

Covarrubias, Miguel. 1999 (1937). *Island of Bali*. Singapore: Periplus Editions.

Djelantik, A.A.M. 1997. *The Birthmark: Memoirs of a Balinese Prince*. Singapore: Periplus Editions.

Eiseman, F. B., and others. 1989. *Bali: Sekala and Niskala*. 2 volumes. Singapore: Periplus Editions.

Geertz, Clifford. 1973 (1972). Deep Play: Notes on the Balinese Cockfight. In *The Interpretation of Cultures* by Clifford Geertz. New York: Basic Books. 412–453.

Lansing, J. Steven. 1995. *The Balinese*. Fort Worth, TX: Harcourt Brace.

McPhee, Colin. 2002 (1944). *A House in Bali*. Singapore: Periplus Editions.

Mead, Margaret. 1970 (1939). The Strolling Players in the Mountains of Bali. In *Traditional Balinese Culture*, edited by J. Belo. New York: Columbia University Press. 137–145.

Slattum, Judy, and P. Schraub. 2003. *Balinese Masks: Spirits of an Ancient Drama*. Singapore: Periplus Editions.

Spies, Walter, and B. de Zoete. 2002 (1938). *Dance and Drama in Bali*. Singapore: Periplus Editions.

Thérèse de Vet

DUNA

GEOGRAPHY AND HISTORY

Speakers of the Duna language live in the Southern Highlands Province of Papua New Guinea. The administrative center for their area is located at Lake Kopiago, where there is a government station and an all-weather airstrip. The Duna language shows close affinities with the Huli language spoken to the southeast and is also related to Bogaiya, spoken by a small population southwest of the main Duna area. Duna speakers number today between 15,000 and 20,000. Immediate knowledge of them focuses primarily on the Aluni Valley, occupied by members of some five named groups that are called "parishes" and numbering fewer than a thousand persons in all.

The Aluni Valley, like the wider Duna area, is marked by numerous limestone sinkholes, subterranean streams, and dense forest stands interspersed with pockets of gardens. The people use the forests for hunting marsupials, birds of paradise, and cassowaries and for gathering wild green vegetables, mushrooms, and tree bark used in manufacturing rope. Bird plumes are prized for their use in decorations worn at periodic dances, held in the past for a variety of ritual occasions and presently for national independence day celebrations. The upper forest areas provide habitat for wild nut-pandanus trees, highly valued for seasonal consumption. In the grasslands near the Strickland River that marks the boundary of the Duna language area with Oksapmin, people burn the grass at dry times and shoot wild pigs as they flee from the flames. Men hunt,

A senior man of the Hagu settlement in the Aluni Valley dressed in traditional clothing. He holds a decorated fighting pick tipped with a cassowary claw and a necklace of cowry shells. (Photograph by Pamela J. Stewart)

At the occasion when a bride-price is to be paid, people bring up a pig, which will be part of the payment, for inspection. (Photograph by Pamela J. Stewart)

while both men and women gather forest produce. The staple crop is the ubiquitous sweet potato, tended in mounds prepared usually by women. Men sometimes make their own gardens in high areas and harvest and consume the produce from these themselves. A variety of greens and other crops is also grown, mostly *Colocasia* and *Xanthosoma* taro, pumpkins, bananas, and fruit pandanus.

The whole landscape and environment are imbued for the Duna with ritual significance as the dwelling place for spirit forces such as the Tindi Auwene, or male spirit, and the Payame Ima, or female spirit, whose domains encompass both the high forest and the Strickland grasslands; the Tsiri, a male spirit of waterways who is thought to throw ashes at disrespectful passersby; and the human ancestors whose bones lie in secondary burial places in the forest. The spirits of prominent people from the past are thought to emerge several generations after their death to the surface of the ground, appearing as *auwi*, (round black volcanic ironstones). In the recent past these *auwi* were honored as central objects in cults directed toward ensuring the benevolence of the spirits and the fertility of the land. A complex of rituals was dedicated overall to maintaining the fertility of each parish and to staving off an expected decline of the land and an ending of a particular historical period. This ritual complex was known as *rindi kiniya*—"straightening out" or "repairing" the earth.

Australian colonial government came into the Duna area in the 1960s after earlier explorations in the 1930s. Christian missionaries soon followed. In the Aluni Valley in the 1990s the major churches where the Sovereign Grace Baptists, the Seventh-Day Adventists, the Apostolics, and the Evangelical Church of Papua New Guinea. The Baptists mounted a vigorous campaign against indigenous rituals, urging people to throw away their sacred stones and obliterate their cult sites, which would be replaced with churches. By the 1990s Christianity was well established, but ritual ideas about the land, concerns over witchcraft—seen as a recurrent problem within communities—and adherence to a wide range of notions encapsulated in group origin stories (*malu*) were also strong. Economic practices of subsistence continued, and each family reared numbers of pigs, fed largely on sweet potatoes, and used these animals as sacrifices for consumption at death feasts and as important items in bride-price payments made to the kinsfolk of the bride on the occasion of a marriage. Sacrifices of pigs were and essentially remain a prime means of communication with the spirit world. Like people, pigs are said to have their own life-force spirits (*tini*), and this life force is offered to the spirits of the land when people sacrifice pigs. The renewal of life force within a cosmos, consisting of the environment and all its living creatures, is the fundamental aim of the indigenous worldview in the Aluni Valley as expressed historically in the *rindi kiniya* ritual cycle.

MEDICINE AND RITUAL

Ritual and medical practices were closely intertwined, because all rituals were designed to ward off ill health and death. Or after a death rituals were performed to reestablish the *tini* in a new realm of being. Spirit forces were thought to cause sickness as a way of demanding sacrifices; divination was practiced to discover which spirit might be causing an illness. For example, the practice of *ita kuma saiya* involved killing a pig and letting its blood drip into a receptacle. By peering into the blood, an expert could determine whether the spirits of the mother's or the father's kin were responsible for the sickness and could recommend appropriate sacrifices of appeasement. While some herbal remedies were used, the main emphasis in counteracting sickness lay in ritual. With the advent of biomedicine introduced since the 1960s, people readily have recourse to treatments when these are available at the Aluni Aid Post or the Health Center at Lake Kopiago station. These treatments are described as *merasin* (medicine), and people declare that they performed curing rituals previously because "they did not have *merasin*"—suggesting implicitly that they have given up their former rituals because they no longer need them. However, introduced medicines are in short supply, they do not always succeed in curing particular conditions, and they are thought to be ineffective against witchcraft attacks (*tsuwake kono*). Christian prayers may be made asking God to heal the sick, but these prayers are also held to be insufficient for curing the bewitched.

Prior to the advent of missions and formal government in the 1960s, experts were employed to identify witches by divination. They used a special divining stick known as the *ndele rowa*, which had shells of the *Pangium edule* fruit (*liki* in Duna) attached to it. Such experts were thought to have received their powers from the Payame Ima female spirit, who could possess them and heighten their powers to see the effects of spirit actions. Witchcraft itself was thought to have arisen from a male *tsuwake* spirit (the general word for spirit is *tama*) who had sexual intercourse with a human female. Since then, witchcraft powers have been thought to be passed down primarily through females, usually from mothers to daughters, although a son may also become a witch. Those accused of witchcraft are mostly women. In the precolonial past after a witch was identified, she might be forced to commit suicide by hanging herself. No doubt this practice contributed to the banning of divination practices by the administration and mission personnel. In the 1990s as a result of putative cases of death caused by witchcraft, divination was revived and one new practitioner was integrated into the Christian scheme by being described as a "prophet" who could "see" witches and where they hid their victims. A witch is said to desire special foods such as pork and to eat the *tini*, or spirit, of a victim, causing sickness or death. People say that if a witch confesses in time, her victim may recover, and a witch who confesses may name others as her accomplices in killing and eating victims in the spirit realm, thus neutralizing both her own power and theirs. These notions were still operative during the 1990s.

FOLKTALES

The Aluni Valley Duna have a rich repertoire of folktales and folksongs. They describe their group origin stories, or *malu*, as *hapiapo tse* (stories of the origins of things). Outside the category of *malu* folktales are simply *hapiapo* (stories of things that were done in the past). Both men and women have a number of such stories that they can narrate from memory and which they use to entertain one another and their children. *Hapiapo* may include etiological motifs—for example, how dogs once had the power to speak but lost it or how a certain bird got its plumage. They also sometimes involve actions, usually malicious, of spirits such as the Tsiri. They recount tricks played between humans or between humans and spirits and their sometimes humorous outcomes. One story tells how a spirit removed the eyes of a victim and how these were restored. (This motif also turns up in the corpus of folklore from an area far to the east of the Duna among the Melpa speakers of Mount Hagen in Papua New Guinea. Folklore motifs are quite often found widely distributed in this way. As popular stories, folktales are easily transmitted across language areas through trade and general social relations of exchange.) Some *hapiapo* attribute stereotyped characteristics to the early ancestors of particular parish groups such as the Kunai people, among whom a particular ancestor was said to have been always cutting his own legs while trying to chop wood with his stone ax. (Steel axes were brought by colonial explorers from the 1930s onward and rapidly replaced the older stone tools.)

The actions of significant spirit figures presiding over the environment could also enter into *hapiapo*. The Payame Ima is often pictured as two sister figures, and in one *hapiapo* these are named Papumi and Lupumi, whose urine formed the Tana River, which flows between the Aluni Valley and Kopiago station. The same story says that the two have migrated away from the river area and gone to the Oko Mamo mountain, which is equated with Ok Tedi, the contemporary site of a huge copper mine west of the Duna area. These two spirits are thus associated with mineral wealth found by an outside company. Stories of this kind establish an implicit link between indigenous groups and the deposits that companies mine for, giving the people a potential lien on claims for compensation or royalties. In 1999 in response to the arrival of a consortium of mining companies to drill for oil near the Strickland River, Valley leaders developed a set of narratives emphasizing their claims on the area and therefore their rights to money if oil was found. They creatively reshaped their *malu* stories, incorporating the figures of the Tindi Auwene and the Payame Ima into the new scenario that included the attempt to find oil.

Hapiapo often teach moral lessons. In the story mentioned in the preceding paragraph, a man hunting by moonlight for marsupials in the forest comes across the two spirit women (Papumi and Lupumi), and they invite him to come to their place and cook marsupials

A house set into a hillside hollow, flanked on one side by banana trees with chickens scurrying in the front yard. Houses like this may be the setting for telling stories in the evening. (Photograph by Pamela J. Stewart)

there. He goes with them, and they give him a netbag (a female wealth object) filled with meat, telling him to share this with men only, not with women. On the fourth day he is to return to the spirits' place, bringing the netbag with him. His wife, however, discovers some of the meat in the bag, eats it, fills the bag with sweet potatoes, and allows it to become dirty. She accuses her husband of eating from another house and tells him to mend some garden fences. So the man is late in returning the netbag to the spirit women, and the bag itself is spoiled. They upbraid him, and when he comes forward to receive a piece of meat from them, one gives him a fatal wound on the neck. They urinate on his body, and their urine becomes the Tano River. The two of them then leave for Oko Mamo.

Several lessons seem to be encoded in this story. One shows the dangers of a human male's involvement with strange (that is, spirit) women. Their wives may be angry and suspect them of wrongdoing. A second lesson holds that if one makes a promise, it should be kept on pain of suffering. And a third emphasizes the respect that must be shown to the Payame Ima in particular. Otherwise she may take retribution and leave the areas where she presides over the wild and its creatures.

The Payame Ima appears in the *malu* (origin story) of the residential group at Aluni itself in the valley. She takes the form of a particular kind of fruit pandanus tree. An Aluni man hears laughter from the tree and takes hold of it, recognizing it as a spirit woman. She changes into various creatures, then takes human form and agrees to marry the man with the proviso that he never insult her

Two knowledgeable men of the Aluni Valley. One wears a partial headdress of marsupial fur and the superb bird of paradise, the other holds a large *colocasia taro corm*, the potato of the tropics, ready for cooking. Such men are repositories of knowledge of *malu* and *hapiapo*. (Photograph by Pamela J. Stewart)

as a creature of the wild. Years later, the husband holds a pig-killing, and a man from Haiyuwi (a neighboring parish) who is involved in the distribution declines to give the woman the cut of meat she wants. She complains, but the husband takes the other man's side and calls her a wild woman. That night she leaves and takes her children up to the high forest. When the husband comes seeking them, she breaks the children's limbs. The children turn into fruit bats while she changes into a nut pandanus tree. The husband returns home and becomes a type of bird that roams the settlement area emitting sad cries. This is also a story of wrongdoing and retribution.

SONGS AND BALLADS

One of the most striking art forms in the Valley area is the singing of ballads (*pikono*) depicting the adventures of a youth, the "ballad boy" (*pikono nane*), in his quest to grow up and find a bride. *Pikono* often portray the ambiguous interactions

A young girl decorated for a festive occasion. She wears a white marsupial headband topped by cassowary plumes and a miniature reed skirt like the longer one her grandmother beside her is carrying. (Photograph by Pamela J. Stewart)

between humans and a category of cannibalistic giants, *auwape*, who preceded humans in occupying the Valley. The *pikono nane* may defeat these *auwape* with assistance from the Payame Ima. Sometimes the *pikono* protagonist joins the *auwape* and takes up their customs, later paying for this in some way. Only a few knowledgeable men can perform *pikono*, which may last for many hours and are sung in the semi-dark by the fireside in a men's house. Despite many changes this art form is very much alive and appreciated. In the past courting songs, one genre of which is called *laingwa*, were popular and performed at occasions known as *yekeanda*. Youths played jaw's harps at *yekeanda* while girls played mouth bows in response, encoding messages into the music. For dances on pig-killing occasions, both men and women would decorate elaborately with face and body paint and headdresses of plumes from forest birds. Nowadays, as noted above, people perform these dances only for national or provincial days of celebration. At home, in addition to *pikono*, people compose songs (*ipakana*) for particular moments or occasions, notably laments (*ipakana heiya*) for the dead. Women specialize in composing and singing these laments at funerals. Like men's speeches on occasions for paying compensation for killings, these women's laments are full of elaborate vocabulary and imagery, directed toward telling the *tini* of the newly dead to fly away to limestone caves in the forest where the other dead dwell.

BIBLIOGRAPHY

Modjeska, C. N. 1995. Rethinking Women's Exploitation: The Duna Case and the Material Basis of Big Man Systems. In *Papuan Borderlands: Huli, Duna, and Ipili Perspectives on the Papua New Guinea Highlands*, edited by Aletta Biersack. Ann Arbor: University of Michigan Press. 265–286.

Stewart, Pamela J., and Andrew Strathern. 2000a. *Speaking for Life and Death: Warfare and Compensation Among the Duna of Papua New Guinea*, Senri Ethnological Reports 13. Osaka: National Museum of Ethnology.

———. 2000b. Naming Places: Duna Evocations of Landscape in Papua New Guinea. *People and Culture in Oceania* 16: 87–107.

———. 2002a. *Gender, Song, and Sensibility: Folktales and Folksongs in the Highlands of New Guinea*. Westport, CT: Praeger.

———. 2002b. *Remaking the World: Myth, Mining and Ritual Change Among the Duna of Papua New Guinea*. Washington, DC: Smithsonian Institution Press.

Strathern, Andrew, and Pamela J. Stewart. 1999. *Curing and Healing: Medical Anthropology in Global Perspective*. Durham: Carolina Academic Press.

———. 2000a. *The Python's Back: Pathways of Comparison Between Indonesia and Melanesia*. Westport, CT: Bergin and Garvey.

———. 2000b. Accident, Agency, and Liability in New Guinea Highlands Compensation Practices. *Bijdragen* 156, 2: 275–295.

———. 2004. *Empowering the Past, Confronting the Future: The Duna People of Papua New Guinea.* New York: Palgrave Macmillan.

Andrew Strathern and Pamela J. Stewart

IBAN

GEOGRAPHY AND HISTORY

A critical examination of Iban folklore reveals that it contains information about relationships—to the world and all life forms; to Iban society and members of other societies; to oneself and the complex features Western scholars have analyzed as "body," "mind," and "spirit." Ibans are the largest of two hundred pre-state societies living on Borneo, the world's third largest island. Found in all four of the island's political divisions—Kalimantan or Indonesian Borneo, Sarawak, Sabah, and Brunei—Iban number over 600,000 in Sarawak, about 15,000 in Kalimantan, and over 1,000 in Sabah. About 480,000 Iban live in rural areas, a majority in traditional longhouse communities. Approximately 120,000 have moved into the towns and cities of Sarawak, Kalimantan, and Sabah.

The regions where Ibans live are tropical, cut through by the equator as it bisects Borneo. The island was formed about 65 million years ago by plate action in the western Pacific. Subject to varying amounts of rainfall, Borneo is affected by the southwest monsoons that blow over the island from March through August and the northeast monsoons that bring heavier amounts of moisture between October and February, totaling well over a hundred inches annually. The most important features of the rains of Borneo are their unpredictability and uneven distribution. Sometimes flooding occurs during the short inter-monsoon period, while at others times there may be drought in the middle of one of the usual monsoon periods. The principal topographic features of the island have been formed by the weathering of the island's central mountain system. Over millennia, heavy rain and erosion have combined to form middle level hills and the broad deltas that extend seaward with annual deposits of alluvia. The rivers that form from the runoff of rains flow in all directions. Rivulets combine to become small streams through which dugouts can move. Streams flow together to produce the major rivers, some of which are navigable by ocean-going ships. The waterways of Borneo for centuries have been the channels by which Ibans and other indigenes have traveled. Borneo is one of the two richest biomes in the world, the other being Amazonia. Constant high temperatures and humidity provide a hothouse environment in which live thousands of plants, an estimated 20,000 insects, and hundreds of birds and animals. Appreciating the biodiversity of the environment and life processes is essential to understanding the diversity and richness of Iban folklore.

Moving to Borneo about 400 years ago, probably from central eastern Sumatra, Ibans are part of a much larger language family known as Austronesian, or "Southern." Austronesian languages are spoken by people from **Hawai'i** and the **Marquesas Islands** in the eastern Pacific to the Malagasy Republic off the east coast of Africa.

171

Women use hardwood poles as pestles to break husks from rice kernels in a rice mortar. (Photograph by Vinson H. Sutlive Jr. From Vinson H. Sutlive Jr., *The Iban of Sarawak: Chronicle of a Vanishing World* [Long Grove, IL: Waveland, 1988])

The indigenous languages of Indonesia and the Philippines all belong to the Austronesian family. One of the distinctive features of Austronesian speakers is that most, if not all, took up farming early, first of tubers such as yams and taros and then of rice. Rice is an amazing plant, having evolved into more than 22,000 subspecies worldwide. For the Ibans rice is a symbol of life and, in one form—unhusked grains, boiled, popped, fermented—or another, figures in every ritual they perform. Over the past four centuries, Ibans have moved from southwestern Borneo into the more northern state of Sarawak, with smaller numbers moving to Sabah and Brunei. Ibans showed a preference for the primary forests of the middle-level hills of Borneo, where they practiced the swidden cultivation of rice. (Swiddening, also known as "shifting cultivation" or "slash-and-burn," involves the rotation of fields rather than crops. This practice requires access to large tracts of land, most of which is fallowed to permit plant growth before being brought under cultivation again.) The premium placed on new lands brought the Ibans into competition and conflict with other people, in particular the Kantu', who became traditional enemies, and Kayan, with whom they struggled for supremacy in the vast Rejang Valley.

In the nineteenth century, thousands of Ibans moved onto the plains of the Rejang Valley, where they took up wet-rice farming. Adapting to the rich environment of Borneo, Ibans have been surrounded by an abundance of instances of life and death. Plants grow and die. Rice is planted, harvested, stored, and prepared, with major and minor ritual acts marking each stage of life. Like all plants, rice is believed to have a soul. Rice plants must, therefore, be apprised of actions that will affect them. For example, when Ibans begin the annual harvest, they must perform a preliminary ritual intended to alert the rice that its time of harvest is at hand. The harvested panicles of rice are transported to the longhouse, the final basketful being covered with clothing of family members so it will recognize the body smells of its hosts.

Ibans have lived in longhouses, attenuated structures for between eight and eighty families. An estimated 80 percent continue to live in rural areas, predominantly in longhouses, while 20 percent have moved into towns and cities. Each family is responsible for construction of its own section of the house, for production and consumption of its own food, and for participation in the social and ritual activities by which the community maintains order and peace. Historically, each house was administered by a senior member, usually a male, together with senior members of each family. He was assisted by specialists, especially bardic-priests who performed principally non-healing rituals; shamans, who performed healing rituals; augurs, who divined the probable success of travels and farming activities; and dirge singers, who performed the chants by which the dead were moved to the next world or invited back for special occasions. Each longhouse was an independent community, usually linked to nearby communities through kinship and friendship for purposes of defense and rituals.

The most significant historical event for Ibans was the arrival of the British adventurer, James Brooke, in 1839, and his eventual imposition of a state system of government over Ibans and all other people in the region. Some Ibans resisted, leading to punitive expeditions by Brooke, his successors, and their allies. Impressed by what appeared to be the irresistible force of the Brooke Raj, other Ibans submitted themselves to the government to become part of the colonial structure. Begun by the Brookes, the subversion of Iban polity was completed in 1974 by the Malaysian government, which seconded all Iban chiefs as civil servants, thereby removing them from effective political leadership.

PRINCIPLES OF IBAN FOLKLORE

Two principles are important for understanding Iban folklore. First, Ibans employ the familiar techniques of homological and analogical reasoning: things look alike, or things behave alike. They do not, however, think of the Western categories of "inorganic," "organic," and "superorganic," first articulated by Aristotle, as meaning what they do for members of American and European societies. Surrounded by thousands more life forms, Ibans have inferred the existence of life-giving souls (*semengat*) which, when present, convey life and, when absent, may cause illness or death. In the world of Ibans, all plants and animals share the potential for sensate thought and action. None is insignificant, and all must be treated with respect.

Traditional longhouses such as this can house several Iban families. Some longhouses are large enough for hundreds of people to live communally. (© Boyd Norton/The Image Works)

Everything—from the tiniest insect to the tallest tree—is incorporated into the texts performed by men and women. In Iban lore, the shaman (*manang*) has not only the capacity to see human souls; he also may capture and treat wandering souls. Second, anything may become anything, and nothing happens without cause. Iban lore presents trees that talk, bushes that walk, macaques that transform into incubi, and jars that moan when not receiving adequate attention. A cricket determines the sex of human beings. In death, this principle continues to be important, as the Worm Queen, herself a master weaver, opens the door for the company escorting the soul of the dead to the Opposite World, and *Sami*, a chicken, is dispatched as messenger to summon the dead for final honors. In the cycle of life and death, the souls of the deceased are transformed into life-giving dew, which nourishes rice, which is planted, harvested, cooked, and ingested to become human life once again.

ORAL FOLKLORE

The physical habitat and sociopolitical environments have been incorporated into Iban folklore. By folklore, we understand all of the lore of the Iban: knowledge by which they have adapted to the world in which they live, or ethnoscience, including astronomy, botany, zoology, protohistory, and history; behaviors and codes, or *adat*, for relating to one another and to other people; and wisdom for interpreting the ultimate issues of life and death.

Iban folklore is expressed in verbal art forms and rituals such as aphorisms and proverbs, chants and dirges or laments, epics, fairy tales, fables and legends, myths and sagas, motifs, prayers, proverbs, riddles, and songs. Aphorisms and proverbs are part of the collective wisdom of Ibans, who can adduce an appropriate couplet for almost every situation. Epic narratives recall the brave deeds of ancestors and spirit beings who serve as models for Iban men and women. Keling, the masculine role model, and Kumang, his consort, embody the intellect and abilities to be emulated. Conversely, Apai Sali, the **Trickster** or, quite literally, "Father of Foolishness," is featured in dozens of amusing tales, which provide cautions against unwise actions. The epics are complemented with accounts of weavers, the channel for able and ambitious Iban women. Weaving is regarded as a spiritual activity, to which a woman is called by an ancestral master weaver. Mastery of weaving and the ability to identify plants and their combination in the rich indigo and burgundy dyes bring distinction to successful weavers. Legends—stories of culture heroes, many of whom are historical personages—are more important than myths, the sacred narratives of how things began or how they came to be as they now are. The Ibans show remarkably little interest in cosmogony (the beginning of the universe) but much awareness of the practical importance of cosmology (the nature of the universe), in particular seasonal differences connected with various positions of the Pleiades, Orion, and Sirius. Riddles formerly were a favorite pastime. As recently as the 1960s, the government-supported Radio Sarawak played "The Riddle of the Week," posing the riddle on Sunday nights and then a bit more information on each following night, finally giving the answer on Friday nights.

RULES AND RITUALS

Iban *adat* is a vast complex system of prescriptions and prohibitions whose principal purpose is avoidance of violence and encouragement of mutual respect among all people. Like all bodies of customary law, *adat* is dynamic and subject to interpretation and re-interpretation. Recognizing the significance of *adat* in a rapidly modernizing context, Iban leaders established the Majlis Adat Istiadat in 1974, and almost twenty years later, a volume, *Iban Adat 1993*, was published. The topics reveal an overriding concern with responsibilities to one's fellow Ibans.

As fully important as its intellectual content is the place of folklore in behavior, especially in the numerous rituals Ibans perform. Rituals are forms of behavior that are repeated because they are believed to be effective. Rituals have an instrumental priority over other forms of folklore. Rituals represent the end or purpose for which other forms of folklore exist. It is hardly an exaggeration to state that Ibans have created rituals for almost every conceivable undertaking, especially those that have any element of risk. Iban rituals may be divided into three major categories: healing rituals, performed by shamans (*manang*); rituals for farming and warfare, performed by bardic-priests (*lemambang*); and chants to accompany the dead to the Opposite World (*Sebayan*) and to invite them back, performed by senior women or "craftsmen of the dirge" (*tukang sabak*) together with bardic-priests. Sutlive and Sutlive in *The Encyclopaedia of Iban Studies* (2001) identify more than a hundred discrete rituals under *gawai* and "rituals." Dozens more rituals appear in the entry for *pelian* ("healing rituals") with brief descriptions of many shamanic rituals and performances. Rituals are observed with sacrifices and offerings. Depending upon the resources of the host community, several pigs, a water buffalo, and numerous chickens will be sacrificed. Chickens, which are waved in blessing over the head of male guests, are killed and cooked. Likewise, chickens that are wounded in cockfighting, a preliminary event that accompanies many rituals, also are consumed by participants. Until recently cockfighting has been the favorite sporting activity. In rituals relating to visits by the dead, male hosts are said to compete with the dead in the series of cockfights, which are enjoyed by the dead as much as their living descendants.

CHANTS

Iban chants are of three principal types, each created and performed to aid in survival of individuals and the society. These chants are quite lengthy, many requiring a full night or several nights to perform. *Timang* are praise chants performed by a quartet of bardic priests, each beating out the meter with a hardwood staff while taking a turn in leading the chant or participating in a three-man chorus. *Timang* recall deeds of derring-do by warriors who conducted raids or defended the community against enemies. *Pelian* are healing chants, performed either by shaman or bardic-priests in solo performances. *Sabak* are death dirges. The *sabak kenang*, or memorial chant, is performed by a senior woman on the night of a resident's death and expresses the sorrow felt because of the death, final passage through all parts of the house, and a journey with the ancestors to the Opposite World. The *sabak lumbung* is performed as an invitation to all of the dead who have not received final honors to return to the house. The company of the dead bring magical charms in exchange for the offerings presented to them and, in some communities, for the small structures which will be their final residence. Among the chants only *timang* are accompanied by bard-sticks. Neither the *pelian* nor the *sabak* has instrumental support. Instruments of importance to Ibans are drums, with which rhythms are beat out for dancing and the living are able to summon the dead for festivals, and bronze gongs.

STUDIES OF IBAN FOLKLORE

Iban folklore was created long ago and continues to be created and edited as commentaries and as a moral code. It is encyclopedic: there are no experiences of life or death among Ibans that are not referenced in or influenced by their folklore. Both scholars and casual observers have commented on the dignity and self-confidence that Ibans manifest. This strength and self-assurance derives in no small measure from Iban folklore. For all people, the unknown is the single greatest cause of anxiety and fear. Ibans have confronted the unknown in life and death, familiar and unfamiliar, near and far, by transforming it into the known with tools of folklore, comprehending both known and imagined circumstances. A reciprocal relationship exists between Ibans and their folklore. Given that products of the experiences and perceptions of Iban society are encoded in the various literary forms, Iban folklore has a constraining and constitutive effect, as individuals draw meaning from and contribute new meanings to their lore. Iban folklore is unusual for two reasons: First, it remains to the present remarkably intact and integrated. In the words of a leading scholar, Clifford Sather (2001): "Iban oral literature, both sacred and secular, is not only phenomenally rich, but still exists in context to an extent almost unique in Southeast Asia and expresses what remains a coherent, integrated symbolic order and belief system. Its study therefore promises results that can be achieved in few other societies in the world." One of the reasons for the continuation of Iban folklore as "a coherent, integrated symbolic order and belief system" was the publication during the 1960s of 108 volumes by the Borneo Literature Bureau (BLB). A vision and legacy of the British Colonial Government, the BLB series remains an invaluable collection of all forms of Iban folklore. Second, Iban folklore parallels in many ways that of the Greeks and Romans in its accounts of warfare and travel. The late Professor Derek Freeman, a scholar of international renown, observed that "in sheer volume, Iban folklore exceeds that of either the Greeks or the Romans."

BIBLIOGRAPHY

Dundes, Alan. 1994. *The Cockfight*. Madison: University of Wisconsin Press.

Gass, Robert. 1999. *Chanting*. New York: Broadway Books.

Lakoff, George, and Mark Johnson. 1999. *Philosophy in the Flesh: The Embodied Mind and Its Challenge to Western Thought*. New York: Basic Books.

Majlis Istiadat. 1993. *Iban Adat 1993*. Kuching: Majlis Istiadat.

Richards, Anthony. 1981. *An Iban-English Dictionary*. Oxford: Oxford University Press.

Sather, Clifford. 2001. *Seeds of Play, Words of Power: An Ethnographic Study of Iban Shamanic Chants*. Kota Samaharan: The Tun Jugah Foundation.

Sutlive, Vinson H., Jr. 1979. Iban Folk Literature and Socialization: The Fertility of Symbolism. In *The Imagination of Reality: Essays in Southeast Asian Coherence Systems*, edited by A. L. Becker and A. A. Yengoyan. Norwood, NJ: Ablex Press. 105–123.

Sutlive, Vinson H., Jr., and Joanne Sutlive, eds. 2001. *The Encyclopaedia of Iban Studies*. Kuching: The Tun Jugah Foundation.

Vinson H. Sutlive Jr.

KADAZANDUSUN

GEOGRAPHY AND HISTORY

The largest indigenous group in Sabah, Malaysia, situated on the northwest coast of Borneo, the Kadazandusun inhabit a region whose topography is dominated by Mount Kinabalu, the highest mountain in southeast Asia, which is believed to be the resting place for departed souls. Sabah enjoys a sunny tropical climate all year round. Daily temperatures range from 23 to 33 degrees Celsius, and rainfall is common throughout the year, ranging from about 150 centimeters to over 450 centimeters annually. In most parts of Sabah the wetter period occurs during the northeast monsoon season from October to February, with the drier season during the southwest monsoon from March to September.

The term "Kadazandusun" combines the **Malay** word *Dusun*, meaning "orchard" and connoting rural life, and *Kakadazan*, which means "town" or "urban area." The population now designated by this term was estimated in 1998 to be about 610,000 or sixty percent of Sabah's total. Many social scientists and historians regard the Kadazandusun as Sabah's original inhabitants, but theories of origin vary. Some argue that Kadazandusun are of Mongoloid stock similar to the Chinese and that during a wave of migration they moved from **China** to the Philippines, the Indonesian archipelago, Borneo, and peninsular Malaysia. Another theory attributes their origin to Indo-Malayan migrations from South China between 15,000 and 20,000 years ago. The migration legend of the Kadazandusun postulates an origin from a place called Nunuk Ragang, which means "red banyan tree," supposedly situated in the interior of Sabah itself. This legend reinforces Kadazandusun belief that they are the region's original inhabitants.

The Kadazandusun divide into ten main tribes and twenty sub-tribes speaking different dialects and residing in various places throughout Sabah. The main tribes are Tanggara, Rungus, Lotud, Tuawon, Tagaas, Liwan, Bundu, Kwizau, Tindal, Tatana, and Orang Sungai. Despite linguistic differences, they all speak closely related dialects of the Malayo-Polynesian stock.

The Kadazandusun are the principal paddy ricegrowers of Sabah. A typical house is surrounded by coconut, mango, rambutan, and other fruit trees. In addition to rice cultivation, Kadazandusun raise pigs and buffaloes. Until recently, one might see pigs running freely and buffalo grazing in any village. Agricultural products are offered for trade in an open market known as *tamu*.

RELIGIOUS BELIEFS AND RITUALS

Approximately half of the Kadazandusun are now Christian, about a tenth are Muslim, and the rest practice their indigenous religion. Tradition-oriented Kadazandusun believe that every rock, tree, or stream has a spirit that must be propitiated. They also possess a hierarchically organized pantheon of gods similar to that of ancient Greece. The chief god is Kinoingan, who is referred to as *minamangun*, meaning "almighty creator." He has both a wife, Suminundu ("holy and miraculous"), and offspring. Rogon (also known as Logon), one of his sons, is related to the evil spirit that causes illness and bad luck, while his daughter Huminudon sacrificed herself for humans, becoming various nourishing plants. The Kadazandusun believe that Kinoingan and his family reside in heaven but descend to earth when necessary. In addition to these gods, the Kadazandusun also believe in many good and evil tutelary spirits with functions related to daily life. These include Kauulung, whose duty is to prevent incest; Ompuan, the rain god; and Kinoingan Tumanak, a god of the soil.

The Kadazandusun ritual specialist is known as *bobohizan* or *bobolian*. These figures, most of whom are priestesses, are the keepers of traditional beliefs and customs. Before the coming of Christianity and Islam, they played an important role in all aspects of community life. They are responsible for conducting the annual *magavau* ceremony, when thanks are given to the rice spirit, as well as the *mamahuidopogon*, a blessing of the world which occurs only once in every eight or ten years. The *bobohizan* is also an herbal specialist, therapist, consultant to the village head committee, and teacher of customs. According to the Kadazandusun creation myth, the *bobohizan* learned from Kinoingan's daughter the art of curing certain ailments with herbs and roots. The use of traditional medicines remains very much alive among the Kadazandusun. Different types of herbs are grown around the house or gathered from the surrounding forest. These include the roots of the *komburongo* (used for fever and stomachache), the leaves of the *hinias* (which heal skin diseases caused by fungus), leaves of the *solibambang* (for broken bones), leaves of the *gaagabang* (which aids in the clotting of blood), and the *kusur* bulb (used as a poultice and to prevent tetanus). When an illness is believed to be caused by harmful spirits, the *bobohizan* consults her *divato* (spirit guide) about how to cure the patient—through chanting, offering sacrifice, or entering a trance to exorcize the evil spirits. The *bobohizan* has a large repertoire of *rinaits* or mantras to choose according to the specific cause of the sickness.

The Kadazandusn cosmology views the primordial universe as a vast ocean stretching through the darkness with a gigantic rock hanging in the sky. The creator couple of Kinoingan and Suminundu emerged from this rock, which then exploded, and created the universe and all living things. The gods then took their residence in the other world in the sky, which some believe to have many realms or levels. The Dusun Tindal of Kota Belud, for example, believe there are seven levels of the other world, in the highest of which dwell Kinoingan and his wife. Below the earth are two more realms, the first of which is inhabited by dwarves known as *minorit* and the second of which is inhabited exclusively by a race of maidens known as the *tandui*.

MYTHS, LEGENDS, AND FOLKTALES

Kadazandusun myths, legends, and folktales have been circulated orally. The usual time for storytelling is during the harvest, both in the fields and once work has been finished. Some folktales are told by older people during times of ritual feasting such as a wedding or the celebration of a baby's first month of life. Given their use as accoutrements of celebration and entertainment, many traditional stories survive. Foreign anthropologists first published collections of such stories. Ivor Evans, for example, published a large collection from Kadazandusun oral tradition in the *Journal of the Royal Anthropological Institute* in 1913. More recent collections include those from Marsh (1988), King and King (1990), and Rutter (1999). The first two works as well as books by Lasimbang (1990) represent the trend in the latter part of the twentieth century for Kadazandusun to publish collections themselves.

The details and names of the protagonists vary from tribe to tribe in the various versions of Kadazandusun creation myths. The most common creation story has it that the world began when the creator couple bathed, the dirt from Suminundu's body forming the earth while that from Kinoingan became the sky. Initially the sky was smaller than the earth. To make the two correspond, the couple pushed at the earth from both sides, inadvertently forming mountains where it folded. The two gods created humans through a process of trial and error, first using stone and then wood, which produced humans who could not speak. After destroying these prototypes, they tried clay and were able to fashion fully human creatures.

Kadazandusun legends include the migration legend of *nunuk ragang*, the origin of the taboo against laughing at animals, and the heroic story of Monsopiad. The migration story gives three reasons for the migration from Nunuk Ragang to Sabah: an epidemic of *tahi ragang* ("red droppings"), an attack by people from beneath the earth, and the desire to find a more fertile territory. The taboo against laughing at animals originates in a story about a group of drunken villagers who were having so much fun forcing a cat and a dog to amuse them that they did not realize that a flood was imminent. Soon the entire house was submerged, and to this day Kadazandusun do not make sport of animals. The story of Monsopiad combines elements similar to the Western accounts of Achilles and Robin Hood. According to this legend, the **hero**'s father bathed the child Monsopiad with a piece of eggshell from the *mugang* bird to make the boy invulnerable to all weapons. He protected his village from robbers and enemies, killing forty-two men, and the skulls of his enemies still hang from the ceiling of a house whose owner traces his lineage back to Monsopiad. In fact, the story relates to the practice of headhunting, which, before being prohibited in the nineteenth century by the British North Borneo Company that ruled Sabah from 1884 to 1963 was carried out for reasons of religion and masculine honor.

MUSIC

Oral tradition also accounts for the origin of traditional musical instruments such as the gong, *tongunggak*, and *kulintangan*. Huminundon produced the *bobohizan* and taught them to fashion bamboo stalks of seven different lengths, shapes, and sizes to form the *tongunggak*. The *bobohizan* then taught people how to make gongs from bamboo. Bamboo gongs were the norm until the late eighteenth century, when traders from Brunei introduced the brass gong, which began to be arranged into an assemblage of seven similar to the *tongunggak*. The gong is the chief ritual instrument among the Kadazandusun, providing a lively beat for weddings and other festivities and a very solemn beat for funerals. At village, district, and state levels, gong-beating competitions known as *magagung* are held during *Tadau Kaamatan* celebrations.

Legend also relates the origin of another Kadazandusun musical instrument, the *sompoton*. The story goes that in a village lived eight brothers, one of whom was dumb. One day both their parents died, but the dumb brother was left out of traditional lamentation because he could not speak. Before the funeral, he had the idea of making an instrument from eight pieces of bamboo tucked into a hollow gourd with beeswax used to seal gaps between pipes and gourd. He was able to express his love for his parents during the funeral by blowing a sad tune into the *sompoton*. This instrument is now a common sight in souvenir and handicraft shops in Koto Kinabalu, the capital of Sabah.

CELEBRATIONS AND GAMES

As an agricultural society, the Kadazandusun have many celebrations related to the rice cultivation. Examples include *kapampanan do Mangasok*, which celebrates the closing of a village paddy nursery, and *Madasalud*, or the blessing of the newly transplanted rice paddy into the field. By far the grandest festival in Sabah is *Tadau Kaamatan*, the annual harvest festival which is celebrated throughout the month of May in honor of the rice spirit, *Bambaazon*. Rice represents a tremendous sacrifice on the part of the gods, for according to Kadazandusun mythology, Kinoingan and his wife sacrificed their only daughter at the time so that humans, who were starving, might have nourishment. Rice and other edible plants grew from various parts of her body. Among the highlights of *Tadau Kaamatan* are the thanksgiving ritual of *magavau* and *unduk ngadau*, a costume contest carried out at district and state levels in honor of Huminundon. Some Kadazandusun hold open house and invite friends and relatives to join them for the feast. In addition, traditional dances such as *sumazau*, *magunatip*, and *sumandai* are performed to entertain guests. These dances, which are accompanied by the beating of gongs, have strong associations with rituals, paddy planting, and harvesting. They are also performed at weddings.

Cockfighting was once a popular pastime among the Kadazandusun, and a villager carrying a big rooster under his arm was a common sight. Cockfighting was the subject of much folklore. One of the more popular stories among the Dusun of Tambunan centers upon a tobacco salesman named Galit and his great white fighting rooster, Gunsiou. According to legend, Gunsiou was abnormally large when hatched

and once achieved a record of twenty-five consecutive victories. However, Gunsiou mysteriously vanished into the jungle one night while Galit was sleeping. The bird's name is still used synonymously with "brave" and "fine tobacco taste," even though cockfights are now illegal.

ARTS AND CRAFTS

In addition to bamboo musical instruments, Kadazandusun craftsmen produce many other products. Woodcarvers create decorations for homes, sword handles, and newly dug graves. Women weave brilliant headdresses and costumes, which are usually black with splashes of color. A common adornment among the Dusun Tindal tribe is a wide belt that stretches from the waist to mid-thigh. It is formed of rows of antique beads. Other pieces of jewelry worn with this costume include hand-engraved silver bangles, silver earrings, and silver pouches with chains worn around the neck. The Rungus from the Kudat area have long been famous for producing beautiful beaded necklaces. They wear long multi-stranded necklaces crossed over their shoulders to their waists and over their traditional black costumes, which are interwoven with gold thread. Patterns on the strands illustrate ancient fables, and human figures are usually done in brightly hued beadwork. Some Kadazandusun still spin their own thread and color it with dyes that have been in use for over two thousand years.

Kadazandusun are also fond of using bamboo and rattan in various items of daily use such as hats, *bubus* (fishing traps), and baskets. The usual red-and-black color on these items comes from local plant dyes, the red from *mengkudu* (or "dragon's

Basketmaker Radiah Yadong makes a going-to-church basket. Because rattan is getting scarce, she uses *lingkong* or *lygodium* for the outside weaving; however, she still uses rattan for other parts of the weaving. (© Michael J. Doolittle/The Image Works)

blood") root and the black from the common indigo plant. The shapes and patterns of a hat, for example, are clear indicators of its geographical origin. The natives of Papar make hats which are steep, conical, and usually decorated with nature imagery. Hats from Penampang and Tuaran have wider circular bases and geometrical designs.

The *bubu* is a trap used by the headhunting tribes to catch freshwater fish. Traditional Kadazandusun baskets are also very practical and are meant to be strapped to a person's back so that he or she may carry fruit, firewood, and paddy stalks while leaving the hands free. Kadazandusun living at the foot of Mount Kinabulu make a particularly elegant basket called the *wakid*. This back carrier is cylindrical at the base and has a flared top. The body is made of carefully split bamboo pieces that are tightly fitted at the elongated base. The spokes of bamboo flare at the mouth of the basket. The ends are secured by being lashed to two or more rattan hoops using split rattan twine. The body is further reinforced with two or more layers of twine tying the spokes at different heights. The base is laced with rattan on an overlay of thin bark. A circular piece of bark lines the bottom of the basket. The *wakid* is in considerable demand for its style and grace. It serves as a household ornament in addition to being a useful carrier and container.

CHALLENGES OF THE MODERN WORLD

Modernization and **globalization** have had an appreciable effect on Kadazandusun folk traditions. The original meanings behind traditional forms of music, songs, and dances are being replaced by the values of the modern world. Only a few people remember the *hius* and the *rinaits*, traditional songs and mantras. Younger folk have substituted television and video games for the folktales that entertained their forebears. Moreover, the coming of Christianity and Islam has led to a decline in traditional beliefs as well as in the importance of the *bobohizan*. Once every village had at least one *bobohizan*, but now few are left. Those still remaining tend to be very old.

The Kadazandusun Central Association (KDCA), supported by the Sabah state government, has committed itself to preserving the fading practices of Kadazandusun culture. During the month-long *Tadau Kaamatan* celebration in May, the KDCA organizes a cultural carnival where people from all walks of life have the opportunity to observe and take part in the *magavau*, the *unduk ngadau* contest, and traditional dances and games. They may also drink *tapai* (rice wine) and enjoy the *sugandoi*, a singing contest. Along with Museum Sabah and the Sabah Society, the tourism industry has played an important role in preserving the culture through publications and in introducing the world to the traditional lifestyle of the Kadazandusun.

STUDIES OF KADAZANDUSUN FOLKLORE

General sources on Sabah and Kadazandusun culture include Alliston (1966), Hoebel (1997), Leong (1982), Luping (1985), Topin (1981), Tongkul (2002), and Williams (1965, 1969). Appell (1986) focuses specifically on the Rungus Dusun, and Fung (1996) deals with the Tindals. Works dealing with narrative folk traditions are

Evans (1922), King and King (1990), Lasimbang (1990), Marsh (1988), Rutter (1999), and Vivienne (1994). The important figure of the *bobohizan* provides the focus for Lamsimbang and others (2002). Other sources dealing with Kadazandusun belief systems include articles that appeared in the *Borneo Mail* on the paddy spirit (1989) and plant lore (1994). Disimon (1997) deals with the role of gongs in Kadazandusun festival life. An important source on arts and crafts is Alman and Alman (1963). One should also consult these Internet resources: www.fascinating malaysia.com, www/lib.my, and www.e-borneo.com.

BIBLIOGRAPHY

Alliston, Cyril. 1966. *Threatened Paradise: North Borneo and Its People*. London: Robert Hale.

Alman, John, and Elizabeth Alman. 1963. *Handcraft in North Borneo*. Jesselton: Sabah Publishing House.

Appell, G. N. 1986. *Social Anthropological Research among the Rungus Dusun*. Kota Kinabalu: Tun Fuad Stephens Research Library.

Bambaazon—The Paddy Spirit. 1989. *Borneo Mail*, 29 May.

Disimon, Gundohing Paul P. 1997. The Heritage of Gongs. *Souvenir Book of Penampang District Kaamatan Festival*, 20 January.

Evans, Ivor H. N. 1922. *Among Primitive Peoples in Borneo*. Philadelphia: Lippincott.

Fung Lan Yong. 1996. Tindals: True Sabahans Past and Present. *Borneo Post*, 12 May.

Hoebel, Robert. 1997. *Sabah*. Kota Kinbalu: Beaufort International Hotels and Tanjung Aru Beach Hotel.

King, John Wayne, and Julie K. King. 1990. *Sungai / Tombonuwo Folk Tales*. Kota Kinabalu: Sabah Museum and State Archives.

Lasimbang, Rita. 1990. *Pulou Tikus and Lugodingon Om I Kookodu*. Kota Kinabalu: Sabah Museum and State Archives.

Lasimbang, Rita, and others. 2002. Exploring the Art of the Bobohizan—Keeper of Kadazan Rituals and Chants. Borneo Research Council Seventh Biennial Conference, Universiti Malaysia Sabah. 15–18 July.

Leong, Cecilia. 1982. *Sabah: The First Hundred Years*. Kuala Lumpur: Percetakan Nan Yang Muda Sdn. Bhd.

Luping, Herman James. 1985. *The Kadazans and Sabah Politics*. Wellington: Victoria University.

Marsh, Ignatia Olim, ed. 1988. *Tales and Tradition from Sabah*. Kota Kinabalu: The Sabah Society.

Rutter, Owen. 1999. *The Dragon of Kinabalu and Other Borneo Stories*. Kota Kinabalu: Natural History Publications.

Sompoton—Sweet Harmony from Wild Plants. 1994. *Borneo Mail*, 30 May.

Tongkul, Felix. 2002. *Traditional Systems of Indigenous Peoples of Sabah*. Kota Kinabalu: PACOS Trust.

Topin, Benedict. 1981. Some Aspects of the Kadazandusun Culture. Kadazan Cultural Association, 2nd Delegates Conference, 5–6 December.

———. 2003. The Making of the Kadazandusun *Huguan Siou*. *Tadau Kaamatan Souvenir Book*. 22–27.

Vivienne, Anna. 1994. Keeping the Tales Alive. *Daily Express*, 29 May.

Williams, Thomas Rhys. 1965. *The Dusun: A North Borneo Society*. London: Holt, Rinehart, and Winston.

———. 1969. *A Borneo Childhood: Enculturation in Dusun Society*. London: Holt, Rinehart, and Winston.

Low Kok On

KALIAI

GEOGRAPHY AND HISTORY

A political subdivision of West New Britain Province, Kaliai is located on the northwest coast of the island of New Britain in the country of Papua New Guinea at approximately 5 degrees south latitude and 149 degrees east longitude. No roads or bridges link Kaliai villages with each other or with the rest of New Britain. Other than a few footpaths, all transportation is by canoe or boat. The coastal people with whom we have done six periods of anthropological research between 1966 and 2003 speak their own Melanesian language, Lusi, as well as Tok Pisin, Papua New Guinea's national language. They are slash-and-burn gardeners who grow a variety of traditional foods—taro, coconuts, long beans, breadfruit, bananas, sugar cane, and yams—and introduced plants such as sweet potatoes, pineapple, squash, water-melon, tomatoes, and sweet casava.

A chain of volcanoes, some of them temporarily inactive, runs down the 300-mile spine of New Britain. Mount Andewa, a quiescent volcano located in Kaliai, is the site of a village of the dead. People who hunt or explore on the slopes of this mountain report hearing the sounds of the spirit village—dogs barking, pigs squealing, children playing—and smelling cooking fires. However, living humans can see nothing. The story "Akro and Gagandewa" recounts the events leading to the war between humans and their spirit in-laws that resulted in the permanent separation of the two groups.

In the late nineteenth century, before European contact, most Kaliai lived in small hamlets near their gardens in the interior of the island. The hamlets consisted of family houses, where women, girls, and young boys slept, and one or more men's houses, where related men and older boys slept. Today most people live in coastal villages of between two hundred and five hundred people but still maintain garden houses in scattered hamlets. Many of the hamlets also contain a men's house. Today, as in the past, villagers trade with and marry people of nearby communities. Marriages are ideally arranged by the parents of the young couple, usually with their agreement, and are frequently between cousins. As before, men who aspire to political leadership often marry two or more women. This may work well, but more often the wives do not get along, causing their husband grief (or they get along very well, to their husband's dismay). The politics and tribulations of marriage are frequent themes in Kaliai folklore. In "The Story of Gavu" two unrelated groups cement their agreement to live peacefully as neighbors by intermarrying their children. Another story, "Akono and Silimala," explores the difficulties of plural marriage and suggests one way in which the senior wife might solve the problem: by persuading the second wife to commit suicide.

There are two seasons in West New Britain. The relatively dry and cool period occurs between May and December, when the southeast tradewinds blow across the mountain chain that runs down the middle of the island. During this time people make gardens, visit friends and family and collect debts, plan ceremonies to welcome children into their father's kin group, recognize marriages, and celebrate the lives and accomplishments of the dead. The rainy season occurs from December to April, when winds from the northwest bring gales and heavy downpours. It is difficult to travel, garden, or hold ceremonies during the rainy season, so people visit in their houses to play games and tell stories. Storytelling is an important form of education as well as a common and enjoyable evening pastime, and stories, told around the fire after the evening meal, introduce children to their social and physical environment and to their history.

MYTHS, LEGENDS, AND FOLKTALES

The Lusi-speaking Kaliai have three kinds of oral literature: *nasinga*, *pelunga*, and *ninipunga*. A *nasinga* is a true accounting of historical events. The word is derived from the verb *nasi*, which means "to recount." When people say *Nganasi legu nasinga* they are announcing that what follows is history. People may hotly dispute the interpretation of events in a narrative because the events have consequences for modern life. For

A *pura* snake; people must establish and maintain good relations with *pura* beings. (Photograph by D. Counts)

example, a *nasinga* may be used as supportive evidence by a group claiming ownership of a tract of land because their ancestors were the first to settle there. The descendants of Kaoroko Parao, whose arrival is described in "The Story of Gavu," have successfully used it to claim the land on which the village school and church are built.

Pelunga are legends or myths. People believe them to be true even though they have no traceable ties to living individuals or current events. They are about real or mythical persons, events, or places and explain why things are as they are today. Often the primary characters are *pura*, powerful beings who change from human to animal form. These beings often appear as snakes with human faces. If people treat *pura* well, they may generously give their human friends new foods or teach them new technology, but if they are angered, they will destroy entire villages.

Both the natural and spirit worlds are continuously present for Kaliai people. Carvings and paintings remind them of stories that recount historical or mythic events whose consequences are important to living people. For example, one *pelunga* recounts the history of a kin group whose founding ancestor was Kalugesing, a changeling who once lived in the Gesing River. Kalugesing sometimes took the form of a human and sometimes appeared as a barracuda (*kaluvia*). As a woman, she gave birth to human children; as a barracuda, she give birth to barracuda offspring. This story explains why barracuda do not eat their human relatives and why Kalugesing's human descendants should not eat barracuda. The carved door decorations of the men's house built by descendants of Kalugesing remind them of their relationship to her.

Ninipunga are similar to English speakers' notion of folktales or fables. They recount events that neither the storyteller nor the adult audience believe to true. They may be new creations composed by a talented performer. *Ninipunga* are primarily told for entertainment, though many are intended to educate children as well as to amuse them. Several conventions distinguish

The carvings on the door of the men's house remind descendants of their relationship to their founding ancestor, Kalugesing. (Photograph by D. Counts)

ninipunga from other types of stories: (1) the unique characters, found in no other kind of story; (2) the context in which they are told; (3) the formulas that are used to introduce and conclude performances; and (4) songs.

Ninipunga are the only stories in which anthropomorphized animals sing, dance, talk, and interact with humans and each other. The human characters are also unique to *ninipunga*. A *ninipunga* will usually have one or more of the following: a generic central character named Akono (male) and/or Galiki (female) and/or a villain called Vohoku. Akono and Galiki may be orphans or the youngest of sets of same-sex siblings. Vohoku is a monster character. He has human form but eats human flesh and is distinguished by his long, uncut hair and fingernails and large canine teeth. Vohoku is usually a powerful but stupid creature, often outwitted by a clever child and is reminiscent of the giant in "Jack and the Beanstalk" or the witch in "Hansel and Gretel." There is one fascinating exception to the rule that vohoku only appear in *ninipunga*. One Kaliai kin group tells a *nasinga* that traces their line back to an ancestor who was a wild man, a vohoku. In addition to recounting the history of a kin group, this story explores the boundaries of humankind. It describes how Vohoku was caught, cleaned up, and taught to speak the language of his captors. After he had been turned into a true human being, he was given a wife and brought into human society. In exchange he gave his new in-laws a new variety of taro, a valuable food.

While other types of stories may be told at any time, *ninipunga* should only be told after dark and in a public performance. The stories will usually be introduced with the phrase *tin tin tavore*, something like the familiar "Once upon a time." *Tin tin* is a meaningless ritual phrase, but *tavore* means "Let's draw [a picture]." The performance of a *ninipunga* is likely to end with *Tamburo sapini natnatu na tamburo Samuro ngapura*, an invitation to children (*natnatu*) to dive into the sea and emerge at Samuro, a very special islet off the Kaliai coast. Samuro marks the boundary between a strip of territory that belongs to ancestor spirits and land belonging to humans. Small and composed of white coral and shell sand, it contrasts dramatically with the dark volcanic sand beaches of much of the New Britain mainland. It is a lovely spot for a day's outing, and children delight in playing with the fine white sand. People passing by the islet or picnicking there often bring home a container of sand as a treat for their youngsters. The closing phrase, then, is the equivalent of "and they lived happily ever after." The use of stylized introductory and concluding phases is optional. Some storytellers seldom use them. Most feel that without them the story is incomplete and improperly told. The use of these formulas is, then, a matter of individual style.

SONGS AND MUSIC

Song is another feature characteristic of *ninipunga*. Other types of stories may contain songs, but they are most common and of greatest importance in *ninipunga*. If a *ninipunga* has an associated song, performers consider it to be an essential and integral part of the presentation and refuse to tell the story if they do not know it. The song in a *ninipunga* is often part of the story's plot. Characters in trouble sing of their plight, are heard, and are rescued. Critically wounded people or those who are committing suicide sing so that others will know that they are dying and why. Vohoku sing of what they will do to their victims. Other characters sing just because they are happy.

Music is an important aspect of Kaliai life, quite aside from its role in *ninipunga*. Children sing while they play, and adults sing as they work. People sing for joy or to give them strength to complete a difficult task. They sing to attract the opposite sex; a young man who sings well is especially attractive to young women. They also sing their grief when death has come, as it often does, to a person in youth or middle age. Death songs, haunting in melody, lament the loss felt by those left to grieve. Yet another occasion for song occurs when ancestral spirit beings (*aulu*), celebrated in legend, take form as physical beings and visit Kaliai villages to dance in honor of children or in celebration of the memory of the dead.

People compose songs about their own experiences or the adventures of ancestors and cultural heroes. One *ninipunga* tells the story of an orphan boy who was abused and neglected by his fellow villagers who drove him away when he asked for food. Angered by this treatment of the child, ancestral spirits rescued him, taught him their song, and then caught and began to eat the villagers. The slaughter ceased only after the leader of the village begged for forgiveness and gave the boy his daughter in marriage. The story ends with the leader of the *aulu* telling the boy, "Treasure these masked figures, for they are the spirits of your ancestors. From now on you must make these designs on the masks. They are yours forever." The masks with these designs and the *aulu*'s song remind the audience of their obligation to care for dependent members of their community.

STORYTELLING

Although anyone can tell a story, there are standards of excellence that set some storytellers apart as especially knowledgeable and skilled raconteurs. The criteria by which people judge the merits of a storyteller are the cultural accuracy and internal consistency of the tale and performance style. It is essential that the events recounted in *nasinga* and *pelunga* be considered historically accurate for they, together with genealogies, serve as charters of inheritance rights. Furthermore, care must be taken lest the members of a kin group be insulted by a version of historical events that makes uncomplimentary reference to the courage, generosity, or ability of an ancestor.

All stories, even those that are not considered historically accurate, should be realistic and internally consistent. If stories are not logically coherent, if descriptions of places are inaccurate, and if the details are not believable, then the audience will consider it to be a poor story and ignore any message it contains. There is, however, allowance for poetic license and a suspension of disbelief. In Kaliai stories, beings change form, people fly, the dead return to life, and humans interact with animals and spirits. People are not disturbed by this type of fiction. Nobody expects coconuts or cucumbers to turn into women, animals to talk, or dead bodies to reanimate themselves. These events do not make the stories less true, nor do they diminish the impact of a message about greed, envy, and the difficulty of human relations. It is essential that a good story accurately describe geographical locations and that it be culturally true: that it be consistent with customary belief, practice, and experience. All bays, reefs, rivers, and other landmarks in Kaliai are named, and people are intimately familiar with the physical geography of their homeland. So if people in a story voyage from one point to another, or if a hunt occurs on a named tract of land, then the details of preparing for and executing the trip or the hunt must be accurate, and the features attributed to the named places must be accurately described, even if the events recounted are fantastic.

A story should be internally consistent as well as accurate in detail. Poor performers of *ninipunga* may attempt to fit together incomplete bits and pieces of unrelated stories. The result is often a conglomerate of unconnected themes and a confusing number of characters who are irrelevant to one another or to any central story theme. An accomplished storyteller may be creative and innovative in combining themes from several stories, but the result must be coherent and internally consistent.

A Kaliai storyteller is a performer as well as a store of knowledge. If raconteurs are to hold an audience's interest, they should not break the continuity of the story or cause the audience to be conscious of their presence by pausing to search for names or facts, by laughing at the humor in the story, or by engaging in extraneous conversation or commentary. Furthermore, accomplished storytellers use more than language to communicate the events of the tale to their audience. *Pelunga* and *ninipunga*, particularly, are performed as one-actor dramas. Storytellers do not paraphrase their characters' speeches but speak for them in the appropriate voice. They may use exaggerated body language to convey actions such as swimming, climbing, or peering into the distance and accompany songs with rhythmic drumming, tapping, or even dance. All these actions draw the audience into a well-executed performance.

THEMES IN FOLKTALES

Although some folktales recount fantastic events, they also emphasize themes that are socially important: sharing food, the significance of premonitions, and the causes and consequences of suicide. Sharing food is basic to Kaliai social interaction and is a right of kinship. People who are related through women share foods that do not require cooking, especially coconuts, bananas, and sugar cane—foods loved by children. People who are related through men share root crops, especially taro—foods that gives strength. The obligation to feed visitors is a topic of speeches made by village leaders and is a theme that runs through many stories. Folktales also teach that a considerate, generous person will attract a mate and allies, while everyone will avoid a stingy, greedy, thoughtless person.

One tenet of Kaliai wisdom is that people should respect strong premonitions and should not pressure others to ignore them. In stories, when one is insensitive to and overrides the strong negative premonitions of another, the result is often injury, violent death, or suicide. A person who commits suicide is a victim of the acts of others. This is expressed in the phrase that people often use to describe a suicide: "She was killed by talk." In real life and in stories, a person who has been shamed, abused, or slandered by her in-laws may kill herself. Suicide is not common in Kaliai, but when it happens, it has significant impact on the community. Customarily a person may kill himself by hanging or by drinking a poison made from vines or household bleach. If the suicide victim is thought to have been "killed with talk," the person held culpable must pay compensation to the dead person's relatives. Alternatively, the community may judge that a suicide victim's own relatives bear some responsibility for the death. The idea that a person's kin may be culpable in a suicide's death is specifically expressed in tragic folktales when a character who is about to die asks, "Brother (or Sister, Father . . .), why you have killed me?"

CHALLENGES OF THE MODERN WORLD

Until the middle of the twentieth century, almost no Kaliai were literate, and there was no formal system of education. Today's schools teach the curricula of the developed world. In the past children learned their society's history, ethical norms, and rules of appropriate human behavior informally and often through entertainment. Transmission of Kaliai culture depended on elders passing their memories and stories to the young. This process continues. As entertainers, historians, and teachers, storytellers were and still are critical to the preservation of Kaliai society and culture.

In addition to our publications, one can find information on Kaliai folklore on the web. See, for example, the site www.arts.uwaterloo.ca/ANTHRO/rwpark/WNB/WestNewBritain.html for full texts of "The Story of Gavu" and "Akono and Silimala" as well as other stories.

BIBLIOGRAPHY

Counts, Dorothy Ayers. 1980. Akro and Gagandewa: A Melanesian Myth. *Journal of the Polynesian Society* 89.1: 33–65.

Counts, Dorothy Ayers, and David R. Counts. 2003 (1982). *The Tales of Laupu*. Boroko, PNG: Institute of Papua New Guinea Studies.

Dorothy Ayers Counts and David R. Counts

KEWA

GEOGRAPHY AND HISTORY

The Kewa people number some 50,000 and live in dispersed nucleated settlements in the Sugu River Valley in the Southern Highlands of Papua New Guinea. The climate here is tropical, but the high altitude makes for a comfortable range of temperatures. There is no marked rainy or dry season, though there are wet periods during which torrential rain may fall for days at a stretch. Sweet potato is the staple, supplemented by taro, plantains, bananas, greens, and many varieties of grasses, wild fruit, and nuts. Small game abounds in the area, but larger marsupials and birds, especially cassowaries, are no longer so commonly found. Bush rats and small birds provide a good source of protein, as do wild fowl eggs and fresh river fish. As in other parts of the highlands, the pig is the domesticated animal.

The Kewa are organized in patrilineal clans within overarching tribes. Clans and tribes are the land-owning units, though plots of garden land are held in the name of individual men. War was endemic in the past, driving clans out of their land and into alliances with friendly clans who made their own land available to them. In this egalitarian but intensely competitive society which lacks inherited chiefly offices, any man may achieve the status of "big man" if he displays the required personal qualities, but he will lose that status if his followers abandon him. Being a "leader among equals," a Kewa big man must maintain the kinship ideology of the equality of all clan brothers, and this requirement acts as a check on overbearing leaders. Women may not achieve the leadership status open to men, but "strong" women have enhanced reputations and are treated with respect. Men may take several wives, for whom they must offer brideprice. Residence is patrivirilocal, which means that on marriage women are expected to move to their husband's village and make gardens on his land.

New Guinea was administered by **Australia** until its independence in 1975. The Kewa area became pacified in the 1950s, and Christian missionaries followed on the heels of government outstations. People tell of how the "little Father" sprinkled holy water on the spirit houses, which he said they must pull down and never rebuild. The Evangelical Church of Papua is now strong in the area, though Catholic, Methodist, Lutheran, and Seventh-Day Adventist churches are also well-represented. The indigenous religions, based on ancestral cults (*rimbu*) and malevolent bush sprites (*rarinelli*) as well as a pantheon of fertility and sky deities, have all but disappeared, though some beliefs in witchcraft and magic (especially divination and the possibility to harm others by bearing grudges) remain.

The central event in the Kewa social cycle is the periodic pig feast, when pigs are killed and pork is exchanged in ceremonial presentations which establish the names of big men and clans. Traditionally the event brought together religious beliefs and political concerns, affirming clan ideologies while discharging war debts to allies and obligations to relatives by marriage. While pig kills may now be held to inaugurate new church buildings rather than cult houses and are reported to be smaller in scale than formerly, they nevertheless remain vehicles for prestige. Their orchestration concentrates and distributes resources while extending political relations. All the

A pig feast, the central event in the Kewa social cycle. (© Danny Lehman/CORBIS)

verbal art forms described in the following sections contain references to the pig kill as a core metaphor for Kewa cultural values.

MYTHS

Kewa myths, known as *lindi*, deal with both social and cosmological themes. They tell of the origin of the earth, sky, water, flora and fauna, and humans and society and comment on social roles and the crucial human cycles such as birth, death, and maturation. They narrate fantastic events of people who turn into mountains, birds, or marsupials, die and come back to life or conceive by swallowing wasps, or magically conjure up pigs and pearlshells. They depict men and women who, despite their magical powers, abide by the real-life Kewa sexual division of labor, yet men do not dominate women and are punished if they offend their wives. With the exception of myths that juxtapose proper with improper behavior through a good wife and a bad wife, most myths depict marriage as monogamous. The dyad is the crucial cultural unit. Some myths tell of two brothers who desire to marry the same woman. They pull her in opposite directions until she is torn in two, then they turn into birds and fly away. Cosmological messages are thus inextricably intertwined with social ones.

The two key themes of Kewa myths are **gender** relations and broader relations of power. In relation to the latter, *lindi* suggest that ascribed statuses are no less contingent than achieved ones. They question the legitimacy of any hierarchy by showing that those in charge of the stability of social organization may in fact jeopardize it, whether through incompetence, weakness, pride, insatiability, or just bloody-mindedness. They show that older brothers are not necessarily wiser or better than younger brothers and that parents can be ogres that kill and eat their children. Concerning gender relations, *lindi* suggest that claims to self-sufficiency by one sex, such as assertions that one sex is capable of fulfilling all the requirements of ritual and social reproduction, will have catastrophic effects and that failure properly to "complete" the opposite sex (through courting songs and marriage practices) will result in a barren single-sex world and eventually the end of the human species.

Myths thus encode alternative social structures that both reinforce and threaten order. Intergenerational conflict, fraternal antagonism, and treachery in gender relations emerge as arenas in which order as a particular configuration that does not represent all interests may be challenged. In effect, myths expose order as a fiction that is menacing rather than comforting, upholding a hierarchy whose ultimate weapon is the teeth of the ogre rather than the wrath of the gods. Here the spirit world is humanized and human abilities are exaggerated, the gap between spirits and humans is narrowed, and the contest between them is transposed to a political rather than a celestial realm.

Out of this rich corpus people create specific cultural meanings in *re agele* (base-story). *Re agele* are treated as true accounts, yet they narrate events no less fantastic than *lindi*. The very same stories are told as *lindi* on one occasion and *re agele* on another, when the narrator wishes to establish a claim to land or a special relationship to other clans. These origin stories, inoffensive when told as myths, now become contestable. For example, the story of Rau concerns a self-contained man with no anus who is tricked by his future brother-in-law into sitting on a sharp piece of bamboo, making an opening in his body. As a *lindi*, this is a story of the origin of social relations. But when Rau becomes a man of clan X and his brother-in-law a man of village Y where the operation takes place, the clan X narrators who are telling the story are making a political claim that clan Z (which also traces a link to village Y) will immediately counter. Another myth tells of two or three sisters who become impregnated when they sit on the cool roots of a large shade tree. One sister then marries the other sister's son and begets many clans. The details of place, clan, and number of sisters and sons depend on who is telling the story and for what purpose. Telling it as a *re agele*, a narrator of clan M who is friendly with clan N but has differences with clan O will omit reference to the shared arboreal birth of clan O ancestor, while clan O may argue that clan M has transposed the episode to N's village out of a desire to invent a kinship link with that clan. *Lindi* and *re agele* thus illustrate the vital transformational qualities of folklore.

Songs

Threnodies, pig-killing songs, and war-decorations songs show the continuity and transformation between *temali* (cry-song), *tupale* (clan songs) and *au yaisia* (war-decorations songs). *Temali* are threnodies composed on a death (or to mark an unhappy event). As they arise directly out of personal experience, they have an immediate poignancy for everyone. They stress the beauty, strength, and clan territory of the deceased, but as personal attributes rather than group ones. What is highlighted is the love and care that went into the creation of that individual. The excerpts below are from *temali* composed by a middle-aged woman.

On her mother's death:

> My mother, at your ground at Kalepenalo
> I did not come to drink your breast milk;
> I tarried in a foreign place.
> My mother's clan, my brother's iron roof,
> the thatched roof at my mother's ground at Korame,
> I did not come to drink your breast milk.
> I am a woman and couldn't. . . .
> A daughter of Sugu Maliesi clan,
> I burn areca palm bark at our ground of Ai.

On her foster father's death:

> At his ground in Yone my father
> protected this stray possum, this waif. . . .
> At my father's land at Pererekepa
> I burn the bark of trees.
> My thoughts fasten on him. . . .
> the thatch roof, the sides
> of Tiarepa son's houses burn.
> I still see the feasts.

The daughter foregrounds the nurturing abilities of her mother, but the word "breast" is prefaced by *worua*, an inedible banana thought to provide food for the spirits. Thus the mother is envisioned as nurturing her child from her own body but by magical means, while the father feeds the child with conventional food outside his own body. In both songs the singer's relationship with the mourned person is stressed. Both songs contain references to the burning of treebark, which is a metaphor for holding a ceremonial pig kill. The foster father's song stresses his kindness in looking after the singer, who refers to herself as a stray possum protected by a big man. Cassowaries, marsupials, and other wild game were traditionally given by the bridegroom to the bride and her parents, and women are often referred to as marsupials or cassowaries.

The singing of *temali* has the power to alter the framing of interactions. Some weeks after a man had left his prospective bride to lodge with his brother while he tried to collect the brideprice, his brother tired of the extra burden and asked the woman to leave. On her way out of the settlement she broke down and wept at the spot where the two men's father's coffin had recently lain. Her prospective brother-in-law, recalling the threnody she had sung for his father at the time, was moved and called her back.

Temali have exactly the same melodic line as *tupale*, "clan songs," their cultural meaning differentiated only by the context of their performance. *Tupale* are sung on public occasions, when the group presents itself as a line of brothers killing pigs for the glory of their name. Men in full decorations and carrying axes and maracas arrange themselves in groups of four and enter the men's house. One pair facing the other, they dance in formation while singing their *tupale*. The singing is competitive, not punctuated by tears as in its original *temali* form. The soloist begins by singing the first couple of lines in the high-pitched head voice used in all singing. Then the chorus joins in. The last word of the stanza leads to a long drawn out "ooo," which is dropped and picked up again with a sharp, short ending. The prized voice must sound sweet and melodious while pitched at a high note without switching into falsetto, and the words must be well-enunciated and audible.

The *temali* and *tupale* songs trace a continuum from undisguised grief at the death of a relative to concerns with prestige and social standing. *Au yaisia* complete the cycle. These are pig-killing songs, impersonal claims of the clan's strength. When a clan holds a pig kill, it must discharge debts to allies who have helped in past wars. The host, adorned with black war paint, dance four abreast, interspersed with rows of very young girls with bodies and faces painted red. The men swing their axes as they sing the *au yaisia* that recall old traditions and contain self-congratulatory sentiments for obligations fulfilled. When the allies arrive, they crouch at the bottom of the hill. The hosts group themselves at the top of the hill, where the pigs are lined up and the pearlshells and bank notes are displayed on bamboo sticks, and their spokesman calls out the name of the group which is to receive pigs. Those summoned charge up the hill with war cries and brandishing spears and axes. One of them throws the proffered pig over his shoulder, and the whole group runs down again to the men's house. Below is a sample of the *au yaisia* sung on this occasion.

HOSTS: We are like small quail
sitting in abundant grass.

ALLIES: Orphan boy, as many men
as there is wild cane in the bush
come to see you.

Orphan boy, I planted you
and you grew.

HOSTS: I follow in my father's footsteps
and compensate with cassowaries.

We are just ten men; yet we have made a fence
and cultivate gardens.

Strong armlets of those long buried
this now I will do.

The longhouse pig killing
I have learned from my father.

Brother, fetch the leaf of the *arimuka*;
We shall cook something.

Only fathers, sons, men appear here. The songs have been abstracted, and the message is that the related group of males manages the events being commemorated. The affective, emotional matters of the kin group and domestic unit have no place here. The allies claim full credit for the host's social reproduction ("Orphan boy, I planted you / and you grew"), while the hosts stress their achievements through link to their male ancestors. Alongside this political transformation of meaning and reference, a musical transformation has also occurred. While *temali* and *tupale* are sweet, plaintive songs sung in a high-pitched voice, *au yaisia* have a warlike, blood-curdling sound. They can be seen as examples of formalized language whose purpose is not to communicate but to make a statement about authority and intent.

Each sex has its own courtship songs, traditionally performed at pig-killing celebrations. The power of men's *rome*, which are spoken rather than sung, hinges on their ability to affect feeling and, through feeling, actions. Their task is to persuade the listener that the scenario they describe (the sexual union of singer and listener) is desirable. Men stress the power of their *rome* as something they have willed and which is important to their description as men. What attracts women, they say, is the power of the words they use.

I look at your face
and it is as if I am looking
at a parrot or a *yarity* bird.
The stars shake my ground at Yone;
I must go, farewell.

I tell this *rome* to you and you listen.
By the fence the sugar cane ripens quickly.
We have ripened like the sugar cane.
What shall we do?

Up there by the bank in the glade
the river Yaro makes a lapping noise.
Your head my head we put together as one.
Now what shall we do?

I tell this *rome* to you and you listen.
Many *wano* trees with teeth like little birds
are close to the house.
The Kewa child comes close to the house.
Sugar cane and pitpit
are almost at the house.

While men stress the power of words, women emphasize their bodies and performance. They insist that the power of their courtship songs to bring off love matches lies in the quality of each individual woman's performance, enhanced by her beautiful, decorated body. Women have to be looked at and their dancing admired. Its power coerces men to make gifts of shells and money to them.

The special cooking leaves are ready
but where are you?
Where has my netbag gone?
You've gone somewhere they say.
Where have you gone?

In our gardens at Yamu
Cordyline leaves grew in profusion,
But now they have been replanted
by the water at the coast.

As among the casuarinas,
so among the many men of Wata.
Their great shadows obscure the place
Yet Rame still stands out among them,
oil pours down his body.

Where many casuarinas cast shadows,
it becomes dark.
Though a man, I cannot call you so,
for at Yamu the areca palms are few.
Answer me!

At Yamu a new banana
will always replace the plucked one.
So just look, and go.

Red sugar cane at Yokere, if I cut you
it will be with a heavy heart.
So let the wind break you off
and lay you down before me.

This *wena yaisia* laments the disappearance of young men ("cordyline leaves"), who have gone to the coast as migrant laborers. By a metonymic substitution the netbag, a euphemism for the vagina, here refers to men, while the banana, a male crop, denotes women. The shortage of men is counterposed to the plenitude of women ("a new banana / will always replace the plucked one"). Dearth and plenty are juxtaposed in these songs; bachelorhood is barren and marriage fertile. Women subordinate the pig-killing imagery of the big man to the imagery of the sexually attractive husband. Their task is to "complete" men by a description of what would make them desirable marriage partners. While men propagate an image of themselves as persons with *rome* power that resides in strong words that achieve a social outcome by describing it, women complete this image by fusing and reaffirming men's various social, cultural, and reproductive roles.

CHALLENGES OF THE MODERN WORLD

By the 1990s, the influx of new genres and practices was altering these art forms in significant ways. Two new forms of technology have revolutionized local music making: the guitar and the transistor radio/cassette recorder. Though the songs sung to the accompaniment of the guitar tend to be church songs, the fact that they draw young people together means that they also function as courting songs. Three new narrative genres reflect attempts to grapple with new world orders and worldviews: Bible stories, the recounting of dreams, and mythologized accounts of historical events. The first genre is disseminated through abridged versions of the Bible, liberally illustrated with devils and the fires of hell. Kewa people appropriate these stories, as one big man did in his account of Noah's flood as a catastrophe caused by the pig-headedness of some young men, who had been to Mount Hagen (the largest Highlands town) and thought they knew everything.

For some Kewa men conversion to Christianity is mediated by powerful dreams which shake the old world to its foundations, maim the dreamers' physical bodies, and refashion them with a strength whose provenance is beyond the old Kewa world. Conversion thus becomes a transformation of the Bible message, empowering the dreamers as the chosen who receive life and become messiahs for those still benighted. While the traditional role of dreamers was to see into the future, the new dreaming is apocalyptic and transforms the dreamer.

Some mythologized accounts allude to the activities of rascals, gangs that seriously threaten public safety in Papua New Guinea. In one account a big man brings to heel a rascal who threatens the security of the village. The rascal behaves like the *lindi* trickster or skin changer, whose power the modern political leader neutralizes by appropriating the authority of the police force.

Two new types of heroes emerge from the last two genres, the religious visionary and the political leader, and their stories show them taking the Kewa into the twenty-first century. Women, meanwhile, make use of new political and educational opportunities to transform gender relations and claim a new kind of independence. The appearance of these new persons and leadership roles demonstrates that folklore is not a static category of outdated remnants from past eras. It can also be a vital force of a living culture, active in cultural transformations that incorporate and appropriate new practices and beliefs.

BIBLIOGRAPHY

Feld, Steven. 1990 (1982). *Sound and Sentiment: Birds, Weeping, Poetics, and Song In Kaluli Expression*. Philadelphia: University of Pennsylvania Press.

Josephides, Lisette. 1982. *Kewa Songs and Myths*. Boroko, PNG: Institute of Papua New Guinea Studies.

———. 1985. *The Production of Inequality: Gender and Exchange Among the Kewa*. London: Tavistock.

———. 1998. Myths of Containment, Myths of Extension: Creating Relations Across Boundaries. In *Fluid Ontologies: Myth, Ritual, and Philosophy in the Highlands of Papua New Guinea*, edited by Lawrence R. Goldman and Chris Ballard. Westport, CT: Bergin and Garvey. 125–141.

Leroy, John. 1985. *Fabricated World: An Interpretation of Kewa Tales*. Vancouver: University of British Columbia Press.

Lisette Josephides

MALUKU

GEOGRAPHY AND HISTORY

An arc of islands in eastern Indonesia, Maluku, or the Moluccas, lies between the larger land masses of Sulawesi to the west and New Guinea to the east. Maluku is a seafaring society. The population of around two million is scattered over dozens of islands and hundreds of miles of deep sea. The Banda Sea has some of the deepest trenches in the Pacific. The islands themselves are characterized by substantial variation in topography and culture. The larger islands of Halmahera, Buru, Seram, and Tanimbar have a mountainous hinterland covered with dense forest. Population is concentrated around the coast. Most of the other islands, many of them volcanic, are much smaller. The tropical climate ensures high rainfall in the rainy season, during which time the generally calm seas become rough, and travel and fishing are difficult. Partly as a result of this potential for isolation, cultural tradition varies among individual islands or island groups. This essay will give a sense of general significant elements in this diversity of tradition and will focus primarily on central and southeast Maluku.

Most rural Moluccans are fishers and/or subsistence farmers. The staple foods are traditionally sago palm and root crops such as cassava and sweet potato. The Spice Islands of European legend, Maluku is also a source of cloves and nutmeg, which are still grown primarily as cash crops, but no longer on the large scale of the colonial period. For coastal residents, the sea provides an astonishing variety of fish and other marine resources and plays a central part in the practical and cultural life of those communities.

In many parts of Maluku the most significant unit of political organization is the village. Individual villages may have their own versions of local origin myths, songs, and dances. Within the village, the most significant category is the *soa*, the definition of which varies between areas but which is generally understood as a descent category related to land rights.

Examples of broader units of alliance occur. In North Maluku during the precolonial period, the sultanates of Bacan, Jailolo, and especially Ternate and Tidore—known as the four mountains of Maluku—formed a powerful federation that exercised some degree of control or influence over large areas of north and even central Maluku. Colonial policy, followed by Indonesian government centralization, has reduced the official power of these positions to a minimum, though the sultans of Ternate and Tidore remain powerful symbolic figures.

Another form of regional identification is the *Siwa-Lima* moiety system, based on the numbers nine and five. It is thought to have encompassed all societies in central and much of southeast Maluku and provided opportunities for a successful leader to claim control over all local groups affiliating with the same moiety. *Lima* villages are associated with resistance to the Dutch and an affiliation with Islam, while *Siwa* villages were converts to Christianity who had a closer relationship with the Europeans. This system has largely ceased to function, but remnants of the *Siwa-Lima* alignments remain in some ritual performance and in intervillage relations.

Maluku is home to dozens of distinct oral languages as well as several dialects. In many areas of central Maluku, especially closest to the city, local languages, or *bahasa tanah* (literally, "language of the land"), are largely forgotten. Although fragments of the old languages may remain in ritual chants or songs, it is common for the meaning of the words to have been lost. Neighboring villages may share a common language, but this is no guarantee of peaceable relations. Long-running, often bitter arguments between villages, commonly with a focus on border disputes, characterize the region. A system of intervillage alliance, known as *pela-gandong*, links villages in a quasi-fraternal relationship, often as a result of earlier conflict. Many myths explain the foundation of villages in terms of a group of siblings going their separate ways: a younger sibling-older sibling relationship between villages therefore can affect the way their inhabitants view each other.

Despite their liminal, even isolated position, the Moluccan islands have a long and colorful history of contact with a range of outside interests. Chinese, Javanese, and Arab traders have long been aware of the attractions of the locally grown spices. References to spices appeared in Chinese courts two thousand years ago. However it was the arrival of the Europeans in the sixteenth century and the subsequent gradual increase in European cultural influence (especially from the Portuguese and subsequently the Dutch, who ruled Maluku for over 350 years) that have had the most significant impact on local tradition and folklore. In most cases colonial influence extended to missionary activity, administration, and education, but Maluku has also been the scene of violent confrontation between natives and settlers. In the Banda Islands, the center of the nutmeg trade, for example, a Bandanese revolt against Dutch exploitation and brutality in 1621 resulted in the bloody slaughter or exile of almost the entire indigenous population of the islands. The nutmeg groves were quickly repopulated, mostly with indentured labor from Java, **Bali**, and elsewhere. Bandanese culture nowadays retains some elements of indigenous cultural tradition, though its practitioners are unlikely to be direct descendants of the pre-massacre inhabitants.

Since Indonesia became independent in 1945, Maluku has been subject to a new external authority in Jakarta. Under President Suharto's drive to develop the country, official rhetoric condemned many nomadic forest peoples in Indonesia as backward and primitive. Government policy encouraged these groups to settle permanently in coastal regions. A program of migration of people from overcrowded Java and Bali to less densely populated regions in the outer islands led to substantial numbers of newcomers settling in Maluku, especially in Seram and Halmahera. As development progressed, the largest town in Maluku, Ambon, grew to be a bustling regional center and attracted urban migrants from other parts of Indonesia, especially Sulawesi. The result is in many places a mixed population with a range of cultures and traditions.

RELIGIOUS BELIEF

According to official Indonesian sources, almost the whole of the population of Maluku follows Islam, Protestantism, or Catholicism. Islam arrived around the thirteenth or fourteenth century, and Catholicism followed soon after with the arrival of

Portuguese traders in 1512. Protestantism, which is today the predominant Christian presence in Maluku, was brought to the islands in the seventeenth century by Dutch missionaries.

In practice, particularly in rural areas, traditional customs and beliefs intersect readily with the ritual calendar of a major religion. The central role of the village founders and other ancestors in shaping ritual practice and traditional law has not been completely superseded by the teachings of Christianity or Islam. An origin myth from North Maluku relates how a Muslim leader married a woman who was actually a representative of indigenous spiritual power, thereby uniting external political authority with local forms of authority. In Maluku today this division is often exemplified in the roles of *kepala desa* (village head—a central government imposition) and *tuan tanah* (an indigenous landlord). While two belief systems may operate apparently harmoniously in many cases, greater authority may be attributed to one or the other in different areas of social life. For example, in Tanimbar, offerings to ancestors are made before a sago palm is harvested or before certain areas of the forest are entered. However, a curse on one village causing many children to fall sick was exorcised by the Protestant priest, and periodic prohibitions on the harvest of certain sea produce are marked with a joint ceremony officiated by both priest and *tuan tanah*.

In 1999, a simple argument on a city bus sparked widespread violence and plunged Maluku into a bloody conflict, pitting Christians against their Muslim neighbors and indigenous Moluccans against migrants. Over 7,000 people died, and hundreds of thousands of people fled their homes. The violence extended even to tiny islands and remote communities. It is widely accepted that external elements, among them a Muslim jihad force, Christian gang leaders, and the Indonesian government and security forces themselves, were involved in precipitating and prolonging the conflict. By late 2003, the situation had stabilized enough for the state of civil emergency to be lifted in central Maluku, though sporadic violence has continued. The long-term implications of the violence have yet to be properly determined, but it is clear that these events will shape people's understanding of local cultural heritage and ownership in dramatic ways.

MYTHS

Myths of origin are a central part of Maluku folklore. Due to their localized nature, generalizations are difficult to make. In central Maluku, the island of Seram is seen as *Nusa Ina*, the mother island, from which all people in the region originated. One version of the story has much in common with origin myths from other areas and includes an account of the origins of the Siwa-Lima moiety. Nunusaku was a mountain in west Seram where a banyan tree with three branches grew. Three brothers survived a great flood by climbing the mountain. When the waters receded, they made their way down the mountain, each walking in the direction indicated by one of the branches of the tree. These were the areas of the three rivers, Tala, Eti, and Sopalewa. It is said that all the people of Seram descend from these three brothers. The Ulisiwa (Patasiwa) people descend from the oldest brother, the Ulilima (Patalima) from the second brother, and the Uliassa from the youngest. The Uliassa people settled on the islands just south of Seram, now known as the Lease Islands. Another myth, collected by the Portuguese in north Maluku around 1544, has the line of kings of Maluku originating from four serpent eggs which hatched to produce leaders, not only of Moluccan islands, but of parts of Sulawesi to the west and Papua to the east. This indicates the extent to which, despite their apparently remote location, the people of Maluku have long had connections with other areas.

Myths of origin do not relate solely to indigenous inhabitants of Maluku. A story from Buru, also in central Maluku, explains why many leaders on the island are descended from migrants from Sulawesi. A leader from Buton (in Sulawesi) suggested to an indigenous Buru leader a way to decide who would be *raja*: each would collect a bucket of sand, and whoever had the heaviest bucket would be *raja*. He then added, "Because you are from the land, you walk landward to get sand, and because I am from the sea, I will walk seaward." Of course, the wet sand nearer the sea was heavier, and the Butonese leader became *raja*.

MUSIC, SONG, AND DANCE

Music and song play an important role in everyday life as well as in traditional art forms. In general, musical performance is not restricted to any particular group within the population, and Moluccans are known for their excellent singing voices. In Ambon, before the recent conflict, a thriving local recording industry ensured that both traditional folksongs and more recent compositions were widely known. Many folksongs in Ambon with lyrics in Ambonese **Malay** speak of homesickness for these beautiful islands on the part of people who are away from home. Images of sailing and the sea are therefore common. Other themes explored through these songs include *kawin lari*, a traditional form of marriage similar to ritualized elopement. Many of the songs evince a strong sense of location. Some are little more than a list of place names.

Dance also forms an important part of folk tradition in Maluku. There are a number of distinctive dances, including the *sulureka-reka*, where two pairs of bamboo poles (*gaba-gaba*) are held at right angles to each other, banged on the ground, and snapped together rhythmically while successive dancers try their skill at skipping in the gaps between the poles. Several other dances or physical rituals are performed under trance, including the well-known *bambu gila* in Ambon, which involves a magic bamboo pole bucking and diving, and the Combalele from Haruku, where participants are stabbed with daggers or spears but appear to suffer no lasting injury. In modern-day Indonesia it is common to see some of these traditional dances performed on state occasions such as Independence Day or in performances for tourists. They may also form a part of *panas pela* ceremonies to "warm," or reaffirm, *pela* connections between villages.

Cakalele is a family of related dances performed throughout north and central Maluku and in the Minahasa region of north Sulawesi. The name *cakalele* is said to derive from a Minahasan word for "shout," and these dances are considered to be war dances, perhaps connected previously with headhunting traditions. In Banda the dancers are known by military titles. The dance is usually performed by men (in Seram, the dancers are said to be under possession by spirits) carrying a *parang*

A group of dancers carry old Portuguese armor, which they use in their performance. Banda Islands, Maluku, Indonesia. (© Jack Fields/CORBIS)

(machete-style knife with a curved blade) or a spear and a narrow *selawaku* shield. The dancers are accompanied by drums, small gongs, and a series of chants. In Banda, each of the recognized *adat* villages—that is, the traditional settlements— has its own *cakalele* troupe, with a different costume and either five or nine dancers, according to whether the village is associated with the *siwa* or *lima* moiety.

It would be a mistake to assume that the *cakalele* relates exclusively to indigenous symbolic systems. In Banda, some dancers wear a Portuguese-style helmet, called a *kapsete*, and one dancer is given the title *kapitan*, relating to Portuguese military rank. In some Bandanese villages—those with a strong link with Islam—the *cakalele* dancers are accompanied by the *maruka*, young girls clothed in white and said to symbolize the purity of Islam. In the mid-1990s, a hotelier in Banda presented the *cakalele* as a re-enactment of the 1621 massacre of the indigenous population by the Dutch. This same hotelier, however, was also involved in the resurrection of *cakalele* and *kora-kora* performances in the 1970s, after they had lapsed during the war, particularly for tourist performances. Certainly, *cakalele* today tends to have a less sacred character than it seems to have had in the past. This incorporation of European forms and meanings exemplifies both the characteristic religious syncretism of Moluccan cultural life, and the strategic, not to say political, aspect of the interpretation of folk traditions in contemporary Maluku.

ARTS, CRAFTS, AND ARCHITECTURE

Houses in Maluku are traditionally made of bamboo, palm leaves, and other materials readily available but not especially durable. Architecture therefore is not a major feature of Maluku culture. In Tanimbar in southeast Maluku, ethnographers in the mid-twentieth century documented the tall houses constructed on stilts from the hardwoods of the forest areas. These, however, are no longer seen and are poorly remembered, as are the intricately carved designs with which Tanimbarese and the inhabitants of the islands at the far southwest of the archipelago would adorn the prows of their sailing boats and altars in their houses. These can now be seen only in museums in other parts of Indonesia and in **The Netherlands**. However, memories survive of the designs of wooden ancestor statues carved in Tanimbar, often from ebony, and placed at sacred sites in the forest around the village. These stylized figures have influenced new, more naturalistic statue designs in recent years aimed at the souvenir market, which has enabled traditional carving skills to endure.

Other aspects of visual art are significant in Maluku culture. In traditional Seram societies, boys from the *Patasiwa* moiety were subject to initiation into secret societies called *kakean*, after which they would be tattooed with signs relating to their tribe. Women also received tattoos relating to initiation. Although prohibited by the Dutch, tattooing was still practiced secretly for some years and *kakean* tattoos were observed in Seram as late as 1970. The motifs used varied slightly from tribe to tribe but often consisted of a series of curved lines and dots often symbolizing a frigate bird. Other common motifs were the sun, moon, stars, and other designs that are thought to have been related to headhunting traditions. It is uncertain whether the custom continues today, though tattoos with designs relating to contemporary political conditions are common among young Christian men. Although other areas of eastern Indonesia are better-known for their weaving traditions, distinctive *ikat* designs can be found in several parts of Maluku. In Tanimbar, both antique and modern *ikat* pieces are prized family possessions and an important part of kinship exchange cycles.

Because it is an archipelago, boats and sailing craft are important in many Maluku societies, both as modes of transport and in symbolic and ritual senses. The practical and symbolic purposes are closely intertwined. In Banda, for example, the stylized Kora Kora war canoe is intricately decorated and used in ceremonies and on special occasions as well as for racing. Kora Kora were also used by the Dutch, who at the height of the Moluccan spice trade sent out fleets of the boats to find and destroy "illicit" clove and nutmeg trees that threatened their monopoly. In Tanimbar, village government structures are imagined as parts of a boat and its crew: captain, lookout, mast, and quartermaster, for example. In the village of Sangliat Dol, a huge stone boat at the top of a flight of steps is the only remaining physical representation of an image that has strong figurative associations in many other Tanimbarese villages. In the village of Ilngei, this "*adat* boat" has a name, Sori Wolanalan, and though nowadays a symbolic, rather than physical presence, the boat is supposed to be that on which the founders of the village first arrived from a neighboring island.

CHALLENGES OF THE MODERN WORLD

These examples suggest that much of Maluku's folklore is today less widely practiced and remembered in the islands than it was half a century ago. One place, however, where many traditional practices are carefully documented and passed on to subsequent generations is in the Netherlands. A population of around 50,000 Dutch Moluccans, descended from migrants who arrived shortly after Indonesian independence around 1950, observe strictly the taboos and regulations surrounding relationships between people from villages linked by the bond of *pela-gandong*, which is less widely heeded in Maluku itself. Similarly, young third-generation Dutch Moluccans have a strong interest in "tribal" tattoos, heavily influenced by traditional designs from Seram. Any study of Moluccan folklore should take into account the development and interpretation of traditional stories, songs, and art within the Dutch Moluccan population.

It is impossible to identify clearly a time when indigenous tradition existed independently of wider forces. In fact, Maluku has been at the center of global trade and cultural exchange for many centuries. The region's rich cultural resources derive from constant interaction with an eclectic range of influences. Under the New Order, state occasions were increasingly the context within which folk traditions were performed, and represented a shift from a focus on local histories and meanings to a national framework within which Maluku folk tradition is but one example of centrally prescribed Indonesian cultural diversity. In view of the recent conflict, it is certain that cultural traditions and what they contribute to a sense of identity and belonging will be examined in a new way. What is less certain is how this will affect the folk heritage of the region in the future.

BIBLIOGRAPHY

Andaya, Leonard Y. 1993. *The World of Maluku: Eastern Indonesia in the Early Modern Period.* Honolulu: University of Hawai'i Press.

Bartels, D. 1977. *Guarding the Invisible Mountain: Intervillage Alliances, Religious Syncretism and Ethnic Identity among Ambonese Christians and Moslems in the Moluccas.* Ithaca, NY: Cornell University Press.

de Jonge, Nico, and Toos van Dijk. 1995. *Forgotten Islands of Indonesia: The Art and Culture of the Southeast Moluccas.* Singapore: Periplus Editions.

Valeri, V. 1989. Reciprocal Centers: the Siwa-Lima System in the Central Moluccas. In *The Attraction of Opposites: Thought and Society in the Dualistic Mode*, edited by D. Maybury-Lewis and U. Almagor. Ann Arbor: University of Michigan Press. 117–142.

Visser, L. E., ed. 1994. *Halmahera and Beyond: Social Science Research in the Moluccas.* Leiden: KITLV Press.

Nicola Frost

MOLUCCAS. *See* Maluku

TAIRORA

GEOGRAPHY AND HISTORY

During the earliest phase of contact with the outside world in the 1920s, speakers of the language now called "Tairora" (currently about 14,000 living in the Kainantu District of the Eastern Highlands Province of Papua New Guinea) received their label from European gold prospectors and colonial administrators who applied to all groups the name of one settlement. People, perhaps ancestral to Tairora, had occupied the region for at least 18,000 years first by hunting and gathering, then from

A Tairora hamlet with traditional house. (Photograph by Terence E. Hays)

about 5,000 years ago by settling and adopting horticulture. In general, oral traditions point to Tairora homelands to the west and southwest, but their territory abuts those of other language groups on all sides, and many different sources have contributed to their current population and culture through intermarriage and extensive trade systems.

Tairora terrain is highly diverse with the north dominated by large, open grasslands at elevations of 1,625 to 1,880 meters above sea level and steep forest- or grass-covered ridges in the south, where the Kratke Mountain Range culminates in Mount Piora at 3,450 meters. The climate is fairly uniform throughout the region with cool nights, warm days, and relatively wet and dry seasons that alternate with the southeast and northwest monsoons, respectively.

In the north, settlements are generally closer together and more nucleated than in the south, where they tend to be hamlet clusters about a half-day's walk apart. Most settlements are found at elevations between 1,500 and 1,900 meters and, until recent population surges, typically had 200 to 250 residents. Traditionally, elevated or ridge-top locations were preferred for defensive purposes. Except for a few groups living in the open grasslands of the north, settlements were surrounded with high palisades for the same reason. Until the 1960s in the north, and later in much of the south, Tairora settlements focused on one or more large men's houses, with women's houses clustered downslope and seclusion houses—used by women during menstruation and childbirth—separated from living areas and usually surrounded by their own fences.

Although in recent decades Tairora have adopted imported Western foods obtained from markets (especially in the north), most people still depend on a wide variety of gardens for their subsistence. Sweet potatoes are the dominant crop, though yams and taro are also important, especially in the south. Tairora are sophisticated horticulturalists, employing fallowing, mounding of sweet potatoes, and ditching of gardens. Other crops include legumes, maize, bananas, sugar cane, and leafy greens. Tree crops include pandanus nuts and, in some areas, betel nuts. Domestic pigs are a major source of protein, but they generally are killed and the pork distributed only on ceremonial occasions. Hunting and collecting also yield food, especially in the more heavily forested south where both game and wild plant foods are more abundant. Everywhere, however, game has special salience in rituals and ceremonial gift-giving. The forests, and to a lesser extent the grasslands, also serve as the sources of countless raw materials for manufacture, medicines, and ornamentation.

Traditionally, people had no occupational specializations, with each man able to build houses and fences, clear garden land, hunt, and fashion his own weapons and implements just as all women were gardeners and skilled in making string bags, sleeping mats, and items of clothing for both sexes. Construction tasks are still assigned as male responsibilities as are clearing garden land, fencing, and ditching. Women are charged with planting, weeding, and harvesting crops, with the exception of tree crops, bananas, sugar cane, yams, and taro, which are the province of males. Both sexes collect wild plant foods opportunistically.

All land, whether used for settlements, gardening, or its resources, is held by patrilineal descent groups. At birth, membership in one's father's lineage and clan is established, though residence in itself can blur such distinctions, especially in the north, where immigrants (such as refugees in time of war) were absorbed into existing groups. Clan members seldom act as a unit in ceremonies, exchange, or warfare. More often, it is the co-residents of a settlement who act as such. An egalitarian ethos pervades social life with an emphasis on individualism, though associations are strong among age mates of either sex.

Marriages are arranged through negotiations between clans and involve the payment of bridewealth to the woman's clan members. Settlements have high rates of endogamy, but substantial numbers of women in-marry from neighboring (often enemy) groups. Individuals of both sexes typically are assigned likely spouses while still in childhood, with formal betrothal deferred until young adulthood. A new bride usually moves into the house of her groom's mother while her husband builds a separate house for her. Polygyny is allowed, though few men have more than one wife. Co-wives typically live in different hamlets and usually object strongly to their husbands' polygyny. There are very few permanent bachelors, and virtually no women apart from albinos and lepers go through life unmarried.

Until recently out of concern for the supposed weakening effects of contact with women, all males past the age of ten or twelve lived together in men's houses. A woman's household would include one or more adult women (sometimes a mother and daughter or sisters), their uninitiated sons, and unmarried daughters. Responsibility for nurturing and socializing young children primarily falls on the women and older girls of a household, but once male children moved into their fathers' men's houses, these tasks were largely taken over by adult males. Girls work side by side with their mothers from an early age, while boys are allowed to roam freely with age mates until adolescence. Distraction and scoldings are used rather than physical punishment for young children, but older boys were sometimes disciplined severely in the men's house.

Traditional leadership was of a big-man type with individuals attaining stature through warfare and management of affairs between communities. Disputes—most often over sorcery accusations, failures to meet social obligations, marriage arrangements, land, and depredations of pigs—were settled in informal moots with the affected parties supported by kin and age mates. Traditionally, warfare was endemic throughout the Tairora region. Each settlement had traditional enemies among its immediate neighbors, though periods of peace were effected through formal ceremonies that often included intermarriage.

RELIGIOUS BELIEFS AND RITUALS

Tairora men decorated for a festival. (Photograph by Terence E. Hays)

The Tairora cosmos is filled with supernatural beings of a wide variety, including ghosts, monstrous human-like figures, nature spirits, and animal-like forest spirits, all of which figure prominently in folklore. Men's house rites drew on a generalized force available through ancestors, and individuals employed diverse types of magic. Knowledgeable elders of both sexes conducted rituals and ceremonies at the settlement level, and some individuals were noted diviners and shamans. Most individuals obtained and administered medicines from local materials themselves, though some individuals of both sexes were renowned diagnosticians and healers.

Life cycle ceremonies traditionally included feasts for babies after they emerged from seclusion houses and septum- and ear-piercing (for both sexes). First-menstruation and puberty rites and a two-stage sequence of male initiation ceremonies were occasions at which the recital of myths and folktales assumed an important role. Weddings were fairly casual affairs, mainly involving the transferal of bridewealth payments and feasting. Wakes, in contrast, were held for several days, at the conclusion of which the ghost possessed a local resident who transported it out of the settlement to begin its journey to the land of the dead, traditionally located to the northeast in the Markham River Valley, where it would live a life that replicated the ordinary world, complete with gardens and pigs. The corpse left behind was traditionally buried in a fenced grave on clan land.

MYTHS AND FOLKTALES

Several genres of oral literature provided evening household entertainment and instruction during ceremonies. Although much of it exists now only in the memories of elders, the Tairora possess a rich oral literature and traditionally told each other stories for a wide variety of reasons. All stories are called *huri*, but several different types can be distinguished.

Some stories, which we might call myths, have a sacred character and were told only under special circumstances to restricted audiences. Usually they deal with events that took place in a remote past when life was very different from that of contemporary times. The main purpose of these stories is to account for origins. For example, when a man and woman were about to marry, they were told myths that explain the origins of various customs they would be expected to follow after marriage, such as sleeping apart due to the dangers to men of too much contact with women. These stories were told to them separately in a men's house or women's seclusion house and were not to be repeated in the presence of young unmarried people. Similarly, at various stages of initiation for young men and during a puberty ceremony for young women, myths might be told to help them understand various rules they must observe in the next phases of their lives. These stories too were restricted to those people who were already at or beyond that stage in the life cycle.

Other stories were more public but tended to be told on particular occasions. These tales, which may be called legends, are placed in the past and often involve the activities of individuals who are thought to be direct ancestors of living people. These individuals may be presented as being responsible for establishing certain customs such as creating the longstanding salt trade with people to the south or for beginning particular settlements or lines of descent. Thus, like myths, they may deal with origins, but whereas a myth might explain how people first began to reproduce, a legend would account for the origins of a specific clan or its claims to a particular plot of land. Legends might be recounted as people tried to settle a dispute over garden land, providing anecdotal evidence that a given clan's ancestor had originally settled on that plot of ground.

A Tairora initiate decorated for presentation to his community. (Photograph by Terence E. Hays)

A third major type of *huri* is what may be referred to as folktales. These were the most public of all stories, often told for their entertainment value. While sitting around the fire at night, children might be told folktales to amuse them. But such stories also were used to teach various lessons at the same time they entertained the hearers. Folktales usually have simple plots with little elaboration of details, and they often employ humor to get across their messages.

Folktales sometimes mix together realistic and fanciful elements. For example, animals may be used to tell a story that could be about people, as when a flock of birds help a young boy stuck high in a tree only to be shot at by children; this is why birds fear people now. Whether people or animals are the main characters, folktales generally teach lessons about getting along with others, though these lessons are seldom stated explicitly. For example, some stories are basically about helping other people, whether such help is rewarded directly or not. In one such tale a man cures a woman of blindness and teaches her how to eat "real food" (that is, sweet potatoes and pork) after she had always lived on earthworms. His reward is that she marries him. In another, however, a man teaches another who only eats stones how to eat "real food" after removing the accumulated stones from his stomach. Here, the stone-eating man's improved state seems to be reward enough. Sometimes, help is given, but, due to the unthinking reactions of some, it is not likely to be offered again, as with the birds who rescued the boy stuck in the tree. Others give examples of how people can lose valuables by reacting without thinking about consequences or the feelings of others. In one tale, which resembles the "Swan Maiden" tale elsewhere in the world, a clump of wild ginger plants high in the forest turns into five young women, who take five young men as their husbands. Later, after one has given birth to a son, the boy's father in anger tells him he is "only the child of a flower." The mother and the other women take the boy back to the forest, where he transforms into a wild ginger plant and the women into pandanus nut trees. Obligations to others might be stressed along with the bad consequences of not living up to one's responsibilities, as when an old woman, left by her son to live alone, has her fire go out and follows a column of smoke to an old man's house, where she steals his fire. The old man finds her and beats her badly, and the shamed son takes her to his wife's house, finally living up to his obligations.

One of the most important obligations people recognize is that of sharing food, and this is a common theme in Tairora folktales. One example concerns a man who does not share his sugar cane with the others in his men's house. In retaliation, they invite him on a hunting trip, during which they leave his catch out of the distribution of the game animals. With his selfishness visibly portrayed and deeply shamed, he changes into a stalk of sugar cane.

A Tairora woman looping a string bag. (Photograph by Terence E. Hays)

ARTS AND CRAFTS

Crafts practiced by the Tairora are most evident in the fashioning of weapons (bows, arrows, clubs, spears in the north, and shields); implements (digging sticks, wooden spades in the north, adzes, knives, and daggers); and string bags, pandanus sleeping mats, and bamboo cooking tubes (with wooden cooking cylinders also manufactured in the north). Locally made traditional clothing for both sexes includes skirts or sporrans made of pounded bark strips or rushes and, in the north, wooden "codpieces" for men. Plastic arts play a limited role in Tairora expressive life. Apart from individual costuming and ornamentation on ceremonial occasions, which can be spectacular, decoration is largely restricted to string bags, arrows, and shields, though in the north in the past men wore wooden frames on their heads with painted bark panels on occasions of public dancing. Jew's harps are played occasionally as private entertainment. Otherwise only hourglass drums supplement the human voice in songs that are almost always very simple and melodic but possess highly repetitive refrains, rarely telling a story.

CHALLENGES OF THE MODERN WORLD

Much has altered in the everyday life of Tairora in recent decades following the establishment of an Australian administrative post in 1932 and an agricultural experimental station in 1937, both in the north, which began the processes of pacification and economic development; these processes started in the 1950s in the south. In addition to the importation of Western foods, various cash crops have been tried with coffee being the most successful. In the north, cattle raising has also become an important source of income, increasingly necessary for life in the modern world. Old trade networks have been abandoned and with them regular contacts with some neighbors, while contacts with the towns of the north have increased.

Since 1940 in the north and the 1960s in the south, a variety of Christian missions have operated, and many settlements now have resident mission catechists. The traditional big-man type of political leadership has largely given way to appointed, then elected government officials, and dispute settlement has increasingly occurred in official courts. However, since the independence of Papua New Guinea in 1975, government services and attention, especially in the south, have been curtailed sharply, and old enmities again erupt occasionally into sorcery accusations and battles.

The very tone of village life has altered along with these larger changes. Increasingly, especially in the north, Tairora are adopting the practice of nuclear families residing in a single household.

A Tairora woman decorated for a ceremony, holding an hourglass drum. (Photograph by Terence E. Hays)

The traditional institution of the men's house and segregation of the sexes have disappeared in the north and are rapidly doing so in the south. With their loss, largely under the influence of missionaries and younger people wanting to be "modern," most ceremonial life has also disappeared or been vastly transformed, incorporating Christian elements in weddings and funerals, with initiation and puberty ceremonies no longer practiced in most areas. In the north, public community dance festivals have become a source of income with outsiders being charged admission. At these festivals, but also just for entertainment back home, songs heard on the radio are nowadays regularly sung, enhancing the traditional repertoire of music, which was never extensive. Oral literature, on the other hand, has, for the most part, been replaced rather than supplemented by modern forms.

Myths and legends are disappearing among the younger generations as their usual contexts of recital have themselves gone. In the 1960s and 1970s, foreign objects and themes (for example, airplanes and imprisonment) began to be incorporated into traditional folktales. But with increasing and longer-lasting visits to and residence in towns and on plantations, young men have brought back to their villages many motifs and stories from other parts of Papua New Guinea, just as Bible stories are now the most frequently elicited ones from younger people.

STUDIES OF TAIRORA FOLKLORE

Little of Tairora folklore has been published (Hays 1985), but rich descriptions of ceremonial life and beliefs about the body and illness are available (Hays and Hays

1998, Mayer 1982). A general description of Tairora society (Hays 1991) is supplemented by a more extensive study of the northern areas (Watson 1983) and an excellent, sensitive biography of a Tairora woman (Watson 1997).

BIBLIOGRAPHY

Hays, Terence E. 1985. Folktales from Habi'ina, Kainantu District, Eastern Highlands Province. *Oral History* 13.1: 31–41.

———. 1991. Tairora. In *Oceania. Encyclopedia of World Cultures, Vol. 2*, edited by Terence E. Hays. Boston: G. K. Hall. 307–310.

Hays, Terence E., and Patricia H. Hays. 1998. Opposition and Complementarity of the Sexes in Ndumba Initiation. In *Rituals of Manhood: Male Initiation in Papua New Guinea*, edited by Gilbert H. Herdt. New Brunswick, NJ: Transaction Publishers. 201–238.

Mayer, Jessica R. 1982. Body, Psyche and Society: Conceptions of Illness in Ommura, Eastern Highlands, Papua New Guinea. *Oceania* 52: 240–260.

Watson, James B. 1983. *Tairora Culture: Contingency and Pragmatism*. Seattle: University of Washington Press.

Watson, Virginia Drew. 1997. *Anyan's Story: A New Guinea Woman in Two Worlds*. Seattle: University of Washington Press.

Terence E. Hays

Central and East Asia

China and East Asia

CHINA OVERVIEW

GEOGRAPHY AND HISTORY

The fourth largest country in the world (slightly smaller than the United States) in terms of landmass, China is first in population. Such a large area exhibits considerable variances in topography, climate, and natural resources. Northeast China (once known as Manchuria) is a northern temperate zone of vast forested river valleys bordering **Siberia**. The Yellow River courses across the dry northern plains of central China, draining into the Yellow Sea along the eastern coast. The mighty Yangzi twists through the broken uplands and rice-rich drainages of southern China, emptying into the sea not far from the mega-metropolis, Shanghai. In southern China, the regions of Guangdong and Guangxi border the warm South China Sea. Limestone karst formations in magical shapes are among the most striking feature of the landscape in the southern uplands, where flat land is a premium. Snow-capped mountains rise around the fertile basin of Sichuan province, north of the upper

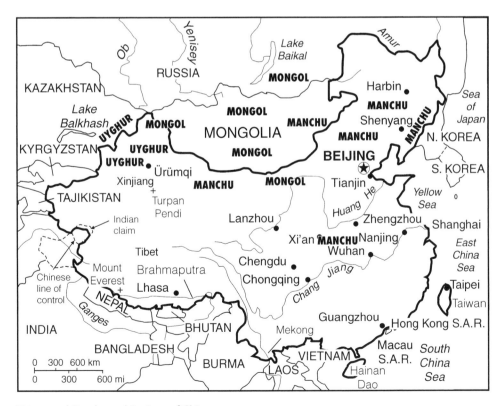

Taiwan and Peoples and Regions of China.

reaches of the Yangzi. Across Sichuan's southern border lies Yunnan province which borders on tropical Southeast Asia and the Tibetan highlands, which are a vast, cold, thin-aired desert lying to the north of the Indian subcontinent. China's northwest is a vast land of deserts and scorching basins, dotted with ancient oasis cities along the old Silk Road. The rolling, grassy steppe-land of Inner Mongolia spans the northern edge of the country. These differences in topography are reflected in the human adaptations to these environments, resulting over time in considerable cultural diversity among the many peoples of China.

Historically China has been an agricultural country, though industrialization has changed the economic landscape over the last century. Wheat and millet are the primary grain crops in northern China, while wet rice farming is the economic staple of southern China. Buckwheat, maize, and tobacco are raised in the uplands of southwest China, and barley is grown in Tibet. Herding sheep and horses is traditional on the northern steppes and parts of the Tibetan plateau. Grapes, melons, and other oasis crops are raised in the northwest desert regions, while fishing and hunting, supplemented by farming and herding, were followed into modern times in the forests and steppes of the northeast. After a series of important kingdoms, the imperial system began in 221 B.C.E. with the reign of Emperor Qinshi Huangdi and lasted with various modifications nearly two thousand years until the Republican Revolution in 1911. The system was based on a hierarchy of power with the emperor at the top, presiding over a huge bureaucracy that extended to the county level over the entire country.

For much of Chinese history landholding aristocrats provided order below the county level. Qualified males filled civil posts via an examination system based on knowledge of the Confucian classics held at local, provincial, and national levels. The basic social unit was the extended family and clan, the patrilineal model being most common. Kinship systems differed somewhat between north and south China, and marriage customs were freer in some areas of southwest China than in regions dominated by Confucian ideology. Elite, urban society was comprised of aristocrats with imperial connections, bureaucrats, craftsmen, military personnel, and tradespeople. The world outside the home was the realm of men, while the women's sphere was the home, often the site of cottage industries such as weaving. Landed aristocrats, farmers, and sharecroppers peopled the rural areas. Rural women, especially in southern China, tended to have more mobility outside the home than in the north, and in some areas of the southwest women were excellent traders. After the fourteenth century the position of merchants rose in the society, especially in cities in the Yangzi delta, along with an explosion of book printing and popular culture. Mainland China has been a socialist country since 1949 and is now reinventing itself as a sociopolitical unit as it enters the global economy.

The ethnic makeup of China has historically been complex, and the government today recognizes fifty-six ethnic groups, some with dozens of subgroups. The majority group is the Han Chinese, which makes up slightly over 90 percent of China's population. The Han nationality is comprised of a number of regional subgroups differentiated by custom and language topolect. Although certain cultural features such as Confucianism, writing, and aspects of social and material culture are "pan-Han," local features are still strong in many areas. Prominent local Han cultures include northern and southwestern Mandarin-speaking cultures, the "Wu" cultures of the Yangzi delta, the Cantonese cultures of southeast China, and the Fujianese and Hakka cultures of the southeast coast and parts of **Taiwan**. The largest populations of the "minority nationalities" (or "ethnic minorities") are found in China's border regions, most in five province-sized "autonomous regions." The northwest autonomous regions of Xinjiang and Ningxia as well as Gansu province are home to Islamic peoples such as the **Uyghur**, Salar, **Kazakhs**, and Hui. Many **Mongols** inhabit Inner Mongolia, and **Manchus**, Koreans, Daur, and small forest-dwelling groups such as the Ewenki (Evenki) live in the northeast. Various Tibetan groups live on the Tibetan plateau in the Xizang Tibetan Autonomous Region and contiguous areas in Gansu, Qinghai, Sichuan, and Yunnan. The southwestern provinces of Sichuan, Guizhou, Yunnan, and the Guangxi Zhuang Autonomous Region are home to dozens of ethnic minorities: the Dai (Tai) of steamy southern Yunnan; the Bai and Naxi on the road toward Tibet in northern Yunnan;

In a village near Nanning, Guangxi Zhuang Autonomous Region, a Han woman makes firecrackers on a handmade wooden roller. Firecrackers are used in many festivals and rituals in China. (Photograph by Mark Bender)

dozens of sub-groups of Yi (Nuosu, Nisu, Lolopo, Lipo, and others) and Miao (for example, Hmong and Hmu) living throughout the southwest mountains; and the Zhuang and Dong (Gaem or Kam) of the karst areas of Guangxi and Guizhou. During various times in Chinese history non-Han peoples have ruled the country, particularly during the Mongol occupation in the thirteenth and fourteenth centuries and the Manchu era from 1644–1911.

RELIGIOUS BELIEFS

Belief systems include elite traditions of the "Three Teachings": Confucianism, Daoism, Buddhism (the latter imported from **India** on the Silk Road). In northwest China, Islam has been popular since at least the twelfth century. Judeo-Christian influences were felt as early as the Tang dynasty, but had little impact until the Christian missionary movements of the late nineteenth and early twentieth centuries garnered local followings in parts of northeast and southern China. Local syntheses of complementary aspects of the Three Teachings, animistic beliefs, shamanism, and ancestor reverence characterized popular religion. The theory of complementary opposites represented in the yin-yang diagram and the divination equations of the *Book of Changes* (*Yijing*) permeate worldview as exemplified in interpretations of the Three Teachings, popular religion, architecture and home arrangements, the life cycle calendar, and traditional medical, healthcare, and eating practices. Since the early twentieth century, the influences of Western science, economics, and political ideas have had strong effects on Chinese worldview. Although at times traditional beliefs have been suppressed, today elements of the older belief systems continue as part of a dynamic and synthetic system that allows for the co-existence of several "teachings" and "ways" within a greater **worldview**.

PRESERVING CHINESE FOLKLORE

These elements of geography, culture, history, and belief provide a framework for a discussion of folklore in China. It should not be surprising that in such a diverse land dealing with folklore presents challenges. Yet the Chinese have taken a very active hand in collecting and organizing every facet of folk culture all over China since 1949, though these efforts have at times been impeded by periods of political unrest. In the 1950s and 1980s the Chinese government sponsored massive folksong and folkstory collection projects, resulting in over 1.8 million stories and over 3 million folksongs gathered from all fifty-six ethnic nationalities. Collecting and study projects are still carried out by folklore workers and scholars at local, regional, and national levels. In recent years, scholars in research institutes and universities such as the Chinese Academy of Social Sciences (*Zhongguo shehui kexue yuan*), Beijing University (*Beijing daxue*), and the Central Nationalities University (*Zhongyang minzu daxue*) have experimented with new approaches to folklore analysis and **fieldwork**, influenced to some degree by Western trends.

ORAL FOLKLORE TRADITIONS

A vast array of orally delivered verbal art traditions can be found across the Chinese landscape. Although local tradition-bearers have their own terminology for forms of verbal art, Chinese folklorists categorize these traditions with a number of specialized terms, most derived from nineteenth- and early twentieth-century Western folklore studies (in a situation similar to **Japan**). Folk narratives include folktales (*minjian gushi*), myths (*shenhua*), legends (*chuanshuo*), animal tales (*dongwu gushi*), and so forth. Prosodic narratives include epics (*shishi*) and narrative poems (*xushishi*) similar to long ballads or lyrical fairy tales. There are numerous terms and divisions for folksongs (*minge* or *minjian geyao*), including love songs (*qingge*), drinking songs (*jiuge*), wedding laments (*kujiage*), and worksongs (*laodongge*). Some oral forms such as epics are found only among some of the ethnic minority groups, though other types are very widespread. In some instances, several ethnic groups may share very similar traditions, especially certain of the antiphonal folksong traditions of the northwest and southwest. Other categories include proverbs (*yanyu*) and jokes (*xiaohua*).

Special terms denominate forms of storytelling and drama. The general term "art of melodies" (*quyi*) is applied to a diffuse body of musical narratives (though a few have relatively little music) that were practiced by professionals and in some cases avocational or amateur performers. Once numbering over 300 styles, these local varieties were popular throughout the Han Chinese areas. A few forms are also recognized among some ethnic minority groups such as the Manchus of northeast China and the Bai nationality of Yunnan province. Many storytelling and local drama traditions were associated with urban entertainment districts, markets, temple fairs, or teahouses, and in some cases had written correlates in vernacular literature. Existing local drama traditions (*difangxi*) tend to be more "literary," professional, and urban than folk operas (*xiaoxi*), which are usually closely related to rural song and dance traditions. Whether to classify many of these forms as "folk" or "popular" entertainments is debatable. Similar questions exist about the classification of local musical styles and material culture.

The following sections will introduce major bodies of tradition, often at regional or local levels. As reflected in the preceding paragraphs, core categories of folklore are sometimes different from those based on European models, though many categories do readily overlap, sometimes with qualifying definitions. In some instances native terms have been utilized. Given the huge corpus of folklore in China, it is difficult to give a comprehensive picture in limited space. The goal here is to present an overview that will allow some sense of the big picture, while illuminating a few representative local traditions drawn mostly from southern and southwestern China.

Myths

Accounts of Han Chinese myths date to records such as *The Classic of Mountains and Seas* (*Shan hai jing*), based on material compiled between the third century B.C.E. and the second century C.E. These early texts include accounts of the creation of the earth and cosmos out of chaos and tell of the creator Pan Gu, whose body transformed into the myriad phenomena of the natural world. Among the early beings are the male Fuxi and the female Nü Wa, who shaped humans from clay and patched holes that had formed in the sky. Another figure, Hou Yi, is an archer who at the bequest of Emperor Yao shoots down nine of the ten suns overheating the earth. Important gods that figure in many myths and other stories and folk beliefs include the Jade Emperor, Queen Mother of the West, and the Yellow Emperor. A favorite of these early accounts is associated with the Mid-Autumn Festival (*Zhongqiu jie*), held on the fifteenth day of the eighth lunar month. The archer Hou Yi meets a charming young woman named Chang'e. Wishing to live with her forever, Hou Yi convinces the powerful Queen Mother of the West (who controls the peaches of immortality) to give him a special elixir. Versions differ over what happens next, but eventually Chang'e drinks the elixir, becomes an immortal, and flies up to the Moon, where she lives today with her pet rabbit. A number of Han myths have parallels in the folklore of many ethnic groups in southern China, and some of the myths (such as that of Pan Gu) may be of ancient southern origin.

In recent decades lengthy epics charting creation have been collected among Miao, Yao, Yi, Hani, Lahu, Dong, Drung, Dai, and other ethnic groups in the south and particularly the southwest of the country. Common motifs include separation and coalescence of heavy and light material out of chaos, measuring the seam between the resulting heaven and earth, sewing the sky and earth together, propping up the sky with pillars, creation of living things, early generations of proto-humans or giants, destruction of life by a great flood, re-peopling of the earth (often by a female creator or as a result of incest between a brother and sister), the distribution of the peoples of earth (often the historic ethnic groups within a particular region), and sometimes the acquisition of language, agriculture, marriage, and so on. A calabash gourd figures in many of the southern minority epics, especially as an ark to carry the brother and sister who escape the flood. In one Miao epic from Guizhou province an important creator figure is a butterfly called Mais Bangx (Mother Butterfly), who lays eggs that hold the early ancestors of humans, tigers, dragons, mythical birds, and so on in a sacred sweet gum tree that later splits into myriad living beings.

Narrative Poems

Narrative poems ranging from a few dozen lines to some of the world's longest epics are found in the northern border regions and the mountains of the southwest. The northern epics include the Kirgiz epic *Manas* (claimed to be the longest epic poem in history), the Mongol epic *Janggar*, and the epic of the Tibetan hero, Gesar. All three epics feature divine, exemplary heroes who win contests, take beautiful brides, fight evil forces, build kingdoms, and lead armies of highly skilled warriors. Flying and talking horses, shapeshifting, and battles with enemies (human and monster) are typical themes. Multi-headed anthropomorphs known as *manggus* are typical foes in the Mongol *Janggar* epic as well as Mongol versions of *Gesar*. A singer or relays of singers recite the epics in the open air at festivals. Some Tibetan singers employ the convention of "paper-singing," in which a singer holds a blank sheet of paper in front of him as if reading as he recites the epic. In recent decades singers have included both men and women. Heroic epics and fairy tale-like narrative poems circulate among several Yi sub-groups in the southwest. Typical is the story of Zhyge Alu, a Yi martial hero whose exploits are told among the Nuosu of northern Yunnan and Sichuan. An illegitimate child, he was born after drops of blood from a flying eagle stained his young mother's skirt. Left in the wilds, the child was raised by dragons. Later, Zhyge Alu is said to have shot down the excess suns and moons in the sky. Among the Sani of the Stone Forest area of Yunnan, narrative poems are sung about Ashima, a lovely, hard-working young woman who was captured and imprisoned by an evil landlord. Her brother (in more recent versions, her lover) Ahei rescues her, but on the way home she is killed by a sudden flood. Her inspiring echo is still said to resound in the strange limestone formations in the region. The epic tradition of the Dai, a people located in the Xishuangbanna (Sipsongpanna) area of southern Yunnan province, has been strongly influenced by Theravada Buddhism.

Folktales and Legends

Folklorists, such as the eminent Zhong Jingwen (1903–2002), have researched folktales throughout the land and identified several as being especially widespread among the Han and some minority groups, existing in oral performance and written media. These include the story of Liang Shanbo and Zhu Yingtai, star-crossed young lovers, the latter of whom is a young woman who dresses as a male student; the Weaving Maid and Cowherd (*Niulang zhinu*), divided lovers who by celestial mandate meet once a year on a bridge of magpies in the sky; and Meng Jiangnu, the tale of a woman who searches for the bones of her husband who was conscripted to work on the Great Wall.

Local folk story traditions include southern tales common to many ethnic groups of a snake who marries a virtuous young woman and later changes into a prince. The

trickster Effendi (Afanti) is the clever **hero** of many Uyghur nationality tales from the Xinjiang Uyghur Autonomous Region in northwest China. Tales of capable hunter-heroes called *mergen* are told among the Daur, Oroqen, and Hezhen nationalities who live in and near the forests of the northeast. Tales of frightful mountain-dwelling Cannibal Mother (*Coqot Amat*) are still common among the Nuosu sub-group of Yi in the Liangshan Mountains of southern Sichuan. Many animal tales have been collected all over China.

Virtually every mountain, hill, unusual rock, stream, river, pool, cave, gorge, grove, ancient tree, temple, bridge, city wall, and other features of the inhabited terrain have one or more legends connected to them. A prime example is the Li River near the tourist site of Guilin in the Guangxi Zhuang Autonomous Region. Popular with tourists since at least the Tang period (618–907 C.E.)—many scholar-poets having left their poems carved on mountain or cave walls—this site has inspired legends about nearly every one of the oddly shaped karst mountains lining the river, beginning with Elephant Trunk Hill near the city.

Many regions, cities, and towns have legends associated with exemplary inhabitants, unusual characters, and benefactors, some of whom are local gods. For instance, many legends surround the Huaqing Pond in the Tang dynasty capital of Chang'an (today's Xi'an), where the incomparably lovely concubine Yang Guifei was said to have bathed and cavorted with Emperor Xuanzong. In the ancient Yangzi deltal city of Suzhou, stories about the sixteenth-century poet-painter Tang Bohu are still part of local storytelling as well as many drama traditions. In the nearby city of Yangzhou, many legends exist about the eight unusual painters in the eighteenth century, still known as the "Yangzhou Eight Eccentrics" (*Yangzhou baguai*). Bai nationality towns in western Yunnan have legends about their *benzhu*, or beneficent ancestor, whose spirit looks over the welfare of the populace.

One Bai legend is associated with a natural feature called "Butterfly Spring" near the small town of Zhoucheng. According to a version told by Zhang Qisheng, a hunter named Du Chaoxuan heard that a giant, supernatural snake was eating local people. Surprising the snake, he managed to shoot it with an arrow before it escaped. The next day, Du went to a nearby spring and saw two young women washing a bloodied cloth on a rock. Though at first he suspected they might be incarnations of the giant snake, they told him how they had been forced to become the wounded snake's wives. They then helped Du steal the snake's magic sword, whereupon he sliced the creature into three parts. Although the women begged to become his wives, he left them behind to go hunting in the mountains. The women were so distraught that they drowned themselves in the spring. Returning from the mountains the next day, Du heard of the women's fate. Wracked with grief, the snake-killing hero jumped into the spring and drowned. Soon after, three butterflies, two leading and one following behind, emerged from the spring. Today many colorful butterflies gather on an ancient tree nearby.

Popular religion in China continues to be a source of legends about spirits (*shen*), immortals (*xian*), bodhisattvas (*pusa*), and wise men, many of whom are regarded as being actual people in earlier ages. The "Eight Immortals" of popular Daoism are especially well represented in oral traditions, dramas, and festival parades. The Ming dynasty vernacular romance, *Tales of Gods and Spirits* (*Fengshen yanyi*), includes many legends associated with historical figures such as an early adviser of the Zhou dynasty kings, Jiang Taigong (who learned patience while fishing without hooks), which have correlates in oral tradition. In certain areas of Guizhou, the work is the basis of productions of folk ritual-drama. In recent years, images of legendary leaders of the communist party, including Mao Zedong, have been integrated into local religious beliefs in some rural areas.

Folksongs

China has one of the world's richest heritages of folksongs, written records beginning with the fifth century B.C.E. collection, the *Book of Songs* (*Shijing*), based in part on local folksong traditions, and the *yuefu* folk ballads dating to the Han dynasty (220 B.C.E.–220 C.E.). Large collections of folksongs by literati such as Feng Menglong date to the Ming dynasty (1368–1644 C.E.). Large-scale collection by modern intellectuals began around the time of the May Fourth Movement in 1919 and continued into the 1930s. During this time, Western folklore methods began to be utilized by young intellectuals like Liu Fu, Gu Jiegang, Zhou Zuoren, and Zhong Jingwen. In the 1950s and 1980s the government of the People's Republic of China launched massive folksong collecting projects. Huge cadres of folksong collectors (many of whom were students) were mobilized at national, provincial, and county levels all over the country, resulting in collection, editing (sometimes for political correctness), and publication in both public and "inner-circulating" print media.

Folksongs in China include courting songs, bridal laments (sung by brides leaving home), hosting songs, drinking songs, ritual songs asking for blessing and good luck, funeral songs and chants, worksongs (sung in rice fields, on fishing boats, and at the loom), lullabies, and other themes. While many folksongs are associated with rural cultures or labor, a kind of refined lyrical singing tradition called *xiaodiao* (small tunes) was common in urban settings all over China, sometimes performed by professional singers. Receiving and sending off guests are important acts in Chinese social interaction. In many parts of China (particularly in the ethnic minority areas today) hosts and guests traditionally exchange songs of welcome and departure. Among some ethnic groups, songs may also be sung during banquets in praise of guest or host and conveying good wishes and praise.

Young Yi women (Nuosu subgroup) from Mianning County, Liangshan Xi Nationality Autonomous Prefecture, Sichuan Province, sing a welcoming song to guests from afar. Such singing is an important part of social protocol. (Photograph by Mark Bender)

Drinking songs may also be part of banquets, drinking parties, and festivals, depending on the ethnic group. Various forms of distilled alcohol made from rice, wheat, maize, and millet, as well as thin beer-like beverages made from fermented rice, buckwheat, barley, and other grains or vegetables, figure importantly in the social cultures in many parts of China. Drinking is usually associated with eating, and singing may be a part of home and public banquets or after-banquet activities (impromptu sings or karaoke sessions) all over China. Drink also plays a role in many rituals, in which alcohol is offered along with songs and chants to various gods, local nature spirits, or ancestral spirits in order to gain blessings.

Although arranged marriages were for millennia the norm for Han Chinese, many ethnic groups allowed young people to engage in courting activities from the early teen years until marriage. Popular activities in the courting process were singing gatherings or parties in which young men and women sang antiphonal folksongs to each other. The antiphonal style, in which songs are traded back and forth between singers in a kind of song talk, was an important social skill. Today in many areas of northwest and southwest China, courting songs are still sung in gatherings by both unmarried and married people. In some areas, the best singers are middle-aged or older.

In northwest China, a common style of folksong among many ethnic groups, including Han, Salar, Hui, Dongxiang, Tu (Monguor), and Yugu is the so-called *hua'er* or "flower songs," known in some places as *shaonian* (often translated as "courtship songs"). Rural people in Shanxi and Shaanxi sing a style of song known as *xintianyou* while working in the vast "yellow earth" areas of north-central China. In many parts of China, short lyrics, often sung in antiphonal form, have for centuries been called *shan'ge* (mountain songs) as well as by many local terms. Such songs were especially popular in the Yangzi delta and all across southern China. Today they are still popular in parts of Fujian, Hunan, Guizhou, Guangxi, and Yunnan, though in many places fewer young people know how to sing.

In the area of Liuzhou, a small city in northern Guangxi, mountain songs are a pan-ethnic phenomenon. Singers from Zhuang, Dong, Mulam, Maonan, Han, and other groups sing similar songs in their own languages as well as in Chinese. Song contests are still held during the Mid-Autumn festival at Carp Peak (*Yufeng shan*) in Liuzhou city, where most songs are sung in a southwest version of Mandarin

Covered bridge, Sanjian County, Guangxi Zhuang Autonomous Region. Such bridges are found in a number of Dong (Gaem) nationality villages in southwest China. The wooden bridges are a favorite spot for young people to meet and sing antiphonal folksongs in the evenings. (Photograph by Mark Bender)

Chinese. A common singing style features two male singers simultaneously singing in turn with two female singers. Such antiphonal lyrics are filled with nature imagery (often stressing reproduction) and feature similes, metaphors, and sometimes riddles. In the past, young people got to know each other through lengthy song exchanges, and lovers or spouses were chosen by the mental dexterity and skill exhibited by the singers. Today groups of older singers gather in parks or at riversides to limber their voices and minds in impromptu tests of singing skill.

The following excerpt from a song exchange comes from the Dong nationality of the Guizhou and Guangxi borderlands. Songs are sung on intricately constructed covered wooden bridges, near ancient trees, stream banks, and springs, or in other special places. The reference to "black rice" is a metaphor for eating a dark variety of rice in the marriage ceremony. The singers were Wu Jinsong and Lu Jinmeng:

> FEMALE: You early on had steady lovers,
> Why do you still use such flowery, tricky words?
> You don't dare to talk straight,
> But last year we already heard
> That a lovely maiden
> Already ate your home's "black rice."
>
> MALE: I have no lover,
> I'm really telling you the truth;
> My house has no cooking smoke,
> There's no fire inside,
> At dawn no rice treadle sounds,
> At dusk no happy spinning-wheel songs.
> If you wish to say I have a lover,
> Then that lover is you.
> The lovers are, in fact, we two.

Folksongs have been incorporated into local-color films, orchestral music, and other media. The 1961 film *Third Sister Liu* (*Liu Sanjie*) featured romanticized versions of Zhuang antiphonal singing. Over thirty years later, a musical version, produced by renowned film director Zhang Yimou in 2003, was staged live in natural settings in scenic Yangshuo, Guangxi. The film *Ashima* (1964) featured artistically enhanced folksongs of the Yi sub-group called Sani. In the early 1980s, folksongs from the barren northern Shaanxi (Shaanbei) area were interwoven into the script of the innovative "Fifth Generation" film *Yellow Earth* (*Huang tudi*), which featured more folksinging than dialogue. Folksongs and music from various ethnic groups have influenced composers such as Nie Er in the 1930s and 1940s. More recently, composer Bright Sheng has drawn on folksongs and music in northwest China in his orchestral compositions. Urban folksinger Yang Yi has recreated rural folksongs under the influence of American singer Bob Dylan. Yi (Nuosu subgroup) minority poets such as Jidi Majia and Aku Wuwu have drawn extensively on folksongs, myths, chants, and customs in their poetic works.

Storytelling and Musical Performance

A vast body of narrative styles that often combine music and speaking is known as *quyi* (art of melodies). These styles, performed by professional or avocational performers, range in length from a few dozen lines to stories that can be told two hours a day for up to a year. A number of regional styles and hundreds of local traditions are most common among the Han Chinese. Many of these traditions were performed primarily in urban entertainment venues. Relatively few survive today.

Several closely related traditions of musical storytelling have been popular in the Yangzi delta region of eastern China for several hundred years. Similar traditions such as the Cantonese "wooden fish" (*mukyu*) style range through ethnic Han cultures southwards along the coast. Incarnations of these traditions today include the *tanci* (plucking lyrics) storytelling styles, sometimes translated as "chantefable" or "story-singing," still performed in and around the cities of Suzhou, Wuxi, Yangzhou, and Hangzhou in the Yangzi delta. Performances are presented in two-hour sets in special story houses as middle-aged and older patrons sip tea while they listen to the stories unfold in a mixture of singing, narration, and dramatic roles. Stories are usually delivered by a pair of storytellers (either same or mixed gender) who accompany themselves on the three-stringed banjo (*sanxian*) and the *pipa* (a pear-shaped lute). Performances of storytelling without musical accompaniment called *pinghua* or "straight storytelling" (called *pingshu* in Beijing and Sichuan) are held in the same story houses and usually delivered by solo performers. Together the two storytelling traditions, which share many stylistic features and history, are called *pingtan*.

Traditional love stories between "gifted scholars and talented beauties" such as *Pearl Pagoda* (*Zhenzhu ta*), *Jade Dragonfly* (*Yu qingting*), *Etched Gold Phoenix* (*Miaojin feng*), *Three Smiles* (*Sanxiao*), *Pair of Pearl Phoenixes* (*Shuang zhufeng*), and *West Wing* (*Xixiangji*) have been a major component in the *tanci* repertoire since at least the early nineteenth century. A number of these stories are also represented in local drama traditions. Stories in the *pinghua* repertoire are often about outlaw or martial heroes and tend to involve amazing displays of stylized gestures and verbal agility, which may include rhyming, folk ditties, and paralinguistic sounds of everything from firecrackers to a fritter rolling on the floor. Stories include heroes such as the twelfth-century patriot Yue Fei and episodes from works of vernacular fiction such as *Three Kingdoms* (*Sanguo yanyi*), *Journey to the West* (*Xiyouji*), *Outlaws of the Marsh* (*Shuihu zhuan*), and *Three Heroes and Five Gallants* (*Sanxia wuyi*). The Yangzhou

Suzhou chantefable (*Suzhou tanci*)—style storytelling, Jiading, Jiangsu Province. Note the extra three-string banjo (*sanxian*) leaning on the lead storyteller's high chair. Performances mix speaking and singing roles. (Photograph by Mark Bender)

pinghua story about the outlaw hero Wu Song and his fight with a tiger high on a mountain ridge after a drinking bout in a tavern is among the best known of the *pinghua* narratives. *Tanci* performances usually begin with a lyrical ballad known as a *kaipian* (opening piece), many of which are also sung at informal gatherings of amateurs or by professionals in contests.

Storytelling traditions (with written vernacular correlates) known as precious volumes (*baojuan*) were once widespread, some with ritual components incorporating Buddhism and other beliefs. A surviving tradition from the Yangzi delta is known as *Jingjiang jiangjing* (Jingjiang telling scriptures). Stories of local gods and devotees as well as more secular tales are told in lengthy "services" combining narration and singing in performances led by a specialist known as a "Buddha-head" (*fotou*) and enhanced by a special chorus comprised of older audience members.

A number of related styles of rap-like ballads known as *kuaiban* (clapper-tales) and *kuaishu* (fast-story) exist in northeast China. Performers sing stories to the beat provided by bamboo, wooden, or metal clappers, depending on the tradition. Very short in comparison to some of the southern forms like Suzhou *tanci*, these story songs include humorous anecdotes and condensed tales of heroes from vernacular literature such as Wu Song. Styles of narrative using drums, sometimes in concert with stringed or other percussion instruments, include the *dagu* (big drum) traditions of Beijing and the extinct form of Manchu (Manju) drum storytelling known as *zidishu* (bannermans' songs). Some *zidishu* texts relate passages from works of vernacular fiction, including the famous eighteenth-century novel-length work, *Dream of the Red Chamber* (*Honglou meng*). Many similar storytelling traditions using a variety of instruments are found in Han areas all over China, though in some areas traditions are a mere shadow of what they were in the past.

MUSIC

The local traditions of Han instrumental music vary significantly from north to south, region to region, and, as Stephen Jones (2004) notes of the southeast, "county to county," with potentially wider variation among the minority nationalities. Still understudied, Han folk music traditions can be roughly divided into ensemble music played without lyrical accompaniment designed to accompany drama, storytelling, and various entertainments and music for weddings, funerals, and temple festivals. "Literati" music such as "silk-and-bamboo" (*sizhu*) chamber music ensembles of the lower Yangzi delta are more closely linked to the traditions of court and ceremonial music in the urban centers. Among the Han, men were the traditional music-makers (with exceptions such as the zither-like *qin* and *pipa*-lute), though since 1949 women in a some areas have become increasingly involved in music-making. In the southern Fujian vocal and instrumental tradition of chamber music called *Nan guan*, women have nearly supplanted men as tradition bearers.

Musical instruments—classified as percussion, string, and aerophonic—are used by small bands or ensembles in combinations of melody and percussion instruments. Jones has noted that Chinese instrumental music is melodic, utilizes a pentatonic scale, and is played in "heterophony" rather than harmony. In this style of playing, the different instruments decorate "the same basic melody in different ways according to the idiom and technique of each instrument." One instrument tends to act as a lead (usually a wind instrument in northern China and a stringed one in the south), though during the course of a performance other instruments may be highlighted. In rural ensembles in northern and western regions a sort of reed-trumpet called a *suona* or *shawm* is the lead instrument. The silk-and-bamboo tradition combines music of the "silk" (*pipa*-lute, the three-stringed banjo [*sanxian*], the two-stringed fiddle [*erhu*]), and other stringed instruments, the "bamboo" (several types of flutes), and a minimum of percussion instruments (woodblock, clappers, or small drum). Farther south is a complex bounty of ensemble traditions. These include the *Nan guan* traditions in Fujian, musical clubs in Guangdong associated with Chaozhou (Teochew) musical traditions, and traditions among the Hakka people (who live in various areas in the southeast). Such musical clubs feature music by a variety of percussion, aerophonic, and string instruments including the plucked zither (*zheng*) and *pipa*-lute. A number of these traditions have followings in Taiwan, Singapore, Thailand, and elsewhere.

An ethnic minority musical tradition that has gained an international following is the *Dongjing* orchestral music of the Naxi nationality in Lijiang, Yunnan, which is also home to one of the best examples of vernacular wooden architecture in China (though somewhat overwhelmed by the burgeoning tourist trade) and a unique tradition of *dongba* ritual writing. The *Dongjing* music tradition has been resurrected and expanded in the tourist trade, and daily performances by mixed-gender ensembles are held in the old city, in a modern theater, and in Black Dragon Pool Park. Instruments include *pipa*-lutes, flutes, three-stringed banjos (*sanxian*), drums, and gongs seen all over China and a number of local stringed instruments.

Many of China's stringed instruments such as the *pipa*-lute had their origins in the Middle East and Central Asia, entering China along with foreign music on the Silk Road up through the Tang dynasty. Today the influence of Central Asian music and instruments continues in the musical traditions of the Turkic-speaking Uyghur nationality of the Xinjiang Uyghur Autonomous Region in northwest China. In the mountains of southwest China a bamboo pipe instrument known as a *lusheng* in Chinese is especially popular among Miao, Dong, Shui, and other ethnic minority groups. Using a "free reed" that vibrates within the instrument, the sound resembles that of Scottish bagpipes. Large festivals with hundreds or thousands of participants feature *lusheng* of many sizes used in a variety of group and individual dances, sometimes in contexts that feature antiphonal singing. Among Yao, Shui, Zhuang, and other southwestern groups, musicians hang a series of different-sized brass drums on frames. Besides striking the drums, players sometimes move wooden buckets in and out of the bottoms of the drums to add extra musical effect. Among the Dong nationality, large banjo-type instruments called *pipa* (different from those above) come in several tones and sizes. Some men among the Sani people in Yunnan dance with gigantic three-stringed banjos with sound chambers the size of five-gallon buckets. Traditions of ritual music are associated with Buddhist, Daoist, and various local beliefs all over the country. Examples include the shaman chants, accompanied by leather-headed hand drums, of the Manchu, Mongol, and Daur nationalities in northeast China and Inner Mongolia. Among many nationalities in China, folk music, folksongs, and folk dances often meld during festival activities.

OPERA

Images of Beijing opera tend to dominate perceptions of Chinese traditional drama. While that particular dramatic form rose to the level of a national art in the late twentieth century, its roots are in local forms of drama that coalesced in Beijing during the early nineteenth century. Besides the Beijing tradition, many regional forms still have followings today, including the Cantonese *Yueju*; *gezaixi* (*gezai* opera) of southern Fujian, Taiwan, and Chinese communities in Southeast Asia; *Kunju* (from Kunshan in Jiangsu province) and *Yueju* (also known as Shaoxing opera) of the Yangzi delta; and *bangzi qiangxi* (named for the wooden clappers used in musical accompaniment) in northern China, including Shanxi, Shaanxi, Shandong, and parts of southwest China. Sichuan opera (*Chuanju*) is famous for the convention of "face changing" (*bianlian*), in which layers of paper-thin silk mask allow actors to change faces in an instant. While the northern forms tend to be robust and emphasize martial skills and acrobatics, the southern forms are more gentle and elegant. Such local drama traditions were once performed by professional actors in private troupes, though many traditions on the mainland became state-supported after 1949. Groups of avocational hobbyists often gather in public parks or other venues, including concert halls all around China to sing opera arias or perform sections of plays. Yueju troupes comprised of female actors are still active in parts of Zhejiang province.

Stories from traditional opera include themes of heroes and historical battles, court cases, love intrigues, and affairs of the imperial court, all with entertainingly moral messages. Some stories such as *Peony Pavilion* (*Mudan ting*) are widespread, while others may be of a local nature. Historically, vernacular literature and styles of oral narrative have influenced local operas and vice versa, creating a situation in which a story may exist in several genres.

DRAMA

Although the convention of painting the faces of major characters is one of the most recognizable features of Chinese drama, in recent decades ethnographers have discovered traditions of local drama in southern China where performers wear carved wooden masks. Many of the masked-opera traditions are known as *Nuo* or *Nuotangxi* (Nuo hall opera). In parts of Guizhou province, where Nuo traditions are especially strong, Nuo performances are an important part of New Year ritual activities. Dozens or hundreds of masks are assembled and worshipped at the beginning of the rituals. Amateur troupes of actors (which may include shamans and men who grow long hair to play women's roles) enact the plays, accompanied by percussion instruments. A common play concerns Kaishan, a mythical figure who loses his ax in a river and must go to the Dragon King's palace to retrieve it. Another wooden mask tradition, known as *Dixi* (local, or "earth" opera), is associated with the Anshun area of Guizhou. Featuring colorful masks and elaborate costumes, the song and dance dramas utilize a narrator and present martial themes from the classic fictional work *Three Kingdoms* (*Sanguo yanyi*) and similar stories. In ritual dramas once common throughout China, actors enacted scenes from the Buddhist story of Mulian, who descends to Hell in order to rescue his suffering mother. Harvest festival dramas in the

Tibetan regions of China enact stories from Tibetan history, including stories of the ancient king Srongsam-gampo.

Traditions of puppet drama include shadow puppet drama (*piyingxi*) in cities such as Tangshan in northeast China and cloth hand puppet drama (*budaixi*) in Taiwan. The shadow puppets are intricately cut from specially treated mule hide and manipulated by puppeteers behind a backlit curtain. Laser lights, digital music, and clouds of dry ice often enhance puppet performances in Taiwan today. Puppet stories parallel those in traditional Chinese opera, and some researchers have even suggested that puppet movements have influenced the stiff movements of human opera performers.

Yi nationality (Nuosu subgroup). A village beauty contest in Butuo County, Liangshan Yi Nationality Autonomous Prefecture, Sichuan Province. Such contests are commonly held at local festivals such as the Torch Festival. The young women dress in their finest traditional clothing and carry yellow umbrellas to enhance their complexions. (Photograph by Mark Bender)

Several styles of drama known as "little opera" (*xiaoxi*), some with strong elements of folksong and dance, are performed in both rural and urban areas across China. These traditions, whose practitioners are often part of the local communities, include various forms of "rice-sprouts" (*yang'ge*) dramas (the most famous from Dingxian county in Hebei province); Huangmei opera (*Huangmei xi*) from the border of Hubei and Anhui provinces; "Hunan flower-drum" opera (Hunan *huagu xi*); "flowery-lantern" dramas (*huadeng xi*) found all over southern China; "flower song" dramas (*huae'er xi*) among Hui and other ethnic groups in northwest China; and certain ethnic dramatic traditions (some quite recent) such as Yi and Dong drama (*Yiju* and *Dongju*, respectively) in the southwest. Performances are held at appropriate times during the agricultural cycle, many associated with Spring Festival and planting, harvest, or mid-summer celebrations (such as the Yi nationality Torch Festival).

SPORTS AND GAMES

Traditional sports differ across region and nationality. The rough-and-tumble "manly arts" of the northern steppe appear at events like the Nadam Fair of the Mongols and include wrestling, archery, and games on horseback. One popular contest among the Zhuang and Dong in the Guizhou/Guangxi borderlands involves two huge teams of area youths who chase each other back and forth in muddy rice fields, attempting to gain control of a small iron ring that is fired high into the air with a small black powder signal cannon. Similar in spirit are the contests held among several ethnic groups in northwest China in which participants on horseback struggle for the possession of a goat carcass while galloping full speed across the steppe. Long wooden "dragonboats" rowed by teams of men (and in recent years women) are a high point in *Duanwu* festivals held in late spring among the Han in southern China. The Dai of Yunnan have similar dragon boat contests during the annual "Water-Splashing" festival, in which crowds of people drench each other with pans of water, along with huge displays of handmade fireworks, folk dancing, singing, and games of skill for children.

In recent years, competitions featuring traditional ethnic minority sports have been held in the all of the ethnic autonomous regions. In some cases traditional folk activities have been modified as sports. One example from Guangxi involves teams of young men and women throwing embroidered balls with cloth tails (*xiuqiu*) back and forth through a hoop at the top of a long pole. This sport is a direct adaptation of a traditional courting game of the Zhuang and related groups, in which young people sang antiphonal songs and young women tossed the handmade balls to prospective lovers.

Folk games, again differing by region and ethnic group, include children's games, contests, festival entertainments, song and dance plays and routines, knowledge games, word games and songs that play on features of language, small animal tricks, cards, and board games. Lantern parades and fireworks are part of the Spring Festival in Han areas. Wooden swings were once popular in many parts of China, especially with young women. Swings are still part of festival events in some Yi communities in the southwest and ethnic Korean communities in the northeast.

Popular children's games of the Han people include Eagle Catches the Chicks (*laoying zhua xiaoji*). To play, an "eagle" attempts to catch the "chicks" hiding in a line behind a vigorously protective "hen." Another common activity involves kicking small bundles of old coins trimmed with feathers (*tijianzi*) that are kept in the air as long as possible by multiple kicks, sometimes between more than one player. Other games include the popular girl's activity of dancing between long strings of rubber bands (*tiaopiji'er*) and grabbing games involving stones (*zhuashizi*) or painted pig knuckle bones (*chuagu*), similar to the Western game of jacks.

Historical records from very early times note contests between various creatures at festivals and private gatherings. In recent decades, these have included struggles between water buffalo, rams, goats, chickens, ducks, birds, dogs, and ants, especially in certain areas in south and southwest China. Crickets have long been favorite pets all over China, and special breeds are used in fighting contests.

Paper playing cards seem to have been invented in China by the Song dynasty (960–1279 C.E.), and long and thin cards are still found in some areas. All over the country Western and Chinese card games as well as traditional table games such as mahjong and *xiangqi* (go) are extremely popular pastimes.

ARTS, CRAFTS, AND ARCHITECTURE

The material folk arts of China appear in a wide variety of mediums and styles according to geography and culture. Wood, bamboo, clay, paper, lacquer, indigo, cotton, silk, hemp, rattan, birchbark, tree leaves, jade, marble, turquoise, coral, natural stone, amber, bone, brass, iron, silver, gold, tin, fruit, seeds, butter, wheat dough, rice flour, sugar, felt, leather, fur, hair, horn, antler, teeth, fish skin, ivory, beads, foil, plastic, and other materials have all been mediums for artistic expression in the folk world. Items include the architecture of homes, shrines, temples, bridges, and community buildings; seasonal and event-specific clothing and accessories; tools for agriculture, hunting, gathering, and herding; weapons such as swords, crossbows, muzzle-loading muskets, and powder horns; brush-writing implements; jewelry; festival decorations and costumes; objects used in life cycle rituals (births and child protection rites, courting and wedding rituals, important birthdays, and funerals); charms and good luck tokens; musical instruments and implements used by sto-

A Lipo child's toy horses, Mayou Village, Chuxiong Yi Nationality Autonomous Prefecture, Yunnan (Yi nationality group). (Photograph by Mark Bender)

rytellers; accoutrements of ritual specialists and personal worship; boats, carts, and sleds; eating utensils and household furnishings; tea drinking implements; smoking tools; alcohol stills; personal hygiene items; sewing and weaving tools; tattooing equipment (in southwest China); and many others.

The styles of vernacular architecture are easy to see on train or bus rides through rural China. They range from round communal compounds (*tulou*) holding 300–500 people in Hakka areas of the Fujian-Guangdong border areas to wooden homes of the Naxi nationality in Lijiang, Yunnan, and the elaborate wooden post and lintel architecture of the Chenyang Wind and Rain Bridge and drum towers in the Dong ethnic region of Sanjiang in northern Guangxi. There are hewn granite homes in the Bouyei nationality regions of Guizhou and the Bai of Dali, Yunnan. Rammed-earth and adobe-walled towns and courtyards featuring heated brick beds (*kang*) are found across northern China. Skillfully excavated cave homes appear in parts of the northwest. Adobe compounds with low roofs pitching down into central courtyards are found in the oases of Gansu and other northwest desert areas, while white-washed brick cottages with black tile roofs line some canals in the lower Yangzi. Felt *ger* (yurts) are still seen on parts of the northern grasslands, though birchbark wigwams once used in the northeast forests would be difficult to find. Expansive timber and adobe Tibetan homes with peaked roofs in the Shangrila region of northwest Yunnan contrast with flat-roofed Tibetan homes in other areas. Qiang nationality dwellings and watchtowers in the Aba Tibetan and Qiang Autonomous Prefecture of Sichuan province are skillfully built of irregular broken rock and timbers. Bamboo and wooden stilt houses of the Dai and Jino nationalities are common in rural areas of the Xishuangbanna region of southern Yunnan. Within the homes of the matriarchal Moso people around Lake Lugu on the Yunnan-Sichuan border, dwelling and eating areas are designated according to age and gender.

Stylized patterns, decorations, and symbols, sometimes with almost universal meaning in China and other parts of East Asia, manifest themselves in many regions and mediums. Examples are images of cranes, bamboo, evergreens, lotus, peaches, plum blossoms, chrysanthemums, peonies, pear wood, dragons, phoenixes, mythical beasts, and pairs of ducks, fish, fowl, butterflies, and the Chinese characters for "double-happiness" or "long life"—all with auspicious meanings related to wealth, status, health, harmony, longevity, offspring, and marital bliss. In other cases, items are regional or local in occurrence. Weaving and embroidery patterns from Miao, Zhuang, Bai, and other ethnic minority groups include many of the images just mentioned as well as mountains, rivers, local water plants, and algae.

PAPER CUTTING

China invented paper by 105 C.E., and paper cuts have been traced to as early as 207 C.E. in northern China. Many paper arts are still current, including elaborate grave offerings burned at funerals and a wide variety of good luck charms and decorative items. Mulberry bark, rice straw, wood, or rags are among the materials used to make paper. The art of paper cutting is still practiced in many areas and has a commercial market, especially for weddings and Chinese New Year. Thin sheets of paper, colored on one side, are stacked in a specially prepared wooden box frame, the bottom tempered with a mixture of fat, charcoal, and beeswax. The auspicious color red is very traditional, though many other colors or mixtures of colors are used. In some styles, ten to fifty sheets of paper are cut at one time, using sharp knives driven down through the paper. Other styles employ large-handled, fine-bladed Chinese scissors. Designs may be cut freehand or transferred to the paper by the use of patterns outlined in smoke or chalk. Themes include good luck items such as peaches, pairs of fish or ducks, scenes from Chinese opera, or daily life. Once cut, paper cuts can be placed on walls or windows or mounted on white paper.

All over China carved woodblocks were used to print images of protector gods and spirits, magic tokens, and good luck pictures displayed at the New Year (*nianhua*). Flourishing by the Song dynasty, pictures were produced on various grades of paper and sometimes in several colors applied with a series of different blocks. In rural areas, doors are often guarded by colorful paper posters of ancient generals known as "door gods" (*menshen*) who are pasted on the outside doors to protect the families from unlucky forces.

CLOTHING STYLES AND FOOD

Age, gender, and locale have traditionally governed vernacular clothing styles. Local cultures, foreign invasions, trade, and dynastic shifts have all influenced Chinese clothing patterns, which evolved over time and in turn influenced surrounding cultures in **Korea**, Japan, and Vietnam. The invasion of the Manchus in the seventeenth century brought widespread changes in clothing patterns, especially styles of side-fastening tunics, still reflected in many colloquial dress styles throughout the country. By the 1930s, the form-fitting, side-fastening, and side-slit *qipao* (cheongsam) based on Manchu style became emblematic of Chinese women's clothing in urban areas such as Shanghai. Highly embroidered bibs and tunics, worn with short skirts and leggings or trousers, are common among women's dress in several ethnic minorities in southwest China, indigo being a common dye for the cloth. Felt cloaks in a variety of shades and styles are still commonly used among the Yi nationality in the Liangshan Mountains of Sichuan. In many rural areas costume and hairstyle can still convey a woman's age-group, marital status, and cultural area.

Foodways, a central focus of activity in all societies in China, vary widely by region and ethnicity. Popular foods in the north include steamed or fried wheat breads, noodles, dumplings, grapes, melons, preserved vegetables, and mutton. Common in the south are rice (of varying gluten content and color), green vegetables, citrus fruits, fish, and pork. A variety of seafoods including shrimp, clams, oysters, scallops, and more exotic fare is popular in coastal areas. An example of the local diversity of foodways is Sichuan province. The cuisine of the Han Chinese living in the Sichuan basin around Chengdu is one of the most varied in China, featuring hot, peppery dishes composed of combinations of meat (pork, chicken, duck, beef, and occasionally rabbit), fish, soybean curd, and many sort of vegetables. Temperate-climate fruits are also available, and a rich variety of local snacks (*xiaochi*) sold from street stands and special snack restaurants. In the Tibetan areas of northern and western Sichuan, yak meat, roast barley (*tsampa*), butter tea, yogurt, and a variety of fruits, vegetables, and grains that can be grown at higher altitudes comprise the diet staples. Hand-pulled noodles (*lamian*) are a specialty of Hui nationality restaurants located in many Han and Tibetan areas of the province. In the Yi nationality areas of southern Sichuan, a typical meal consists of plain boiled chicken, potatoes, maize, and buckwheat pancakes.

CHALLENGES OF THE MODERN WORLD

The effects of **modernization** on Chinese folk traditions on the mainland and on Taiwan have taken somewhat different tracks, though there are similarities. While Taiwan was spared the political movements that wracked the mainland periodically from 1949 to the late 1970s, the effects of mass culture and modernization were already being felt in the early 1970s as audiences and practitioners were drawn from traditional entertainments and mediums of expression by increased urbanization, mechanization, and competition from electronic media. In some instances, however, past has melded with present, as exemplified by Taiwan puppet operas featuring laser lights and dry ice and shortened and revised Beijing opera performances (many featuring the lively Monkey King) in tourist venues in Beijing.

On both the mainland and Taiwan tourism has appropriated, adapted, reworked, revived, recycled, recreated, and invented folk traditions to draw in audiences comprised largely of non-locals. The commodification of ethnicity has been especially pronounced in ethnic minority venues. Examples

A young woman of the Bai nationality in Dali, Yunnan Province, sings the lyrics to a "great volumes tune" (*dabenqu*) with accompaniment by a large three-stringed banjo (*sanxian*). Such performances, linked to a local style of storytelling, have become part of the tourist trade. This image dates from 1985, when tourism was just beginning in the region. (Photograph by Mark Bender)

229

include dances and songs performed by Ami people at Taroko Gorge in Taiwan, Mongol riding and wrestling exhibitions in Inner Mongolia, folksinging, traditional architecture, and marriage re-enactments among the Miao, Zhuang, and Dong peoples in Guizhou and Guangxi. Full-scale promotions of ethnic culture are pervasive in Yunnan, a province in southwest China where ethnic tourism has become a major source of local and regional income. Aspects of Bai, Naxi, Dai, Yi, and Tibetan performance, foodways, folk costume, music, and architecture are available through short tours, home visits, and overnight stays. Recently tourist growth in Yunnan and neighboring areas has been promoted as part of an "opening of the West" development project and aided by the infrastructure of new road systems, tourist buses, convenient lodgings, and digital technology.

An outstanding example of ethnic tourism is the song-and-dance extravaganzas and laser light shows in the Stone Forest, south of Kunming, Yunnan, where versions of the story of the Sani people's folk heroine Ashima are presented alongside re-enactments of rituals by actors dressed as priest-shamans called *bimo*. Shops are filled with ethnic costumes (sometimes of other ethnic groups), batik wall-hangings, jewelry, carvings, and other folk arts. The Ten-Month Solar Calendar Park in Chuxiong, Yunnan, is a large-scale park artistically introducing aspects of myth, legend, song, dance, and material culture of Yi groups in Yunnan. Statues representing folk figures such as the song goddess Liu Sanjie (Third Sister Liu) in Liuzhou, Guangxi, and the Yi hero Zhige Alu in Ninglang, Yunnan, are sometimes encountered in small cities throughout the ethnic minority areas of China. Variety shows presented to huge audiences on national television often feature increasingly elaborate and abstracted performances of ethnic minority folksongs, folk dances, and rituals to audiences with little or no understanding of the particular local cultures represented.

While tourism provides new and sometimes radically altered contexts, contents, and mediums of folk expression, audiences and performers in more traditional situations are in many instances fading. In some areas of southwest China, for instance, the number of folksingers under the age of thirty has fallen dramatically in the last two decades. Audiences are also shrinking for the daily storytelling sessions in story houses and local opera houses, though in some places new venues have grown in or near senior citizens' complexes. Like folk traditions throughout time, the situation is dynamic, and while some forms may disappear without practitioners and audiences, new or modified forms may emerge over time—one example being the widespread growth of the "rice-sprouts (*yang'ge*) street dancing and drama among middle-aged women and men throughout the 1990s in many urban areas in northern China. Some folk forms may also receive new attention as modern audiences search their collective past for their roots in Chinese culture.

Numerous national, provincial, and local **museums** all over the country preserve and interpret folk culture. These include the huge Ethnic Palace Musuem (*Minzu gong*) in Beijing; the Suzhou Folk Culture Museum (*Suzhou minsu bowuguan*) in Suzhou, Jiangsu province; the Yunnan Ethnic Minorities Museum (*Yunnan minzu bowuguan*) and Ethnic Minority Village park (*Minzu cun*) in Kunming; Museum of the Liangshan Yi's Slave Society (*Liangshan Yizu nuli shehui bowuguan*) in Xichang, Sichuan; a folklore museum of Shanxi folk culture in the huge late-Qing dynasty residential architectural complex known as "Qiao Family Castle" (*Qiaojia dayuan*) in Taiyuan; the County Museum (*Xian bowuguan*) in the ancient Silk Road town of Dunhuang, Gansu province; the Inner Mongolian Historical Museum (*Nei Menggu lishi bowuguan*) in Hohhot, Inner Mongolia; and the Tianjin Folk Museum (*Tianjin minsu bowuguan*), built on the site of an ancient temple to the sea goddess, Mazu, in Hebei province.

STUDIES OF CHINESE FOLKLORE

Massive numbers of books, articles, and journals devoted to folklore studies printed at national and local levels have appeared in China since 1949, with the number of publications increasing every year since the 1980s. The journal *Studies of Ethnic Literature* (*Minzu wenxue yanjiu*) published by the ethnic literature division of the Chinese Academy of Social Sciences is particularly noteworthy for studies of folk literature. Younger scholars who innovatively incorporate Chinese and Western folklore theory into their research include the student of the Mongol epic Chao Gejin (Chogjin) and Yi (Nuosu) epic scholar Bamo Qubumo. Works by foreign scholars and missionaries on local folk customs began to appear in the nineteenth century. In the 1950s and 1960s, David Crockett Graham and Wolfram Eberhard edited collections of Chinese folktales collected in the 1940s from local regions in China. After 1949 access to mainland China was severely limited, and many folklorists and anthropologists could work only in peripheral Chinese culture areas. By the late 1980s, however, books and articles by European, Japanese, American, and Korean scholars increased as China began to re-open. Among recent works in English are studies of Yangzi delta folksongs by Antoinette Schimmelpenninck, northwest minority stories and songs collected by Kevin Stuart and local collaborators, Naxi folk music by Helen Rees, and Yangzhou and Suzhou professional storytelling by Vibeke Bordahl and Mark Bender respectively. More recent anthropological studies include those on folk cultures of the Yi (Nuosu) in Sichuan by Steve Harrell, Bamo Qubumo, and Ma Erzi; Yi (Lolopo) in central Yunnan by Eric Mueggler; and Miao in southeast Guizhou by Louisa Schein. Important English-language journals for the study of Chinese folklore include *Asian Folklore Studies* (published in *Najoya*, Japan), *Asian Music: Journal for the Society of Asian Music*, CHIME (journal of the European Foundation for Chinese Music Research), *Chinoperl Papers*, and *Oral Tradition* from the Center for Studies in Oral Tradition at the University of Missouri, Columbia. *See also* **Chinese Abroad**.

BIBLIOGRAPHY

Bamo, Qubumo. 2001. Traditional Nuosu Origin Narratives: A Case Study of Ritualized Epos in *Bimo* Incantation Scriptures. *Oral Tradition* 16.2: 453–479.

Bender, Mark. 2001. A Description of *Jiangjing* (Telling Scriptures) Services in Jingjiang, China. *Asian Folklore Studies* 60: 101–133.

———. 2003. *Plum and Bamboo: China's Suzhou Chantefable Tradition*. Urbana: University of Illinois Press.

———. 2004. Hunting Nets and Butterflies: Ethnic Minority Songs from Southern China. In *The Poem Behind the Poem: Translating Asian Poetry*, edited by Frank Stewart. Port Townshend, WA: Copper Canyon Press. 39–54.

Birrell, Anne. 1999. *The Classic of Mountains and Seas*. London: Penguin Classics.

Bordahl, Vibeke, ed. 1996. *The Oral Tradition of Yangzhou Storytelling*. Nordic Institute of Asian Studies Monograph Series, No. 73. London: Curzon.

———. 1999. *The Eternal Storyteller: Oral Literature in Modern China*. Nordic Institute of Asian Studies. Surrey, England: Curzon.

Chao Gejin. 1997. Mongolian Oral Epic Poetry: An Overview. *Oral Tradition* 12.2: 322–336.

Drums of the Ancestors: Manchu and Mongol Shamanism (film). 1995. The Foundation for Shamanic Studies.

Duan Baolin. 1985. *Zhongguo minjian wenxue gaiyao* (Outline of Chinese Folk Literature). Beijing: Beijing daxue chubanshe.

Eberhard, Wolfram, ed. 1965. *Folktales of China*. Chicago: University of Chicago Press.

Guo Panxi. 1996. *Zhonguo minjian youxi yu jizhi* (Chinese Folk Games and Sports). Shanghai: Shanghai sanlian shudian, Xuelin chubanshe.

Harrell, Steven, Bamo Qubumo, and Ma Erzi. 2000. *Mountain Patterns: The Survival of Nuosu Culture in China*. Seattle: University of Washington Press.

Hung, Chang-tai. 1985. *Going to the People: Chinese Intellectuals and Folk Literature 1981–1937*. Cambridge: Harvard University Press.

Johnson, David. 1995. *Mu-lien in Paochuan: The Performance Context and Religious Meaning*. In *Ritual and Scripture in Chinese Popular Religion: Five Studies*, edited by David Johnson. Publications of the Popular Culture Project 3. Berkeley, CA: IEAS Publications. 55–103.

Jones, Stephen. 2004. *Plucking the Winds: Lives of Village Musicians in Old and New China*. Leiden: CHIME Foundation.

Limusishiden and Kevin Stuart, eds. 1998. *Huzhu Mongghul Folklore: Texts and Translations*. Munich: Lincon Europa.

Mair, Victor. 1997. The Prosimetric Form in the Chinese Literary Tradition. In *Prosimetrum: Crosscultural Perspectives on Narrative in Prose and Verse*, edited by Joseph Harris and Karl Reichl. Rochester, NY: D.S. Brewer. 365–385.

Mueggler, Eric. 2001. *The Age of Wild Ghosts: Memory, Violence, and Place in Southwest China*. Berkeley: University of California Press.

Rees, Helen. 2000. *Echoes of History: Naxi Music in Modern China*. Oxford: Oxford University Press.

Schein, Louisa. 2000. *Minority Rules: The Miao and the Feminine in China's Cultural Politics*. Durham: Duke University Press.

Schimmelpenninck, Antoinette. 1997. *Folk Songs and Folk Singers: Shan'ge Traditions in Southern Jiangsu Chinese*. Leiden: CHIME Foundation.

Siu, Helen F. 1989. Recycling Rituals: Politics and Popular Culture in Contemporary Rural China. In *Unofficial China: Popular Culture and Thought in the People's Republic*, edited by Perry Link, Richard Madsen, and Paul Pickowicz. Boulder, CO: Westview Press. 121–137.

Swain, Margaret. 1989. Development Ethnic Tourism in Yunnan, China: Shilin Sani. *Tourism Recreation Research*. 16.1: 33–39.

Temko, Florence. 1982. *Chinese Paper Cuts: Their History and How to Make and Use Them*. Beijing: China Books and Periodicals.

Ting, Nai-Tung. 1978. *A Type Index of Chinese Folktales*. Folklore Fellows Communications No. 223. Helsinki: Academia Scientiarum Fennica.

Wu, Sue-mei. 2003. Hand Puppet Theater Performance: Emergent Structures and the Resurgence of Taiwanese Identity. In *Religion and the Formation of Taiwanese Identities*, edited by Paul R. Katz and Murray A. Rubenstein. New York: Palgrave.

Yang, Gladys. 1957. *Ashima*. Beijing: Foreign Languages Press.

Yang Guoren, ed. 1988. *Dongzu zuoye ge* (Dong Nationality Courting Songs). Giuyang: Guizhou minzu chubanshe.

Yung, Bell. 1989. *Cantonese Opera: Performance as Creative Process*. Cambridge: Cambridge University Press.

Zhang Daoyi, and others, eds. 1990. *Minjian muban hua* (Folk Woodblock Pictures). Nanjing: Jiangsu meishu chubanshe.

Zhongguo dabaikequanshu chubanshe bianjibu (Chinese encyclopedia editorial board), ed. 1983. *Xiqu quyi* (Drama and storytelling arts). In *Zhongguo dabaikequanshu* (Chinese encyclopedia) series. Beijing: *Zhongguo dabaikequanshu* chubanshe.

Mark Bender

CHINESE ABROAD

HISTORY

Huaqiao or *haiwai huaren* (Chinese abroad or overseas) is a general term referring to the Chinese living outside of China. The overseas Chinese communities around the world are often more diverse in language, ethnicity, and belief than those in **China**. Waves of emigration from different regions of China over different periods of history have added layers of meaning to these communities. The study of overseas Chinese folklore is an emerging field, for which much of the data has yet to be collected, categorized, and analyzed, especially with regard to communities in continental Europe, Latin America, Africa, West Asia, South Asia, and the former Soviet Union. Although in many ways not comparable to the variety and richness of folklore in China, the folklore of the overseas Chinese has played a crucial role in maintaining their tradition and identity. This transformed folklore can only be sketched here by providing its ethnohistorical and sociocultural contexts—with the examples in the United States, major expressions of the fundamental belief system, and its changes during this era of **globalization**. Though the Chinese have been emigrating from their "Middle Kingdom" since the third century B.C.E., reaching as far as the east coast of Africa and Rome by the twelfth century C.E., Chinese communities in the United States will represent their counterparts throughout the world in the manner in which they have sought to preserve their distinctive cultural identities.

Chinese laborers who came to the United States before 1850 numbered less than fifty, and their influence was insignificant. Thereafter, wars (for example, the Opium War in 1840 and the Taiping Rebellion in the 1850s

The Chinatown gate in Portland, Oregon. (Photograph by Juwen Zhang, 2004)

and 1860s) and other social upheavals in China, as well as the Gold Rush in California and the construction of the transcontinental railroad, made Chinese migration to the United States increasingly attractive. However, waves of would-be Chinese immigrants (in particular, women and children) were blocked by discriminative legal exclusion acts from the 1890s until the 1960s. Those who were allowed to stay and who were smuggled into the United States were mostly poor and illiterate rural laborers known as "coolies" (from the Chinese *kuli*—"hard labor") from Canton and Fukien (the provinces now known as Guangdong and Fujian), and they formed male-only communities. This unnatural situation, also common in Southeast Asia, limited the practice of customs that were based on the family unit. However, eventual intermarriages with non-Chinese helped the spread of Chinese customs outside of China.

By the turn of the twentieth century, the "sojourner" mentality of the early emigrants started to change. The proverb, "Falling leaves return to their roots" (*luoye guigen*), was gradually replaced by another one, "Falling seeds take root" (*luodi shenggen*). The saying, "Once a Chinese, always a Chinese," no longer adequately described developments in the immigrant experience. It was, however, only after the mid-twentieth century that the "settler" mentality of taking root in a new location began to replace the sojourner mentality. In 1940, only 4,928 Chinese remained in the United States after the peak of 123,201 in 1880. By 1970, the population increased to 34,764 after the end of legal exclusion. Thirty years later the number in the United States jumped to 3 million, including 2 million speaking Chinese at home, along with those local-born generations or adopted individuals with Chinese ancestry. At the same time the total number of overseas Chinese worldwide, beyond China, **Taiwan**, and Singapore, rose to more than 30 million.

The complex background has shaped the characteristic diaspora folklore of the overseas Chinese, which is little studied. Material folklore such as food, housing, and festival objects, for example, is practiced more than verbal arts. The complex ethnicities of the overseas Chinese community may be categorized in several different ways, but language (that is, dialect) and regional identity, two inseparable markers, are a good place to start. A menu from a Chinese restaurant in virtually any overseas community may be seen as an example of the diversity of the overseas Chinese populations: Hunan chicken, Sichuan bean-curd (*doufu* or *tofu*), Cantonese dim-sum, Yangzhou fried rice, and Beijing duck. Distinct regional identities are most apparent among the first generation of the overseas Chinese. Their use of hometown dialects distinguishes regional identity, which is seen in their forming or joining associations known as *hui*, *huiguan*, *gonghui*, or *gongsuo*, which are based upon their places of origin back in China. Nostalgia for home is somewhat alleviated by joining these associations. These linguistic/regional distinctions and nostalgia tend to fade in later generations.

What does it mean to be "overseas" Chinese in the new millennium? The philosopher Tu Wei-ming (1994) proposes the notion of "Cultural China," which refers to three groups of "Chinese" people: those who live in China, Taiwan, and Singapore; those who live outside those regions; and those who intellectually self-identify as Chinese. The anthropologist Yih-yuan Li (1995) has developed this notion to emphasize the everyday practices of ordinary people. He contends that three key markers identify an "Overseas Chinese": (1) family relationships and ties, characterized as Confucian; (2) traditional diet; and (3) the practice of fortune-telling and *feng shui* (geomancy). Indeed, these markers, which are expressions of the fundamental belief system, are also the basis of their distinct folklore.

RELIGIOUS BELIEFS

Overseas Chinese carry with them an inclusive and polytheistic belief system that does not clearly distinguish between the religious and the non-religious, the official (elite) and the unofficial (folk). This system holds that the origin of the universe is the Great Ultimate (*taiji*), from which *yin* (lunar, female, etc.) and *yang* (solar, male, etc.) are engendered. *Yin* and *yang* then interact to generate the Five Elements or Phases (*wuxing*—water, metal, earth, fire, and wood), which are the components of all things in the universe. The ancient Chinese believed that the cosmos could be understood through the correlation of numbers, signs, colors, directions, and patterns. These were reduced to the Eight Trigrams (*bagua*) that combine to make the sixty-four hexagrams of the *I-Ching* (*Yi Jing*), which may be interpreted to explain all things. The ancient Chinese tendency toward correlative thinking about the cosmos may appear to be simple at first glance, but the underlying philosophical concepts are extremely complex. Because complex cultural concepts are invariably expressed in concrete customs and practices, the study of these customs and practices will help us understand how the Chinese belief system has been modified overseas. The following four concepts, therefore, characterize the belief system of overseas Chinese:

1. The immortality of the soul (*linghun bumie*). Gods, ghosts, and souls of the deceased exist in a realm that mirrors the human world. The two parts of the human soul—the *hun* and the *po* (*yin* and *yang* aspects)—combine to make a life and separate at its death. Ancestor worship stems from the believed continuation in another realm of these spiritual components of a human being. During a funeral, material needs are transferred to the spirit by means of offerings and by burning symbolic paper representations of such items as cars, houses, and money.

2. The unity of nature and man (*tianren heyi*). Supernatural beings possess the power to affect human affairs. Man is one component of the eternally changing universe. Spirits and humans can help each other through the proper conduct of appropriate rituals. When natural disasters and human conflict occur, rituals are carried out to appease gods and ghosts and to alleviate human suffering.

3. The Great Unity (*dayitong*). Diverse practices are acceptable, as long as common goals are maintained. In other words, various local or imported beliefs and behaviors may be practiced if officially sanctioned ideas are preserved. Indeed, just as the syncretic tendency of Chinese thought and practice has operated in Chinese culture throughout history, it continues to underlie the beliefs and practices of overseas Chinese.

4. The pursuit of good-fortune (and harmony) and avoidance of misfortune (*quji bixiong*). One's fate (*ming*) and luck (*yun*) determine one's life. However, fate is changeable with the help of gods and ghosts, who can be moved through ancestral worship, divination, and the proper conduct of rituals.

These beliefs have been well expressed through the practice of "Follow the local customs" (*ruxiang suisu*) and "Falling seeds take root," an important virtue in Chinese and overseas Chinese cultures. Indeed, these traditional concepts were effectively translated into an ethical system by Confucius (551–479 B.C.E.) and his followers, and with modifications for political expediency, the system has been the dominant worldview of the Chinese for two millennia. This pragmatic ethical system, based on the two keystones of *xiao*, respect for parents and elders, and *zhong*, loyalty to family or group, stresses five constant virtues in everyday life: *zhi*, the wisdom that comes from self-cultivation and education, which leads to improving the social status of oneself and family; *yi*, concern for social justice that results from wisdom; *xin*, good faith and trust, which leads to power; *li*, the rituals that properly order relations among human beings and between the natural and supernatural; and *ren*, benevolence, humaneness among people and harmony between man and nature and man and the heavens. Daoist, Buddhist, Christian, Islamic, and various local beliefs have been integrated alongside Confucian ethics into the folklore of the Chinese people, whether in China or overseas. For example, those in Europe and North America have adapted themselves to Christian culture, while those in other places, such as Thailand and Malaysia, have adapted to Buddhist and Islamic cultures. Evidence that these adaptations have become inseparable from the local cultural landscape of overseas Chinese is seen in the temples, churches, fortunetelling stands, restaurants, groceries, Chinatowns, jokes, modified traditional tales, Disney films, and Kung Fu (*gongfu*, martial arts) movies of these communities.

That the overseas Chinese appear to integrate diverse beliefs and practices so easily is not surprising because Chinese philosophy and tradition from the earliest times has been characterized as syncretic. Indeed, it is this tendency toward syncretism that distinguishes the Chinese way of looking at the world from the exclusivity of Judeo-Christian and Islamic traditions. This tendency helps to explain why overseas Chinese accept and absorb whatever beliefs and customs they consider to be useful, while rejecting others. The folklore of the overseas Chinese is a further testament to the inclination of the Chinese people, wherever and whenever they have lived, to find harmony in diversity and create order out of chaos. This is most apparent in their ritual life.

RITUALS, FESTIVALS, AND CELEBRATIONS

Along with folk customs, life cycle rituals (rites of passage), which include births, initiations, weddings, and funerals, are the best expression of a society's belief system. For the overseas Chinese, birth and initiation rituals are often held within families, while wedding and funeral rituals are elaborately performed as public events and key markers of group identity. Transforming changes are seen at various levels. For example, the custom of "sitting the month" (*zuoyuezi*) at birth, with which the new mother should stay inside the room with the baby for a month, following various taboos and a special diet, is rarely practiced. However, the long-life noodles (*changshou mian*) served at traditional birthday celebrations easily accompany the birthday cake.

Weddings in a Chinese community, especially in a sizeable Chinatown, are usually held on weekends, unless otherwise determined by a fortuneteller or traditional calendar. A typical wedding may have some or all of the following components: announcement of the wedding in a local Chinese newspaper; a visit to a local temple; a service in a church; a banquet in a restaurant; receiving guests and their gifts at the banquet; respectful bowing (traditionally the more serious *ketou* or kowtow, knocking of the head on the ground), directed by a ritual host to heaven and earth, the ancestors, and parents; the offering of tea or wine to the parents; traditional Chinese dress for the ceremony, then changing two or three times during the banquet, sometimes into Western dress; formal thanking of the guests by offering wine and food; well-wishing of guests for many children (for example, offering peanuts to represent the birth of many children) and a harmonious marriage (for example, Mandarin ducks). No taboo words are to be uttered at any time. Traditionally, all the decorations and the bride's dress were red, the auspicious color of folk belief. During the banquet, a lion dance might be performed, and firecrackers might be set. This promotes the auspicious and drives away the inauspicious. In terms of language used, English and Chinese may be naturally mixed, although the younger generations may be inclined to use English. At a wedding banquet, the presence of some non-Chinese spouses and friends is common and seen as a pleasant addition to the ritual. In fact, intermarriage is increasingly popular. Love marriages are replacing traditional marriages arranged by parents. The early practice of polygyny (one husband with more than one wife) in China and abroad is rarely seen among current overseas Chinese for a variety of reasons, among them lack of adequate means, better education, and the desire to adapt to the judicial norms of their chosen locales.

Funerals are a key marker of cultural identity for Chinese both in China and abroad. Among the early overseas Chinese from South China, "secondary burial" was common, a practice of burying the dead in a temporary grave for a few years and then re-burying the remains in ancestral graveyards in China. In the 1960s, for instance, thousands of urns from all over the world were shipped back to China. However, many urns, like those still in **Hawai'i**, were not shipped back and remain overseas due to the community's affordability and broken kinships. Thus, the name "without-ancestor-graves" (*wuzufen*) was given to the graves of those early laborers buried far away from ancestral homes, and, in overseas Chinese communities such as that in Philadelphia, the new generations hold annual sacrificial rituals on the *Qing Ming* Festival on 5 April. In one cemetery there, where the earliest extant Chinese graves date from the 1900s, the most common gravestone until the 1950s was a small piece of marble bearing the name, date of death, and hometown of the deceased. Gradually, not only did the size and quality of the gravestones change, but also the format of the inscription, which came to include both traditional Chinese epitaphs and the English names of the deceased. Combined graves of husband and wife, in addition to the single graves of women, could also be found. Since the 1990s, the elaborate funerary, burial, and sacrificial rituals carried out in good *feng shui* locations have been dramatically different from the rituals conducted decades earlier. Thus, the ways in which burial rituals are carried out and gravestones selected and inscribed are clear indicators of the improving socioeconomic conditions of the overseas Chinese and the change from "sojourner" to "settler" mentality.

A 1990-era Chinese grave from a cemetery in Philadelphia, Pennsylvania. (Photograph by Juwen Zhang, 1999)

When conducting a funeral ritual, until the early part of the twentieth century in the United States, fellow villagers of the deceased would put a penny or nickel in the mouth of the corpse, offer a chicken as sacrifice, put a sealed bottle with the name of the dead in the coffin, and bury him in the grave purchased by the village-based association to which they belonged. Today in large communities, funeral homes operated by Chinese have sprung up. Self-sufficient associations are still the major resources for many families, especially those in Chinatowns, when they need to conduct a decent burial at an auspicious gravesite (for example, sites on a slope in a cemetery were usually cheaper, but might be thought to have good *feng shui*). Indeed, the selection of an auspicious gravesite is essential to give the funeral ritual meaning, and this is consistent with the Chinese belief system. There are still times—as with the spreading and burning of paper money—when the Chinese seek strategically to accommodate their cultural need without violating local government laws. In some communities, the procession may even pass by the house of the deceased, which tends to ritualize a local practice. In reality, the family, directors of the funeral home, and the cemetery can often make adjustments so that everyone is satisfied that the rituals are being conducted in accordance with their remembered tradition. This contributes to affirming the nostalgia and the sense of identity of the overseas Chinese. Overall, modifications in funeral ritual must be seen to represent to a certain extent changes in traditional beliefs, but without these modifications and adaptations, it is likely that the ritual might become obsolete.

Sacrificial rituals have equal importance. Communication with deceased ancestors, ghosts, or supernatural beings occurs during such events as the *Qing Ming* Festival and anniversaries of the deceased family members. The traditional Ghost Festival (*guijie*) on the fifteenth day of the seventh month in the lunar calendar and similar festivals, however, are often practiced as family events. The rituals may take place at home or the grave. In a public event directed by a ritual host, the process may start by offering incense and food to the Earth God (*tudigong*), offering eulogies, and bowing to the tablets or pictures of the gods or deceased. Then individual families will share a meal with the dead by putting a pair of chopsticks or a bowl upon the grave in the fashion of a picnic.

Despite the relatively short history of immigration from China, the United States has witnessed an increasingly palpable practice of multi-belief worship in Chinese communities. Owners of businesses in Chinatowns may worship at Christian churches or Buddhist temples on holidays. At the same time, they may also make offerings to the Treasure God (*caishen*) at shrines located in their own places of business or offer sacrifices to the Earth God at graves of family members. One traditional funeral service in Philadelphia Chinatown in 1999 epitomized the Chinese tendency to syncretize beliefs and practices when appropriate and useful: Buddhist monks chanted at certain intervals, a Catholic priest came to pay last respects to his congregant's deceased parent, and a *fengshui* practitioner selected an auspicious gravesite. In general, the community elders will be consulted to resolve differences of opinion regarding the practice of traditions or rituals. Such a practice always involves various taboos and embraces flexible definitions of fate and luck for their strategic adaptation. For example, early overseas Chinese settlers found it hard to survive and had to give up many of their customary practices. Yet they would not give up their offering of ritual food to gods and ghosts, nor would they stop seeking auspicious locations for gravesites. They also continued to follow the funeral-related taboos by having non-Chinese caretakers deal with corpses. Today, immigrant Chinese continue such important practices as these as well as those related to auspicious decoration of homes, rooms, and places of business and the selection of auspicious locations for houses and gravesites. Furthermore, these practices, primarily related to ancient *feng shui* practices, have become quite popular both in and outside of China. To a great extent, this aspect of the materialist search for wealth or good fortune correlates with the institutional codes of many local governments, which then further promote such practices. While this serves to enrich and spread the practice of traditional folklore, it simultaneously creates a problem: the rise of secular materialism and formal religious institutions (due to the higher education level of the immigrants) has resulted in the

A fortunetelling stand attracts a curious audience at a Spring Festival celebration in Portland, Oregon. (Photograph by Juwen Zhang, 2003)

loss of a sense of spiritual connectedness, fundamental to Chinese beliefs, between the people and the place they inhabit.

As they are celebrated traditionally, festivals are another expression of a people's belief system. Those most commonly maintained abroad are the following: the Spring Festival (Lunar New Year), in which dumplings, spring-rolls, and fish are eaten; the Lantern Festival (fifteen days after the Spring Festival), replete with lanterns, firecrackers, and lion dances; the Mid-Autumn Festival, in which the moon-cake and round fruits symbolize family reunion and perfection; and the early spring *Qing Ming* Festival, in which graves are visited with offerings. The symbolic meaning of the food and objects of the rituals, which may be long forgotten by the practitioners, is, however, of great interest to folklorists. For the overseas Chinese these celebrations serve the important function of integrating their remembered traditions with local customs and festivals, which then become part of their own evolving folklore. One should, however, never underestimate the importance of the seemingly simple pleasure of enjoying the traditional foods.

FOOD AND MEDICINE

Food is one of the most important components of life for a Chinese. While images of the Stove God (*zaoshen*) are rarely seen in kitchens, images of the Treasure God and the character for good-fortune (*fu*) or similar decorations are observable in all overseas Chinese families. Indeed, the overseas Chinese pay so much attention to the kitchen that, in addition to finding an auspicious *feng shui* location for it, they have developed a common practice of modifying their residences with patio-kitchen or garage-kitchen type accommodations.

In the United States, the overseas Chinese have developed their own style of preparing and serving restaurant food, often different from traditional or home cooking: the utensils are fork and knife, though one may request chopsticks. This style functions as a medium for the overseas Chinese longing for tradition as well as for their interaction with non-Chinese. Typical appetizers are three types of soup (won-ton, sweet-sour, and egg-drop), spring roll, or dumpling, with the reversal of the traditional Chinese soup-after-meal custom. Nearly all menus have such dishes as "General Tso's Chicken," *mogu gaipan, chao mein,* and chop-suey, which are among those "invented in America," though they remotely resemble traditional Chinese dishes. The ubiquitous fortune cookie—served at many in lieu of dessert—has become a marker of the Chinese restaurant, which, like Chinatown itself or any other transformed custom, is a compact and complex item of folklore. The cookie is just an attractive, edible pseudo-ethnic marker reifying an exotic "Chinese" experience and providing momentary titillation by prospects of fate control through a demystifying action of exploring one's "fortune." This item functions not only as a bridge between the overseas Chinese and the local population but also as a connection between their real life and their cherished, remembered traditions.

Chinese food and traditional medicine are inseparable, together reflecting the fundamental cosmological and philosophical views about life, body, and the supernatural world. An English proverb says, "You are what you eat." The Chinese equivalent is "What you eat is what you fix" (*chi shenme, bu shenme*). It is not surprising, therefore, that overseas Chinese keep fish tanks or animal cages in restaurants and shop in their special seafood stores or deli markets. Indeed, the Daoist idea of longevity is intimately connected to food. The many folktales, legends, proverbs, and jokes surrounding each dish increase the pleasure of eating and the feeling of well-being. Herbal medicine and acupuncture are becoming increasingly accepted by the public and even some health insurance companies. Chinese clinics, identified by signs of the Daoist Immortals or the Longevity Star (*shouxing*), are no longer limited to those in Chinatowns or those run by Chinese only.

MYTHS AND FOLKTALES

Myths and folktales are no longer commonly spread by word of mouth overseas, while tales, proverbs, and jokes are either retold in different languages or told in a mixture of Chinese and some other language. Books and the Internet are also a source of traditional folklore. Increasingly close and convenient telecommunication with China has made accessible performances of a variety of verbal art genres to new immigrants worldwide. In certain older communities, one can hear and see performances of verbal art genres, *quyi* (art of melodies), by elderly aficionados. More elite but traditional opera genres such as Cantonese musical drama (*yueju*) or Beijing opera (*jingju*) are also popular in overseas communities. New York boasts one of the largest and oldest Chinatowns, constantly presenting a variety of performances. It is not surprising that a Beijing opera troupe in New York, led by Qi Shufang, a famous opera performer, was awarded a National Heritage Fellowship from the National Endowment for the Arts. Western scholars of *quyi* have brought performers of different folklore and operatic genres to appear in various settings across the United States. Folk drama and acrobatic troupes are increasingly popular in the overseas communities and the locales in which they have chosen to put roots, and serve as an infusion of traditional folklore into modern life. Weekend Chinese schools are sprouting up all over and provide yet another effective way of keeping alive and practicing verbal arts.

Collection and study of the evolving genres of verbal art among the overseas Chinese is still in an embryonic stage. There are few collections of tales and songs and even fewer studies of them. In the late nineteenth century, Steward Culin and his

The decoration of a gospel church at a Spring Festival celebration in Portland, Oregon, uses traditional Chinese folk images. (Photograph by Juwen Zhang, 2003)

colleagues provided some of the earliest reports of Chinese American folklore. One early collection of ballads from San Francisco gives us a description that is stunning in its racial caricature of the Chinese as they were seen at that time:

> You can take a Chink away from 'is hop,
> 'Is lanterns an' gals an' pigs an' chop,
> Yu can dress 'im up in yer Christian clo'es,
> Put texts in 'is head an' hymns in 'is nose,
> But yu'll find, when he's actin' a dead straight part,
> He's a Chinaman still in 'is yeller heart.

When the early Chinese were mostly in the laundry business, a humorous proverb circulated not only among them, but also among non-Chinese: "No tickey, no washy" (that is, without a ticket, one could not get back the washed clothes). Today one hears this line: "They want to be Americans on work days, but they want to be Chinese on weekends." Indeed, ethnic humor, in this case, by and about Chinese Americans, appears to be a distinctive and popular genre of folklore of the overseas Chinese.

SPORTS AND GAMES

Entertainment in the form of sports and games has much to do with socioeconomic conditions. Western sports and mass-produced toys, however, are gradually replacing some of the traditional Chinese pastimes. *Majiang* and Chinese card games, popular among the early immigrants, remain a widespread form of entertainment among the first generation. In the last few decades, ping-pong has become common among Chinese Americans, as more and more of them have become homeowners. For the young generations, traditional sports and children's games are little known, but the Yao Ming (a professional basketball player from China on the Houston Rockets team since 2002) phenomenon has doubtlessly aroused or enhanced their interest in sports. Some folklore forms have been integrated into the popular culture (for example, yo-yos and T-shirt decorative designs). More and more classes or clubs have opened to practice traditional sports or games. Meaningfully, the increasing number of non-Chinese participants in Kung Fu, *taijiquan* classes, or lion dance teams that have sprung up everywhere has demonstrated further cultural integration.

ARTS, CRAFTS, AND ARCHITECTURE

The improving socioeconomic status of the overseas Chinese is also visually demonstrated through the construction of traditional architecture, the plastic arts, and signage in Chinatowns. In the past two decades, arches (gates) have been built at the entrances to most major Chinatowns, where folklore often accelerates business. The statue of Confucius in downtown New York City and the Classic Chinese Garden in Portland, Oregon, not only mark the revival of these old Chinatowns but have also become an important part of the local cultural landscape. In comparing the architecture and decorative motifs in the old Chinatown in San Francisco and the newer one in Los Angeles, one may discover a dynamic cultural continuum.

CHALLENGES OF THE MODERN WORLD

The impact of **globalization** on overseas Chinese is most evident in the evolution and adaptation of folklore and tradition to new environments. Technology has, on the one hand, facilitated communication between the overseas Chinese and their hometowns; on the other hand, it has presented a serious challenge to the effort to preserve the folklore that is the key to identity. The early overseas Chinese relied on oral communication to give meaning to their lives. As a result, they held onto a folklore that, having been taken out of its dynamic context and transplanted overseas, became quickly obsolete to their hometown people. Insofar as it represents an earlier unchanged tradition, this folklore is of intrinsic interest because it has become a key medium of strategic globalization in which cultural identity forms the core. For younger generations, though the old ways are replaced by the new, the practice of certain traditional rituals and customs continues to give meaning to them and their communities. Indeed, the vitality and creativity of any tradition lie in the hands of its practitioners.

In conclusion, we have more questions than answers: How does telecommunication function to maintain folklore in a multi-lingual context? How have intermarriage and interracial adoption expanded the concept of the overseas Chinese beyond "Cultural China"? How has the recent wave of intellectual immigrants affected the decline of traditional Chinese beliefs and the rise of canonical religions? Why do certain folklore forms survive, while others do not? How do practitioners choose a substitute for an item that is not available for a traditional dish, proverb, or festival decoration? These questions can only be answered by field-based research, the collection, categorization, and analysis of folklore materials. In the meantime, the Chinese will continue telling jokes and tales, using traditional recipes, celebrating festivals, carrying out rituals, and integrating whatever new cultural elements give meaning to their everyday actions. They will continue, consciously or not, to keep alive the activities of folklore. Doing so will not only satisfy the longing and nostalgia for tradition but will also reaffirm cultural identity in overseas environments.

STUDIES OF OVERSEAS CHINESE FOLKLORE

In addition to the books, films, and recordings listed below, those interested in overseas Chinese should consult the *Journal of Asian American Studies* as well as these Web sites: The Shao Center (Dr. Shao You-Bao Overseas Chinese Documentation and Research Center) at www.library.ohiou.edu/subjects/shao/main.htm; The National Archives and Records Administration (NARA) on Chinese Immigration and the Chinese in the United States at www.archives.gov/facilities/finding_aids/chinese_immigration.html; The World Huaren Federation at www.huaren.org; and the Chinese American Museum at www.camla.org/index.htm.

BIBLIOGRAPHY

Becoming American: The Chinese Experience (film). 2003. New York: Thirteen/WNET.

Benton, Gregor, and Frank N. Pieke. 1998. *The Chinese in Europe*. New York: St. Martin's Press.

Chan, Wing-Tsit. 1963. *A Source Book in Chinese Philosophy*. Princeton: Princeton University Press.

Chang, Iris. 2003. *The Chinese in America: The Narrative History*. New York: Viking.

Chen, Jack. 1980. *The Chinese of America*. San Francisco: Harper and Row.

Chen, Shehong. 2002. *Being Chinese, Becoming Chinese American*. Urbana: University of Illinois Press.

Cheu Hock Tong, ed. 1993. *Chinese Beliefs and Practices in Southeast Asia*. Petaling Jaya, Selangor: Pelanduk Publications.

Chin, Frank. 1991. *Donald Duk: A Novel*. Minneapolis: Coffee House Press.

Cimino, Michael. 1992. *Year of the Dragon* (film). New York: MGM/UA Home Video.

Constable, Nicole, ed. 1996. *Guest People: Hakka Identity in China and Abroad*. Seattle: University of Washington Press.

Culin, Stewart. 1985. *Chinese Games with Dice and Dominoes*. Washington: G.P.O.

Glick, Clarence E. 1980. *Sojourners and Settlers: Chinese Migrants in Hawaii*. Honolulu: University Press of Hawai'i.

Gold Mountain Dreams (film). 2003. Princeton: Films for the Humanities and Sciences.

Hicks, George, ed. 1993. *Overseas Chinese Remittances from Southeast Asia 1910–1940*. Singapore: Select Books.

Hsu, Francis L. K. 1972. *Americans and Chinese: Reflections on Two Cultures and Their People*. New York: American Museum of Science Books.

Hsu, Francis L. K., and Hendrick Serrie. 1998. *The Overseas Chinese: Ethnicity in National Context*. Lanham, MD: University Press of America.

Irwin, Wallace. 1906. *Chinatown Ballads*. New York: Duffield and Company.

Kingston, Maxine Hong. 1975. *The Woman Warrior*. New York: Random House.

Lai, Him Mark, and others. 1980. *Island: Poetry and History of Chinese Immigrants on Angel Island 1910–1940*. San Francisco: San Francisco Study Center.

Lee, Ang. 1994. *The Wedding Banquet* (film). Beverly Hills, CA: FoxVideo.

Lee, Rose. 1960. *The Chinese in the United States of America*. Hong Kong: Hong Kong University Press.

Li, Yih-yuan. 1995. Notions of Time, Space and Harmony in Chinese Popular Culture. In *Time and Space in Chinese Culture*, edited by C.-C. Huang and E. Zurcher. Leiden: E. J. Brill. 383–398.

Lin, Jan. 1998. *Reconstructing Chinatown: Ethnic Enclave, Global Change*. Minneapolis: University of Minnesota Press.

Look Lai, Walton. 1998. *The Chinese in the West Indies 1806–1995: A Documentary History*. Kingston, Jamaica: University of the West Indies Press.

Pan, Lynn, ed. 1999. *The Encyclopedia of the Chinese Overseas*. Cambridge: Harvard University Press.

Serrie, Hendrick. 1998. Chinese Around the World: The Familial and the Familiar. In *The Overseas Chinese*, edited by F.L.K. Hsu and H. Serrie. Lanham, MD: University Press of America. 189–215.

Sung, Betty Lee. 1990. *Chinese American Intermarriage*. New York: Center for Migration Studies.

Tan, Amy. 1989. *The Joy Luck Club*. New York: Putnam.

———. 1991. *The Kitchen God's Wife*. New York: Putnam.

Ting, Nai-tung. 1974. *The Cinderella Cycle in China and Indo-China*. FFC No. 213. Helsinki: Suomalainen Tiedeakatemia.

Tom, K. S. *Echoes from Old China*. Honolulu: Hawai'i Chinese History Center. Distributed by University of Hawai'i Press, 1989.

Tu, Wei-Ming, ed. 1994. *The Living Tree: The Changing Meaning of Being Chinese Today*. Stanford, CA: Stanford University Press, 1994.

Tung, William L. 1974. *The Chinese in America, 1820–1973: A Chronology and Fact Book*. Dobbs Ferry, NY: Oceana.

Wang, Gungwu. 2000. *The Chinese Overseas: From Earthbound China to the Quest for Autonomy.* Cambridge: Harvard University Press.

Wang, Peter. 1997. *A Great Wall* (film). Los Angeles: Orion Pictures Corp.

Wee, Vivienne, and Gloria Davies. 1999. Religion. In *The Encyclopedia of the Chinese Overseas*, edited by Lynn Pan. Cambridge: Harvard University Press.

Williams, Dave, ed. 1997. *The Chinese Other, 1850–1925: An Anthology of Plays.* Lanham, MD: University Press of America, 1997.

Wong, Bernard. 1982. *Chinatown: Economic Adaptation and Ethnic Identity of the Chinese.* New York: Holt, Rinehart and Winston.

Yap, Melanie, and D. L. Man. 1996. *Colour, Confusion and Concessions: The History of the Chinese in South Africa.* Hong Kong: Hong Kong University Press.

Yung, Judy. 1995. *Unbound Feet: A Social History of Chinese Women in San Francisco.* Berkeley: University of California Press.

Zhang, Juwen. 2001. Falling Seeds Take Root: Ritualizing Chinese American Identity through Funerals. Diss., University of Pennsylvania.

Juwen Zhang

MANCHU

GEOGRAPHY AND HISTORY

The Manchu language belongs to the Manchu-Tungusic branch of the Altaic language community, along with the **Mongol** and Turkic languages. According to the traditional classification based on the territorial location of the Manchu-Tungusic people, Tungusic languages comprise the northern group, while Manchu and its related languages comprise the southern group. To the Manchu group belong the dead written Manchu language and the modern spoken Sibe (Sibo; in pinyin transcription, Xibo) dialect, the language of isolated Manchu groups in Manchurian villages, the dead Dshürchen (Dshürchi), Nanai, Oroch, Orokh, Ultcha, and Udekhe. The majority of the Manchus live in Liaoning province of **China**, although many live in Jilin, Heilongjiang, Hebei, Inner Mongolia, Xinjiang, Gansu, Ningxia, and Shandong provinces and in big cities such as Beijing, Urumqi, and Chengdu. They claim to be the one of the largest nationalities in China (10 million in 2000). The Sibes (their number was 192,000 in 2000) are believed to be descendants of an early Inner Asian nomadic tribal confederation, called Shiwei. They are divided into an Eastern and a Western group. The majority still live in the Northeastern region of China. Forced to migrate westward in 1764–1765 to serve as frontier guard for the newly occupied territories, the Sibes now have their own autonomous county Chapchal (Qapqal) and live also in other neighboring counties mingled with Han, **Uyghur**, and **Kazakh** nationalities. The isolation of Sibe groups who wandered westward helped them to preserve their original ethnic character, culture, and language, thus slowing their acculturation.

Similarly to other Altaic-speaking groups, the Manchus migrated in all probability from their original South Siberian habitat to the lower part of the Amur River. In Siberia they lived traditionally by hunting and fishing and semi-nomadism, but after their migration southwards they learned cultivation, accommodating themselves to the conditions in Northeastern China. The Manchus preserved their original clan

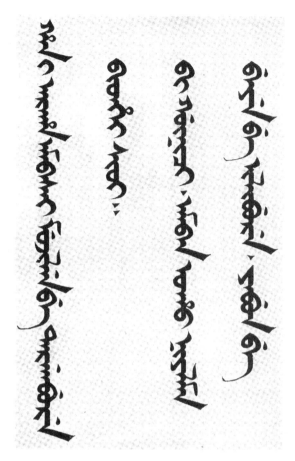

A text in Manchu script, based on the Uyghur-Mongolian writing system.

system (*hala*), and as the successors of the Dshürchen Jin state (1125–1234), they united the Manchu-speaking clans into a confederation under the leadership of the Aisin Gioro clan at the turn of the sixteenth and seventeenth centuries and seized control of the territory of Northeastern China. Simultaneously with the submission of the still powerful neighboring Eastern Mongolian khans and defeating the rebellious Western Mongols in the seventeenth and at the beginning of the eighteenth centuries, the Manchus established their political and administrative system in China and in the newly conquered territory of Inner and Central Asia.

The Manchu clans formed the last and one of the longest ruling Chinese dynasties, the Qing or Dai Qing "Great Ching" (1644–1912), and although the ruling elite became more and more sinicized, they tried to preserve some typical Manchu customs such as clothing, hairstyle, and the sometimes very complicated etiquette. Politically—and hence culturally—the heyday of the Manchu empire coincided with the ruling periods called Kangxi (1662–1723) and Qianlong (1736–1796).

The Manchu script was based on the Uyghur-Mongolian writing system, used by the Mongols since the thirteenth century. The Mongolian script was introduced into Manchu usage in 1599 by Erdeni and Gagai, two learned courtiers of the dynasty founder Nurhachi (1559–1626). However, the Mongolian script did not fit Manchu phonetics, and a group of scholars—among them Dahai—established a variant of the system, adding diacritical marks that made it more appropriate for the Manchu language. (The new system was called *tongki fuka sindaha hergen*— "writing adorned with dots and circles.") Although written Manchu culture was highly developed and in some respects preserved the Manchu language and literature as well as even folklore genres, the influence of Chinese literacy replaced the original forms and system.

During the twentieth century the Manchu-speaking population in northeastern China (Manchuria) almost completely disappeared. However, at the beginning of the twentieth century the ethnologist S. M. Shirokogoroff researched the native cultures of the Amur basin and recorded a Manchu epic tale in 1915. Shirokogoroff wrote down the text of the epic, designated the "Manchu Odyssey," from a female storyteller known as Teptalin Mama, but the text was lost during the Cultural Revolution of the 1960s and 1970s. The noted scholar M. Gimm may have recorded the same epic again, but it has not yet been published. Around the 1980s, the Manchu-speaking population shrank to one or two villages, according to studies by Chinese and foreign scholars. However, perhaps due to political changes in the Inner Asian and Chinese areas, new records, including linguistic transcriptions, relating to remote Manchu groups in Eastern China appeared in the 1990s in Chinese.

PRESERVING MANCHU FOLKLORE

In many respects the system of folklore genres and forms of the Manchu and Sibe populations resembles those of neighboring Tungusic, Mongolian, and Chinese ethnic groups. Although abundant original and translated works of political and administrative documents as well as fiction written in Manchu contain valuable linguistic and culture historical materials, the earliest records of traditional Manchu folklore appeared in the late eighteenth and early nineteenth centuries. A few folksongs have been preserved in Chinese transcription and also in Manchu script from the middle of the nineteenth century. The first records of spoken Manchu and Sibe in transcriptions reflecting the linguistical peculiarities were written down and partly published by Russian explorers and researchers such as V. V. Radloff, A. V. Grebenshchikov, N. N. Krotkov, A. O. Ivanovskij, F. Muromskij, and A. Rudnev; most of them are stored in the archives of the Russian Academy of Sciences. Radloff recorded *Sidi-Kür* (Tales of Bewitched Corps), a Sibe version of a Mongolian tale series—Sanskrit and Tibetan in origin—the *Siditü kegür-ün üliger* in written Mongolian. F Muromskij wrote down numerous texts in spoken Sibe dialect that were published by S. Kałużyński in 1977. Interest in Manchu studies, particularly in the folklore records, grew in the mid-1980s, when Giovanni Stary (Venice), Tatjana Pang (St. Petersburg), L. M. Gorelova and P. Lebedeva (Moscow), and their teams turned to the systematization of the Manchu and Sibe records. Michael Weiers (Bonn) has examined and published Manchu historical documents. Although these administrative documents are not folklore materials, they may contain important information for the study of traditional Manchu life.

Although the folklore genres of Altaic people such as the Manchus, Tungusic groups, Mongols, and South-Siberian Turkic people can be characterized by the terminology used in international folklore studies, the main genres of verbal and performing arts have been systematized from an indigenous perspective.

EPICS AND FOLKTALES

The first record of a Manchu national epic, the *Tebutalin*, disappeared. In the 1990s another epic entitled *Wubuxiben Mama* (in Chinese transcription) was discovered in a remote Manchu village. This epic is also based on shamanic tradition and narrates the story of a female ruler, a shaman, who could unify and govern the 700 tribes of the Dschürchen, the predecessors of the Manchu. The epic includes elaborate descriptions of folk customs and contains fragments of the common mythological heritage of Inner and East Asian and the South Siberian peoples. The origin myth of the Manchu ruling clan, the Aisin Gioro, also includes mythological motifs from the shared tradition. The myth has been preserved for the purpose of legitimatizing the heavenly origin of the ruling class. The ancestor of the ruling clan originates in the upper world, where he was born to a heavenly maiden, Fekulen, who descended from the sky with two other fairies in order to bathe in a lake (Bulhôri) in the middle, human world (a **motif** similar to the "Swan Maiden"). A magpie, the sacred bird of the Manchus, put a fruit on her dress. Swallowing it, she became pregnant and could not leave the human world. Her son, Bukôri jongson, grew up quickly. After his mother—now able to return to heaven—left him alone, he was elected leader by three hostile tribes and brought prosperity to the folk (a common theme among the Mongols—reminiscent of the ancestor of Chingis Khan—and also in **Korea**).

Motifs in Manchu folktales also appear in the official annals and chronicles of the dynasty. There are original plots stemming from the common Inner Asian and Siberian heritage as well as borrowings form the East Asian stock. Recently eleven volumes of Sibe folktales have been published. These cover many traditional types of tales, including animal tales, fairy tales, anecdotes, comic tales, and heroic tales. Among these folktales are also borrowed stories form the neighboring Mongols and Kazakhs.

FOLKSONGS

The majority of folksongs—*uchun* (*ucun*, plural: *ucuri*) in the native language—that survive thanks to early records are epics and lyrics. The songs published by A. O. Ivanovskij at the end of the nineteenth century and songs recorded in the twentieth century among the Sibe in Xinjiang show thematic and poetical similarities that prove the continuity of the tradition. Numerous songs sing of the glorious historical past going back to the establishment the Ch'ing dynasty or the historical events of a particular clan. The historical songs also contain fragments of the Manchu mythical tradition: for example, *Muduri mukdeke ucun* (Song on the Rise of the Dragon) or *Daicing gurun-i Kashigar ucun-i bithe* (Written Song on Kashgar [a city] Belonging to the Dai Ch'ing Empire). The newly and previously collected Sibe songs are classified thematically: festive songs (including songs for wedding ceremonies), love songs (also with motifs of Chinese origin), historical songs, songs for children, religious songs, and "new" songs.

POETRY AND PROVERBS

On the basis of early records, G. Stary (1985a) analyzed the poetic nature of Manchu verses and established different characteristic rhyme types, among which the alliterative four-lined stanzas ending with grammatical rhymes are the most characteristic. The following type of Manchu stanza is found not only in lyric and epic folklore genres but also in official inscriptions. The end rhyme derives from the grammatical endings and, similar to Mongolian poetry, appears in numerous cases to be due to parallelism. The scheme of the typical Manchu stanza is aaba. This is illustrated by a stanza from *Ba nai-i ucun* (Song of the Homeland):

Abkai wehiye-i forgon de sehe.	It was in the time of Emperor Abkai Wehiye.
Amursana be dailame gisabuha bihe.	The rebel Amursana was destroyed in fighting.
Ambarame wargi jecen be toktobufi,	The western frontiers have been established, and
Acalafi ahantume jihe.	People after defeat have submitted.

Stary differentiated eight other poetic categories on the basis of the presence or lack of alliteration and the types of end rhyme. In most cases the lines begin with alliterative sounds, and in certain genres such as sacred shamanic poetry (prayer, invocation, eulogy, and incantation) and proverbs alliteration within the lines is also frequent. Manchu poetry is also characterized by a certain rhythmical freedom. The refrain in Manchu is a decisive part of ritual poetry. Various genres of shamanic rituals contain a refrain, added for magical purposes, at the beginning and end of the lines. The invocations of different spirits require different refrain words and are often introduced with an initial formula.

Among the known Manchu proverbs, many belong to the common treasury of East Asian proverbs, most often borrowed from Chinese sources. However, poetically they are composed according to the Manchu rules. Some proverbs are masterpieces of wordplay and equivocation. They are rich in the various forms of alliteration. For example, *Hir hir serengge hiri hihun; / Her ler serengge leli lergiyen* (The condition called "excited" is just a real weakness; / The condition called "worthy" is the real generosity).

SHAMANISM

The best-documented field of Manchu folklore relates to shamanism, the traditional belief system of the area. However, shamanism was pushed into the background for political reasons. The Ch'ing state converted to Buddhism, and during the seventeenth and eighteenth centuries the emperors Kangxi and Qianlong supported the spread of Buddhism and Buddhist literacy. Nevertheless, the Manchus have preserved their primary animistic religion and shamanism. The term *shaman* (phonetic variants: *haman, saman*) for the religious mediator between the human world and the realm of spirits originates in the Manchu-Tungusic languages (first introduced to the West by Ysbrandt Ydes in the seventeenth century) and means "the one who knows, who sees clearly." It is not surprising that even among the Manchus as well as among the Sibes and even more among their relatives in **Siberia** such as the Nanai, Ultcha, and Oroch, shamanism still exists and, owing to recent political changes, is practiced freely again. For the revival of traditional shamanic customs, the new shamans and their communities drew on the old records, but due to **globalization**, the neo-shamanic tendencies of the West also influence the revival of traditional native shamanism.

Probably the best-known work of Manchu literature, translated into numerous languages, is the

Probably the best-known work of Manchu literature is *Nishan saman-i bithe* (The Story of the Nishan Shamaness).

249

Shaman dance.

Nishan saman-i bithe (The Story of the Nishan Shamaness), a detailed description of the shaman's descent into hell to save the soul of a Manchu nobleman's child. The account is a special treasury of different ritual folk genres—invocations, benedictions, eulogies, prayers, and death-songs—inserted into the narrative. The story of the Nishan shamaness spread among the neighboring people of the Manchus. It has been recorded among Tungusic, some Mongolian, and even Chinese groups. These versions are not simple translations of one another, for there are significant ethnic differences among them. However, some decisive points are common: especially the main motif, the descent of the shamaness into hell in order to liberate the stolen soul of a dead person. As the shamaness's soul travels in hell, she must pass several obstacles and overcomes all of them with sacrificial objects (tofu) and sacrificial animals (dog, cock) and with her cleverness. She meets a number of spirits, the ruler of hell Ilmun Khan, and also the goddess of fertility Omoshi Mama, on whose life tree sit the souls waiting to be born. Finally she bargains for the child from the spirits and returns. In almost all variants she is punished after her return, but the reason differs. The most widespread motif is that she cannot liberate another soul from hell (her former husband or the emperor's daughter, for example). The most elaborate Manchu variant ends with the confiscation of her properties and shamanic objects, while in the version of other Tungusic or Mongolian groups she is punished with death. She is forever known as the first shaman, the ancestor of future shamans.

Several sources describe shamanic rituals and accoutrements. In the newly discovered Manchu epic *Wubuxiben Mama* is found a fairly long depiction of the clothing of the shamaness and the start of the ritual. The following fragment demonstrates the shamaness's soul journey:

> The weight of her whole clothing is a hundred *jin* [0.6 kilograms].
> She sat on her magic drum made of fish skin in the form of a duck
>   egg.
> With her shout
> The magic drum starts gently flying.
> It flew to the sky like a goose feather;
> It made a circle over the crowd of people
> And slowly landed on the waters of the Wumulin *Bira* [a river].

From earlier shaman books, dynastic and clan ritual handbooks, and the newly discovered and published materials, a fairly broad Manchu and Sibe shaman repertoire consisting of many genres of folklore emerges. *Jarin* is usually translated as "incantation," but depending on the ritual circumstances it could also imply elements of invocation and prayer. An important type of *jarin* is the text for invoking gods and spirits for a meal made from the meat of a sacrificed animal (usually a goat). The description of the shaman's route through the eighteen watch-posts of hell is also designated with the same genre name (*jarin*). Incantations are recited on the occasion of an exorcism when the shaman bans the spirit or god that causes the illness of his patient into a paper cutting. (The use of a paper figure as effigy probably derives from Chinese influence.) The following fragment comes from the banishing text of the shamans of the Sibe Nara-Clan. The shaman identifies the cause of the sickness and tries to ban the harmful spirits from the victim. The Sibe text uses categorical imperative forms:

Ucube tucirebe	When you enter the door,
Ujube meite!	Your head should be cut off!
Uli moode	In a plum-tree
Ilifi sindaha!	Should [your head] be put up!
Uli mooci	From the Plum-tree
Alime gaifi	Should [your head] be caught!
Unenggi bade	On a real place
Isibume beneki!	Should one go and place [your head]!

Songs called *ucun* are also used in the shamanic repertoire for eulogizing the supreme god (*dergi abka,* "Above sky") or other deities. Special prayers known as *bairennge* or *uculehengge* are recited for different ritual purposes such as the first clothing of the shaman candidate and the ritual of erecting the shaman's birch ladder (*cakôran,* an important symbol of the soul journey between the world layers for the shaman's soul and the spirits and gods). The *tuitumbi* is a ritual and also the genre of the ritual text, addressed in darkness to female deities.

DANCE AND DRAMA

The Manchus have been considered as a people with a special flair for the performing arts and theater. Considerable material deals with their dance (*maksin*) traditions. The dances have been frequently accompanied by songs and stringed instruments. The dances represented such activities as hunting—with the dancers wearing leopard skins—or fighting, during which they would imitate riding on tigers and leopards. The dances functioned also as rituals for summoning good fortune. The epic *Wubuxiben Mama* contains information on ritual dances that are named after imitated animals (fish, bird, and serpent dances), certain body parts (head, breast, and shoulder dances), or spirits and gods (sea spirit dance).

BIBLIOGRAPHY

Gimm, Martin. 1984. Die Literatur der Manjuren. *Neues Handbuch der Literaturwissenschaft.* 23: 193–216.

Ivanovskij, A. O. 1893–1895. *Many'chzhurskaia hrestomatiia.* 2 volumes. Sanktpeterburg: Tipografija Imperatorskoi Akademii Nauk.

Laufer, Berthold. 1908. Skizze der manjurischen Literatur. *Keleti Szemle* 9: 1–53.

Nowak, Margaret, and Stephen Durrant. 1977. *The Tale of the Nishan Shamaness.* Seattle: University of Washington Press.

Pang, Tatjana A., and Giovanni Stary. 1994. On the Discovery of Manchu Epic. *CAJ* 38.1: 58–70.

Pozzi, Alessandra. 1992. *Manchu-Shamanica Illustrata*. Shamanica Manchurica Collecta 3. Wiesbaden: Otto Harrassowitz.

Schwarz, Henry G. 1984. *The Minorities of Northern China: A Survey*. Studies on East Asia 17. Bellingham: Western Washington University.

Sinor, Denis. 1968. Some Remarks on Manchu Poetry. In *Studies in South, East, and Central Asia Presented as a Memorial Volume to the Late Professor Raghu Vira*, edited by Denis Sinor. New Delhi: International Academy of Indian Culture. 105–114.

Stary, Giovanni. 1981. Mandschurische Balladen und Lieder als historisches Spiegelbild der Ch'ing-Dynastie. In *Fragen der mongolischen Heldendichtung. Teil. 1. Vorträge des 2. Epensymposiums des Sonderforschungsbereichs 12, Bonn 1979*, edited by Walter Heissig. Wiesbaden: Otto Harrassowitz. 340–359.

———. 1982. Mandschurische Reime und Lieder als Beispiele autochthoner Dichtkunst. In *Florilegia Manjurica in Memoriam Walter Fuchs*. Asiatische Forschungen 80, edited by Michael Weiers and Giovanni Stary. Wiesbaden: Otto Harrassowitz. 56–75.

———. 1985a. Fundamental Principles of Manchu Poetry. In *Proceedings of the International Conference on China Border Area Studies April, Taipei 1985*, edited by Lin En-shean. Taipei: National Chengchi University. 187–221.

———, ed. 1985b. *Three Unedited Manuscripts of the Manchu Epic tale "Nišan saman-i bithe."* Wiesbaden: Otto Harrassowitz.

———. 1988. *Epengesänge der Sibe-Mandschuren*. Asiatische Forschungen 106. Wiesbaden: Otto Harrassowitz.

———. 1992. Das "Schamenenbuch" des sibe-mandschurischen Nara-Clans. In *Altaic Religious Beliefs and Practices. Proceedings of the 33rd Meeting of the Permanent International Conference, Budapest June 24–29, 1990*, edited by Géza Bethlenfalvy and others. Budapest: Research Group for Altaic Studies HAS and Department of Inner Asiatic Studies ELTE. 319–329.

Uray-Kőhalmi, Käthe. 1998. Die Mythologie der mandschu-tungusischen Völker. In *Wörterbuch der Mythologie. 1. Abteilung. Die Alten Kulturvölker 27*, edited by Egidius Schmalzriedt and Hans Wilhelm Haussig. Stuttgart: Klett-Cotta. 3–170.

———. 2003. The Myth of Nishan Shaman. In *Rediscovery of Shamanic Heritage*. Bibliotheca Shamanistica 11, edited by Mihály Hoppál and Gábor Kósa. Budapest: Akadémiai Kiadó. 113–121.

Walravens, Hartmut. 1982. *Aleksej Osipovich Ivanovskij, a Little Known Russian Orientalist*. Hamburg: C. Bell.

Ágnes Birtalan

MONGOL

GEOGRAPHY AND HISTORY

The ethnic designation Mongol comprises numerous folk groups living in a vast territory of the Eurasian continent and numbering approximately 7 million in three states (**Russia, China,** and the Republic of Mongolia). Their linguistic features, which partly coincide with their geographical locations, identify western Mongols (the Kalmyks living in the Russian Federation near the Caspian Sea, the Oirad groups living in Western Mongolia and in China), northern Mongols (the Buriats living in South Siberia in the Russian Federation near Lake Baikal and in Northern Mongolia), southern Mongols (the Khalkha in the Republic of Mongolia and several groups such as the Chakhar, Tümet, Kharchin, Khorchin, Üdshümchin, and Ordos-Mongols living in the Autonomous Territory of Inner Mongolia in China), and groups of Mongols that speak archaic languages such as the Dagur, Monguor, Tunghsiang, Shera Yögur, Santa, and Pao-an in Northern China and the Moghols. The majority of the population in the Republic of Mongolia is Khalkha, whose language is Mongol proper. The Mongolian languages are related to the Turkic and **Manchu**-Tungusic languages of the Altaic language family (though its affiliation with **Ainu**, Japanese, and Korean has not yet been definitively proven).

The Mongol as ethnic or political designation (name of a tribal confederation) occurs in Chinese sources of the seventh century C.E. The Great Mongol Empire that had world historical significance was established at the beginning of the thirteenth century under the leadership of Chingis Khan, whose descendants from the time of Khubilai (1260–1294) ruled China as the Yuan dynasty. (The Venetian merchant, Marco Polo, wrote a detailed description about Khubilai's court.) Unlike their numerous nomadic predecessors, the Mongols had not become acculturated to the Chinese culture and, after the collapse of their rule in China, withdrew to the Inner Asian steppes, their original homeland (the approximate territory of today's Mongolia). Although their original clan and tribal structures dissolved with the establishment of the empire, individuals preserve an awareness of belonging to a particular clan.

The Mongols of the Republic preserve the traditional several-thousand-year-old nomadic way life based on cattle breeding. They pasture five sorts of livestock: horses and sheep being the most important, followed by cattle (or yaks), camels, and goats. The cattle provide the felt for their tents as well as food in the form of milk products and meat. However, some members of the younger generation prefer to live in the capital city Ulaanbaatar, where they have abandoned the traditional way of life. Mongols living in China and Russia preserve their language and features of their traditional culture, but the majority have adapted to an agricultural economy.

The folk culture of the Mongols is well documented. From the time of the establishment of the Great Mongolian Empire, there are records of different folklore genres and verbal art and descriptions of customs and habits. Besides the reports of the thirteenth-century Christian missionaries such as Rubruck and Plano Carpini and travelers such as Marco Polo, a valuable source in Mongolian dates probably from 1252, known today as *The Secret History of the Mongols*. Although it is a chronicle of Chingis Khan and his first successo, Ögödei Khan, it contains numerous fragments of folk

A Mongolian family and their *ger*, the traditional house. (Photograph by Ágnes Birtalan)

poetry, **motifs** of epics, tales, stanzas of folksongs, riddles, proverbs, and sacred poetry, all of which are still reflected in contemporary folklore. The ancient narrative and lyric folk tradition also survived in written historical and Buddhist literature of the next centuries. The interaction between folk tradition and written literature became especially intensive after the so-called second conversion to Buddhism in the seventeenth century, when Buddhist missionaries incorporated numerous oral folk religious texts into the written Buddhist ritual texts. **Uyghur** (early thirteenth century) and later the Indo-Tibetan and Chinese Buddhism (late thirteenth century) also influenced folk literature by providing numerous new stories and literary forms.

The first transcriptions of original Mongol folk literature appeared in the eighteenth century, when researchers and travelers, such as P. S. Pallas, G. Tymkowski, and A. Potanin, recorded materials mostly in Russian and German translations, but also preserved a few texts or fragments in such Mongolian languages as Khalkha, Buriat, and Kalmyk. In the nineteenth and twentieth centuries more systematized **fieldwork** aiming to collect materials in the original language, written in elaborate lingusitical transcription, began.

HEROIC EPICS AND FOLKTALES

The best known Mongolian folklore genre (also commonly known and performed among the nomads of Inner Asia and the hunters and fishers of Siberia) is the heroic epic (in Khalkha, *tuuli*; in Buriat, *üliger, üliger ontoxon*; in Kalmyk, *tuuj*), which usually consists of several hundred or in many cases several thousand lines and is performed by professional epic-tellers (Khalkha *tuulič*). The performance of heroic epics requires special circumstances (at night, on definite days, only for a large audience) and is considered to have magic and even healing effects. The protagonist of the epic is an extraordinary hero who is born in miraculous circumstances (for example, the motif of petrogenesis, or birth from a rock) and grows up quickly (maturing several years in a few days). He departs on a journey in order to seek a fiancée or to exact revenge against his antagonist, who appears either as the dragon-like *mangas* or as a human being. In some stories, the hero's wife appears as the betrayer of her husband and is punished at the end. Numerous epic tales have been translated into European languages. The most widely known epics are the *Geser*, which has Tibetan connections, and the *Jhangar*, collected among the Kalmyks and Oirats in its most elaborate form. Both epics are named after their main heroes. Geser (among the Buriats, Abai Geser) has a heavenly origin and is sent to defend the world from harm, sickness, and pain caused by harmful gods. Jhangar is an orphan who builds the perfect kingdom similar to the Arthurian traditions: his **heroes** sit in a circle, and a wise soothsayer, Altan Ceej, helps him to rule.

An *oboo*, the world axis where earth and heaven meet. (Photograph by Ágnes Birtalan)

The tales (Khalkha *ülger*, Buriat *ontoxo*, and Kalmyk *tuuli*) are closely connected to the heroic epic. Heroic tales have in most cases epic parallels. For example, the tale "The Rabid Red Hero with One Hair" and the epic *Darkness khan* have similar motifs. The Mongols classify tales according to their topics: tales about animals and plants (Khalkha, *adguus amitnii ülger*), heroic tales (Khalkha, *baatarlag ülger*), tales that contain elements of magic which include animal or human characters with magic power and magic objects (Khalkha, *šidet ülger*), and humorous tales (Khalkha, *šog xošin ülger*). The tales about animals are short and borrow extensively from Indo-Tibetan tale collections of pre-Buddhist and Buddhist origin such as the *Tales of the Bewitched Corpse* or the *Pancharaksha*. The Buddhist tales end with a moral point. The humorous tales aim to expose and ridicule mostly the morals of wandering monks (Khalkha, *badarčin*) or the greed of nobles. A typical hero of such a story is the Dalanxudalč, "Seventy Liar," who is similar to the Turkic Nasreddin Hoja.

A special group of tales in the Mongol narrative tradition is etiological myths or legends (Khalkha, *ülger domog*), which explain the origin of such phenomena as astral objects such as the sun, moon, and various constellations, aspects of nature such as animals, plants, mountains, and rivers, traditional customs and habits (for example, why Mongols prepare milk brandy or why Mongol shamans have only a half shaman-drum), and different ethnic groups. One of the best known *domogs* explains the origin of the favorite booty of Mongolian hunters, the *tarbagan* (marmot), who was originally an archer. He vowed to shoot all the nine suns from the sky, for they tortured living beings with their heat. When he took aim at the last one, a swallow diverted his arrow (for which the swallow has a forked tail) and, according to his oath, he cut his thumbs and turned into the *tarbagan*.

SONGS AND POETRY

According to the travelers' observations, all Mongols are able to sing, and many of them can even compose original songs. Mongols classify folksongs in several ways. The most widely known classification system is based on the manner of performance. Festive and thematically elevated songs (songs about the motherland, songs to the mother and parents, song to beloved persons, songs about historical heroes, and songs with Buddhist philosophical content) are performed slowly and gravely with many grace notes. They are called "long songs" (Khalkha, *urtiin duu*). Songs that depict the pleasure of love and those that mock certain members of the community or another ethnic group are performed more spiritedly and are called "folksong" (Khalkha, *ardiin duu*). These are thematically the most

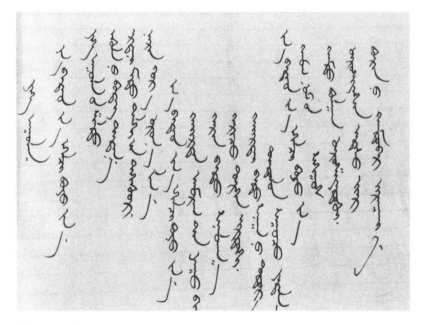

Folksong text.

important groups, but Mongols also categorize songs according to temporal circumstances and the occasion of singing: for instance, songs for the beginning of a feast such as the Lunar New Year or a wedding ceremony), for celebrations such as a child's first haircut, and songs for the end of a feast, which could be polite send-offs of guests. Songs are also differentiated according to the audience for whom they are performed (for example, to mother, father, maternal aunt, fiancée, or the superior of the district).

The most typical poetic features of Mongolian poetry are alliteration and parallelism. The first stanza in the long songs could be independent from the following ones. The most typical structure—based on parallelism—begins with two lines of nature description and ends with two lines introducing the feelings of the singer. The stanzas consist of four (though occasionally two) lines. For example, the second stanza of a song for ending celebrations goes as follows:

Burgaastain čini dawaag	The pass with willow-trees
Bulgan xaraaraa dawyaa!	I will pass on my black horse with white stockings!
Buyantai buural eejiidee	My virtuous gray-haired mother,
Bucaj irj jolgoyoo!	I will meet [you] when I return!

Xoton musician. (Photograph by Ágnes Birtalan)

A special group of songs are called "dialogue songs" (Khalkha, *xarilcaa duu*). These are considered the primary forms of Mongolian drama. Thematically, most dialogue songs belong to the category of love songs and are performed in the mood of the long songs. For example, in "Aligermaa" the chanted story tells of the tragic destiny of the daughter who is forced to marry somebody whom she does not love (usually a rich, old man). The highly dramatic roles played by several singers provide a good opportunity to show the performers' talent. Especially widespread dialogue songs include the philosophical "The Old Man and the Birds" (Khalkha, *Öwgön, šuwuu*), a poem by the nineteenth-century poet, Dulduitiin Rawjaa (1803–1856). This is chanted as a folksong at the beginning of feasts. Another popular dialogue song is the epic story of Chingis's two stray stallions, in which the dialogue occurs between an older modest horse and a younger hot-blooded companion. This latter song also has its origin in the written tradition.

RELIGIOUS BELIEFS

The original belief system of the Mongols (similarly to their Inner-Asian and Siberian neighbors) is based on the animistic comprehension of the world. According to that system, living beings have two or three souls. One of them can wander freely (for example, in dreams), but only shamans are able to direct the movements of their souls during ritual trances. Buddhism spread among the Mongols since the establishment of the Great Empire but only became the real state religion during the Yuan dynasty (1280–1368) and, later, after the collapse of the Mongolian Empire. The folk religion of the Mongols is still based on the animistic beliefs but is strongly combined with Buddhism. (Among the Buriats and the Kalmyks the influence of Christianity is also significant.) The recitation of texts of various genres accompanies large-scale folk religious rituals. Some sacred texts can be recited or chanted by shamans; however, the majority of the rituals could be performed by other authoritative persons in a community. The most characteristic shamanic text is the invocation (Khalkha, *duudlaga*; Buriat, *duurdlaga*), which consists of calling for the attention of the gods and spirits, followed by enumerating the offerings and requesting a boon such as good fortune or averting harm and sickness. The invoked spirits are described in detail in this text from an Oirat informant in Western Mongolia:

Gal mogoi tašuurtanguud,	You, who have a fire snake for a whip,
Galjuu čonon xölögtengüüid,	You, who have a rabid wolf for a mount,
Xüünii maxan xünestengüüid,	You, who have human flesh for aliment.

The ritual texts are sometimes performed at great feasts by professional performers such as those who undertake the blessing (Khalkha, *yöröölč*). A really effective curse also requires a professional curser (*xaraalč*). The blessing (Khalkha, *yörööl*), the praise (Khalkha, *magtaal*), and the anointing (Khalkha, *myalaalag*) are the most common ritual texts recited at family or communal celebrations. These sacred genres have specific structures, including a long description of the blessed phenomenon (a foremost wrestler, a good racer or any other livestock, new clothes, a new tent, or a new saddle, for example). In the case of the blessing the ending lines contain the "active" part of the text: the request for blessing, good luck, and averting harm and misfortune. This brief conclusion can stand alone as an independent genre (Khalkha, *beleg dembereliin üg*: literally, "saying for good fortune"). Numerous nomadic activities such as felt making, castrating sheep and goats, and preparing milk brandy are accompanied by such sayings. The following is said to prevent the wind from blowing the wool that has been laid out for felt making:

Performing a blessing. (Photograph by Ágnes Birtalan)

Xun šig cagaan,	Become white like the swan,
Dun šig xatuu,	Become hard, like the shell,
Xuigüi xurdan,	Become quickly [felt] without whirlwind, and
Salixgüi saixan boltugai!	Beautiful [felt] without wind!

The nomads are in continuous mutual interaction with the world of spirits that reside in the human world (called "the Lords of Territories") and perform for them a daily libation (Khalkha, *cacal*) ritual with milk, milk brandy, or koumiss (fermented milk). The first milk of day will be sprinkled by the housewife to the four cardinal points and to the earth and the sky, while intoning a simple ritual text. On the altars erected for the Lords of the Territories, the male members of the community offer sheep, burn certain parts of the sacrifice with juniper, and recite special prayers (Khalkha, *jalbiral*), accompanied by circling movements in order to summon good fortune (Khalkha, *dallaga*). Incense offerings (Khalkha, *sang*) are frequently made on other occasions too and could be performed by shamans and Buddhist monks.

PROVERBS AND RIDDLES

Mongols like to quote proverbs (Khalkha, *cecen üg*). Their proverbs and wise sayings cover a range of natural phenomena and social, religious, and cultural life. The most important elements in the structure and poetry of proverbs are the alliteration and parallelism that dominate other genres of folk poetry. Mongolian researchers have collected more than ten thousand proverbs in a collection called *The Ocean of Wise Sayings*. Examples include *Agtiig baixad gajar üj!* / *Aawiig baixad xüntei tanilc!* (While you have a steed, go around the world! / While you have a father, get to know people!), and *Töröögüi xüüxded* / *Tömör ölgii beltgex* (One prepares a metal cradle / For a child that is not born yet).

The Mongols tell riddles (Khalkha, *onisog*) only on special occasions, in larger company, and in groups that compete with each other. According to tradition, the losers in competitions could be subjugated. An example of a typical Mongolian riddle asks, *Teer deegüür* / *Temeenii nüüdel* (Far away above / Migration of camels). The solution is *Üül* (Clouds moving across the sky).

DANCE, CRAFTS, AND FESTIVALS

Although today all the Mongolian ethnic groups have their own folk dances, according to researchers only the circle dance of the Buriats (Buriat, *yoohor*) and the pantomime dance of the Western Mongolian Oirats (Oirat, *biilge*) are considered to be native folk dances, while all the others originated during the Manchu epoch from the court dances and the culture of the elite. Folk dances and long songs are often accompanied by a special two-stringed instrument called *morin xuur*, which is a horse-headed violin that has a wooden sound box and a scroll carved in the form of a horse's head. The Western Mongols play the *towšuur*, which is similar to a stringed instrument of the neighboring **Kazakhs**.

Mongol nomads use a wide variety of ornaments to decorate the wooden parts of their felt tents, their furniture, and their garments. Favorites include the variants of the *öljii* ("the endless happiness") and of

Playing the *morin xuur*, a two-stringed, horse-headed violin. (Photograph by Ágnes Birtalan)

the swastika. Smithing is highly developed among them. Smiths (Khalkha, *darxan*) had a special status in Mongolian society and worked usually with silver for women's hair ornaments, men's daggers, bowls, and saddlery.

The most important festival of the Mongols is *naadam*, once a fighting practice for the warriors in peacetime (similarly to battue hunting). Today as a remembrance of the People's Revolution in 1924, a national festival is celebrated in Mongolia where the "three games of men" are staged: horse races, wrestling, and archery. These games can accompany other national or communal events such as religious feasts and the Lunar New Year.

BIBLIOGRAPHY

Bawden, Charles. 1963. The Mongol Conversation Song. In *Aspects of Altaic Civilization*, edited by Denis Sinor. (Ural and Altaic Series 23.) Bloomington: Indiana University. 75–86.

Birtalan, Ágnes. 1987. Zwei kalmückische Volkslieder aus dem XVIII. Jahrhundert. *AOH* 41: 53–74.

———. 2001. Die Mythologie der mongolischen Volksreligion. In *Wörterbuch der Mythologie*. *I. Abteilung Die Alten Kulturvölker* 34, edited by Egidius Schmalzriedt and Hans Wilhelm Haussig. Stuttgart: Klett-Cotta. 879–1097.

Birtalan, Ágnes, and János Sipos. 2004. "Talking to the *Ongons*": The Invocation Text and Music of a Darkhad Shaman. *Shaman Spring/Autumn* 12.1–2: 25–62.

Gâdamba, Š., and D. Cerensodnom, eds. 1987. *Mongol ardiin aman joxioliin deej bičig* (*The Best of Mongolian Folklore*). Ulaanbaatar: Ulsiin Xewleliin Gajar.

Hangin, John Gombojab, and others, eds. 1998. *Mongolian Folklore. A Representative Collection from the Oral Literary Tradition*. Bloomington: Indiana University Press.

Heissig, Walter 1988. *Erzählstoffe rezenter mongolischer Heldendichtung I–II*. Asiatische Forschungen 100. Wiesbaden: Otto Harrassowitz.

Jackovskaja, K. N. 1988. *Narodnye pesni mongolov*. Moskva: Nauka.

Kara, György. 1970. *Chants d'un barde mongol*. Budapest: Akadémiai Kiadó.

Laufer, Berthold. 1907. Skizze der mongolischen Literatur. *Keleti Szemle* 8: 165–261.

Lörincz, László. 1979. *Mongolische Märchentypen*. Budapest: Akadémiai Kiadó.

Mostaert, Antoine. 1937. *Textes Oraux Ordos*. Monumenta Serica Monograph Series No. 1. Peip'ing: Cura Universitatis Catholicae Pekini.

Poppe, Nikolaus. 1955. *Mongolische Volksdichtung. Sprüche, Lieder, Märchen und Heldensagen Khalkha-mongolische Texte mit deutscher Übersetzung, einer Einleitung und Anmerkungen*. Wiesbaden: Franz Steiner Verlag GMBH.

Pozdneev, A. 1880. *Obrazcy narodnoi literatury mongolyiskih plemen. Narodnye pesni mongolov*. St. Peterburg: Tipografija Imperatorskoi Akademii Nauk.

Ramstedt, Gerhardt, and Harry Halén. 1974. *Nordmongolische Volksdichtung II*. Helsinki: Academia Scientiarum Fennica.

Vladimircov, B. Ja. 1928. *Obrazcy mongolyiskoj narodnoi slovesnosti. (S.-Z. Mongoliia)*. Leningrad: Institut Zhivyh Vostochnyh Jazykov imeni A. S. Enukidze.

Xorloo, P. 1981. *Mongol ardiin duunii yaruu nairag* (Poetics of Mongolian Folk Songs). Ulaanbaatar: Šinjlex Uxaanii Akademiin Xewlel.

Zhamcarano, C., and A. D. Rudnev. 1908. *Obrazcy mongolyiskoi narodnoi literatury*. St. Petersburg: Tipo-litografija B. Avidona.

Ágnes Birtalan

TAIWAN (REPUBLIC OF CHINA)

GEOGRAPHY AND HISTORY

A subtropical island located in the Pacific Ocean, Taiwan is separated from the coast of **China** by the Taiwan Strait. Outlying smaller islands of the Penghu Archipelago (the Pescadores), the islands of Matsu and Kinmen (Quemoy) in the Strait, and Lanyu (Orchid Island) and Lutao (Green Island) off the eastern coast are also part of the territory of the Republic of China. The main island is 250 miles in length and eighty miles wide with agriculturally rich lowland areas and a sparsely populated central mountain range that reaches to heights of more than 10,000 feet above sea level. Jade Mountain is the highest mountain with an altitude at its highest peaks of 13,114 feet. The location of the main island has made it ideal for fishing and rice farming. However, currently the competitive high-tech semi-conductor industry is the mainstay of the Taiwanese economy, involving it deeply in international trade. The island's authorities maintain a high level of ecological awareness because typhoons and earthquakes occur frequently; both cause earthslides in overly cultivated mountainous areas. The seaports of Keelung, Kaohsiung, and Taichung are the access points for Taiwan's increasing globalization and the foundation of trade and cultural links with China. The major international airport is the International Chiang Kai Shek Airport. The plum flower that blooms in late winter is the national flower. It symbolizes the ability of Taiwan to endure hardship.

Taiwan has a culturally pluralistic society with a long history of migrations from mainland China. The 2004 population reached 22,668,000. Indigenous tribal Austronesian peoples have inhabited the island for at least ten thousand years. The Amis, Atayal, Bunun, Kavalan, Paiwan, Peinan, Puyama, Rukai, Saisiyat, Thao, and the Tsou now live in the mountain areas of central Taiwan. The Dawu live on Orchid Island. People in these tribal areas combine traditional living with state education mandated by the central government.

Minnan and Hakka peoples from Fukien and Kuangtung Prefectures in China compose two of the main population groups. During the Ming Dynasty (1368–1644), major migrations of Minnan people from coastal villages led to significant agricultural settlement along the western lowland areas of the island. The little town of Lukang along the central coast, dating from the 1600s, shows the folk history of the Minnan immigrants. Ethnic Hakka peoples migrating first from Hunan and Kuangtung also settled in Taiwan during this period. The early settlement of Meinung in what is now Kaohsiung County dates from 1736, the first reign of the Emperor Chien Lung of the Ching Dynasty. Today the majority of Hakka peoples live in areas near the central mountain range including the counties of Miaoli and Hsinchu.

Another major population group consists of mainland Chinese refugees who came with Chiang Kai-shek in 1949 in retreat from Communist rule. Alongside the **globalization** of markets, marriage of Taiwanese businessmen with brides from the mainland and other Southeast Asian countries is effecting a demographic change with an impact on the ethnohistory of the area.

Global communication with other areas of the world began with colonization. Portuguese, Dutch, and Spanish trading companies found the island to be a convenient stopping place along the China coast for the transportation of goods. During this period of European colonization, the Dutch East India Company was the most active in its efforts. It levied taxes on local people and controlled trade when it drove out the Spanish in 1642. The most recent colonization was that of the Japanese between 1895 and 1945, during which the authorities introduced Japanese education. Older Taiwanese people therefore still know some Japanese and watch Japanese television programs on cable networks (see **Japan**). Traces from each of the colonization periods can be found mainly in architecture and food traditions.

RELIGIOUS BELIEFS AND RITUALS

Solar and lunar calendars are both used to regulate life activities in Taiwan. While the Western solar calendar is the main official calendar, the lunar calendar is more important for the traditional observances associated with religious belief. The migration history is reflected in religious plurality. Various sects of Buddhism and Taoism make up the dominant religions. In popular religious belief throughout Taiwan, popular Buddhism and Taoism are syncretized. It is mainly the highly learned and those practicing Zen or one of the higher forms of Taoism who make esoteric distinctions. Islam as well as Catholic and Protestant Christianity have a smaller number of followers. Confucius is honored in temples throughout the island and is especially venerated by scholars and students. This philosopher's birthday is celebrated on 28 September with elaborate ceremonies transmitted from ancient times.

While following religious precepts and Confucian ethics, most families also honor their own ancestors, whose names and sometimes pictures stand on a family altar next to or below the deities worshipped in the Taiwanese home. Here the Bodhisattva Kuanyin, Matsu, and Tikong as well as other deities are enshrined. A dream by a prominent member of the family in which he or she saw or heard which deity wanted to receive the family's worship often determines which deified persons assume places on the family altar. For instance, the Sung Dynasty official Pu An was chosen for one family's altar in the southern town of Chiayi because of a dream of the family patriarch. When he died, the altar moved to the home of his oldest son in the town of Lungching in central Taiwan. In traditional Hakka families, one usually finds the Three Kings of the Mountains. These deified kings have been worshipped from the time that this people inhabited the mainland, and they are also found in major Hakka temples.

A symmetrical arrangement of blessings written on red strips of paper is placed over the top and the sides of doorways to the home, at the local earth god shrines, and at other places of importance. These sayings are termed *tui-lian* and are renewed each year. More permanent versions of the *tui-lian* are engraved into the wood of the gateways to temples.

On major holidays, food sacrifices, including the three meats of fish, pork, and chicken as well as fruit, wine, and other offerings, are made to the deities, along with the burning of paper "money" consisting of square pieces of gold and silver foil pasted on paper. The times of sacrifices vary with regions and occupations. For instance, the owners of small businesses offer food sacrifices and burn paper money in front of their businesses on the fifteenth day of each lunar month. Even larger companies may maintain this tradition.

Folk shrines dot the landscape of the countryside. They range in size from the small ones at the edge of rice paddies which house the local earth deity to larger ones housing the god, the table for offerings, an incense burner, and other religious objects. One of the indicators of a propitious earth god site is the banyan tree, also important for its connection to Buddhism. It was under the *bodhi* tree that Gautama Buddha received enlightenment. Legend tells that a large snake is living in the hollows of very ancient trees beside the temples to the earth god.

The local earth god who receives the offerings influences the lives of the believers through a process of divination. After presenting the offerings and burning the incense, the worshipper addresses a question silently to the god. Then two crescent blocks of wood, one with flat and one with rounded side, are cast to the floor. If one flat and one rounded side are facing upwards, the god has given a positive answer to the question.

In larger temples this process is more complex. The answer from the god is in the form of a lot from the *I-Ching*, a classical Taoist text. A temple guardian can provide further interpretation if the devotee does not feel that he or she understands what is written on the slip of paper. In popular belief, asking advice from the deity of a temple at the beginning of a New Year or when engaging in a new business, getting married, having children, or taking an important examination is an important step. If a new couple has not given birth to a child, they may ask the god to help them. A person's fate is said to follow the birth year according to the zodiac cycle of twelve years named for the animals: mouse, ox, tiger, rabbit, dragon, snake, horse, sheep (or goat), monkey, chicken, dog, and pig. When one's zodiac animal comes round, the temple authorities can light a candle and set an astrological charm so that the dangers of this year can be lessened. When a boon is granted by the god, such as when a couple has been granted a child, a thanksgiving offering must be given. Usually this sacrifice takes the form of a pig, but with globalization, recently thanksgiving offerings have even included an ostrich.

Marriage ceremonies preserve folk traditions according to the parents' and the couple's wishes. The arrangement of marriage by parents, a practice of traditional Chinese culture, is largely a thing of the past, though sometimes a person interested in helping a friend to find a suitable mate will assume the role of matchmaker. Observances for engagement—such as the future groom buying cakes for distribution to his fiancée's relatives and friends, and the ceremony of her offering cups of sweet tea to members of the future groom's family who, in return, give her money in red envelopes—are still frequently practiced. A feast for a large number of guests is the norm for all ethnic groups.

In the past a bride was supposed to lower her head and cry on the day of her wedding, but now it is said that she talks and smiles. In a Hakka marriage, stalks of sugar cane are attached to the vehicle used by the couple. This simplifies a former tradition of carrying chickens on sugar cane stalks when the bride returns on foot to her home three days after the marriage. Whether in the past on the day of return or, as at present, on the wedding day itself, the bride's family offers sweet sticky rice to the groom.

At the birth of a baby, the mother eats special herbal chicken stewed in rice wine, often made by the mother-in-law, and does not leave the home. After the first month, the couple distributes gifts of painted eggs and a special sticky rice cake to relatives and friends. In the past the egg was only given when the baby was a male, but with increasing awareness of women's equality, the egg is given for boys and girls alike.

Among the rites of passage, the most traditional is the funeral. The folk arts associated with funeral rites include making miniature houses and even appliances and automobiles out of paper. These elaborate furnishings are then conveyed through burning to the other world so that the deceased may live in comfort. Wreaths of flowers, now artificial, are distributed in the vicinity of the home of the deceased. Musical entertainment may also be arranged for the guests who attend a funeral feast. After the funeral, food offerings are given to the deceased every seven days for seven times. Recently, to accommodate busy life schedules, some make these food offerings seven times within one day. The departed often returns in dreams to make requests of the living.

All the ancestors of the family are honored on Tomb Sweeping Day. Minnan and recent immigrants from the mainland celebrate this holiday on the fifth day of the fourth solar month. Relatives gather at the family gravesite to clean the stone monuments and cut away the overgrown grasses and weeds. The Hakka celebrate this festival at an earlier date determined by the elders of each local region.

Many beliefs and legends surround the use of *feng shui*, literally "wind and waters." *Feng shui* is a system of belief about the environment concerning placing buildings on the land, the directions one faces when engaging in various activities, and finding ideal burial sites. Often discord in the family, an accident, suicide, bankruptcy, and other unfortunate events are attributed to a lack of consideration of the *feng shui* of the place where the person lives or works.

SONGS

Ethnic singers and amateur groups maintain the traditions of Hakka Mountain songs, which are also used in the Hakka operas. Pi-hsia Lai, a singer of Hakka Mountain songs who has won national recognition through local contests, explains that one type of these mountain folksongs, the call-and-response songs, reflects the life of the mountain people. In the past, they would try to communicate across great distances while picking tea or doing other agricultural work. The initial word *wei* can be sung out and held at indefinite length before beginning the address to a relative, a lover, or neighbor's family member across the mountainside. Innuendo and metaphor pervade the content of the composition. Once the style and form are learned, the words can be improvised freely as long as the rhythm and rhyme of the seven-character matching phrases, sung in units of four for each response, are maintained.

OPERA

The troupe tradition for Taiwanese opera is said to have started in Ilan, a town on the eastern coast, and spread to all of Taiwan. Semi-professional folk groups continue this tradition. Actors and actresses dress in costumes from the Ching Dynasty, when Minnan immigrants came to Taiwan. They perform traditional legends and myths from Chinese history and are accompanied by instruments deriving from the ethnomusical traditions of southern China. Many kinds of folksongs and even popular songs can be incorporated into a performance. The topics of the plays performed, the stylized movements, and the instrumentation are distinguished as being either *wen* or *wu*. The former term refers to plays concerning romantic topics, to the peaceful actions of the literati, and even to the plucked (*hu-chin*, *er-hu*, and *san-hsien*) and blown instruments (flute, *so-na* trumpet) used to accompany the singers in this type of opera. The latter term refers to plays about traditional warriors and martial dance movement as well as to the percussion instruments that resound during the performances of this type of opera. The folk versions of these operas are commissioned for the birthdays of the deities of local temples and on other special days such as giving thanks for a boon granted to a family. Besides having a function in religious observances, this local art is cultivated by professionals for national performing arts' venues. Actors and actresses travel abroad to perform for overseas Minnan and Hakka audiences of Taiwanese emigres and foreigners. The opera brings a vivid sense of homeland identity to ethnic groups worldwide.

PUPPET PERFORMANCES

Hand puppet performances of Chinese historical legends and the legends of Taiwanese local **heroes** and **tricksters** are a traditional art that has been maintained in various media. In the 1960s these performances were still frequently performed on outdoor stages in front of temples as an offering to one of the deities inside on his or her birthday. Although puppeteers may still be asked to perform for temple celebrations, their shows are now a part of regular television programming. Traditional roles for the puppets survive, but this folk history is "electrified" through elaborate lighting techniques synchronized with sounds to emphasize the power of the heroes in battle scenes. The folk arts of woodcarving, embroidery on the costumes on the puppets, folk tunes, and the stories themselves reflect the long tradition of this form. The entertainment function, however, has taken priority over the religious function in such popular contexts.

Another genre of popular traditional performance in Taiwan is *shang sheng*. Brought to Taiwan by mainlanders who came in 1949, it is a quick witty repartee in which anecdotal humor, puns, and other language play are conveyed in rhythm accompanied by a clapper held by one of the performers or by a small drum. One of the speakers plays a straight role, while the other initiates the humor. The techniques of this traditional art are now being used in education—for instance, to alert children in a humorous way to the dangers they might encounter in modern society.

ARTS AND CRAFTS

In a tradition reaching back to ancient Chinese villages in which the inhabitants of one or two clans devoted themselves to a special craft such as pottery or woodcarving, one finds the phenomenon of one locale stressing the traditions of one craft. Three villages in particular have international customers for the crafts made by their people: Sanyi, an ethnic Hakka town in central Taiwan known for its woodcarving; Yingge, a Minnan town near the city of Taipei in the north known for its pottery crafts; and Meinung, a Hakka village which has become famous for its waxed and decorated umbrellas.

The town of Sanyi has a history of using local camphor wood to make traditional Chinese furniture, especially tables. A particularly old tree is selected for its shape and the size of its trunk and branches. The original shape of the trunk or branch is maintained as the wood is finished and covered with lacquer. Wooden stools from smaller trees are molded to match the ta-

A Chung Kuei figure by the artist Jung-chou Huang. (Photograph by Patricia Haseltine)

bles. The carpenters of the area also make cabinets and other furniture. Another facet of the work of the craftsmen of this village is to carve images of Buddhist and Taoist deities and of legendary monks or scholars. The artist-craftsman Jung-chou Huang specializes in carving the figure of Chung Kuei, who is said to cross between the world of men and underworld spirits at will. The deity's image is used in entrances to ward off harmful influences.

During the Japanese occupation, making decorative articles for export to Japan globalized the economy of the town. Later, as the mainland forces of the Republican Army supported by United States forces retreated to Taiwan, smaller, more portable decorative carvings were made for Western customers. Currently, many of the craftsmen have taken their expertise to the mainland, where objects imitating traditional ones can be made to fit increasing demand more cheaply. In the past most of the work was done by hand with traditional carving tools. However, this craft is now highly mechanized. Currently, unlike the craftsmen, creative artists tend to carve secular motifs such as animals or insects, using the major artistic themes found in Chinese figure painting. A similar history of a native craft entering the international market and influencing the development of the themes and styles is found for the porcelain making town of Yingge in northern Taiwan.

MEDICINE AND FOLK ARTS

Herbal remedies for many types of ailments are readily available as an alternative to the medicine derived from the West that is practiced in the major hospitals. Traditional pharmacies are found in every small village. In the countryside, too, ordinary people find plants that will relieve pain, thin the blood, and provide added nourishment at the dining table. Currently, university laboratories are studying the healing properties of herbal remedies to ascertain their compatibility with

Western medicines. Herbal medicines are packaged and prepared for international distribution.

Besides their healing power, plants also have divining properties. For example, in the late spring and early summer, one can examine "typhoon grass" to discover the number and strength of the typhoons during the coming summer and fall seasons. One counts the number and depth of the lines crossing the stalk of the leaf to make this amazingly accurate prediction.

Since the lifting of martial law, which put some restrictions on public gatherings and the formation of popular associations, the folk arts have been flourishing, especially those associated with folk religious temples. With the democratization of Taiwan, ethnic groups can speak their dialects in schools and public venues and can form amateur groups to revive and cultivate folk arts that have been somewhat in decline. Professional and semi-professional drama troupes such as dragon and lion dance clubs have preserved Taiwanese and Hakka language and performance arts.

FOOD

In Taiwan, towns and cities are distinguished by the food traditions offered by the snack vendors located in local street markets or along scenic streets. For instance, the old town of Lukang has oysters and a specialty called ox tongue cake—its name referring to its shape. In the city of Tainan, one finds the square coffin-bread. Taichung is famous for its round Sun Cakes. Most of these traditions date to the time of original settlement of these towns. Other food traditions are associated with festivals: examples include the Moon Cake with blessings inscribed on the top for the Mid-Autumn Moon Festival and the Wealth and Good Fortune Cake made of yeast flour and a sticky rice cake for the Chinese New Year.

FESTIVALS

The Chinese New Year determined by the lunar calendar is the most important festival of the year with various celebrations lasting for five days. On New Year's Eve, families gather for a special dinner. In the early morning of the New Year, firecrackers resound from almost every household. The firecrackers are traditionally set off to scare away evil spirits that might be lurking nearby. The ancestors are considered present with the family during this period, and lights may be left on at night in the home. In this still mainly patriarchal and patrilocal society, extended families gather in the oldest male's home to celebrate the New Year. However, on the second day of the New Year, each nuclear family travels to the home of the mother's family for a dinner with her relatives. On the third and fourth days, people can visit friends, go mountain climbing, visit a hot spring, see a movie, or even travel abroad. The fifth day is the day that shops, companies, and offices, which have been closed since New Year's Eve, open again for business.

The Lantern Festival falls on the fifteenth day after the New Year at the full moon. This festival is celebrated with the lighting of lanterns, and children receive small lanterns to carry through the streets. Traditional riddles or blessings are written on lanterns of various sizes and shapes found in temples all around the island. The Lungshan Temple in Taipei and the Matsu Temple in Tachia have especially elaborate displays. Groups of people write their wishes for the New Year on a larger type of lantern called a sky-lantern. As a fire is lit inside the sky-lantern, it flies like a kite into the air. In the winter skies of February under a full moon of the fifteenth day of the lunar month, it is a warming sight to see the lanterns floating in the sky above. To celebrate the Lantern Festival in Taipei, a parade of large-scale plastic lanterns is lighted by electricity, showing how this tradition has become modernized. Theme floats, with lighted representations of the zodiac animal of the year and picturesque landscapes, surround the magnificent plaza of the Chiang Kai-shek Memorial building complex to celebrate the Lantern Festival. Community groups, international airlines, and other businesses compete against one another with these lighted floats. People wanting to view this colorful sight gam the highways and city streets.

Other important traditional festivals that continue to feature folk arts, performances, myths or legends, and even traditional sports include the Dragon Boat Festival, which memorializes the death of the famous poet Chu Yuan with dragon boat racing. Teams of rowers spurred on by the beating of a drum are found on many of the rivers in Taiwan and mark the beginning of summer. Other traditional occasions are the Midsummer Putu Festival, when the ancestral spirits and other departed spirits return to the earth for fifteen days at the summer solstice, and the Mid-Autumn Moon Festival, which occurs at the full moon of the tenth lunar month. On this date, people recall the myth of the archer Hou Yi, who shot down seven suns from the skies, and his wife Chang O, who stole his pill of immortality and was banished to the moon, where she is said to reside today. Since ancient times young and old have taken to the streets and gone to the countryside to appreciate the moon on the evening of this date; it is also a time of outdoor barbecuing.

A lantern for the Lantern Festival. (Photograph by Patricia Haseltine)

A religious tradition that has recently become quite significant is the annual Matsu Pilgrimage. Matsu is a local deity of the Minnan area of Fukien and Taiwan. Her legend tells that in a dream the goddess Kuanyin recommended a particular medicine for the mother to take to help her become pregnant. The mother followed the advice and gave birth to the girl Matsu. The child was precocious and very pious. Once when her father and brother went out to sea and encountered a storm, they almost drowned, but at that moment Matsu entered a trance and sent her soul to save them.

The Matsu in Fukien is considered the oldest, but she is also worshipped in temples throughout Taiwan. Customarily one temple's Matsu visits another temple's Matsu accompanied by pilgrims. The Peikang Matsu receives her guests from all over Taiwan during the period after the New Year. A major annual pilgrimage on foot from the Tachia Matsu to the Hsinkang Matsu is held in the third lunar month. The

Lantern Festival at Matsu Temple. (Photograph by Particia Haseltine)

route today covers over 300 kilometers, and pilgrims visit more than fifty local temples. The pilgrims begin at midnight and walk until noon each day. Along the route local residents greet them with firecrackers and food and drink. An opera or a puppet show is arranged to honor the visit of the Tachia Matsu and entertain the visitors at each local stop. Stilt-walkers and other performers also cavort especially to entertain the children. As the procession of the sedan chair carrying Matsu followed by a retinue of soldiers in Ming Dynasty costume passes, people who want to be cured of various illnesses or who have a special wish crawl under the chair. They hope that the goddess will grant them their wishes. The pilgrimage is a fine opportunity for relatives and friends to gather together for feasting and to share stories, some of which are miracle legends. As at other temple celebrations for various deities, spirit possession by shamans also occurs during this festival. When the deity enters the body of the shaman, he writes on a special red paper in a script that must be interpreted by the Taoist priest.

Another important festival is the Ghost Festival held on the fifteenth day of the seventh lunar month. During the entire seventh lunar month, the spirits of all the departed return to earth to be feted with sacrifices. This celebration commemorates the journey of the Buddhist monk Mu Lian to the underworld to save his mother from punishment. Because so many spirits—some of whom are hungry because they have no relatives to care for them—are wandering about, it is dangerous to move from one dwelling to another and to travel, especially near the water, during this month.

With recently increasing international contact, Taiwan has become the site of several folk festivals. Yearly in the summer on the central eastern coast of Taiwan at Ilan, a folk celebration of international scale is held. Folk dancers and other performers from all around the world are invited to a month-long round of festivities. Games and various contests are held, and in this hot climate participants and guests enjoy a number of water sports in specially designed pools close to the performance sites. Also on the eastern coast, but in the south, there is an annual international aboriginal festival. Indigenous peoples from New Zealand, Australia, and other countries join the tribes of Taiwan to display their arts of weaving and handicraft and to share their dance and music traditions. These indigenous people also meet to discuss the problems they share in their relations with the dominant ethnic groups in their respective countries.

STUDIES OF TAIWANESE FOLKLORE

The sources for folklore on Taiwan are mostly in Chinese, although a number of theses and dissertations in the United States and other countries have been written on this topic. In the early years of the Republic, Taiwanese folklore study was carried out by Lo Tze-kuang, who published a number of volumes. Min-hwei Chen studied the Matsu pilgrimage when the Tachia pilgrims journeyed to Peikang. Emily Ahern has investigated Hakka traditions in the Sanhsia area. Wolfram Eberhard published a volume on the tales he collected in Taiwan. A good study by Eberhard (1989) treats versions of "Grandaunt Tiger," a tale with motifs in common with "Red Riding Hood" in which the predator is a tiger instead of a wolf. Research on Hakka Mountain songs began in the 1960s, when songs were assiduously collected and notated. The study of these songs was written and published by Chuan-hsiung Hu in 2003. Many earlier works on Chinese myths and folktales are also of use to scholars interested in the Han immigrants to Taiwan. Tales of the aboriginal tribes are now being published in bilingual English-Mandarin format (www.thirdnature.com.tw). Research institutes and **museums** have collected and done research in **ethnography**, linguistics, and folklore for over twenty years. Researchers may contact the Ethnographical Institute of the Academia Sinica in Nankang, the National Science Museum in Taichung, the Museum of Pre-History in Taitung, and the Shung Ye Museum of Formosan Aborigines.

Statistics for Taiwan can be found at www.moio.gov.tw/W3/stat. A brief introduction to the Taiwanese opera of the Lan Yang Troupe can be found at www.ilccb.gov.twl/lytoc.media/news. Folktales are translated at the following site: www.taiwandc.org.folk.htm. Historical information in English can be found at the New Taiwan, Ilha Formosa site at edir.yam.com/cult/folk. Information on festivals can be found at www.gio.gov.tw/info/festival.

BIBLIOGRAPHY

Ahern, Emily Martin. 1981. The Thai Ti Kong Festival. In *The Anthropology of Tawainese Society*, edited by Emily Martin Ahern and Hill Gates. Stanford: Stanford University Press. 397–425.

Chen, Min-Hwei. 1984. A Study of Legend Changes in the Ma Tsu Cult of Taiwan: Status, Competition, and Popularity. Thesis, Indiana University.

Eberhard, Wolfram. 1989. The Story of Grandaunt Tiger. In *Little Red Riding Hood: A Casebook*, edited by Alan Dundes. Madison: University of Wisconsin Press. 21–63.

Patricia Haseltine

Japan and Korea

JAPAN OVERVIEW

GEOGRAPHY AND HISTORY

The islands of Japan extend approximately 1,200 miles in a northeast to southwest direction with the nearest points of contact about 100 miles from the Korean peninsula and 500 miles from Mainland **China**. This separation from mainland Asia was important in the early history of Japan because it was far enough away to make it difficult to mount an invasion of Japan (two were attempted in the thirteenth century) but close enough that contact and the introduction of (mostly) Chinese culture were possible. The four main islands are Honshu, Hokkaido, Shikoku, and Kyushu. The total land mass of Japan is under 150,000 square miles.

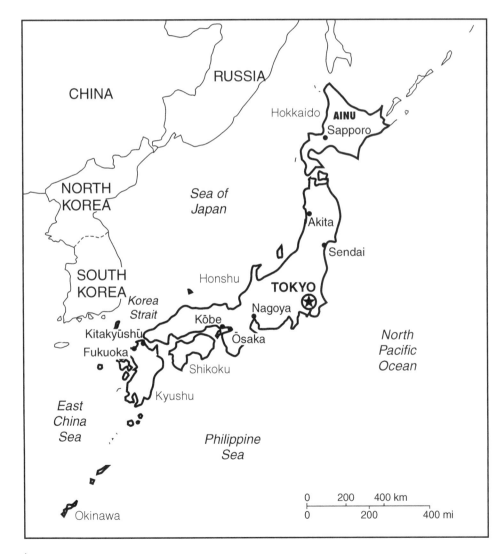

Japan.

Four Japanese men on one of the many steep mountains, looking out over a valley, 1905. (Courtesy Library of Congress)

A number of topographical features of Japan have helped shape the history and culture of the country. The islands are composed of steep mountainous areas that occupy over two-thirds of the total land mass. Honshu, the main island, has three large plains centered on the modern cities of Tokyo, Osaka and Kyoto, and Nagoya. Today the first two areas (Tokyo, Osaka and Kyoto) each comprise about 2 percent of the total land mass but contain approximately 25 percent and 15 percent respectively of the total population.

Many of the mountains in Japan are or have been volcanoes. One hundred eighty-eight volcanoes, of which over forty are still active, have been recorded on the islands. The land mass of the islands also drops off precipitously into the surrounding waters in geologic formations called trenches and troughs. These two features, volcanic action and the incredible change in elevation, lead to one of the most important characteristics of the land: its instability. Volcanic activity and earthquakes, along with the uncertainty and destruction they bring, are a part of everyday life.

The steep mountains and powerful rivers flowing through the gorges made travel difficult until recent times. The geography therefore hindered attempts to conquer, unify, and control the country under a single powerful ruler. Outlying areas away from the capital, even up to the nineteenth century, could be ruled with relative autonomy from the central power. These centers of political power and culture, which were also the centers of rice-growing agriculture representing economic power, for the past 1,600 years have been located in the urban areas on the major plains, most notably Nara, Kyoto, and Tokyo. Almost all major wars were fought in and over these areas.

Various theories have been advanced to explain where the people who inhabit the Japanese islands came from. One of the most comprehensive culture-complex hypotheses was formulated in 1933 by Oka Masao. Oka argued that a number of major components in prehistoric and early historic Japanese culture, myth, religion, and social structure were found in three different ethnic groups from mainland Asia. These were certain ethnic groups from South China and Southeast Asia with some Melanesian cultural and religious traits—for example, secret society systems, female shamans, mythical motifs of brother-sister deities, initiation rites, and the cultivation of rice; a Tunguz group originally from **Siberia** or Manchuria (see **Manchu**) who had a patrilineal clan system and believed in deities who descend from heaven to mountain tops, trees, or pillars; and an Altaic pastoral tribe who had subjugated other tribes in Manchuria and **Korea** and had an efficient military organization,

Siberian shamanism, and a patriarchal clan system. Oka believed that the first group may have come by sea from the south, that the latter two groups crossed over from Korea to Kyushu, and that the most powerful clan from the last group eventually emerged as the imperial family in the historic period. Other scholars have proffered other explanations, but many seem to include much of Oka's thinking.

The first recorded information about Japan occurs in the Chinese dynastic histories in 57 C.E. At this time Japan was composed of over 100 tribal communities. From the Chinese *History of the Kingdom of Wei* (297 C.E.) we learn that the consolidation of power occurred slowly, because after a little more than 200 years only forty communities existed. Mention is also made of death rituals, the importance of purification, rank, and family, the use of divination, and the rule of Japan by a female shaman along with her brother. The Chinese histories claim that by the fifth and sixth centuries C.E. the Yamato clan had become preeminent among all of the clans and established hegemony over them. This marks the beginning of the emperor system in Japan, which has continued unbroken for approximately 1,600 years.

The Chinese chronicles record the consolidation of power into the hands of fewer clans (*uji*) over time. The importance of *uji* cannot be overstated. Not only were these family/clan units, but they were also centers of military, economic, and spiritual power. The head of the *uji* was referred to as the *ujigami*, and this word could be written with different Chinese characters so that it could refer both to the head of the clan and to a god. Many scholars argue that this was the beginning of the native religion Shinto, which literally means "the way of the gods." The emperor, as the head of the most powerful *uji*, was not only the leading political figure, but also was seen as being an *ikigami* (living god), a direct descendant of the sun goddess Amaterasu, responsible for the performance of important religious rites to ensure the abundance of the rice harvest. In addition to *uji*, rural sociologists have noted the importance of three other kinship groupings in Japanese society. The first kind of village community is known as *miyaza* (*miya* meaning shrine and *za* referring to guild or group). In *miyaza* type villages all of the households take care of the village Shinto shrine at defined intervals. Often there is a distinction between superior and inferior households, with the former having greater responsibility for certain important rituals conducted during festivals, during rites of passage, or before the gods. The second type of village community is referred to as *kō-kumi*. The households in *kō-kumi* villages are considered to be socially and economically equal, and therefore mutual aid and the bonds of community outweigh kinship ties in social affairs and community activities. The final village grouping is the *dōzoku* type, which consists of a hierarchical group of households connected by kinship ties. In such a system a main house is ideally passed down from eldest son to eldest son, and branch houses are established by other sons and cousins.

PERIODS OF CULTURAL HISTORY

For the sake of simplicity, recorded Japanese cultural history can be divided into four periods: (1) fifth to twelfth century, when the imperial family and noble families rule and are the creators and purveyors of artistic taste; (2) late twelfth to mid-seventeenth century, when warrior clans rule and determine artistic taste and culture;

(3) mid-seventeenth to mid-nineteenth century, when warriors rule but now the rising merchant class becomes the leader in the creation and consumption of art and culture; and (4) late nineteenth century to the present with the development of mass culture.

The earliest written records in Japan are the *Kojiki* (712 C.E.), the *Nihon shoki* (720 C.E.), and approximately sixty *fudoki* from the eighth century C.E. The *Kojiki* (Records of Ancient Matters) includes myths of the creation of heaven, earth, and Japan and of the descent of the gods to Japan. It provides an explanation of the relationship between certain gods and the imperial family and other powerful clans and presents legendary and historical data covering the first emperor Jimmu to the fifth century emperor Ojin. Concerned that the oral reciters of this material were forgetting or corrupting the stories of the foundation of Japan and the connection between the imperial family and the gods, the emperor ordered the compilation of the *Kojiki* in the late seventh century. A written record would fix the history and pedigree for all times.

The *Nihon shoki* (Chronicle of Japan) is a history of Japan from the mythical age of the gods to the empress Jito, who ruled in the late seventh century. While it covers much of the same time period as the *Kojiki*, the *Nihon shoki* focuses much more on the day-to-day activities of the emperors and empresses. This early history is also of interest because it provides multiple versions of many of the myths, legends, and stories.

Approximately sixty *fudoki* were compiled in the eighth century by order of the emperor. Each of the *fudoki* focused on a specific geographical area and reported on the local topography, etymologies of place names, natural resources, local legends, folktales, deities, and folk beliefs. Of the sixty original *fudoki* only five have survived in a form close to the originals.

Most of the records that have come down to us from the Nara (710–784 C.E.) and Heian (794–1185 C.E.) periods derive from aristocratic life. Some of these materials provide information about local legends and folktales and often contain a wealth of information about the folk belief system. An excellent example is *The Tale of Genji*, written in the eleventh century by Murasaki Shikibu (978–ca. 1016), a lady-in-waiting to the empress. *The Tale of Genji*, which is often cited as the first great novel in world literature, contains a number of episodes of spirit possession, still a commonly held belief in Japan. The two most famous episodes of possession relate to the death of Genji's young lover Yugao and then eventually the death of his pregnant wife Aoi. Both occur at the hands of the possessing spirit of an earlier jilted lover. Recently, Doris Bargen (1997) has done a detailed study of these possession episodes, comparing and contrasting male-centered and female-centered interpretations of these spirits.

The Heian and Kamakura (1185–1333 C.E.) periods mark a high point in the collection and publication of Buddhist and secular tales including almost fifty different titles. The *Nihon ryoiki*, which contains 116 Buddhist tales and legends, was compiled in the 820s. Many other collections of Buddhist tales exist—two of the most important being the *Dainihonkoku Hokekyōkenki*, which was compiled in the mid-eleventh century and contains 129 tales, and Muju Ichien's *Shasekishu*, which was compiled in the late thirteenth century. A number of collections contain mixtures of Buddhist and secular tales. The two most important are the *Konjaku monogatari*, which was compiled in the early twelfth century and is one of the great tale collections in the world containing 1,039 tales, and the early-thirteenth-century *Uji shūi mono-gatari*, which contains 197 tales. These tale collections were compiled for a number of reasons, but the two most important are for the compiler to gain merit for his next rebirth and for use by itinerant priests who traveled the countryside to spread Buddhist teachings and collect donations for the construction of temples and statues.

The recitation and eventual transcription of the great Japanese war epic, *The Tale of the Heike*, occurred during the Kamakura and Ashikaga (1338–1573) periods. This collection of martial exploits and legends is based on the great civil war between the Heike and Genji clans, which took place from 1180 to 1185, and is one of the most powerful examples in Japanese literature of the Buddhist concept of *mujō* (impermanence/change). A tradition arose of mostly blind itinerant jongleurs (*biwa hōshi*) who traveled the countryside singing and reciting famous episodes from this war. Eventually a longer version of the tale recited by the great *biwa hōshi* Kakuichi was recorded in 1371 and quickly became the standard text for reading and recitation. Many of the individual stories and legends have been used by dramatists to write plays of great pathos. Some of the most moving examples are the warrior ghost plays in the Noh theater, which not only relate famous tales but also illustrate Buddhist ideas and ideals of death and the afterlife as well as belief in spirits of the dead and their ability to interact with the living.

During the Edo (1600–1868) period a group of scholars began to study Japanese classical literature and ancient writings in a search for the true Japanese spirit (*Yamato gokoro*). The scholars of note in this investigation of Japanese thought and culture, called *kokugaku* (National learning), were Kada no Azumamaro (1669–1736), Kamo no Mabuchi (1697–1769), Motoori Norinaga (1730–1801), and Hirata Atsutane (1776–1843). By means of philological studies of the classics, including the *Manyōshū* (an eighth-century poetry collection), the *Kojiki*, the *Nihon shoki*, and *The Tale of Genji*, these scholars attempted to identify the roots of Japanese culture before the introduction of Chinese influence in the sixth to ninth centuries. While their focus varied, an underlying ideological foundation came to support a very nationalistic view of Japan and Japanese history in the nineteenth century. The influence of *kokugaku* thought on the eventual overthrow of the Tokugawa family and military rule in Japan in 1868 and the "restoration" of the emperor to his rightful place as ruler of Japan cannot be underestimated. An underlying problem that they faced, and one that has interesting parallels elsewhere in the world (for example, the Grimm brothers in **Germany** and Lönnrot in **Finland**), was the fact that all of the classical documents studied from earlier times were written in a script borrowed from China. How could the true Japanese spirit be expressed and discovered in a foreign language?

RELIGIOUS BELIEFS

Buddhism and Confucianism were introduced to Japan from China in the sixth century. Both had a profound effect on Japanese culture. Buddhism introduced elite Japanese to higher Chinese culture. A close connection between Buddhism and the state also developed over time with imperial support of priests and temples. A system of *kokubunji* (country protecting temples) was constructed in the eighth century by

眾瞽
探象之圖

Ukiyo-e print illustration from a Buddhist parable showing blind monks examining an elephant. Buddhism introduced the Japanese elite to higher Chinese culture. (Courtesy Library of Congress)

order of the emperor. Strong ties between families and clans also developed initially with aristocratic families building their own temples and later (from the seventeenth century) with most families establishing family gravesites at a particular temple. Another area of interest was the esoteric side of Buddhism, which along with the shamanistic elements already in Japan is still popular today. These practices connect practitioners to the world of spirits, ancestors, and *genze riyaku* (this world benefits).

Finally, Confucianism has had tremendous impact on Japanese society. The dissemination of this Chinese import has been promoted by most Japanese governments and elite society because it makes a very strong argument for a hierarchical society in which everyone must understand his or her place. When people understand their places, live according to their stations in life, interact with those above with deference and with those below with kindness and forbearance, then all will be well in Heaven, in nature, and among humans. If strictly practiced, Confucianism argues against social change and for the status quo.

The fifth through the eighth centuries C.E. saw a tremendous Chinese influence on Japanese culture. Prior to this time the Japanese did not have a written script and therefore borrowed the Chinese writing system. The Japanese also borrowed and modified Chinese historical writing, legal codes, layout of the capital city, Buddhism (with all of its attendant art, literature, and architecture), Confucianism, Daoism, painting, and poetry among other aspects of culture. The influence is of such major proportions that a movement that lasted from the seventeenth to the nineteenth centuries aimed to eliminate Chinese cultural influence and discover the true Japanese spirit (*Yamato gokoro*).

FOLK RELIGION AND PERFORMING ARTS

Another area of intense interest is *minkan shinkō* (folk religion, folk belief). The formal study of *minkan shinkō* can be traced back to the Edo period and the early *kokugaku* scholars. In their attempts to discover the original Japanese spirit they focused on indigenous belief systems and practices. Along with the indigenous beliefs there were many accretions from foreign belief systems, most notably Buddhism, Daoism, and Confucianism. The study of *minkan shinkō* has focused on a number of areas: *kami* (gods) and spirits, divine chastisement and protection, worship and taboos, annual observances (Miyake [1972] lists fifteen), rites of passage (Miyake lists six), superstitions, connections to social organization, and the relation to new religious movements which have arisen since the early nineteenth century.

Minzoku geinō (folk performing arts) have also been studied extensively. Many such performances have their basis in the distant past and can be studied historically, especially their close connections to the agricultural cycle (most notably rice planting and harvesting) and the local festival and religious context. Honda Yasuji established a classification system for *minzoku geinō* that includes three major categories: *kagura* (dramatic singing and dancing performances usually performed at Shinto shrines for the protection of human life), *dengaku* (performances focusing on the

Kagura are dramatic singing and dancing performances that are usually performed at Shinto shrines for the protection of human life. (© Takashi Hirowatari/HAGA/The Image Works)

production of rice and guaranteeing enough of this staple grain to sustain human life), and *furyū* (a performance in which harmful spirits are banished thereby driving away evil influences that threaten human life). All three categories center on protecting and sustaining the lives of human beings and demonstrate the close connection that exists between *kami* and humans and the avenues of communication that are open between them through the performing arts. The study of festival, which combines elements of *minkan shinkō* and *minzoku geinō*, has also been a rich field of study in Japanese folklore with numerous field reports from throughout the country being written.

Sports and Games

Before the war, sports and games were studied as part of the larger research on rural village life encouraged by Yanagita. After the war, the study of games and sports received modest attention. Earlier studies were searched for references to children's games, which were then examined for the light they might shed on such practices, especially on lost traditions. One of the most interesting reports dating from the 1930s was from the diary kept by Ella Embree while her husband John Embree was conducting anthropological research in a small Japanese village. From her diary we learn of the places where games were played, the kinds of games, the gendered nature of certain games, and the importance in many of the games of imitating adult behaviors. Many scholars have lamented that because of the *juku* (cram school) system of education now in place children do not have time to interact and play with their peers. The play that they do participate in is often limited to computer games. Sports, especially baseball, sumo, and the martial arts, have received more attention. Robert Whiting has written about the history and peculiarly Japanese way of playing baseball, which is arguably the national sport. He has clearly shown that cultural factors are very important in sport and can alter the way a game is played in important ways. Sumo and the other martial arts, which are often considered quintessentially Japanese, have also been widely studied. Some of the recent scholarship, taking their cue from Benedict Anderson, looks at these sports and their histories as forms of invented tradition.

ARTS, CRAFTS, AND ARCHITECTURE

Folk architecture, most notably *minka* (farm houses) and *kura* (storehouses), has been widely studied. The basic areas of interest are the materials used in construction, floor plans, basic structural features (for example, foundation, floor, posts and framework, beam systems, and roof trusses), and regional styles—especially of the roofs.

Finally, the subject of *mingei* (folk crafts), initially under the direction of Yanagi Muneyoshi, was widely studied and promoted. An incredible amount of research related to pottery, textiles, woodworking, shop signs, and numerous other crafts has been published. Numerous small specialty retail stores sell *mingei* throughout Japan and most large department stores have a *mingei* section. One of the best (some say the best) specialty stores is Bingoya, which is located in Tokyo and stocks an incredible selection of *mingei* from all over Japan.

MEDICINE

Since the 1970s, there has been a surge of interest in the study of East Asian medical systems. Many of these studies look at the range of medical practice that patients have to choose from when they feel the need to consult a specialist. Margaret Lock (1980) outlines four systems that are available in Japan: cosmopolitan (Western, modern, scientific) medical system; East Asian medical system or traditional Chinese medicine; folk medical system that is not related to a scholarly tradition; and popular medical system which individuals and/or families provide. As Lock demonstrates in Japan and Arthur Kleinman (1979) in China, except for the first one, these differing medical systems have long histories in East Asia, and each system is adept at handling certain physical and psychological problems that often cannot be handled by the other systems.

CHALLENGES OF THE MODERN WORLD

After the devastation of World War II, Japan began its recovery in the late 1940s through the 1950s. The beginning of the so-called economic miracle in the 1960s also marked an increase in disposable income and leisure time. At this time a "cultural boom" and later in the 1970s a "nostalgia boom" occurred when Japan experienced an increased interest in the arts (both folk and elite); constructed history and folklore **museums** and clubs throughout the country; and strengthened existing and created new departments of folklore study at the university level, which trained advanced graduate students who went on to teach at universities and work in museums. In 1983 the National Museum of History was opened in Sakura just outside of Tokyo. This museum is the first national museum of history and has four research sections: history, folklore, archeology, and museum science. Every major town and city in Japan has its own history and folklore museum, and cities the size of Tokyo usually have history and folklore museums in each ward of the city. These museums have very active exhibition schedules, publish a plethora of material on the history and folklore of the area, and have outreach programs aimed at students and local residents.

Along with the increased interest in the academic study of folklore, a concomitant interest in creating or recreating local festivals grew as part of the nostalgia boom. Villages, towns, and cities vied with each other in marketing their "traditional" crafts and festivals as tourist attractions. The Japanese National Railway (JNR) recognized this trend early in its development and began to take an active interest in the promotion of such activities in an attempt to increase their revenues through increased travel. JNR began national advertising campaigns, created by Dentsu (the largest advertising agency in the world), which were aimed at encouraging people to travel from large metropolitan areas back to the countryside to discover and participate in "traditional Japan" firsthand. This was seen as a way to reconnect with the true Japanese spirit, which seemed to have gone awry during the brutality of the war and the focus on materialistic aspects of life during the subsequent recovery. This phenomenon led to further academic study of tradition and the invention of tradition.

MODERN STUDIES OF JAPANESE FOLKLORE

Some scholars see the founding of modern folklore studies (*minzokugaku*) in Japan in the early twentieth century as an attempt to find a solution to this problem and provide a continuation of *kokugaku* studies. The three founders of modern folklore studies in Japan were Yanagita Kunio (1875–1962), Yanagi Muneyoshi (Sōetsu; 1889–1961), and Orikuchi Shinobu (1887–1953). Yanagita was initially a government bureaucrat and then a journalist who traveled extensively around Japan. He eventually became interested in the folk, their way of life, stories, and the notion that the uneducated masses, who had not been influenced by Chinese cultural importations as much as the elites, expressed in their daily life the true Japanese spirit. His first collection of tales entitled *Tōno monogatari* (1910) demonstrated clearly that ordinary farmers were not concerned with national events and the emperor, but rather told stories about ghosts and spirits and the potential dangers of country life. From around 1930, Yanagita worked full-time trying to lay a foundation for folklore studies. He encouraged fieldwork studies of rural areas, focusing on folk religion, oral narratives, local festivals, and social organization. In 1934 Yanagita published his *Folklore Handbook* as a guide for young fieldworkers who were instructed how to go into rural farming and fishing villages to collect the one hundred items of data listed in the *Handbook*. At this time (1957) he also wrote a history of the Meiji period (1868–1912) in which he did not use one proper name, in order to make the point that history could be written from the perspective of the nameless masses. Yanagita's major writings were collected in thirty-six volumes in 1985.

Yanagita's relative lack of interest in folk material culture was addressed by Yanagi Muneyoshi, the driving force in the folk craft (*mingei*) movement, which began to take shape in the 1920s. Yanagi was not only a collector but also a sponsor and mentor of traditional crafts and craftsmen. The artists most prominently associated with Yanagi's attempts to revive folk crafts were the potters Hamada Shōji, Kawai Kanjirō, and the English potter Bernard Leach, the woodblock print artist Munakata Shikō, and the textile designer and dyer Serizawa Keisuke. In the early 1930s Yanagi began publishing a journal focusing on the decorative arts, and in 1936 he established the Japan Folk Crafts Museum to preserve and display traditional folk crafts. A visit to this museum, located in Komaba in Tokyo, illustrates his principal areas of interest: textiles, ceramics, objects made of wood, lacquer, and metal, and pictorial art. In his writings Yanagi attempted to explain the appeal of everyday objects made by the hands of skilled craftsmen. The appeal was not only esthetic but also religious in nature and, if made properly and approached properly, could enrich one's life in innumerable ways. Yanagi's major writings are collected in ten volumes.

The third great figure in the early development of folklore studies in Japan was Orikuchi Shinobu. Orikuchi, a scholar of classical Japanese literature and a poet, focused his folklore studies on literary-philological approaches; that is, in many ways he was continuing in the *kokugaku* tradition. Orikuchi's approach has often been said to be the opposite of Yanagita's because Orikuchi studied ancient sources first and then searched for modern remnants, while Yanagita began with the present tradition and then tried to relate it to the past. His major works are collected in eighteen volumes.

During the Pacific War (1937–1945) it was difficult for most scholars to undertake serious research. The government encouraged folklorists to continue their work, however, because it was seen as an investigation of the Japanese spirit, which the government was interested in promoting for the war effort. Some folklorists were also sent overseas, especially to Korea and China, to conduct fieldwork among the subjected peoples. During this period of military expansionist policies in Asia, folklore—in particular folk narrative—was put to use by the government to further their policies. One of the most prominent examples is the use of the famous folktale of Momotarō (Peach Boy), who is born into humble origins, grows up to be a paragon of virtue and filial piety, and with some animal helpers encounters and defeats some ogres and devils who are plaguing the virtuous peasants. Making the connection between Momotarō and the Japanese, who were attempting to free enslaved Asians from the American and European imperialist powers, and between the ogres and devils and the imperialist West was easy.

The thought of Yanagita, Yanagi, and Orikuchi dominated Japanese folklore studies through the 1960s and beyond. One of the major problems for later scholars was distancing themselves from these founders without appearing to disrespect their life's work. The collection and analysis of folklore materials in the twentieth century focused on a number of areas. One main area of interest was oral narratives—especially the folktale. In 1936 Yanagita published a handbook with one hundred representative folktales for collectors, including blank pages for them to record similar tales from informants. This handbook was mailed to collectors throughout Japan, who were asked to fill in the books with tales and return them to Yanagita for study. The books were so popular with the collectors that not one was returned. Many tales, however, were collected, and numerous journals began to publish them, thereby encouraging others to begin collecting. In 1958, one of Yanagita's assistants, Seki Keigo, published a collection of over 8,600 tales that he divided into seven hundred types. He established his own classification, making it difficult to use his work for comparative purposes with the type index of Antti Aarne and Stith Thompson. In 1971 Ikeda Hiroko published *A Type and Motif Index of Japanese Folk Literature* modeled on the Aarne-Thompson type and motif classification system. In addition to the tales themselves, the use of themes from oral narratives in the graphic arts is widespread. A classic of folklore study in Japan was the publication in 1908 of Henri L. Joly's *Legend in Japanese Art*. This text is a treasure trove of legendary tales with examples of their use and appearance in an incredibly wide variety of Japanese art forms. Many Japanese legends deal with the supernatural, which has also been a popular theme in various Japanese arts. The 1980s saw a boom in peasant studies in Japan. One area of particular interest was the study of peasant histories, including themes of peasant protest, early modern economic history and the plight of the peasants, martyrdom, and the narratives that developed around these heroes who sacrificed their lives for the masses. Research has also been conducted on the use of personal experience narratives (*taiken*) in new religions in Japan. Adherents are encouraged by the religious organizations to relate *taiken* in front of large groups of people, telling them of the benefits they have received by joining the group and internalizing and practicing their way of living. These narratives are often recorded and published in monthly newspapers and magazines and are considered to be one of the best recruitment tools for gaining new members.

Another popular area of study was folksong (*min'yō*). Before the age of television and mass communication there were very clear regional differences (dialects, scale structures) in *min'yō* which became less pronounced in the late twentieth century. The classification of the songs by function usually includes four specific headings: (1) religious songs used in Shinto rites and local festivals; (2) occupational songs used especially during the planting and harvesting of rice and for other agriculture-related activities; (3) songs for specific social gatherings, especially rites of passage; and (4) children's songs including both songs sung to and by children. Large collections of *min'yō* exist, and many of the field recordings have been released on record and compact discs. *See also* **Ainu (Japan)**.

BIBLIOGRAPHY

Addiss, Stephen, ed. 1985. *Japanese Ghosts and Demons: Art of the Supernatural*. New York: George Braziller.

Anderson, Richard W. 1992. To Open the Hearts of People: Experience Narratives and Zenrinkai Training Sessions. *Japanese Journal of Religious Studies* 19.4: 307–324.

———. 1995a. Social Drama and Iconicity: Personal Narratives in Japanese New Religions. *Journal of Folklore Research* 32.3: 177–205.

———. 1995b. Vengeful Ancestors and Animal Spirits: Personal Narratives of the Supernatural in a Japanese New Religion. *Western Folklore* 54.2: 113–140.

———. 1999. Religious Tales and Storytelling in Japan. In *Traditional Storytelling Today: An International Sourcebook*, edited by Margaret Read MacDonald. Chicago: Fitzroy Dearborn Publishers. 114–118.

Aoki, Michiko Yamaguchi. 1971. *Izumo Fudoki*. Tokyo: Sophia University.

Araki, James T. 1978. *The Ballad-Drama of Medieval Japan*. Rutland: Charles E. Tuttle.

Aston, W. G., trans. 1972. *Nihongi: Chronicles of Japan from the Earliest Times to A.D. 697*. Rutland: Charles E. Tuttle.

Averbuch, Irit. 1990. Yamabushi Kagura: A Study of a Traditional Ritual Dance in Contemporary Japan. Diss., Harvard University.

———. 1995. *The Gods Come Dancing: A Study of the Japanese Ritual Dance of Yamabushi Kagura*. Ithaca: Cornell University East Asia Program.

Bargen, Doris G. 1997. *A Woman's Weapon: Spirit Possession in* The Tale of Genji. Honolulu: University of Hawaii Press.

Blacker, Carmen. 1975. *The Catalpa Bow: A Study of Shamanistic Practices in Japan*. London: George Allen and Unwin.

Bock, Felicia, trans. 1970, 1972. *Engi-Shiki: Procedures of the Engi Era*. 2 volumes. Tokyo: Sophia University.

Bonnefoy, Yves. 1991. *Asian Mythologies*, translated under the direction of Wendy Doniger. Chicago: University of Chicago Press.

Brandon, Reiko Mochinaga. 1986. *Country Textiles of Japan: The Art of Tsutsugaki*. New York: Weatherhill.

Butler, Kenneth Dean. 1966. The Textual Evolution of *The Heike Monogatari*. *Harvard Journal of Asiatic Studies* 26: 5–51.

———. 1969. *The Heike Monogatari* and the Japanese Warrior Ethic. *Harvard Journal of Asiatic Studies* 29: 93–108.

Chingen. 1987. *Miraculous Tales of the Lotus Sutra from Ancient Japan*: The Dainihonkoku Hokekyōkenki *of Priest Chingen*, translated by Yoshiko K. Dykstra. Honolulu: University of Hawai'i Press.

Cort, Louise Allison. 1992. *Seto and Mino Ceramics: Japanese Collections in the Freer Gallery of Art*. Honolulu: Freer Gallery of Art and University of Hawai'i Press.

Czaja, Michael. 1974. *Gods of Myth and Stone: Phallicism in Japanese Folk Religion*. New York: Weatherhill.

de Bary, Wm. Theodore, Donald Keene, George Tanabe, and Paul Varley, eds. 2001. *Sources of Japanese Tradition: From Earliest Times to 1600*. 2nd edition. New York: Columbia University Press.

Dorson, Richard. 1961. *Folk Legends of Japan*. Rutland: Charles E. Tuttle.

Dower, John W. 1986. *War Without Mercy: Race and Power in the Pacific War*. New York: Pantheon.

Gordon, Andrew, ed. 1993. *Postwar Japan as History*. Berkeley: University of California Press.

Guttman, Allen, and Lee Thompson. 2001. *Japanese Sports: A History*. Honolulu: University of Hawai'i Press.

Heineken, Ty, and Kiyoko Heineken. 1981. *Tansu: Traditional Japanese Cabinetry*. New York: Weatherhill.

Hickman, Money, and Peter Fetchko. 1977. *Japan Day by Day: An Exhibition in Honor of Edward Sylvester Morse*. Salem: Peabody Museum of Salem.

Hori Ichirō. 1968. *Folk Religion in Japan*, edited by Joseph M. Kitagawa and Alan L. Miiller. Chicago: The University of Chicago Press.

Ikeda Hiroko. 1971. *A Type and Motif Index of Japanese Folk-Literature*. Helsinki: Folklore Fellows Communications No. 209.

Inoue Shun. 1998. The Invention of the Martial Arts: Kanō Jigorō and Kōdōkan Judo. In *Mirror of Modernity: Invented Traditions of Modern Japan*, edited by Stephen Vlastos. Berkeley: University of California Press. 163–173.

Itoh Teiji. 1973. *Kura: Design and Tradition of the Japanese Storehouse*. Seattle: Madrona Publishers.

Ivy, Marilyn. 1995. *Discourses of the Vanishing: Modernity, Phantasm, Japan*. Chicago: University of Chicago Press.

Japanese Folk Crafts Museum, ed. 1991. *Mingei: Masterpieces of Japanese Folkcraft*. Tokyo: Kodansha International.

Joly, Henri L. 1967 (1908). *Legend in Japanese Art: A Description of Historical Episodes, Legendary Characters, Folk-Lore, Myths, Religious Symbolism Illustrated in the Arts of Old Japan*. Rutland: Charles E. Tuttle.

Kawashima Chūji. 1986. *Minka: Traditional Houses of Rural Japan*, translated by Lynne E. Riggs. Tokyo: Kodansha International.

Kelsey, W. Michael. 1982. *Konjaku Monogatari-shu*. Boston: Twayne.

Kitagawa, Joseph M. 1966. *Religion in Japanese History*. New York: Columbia University Press.

Kleinman, Arthur. 1979. *Patients and Healers in the Context of Culture: An Exploration of the Borderland Between Anthropology, Medicine, and Psychiatry*. Berkeley: University of California Press.

Kobayashi Hiroko. 1979. *The Human Comedy of Heian Japan: A Study of the Secular Stories in the Twelfth-Century Collection of Tales*, Konjaku Monogatarishu. Tokyo: Center for East Asian Cultural Studies.

Koschmann, J. Victor, Oiwa Keibo, and Yamashita Shinji, eds. 1985. *International Perspectives on Yanagita Kunio and Japanese Folklore Studies*. Ithaca: Cornell University China-Japan Program.

Kyōkai. 1973. *Miraculous Stories from the Japanese Buddhist Tradition*: The Nihon Ryoiki *of the Monk Kyōkai*, translated by Kyoko Moromochi Nakamura. Cambridge: Harvard University Press.

Leach, Bernard. 1975. *Hamada, Potter*. Tokyo: Kodansha International.

Levy, Dana, Lea Sneider, and Frank Gibney. 1983. *Kanban: Shop Signs of Japan*. New York: Weatherhill.

Lock, Margaret M. 1980. *East Asian Medicine in Urban Japan*. Berkeley: University of California Press.

Malm, William P. 2001. *Traditional Japanese Music and Musical Instruments*. Tokyo: Kodansha International.

Mayer, Fanny Hagin, ed. and trans. 1985. *Ancient Tales in Modern Japan*. Bloomington: Indiana University Press.

McCullough, Helen Craig, trans. 1988. *The Tale of the Heike*. Stanford: Stanford University Press.

Mills, D. E., trans. 1970. *A Collection of Tales from Uji: A Study and Translation of* Uji Shūi Monogatari. Cambridge: Cambridge University Press.

Miyake Hitoshi. 1972. Folk Religion. In *Japanese Religion: A Survey by the Agency for Cultural Affairs*, edited by Hori Ichirō, Ikado Fujio, Wakimoto Tsuneya and Yanagawa Keiichi. Tokyo: Kodansha International. 121–143.

Moeran, Brian D. 1981. Yanagi Muneyoshi and the Japanese Folk Craft Movement. *Asian Folklore Studies* 40: 87–100.

———. 1984. *Lost Innocence: Folk Craft Potters of Onta, Japan*. Berkeley: University of California Press.

Mujū Ichien. 1985. *Sand and Pebbles* (Shasekishu): *The Tales of Muju Ichien, A Voice for Pluralism in Kamakura Buddhism*, translated by Robert E. Morrell. Albany: State University of New York Press.

Mullins, Mark R., Shimazono Susumu, and Paul L. Swanson, eds. 1993. *Religion and Society in Modern Japan*. Berkeley: Asian Humanities Press.

Murasaki Shikibu. 1982. *The Tale of Genji*, translated by Edward G. Seidensticker. New York: Knopf.

Okada Shigehiro, Torao Toshiya, Tsukamoto Manabu, and Iwai Hiromi. 1989. *National Museum of Japanese History: English Guide*, translated by Furuta Gyō and Paul F. Shepherd. Sakura: National Museum of Japanese History.

Ōtsuka Minzokugakukai, ed. 1972. *Nihon Minzoku Jiten* (Dictionary of Japanese Folklore). Tokyo: Kōbundō.

Philippi, Donald, trans. 1968. *Kojiki*. Tokyo: University of Tokyo Press.

Provine, Robert C., Tokumaru Yoshihiko, and J. Lawrence Witzleben, eds. 2001. *East Asia: China, Japan, and Korea (Garland Encyclopedia of Music vol. 7)*. New York: Garland.

Reader, Ian, and George J. Tanabe. 1998. *Practically Religious: Worldly Benefits and the Common Religion of Japan*. Honolulu: University of Hawai'i Press.

Roberts, Laurance P. 1987. *Roberts' Guide to Japanese Museums of Art and Archaeology*. Tokyo: The Simul Press.

Robertson, Jennifer. 1991. *Native and Newcomer: Making and Remaking a Japanese City*. Berkeley: University of California Press.

Sasakura Gensho. 1987. *Tsutsugaki Textiles of Japan*. Kyoto: Shikosha.

Segi Shinichi. 1985. *Yoshitoshi: The Splendid Decadent*. Tokyo: Kodansha International.

Seki Keigo. 1966. Types of Japanese Folktales. *Asian Folklore Studies* 25: 1–220.

Seki Keigo, ed. 1963. *Folktales of Japan*. Chicago: University of Chicago Press.

Shimazaki Chifumi. 1993. *Warrior Ghost Plays from the Japanese Noh Theater*. Ithaca: Cornell University East Asia Program.

———. 1995. *Restless Spirits from Japanese Noh Plays of the Fourth Group*. Ithaca: Cornell University East Asia Program.

Smith, Robert J. 1974. *Ancestor Worship in Contemporary Japan*. Stanford: Stanford University Press.

Smith, Robert J., and Ella Lury Wiswell. 1982. *The Women of Suye Mura*. Chicago: University of Chicago Press.

Stevenson, John. 1983. *Yoshitoshi's Thirty-Six Ghosts*. New York: Weatherhill.

Takashima Taiji. 1981. *Kotowaza no Izumi* (Fountain of Japanese Proverbs [in Japanese, English, French, and German]). Tokyo: The Hokuseido Press.

Thompson, Lee A. 1998. The Invention of the *Yokuzuna* and the Championship System, Or, Futahaguro's Revenge. In *Mirror of Modernity: Invented Traditions of Modern Japan*, edited by Stephen Vlastos. Berkeley: University of California Press. 174–187.

Ury, Marian. 1979. *Tales of Times Now Past: Sixty-Two Stories from a Medieval Japanese Collection*. Berkeley: University of California Press.

Vlastos, Stephen, ed. 1998. *Mirror of Modernity: Invented Traditions of Modern Japan*. Berkeley: University of California Press.

Walthall, Anne. 1991. *Peasant Uprisings in Japan: A Critical Anthology of Peasant Histories*. Chicago: University of Chicago Press.

Yamamoto Yoshiko. 1978. *The Namahage: A Festival in the Northeast of Japan*. Philadelphia: Institute for the Study of Human Issues.

Yanagi Sōetsu. 1972. *The Unknown Craftsman: A Japanese Insight into Beauty*. Tokyo: Kodansha International.

Yanagita Kunio. 1957. *Japanese Manners and Customs in the Meiji Era*, translated by Charles S. Terry. Tokyo: Obunsha.

———. 1970. *About Our Ancestors*, translated by Fanny Hagin Mayer and Ishiwara Yasuyo. Tokyo: Japan Society for the Promotion of Science.

———. 1975. *The Legends of Tōno*, translated by Ronald A. Morse. Tokyo: The Japan Foundation.

———. 1986. *The Yanagita Kunio Guide to the Japanese Folk Tale*, edited and translated by Fanny Hagin Mayer. Bloomington: Indiana University Press.

Richard W. Anderson

AINU (JAPAN)

GEOGRAPHY AND HISTORY

The Ainu are the aboriginal people of **Japan** and live on the island of Hokkaido. Their homeland, however, formerly included southern Sakhalin Island and the Kuriles. Ainu culture and language were highly diversified, showing regional variations among the Hokkaido, Sakhalin, and Kurile Ainu. The focus here is on Ainu folklore and culture on Hokkaido.

Hokkaido is located north of Honshu, Japan's largest island. The northern end of Hokkaido is about twenty nautical miles south of Sakhalin, while the Kurile Islands stretch northeast toward the Kamchatka Peninsula. Hokkaido's climate ranges from sub-arctic to cool temperate with a long snowy season from December to March in the coastal areas. The island was once well wooded with fir, spruce, birch, oak, and elm. Grizzly bears and deer are found in the mountains, and salmon run in most rivers from August to December. These provided the Ainu with rich food resources. Most of the rivers flow from a mountain range that bisects the island from north to south. Rivers and mountain ranges used to constitute natural boundaries between local areas of the Ainu.

The genealogy of the Ainu once attracted the interests of Europeans because of speculation that they were of Caucasoid origin. Recent anthropological studies, however, have proven that the Ainu population belongs not to the Caucasoid but to the Mongoloid family. Prehistoric remains show that Hokkaido has been populated since the Paleolithic period. An archeological site in the southern part of Hokkaido dating to 5500 B.C.E. with more than 600 dwellings shows the prevalence of the Jomon culture (the oldest earthenware culture of Japan). The ethnic origin of the Ainu is still in dispute. It has not yet been determined whether they are of the same stock as the Okinawan and Jomon people, since they differ from other peoples arising from a mixture of proto-Japanese with immigrants. However, it is clear that the Jomon culture once prevailed throughout Hokkaido. The Jomon culture subsequently developed through the post-Jomon culture and Satsumon culture into Ainu culture, the full formation of which is generally considered to have started between the late fourteenth and early fifteenth centuries on Hokkaido.

The Ainu traditionally subsisted by hunting, fishing, and gathering. Deer and salmon (dog salmon) were their major food sources. Bears were also important game not only for food but also for ritual purposes. Moreover, the Ainu have engaged in trading with both mainland Japan and the eastern coast of Siberia since 1350 and in cultivating several types of millet such as the barnyard grass millet and foxtail millet since 1790 at the latest. In particular, Ainu who lived along the coast practiced small-scale slash-and-burn cultivation, which was probably introduced through contact with Japanese. Generally, women were responsible for crop cultivation. Once a plot of land had been cultivated by a person, that land was acknowledged as belonging to her or him. Thus, the cultivator had the usufruct of the plot until it was abandoned.

Social structure differed from region to region but generally consisted of the same basic units: the settlement group (*kotan*), the local group, the *shine-itokpa* group (a group possessing the same mark of male ancestry), and the river group. The basic social unit was the nuclear family. A group of families formed a settlement (*kotan*), though the number of families in a settlement varied from one to over twenty. Settlements were set up near rivers, and sites were usually chosen for their proximity to fishing grounds, especially the spawning grounds of the dog salmon. The local group was a sociopolitically integrated territorial unit, which consisted of one or several settlement groups under a common headman. The unity and integrity of a settlement group were expressed by the common ownership of salmon spawning beds, and the local group participated collectively in the river deity ceremony before the start of salmon fishing.

Aming the Upper Tokapchi Ainu especially, members of the local groups regarded the river valley as their territory and had exclusive rights to exploit its resources, which they defended against the trespass of outsiders. For all economic purposes, the local group was self-sufficient. Several local groups living adjacently along a river formed a *shine-itokpa* group. The group had neither a single authority nor common territory but functioned as a collective unit only for the bear ceremony, the sending-off ritual for the bear cub. The river group recognized the total area of a river basin as common territory, or *iwor*, which means "the area in which deities are." The term was used to signify a hunting, fishing, and gathering ground. The river group was an aggregation of all the local groups along a river and held collective rituals to ward off catastrophic natural phenomena.

The Ainu were not an isolated population but had a long history of contact with neighboring peoples. A mid-fourteenth-century document tells of their often coming to the shore of the Tsugaru district (the northernmost area of mainland Honshu) to trade. There the Ainu were recognized as a distinct ethnic group, different from other Japanese. Contact between Ainu and Japanese through trading occasionally resulted in the revolt of the former against the latter. After the 1669 revolt of Shakushain against the Matsumae feudal clan, who were granted exclusive trading rights with the Ainu by the Tokugawa Shogunate, Hokkaido Ainu remained fully under the control of both the Matsumae clan and the Tokugawa Shogunate throughout the Edo period.

The Meiji Restoration in 1868 fully integrated Hokkaido into the nation state of Imperial Japan, and the Meiji government began to promote the colonization of Hokkaido. Accordingly, the Ainu population, estimated at between 18,805 and 23,797 during the Edo period, began to decrease drastically, especially due to infectious diseases that spread throughout Hokkaido. More tragic, though, was their gradually becoming a minority population due to the influx of new Japanese settlers in Hokkaido. The percentage of the Ainu population in Hokkaido decreased from 12.1 percent in 1872 to 0.6 percent in 1925. According to the census conducted by the Hokkaido local government in 1999, the total population of the Ainu was 23,767, constituting only about 0.4 percent of Hokkaido's population.

Following the Meiji government's colonization policy, the new settlers initiated salmon farming, agriculture, cattle farming, forestry, and mining operations. Accordingly, the land where the Ainu hunted and gathered began to be reduced. They were even forbidden to fish salmon in the rivers. From 1884 onward, the Meiji government encouraged the Ainu to take up agriculture, and each household was allotted a plot of land, given agricultural implements and seeds, and taught agricultural techniques by Japanese officials. The basis of Ainu livelihood thus drastically changed after the Meiji Restoration.

RELIGIOUS BELIEFS AND RITUALS

Although the daily life of the Ainu today differs little from that of other Japanese, the Ainu traditional cosmology or worldview has been handed down by their well-developed oral tradition, which includes a rich variety of genres: *tus-shinotcha* (shaman's oracle), *kamui-yukar* (epic songs concerning nature deities), *oina* (epic songs especially concerning the Ainu cultural hero, the deity Oina), *yukar* (epic songs concerning Ainu heroes), *kamui-uwepeker* (prose stories concerning nature deities), *ainu-uwepeker* (prose stories concerning headmen), *upaskuma* (teachings or ancestor tales), and lyrics.

Tusu-shinotca is the melodious oracle of a shamaness possessed by the snake deity, from which *kamui-yukar* is believed to originate. Epic songs about deities or heroes are characterized by first-person narration and a style of singing that features the insertion of particular refrains (*sakehe*). The narration of a goddess, for example, generally starts with the phrases such as "[I] have lived by devoting myself to embroidery and keeping an eye on one place. . . ." Refrains are mostly incomprehensible, but some represent the barking of the embodied animal of a hero deity. Many items of oral tradition have been transcribed and translated into Japanese by scholars since the Meiji period.

The Ainu belief system and religion is animistic. Ainu believe not only human beings but all things in the universe, animate and inanimate, have *ramat* (soul—literally "heart"). They also believe in supernatural beings with spiritual powers of a divine nature called *kamui* (deity or spirit). We can see that the concept of deities was fundamental to Ainu cosmology and that belief in deities was essential to their religion. Despite the linguistic relationship between the Ainu *kamui* and the Japanese *kami* (god), careful examination of legends and myths such as *kamui-yukar* and *kamui-uwepeker* reveals that these two concepts are not the same.

Ainu theology includes a few deities such as Kanto-kor Kamui (Master of the Heaven) and Yuk-kor Kamui (Master of the Deer) which have no incarnation

Men and women sit around the sunken hearth where the Fire Goddess resides to offer prayers to her. (Photograph by Takako Yamada)

in the real world. Most deities, however, are embodied in living beings, natural objects, or natural phenomena. For example, Tokap-chup Kamui (Day-Shining Deity) is incarnated as the sun; Kim-un Kamui (Mountain-Inhabiting Deity) as a bear; Wose Kamui (Howling Deity) as a wolf; Surku Kamui (Aconite Deity) as aconite; Ape Huchi (Fire Grandmother) or Kamui Huchi as the fire; Onne Chip Kamui (Old Ship Deity) as a ship; and Porosir-un Kamui (Mt. Porosir-Inhabiting Deity) as Mt. Porosir. Furthermore, some sicknesses are considered as omens of the visits of certain deities. A cold, for example, is believed to be caused by a visit from Sio Kamui (Cold Deity). The Ainu thus regard various entities as deities or the manifestation of deities. Moreover, the dead are believed to become deities, having been inspired by divine souls. However, not all things in nature are designated as deities. The bear represents a deity, while the salmon is not regarded as a deity but as the divine fish sent from the divine world; the same applies to the deer.

The Ainu's animism derives from their view of the universe as composed of two divisions: *kamui-moshir* (literally, "the divine world"), where deities or the dead live, and *ainu-moshir* (literally, "the human world"), where all living beings reside. They believe that deities live in the divine world just as human beings do in this world. Backed by their human-like figures, deities are also characterized like human beings: for example, they are attributed with **gender** as well as master-servant relationships. They are also contrasted as good or evil and important and dignified or less important and thoughtless. The differentiation among deities according to the moral standard of good and evil is not absolute, but relative. As good deities cannot be always good, evil deities cannot be always evil. Moreover, the relationship between humans and deities is considered as complementary and reciprocal. Deities bestow their temporary incarnations as animals and plants as gifts. In return, human beings entertain deities with food and *tonoto* (sake) and give them *inau* (ritual sticks with special shavings) as presents. Rituals are occasions when Ainu confirm this reciprocal and complementary relationship with deities.

Based on these ideas, Ainu performed a variety of rituals throughout a year: the bear ritual (*iyomante*); New Year's ritual (*ashirpa-ek kamui-nomi*) in January; prayers for a rich harvest (*harue-nomi*) in spring; a sending-off ritual for wasted tools (*iwakte*) when necessary; the river deity ceremony (*pet kamui-nomi*) before the start of salmon fishing; a ritual for the first salmon (*ashirchep-nomi*); a ritual for the hunt in the mountains (*kimun-iramante kamui-nomi*); and a ritual for fishing in the sea (*repa kamui-nomi*). Furthermore, a ritual for worshipping ancestors (*icharpa*) was performed not only at prescribed times in January and August but at every ceremonial occasion.

Ritual sticks and food are offered to the ancestors. (Photograph by Takako Yamada)

Because salmon fishing was the most important subsistence activity, the river deity ceremony was one of the most important rituals. A splendid ritual of welcoming the salmon had always been performed by each village before commencing full salmon fishing in the river. The Ainu would construct a *nusa-san* (altar) near the river for deities who watched over river fishing. There they offered prayers to these deities and performed dances and songs to entertain them. Moreover, when they fished during the first salmon run, they offered the first salmon to the fire goddess of their family and then distributed it to all their neighbors.

The bear ritual can be distinguished into two types. One is the "sending-off the hunted bear," which is performed after hunting bears in the mountains. The other is the "sending-off the reared bear cub," which is the most important group ceremony because it made the Ainu reconfirm their solidarity with a common *shine-itokpa* group. The ritual was performed in a village in January or in February before the start of spring bear hunting in a village by ceremonially killing a bear cub, which was captured alive and raised for one to two years in the village, in order to return the bear's soul to the divine world.

Besides offering prayers to the deities (*kamui-nomi*), Ainu used ritual sticks at every ceremony. They were considered not only as the most important and essential offerings to the deities but also as the symbols of their

Nusa-san, an altar for the Ainu, where deities are enshrined. (Photograph by Takako Yamada)

Iyomante, the Ainu bear-sending ritual, Hokkaido, Shiraoi. (© Yashiro Haga/HAGA/The Image Works)

presence at a ritual. Various types of ritual sticks were newly made for high deities invoked at each ritual. Also, outside a large house, opposite to the sacred window, a cluster of ritual sticks was usually set up like a fence and was called *nusa-san* (altar). Offering prayers and sake to deities embodied in the altar was essential in every ritual, and subsequently the Ainu were virtually obliged to enjoy themselves with songs and dances.

The bear ritual clearly represents this reciprocal and complementary relationship, which is described in an epic song, "The Master of the Mountain (the Bear God)." This song tells that the bear is a temporary form of the bear god in the divine world visiting the human world. Sometimes the bear god or his family wants to visit the human world. When he does, he brings bear meat and hide as gifts. After being

Inau (ritual sticks) are offered to the Fire Goddess who resides in the sunken hearth. (Photograph by Takako Yamada)

entertained with food and wine by humans, he returns to the divine world laden with presents, including ritual sticks with special shavings, sake, and millet rice cakes, and invites all the deities here and there to feast on what he has brought back from the human world. Bears cannot return to the world of the gods from a visit to the human world until a human kills them. Therefore, at the bear festival, killing a bear cub is indispensable for sending the bear's soul back to the divine world where it belongs.

The Ainu contrast human beings with deities by perceiving the gods as mirror images: a *kamui* (deity) is a human, and a human is a *kamui*. Deities exist in the form of "man" in the divine world, and they only appear as "deified" animals or plants when visiting the human world. In contrast, men are men only in the human world, and after death they become deities. The Ainu also perceive an equality between humans and deities, which can be known through ancestor worship (*icharpa*). This ritual was done first by invoking the fire goddess and giving an offering of prayers and sake to all the deities enshrined in the altar outside. Then women offered prayers and food to ancestors. After that, all who participated in the ritual enjoyed themselves by singing songs (*upopo*) and dancing (*rimse*). The procedure suggests that although this is done for the ancestors, not only ancestors but also deities are invoked to be entertained, thus demonstrating their equal status.

CHALLENGES OF THE MODERN WORLD

Following the introduction of so-called "school education" in 1872, the Japanese government-mandated education system gradually spread among the Ainu. As a result, by the late 1910s most Ainu in Hokkaido had become bilingual, and only a few older Ainu spoke Ainu exclusively. Today almost all Ainu are monolingual in Japanese, and very few can understand fully the Ainu language. Furthermore, the performance of rituals has been gradually discarded. In 1950s the bear ritual began to be criticized by humane organizations for killing a live bear cub at the climax of the ceremony. However, the rise of Ainu political movements since the 1970s has begun the revival of traditional culture and rituals. In 1983 a Mr. Kayano privately opened the first Ainu language class at Nibutani in Biratori Town. Cultural revitalization movements were also developed by the Corporation Hokkaido Utari Association (CHUA), resulting in the founding of Ainu language schools in Biratori and Asahikawa in 1987, in Kushiro and Urakawa in 1989, and in Sapporo and Shiraoi in 1990, for example. Ainu language schools serve as facilities not only for learning Ainu language but also for learning the culture in general. By attending Ainu language schools, Ainu have come to understand and appreciate their culture and have even forged intimate friendships with one another. Ainu language schools have thus operated to strengthen social solidarity.

By opening classes for learning Ainu embroidery, weaving meshed bags, and making netted cord for carrying goods, CHUA has been able to advance the transmission and popularization of Ainu traditional crafts. CHUA has held the Ainu Cultural Festival annually since 1989 to offer opportunities for Ainu people to become familiar with their own culture. By preparing for and participating in the festival, Ainu can learn their language, ethnic dances and songs, how to play the *mukkuri*, how to make ethnic costumes, and how to recite Ainu oral traditions such as *yukar* (epic songs). Furthermore, contemporary Ainu movements have transformed the negative image of Ainu identity to one more positive. The revival of ritual ceremonies has been forwarded by each branch office of the CHUA. In 1996, for example, one year prior to the enactment of the new Ainu law, cultural revitalization climaxed with twenty-one out of fifty-six branch offices in Hokkaido holding one or two religious events.

Many of these events have a long history, while others are recent developments. For example, the Marimo Festival held in Akan, one of the most famous resorts in Hokkaido, has a history of more than forty years. The *marimo* is a ball-shaped freshwater weed grown in Lake Akan. The festival was originally held as a tourist attraction. The inviting and sending-off rituals of the *marimo* that are performed during the festival were not purely traditional but were newly invented, because the *marimo* had no religious value for the Ainu. Now, though, the festival has become fairly traditional even for the Ainu. The ritual festival for a good catch of smelt held in Monbetsu also has a long history. Monbetsu lies at the center of an area that is famous for its good catch of smelt, and smelt fishing has been a major subsistence practice in this area. The *chip-sanke* (a launching ritual) held in Biratori has a history of more than twenty-seven years. Ainu in Biratori—known as the Saru River Ainu—have played a leading role in the cultural revitalization movement. The *chip-sanke* was originally a launching ritual for a new dugout canoe but was also performed every year before the canoe was used for the first time. After the craft of making a dugout canoe was revived, the launching ritual was also revived.

As of 1996, no branch office of the CHUA had performed the bear ritual (*iomante*), which was the most important ritual conducted by the *shine-itokpa* group. However, rituals related to salmon fishing such as the *ashir-chep-nomi* (the first-salmon ritual) and the *raomap kamui-nomi* (prayer for the salmon trap) have been revived regularly in recent years. The *ashir-chep-nomi* held in Sapporo has gradually become one of the most important cultural events not only for Ainu in Sapporo, but also for Ainu in other regions. Compared to bear hunting, salmon fishing has been of great significance as a symbol of indigenous subsistence practices. Moreover, by performing ceremonies related to salmon fishing, Ainu have tried to make an appeal for their ancestral right to fish for salmon in the rivers. Because the government permits salmon fishing only in the sea due to the salmon farming, the Ainu—like other Japanese—cannot fish for salmon from the rivers. Thus the revival of the first-salmon ritual involves a political dimension. The revival of rituals can be based also on other motives, as indicated by recent performances of ancestor worship (*icharpa*) or memorial services. These ceremonies were mostly revived because some Ainu felt sorry for their ancestors who had not received traditional reverence, only Japanese-based ancestor worship.

Performances of ritual festivals today follow almost the same process. Preparations begin several days beforehand: women prepare food and sake, while men carve a variety of ritual sticks with shavings and set up the sacred altar. The festival opens with prayers to the deities. Men sit around a square, sunken hearth where the Fire Goddess, to whom the first prayer is directed, resides. While the rest of the men sit around the hearth, one elderly man taking the role of priest approaches the altar and begins to recite prayers, offering sake to the deities one by one. After the prayers to all the deities enshrined in the altar, the women begin the ritual of *icharpa*, which is the only religious ceremony in which women can participate. At the left corner of the altar, each woman, taking food and *inau* with her as offerings to ancestors, sticks her *inau* into the ground, recites the ancestors' names, and offers food to them. Following the prayers, various Ainu ethnic dances are performed.

The revival of Ainu rituals is not simply the revival of formal aspects but also results in revitalizing the language, traditional handicrafts, performing arts, manners, and even worldviews. For example, prayers to a deity, whose phrases differ depending on the god's character, must be performed by men. Because very few elderly men know the prayers precisely, most have to recite the prayers by referring a book. But some men have begun to learn Ainu to fulfill their responsibility to revive ritual prayers. It is also necessary to make a variety of shaved sticks to offer deities for every ritual. Making these used to be done by men, and consequently men have begun to revive traditional wood-carving technology.

Moreover, dances were always performed during religious ceremonies and feasts as well as at special festive occasions for each family. The dance was a form of entertainment for both people and deities. Some dances had their own religious meanings: *iyomante rimse* for the bear ritual; *emushi rimse* (sword dance) and *ku rimse* (bow dance) for exorcising evils; *hunbe rimse* (whale dance) to wish for a large catch; *han chikap rimse* (waterfowl dance) and *sarorun-chikap rimse* (crane dance), which imitate birds' behaviors; and *tapkar* (dance with a howl performed by men). Each variety of dances is generally accompanied by its own song, mostly performed by women. Women thus learn the Ainu language through singing. Performances also require the revival of the art of making ethnic costumes and accessories. Women have learned Ainu embroidery by copying traditional patterns and colors of old ethnic costumes preserved in museums, and they now make costumes themselves, becoming experts in Ainu handicrafts in the process.

The revival of rituals originally had a definite political intention. However, the efforts of the cultural revitalization movement have led to a gradual revival of a variety of rituals associated with nature-worship. And now through the revival of these rituals, Ainu ideas of respecting nature, of nature conservation, and of the symbiosis of humans with nature are also spreading not only among Ainu but also among non-Ainu Japanese.

Today the revival of language itself seems to be treading a difficult path, because the majority of Ainu are monolingual in Japanese; they have to learn Ainu just as they would a foreign language. However, men and women now have opportunities to learn more about their language and culture by participating in ritual ceremonies and attending Ainu language schools. Moreover, to know and speak even a few Ainu words makes an Ainu person feel a sense of cultural identity. Consequently, learning Ainu and participating in ceremonies have become very fundamental for the orientation and sense of belonging of the Ainu. Ainu folklore is thus an integral part of their life in contemporary Japan.

STUDIES OF AINU FOLKLORE

Ainu folklore studies have an interesting history, starting during the Edo period with official explorations to "Ezo" (renamed Hokkaido in the Meiji period) organized for specific purposes: the exploitation of mining or the defense of the national boundary against invasion from the north. Explorers left fine geographical and cultural descriptions of the Hokkaido region and the Ainu. Later by studying systematically the pre-Meiji archives together with archeological materials and ethnographic documents since the Meiji period, Takashi Irimoto was able to present a detailed monograph on the society and culture of the Ainu of the Saru River region during the Tokugawa Shogunate from circa 1300 to 1867. This academic tradition during the Edo period was followed by a new trend of Ainu studies during the Meiji period.

Ainu studies in the Meiji period were stimulated by European scholars interested in the ethnic origins and folklore of the Ainu. In particular, John Batchelor, who settled in Hokkaido as a missionary in 1877, studied the Ainu language, began to collect myths, legends, customs and manners, and beliefs, and published the first full-scale **ethnography** of Ainu life in 1901. Neil G. Munro, who arrived in Yokohama in 1891 and settled in Nibutani in the Hidaka district in 1930, posthumously published a valuable ethnography of the beliefs and rituals of the Ainu in 1963. Kindaichi Kyosuke was one of the first prominent Japanese linguists to take an interest in the rich folklore tradition of the Ainu. His system for publishing oral epics with a text transcribed in *kana* and alphabetic forms together with a literal translation into Japanese became the model for later folklore studies. The studies begun by Kindaichi were continued by his students Chiri Mashiho, himself an Ainu, and Kubodera Itsuhiko. As they continued to collect and record Ainu oral traditions and to analyze the beliefs and worldview of the Ainu, folklore became the mainstream in Ainu studies. While Kindaichi's studies focused especially on heroic epics (*yukar*), Chiri moved on to explore a variety of genres of oral tradition, including narratives, stories of origins (*upaskuma*), riddles, prose stories (*uwepeker*), and epics of deities (*kamui yukar*). He positioned Ainu oral tradition as Ainu literature. Meanwhile, Kubodera Itsuhiko, who first visited Biratori in the Hidaka district in 1923 with his professor, Kindaichi, was engaged particularly in the study of oral tradition in the Saru River region. He published monographs on funeral rites and customs and the worship of the souls of the ancestors. His most important work (1977a) includes eighteen examples of *oina* and eighty-six examples of *kamui yukar* with alphabetic transcriptions, literal translations into Japanese, and fully detailed annotations. This is one of the most monumental folklore studies of the Ainu.

Descriptive studies of traditional beliefs and rituals remained a major concern in Ainu studies until the 1950s, when ethnological studies of the Ainu began to be carried out. Until recently, little research was carried out on the social aspects of Ainu culture, especially the traditional social organization. However, a full-scale ethnography of the Ainu was published in 1970 and recent ethnological studies from the viewpoints of ethnoscience and cognitive anthropology have contributed to providing a new framework for understanding Ainu **worldview**. Yamada's work (1994, 2001) is one of these studies. It analyzes Ainu worldview through an examination of published materials on oral tradition, particularly that of the Saru River and Iburi regions.

Useful Web sites for Ainu studies include the Ainu Museum: www.ainu-museum.or.jp/english/english.html and the Foundation for Research and Promotion of Ainu Culture: www.frpac.or.jp/.

BIBLIOGRAPHY

Ainu Bunka Hozon Taisaku Kyogikai. 1970. *Ainu Minzokushi* (The Ethnography of the Ainu). Tokyo: Dai-ichi Hoki Shuppan.

Batchelor, John. 1901. *The Ainu and Their Folklore*. London: The Religious Tract Society.

Chiri Mashiho. 1955. *Ainu Bungaku* (Ainu Literature). Tokyo: Gengensha.

Irimoto Takashi. 1987. Saru-gawa Ryuiki Ainu nikannsuru Rekishiteki-shiryo no Bunkajinruigakuteki-bunnseki: c. 1300–1867 (A Cultural Anthropological Analysis of Historical Data on the Ainu of the Saru River Region: c. 1300–1867). *Bulletin of the Institute for the Study of North Eurasian Cultures Hokkaido University* 18: 1–218.

Kindaichi Kyosuke. 1931. *Ainu Jojishi: Yukar no Kenkyu* (Ainu Epic: A Study of Yukars). A Collection of Toyo Bunko, No. 14-1, 2. Tokyo: Toyo Bunko.

Kubodera Itsuhiko. 1977a. *Ainu Jojishi: Shinyo, Seiden no Kenkyu* (The Ainu Epics: A Study of Kamui Yukar and Oina). Tokyo: Iwanami Shoten.

———. 1977b. *Ainu no Bungaku* (Literature of the Ainu). Iwanami Shinsho, vol. 989. Tokyo: Iwanami Shoten.

Munro, Neil G. 1963. *Ainu: Creed and Cult*. New York: Columbia University Press.

Yamada Takako. 1994. *Ainu no Sekaikan* (The World View of the Ainu). Tokyo: Kodansha.

———. 2001. *The World View of the Ainu: Nature and Cosmos Reading from Language*. London: Kegan Paul.

———. 2003. Anthropological Studies of the Ainu in Japan: Past and Present. *Japanese Review of Cultural Anthropology* 4: 75–106.

Takako Yamada

KOREA

GEOGRAPHY AND HISTORY

The peninsula of Korea is located in northeastern Asia, situated between **China** and **Japan**. More than 70 percent of its territory is mountainous, and thus nearly every city in Korea is surrounded by mountains. In the agricultural regions, many kinds of crops, though mainly rice, are produced, and a variety of fish and seafoods come from the sea. Some limited mountainous land is made arable by the slash-and-burn method. As the main source of food, land is very important in Korean society. In particular, the staples in the Korean diet are rice, barley, and other crops, so owning cultivated land has been regarded as a symbol of Koreans' fortunes.

Superficially Koreans bear a physical resemblance to other Asians. Therefore, some Westerners may think that Korean culture is not much different from that of other Asian cultures, yet it is very distinctive. For instance, *hanbok*, the elementary form of traditional Korean costume, mainly consists of two sections: an upper part called *chogori* (Korean-style short coats) and a lower part called *paji* (Korean-style trousers). This traditional costume is still worn during festival days, ceremonies, and other special occasions. Also the traditional Korean floor heater, named *ondol*, is still very popular, and even in modern apartments people prefer folk-style floor heaters to heating by radiator.

Koreans are proud of their nearly 5,000 years of history. Their sense of the past derives mainly from *Tangun* mythology, and it has affected various aspects of Korean folklore. The *Tangun* myth is popular probably because it tells how the Korean people originated. According to the myth's outline,

Once a Son of God in the sky world, named *Hwanung*, looked around the earth and wanted to live there. His father, named *Hwanin*, realized his son's will and searched for a proper place. Eventually, he found a beautiful and peaceful place where there were plenty of animals, trees, and flowers for his son. When *Hwanung* descended to *Taebak* mountain from the sky world, his father (*Hwanin*) sent three thousand of his followers, including the gods of wind, rain, and cloud, to assist his son. One day a tiger and a bear living in a nearby cave came to *Hwanung* and told him

North and South Korea.

that they wanted to be human. Then *Hwanung* told the two animals to follow him to a secluded retreat with only some water and a bunch of garlic and mugwort and to stay inside the cave for a hundred days. If they followed these regulations, then they would transform into humans. As soon as they began their retreat, the tiger couldn't endure the restrictions and ran away. However, the bear tried to fulfill these regulations and stayed for twenty-one days and then suddenly transformed into a beautiful woman. Her name was *Ungnyo*, and she wanted to have a baby, yet she didn't have a partner. So she prayed nearly everyday to have a baby. *Hwanung* accepted her request and married her. Soon after, she had a baby named *Tangun*. Later on, about 2333 B.C.E., *Tangun* established the first state on the Korean peninsula, called *Kojosun*, and its capital was *Pyongyangsung*. He governed *Kojoson* for 1500 years. Then he retired and entered *Asadal* and lived there for 308 years. He became a mountain god.

This myth is deeply embedded in Korean people's minds as well as in Korean folk religion and grassroots culture.

ANCESTOR WORSHIP AND FUNERAL RITUALS

One of the most distinct characteristics in Korean culture is ancestor worship. Today it is ironic that the rapid spread of industrialization and urbanization is changing Koreans' traditional way of life, and yet many Koreans still stick with long-lasting traditions such as ancestor worship. The French folklorist Arnold Van Gennep described the process of rites of passage as three main stages: separation, liminality, and reincorporation. In Western society these rites of passage are mainly applicable in the significant processes of human life such birth, initiation, marriage, and death. In Korean society, rites of passage are more applicable to *kwanhonsangje* (initiation, marriage, funerals, and sacrificial rites).

Koreans practice three kinds of rites for ancestors: *kijesa* (annual rites that are held on the day of the ancestors' death), *charae* (rites that are held at the Lunar New Year and *chusok*, a full moon festival in August), and *sije* (held in October of the lunar calendar for worshipping ancestors who are more distant than four generations). The literal meaning of *charae* is "offering tea for ancestors," because in olden times people worshipped their ancestors with tea. Some scholars suggest that this tradition originated from Buddhist rituals. Today in *charae*, people use alcohol rather than tea.

Charae is held in the morning, usually at eight or nine o'clock, even though the exact time varies from household to household, while *kijesa* is normally held at night. *Charae* is the time when deceased ancestors and their descendants meet together. Hence, in the *charae* ceremony people sincerely offer various foods to dead parents, grandparents, great-grandparents, and great-great-grandparents. Today people may offer food to dead parents and grandparents only for convenience.

When food is offered at rituals like *kijesa* and *charae*, a certain order is followed. For example, fish is located to the east and meat is placed to the west. The head faces east, while the tail is put toward the west. From the standpoint of those who are making the offering, dried meat is located to the left and pickled or salted fish is placed to the right. For the ancestral tablet, father is to the west and mother is to the east. Dates are placed to the east and chestnuts are put to the west. Red-colored fruit is located to the east and white-colored fruit is placed to the west. This tradition differs slightly from region to region and from family to family.

Ancestral tablets used in sacrificial rites. (Photograph by Hwan-Young Park)

The folkloric aspects of burial customs in Korea today mostly involve inhumation, cremation, and the laying of a person's ashes to rest as well as sacrificial rites for dead ancestors. Yet these current burial customs are also closely linked to previous traditions, which to some extent have weakened but are still visible in many parts of the Korean peninsula. In Korea, the main burial customs today are inhumation and cremation, though the latter is increasing in popularity. In general, funerals in Korean society are mostly influenced by Confucianism with basic elements of Buddhism in the background.

In Korean society funeral customs may involve dolmens, *pungjang* (aerial sepulture), inhumation, cremation, and "double burial customs" such as *chobun*. Also, Koreans have traditionally had special rituals like *kyejang* (reinterment) or *segol* (cleaning the bone), which reflect the importance of the proper treatment of bones and filial duty toward ancestors.

Chobun is a kind of double-burial custom. First, the corpse is covered with rice-straw before being buried in the earth. After some years, only the bones remain, and these are then purified ritually and reburied. This tradition is mainly found along the southwest coast of the Korean peninsula, particularly on Jin and Cheongsan islands. Some evidence suggests that *chobun* is connected to Bronze Age dolmens. Also, several historical texts mention burial customs such as *chobun*. For example, in *Koguryo*, a record states that "once a person dies, then the body is usually left in the house for three years." Also, the chronicles of the *Yi* dynasty contain several records indicating the existence of *chobun* culture. There is some connection between *jindo sikkimgut* (a ritual in Korean shamanism) and *chobun*. Elements of *chobun* survive in shamanic rituals such as *jindo sikkimgut*, which is performed when the purified bones are reburied at the new site based upon a division by configuration of the ground. The popularity of *chobun* customs is reflected in some rituals in Korean shamanism. In particular, *sikkimgut*, which is mainly practiced on the southwest coast of the Korean peninsula, is closely linked to the folk tradition of *chobun*. Also, the *chobunjang sikkimgut* indicates the combination of *chobun* and Korean shamanism.

In traditional Korean society, the proper funeral ritual usually continued for three years. It meant that close relatives, in particular children of the deceased, had to perform three-year-long funeral rites, which may symbolize the period of being raised by parents. Koreans say that it takes three years at least for a baby to learn how to eat and be toilet trained without the parents' help. Symbolic woods are used for deceased parents: bamboo for the father's funeral and paulownia tree for the mother's. During the funeral rites for the deceased father, for example, close kinsmen carried bamboo sticks. Usually guests know whose funeral

Chobun, the double-burial custom. (Photograph by Hwan-Young Park)

297

it is, and yet on some occasions—for example, unexpected visits to funerals—guests also can precisely tell the proper situation from the unveiled symbols. In the traditional concept, a bamboo tree is round like the sun and high like the sky. Hence a bamboo tree shows symbolically the image of the father. In the case of the paulownia tree, its Korean pronunciation is similar to *dong*, which means "the same." On the one hand, the father's funerals are differentiated from the mother's funerals, but on the other, they are treated equally, having the same (*dong*) importance.

A god of earth (*Tojusin*) in the inside yard of a house. (Photograph by Hwan-Young Park)

RELIGIOUS BELIEFS

Traditionally, Koreans believed that various gods resided in different parts of the house. For instance, in the main gate there is a god of the gate (*Munsin*), while there is a god of earth in the yard inside the house (*Tojusin* or *Jisin*). Also, under the girder in the building, which is the center of the house, is a god of *songju* (*Songjusin*), and in the kitchen there is a god called *Chowangsin*. Even in the toilet there is a god called *Pyonsogaksi*. In addition, on the wall shelf in the inner room, *Samsin* is usually worshipped as a god. *Samsin*, in particular, is widely observed among Korean women, because this god is believed to be female. *Samsin* is often called *Samsinhalmae* (a grandmother god). *Samsin* possibly means three (*sam*) gods (*sin*): a god of bearing babies, a god of giving birth, and a god of bringing up a baby until a certain age. Some people argue that *Samsin* especially governs the sphere of giving birth because this matter can be is painful and dangerous.

A traditional story concerns the relationship between *Samsin* and the "Mongolian spot." It is believed that Grandmother *Samsin* is usually actively involved in the process of a safe and painless delivery of a baby and makes a mark on the hips of the baby indicating a slap by her hand. She hits the newborn baby's hips to make him or her emerge from the mother's womb without delay. Hence, Koreans often say that most Korean children have this mark, called the Mongolian spot, from their delivery by Grandmother *Samsin*.

Many gods inhabit the house, and in many villages people worship a guardian god for their community. In general, this god is a mountain god (*Sansin*) for agricultural and mountainous villages, while it can be a dragon god (*Youngsin*) or a sea god (*Haesin*) for fishing villages. Also some villagers worship a god called *Sonagsin*, who has several forms such as a big tree or a heap of stones. This folk belief is one of the most distinctive in Korean culture, and in some places in the Korean countryside there is a small, sanctified house for *Sonagsin*.

In addition, the devil post (*changsung*) and *sosdae* are unique folk beliefs in Korea. In general, two devil posts (one for male and another for female) stand in the main entrance to local villages, though in some villages devil posts stand in the four cardinal directions surrounding the village. The principal role of devil posts is both to mark the village boundary

A mountain god (*Sansin*). (Photograph by Hwan-Young Park)

and to protect from evil spirits that live outside the village. Similarly, *sosdae* consists of a tall pole with a wooden bird on the top. As a guardian god for villagers, it gets rid of evil spirits, produces a good harvest, protects from fires, and performs other beneficial functions.

Shamanism is Korea's indigenous religion. There are traditionally two kinds of shamans in Korea: inherited shamans and possessed shamans. Most shamans are women, and yet traditional musicians who assist shamans in the performance of shamanic rituals are usually men. The key role of the Korean shaman can be to mediate between common people and the gods. In fact, Korean shamans worship various gods such as ancestor gods and famous historical figures.

Buddhism has also been very influential on Korean folklore. This is because the history of Buddhism in Korea is more than 1,600 years old, officially coming into Korea about 372 C.E., when a Chinese monk named Sundo brought it to the northern Korean Kingdom of Koguryo. In 384 Buddhism spread to the southwestern Korean Kingdom of Paekje by a Chinese monk named Marananta, and after about 530, Korean Buddhist monks traveled to Japan and spread the religion there. In the southeastern Korean Kingdom of Silla, Buddhism was officially introduced around the sixth century C.E. During the reign of King Pobhung (514–540) in the Silla Kingdom, a Korean martyr Ch'a-don Lee played a crucial role in publicly introducing Buddhism to the people.

The devil post (*changsung*). (Photograph by Hwan-Young Park)

The story goes that a court official named Ch'a-don Lee, who petitioned the Silla court to accept Buddhism, was viewed with disfavor and sentenced to death. When he was decapitated, he bled white, giving credence to the power and legitimacy of Buddhist truth. This led to Buddhism being adopted as the Silla Kingdom's principal religion.

One of the most important Buddhist festivals in Korea is the birthday of Sokkamoni, which is normally celebrated on 8 April on the lunar calendar. In this festival, many people gather at temples and celebrate Sokkamoni's birthday, while trying to purify their accumulated sins. In order to receive blessings, people also make a circle around the Buddhist pagoda either inside or outside the temple.

Some basic ideologies behind Buddhism and Korean shamanism are in accord, leading to many aspects of shamanism being incorporated into Buddhism. For example, Buddhist temples were built on mountains that were believed to house gods in pre-Buddhist times. In particular, some elements of traditional shamanism are held inside Buddhist temples, called either *Samsunggak* or *Sansingak* after a mountain god, a god of seven-stars, or a god of the self-enlightened monk. These three gods illustrate the blending of the folk religion, shamanism, with Buddhism in Korean culture and folklore.

MUSIC

Traditional music in Korea can be divided into two major categories: *jongak* for nobles' music and *sanak* for that of commoners. *Jongak* is music for calm and appeasement, whereas *sanak* induces excitement and stimulation. Hence, the former is rather rational, while the latter is emotional. In other words, *jongak* is characterized by

Nongak, Korea's distinctive traditional music. (Photograph by Hwan-Young Park)

subdued melodies and a slow formal tempo, as befits the Confucian mindset. Hence, *jongak* mainly consists of ceremonial music for court banquets and formalized ritual music such as Confucian music and royal shrine music.

Sanak is best represented by *pansori* and *nongak*. The former is probably Korea's most distinctive musical-dramatic form. It is normally performed by two people, a singer and a drummer. While it is not really clear how *pansori* developed, some people argue that it emerged from ritual songs performed by shamans in the southern part of Korea. Others suggest that it originated from the chanted recitation of classical literature. Regardless of the origin, *pansori* became very popular in the nineteenth century, when Jae-hyo Shin (1812–1884) revised and rewrote six of the major *pansori* narrative texts, five of which are still performed today.

Nongak is the music of farmers. It is performed by a group of musician-dancers led by the gong-playing *sangsoe*. This type of music developed as a means for enhancing efficiency by easing farmers' fatigue and cultivating a spirit of cooperation within the village community. Therefore, *nongak* is linked to farmers' economic activity. It is generally performed on important seasonal days for farmers such as New Year's, the Big Full Moon, and the Harvest Moon Festival.

DANCE

Religions such as Buddhism, Confucianism, and shamanism have contributed to the development of traditional Korean dance. For instance, Buddhism brought a variety of musical and dance genres to Korean culture, including *nabichum* (the butterfly dance) and *parachum* (the cymbal dance). In *nabichum*, man is epitomized by the metamorphosis of the butterfly, while in *parachum* two or four monks swing large brass cymbals when they dance. These dances were a part of traditional Buddhist rituals and are laden with rich Buddhist imagery. In addition, some influence of shamanism on Korean folk dance can be seen in the performance of the *kut*, *salpuri chum* (dance for getting rid of an evil spirit), and *puchae chum* (fan dance).

Ganggangsuwolrae, a traditional Korean dance. (Photograph by Hwan-Young Park)

As part of various rituals, shamans perform dances too. These dances function as ritual and entertainment, and this kind of dance is usually characterized by a hopping and whirling motion with the arms outstretched. Korean shamans usually carry a folding fan, bell, five colors of flags, and sometime a sort of shaman tree. During the ritual dances, the shamans' movements become increasingly wild and active as they reach an intensified state of ecstasy.

The circle dance called *ganggangsuwolrae* accompanies the folksong *ganggangsuwolrae* and originated in the southwestern provinces. It is usually performed on the evening of the full moon of the first and eighth months of the lunar calendar. In the course of this dance, young women of local villages dress in *hanbok*, the Korean traditional costume, and gather in an open field to dance. They join hands in a circle facing the center and slowly move around the circle to the beat of the song. Gradually the pace quickens, and the dance ends in a whirling climax.

FESTIVALS AND CELEBRATIONS

Annual customs of Korea are usually based on the lunar calendar. This is because traditionally Korean people were involved in their day-to-day lives mainly in the spheres of agriculture and fishery, even though they were also involved in subsidiary activities such as hunting and forestry depending upon the regions. This folk culture calendar is divided into four seasons and then subdivided into twenty-four seasonal divisions.

Koreans traditionally celebrate the beginning of the new year, called *Seol* or *Seolral*. On the day before *Seol*, people are busy with cleaning their houses and preparing food for ancestors, relatives, and other guests. A folk belief held that if someone slept on that night, his or her eyebrows would turn white. Hence, in the Korean countryside local people used to turn on the light in every room and sometimes in the kitchen. This custom may reflect the fact that every member of the family was very busy in preparing for the celebration, and thus they hardly had time to sleep. On *Seol*, Korean people usually get up early in the morning, take a bath and put on new clothes, called *solbim*. *Solbim* are especially prepared to wear on New Year's Day and often follow the model of the Korean traditional costume, *hanbok*. Then every member of the kin group gathers in the house of the eldest son of the

At Songmyo, Koreans visit the graves of ancestors to inform them of the new year. (Photograph by Hwan-Young Park)

head family through the paternal line to attend the ritual for ancestors, *charae*. After the *charae* is over, kinsfolk have breakfast with the food offered at the ancestor ritual. Then younger members bow to their elders, wishing them health, a long life, good blessings, and prosperity throughout the whole year. This special form of bowing on New Year's Day is called *sebae*. To perform *sebae*, a man brings his hands together in front of his eyes and sits on his knees touching the floor. He then bows his head to his hands, which touch the floor. A woman sits with her hands brought together in front of her eyes. She sits down with her hips instead of her knees on the floor. Traditionally, elders give some money called *sebaeddon* (literally, "money generated from *sebae*") to younger people in response to their obeisance. The most distinctive food for New Year's Day is probably rice cake soup, called *ttokgug*. It is mainly made from rice cakes with meat—traditionally pheasant, though beef is used today. The round shape of the sliced rice cake symbolizes a coin and thus wealth. Consequently, if someone eats a huge portion of *ttokgug* on New Year's Day, he or she will become rich.

Chusok is probably the most popular festival in Korean culture. It falls on 15 August of the lunar calendar. During the *Chusok* holidays, Koreans who are away from home usually visit their hometown to meet their extended family and relatives as well as to pay respects to their ancestors. For this reason, around *Chusok* most highways are very crowded with travelers. Many Koreans do not mind facing long delays and inconveniences in travel because they are so excited about getting together with their family members and relatives.

Chusok was one of the four main traditional festivals in Korea. The others are the Lunar New Year (*Sornal*), *Hansik* (5 April on the lunar calendar), and *Dano* (5 May on the lunar calendar). However, today only the Lunar New Year and *Chusok* are still widely celebrated, while the other two occasions are rapidly losing their previous popularity. Probably *Chusok* has been continuously the most important festival among ordinary Koreans who are either directly or indirectly engaged with agriculture because it is a kind of thanksgiving.

The origin of *Chusok* can be traced back to the Silla dynasty. According to "The History of the Three Kingdoms" (*Samguksaki*), people in Silla during the reign of King Yuri were divided into two groups and competed in weaving from 16 July until 15 August. At the end of the competition, the king and queen assessed the results. The losers provided food and drink for the winners, and everyone celebrated with songs, dances, and plays. It is said that this event developed into the present *Chusok*. There are two widely accepted interpretations regarding the meaning of *Chusok*. First, *Chusok* is also called *Jungchujol*, which means the central period of autumn. Second, *Chusok* also can be understood as a payback for the gods' and ancestors' blessings.

In the process of agriculture, *Chusok* indicates that the harvest season is approaching. Because *Chusok* falls in the middle of autumn, the weather is neither hot nor cold. Hence, farmers who are ready to harvest feel pleasant and are full of hope. It is the right time to offer newly gathered fresh food to the nature gods and ancestors, for people believe that a good harvest is due to generous protection from the nature gods and their ancestors. This offering is called *chonsin*. After the *charae* ceremony, kinsmen get together and visit their ancestors' tombs. This is called *songmyo*. During this journey, the elder kinsmen often tell stories about their ancestors to the younger kinsmen. In the cool and clear autumn weather people open their minds and feel the relationship between ancestors and descendants. The awareness of sharing common ancestors reaffirms strong kinship solidarity.

Songpyun, a rice cake steamed with pine needles, is the most popular food at Chusok, a harvest festival. (Photograph by Hwan-Young Park)

Songpyun, a kind of rice cake steamed with pine needles, is the most popular food at at *Chusok*. Koreans say there are two reasons for steaming *songpyun* with needles. First, in the process of steaming rice cakes, they can become very sticky and often stick to the steamer. Pine needles prevent stickiness. Second, some elements in the pine needles are nutritious and help keep the cakes from rotting. At *Chusok*, *songpyun* must be offered to the ancestors. Offering *songpyun* makes *Chusok charae* special and different from *kijesa*. The distinctive point of *Chusok* is that food is made from the new crop. *Songpyun* is a very nutritious food made from rice, beans, red beans, chestnuts, dates, and other ingredients. It is usually shaped like a half moon rather than a full moon, because a half moon symbolizes growth and progress while a full moon is filled up and symbolizes decline. For this reason people prefer to eat half moon *songpyun* to encourage a better harvest in the upcoming year. Like other food, making *songpyun* requires much care and sincerity. This is because Koreans believe that the ancestors who eat these foods will give good blessings. Also, after the offering to the ancestors, these foods are consumed by all kinsmen who attend the *Chusok charae*. Hence, *Chusok* food plays an important role in bridging between ancestors and descendants as well as between relatives.

Koreans connect *songpyun* to fortune telling. For example, if you make nicely shaped *songpyun*, you will have a handsome husband or a pretty baby. In addition, a woman who is expecting a baby can tell whether it will be a son or a daughter. To do this, people insert a pine needle inside one *songpyun* before steaming it. When the woman finds the *songpyun* with the pine needle, she bites it. If she bites the sharp end, then she might have a son, while if she bites the thick end, she might have a daughter. This sociable custom makes for a pleasant atmosphere in the domestic workplace. If people are happy and sincere in preparing the *Chusok* food, then the food offering will surely be well accepted by the ancestors.

FOOD

The most distinctive and characteristic food in Korean society is probably *kimchi*. A traditional saying, *"hajang dongjo,"* recalls making soy sauce during summer while one makes and ferments *kimchi* in the winter, emphasizing how essential they both are in the daily lives of Koreans. In general, the tenth month of the lunar calendar is the month for harvesting vegetables, and most Koreans traditionally make a huge amount of *kimchi* to satisfy the need for vegetable consumption during the winter period. Hence, during this time of year especially, Korean women in every household are busy making *kimchi*. As a mutual aid association, the *kimjanggae* (a benefit club for making *kimchi*) was traditionally established, allowing women to share their labor efficiently.

It is not known exactly when *kimchi*-making began. Nevertheless, its development can be traced to myths like that of *Tangun*, which is more than 4,000 years old. It is remarkable that in the *Tangun* myth a bear endured a secluded retreat inside a cave by only eating some garlic and mugwort in order to be human. Garlic is the most essential ingredient in making *kimchi*, and mugwort is similar to Korean-style cabbages.

Kimchi formally developed during the agrarian culture of the Three Kingdoms era in Korea. Due to the cold weather during winter, the Korean people had to come up with a storage technology for vegetables, and one of the most traditionally successful methods is salting as a means of preserving food. Thus, at this earlier stage, *kimchi* was just salted vegetables. During the twelfth century a new type of *kimchi* with some spices and seasonings developed. Around the seventeenth and eighteenth centuries, hot red pepper became one of the major ingredients for *kimchi*. The name *kimchi* probably originated from *shimchae*, which means "salting of vegetables." Then, through phonetic changes, *simchae* became *dimchae*, later *kimchae*, and finally *kimchi*.

Kimchi has become a symbol of Korean food and is now popular around the world. The major ingredients include Korean-style cabbage, radish, red pepper, and garlic. But there are many varieties of *kimchi* in Korea, varying from region to region where different ingredients are added. Depending upon the region, one may also include dried and salted shrimp, anchovy paste, oysters, and other sea foods. Fermentation takes approximately one month, depending upon weather conditions. For the purpose of good and proper fermentation, traditional *kimchi* pots are stored either entirely or partially underground inside cellars or sheds built for this function.

BIBLIOGRAPHY

Andrews, R. C. 1919. Exploring Unknown Corners of the "Hermit Kingdom." *National Geographic* 36.1: 24–48.

Biernatzki, W. E. 1967. Varieties of Korean Lineage Structure. Diss., St. Louis University.

Brandt, V. S. 1971. *A Korean Village Between Farm and Sea.* Cambridge: Harvard University Press.

Chai, A. Y. 1962. Kinship and Mate Selection in Korea. Diss., Ohio State University.

Chang, Ch. S. 1984. *Initiation, Marriage, Funeral and Sacrificial Rites in Traditional Korean Society.* Seoul: The Academy of Korean Studies.

Choe, S. S. 1983. *Annual Customs of Korea.* Seoul: Seomun-dang.

Choi, C. M. 1987. The Competence of Korean Shamans as Performers of Folklore. Diss., Indiana University.

Chun, K. S. 1984. *Reciprocity and Korean Society: An Ethnography of Hasami*. Seoul: Seoul National University.

Cultural Properties Adminstration (The Republic of Korea), ed. 2001. *Korean Intangible Cultural Properties: Folk Dramas, Games, and Rites*. Seoul: Hollym.

Dallet, C. 1954 (1874). *Traditional Korea*. New Haven: Human Relations Area Files.

Ha, T. H. 1970. *Maxims and Proverbs of Old Korea*. Seoul: Yonsei University Press.

Han, S. B. 1972. *Korean Fishermen: Ecological Adaptation in Three Communities*. Seoul: Seoul National University Press.

Janelli, R. L. 1975. Anthropology, Folklore, and Korean Ancestor Worship. *Korea Journal* 15.6: 34–43.

Janelli, R. L., and D. Y. Janelli. 1982. *Ancestor Worship and Korean Society*. Stanford: Stanford University Press.

Kendall, L. 1977. Caught Between Ancestors and Spirits: A Korean Mansin's Healing Kut. *Korea Journal* 17.8: 8–23.

Kendall, L., and G. Dix, eds. 1987. *Religion and Ritual in Korean Society*. Berkeley: East Asian Institute, University of California.

Kim, H. K. 1999. *Korean Shamanism and Cultural Nationalism*. Seoul: Jimoondang.

Kim, K. O. 1994. Rituals of Resistance: The Manipulation of Shamanism in Contemporary Korea. In *Asian Visions of Authority*, edited by C. Keys, L. Kendall, and H. Hardacre. Honolulu: University of Hawaii Press. 195–220.

Lee, K. G. 2000. *Overseas Koreans*. Seoul: Jimoondang.

Moon, O. P. 1990. Urban Middle Class Wives in Contemporary Korea: Their Roles, Responsibilities and Dilemma. *Korea Journal* 30.11: 30–43.

Park, H.-Y. 2003. The Folkloric Study of Proverbs and Riddles Concerning Korean Family and Kinship. *Kwangwon Minsokhak* 17: 311–334.

Saccone, R. 1994. *The Business of Korean Culture*. Seoul: Hollym.

Sorensen, C. W. 1981. Household, Family, and Economy in a Korean Mountain Village. Diss., University of Washington.

Wagner, E. W. 1972. The Korean Chokpo as a Historical Source. In *Studies in Asian Genealogy*, edited by S. J. Palmer. Provo, UT: Brigham Young University Press. 141–152.

Wilson, B. 1983. The Korean Shaman: Image and Reality. In *Korean Women: View from the Inner Room*, edited by L. Kendall and M. Peterson. New Haven, CT: East Rock Press. 113–128.

Yim, D. H. 1990. *Sacrificial Rites for Ancestors*. Seoul: Taewonsa.

Hwan-Young Park

Central Asia and Siberia

KAZAKH

GEOGRAPHY AND HISTORY

Located in the center of the Euroasian continent, Kazakhstan stretches from the lower Volga in the west to the Altai in the east for 3,000 kilometers and from the Western Siberian plain on the north to the Tian-Shan Mountains in the south for 1,600 kilometers. Thus, the territory of Kazakhstan occupies the central and southern latitudes of the moderate climate zone, bordering the subtropic zone in the south. The borders of the newly independent Kazakhstan comprise more than 15,000 kilometers, 3,000 of which touch the Caspian and Aral Seas. In the west, north, and northwest the republic borders the Russian Federation, and in the south and southwest its neighbors are the other Central Asian republics: Turkmenistan, Uzbekistan (see **Uzbek**), and Kyrgyzstan. In the east and southeast Kazakhstan

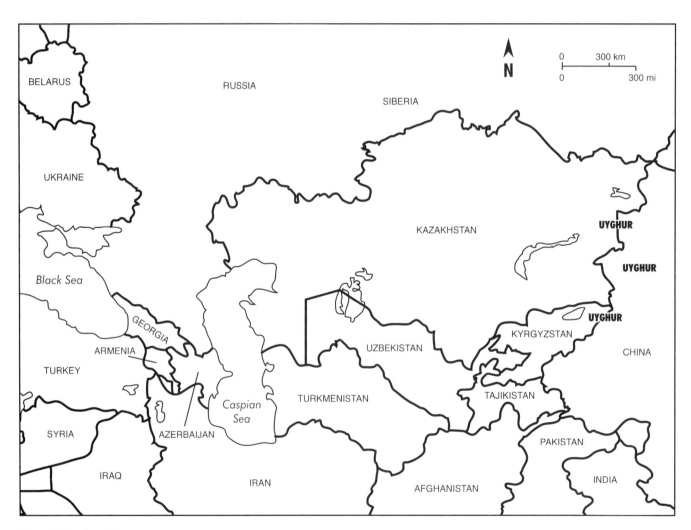

Central Asian Republics.

A baazar in Kazakhstan (ca. 1885–1886). Located between Europe and Asia, Kazakhstan has long been an arena of brisk economic, cultural, and political relations between European and Asian peoples. (Courtesy Library of Congress)

borders the People's Republic of **China**. Located between Europe and Asia, the territory of Kazakhstan has long been an arena of brisk economic, cultural, and political relations between European and Asian peoples.

The landscape of Kazakhstan is extremely diverse. Its distinguishing features are the high mountain ranges that fringe it to the south and east and whose highlands comprise some 10 percent of the territory (the Altai, Zhungar, and Tian-Shan regions). Most of Kazakhstan is plains. Climatic conditions vary considerably on these extensive open spaces. From north to south is a gradual transition from a steppe zone (with small islet forests in the extreme north) to a zone of deserts in the south. These conditions have been an important determinant of human activities throughout the ages.

During the Bronze Age, the Kazakhstani steppes, known as Ariana Vaedzha, were home to the semi-nomadic Indo-Aryans. Their descendants, the east Iranian Sakas, were also semi-nomads. But the Sakas of the Syr-Darya area had cities and were sedentary farmers. The first Turkic-speaking semi-nomadic tribes in the territory of southeast Kazakhstan (Zhetisu, or Seven Rivers) were the Hsong-nu tribes. They mingled with the Sakas, who adopted the Turkic language. Their myths, religious beliefs, material culture, and vocabulary became a part of Turkic culture.

The Sun was a main god of the Sakas, and they sacrificed horses to him. The Turks worshiped Tengri (Heaven), Yer-Sub (Earth-Water), and Umai (patroness of hearth, home, and child). The Kams (shamans) were mediators between gods and men. Since the seventh century C.E., the Turks of this region used a runic system of writing, and many of their myths, including creations stories, are preserved in runic texts. Buddhism, Manichaeism, and Christianity came to cities of South Kazakhstan via the Great Silk Road. Some tribes (Kereits and Naimans) adopted Nestorian Christianity. Later these tribes were included among the Kazakhs. Satuk, the ancestor of the Karakhanid dynasty, adopted Islam in the beginning of the tenth century. His son Bogra-khan proclaimed Islam the state religion. Sufism was particularly popular among nomads as it assimilated many elements of regional belief systems, and many Sufi preachers were reputed to be saints. The most famous of them were Khodzha Akhmad Yassawi and his teacher Arstanbab. People told many legends about theirs lives and wonders.

The thirteenth-century **Mongol** invaders adopted many elements of the Turkic culture present in Kazakhstan, among them the script and political institutions, and, in turn, influenced the Turks, most notably with the ideology of Chingisizm, which held that Chingis-khan and his descendents ruled by the power of God. The Khan must always be originally from the Chingizid clan. In the territory of Kazakhstan, the descendants of Chingis-khan formed many khanates. Two of them, Dzhanibek and Kerey, separated with many of their people from the Uzbek khanate in 1459 and became Kazakhs—that is, "free men." The territory of the Kazakh khanate included the steppe zone and the cities on Syr-Darya. Facing many different invaders throughout the years, the Kazakh khan, Abulkhair, asked **Russia** for assistance in defending his land, thus marking the beginning of the penetration of Russians into this region, a process that was, for the most part, completed by 1864, adding another ethnic dimension to the country. Now, speakers of different Indo-European, Turkic, Mongolian, and Finno-Ugrian languages lived in relative proximity and have influenced each other's culture.

MYTHS AND LEGENDS

Myths and ethnogenetical legends are of significant importance in the folklore of the Kazakhs, relating, among other things, their understanding of the social structure: for example, the division of Kazakhstan into three Hordes (*zhuzes*). Although such a political structure was quite practical—given that the steppe contained three natural geographic regions and that such a division brought stability during an absence of centralized authority—the mythology often provides a different take on the matter. One myth explains as follows: "Give the Eldest Horde a stick for grazing a herd; give the Middle Horde a pen; give the Junior Horde a spear." This speaks to the people's understanding that each Horde executes a different societal function: sacral, military, or economic. Such division existed among the Indo-European peoples, including the East Iranian and Scythes. Ancient Turkic myths about the creation of the universe remaining in Kazakh folklore also imagined all creation existing in a tripartite division of Heaven (upper world), Earth (middle world), and an underground world. Baiterek (the World Tree, or *Arbor Mundi*) connects these zones. Its roots are in the underground world, trunk in the middle zone, and top in Heaven. Baiterek grows on the World Mountain, Kok-Tube. Since the Xiongnu Dynasty, the Turks marked the sides of world with different colors: the East was blue, the North black, the South red, the West white, with the center either of mixed or golden color.

Myths speak of the origin of both the mundane and the fantastic. One fifteenth-century *epos* of the Orguz tribe relates the story of the first shaman, Korkut, who was a patron of shamans and singers and the inventor of the *kubyz*, a musical instrument that resembles the Jews' harp. Korkut saw in his dreams men who were digging a grave for him. Wanting to escape from death, he ran away, but this dream followed him everywhere. Deciding that death would find him only on the earth, he floated a blanket on the Syr-Darya River and began to play the *kubyz*. When he slept there, he dreamed of death in the form of a snake that stung him. Korkut's music remains a staple of Kazakh culture, though he lived long before the formation of the modern state, and people still honor his grave.

Myths explaining the origins of tribes are quite common and important for keeping up with one's ancestors. The Kazakh people must keep track of the previous seven generations of their ancestors to determine whom they can and cannot marry among other reasons. Tribes often took the names of their mythical progenitors. Thus the Oguz tribe traces its lineage back to Oguz-khan. The Kipchaks have also taken the name of their founder. And even though history has largely forgotten them, the Kazakhs still tell stories of the Wusun, an ancient Central Asian people whose future king was saved from hunger by suckling a she-wolf.

The formation of the Kazakhs has also been reflected in myths. Accordingly, the khan had a little son, Alash, whose skin was of many colors. Though put in a trunk and thrown in a river, Alash was saved by a hunter, who then raised him. Alash grew up to become a famous knight, and his father sent a hundred warriors to bring his son home. Those warriors remained with Alash, and so the khan sent two more sets of one hundred warriors each. They too stayed with Alash and thus formed the three Hordes of the Kazakhs. As mentioned above, each fulfilled a specific function, and Alash as king combined those three functions, as symbolized by the colors of each of the Hordes coming together in Alash, whose name literally means "mixed color."

The Three Hordes were subdivided further into "white bone" (*ak suyek*) and "black bone" (*kara suyek*), names given to the two basic Kazakh social groups. The white bone was made up of the khans of the Chingis dynasty as well as *sayyids* and *hodjas* (the aristocracy), while the black bone included everyone else. While the people of the black bone were subdivided into many clans and tribes, the white bone aristocracy recognized only two tribal distinctions: the Tore (descendents of Chingis-khan's eldest son Dzhuchi) and Khodzha (descendents of the prophet Muhammad and his fellow campaigners). Kazakhs have different legends about Muhammad and Chingis-khan, which exist in quite a few variants—some among the Turkic peoples, such as the *epos* of Edige and Alpamys, and others among the Uzbeks, Kara-kalpaks, Bashkirts, and Nogais. The chief differences among these versions relate to the individual history of the tribe or nation producing them. For example, after the 1723 invasion of Kazakhstan by the Jungars (during which the Kazakhs lost 40 percent of their population), all enemies in any legend or folktale were referred to as Jungars-Kalmyks. Much of Kazakh folklore deals with this seminal event.

FOLKTALES

Scholars divide Kazakh tales into three genres: fairy tales, animal tales, and tales about life. Fairy tales have their origin in ancient myths. Stories of the wicked witch

Zhezturnak, who has sharp nails made of copper, come from the Bronze Age when that metal was in common use. Many fairy tales depict the structure of the universe as a hero travels through it. Usually, a tale will begin with an old couple who do not have children and to whom God gives a son who is not quite ordinary: he will grow up faster than most boys and, when still young, accomplish many exploits, demonstrate courage, and be a wise ruler. Ordinary herdsmen are clever and quick-witted heroes; they travel to different countries, encounter miracles, fall in love with beautiful princesses, and have other adventures. In animal tales, animals stand in for people, often as symbols of such characteristics as courage, cowardice, and nobility. These tales are important in childrearing. Tales about life have contrary characters and may be comic or satirical or broach the subject of true wisdom. Many tales reflect ancient nomadic life. Kazakhs are fond of tales about the different Turkic tribes who formed the nation. Some motifs were borrowed from the Mongols, but many characters (such as the *peri*, *dev*, and the dragon Aidakhar or Azhi-dakhako, among others) came into Kazakh folklore from Iran and Arabic countries. Such tales were fairly widespread from the fifteenth to the eighteenth centuries.

In keeping with its multicultural population, Kazakh verbal art has been tremendously influenced by outside sources such as the tales of the Arabian nights and various European authors, but at the same time it still holds to its ancient Turkic roots, which are especially noteworthy with regard to its proverbs and puzzles, most of which date back to the eleventh-century book *Divani Lugat-at-Tiurk* (Collection of Turkic Language) by Makhmud Kashgari.

SONGS

Many songs, composed in the form of *koshtasu* (a song of parting) tell of Kazakhs fleeing their homeland and the difficulties they faced. Other songs (*Kara-kerei Kabanbay*, *Bogenbay*, *Shakhak Zhanibek Banyr*, and *Olzhabay Batyr*, for example) are devoted to *batyrs* (knights) who led the resistance against the Jungars, while still others detail the struggle of Kazakhs for freedom throughout history, linking the fight against the Jungars with the rebellions of Kenesary-khans, Makhambet Utemisuly, Isatai Taimanuly, Syrym Datuly, and others against the Russian Tsar. Kazakh historical songs of the nineteenth century centered on the figures of Zhankhodzha and Beket. The songs about Zhankhodzha, for example, describe the battle of the Syr-Darya Kazakhs with the Kokand invaders. Other historical events such as World War I, the Russian Revolution, and World War II have also become the subject of songs.

A popular form of verbal folklore is the *aitys*—an improvised, poetic song that may be part of a discussion, dispute, speech competition, or intertribal litigation. During the *aitys* the performer expresses his own ideas in poetical form while playing the *dombra*, a stringed instrument. All of his songs are improvisations. Listeners are divided into two groups. Each tribe sends forth its best *akyn* to perform the *aitys*. The people consider *aitys* a demonstration of poetical skills and know the names of very famous *akyns* from the past: Zhanak, Tubek, Sabyrbay, Orynbay, and Dzhambyl. The speeches are considered a kind of oratorical art form which may broach such subjects as philosophy, social relations, humorous musings, or simply dedications for something or someone. Debates might address the division of livestock, the care for land or widows, punishment for crimes, revenge, and similar topics.

Songs also accompany the various rites that mark Kazakh life. As an important transition, a wedding provides a context for singing—before, during, and after the actual ceremony. One song known as *toy-bastar* is sung in the home of the bride's parents before the wedding feast. An improvised piece, it congratulates the couple and wishes them great happiness. When the bride leaves her parents' home, she sings *synsu* or *tanysu*, saying good-bye to her family, friends, and native place. *Synsu* itself is often melancholy, with the bride taking umbrage at going so far from her native home and with her parents' selling her to a strange man for cattle. The inequality of women and men is a recurring motif. Singing *bet-ashar* before his family, the groom draws an ideal picture of the bride, introducing relations to whom she bows during the course of the song. *Zhar-zhar* is a song performed by two duets, composed of girls from the bride's family and boys from the groom's family. The boys will offer congratulations to the bride and sing of the joys of her new family, while the girls will respond with declarations that nothing can take the place of parents or homeland.

Many songs also touch upon death: pieces for notifying people of a recent death (*estirtu*), condolence (*konil-aitu*), consolation (*zhubatu*), and mourning (*zhoktau*). When notifying relations with *estirtu*, the singer uses many symbols and metaphors, speaking of a swan flying to a lake or a falcon flying to a steppe. With the mention of the dead person's name, the song becomes *zhubatu*, which is filled with many allegories which present death as our common fate: for example, just as a skilled workman does not create anything eternal, so God does not create man eternal. *Zhoktau* is the actual song of mourning. In Kazakhstan before the Russian Revolution, widows engaged in *zhoktau* three times a day for the course of a year. Death is idealized even as musicians enumerate the qualities of the departed. Related to such mourning songs are *koshtasu*, which speak of parting and separation, such as when one leaves his or her native land. Some remarkable examples of this art form come from the time of the Jungar invasion, while more modern ones have addressed exile into **Siberia**. *Koshtasu* are often included in many genres of poetry.

MUSIC

Music is important in Kazakh culture. The Kazakhs have more than twenty musical instruments with legends about the origin of some of them. Some instruments are very simple (*sherter*, *sazsyrnai*, *kepshek*, *shankobyz*, *dangyra*, and *asataiiak*, for example), while others such as the *dombra* are more sophisticated. The *dombra* has two or three strings made from the sinews of animals stretched over a flat, oval resonating box. The *kobyz* (or *kylkobyz*) is a bowed, two-stringed instrument with a hollow wooden body and a curved neck. It was often used by shamans. The *sybyzgy* is a wooden, reed, or metal flute with four or six fingerholes. The *dauylpaz* is a kind of drum in the form of a little wooden or metal boiler covered by skin. Larger versions are used in the army. Later the Kazakhs became acquainted with the two-rowed accordion from Russia.

The songs and *kiuis* (instrumental pieces) might begin a wedding, entertain a gathering of *aksakals* (old men), or mark the migration to *dzhailiau* (summer quarters) and the return to *kystau* (winter quarters). Some songs were devoted to hunting birds and famous racehorses. *Khabarshi* (heralds) rode about and informed people of significant news through song. Women sang as they constructed yurts, milked cattle, shook up wool, wove carpets, rolled out the *coshma* (felt carpets), and nursed children. The *zhubatu* is a song of sorrow, while the *suiunshi* is a song of joy. The eighteenth century saw singers and *akyns* performing professionally, playing heroic and lyrical epics and songs about ancient times and important men such as Koblandy-batyr, Aksak-kulan, Zhoshy-khan (Chingis-khan's son Dzhuchi), Eskendir (Alexander the Great), and Amir aksak (the Central Asian ruler Timur). The famous folk composer Kurmangazy Sagyrbayev (1806–1879) devoted his musical piece, *Kishkentai*, to the revolt of Isatai Taimanov. Another piece, *Syrym sazu* (Syrym's Thoughts), is devoted to Syrym Datuly. The invasion of the Jungars is also reflected in the musical heritage of Kazakhs. *Akyn* and composer Baizhigit from the Kerei tribe created a piece about the milking of a birch tree, whose sap men drank during those times of starvation. The representatives of different people contributed to Kazakh music and culture. A Russian girl, Maria, wrote the song "Dudarai," which deals with her love for a Kazakh youth. Kazakhs love the songs and music of Nadezhda Lushnikova. One Polish song has become a Kazakh folksong.

SPORTS AND GAMES

Many sports and games are connected to the nomadic life. Many of these, such as *baiga* races, are played while on horseback. *Zhamby atu* is a game in which riders throw down and have to retrieve silver or gold ingots. *Kyz kuu* is a race in which a young man pursues a girl. If he catches her, he earns a kiss, but if not, she gets to whip him with a lash. In Kokbar, two teams of riders fight for a goat carcass.

ARTS AND CRAFTS

Kazakh dress is a significant indicator of social status for both men and women. Men's dress fastens on the right side; women's on the left. Poor men usually wear something made of wool and leather, while wealthier men have dresses of velvet and silk. The khans decorated their clothing with golden embroidery and their hats with the plumage of eagles and owls as well as silver, precious stones, and coral. Women's jewelry is made of gold and silver. Women may wear bracelets, earrings, rings, buckles, and buttons as well as various kinds of adornment on their chest.

The saddles of wealthy people are often decorated and adorned with precious stones or carved bone. In addition, musical instruments, furniture (trunks and bed frames, for example), the details of a yurt, carts, and dishes will often feature some sort of carving. This craft was the realm of men, while women were responsible for the production of carpets. Indeed, Kazakhs are renowned for trying to make all things beautiful, even the simple leather bowls that hold milk. One traveler remarked that the yurts of wealthy Kazakhs looked like museums.

ARCHITECTURE

Nomadism also influenced Kazakh architecture. The main style of home was the yurt, built without any nails and designed to be disassembled and moved elsewhere. The most durable part of a yurt is the *shanyrak*, which is difficult to assemble. The *shanyrak* is a wooden circle forming the smoke opening in the yurt. It symbolizes home or family. Instead of speaking about somebody's home or house, Kazakhs refer to somebody's *shanyrak*. The *shanyrak*

Nomadism influenced Kazakh architecture. The yurt is built without any nails and designed to be disassembled and moved elsewhere. (Courtesy Library of Congress)

is made of even, uncracked willow wood formed into a circle with *taspa*, a lace of dressed leather used for sewing. The walls of yurts, *kerege*, have the form of folding lattices. The *kerege* and *shanyrak* are connected by curved sticks, *uyks*. One end of a stick is put in a hole of the *shanyrak*, while the other end is tied to *kerege*. The yurt is covered with felt. Inside the Kazakh yurt are beautifully decorated carpets. The yurt is considered a model of the universe in the form of man's body. The *kerege* is equated with the skeleton, and the holes in *shanyrak* become eyes. The *tor*—the place of honor for a guest—is opposite the door. On the left are housekeeping items for women, while on the right are various tools and weapons for men. In the winter, Kazakhs live in half-underground houses.

Because life is a state of movement, Kazakhs view monuments built in graveyards as the houses of the dead, who do not move. Such monuments may be constructed in the form of sheep (*koitas*) and carved stone pillars (*kulpytas*) with pictures of weapons or tribal symbols (*tanba*). With the adoption of Islam, however, this very ancient tradition is disappearing. In the Bronze Age art of the Xiongnu, the horns of rams are found on many monuments. Some researchers suppose this **motif** to be somehow related to the Tree of the World motif.

FESTIVALS AND CELEBRATIONS

The ancient Iranian holiday Nawryz (new year) is a favorite holiday of the Kazakhs, who renamed it *Ulystyn Uly kuni* (the great day of people). This holiday is accompanied by music and different forms of theatrical performance. On the first day of Nawryz people play holiday games such as *Kaltyrauyk Kamyr Kempir* (Old Woman from Paste) and *Ak Boran* (White Snowstorm), which imitate the conflict between summer and winter. The Old Woman from Paste is a symbol of dying winter. Her motions show the conditions of winter. The main dish of the holiday is *nawryz-kozhe*. It is prepared from seven different ingredients and symbolizes abundance. Two components, milk and grains, are symbols of agriculture and nomadism.

Some rites are connected with the work of a nomad. The rite of hospitality, *Kymyz murundyk* (first *koumiss*), is performed in summer at the time of the first milking of the mares. Rites are usually accompanied by entertainment. Men often sing songs devoted to the patron of horses, *Zhylkyshy ata*, when the milking of the mares is finished at the beginning of autumn. The Badik game was originally a magical game connected with working activity. Badik is a wicked spirit who makes cattle ill, and in the summer the youth will gather at a yurt in order to ridicule Badik, demanding he go away. A shaman takes the lead in exiling the spirit. Players support the shaman by crying, singing, and moving their bodies. The playing of *shaman-baksy* is a rite with theatrical elements. In the home of a sick man, Baksy will go barefoot on sharp stones, lick scorching metal, and perform other feats of endurance to the accompaniment of singing, dancing, and music. This has a palpable impact upon the audience and the sick person. Weddings are also a time of games and theatrical performances. One such is *Khan Zhaksy Ma?* (Is He a Good Khan?). Participants elect a khan, his wife, and counselors. The "khan" then deals with certain issues such as giving orders and considering complaints. It is a game of citizenship that amuses both participants and spectators.

CHALLENGES OF THE MODERN WORLD

Given that all such folk arts stem from the principles of nomadic life, it was a major blow to traditional Kazakhs to endure the collectivization and sedentarization imposed by the Soviet Union in 1930. The nomads had to change their lifestyles, and half of the people and their cattle perished during this experiment. The holidays and songs of the Kazakhs were forbidden, being viewed by those in authority as religious, feudal, and anti-communist. The Soviets forced the Kazakhs to write their language in the Cyrillic alphabet rather than the Arabic script, which separated many people from their folklore and literary heritage. As a result, many Kazakhs did not use their native language. Before the collapse of the Soviet Union, the Kazakh writer Shakhanov introduced the term *mankurt*. Now this term implies a person who does not know the Kazakh language and culture. At the same time, many Kazakhs deny the necessity of knowing their culture, traditions, and language. They claim that in an era of **globalization** it is enough to know English and Western culture. *See also* **Turkey**.

BIBLIOGRAPHY

Kazakh Traditions and Ways. 2002. Almaty: Daik Press.

Nysanbaev, A., E. Arynov, and B. Yesekeyev. 1996. *Republic of Kazakhstan: Five Years of Independent Development.* Almaty: Daik Press.

Olcott, M. Brill. 1987. *The Kazakhs.* Stanford: Hoover Institution Press.

Svanberg, Ingvar, ed. 1999. *Contemporary Kazaks. Cultural and Social Perspectives.* Richmond, Surrey, UK: Curzon Press.

Anuar Galiev

SIBERIA

GEOGRAPHY AND HISTORY

Approximately twenty-six aboriginal tribes and nations now occupy the area from the Urals to the Pacific and from the Arctic Ocean to the borders of Mongolia and **China**. Populations range from Buriat and Tuvans with about 200,000 to 300,000 each to the Orok with only 200. Various tribes have disappeared because of wars, disease, and colonization by **Russia**, but most of all through assimilation and government policies of combining tribes and territories.

Six major Siberian linguistic-cultural groupings are members of three language families. The Altai family consists of these groupings: Turkic (Altai, Dolgan, Khakass, Sakha, Shor, Teleut, Tofalar, and Tuvan), Tungus (Even, Evenk, Nanai, Negidal, Oroch, Orok, Udeghe, and Ulchi), and Mongolian (Buriat-Mongol). The Paleoasiatic family includes these specific ethnic populations: Chukchi, Itelmen, Kerek, Ket, Koryak, Nivkh, Yukaghir, and Yupik. The Uralic language family is comprised of two major groups: Finno-Ugric (Khanti and Mansi) and Samoyedic (Enets, Nenets, Nganasan, and Selkup). These people live in three major geographic zones: tundra, where people herd reindeer and hunt sea mammals on the Arctic shore; taiga forest, inhabited by hunter-gatherer cultures; and steppe, where livestock herding provides the major source of livelihood. Since the seventeenth century most peoples also engaged in trade with Russia and China. The twentieth century saw the growth of cities and industry in the region.

In spite of the role geography plays in folklore imagery, spiritual belief systems and traditions tend to coincide with language groupings more strongly. Siberian peoples have moved over huge distances under pressure from wars and other social factors. For example, the Turkic Sakha people, who formerly lived in the steppes immediately north of Mongolia, moved northward and expanded their territory into the taiga and the Arctic tundra north and northeast of Baikal, carrying lifestyles and folklore images of birds and animals not found in their new home. On the other hand, the Paleoasiatic Nivkh people now live in a small taiga zone on Sakhalin Island and the mainland alongside the Tungus tribes. Their territory was once much larger, including parts of China and the

A Tuvan family beside their yurt in the Erzin District. (Photograph by Kira Van Deusen)

Nivkh dance to accompany the bear ceremony, Sakhalin Island. (Photograph by Kira Van Deusen)

Kamchatka Peninsula with volcanoes that show up in their stories and have been passed to their neighbors. The Tungus-language peoples have moved more widely than any other group: from western Siberia to Chukotka and the Amur region, carrying Central Asian horse imagery and other themes. Geographic neighbors can have quite different cultures and even ways of life. Witness the fact that in the Arctic some people ride domestic reindeer, some use them to pull sleds, some milk them, and others use them only to attract wild reindeer.

Although most Siberian peoples are little known to the outside world, well-documented forces have caused their migrations. **Mongol** Khans forced many people to move northward, spreading tales and folklore motifs that had traveled the Silk Road from distant **India** and China. This process continued until recently with the Tuvans and Buriats, the only Siberian peoples to adopt Tibetan Buddhism. Russian styles, particularly in the late nineteenth and twentieth centuries, have influenced regional folklore. Ancient circumpolar motifs such as raven tales are shared by peoples of the Russian Arctic and their relatives across Alaska, Canada, **Greenland**, and Europe.

Traditional lifestyles were radically altered by communism, which forced the adoption of Russian culture and the creation of new politically based folklore genres such as epics about Lenin and hundreds of Komsomol worksongs. Large dance ensembles were formed with Russian choreography. Circumstances for the older practices of epic telling, holiday celebrations, music, and wearing traditional clothing and adornment were reduced or eliminated along with the nomadic way of life.

RELIGIOUS BELIEFS

The worldview of all Siberian peoples is characterized by animism, the belief that everything is imbued with spirit, including physical objects and intangibles such as songs and stories. Customs developed to help people live in harmony with nature and its spirits. Although most scholars describe a mythic system of three worlds, in fact there are often more, including not only the sky, earth, and underground worlds with their several layers, but also worlds under the water, the land of the dead, and, for some, a world of pure imagination.

Spirits of animals, weather phenomena, rocks, trees, sky, mountains, lakes, rivers, and sacred springs are part of the living essence of the planet. Spirit behavior in relation to people may be good, evil, or changeable. As a fire can warm the home or burn it down, as water can nourish or drown, many spirits can either help or harm human beings, depending on the relationship with them. They can change shape, appearing as anything from a monster with six heads to an animal or a sexually appealing member of the opposite sex. They make themselves known visually, through sound, and as vibrational influences.

People are also affected by the spirits of their ancestors, both genetic and those acquired through reincarnation. Some ancient Siberian spirits have one eye, which connects them with world cyclops folklore. Thus when the story of *The Odyssey* made its way into Tuva, the resonance with the older *shulbus* led to an interesting adaptation of the Polyphemus tale to Tuvan circumstances.

Indigenous Siberians understand the human soul as multiple. Turkic Khakassians call the basic life force *khut*. Although it may leave the body temporarily at night, its final loss means death. The *sür* soul is connected to the physical body, staying with the bones even after death. *Tyn* is the breath. When it leaves the body, it stays attached by a thread. *Chula* is the astral body, or "fire of the eyes," which may leave the body at night. *Sagys*, or reason, stays near the family for forty days after death. *Süne* is the soul of a dead person that stays one year on earth and then becomes a spirit called *üzüt* in the other world. *Sus* is a sun's ray that carries the child's soul to the body. In addition a shaman has another soul called *myg'yra*, located in the clan tree. Every clan has a soul located in a certain kind of tree. It is forbidden for clan members to cut that tree or make things from the wood. In addition, human hair is said to contain a part of the soul.

ANIMALS, NATURE, AND THE SPIRITUAL WORLD

A Paleoasiatic Yupik tale of a woman who married a whale connects with the circumpolar myth of Sedna. Yupik elder Nununa told it to Kira Van Deusen in 1994 in Sireniki, Chukotka. Nununa sang in the old Sireniki dialect, of which she was one of the last two speakers. One of her songs was about the Soviet astronaut Yuri Gagarin, who in April 1961 became the first man to orbit the earth. This was particularly interesting as the Yupik tell tales of flying shamans who traveled among the stars. Nununa had facial tattoos. Girls tattooed each other as they approached puberty, using black soot from a cooking pot mixed with seal fat and applying it with needle and thread. Although it was very painful, they claim it was simply done "for beauty!" Sketches done a hundred years earlier show exactly the same intricate designs. In earlier times the tattoos were believed to give protection from evil spirits and to ensure fertility.

Nununa's story opens with a formula about the earth's creation common in most Siberian epics. It was long ago, when we were not here yet. Things were not yet developed; the land had just started to breathe. The young people went down to the shore together. But the numbers were uneven, and one girl didn't get a husband. Her foot got caught in a hole in a whale bone, which moved into the sea and took the girl with it, turning back into a whale as it went. Quickly the young men set out in their boat. Two moving rock cliffs in the bay opened apart and crashed closed. The brothers got through by following the birds. They followed the shoreline and found their sister, now pregnant. She refused to come home, saying she was married to the whale. All the same, they took her, though she was weeping. The girl gave birth to a baby whale. When he was a year old, she let him go into the sea. His father came often to look at him. This son had a talisman attached near his eye, and hunters didn't touch either the son or the father. But then the mother saw some people from another settlement kill the baby whale with the talisman. They cut it up on the beach. When nothing was left but bones, she gathered them together and slept with them. The father whale overturned the hunters' boat as they were leaving, and all of them died.

Many stories portray people who marry sea mammals, frequently a whale. The distinctive feature of this version is the crashing rocks, which bring to mind the rocks on the beach at Sireniki. The image of clashing rocks is familiar from the classical Greek myth of Jason's quest for the Golden Fleece and is also told as part of a shaman's journey among the Khakass of south-central Siberia. The birds impart an important lesson to sea hunters.

The image of marriage with an animal is basic to understanding the place of humanity in nature. It acknowledges the intimate connection between people and the animals they depend on. When human women marry land animals such as bears and tigers, they give birth to both animal and human children who survive to found new clans. We might expect that to happen here, but those who marry whales give birth only to whales, and the babies die. While the stories about land animals tell of people's origins, the tales of sea mammals, at least in their present form, tell of hunting taboos.

A good part of human activity had to do with gaining an element of control in relations with nature, but this was control through understanding and balance rather than control through destruction. People must kill to live, but by obeying the laws of nature they ensure that their killing is not permanent and that the animals return and stay in balance as in the bear ceremony. Nununu's story expresses this by the woman sleeping with the bones, an image that appears as the point of departure in other stories of resurrection. Bones are connected with shamanic death and rebirth. Earlier story versions may have followed this path.

Certain animals must not be killed at all—in this case the whales marked with the talisman given by the woman who was their mother. Those foreigners who disobeyed this taboo, even through ignorance, were severely punished.

The intimacy of humans' relationship with whales can be seen in the fact that in the earliest times Yupik people lived in houses constructed of whale bones—literally living inside the whale. The jawbone provided the central support, while a shoulder-blade closed the summer door. In winter they used an underground passage, which prevented cold air from entering the house. Smoke exited through a hole in the whale's vertebra.

The placement and set-up of a traditional Turkic or Mongolian yurt reflects the cosmos and the inner spiritual world as well as practicalities of nomadic life. The side of a felt yurt to the left on entering is for the males and that to the right for the females. Places are also set aside for the very young near the door and the very old in the place of honor opposite the door. The yurt is oriented with the door to the sunrise. One can tell the time of day by the movement of sun and shadow over the poles holding up the central roof ring. The roof of a yurt is associated with the Upper World, and it was considered bad luck if a lower world animal such as a dog got onto the roof. A shaman often describes beginning a visionary journey by going out through the smoke hole.

Lassoing, a Chukchi sport. (Photograph by Kira Van Deusen)

The hearth is a similar point of entry to the Lower World. It is also a place of protection for women, who can hide there from attack by people or evil spirits, protected by the goddess of fire. The threshold is an important transitional zone between the inside world of family and clan and the outside world of strangers. The poor and the sick were not allowed to enter beyond the threshold.

In Arctic Chukotka the *yaranga* is not completely symmetrical and orients to withstand high winds. It has similar reference points to the spiritual world. Other dwellings include tents resembling a North American tipi, wooden yurts, and, formerly, semi-subterranean houses in the Arctic.

In the Arctic, sports develop the strength, agility, and skill necessary in reindeer herding. These include weightlifting and elaborate feats with jumpropes and lassoing. Tongue-twisters and riddles are very popular throughout Siberia, and some say they are related to shamanic poetry. Ulchi dolls connect a young girl to the life skills she will need as well as to the shamanic figures that the dolls resemble. The exception is that the shamanic figures are truly alive because they have eyes, while the doll remains eyeless and functions only as a toy. For the most part dance was limited to shamans, though the Evenk, Sakha, and Buriat peoples have a round dance dedicated to the sun, which bears a strong resemblance to Balkan circle dances.

SHAMANISM

The best-known feature of Siberian spirituality is shamanism. The word "shaman" is derived through Russian from the Tungus language family word *sama*. Siberia is considered to be the home of "classic" shamanic features: heredity and selection, initiation including dismemberment, diverse forms of divination, ceremonial functions, spiritual journeys for soul retrieval, and accompaniment of the souls of the dead to the next world. Shamans usually used elaborately symbolic costumes. Their oral poetry and the music of a large single-headed drum with jingling metal pieces inside, a jaw harp, or, further to the west, bowed strings transport them on visionary journeys to worlds in the sky and under the earth and water. Some say that women were the

A Tuvan shaman at a shaman's clinic in the city of Kyzyl. (Photograph by Kira Van Deusen)

first shamans, because the gift in early times was closely connected with fire rituals carried out by women in honor of the goddesses of the hearth and the sun. This is supported by linguistic evidence and the shaman's costume, which befits a female figure. Ancient myths speak of women who received a spiritual gift from heaven and then gave birth to the first male shaman.

Women and men may be selected by the spirits of nature and the ancestors to become shamans as well as storytellers and other kinds of healers, diviners, and ceremonial leaders. One characteristic of Siberian shamanism and spirituality is its lack of dogma; its flexibility is based in oral tradition. Shamanism adapts to new conditions, interacting with Christianity and Buddhism from the sixteenth to the nineteenth century. In the post-Soviet period shamans have developed urban clinics and new practices. Always highly competitive, shamans compete today for the international spiritual market.

Shamanic spiritual initiation involves experiences of death and rebirth, with bones taken apart and counted before being reassembled. Most novices suffer from what is called the "shaman's illness," which can be diagnosed and cured only by a shaman. It takes forms that appear similar to both physical and psychological disturbances. The healing results in the new shaman becoming ready to practice. During their initiation they make contact with helping spirits and learn to bring back souls stolen by evil spirits or driven from the body by shock. They may also remove foreign energies with drumming or fanning. Unlike shamans from other parts of the world, most traditional Siberians made little if any use of hallucinogens. They did not study with a shaman mentor beyond this initial healing, which sometimes included a short period of instruction about specifically shamanic language and ritual. Today some shamans describe a longer period of study, as did a minority in the past. In Tuva the shaman's association offers courses of study to new shamans. This has occurred because the younger generation has not been brought up in a traditional way of life, where much needed information would simply have been absorbed in the course of daily existence.

Community support was essential to shamans, who do not work unless invited. People searched out the strongest and most effective shamans, but always with a certain reluctance. Most people would first try other means such as herbal medicine for solving their problems. Much of this reluctance comes from people's fear of sorcery and of those who make connection with the spirits of the dead. No sense of romance surrounds shamans among indigenous Siberian peoples, even today when so much interest comes from the outside.

Shamans did not charge set fees and often gave away the gifts they received. Besides being a drain on the their energies, lengthy ceremonies took time away from their households. The danger springing from contact with spirits is also a reason many resist the shamanic call, though in the Soviet Union politics also played an important role. Shamans were severely persecuted under various regimes because of their community leadership and their opposition to communist institutions.

The story of the first Buriat shaman shows many classic features, including shape-changing. Throughout Siberia the drum is referred to as a riding animal, driven by the shaman with the drumstick. This story appears in the Buriat National Archives in many versions collected in the nineteenth century and in works on shamanism. The first Buriat shaman was the powerful Morgon Kara. He could bring souls back from the dead, and some say he even created a life. Erlik Khan, Master of the Land of the Dead, complained to the great god Tengri in the Upper World. Tengri came down into the Middle World, stole a man's soul, and took it home. He put it in a bottle covered with his thumb and waited. The man got very sick, and his family called Morgon Kara, who took out his drum. Instead of having one head and a narrow frame, as they do today, his drum had a wider frame with a head on each end. Riding on the drum's beat, Morgon Kara searched through the three worlds. At last he saw Tengri with his thumb over the top of a bottle. Morgon Kara turned into a wasp and stung him. Tengri tried to slap the wasp, but Morgon Kara escaped with the soul. Tengri hurled a thunderbolt, splitting the drum in two. Still Morgon Kara got back to earth and breathed the soul into the sick man, who got well. Since that time shamans have not been as powerful as before, and the shaman's drums have only one head. Some say that Morgon Kara was set on a rock and forced to jump in place until he disappeared in the earth. When he disappears completely, there will be no more shamans.

RITUALS

Siberian peoples celebrated many rituals, seasonally and around important life events such as births, marriages, and deaths. The Turkic and Mongolian peoples celebrate major spring holidays (Sakha *Ysykh*) as well as group prayers to the heavens (Khakass *Tigir Taiykh*). The Nivkh and Ulchi people once had a bear ceremony in which a bear cub was raised within a human family for two to three years and then ritually killed. The bear's spirit was to go to the Upper World and report on human behavior, which is why the cub was treated so carefully. In 1992 the ceremony was revived in an Ulchi village for the first time since 1937, but so many people felt sorry for the way the bear was treated that they decided to keep parts of the ceremony without the live bear. The ceremony, not conducted by a shaman, had special music and dance to accompany it. The Udeghe did not perform this kind of ceremony but did have ceremonies to be carried out if a bear had been killed after harming a human, which aimed to make an agreement between bears and humans that they would not further harm each other. The Finno-Ugric Khanti and Mansi also conduct a bear ceremony after hunting, again without raising a bear in the home.

Nunua, a Yupik storyteller with tattoos. (Photograph by Kira Van Deusen)

STORYTELLING

Oral storytelling held a vitally important and respected place in Siberian societies, functioning as carrier of history and life patterns, as the most important tool for education, and as a means for facilitating healing and spiritual growth. Live storytelling walks listeners through geographic and spiritual space. Many tellers say that once they have invoked the spirit of story, they see actions unrolling before their inner eyes and simply relate what they see. Story images map the whole spiritual world from which shamanic practice springs.

Like shamans, certain epic-tellers can call spirits and see beyond the boundaries that divide ordinary life from the worlds of dreams and visions. They have a spiritual initiation and the ability to heal individuals and societies. Shamanic storytelling tradition includes life stories and legends about shamans, stories and songs that are part of a ceremony, and magic tales whose plots follow the course of an initiation and/or healing journey.

Other oral genres include legends, highly developed epics (especially among Turkic and Mongolian peoples), anecdotes, and poetic good-wishes recited at table. The Tungus categorize folklore genres not so much as myth, legend, and tale based on the kinds of plots and imagery they contain, but by the source—passed down "real-life" events, *telungu*, or the product of a vision or dream, *nimanku*. Both are considered true in different ways. *Nimanku* is related to the Nanai words *ningma*, story or shamanic activity, and *ningmachi*, the ceremony of seeing off the souls of the dead. Their root word means "to see with the eyes covered or closed," which again connects the arts of shamanism and storytelling. *Telungu* may also contain shamanic imagery such as shape-changing, death and rebirth, bones, communication with animals, and the use of shaman's tools.

Turkic storytellers are subject to several "rules" related to the spiritual nature of the art. They must not refuse to tell a tale when asked, nor may they leave a story incomplete. Breaks must be taken when the story characters are resting or feasting. If any of these rules are not observed, the story spirits are left discontented in our world and can make trouble for the teller and others. A Turkic Tuvan tale, narrated by Ortaat (born in 1916) to Valentina Süzükei in the 1980s, shows how one man became a storyteller and demonstrates the connection of music with story. His instrument has two strings, a skin head, and a bow, and its sound expresses a sad beauty. Stories with this "Rip Van Winkle" theme appear all over the world. A young man found shelter in a cave, where he heard the sound of an unknown instrument, played by a white-bearded old man, the spirit of the mountain. The young man tried playing the instrument, was entranced by its beauty, and borrowed it to make a copy. When he finally got home, he discovered that instead of a few hours, many years had gone by, and all his friends and family had died. He aged on the spot and from that time became a famous story-singer, whose music was always filled with sadness.

MUSIC AND SONGS

Vocal forms of music in Siberia include epic-singing, many varieties of throat-singing, improvised competitions (Khakass *takhpakh*), invocations, lullabies, and folksongs. Musical instruments include bowed and plucked strings, flutes, the jaw-harp (with a museum in Yakutsk to celebrate its elaborate development in Siberian culture), hunting horns, zithers, and drums. Much of the music uses pentatonic scales. In the Soviet Union large ensembles were formed. Harmony and structures altered from ancient tradition. The Siberian musicians best known in the west are the throat-singers of Tuva.

In a Tungus-Manchu Udeghe tale, told by Valentina T. Kyalundzyuga to Kira Van Deusen in 1993, conversations between the girl and the bear take the form of a song. It is common in Tungus-Manchu storytelling for a storyteller to sing conversations that cross between worlds, between humans and animals, or between humans and deities or spirits while other parts are spoken in prose. The songs lines follow an eight-syllable pattern common in sacred music across northern Asia and related to the rhythm of the Finnish *Kalevala*. A girl lived with her brother as husband and wife. One day when he was away, she began singing, calling the bear, Biatu. She prepared tasty food, and the bear came to live with her. Later the brother came back and killed the bear. The woman was pregnant and gave birth to two bear cubs. Angry with her brother for killing Biatu, she left the children with him. She turned into a bear and disappeared into the forest. In fall the children found a den to sleep in. The brother left an embroidered robe to protect them and show that they had human parentage. Nonetheless, when he came back in spring, the bear cubs had been killed by hunters. He found the hunters, who offered him their sister as a wife so that he would not take revenge on them.

ARTS AND CRAFTS

Largely functional, Siberian visual art forms include embroidery, wood- and stonecarving, metalwork, and fur mosaics. Images dating back to ancient petroglyphs are still in use today. Udeghe women, like their neighbors along the Amur, are masters of an elaborate and very beautiful form of embroidery and applique. Specific to the Udeghe is the art of cutting a design out of treated salmon skin, also used in the past for clothing. The artist stitches over the raised fish-skin, which has the consistency of light leather, with silk threads imported from China to make a raised design. Embroidered designs representing protective spirits have the power to protect human beings from evil spirits, as should have been the case with the bear-children in the story of Biatu.

Tree of Life, embroidered by Nanai artist Lubov Samar. (Photograph by Kira Van Deusen)

CHALLENGES OF THE MODERN WORLD

Siberian folklore has been influenced by Russians in both the tsarist and communist periods as well as by Western television in the recent "market economy" period. As the way of life changed, so did understanding of older folk forms. While some values persist on a very deep level, they have come into conflict with demands of industrialization and consumerism. An example of story lessons that need to be rethought from the Soviet times and clarified for today's students is in an Udeghe tale of the good/bad hunter. This young man was so successful at killing animals that his elderly parents got tired of dragging the take home and decided to kill the boy and send his body down the river in a coffin! Many listeners today laugh at the foolishness of these parents who kill the goose that laid the golden egg and are horrified at the evidence of poor parenting. But before the days when hunters depleted their lands in order to pay tribute to the tsars and before Soviet policies brought the idea of producing the maximum possible at all costs, it was understood that a hunter must not take more than he needed. The land and its resources should stay in balance. The boy had to be stopped from his obsessive killing. A return to life was possibly included in the idea of their putting him in the coffin, because the concept of death does not contain the finality it does in European languages. On his way down the river in the coffin, a young woman eventually pulls the boy to shore and brings him back to life by rocking and singing to his little finger bone, which contains his soul. And after that he becomes a wiser hunter. The story's text is worded in such a way that either interpretation is possible, and what people take from it is in the emphasis provided orally by the storyteller and in the realm of what "goes without saying" in a particular society.

STUDIES OF SIBERIAN FOLKLORE

Siberian folklore was extensively collected and published in Russian in the nineteenth and twentieth centuries. Many of those publications reflect social and political biases. General information on Siberian peoples is available on the Internet at www.eki.ee/books/redbooks/introduction.shtml, and information on languages can be found at the UNESCO site on endangered languages: www.helsinki.fi/~tasalmin/endangered.html. *See also* **Turkey** and **Western Inuit and Yupik**.

BIBLIOGRAPHY

Balzer, Marjorie, ed. 1997. *Shamanic Worlds.* Armonk, NY: M. E. Sharpe.

Bogoras, Waldemar. 1975 (1904–1909). *The Chukchee.* New York: AMS.

Campbell, Joseph. 1988. *Historical Atlas of World Mythology, Volume I: The Way of the Animal Powers.* New York: Harper and Row.

Coxwell, C. F. 1983 (1925). *Siberian and Other Folk-Tales.* New York: AMS.

Fitzhugh, William W. 1998. *Crossroads of Continents.* Washington, DC: Smithsonian Institution Press.

Kurosawa, Akira. 1974. *Dersu Usala* (film). Kino Video.

Leisiö, T. 2001. On the Octosyllabic Metric Pattern and Shamanism in Eurasia. In *Shamanhood, Symbolism, and Epic*, edited by Juha Pentikainen. Budapest: Akademiai Kiado. 89–134.

Levin, T., and Michael Edgerton. 1999. The Throat Singers of Tuva. *Scientific American*, September: 80–87.

Rasmussen, Knud. 1976 (1929). Report of the Fifth Thule Expedition (1921–24). In *Intellectual Culture of the Igulik Eskimo. The Netsilik Eskimos: Social Life and Spiritual Culture*, translated by W. Worster. New York: AMS.

Van Deusen, Kira. 1999. *Raven and the Rock: Storytelling in Chukotka*. Seattle: University of Washington Press.

———. 2001. *The Flying Tiger: Women Shamans and Storytellers of the Amur*. Montreal: McGill-Queens University Press.

———. 2004. *Singing Story Healing Drum: Shamans and Storytellers of Turkic Siberia*. Montreal: McGill-Queens University Press.

Zheleznova, Irina. 1989. *Northern Lights: Fairy Tales of the People of the North*. Moscow: Raduga.

Kira Van Deusen

TAJIK

GEOGRAPHY AND HISTORY

A modern republic in Central Asia bordering **China**, Afghanistan, Uzbekistan, and Kyrgyzstan, Tajikistan is largely mountainous. Mountains cover some 93 percent of the territory, and almost half of them are higher than 3,000 meters. The capital is Dushanbe. The state language is Tajiki, a branch of New Persian, although Russian is widely spoken for international relations. The population of Tajikistan is divided among these ethnic groups: Tajiks (80 percent), **Uzbeks** (15 percent), Russians (2.6 percent), and others (2.4 percent).

The creation of the state of Tajikistan occurred under Soviet auspices by the so-called national-territorial delimitation of Central Asia in 1924. The Tajik Autonomous Soviet Socialist Republic (ASSR), functioning as a part of the Uzbek SSR, consisted of Eastern Bokhara, still then belonging to the Bokharian People's Republic, which until 1920 had been the Emirate of Bokhara and was removed by the above-mentioned delimitation; a part of the Pamirs (since 1895 under Russian dominion); and twelve districts (*volost'*) of the Turkestan ASSR, until 1917 a governor-generalship of **Russia** and also removed by the delimitation of 1924. In October 1929 the province and city of Khujand were added to the territory of Tajikistan, which at the same time received the status of a Union Republic (SSR).

Tajikistan was included in the general development schemes of the Soviet Union such as collectivization and industrialization and became subject to various campaigns, more or less extensively and originally launched in 1927–1928. These included elimination of illiteracy, the changeover to the Latin and then to the Cyrillic alphabet, unveiling and liberation of women, promotion of atheism,

Mural depicting parrots from the Asht District.

resettlement operations, and political purges. The first decade of these policies was marked by waves of emigration (mainly to Afghanistan) and anti-Soviet, traditionalist, armed resistance by the *Basmachis*. After World War II, Tajikistan, one of the poorest republics of the Soviet Union, in a technical sense represented a relatively developed country with a certain amount of industrial and agricultural production, a basic infrastructure, and broad networks of public health and education. At the breakup of the Soviet Union in 1991, Tajikistan declared itself independent but soon fell into a precarious situation. Regional animosities and political quarrels led to a civil war in 1992. These conflicts and their consequences were resolved in 1997.

Tajik folklore has deep roots in the history of **Persian**-speaking people. In ancient Iranian literature such as *Avesta, Bundahishn, Saddar, Shayast na shayast*, and *Khvaday-namak* appear many myths and mythological stories. The great Tajik-Persian poet Firdausi (ninth and tenth centuries C.E.) gathered many myths, legends, folktales, stories, and oral histories from Iranian people in Iran, Afghanistan, and Central Asia. Afterwards utilizing his collected materials, he wrote an epic master-piece poem *Shoh-noma* (The Book of Kings), which consists of 60,000 *bayt* (distich).

In the last decades of the nineteenth century, Russian orientalists and geographers gathered and published examples of Tajik folklore forms. Then in the 1920s and 1930s Tajik and Russian researchers started official work on Tajik folklore. In 1940 one of the first collections of folklore materials, *Namunai folklori tojik* (Examples of Tajik Folklore) by M. Tursunzoda, was published. In the mid-twentieth century, Tajik folklore studies had developed further. A group of Tajik folklorists from the Institute of Language and Literature of the Tajik Academy of Sciences regularly traveled into the field and collected folklore materials in different forms. Today, about 200,000 pages of their material are housed in the Archive of the Institute of Language and Literature.

In the 1950s special courses on Tajik Folklore were created for students at universities and institutes of Tajikistan, which published five guidebooks: *Folklori tojik* (Tajik Folklore) by N. Ma'sumi (1952); *Ejodiyoti dahanakii khalqi tojik* (Tajik Verbal Folk Art) by R. Amonov and V. Asrori (1980); *Zhanrhoi khurdi folklori tojik* (Small Genres of Tajik Folklore) by V. Asrori; *Folklori tojik* (Tajik Folklore) by S. Chalishev (1994); and *Afsona va zhanrhoi digari nasri shifohi* (Folktales and Other Oral Prose Genres) by R. Rahmoni (Rahmonov, 1999). Since 1993, the folklore journal *Mardomgiyah* has been published, focusing on theoretical articles mainly on Tajik folklore and examples of verbal texts.

Tajik folklore occurs in a variety of verbal genres and forms: *ruboi* (quatrain), *dubayti* (double distich), *surud* (folksong), *bayt* (distich), *zarbulmasal* (proverb), *maqol* (saying), *shugun* (omen), *ta'biri khob* (dream interpretation), *chiston* (riddle), *qasam* (oath), *duo* (spelling), *maslihat* (advice), *latifa* (anecdote), *afsun* (charm), *naql* (oral story), *rivoyat* (short legend), *qissa* (legend), and *afsona* (folktale)—to name several of them.

PROVERBS AND RIDDLES

The proverb is called *zarbulmasal*, though another oral form, *maqol* (saying), has many similar features. The Institute of Language and Literature includes 20,160 texts of proverbs and sayings in its folklore **archive**. The themes of Tajik proverbs are rich and colorful, and they are used in different contexts of everyday Tajik life. Some examples are "A man who does not work looks like a fruitless tree"; "A wise enemy is better than a foolish friend"; "I slammed the door, and the wall has broken"; and "Know much and speak little."

The word *chiston* (riddle) is comprised of the words *chist* and *on*, which mean, "What is this?" *Chiston* is one of the widespread genres of Tajik folklore and is used mainly for entertainment. Regional variations in terms for marking riddles among Tajiks include *matali meyoftagi* (Samarkand), *shugi meyoftagi* (Bokhara), *chistun* (Gharm, Darvaz), and *chiston* (Hisar, Kulab). The length of Tajik riddles also varies: some consist of a simple sentence, while others are made up of two to four sentences. For example, "What is a golden nail in the earth?" (Carrot); "It has hands, but no feet. It has stomach but no gut?" (Jug); "Which water in the water? Which pond has two waters? If fair affects, it will be frizzed, but what is its name?" (Egg).

Carved door featuring a horseshoe from the Asht District.

MEDICINE AND RITUALS

Tajik folk beliefs are expressed in the following verbal genres: myths, spells, folktales, legends, dream interpretations, omens, and charms. They also appear in association with celebrations, festivals, seasonal and religious rituals, and traditional medicine.

Traditional medical beliefs comprise a signficant portion of Tajik folk beliefs. Rites of psychological treatment in Tajik traditional medicine such as *alas*, *alavparak*, *nukchamoni*, and *momogi* resemble shamanism. They usually involve fire. Some medical treatments and traditional medical customs are performed with Qur'anic *suras* (quotations), which are considered to be holy texts. Tajik folk medicine relies on well-known physicians from the Eastern tradition such as Avicenna, Zakariyoi-Rozi, and Abdullohi Khorazmshohi. In spite of the development of contemporary medicine, Tajik people continue to treat themselves with plants and traditional pharmaceuticals.

Special actions and rituals allow one to request rain on rainless days. During droughts the ritual for demanding rain called *Ashaglon* will be held in the southern districts of Tajikistan; a similar ritual is called *Suskhotun* in the northern districts. Women in villages select a woman and dress her inside out, put her on a donkey, and have her ride through the village streets. Other women will sing songs devoted to *Ashaglon* and pour water on the head of this woman, a practice that has retained the principles of homoeopathic magic. In some districts people hang a tortoise so that God might hear his prayer and give them rain. Others might hit or kill a frog to bring rain.

There are also some actions for stopping rain when too much has fallen. People might put a mirror to face the sky or women hang trousers in the yard in order to shame the sky into stopping the rain. In some districts people put flat cakes on the ground to achieve the same end.

Many Old Iranian mythological elements survive in folk beliefs. Although Islam prohibits Zoroastrianism and other ancient Iranian religions and considers them as harmful, people still believe in them. They pass orally from generation to generation. In general, Tajik religious beliefs divide into two groups: pre-Islamic beliefs and those connected to Islam. The people give Islamic meaning to the non-Islamic traditional customs and rituals, which allows such beliefs to persist. For instance, women doing a *Bibi mushkilkusho* (literally, "Miracle-worker granny") ritual believe that the soul of *Bibi mushkilkusho* helps them to ease their work. This ritual consists of a "cult of spirits," which the monotheistic religion Islam prohibits. But Tajik women reading the Qur'an and religious books show people that the ritual *Bibi mushkilkusho* has a connection with Islam.

In spite of important changes in the life of the Tajik people, numerous social customs and ceremonies belonging to the traditional culture have been preserved. Specific ethno-genetic features of the Tajiks are displayed in these customs and ceremonies. For example, the wedding ceremony richly manifests such customs and ceremonies.

A man from the Vose' District performs on the *dumbra*. The other musical instruments are the *ghizhak*, *rubob* (another kind of *dumbra*), and *tor*.

MUSIC

Tajik national music encompasses a wide array of genres: epic, labor, customs, lyrical works, and instrumental music. The musical traditions of Tajikistan are both diverse and distinctive. The set of instruments includes stringed instruments (*rubob*, *setor*, *dutor*, *dumbra*, and *tambour*); bowed instruments (such as the *ghizhak*); wind instruments (*nay*, *karnay*, and *surnay*); the dulcimer (*chang*); percussion instruments (*doyra*, *tablak*, *naghora*, and *qayroq* [stone castanets]); and the bell (*zang*).

The musical genre *Falak* (sky) is performed in the southern regions of Tajikistan and Badakhshan province. It divides into two types: *Falaki dashti* (plain *Falak*), which is performed without musical instruments, and *Falaki roghi* or *kuhi* (mountainous *Falak*), which is performed with the *dumbra* or *ghizhak*. *Falak* is a petition to

God. People complain to God, addressing the sky because of the difficulty of life and the harshness of rulers and kings. They ask God for help. *Falak* is performed at the time of farming, wheat mowing, harvesting, and feeding the goats. Now *Falak* is sung at the weddings and other celebrations. The texts of Falak mainly consist of the *ruboi* (a quatrain).

FOLKSONGS AND DANCE

Surud (folksong) is derived from the Persian verb *surudan*—that is, "to sing." Folksongs are referred to in various regions of Tajikistan by different terms: *bayt*, *ghazal*, *mukhammas*, *naghma*, *ashula*, *hofizi*, *qushuq*, *kuchaboghi*, and *she'r*, for example. Tajik folklorists have divided Tajik folksongs into six types: historical, ritual, lyrical, comic, sad, and children's folksongs.

Ritual folksongs are connected with seasonal rituals as well as rites that are performed during weddings and circumcision events. For example, during harvest time farmers sing their popular songs *Man dogh* and *Maydayo*. According to the researcher F. Zehnieva, eight types of songs are performed during wedding ceremonies, most of them accompanied with such musical instruments as *doira* or *daf*, *surnai*, *tor*, *rubob*, and *dumbra*.

In the Mountainous Autonomous Badakhshan Province, funeral folksongs called *maddo* (from the Arabic word *maddah*—"praising") are performed with musical instruments such as *rubabi pomiri*, *tablak*, and *ghizhak* for three days after a burial. The texts of *maddo* include songs eulogizing Allah, the prophet Mohammad, his son-in-law Ali, Shah Nasir (the eleventh-century Tajik poet and philosopher and the founder of Ismailism), and the imams of Ismailism. Other kinds of Tajik folk music include *mavrigikhoni*, sung in the northern districts, and *Shashmaqom* (six makams), associated with classical music traditions. Many folksongs are performed with dancing.

Different folk dances throughout Tajikistan have their own names and requisite attire. Among these dances *raqsi kulobi* (kulabian dance), *raqsi ostin* (sleeve dance), *raqsi zang* (dance with bell), *kordbozi* (dance with knife), *dosbozi* (dance with sickle), *raqsi ravon* (flowing dance), *raqsi shikam* (stomach dance), *aspakbozi* (horse dance), *qayroqbozi* (dance with stones), *raqsi tabaq* (dance with plate), and *raqsi mor* (snake dance). Some mourning dances performed by women at funerals are unique to the Rushan district of the Badakhshan region and differ completely from funeral dances performed elsewhere in Tajikistan. They are called *poyamal*, which means "foot action."

DRAMA

Tajik traditional drama was widespread until the 1920s and 1930s. Traditional dramas were performed mainly in the bazaars, during festivals such as *Navruz*, and at weddings and circumcisions. Tajik traditional drama occurs in the following forms: pantomime theater, doll's theater, *dorboz* (circus theater), comic dances, ritual-cult dances, dances with things, acrobatic dances, *badeha* (duets, in which a song is performed with dances by a man and woman), and folk comedy. Traditional drama has two basic functions. First, it makes people happy through comedy and comic dances so they will forget the problems of life such as the harshness of their rulers. Second, comic actors are able to critique existing social problems through their portrayal of public figures such as local officials and mullahs. For instance, they criticized the mayor in the drama called *Ra'is* (Mayor), and in *Khirsbozi* (Bearhunting) they criticized the judge. Other dramas critized unskilled hairdressers (*Sartarosh* [Hairdresser]) and inept dentists (*Dardi dandon* [Tooth Pain]). Tajik traditional drama was popular until the 1970s, but cinema and professional theater have taken its place. Nowadays some parts of traditional drama are observed in the mountainous districts and villages.

SPORTS AND GAMES

Sports and games, many of which have folkloric and theatrical elements, figure prominently in Tajik life. They usually are placed at the New Year festival and wedding celebrations. Many sport competitions (wrestling, grass hockey, goat snatching, and racing) connected with *Navruz* symbolize the struggle of dying and reviving powers of nature.

Gushtin (wrestling) usually is held during *Navruz*, wedding ceremonies, and *khatnasur* (circumcision) rituals. A powerful *pahlavon* (wrestler) sits in front of the spectators. His behavior means that he has challenged his opponent-wrestler. Another *pahlavon* sits next to him. Wrestling judges declare prizes for winners, old men pray for them, and the wrestling starts. The winner who receives the prize sits down again and challenges another opponent.

Buzkashi (Goat-snatching) is a sports competition that competitors play on horseback. Lasting from two to seven days, *buzkashi* occur at *Navruz* or *khatnasur* ceremonies. The number of *chovandoz* (player-riders) usually ranges from thirty to two hundred. In some competitions even more compete. One of the organizers will throw a goat carcass in the center of playing area. Players try to catch the goat carcass and take it to a certain place. Others try to hinder him and take the object from his hands. The winners will be rewarded with *joma* (a dressing-gown), carpet, televisions, sheep, even cows, horses, cars, and other presents.

Poygah (the race) often takes place in the villages of Garm, Kulab, and Ayni on the last day of wedding and circumcision celebrations. Forty to fifty young men race one to two kilometers. The winner is he who arrives first at the *poygahjo* (finish). Winners are rewarded with presents such as a *ruymol* (kerchief) or a *kurta* (shirt).

ARTS AND CRAFTS

Of all genres of Tajik folk craft, ceramics are the most popular. This is quite appropriate, given that ceramics making is an ancient folk art. The people of Tajikistan, particularly villagers, widely use ceramic vessels of local production. Plates, *kosas* (bowls), *pialas* (tea-bowls), and pitchers can be found in every peasant home. A universal feature of ceramic decor in almost all regions of Tajikistan is its ornamentation using glaze painting with mineral dyes. Tajik ceramics work is reflected in the genre of small plastic souvenirs: tiny pitchers, exact replicas of large vessels, and figures to please a variety of tastes. Ceramic figures may vividly illustrate Tajik character traits by depicting folk types and scenes from everyday life. The traditional forms of ancient folk ceramics have become part of the modern folk decorative art of Tajikistan. Tajik ceramists have been able to find the right combination of the modern with the traditional.

CLOTHING STYLES

Many common features characterize the traditional costumes of the peoples inhabiting Central Asia. Shoulder garments are mostly tunic-shaped. Belts, headgear, footwear, and the type of fabrics and ornaments are also of similar shapes and styles. Characteristic of the traditional costume of the early twentieth century was the similarity of the clothes of the nobility and the common people. They all wore shirts, dresses, robes, headgear, and footwear of the same type. Social differences were expressed in the richness of the fabrics and multiplicity of garments and ornaments that the people wore. Festive or ritual clothes differed from everyday ones in the quality of the fabrics, trimmings, and the completeness of the ensemble. The inhabitants of *kishlaks* (villages), particularly in the mountainous regions, have retained their folk dress.

The female *kurtai zanona* consists of long, white, or colored dresses of cotton or silk and wide trousers (*poyjoma*) tied at the ankles. The types of women's ensembles clearly reveal a difference between girls' and women's dresses. The girls wear dresses with a horizontally cut neckline, while women have a vertical neckline on theirs. The color range and the number of ornaments also vary. Women's dresses from Kulab called *kurtai chakan* are completely covered with embroidery, which explains to some extent the absence of metal jewelry. Earrings, bracelets, and chest ornaments constitute obligatory additions to the

Women's *toqi* (skull caps) and shoes, made with golden threads.

women's costume. The chest ornaments—with their multitude of pendants, chains, coins, and rings of metal, precious and semi-precious stones, and coral—sway, flutter, and flicker when a woman walks.

Specific ethnic features of individual groups are expressed most vividly in headgear. Many Tajiks wear a *toqi* (skull-cap). This was once a cap made from a rectangular piece of cloth with a single seam, slightly gathered in the upper part. Then the small top was transformed into a crown and became more complicated. The skull-cap acquired a more solid form when it became wadded and quilted. *Ruymol* (headscarf) are more often part of a woman's headgear, though men also make use of small kerchiefs, which are folded diagonally and wound turban-like around a skull-cap.

Despite a variety of local features, Tajik dress has a lot in common. Tajiks have retained plenty of archaic elements typical of the pre-class formations. Some of them have preserved certain peculiarities, though others have completely changed. Most clothing elements are indicative of the sex and age of the person wearing them.

FESTIVALS AND CELEBRATIONS

The wedding ceremony, *nikoh*, is a tradition in itself, though it retains a religious character. Weddings, which included a number of celebrations connected with marriage of the son or the daughter, contained the whole system of national customs and

The fire ritual during a wedding ceremony in the Asht District.

ceremonies. *Khostgori* (matchmaking), *fotiha* (engagement), *parchaburon* (preparation of clothes for the bride), and *rubinon* (bride-show) are parts of the wedding process. One important moment is the *sartaroshon* (haircutting of the bridegroom). This ceremony is accompanied by such entertainment as dances, songs, and strewing coins and sweets upon the bridegroom. In Kulab, moreover, the songs are of comic coloring. Not only the bridegroom but the barber as well becomes the subject of jokes and amusements. This ceremony has continued up to present. Another wedding feature is greeting the bride and bridegroom. The bride wears a beautiful dress with numerous adornments, among which are amulets protecting her from evil forces such as the evil eye. Similar measures are carried out for the bridegroom.

The processes of childbirth and childrearing are also accompanied by various, chiefly magical customs and ceremonies. One of these is circumcision. The custom is preceded by a small feast with entertainment such as *gushtingiri* (wrestling), *buzkashi* (goat-snatching), and *poigah* (racing). Although this ritual is considered part of Islam, its origins lie in ancient times.

The custom to enter into a sworn *juragi* (brotherhood) between children of the same sex helped to establish links between neighbors and non-kin families. According to this custom, those entering such a brotherhood would be equal to a blood relation and in some cases valued more than a brother or an uncle. This traditional custom of the Tajiks was one of the social and family phenomena rooted in the remote past. It not only strengthened friendships among members of the family but it also drew together people of different ethnic groups living in the neighborhood.

The holiday of *Navruz* is ancient and widespread in Tajikistan. The word itself literally means "new day" in Persian, and the festival marks the beginning of the solar year and new year on the Iranian calendar as well as the calendars of several other nationalities. *Navruz* traditionally celebrates the awakening of nature and the triumph of good over the oppressive darkness of winter. It is a time to celebrate life when it begins or is renewed on earth. The new year is marked at the instant the sun leaves the astrological sign of Pisces and enters that of Aries. This renewal of nature is the essence of the millennia-old tradition. Originally held as a spring festival, it is believed to have been first acknowledged and named "Navruz" by the mythical Persian emperor Jamshid. Others credit the Achamenian dynasty with the *Navruz* festival. Fairs, concerts, and attractions are everywhere. The solemn approach of the holiday is announced by *karnai* and *surnai*, inviting all to cheerful fun. A traditional dish during this celebration is *sumanak/sumalak*, which the women prepare from germinated grains of wheat. Before dawn, when the dish is ready, seven specially selected stones are thrown into the pot. According to popular belief, they bring health, happiness, riches, and good luck.

Another tradition is the Seven Symbols, a table upon which is placed objects each representing a wish or theme. The names of these seven objects begin with the Farsi letter "S." The table is usually set a couple of weeks before *Navruz* in much the same way families of some Christian cultures erect a Christmas tree. The seven items on the table—*sumanak* (germinated grains of wheat), *sir* (garlic), *sipand* (a kind of plant: *Peganum harmala*), *sirko* (vinegar), *sanjid* (a kind of fruit: *Elaegnus*), *seb* (apple), and *sabzi* (carrot)—represent truth, justice, good thoughts, words, and deeds, prosperity, virtue, and immortality. These are what Zoroaster offered to his deity, Ahura Mazda, on seven trays.

Important Muslim holy days, scheduled according to the lunar calendar, include Ramadan, the month of sunrise-to-sunset fasting; *Eidi Fitr*, the celebrations marking the end of Ramadan; and Kurbon, *Eidi Kurbon*, the feast of sacrifice, when those who can afford to slaughter an animal—usually a sheep, goat, or cow—share it with relatives, neighbors, and the poor.

CHALLENGES OF THE MODERN WORLD

Tajikistan has encountered the influences of **globalization** and **modernization**. These influences are seen in three forms. First, many oral texts—but also some entire genres—no longer have a place in everyday life. For example, in recent decades the epic musical genre *Gurughli* is rarely performed; only a few *Gurughli* performers remain. Second, as a result of globalization some traditions from other countries have made their way into Tajik folklore such as *Foli Hofiz* (divination with Hafiz poems), which passed from Iran; divination with playing cards and divination from palm lines has come from European countries through Russia. At present some new beliefs have appeared among young people. These beliefs are connected with new objects, but they have their roots in simple magic principles. For example, a superstition emerging among the young holds that catching sight of double numbers (22 or 55, for example) means an imminent encounter with a good friend; this omen is known as *vstrecha-udacha*. These words come from Russian, meaning "successful encounter" and demonstrate that young people are creating new "modern" beliefs. Third, people have created new poems and folksongs with new images and subjects. New riddles about modern technologies such as television, telephones, electrical equipment, cars, and airplanes have appeared. Many changes are seen in the content of rituals, wedding ceremonies, and customs depending on new technologies and the changes of lifestyle. Tajik folklorists and ethnographers try to record all of these changes and research them.

BIBLIOGRAPHY

Ahmadov, R. 1978. *Navruzi olamafruz*. Dushanbe: Irfon.

Amonov, R. 1968. *Lirikai khalqi tojik*. Dushanbe: Donish.

———. 1987. *Ruboiyoti khalqi va ramzhoi badei*. Dushanbe: Donish.

Asrori, V. 1990. *Zhanrhoi khurdi folklori tojik*. Dushanbe: Ma'orif.

Asrori, V., and R. Amonov. 1980. *Ejodiyoti dahanakii khalqi tojik*. Dushanbe: Ma'orif.

Braginskiy, I. 1956. *Iz istorii tadzhikskoy narodnoy poezii: Elementi narodno-poeticheskogo tvorchestva v pamyatnikakh drevney i srednevekoviy pismennosti*. Moscow: Izd-vo AN SSSR.

Mills, M., and R. Rahmoni. 2000. *Conversation with Daulat Khalav: Oral Narratives from Tajikistan*. Moscow: Humanitary.

Nurdzhanov, N. 2002. *Tradicinoniy teatr tadzhikov*. Dushanbe: Mir puteshestviy.

Nurjonov, N. 1985. *Dramai khalqii tojik*. Dushanbe: Donish.

Obidov, D. 1978. *Afsonahoi hajvii maishii tojiki*. Dushanbe: Donish.

Qodirov, R. 1963. *Folklori marosimii torevolicionii tojikoni vodii Qashqadaryo*. Dushanbe: Nashriyoti AF RSS Tojikiston.

Rahimov, D. 1998–2002. Bovarhoi ibtidoi dar shugunhoi tojiki. *Mardomgiyah* 1–2: 33–41.

Rahmoni, R. 1997. *Qissaho, rivoyatho va duohoi Bukhoro dar sabti Ravshan Rahmoni*. Dushanbe: Royzanii farhangi Jumhurii islomii Eron dar Tojikiston.

———. 1998. *Skazki i skazochniki persoyazinikh narodov*. Moscow: Derevo zhisni.

———. 1999. *Afsona va zhanrhoi digari nasri shifohi*. Dushanbe: Amri ilm.

———. 2000. *Tajik Women as Folktale Tellers: Tales in Tradition*. Moscow: Gumanitariy.

———. 2001. *Ta'rikhi girdovari, nashr va pazhuhishi afsonahoi mardumi forsizabon*. Dushanbe: Sino.

Shakarmamadov, N. 1975. *Nazmi khalqii Badakhshon*. Dushanbe: Donish.

Shermuhammadov, B. 1973. *Nazmi khalqii bachagonai tojik*. Dushanbe: Donish.

Sufiev, A. 1972. *Chistonhoi khalqii tojiki*. Dushanbe: Donish.

Tilavov, B. 1967. *Poetika tadzhikskikh narodnikh poslovic i pogovorok*. Dushanbe: Donish.

Zehni, T. 1927. Adabiyoti khalq. *Rahbari donish* 4–5: 29–35.

———. 1928. Adabiyoti khalq. *Rahbari donish* 4–5: 27–34.

———. 1929. Adabiyoti khalq. *Rahbari donish* 2–3: 33–41.

Zehnieva, F. 1982. *Surudhoi marosimi tuyi tojikon*. Dushanbe: Irfon.

Ravshan Rahmonov and Dilshod Rakhimov

UYGHUR

GEOGRAPHY AND HISTORY

The Uyghurs of Central Eurasia have a diverse and complex history that is reflected in their many genres and styles of folk music, poetry, dance, arts, and tales. They live in the ecologically diverse heartland of Asia, where peoples and cultures have interacted for millennia. Nomadic herders such as **Mongols** from the north and northeast, Hindus and Buddhists from **India** and Tibet to the south, Han Chinese from the east, and Tokharians, Sogdians, and Iranians from the west have met, traded, and settled in this region. Innumerable people traveled further as traders, migrants, and pilgrims along the so-called "Silk Road," a network of trade routes along which people carried religions, ideas, technologies, and goods from oasis to oasis and among the mountain and steppe regions throughout Central Eurasia.

At present there are roughly 8 million Uyghurs in **China**, living in oasis regions around the Tarim Basin of the Xinjiang Uyghur Autonomous Region, particularly the cities of Kashgar (Kashi), Yarkand (Shache), Khotan (Hetian), Aqsu, Kucha, Korla, and Turpan and Qumul further to the east, and the villages around these cities. North of the Tangri Tagh (Tian Shan) mountain range, Uyghurs live in Ürümchi (Wulumuqi) and Ghulja (Yining) and the surrounding agricultural regions. Some Uyghurs have moved to the areas further north around the Junggar Basin in north Xinjiang to towns in the Tarbaghatay and Altay regions, and roughly 400,000 Uyghurs live in Kazakhstan, Kyrgyzstan, Uzbekistan, and other parts of the Middle East.

The modern Uyghurs descend from horse-riding Turk and Uyghur nomads who expanded from the mountain and grassland of the Orkhon river region in present-day

Mongolia to establish a series of empires (Qaghanates) that dominated the lands north of China and most of Central Asia as far as the Caspian Sea between 551 until 840 C.E. As these empires expanded, many of these nomads began to settle in the oasis towns of Central Eurasia, including the Tarim Basin and Tängri Tagh regions. After the Turk Qaghanate fell to the Uyghurs in 745 and the Uyghur Qaghanate fell to the Qirghiz in 840, these two Turkic peoples founded a number of kingdoms throughout the regions now known as Eastern and Western Turkistan.

In China, the term Eastern Turkistan has been officially forbidden, as has the nationalist name Uyghuristan now used by some Uyghur political activists. The only permissible political term, *Xinjiang*, is a Chinese term that means "new territory." The history of the Uyghur name is also complex, because when the Turks of the western Tarim converted to Islam, the term Uyghur was used to refer to the Buddhist Turks to the east. When the Buddhist Uyghurs finally converted between the fourteenth and sixteenth centuries, the Uyghur name was no longer used until it was revived in 1921 in the Soviet Union. For the purposes of this entry, Uyghur will be used to refer to the settled Turks of the oases in modern-day Xinjiang and their ancestors, while Turkic will be used to refer to the general cultural and linguistic group to which they belong.

The first native record of Turkic folklore in Eurasia can be found in the Orkhon River region in Mongolia where a stone inscription from 716 C.E. records a number of examples of proverbial wisdom as used by Tonyuquq, an advisor to the Turk Qaghan. In one proverb he argues for an early attack on their enemies the Chinese, Qitan, and Oghuz before they unite: "Thin things are easily pierced; small things are easily broken. / If the thin becomes thick it is hard to pierce, if the small becomes big it is difficult to break." Tonyuquq successfully leads the Turks to victory over their enemies and expands the Turk Qaghanate, but a few decades later the vast empire of the Turk Qaghan was conquered by the Uyghurs, who ruled it from 745 until 840. The Uyghur nobility took up the Manichean religion in 762 while still in the Orkhon river area, but after taking refuge from the Qirghiz invaders in 840 and moving into the northeastern Tarim region, they began to adopt Buddhism. Upon settling in the oasis towns, Uyghurs adopted local cultural practices such as agricultural techniques and a new alphabet based on the Sogdian script. Records of folklore from this early period of Uyghur city life include a few examples of proverbs and a book of poetic recitations used for divination, but it is the many religious and civil documents that offer more insight into the complex cultural mixing in these oases.

The Turks of the southwestern Tarim converted to Islam around 950 C.E. and began to interact culturally with Persians and Arabs. In 1077 C.E., the scholar Mahmud Kāshgharī finished his monumental dictionary of Turkic dialects and folklore in an effort to show that Turkic culture was comparable to that of the Arabs and Persians. Because the Turkic literary tradition was very limited, he relied on oral tradition for his examples of epic and lyric poems, proverbs, recipes, crafts, and legends. A number of the roughly three hundred proverbs Kāshgharī includes can also be found in manuscript Uyghur proverb collections from the century before, and one even appears in a Chinese history of the An Lushan rebellion of 752. Kāshgharī also reports legends that describe both Alexander the Great and the Turanian prince Afrāsiyāb, a figure in the Persian *Shāhnāma*, as founders of Turkic culture. Kāshgharī praises the culture and speech of nomadic Turks and rejects the neologisms and mixed dialects of the towns. He values the tough independence of rural Turks and decries urban moral decay. When he describes daily culture, Kāshgharī seems to believe the most important activities are foodways. He describes the preparation of twenty different foods, while providing less vivid discussions of other aspects of daily life, including animal husbandry, medicines, and crafts.

Because they voluntarily joined the Mongols under Chingiz Khan in 1209, the Uyghurs gained authority in the Mongol Empire and its successor states. Uyghurs became the literate officials under the Mongols, and the Mongol vertical script was adapted from the Uyghur alphabet. Among the limited records of Uyghur folklore, one important work is the *Oghuz Nama*, an epic about Oghuz Khan, a culture hero who could speak at birth and quickly gave up his mother's milk in favor of eating meat. Following a gray wolf, Oghuz Khan led the Uyghurs and other Turkic tribes to conquer the Rus, Byzantines, Syrians, Indians, and Tangut among others. His two wives bore six sons, thus establishing the tribal divisions of the Oghuz Turks, among whom are the modern day Turkmen and Anatolian Turks. The *Oghuz Nama* was probably not a vital tradition within Uyghur society, but was perhaps recorded from more nomadic Oghuz Turks by Uyghur scribes during the thirteenth or fourteenth century. In any case, it has since faded from Uyghur oral tradition.

RELIGIOUS BELIEFS

Present Uyghur religious practices vary widely. In the more traditional oasis cities such as Khotan and Kashgar, mosque attendance is considerably higher than in the more cosmopolitan cities of Ghulja and Ürümchi. In addition to conventional Islamic practices, Sufi sects such as the Naqshbandiyya and Kubraviyya also have many followers in Xinjiang. Sufism has influenced many popular beliefs and practices such as festive visits to saints' tombs. These *mazar säyläsi* take place during spring, early summer, and religious holidays and involve music and dancing. Many of the performers are *ashiqs* or dervishes, though such Sufi mendicants are less public now because the present government views them as feudal survivals. These celebrations have long been opportunities for singers and performers from different regions to compare traditions and learn from each other.

The modern Xinjiang government uses some traditional symbols of religious belief to promote Uyghur pride in their cultural history. Tombs and monuments have been built to honor the eleventh-century authors Mahmud Kāshgharī and Yūsuf Khāss Hājib along with the sixteenth-century culture **heroes** Abdurashid Khan and Amannisa Khan. Such figures become the sacred cultural founders of the modern state and help authenticate its claim to a fixed territory and continuous history. The more popular tombs of Muslim saints and leaders such as Satoq Bughra Khan, who converted Turks around 950, and Appaq Khoja, who ruled Kashgar in the seventeenth century, are also officially recognized as monuments to Uyghur cultural and political history rather than to religious history.

Just as Islam and Sufism in particular have become suspect in modern China, the widespread Uyghur use of shamanistic healing practices was marginalized within official Islamic dogma and is now considered a primitive survival. On the other hand, the extensive tradition of Uyghur traditional herbal medicine has become an important part of medical education in Xinjiang, because it is a source of ethnic pride. Emulating the national pride and institutional training in Han, Uyghurs have also formalized their traditional medicine as a valuable indigenous science. However, there has been little study of this formalized tradition outside of China.

SHAMANISM

Of more interest to Western scholars have been the *perikhun* or *bakhshi*, usually described as shamanistic healers, who use diverse means to control spirits and heal patients. In 1892 in Qumul, N. F. Katanov collected the incantations a *perikhun* would use to compel Muslim, *kaffir* (literally, "infidel"), Christian, and Jewish *peri* or spirits to leave a patient: for *kaffir* spirits, the incantation begins,

> I conjure you, oh devils, oh *peris*,
> In this body is no place for you!
> With musk and saffron I have made smoke, oh *peris*!
> With the word of the Lord I have barred you from the mosque!

Upon reciting the incantation, the *perikhun* touches each afflicted part of the body with a knife and says, "Go on, get out!"

More detailed descriptions of healing methods currently used by Uyghur healers can be found in Ildikó Bellér-Hann's detailed description of two Uyghur women in Kazakhstan (see **Kazakh**): both used divination to diagnose and a number of religious symbols and prayers as well as bodily manipulation, knives, and smoke to eliminate negative effects of spirits.

MYTHS AND LEGENDS

The most famous compilation of Islamic legends in Turkic is the *Qisas al-Anbiyā'* completed by Nāsiruddīn Rabghūzī in 1310 in Khwarazm in Western Turkistan. His work was based on both written and oral narrative traditions. It has been very widely copied and distributed throughout Central Asia and used as the source for many oral narratives about Islamic traditional history and the prophets. Dozens of old manuscripts of this work exist in Xinjiang, and oral narratives based on the text have been collected from Uyghurs throughout the region. The longer narratives in this work describe Adam, Nūh (Noah), Ibrāhīm (Abraham), Ya'qūb and Yūsuf (Jacob and Joseph), Ayyūb (Job), Mūsā (Moses), Dāwūt (David), Yūnus (Jonah), Sulaymān (Solomon), 'Īsa (Jesus), Dhū'l-Qarnayn (Alexander), and Muhammad and his family, but there are many shorter narratives about other prophets, saints, and legends. Many of these narratives include oral tales that have no known written source, which suggests that like Kāshgharī before him, Rabghūzī recognized the value of oral sources. In addition to this early and widely copied collection, manuscript knowledge of Islam also circulated in both Arabic and Persian as well as in additional translations into Turkic and came to play important roles in local religious culture as in other parts of the Islamic world. For example, an extensive manuscript legend of the *Ashābu'l-Kahf* (The companions of the cave), considerably more detailed than the version found in Rabghūzī's collection, was available at a *mazar* (Muslim tomb) near Turfan in the nineteenth century to explain the *mazar's* significance to pilgrims. A ruined city nearby was identified with the city Afsūs, or Ephesus, described in this widely disseminated Christian and Islamic legend.

Islamic knowledge also circulates in the form of written romantic *dastans* that alternate prose narrative and poetic dialogue. Folk performers memorize these written texts, especially the poetic songs. Importing these texts from Western Turkistan and Turkey increased in the nineteenth century when printing helped disseminate this genre. The best known of the *dastans* include *Yusuf-Zulaykha*, telling the story of Joseph's unjust persecution by Potiphar's wife, and *Gherip-Sänäm*, describing the orphan Gherip who is forbidden to marry Sänäm, the daughter of Shah Abbas I (1587–1629), and banished to Baghdad, where he is tested with riddles by the Sufi Shaykh Junayd:

> JUNAYD: Who is it that went up into the sky and did not fall back?
> Who is it that entered Heaven and did not leave?
> Who is it that was born and never died?
> My son, if you are an *ashiq*, give me an answer.
>
> GHERIP: The prophet Aysa [Jesus] went up into the sky.
> The prophet Idris went into Heaven.
> The prophet Khizr was born and never died.
> If you are my master, that is my answer.

After long separation and exile, Gherip and Sänäm eventually succeed in getting the Shah's approval for their marriage. Identifying Gherip as an *ashiq* or love-mad wanderer suggests that this story reflects the Sufi quest for union with an unreachable beloved, God. In the more secular atmosphere of modern Xinjiang, the Gherip-Sänäm story has become a favorite story of worldly love and is widely performed on stage as a musical drama.

FOLKTALES AND FOLKSONGS

The most important genres of Uyghur oral folklore recorded over the past two hundred years have been folktales known as *čöčäk*, folksongs with quatrain stanzas known as *qoshaq*, proverbs (*maqal-tämsil*), and humorous anecdotes (*lätipä*). The proverbs, folktales, and most *qoshaq* circulated purely orally, while humorous narratives include both local oral narratives about and by historical figures as well as the international Nasreddin Effendi (*Näsirdin Äpändi*) stories that were disseminated both orally and in writing. Many singers during this period learned some of their *qoshaq*, *ghazal* (a sonnet-like written form), and *dastan* poetry from written sources. In addition to these genres, Uyghur folklore includes riddles (*tepishmaq*) and some less common narratives described as *rivayät* (legend), *hikayät* (anecdote, story), *äpsanä* (myth or legend), or *qissä* (longer tale) that are not felt to fit the more specific *čöčäk* genre.

Important local *dastan* and *qoshaq* genres developed in the nineteenth century celebrating rebels against the **Manchu** Chinese, who conquered Xinjiang in 1758. One of the most famous heroes of these conflicts is Nozugum, a woman who became an outlaw during the Jahangir uprising in 1826. These first-person songs create the image of a persecuted young woman forced to flee her homeland and live in the wilderness:

> Bare-legged I have crossed streams and drunk the waters of the mountains.
> Unable to stand the Qalmaq oppression, I left my loved ones. . . .
> For six months I have slept in the fields and baked bread with straw.
> Weak and delicate in the wilderness, Father, where should I run?

Other songs sing of the warrior Sadir Palwan, who always defeated Manchu soldiers, and of the heroines Gulämkhan and Mayimkhan as well as Jahangir and Yaqub Beg themselves. These songs exist in multiple versions, and they are often performed as *dastan* narratives with the events between the songs described in prose, while the songs tend to reveal conditions and evoke emotions. The songs themselves are also performed alone as *qoshaq* without prose narratives.

The Muslim romantic *dastans* mentioned above constitute a large, diverse genre in Uyghur tradition, but have not been studied adequately because they are both oral and written, composed by known authors and anonymous. Moreover, some are indigenous compositions, while many come from Western Turkistan. Many *dastans* are recreations or reworkings of well-known plots. In the past twenty-five years, many Uyghur *dastans* have been published in Xinjiang, but a broader perspective is necessary to understand them historically, ethnographically, and comparatively. Because there has been little ethnographic and historical study, it is difficult to explain the indigenous perspectives on romantic *dastans* and how they became distinct from the heroic *dastans* more common in nomadic Turkic tradition.

Trickster figures are important heroes in Uyghur traditional culture and can be compared to some Sufi religious figures, especially the poet-singer and *qalandar* Baba Rahim Mashrab (*Mäshräp* in Uyghur). Although originally from the Ferghana region, according to Mashrab's legendary life-story he spent seven years in Kashgar as a disciple of Appaq Khoja, and he remains a popular poet in Xinjiang. While Mashrab violates convention to impart spiritual lessons, other trickster figures, real and imagined, both amuse and provide social criticism. The folklore genre of humorous tales has been well-documented since the nineteenth-century. The international figure of Nasreddin Effendi, known throughout the Turkic-speaking world under the name of Mulla or Hoca Nasreddin and Nasreddin Khoja, has been adopted into Uyghur tradition. Uyghur versions of these Näsirdin Äpändi tales use many of the same plots and humor that appear in Turkish variants, though some stories have been adapted to more recent Uyghur cultural and historical contexts such as Chinese rule. More localized and realistic events are found in stories about the jokers Mulla Zäydin and Säläy Chaqqan from the nineteenth century and Hisamidin in the twentieth century. Stories about these figures are often told at Uyghur social gatherings and have subsequently been published in many popular magazines and books. These stories reinforce a Uyghur self-image of irreverence for those in positions of power and valorize the use of witty retorts and disdain for protocol in public settings. The "hard joking" and willingness of Uyghurs to challenge social conventions have earned an ambivalent respect from Han Chinese, who tend to be more deferential towards authority. Although political dissent is strongly discouraged in Xinjiang, Uyghurs often communicate joking criticisms with less fear of repercussions. The resulting joker image also leads to ethnic stereotypes about Uyghurs because Näsirdin Äpändi stories are so widely translated into Chinese.

Joking monologues and dialogues have long been important performance forms in Uyghur, and many audio cassettes circulate of the performances of these *qiziqchi* or *chakhchaqchi*. Such dialogues appear in the *läpär* dance form as well. The importance of jokes as events can be seen in the value placed on retelling them. Writing in 1908, the prolific Uyghur historian Mulla Musa Sayrami described people's frustration with Yaqub Beg's rule (1864–1877):

> [Near Kashgar] when someone was sowing seed in a field, another person came and asked, "Hey brother! What are you planting here?" The first replied, "What am I planting? I am planting Chinese." The second person smiled and was amused. In less than six months, on that very land Chinese troops camped.

Sayrami explains that it was Yaqub Beg's rigid enforcement of Islamic law and heavy taxation that made resentful Uyghurs nostalgic for Chinese rule. He likens the situation to a story of three ascetics traveling together in the desert when they find some old bones. They are curious to know what animal the bones were from, so the first says a prayer and the bones join together. The second prays and the bones gain meat, tendons, and veins. The third prays and the bones spring to life as a hungry lion that eats the ascetics. "Now the Chinese who were sought and found have become like this hungry lion that came to life," he notes.

MUSIC

The diverse genres of Uyghur folk music have a long history. The most popular instruments are lutes: the *dutar*, a long lute with two silk strings strummed to accompany singing; the *rawap*, a three-to-six-string short lute with wire or gut strings and a small snake-skin covered resonator, played with or without singing; the *satar*, a long bowed lute often used for more meditative songs; and the *tämbur*, a long plucked lute with wire strings, usually played with a plectrum to accompany singing. In addition, the oboe-like *surnay* and *naghra* kettle-drums, the *qalun* dulcimer, and *dap* frame drum are widely used. There are many popular songs and styles of singing, and the traditional folksongs remain important in modern Uyghur recorded music as well. Most Uyghurs enjoy dancing, and many sing or play an instrument. The most popular folksongs are love songs and lyric songs about home and family, followed by longer *qoshaq* narrative songs. Each region of Xinjiang has characteristic songs that are widely recognized as belonging to that region.

Musicians playing atop the mosque during festivities at the end of Ramadan, Kashgar, China. (© David Butow/CORBIS SABA)

One of the most important elements of modern Uyghur music is the song suite known as the Twelve Muqams. Although the *muqam* tradition has been valued for at least five hundred years, it has now become a stage genre performed by conservatory-trained ensembles that has been made the centerpiece of Uyghur cultural traditions. Each of the Twelve Muqams requires more than an hour to perform and includes solo songs, ensemble songs, and song and dance pieces. Each *muqam* is a sequence of twenty to thirty songs that follows a rhythmic progression that is similar for all the *muqams*. Some of the tunes are also similar from one *muqam* to another, but most of the song texts differ. The stability of rhythms and variation of songs reflect the oral tradition in which the *muqams* developed: each master performer would establish his or her own repertoire of song texts and tunes, but the rhythms, performed by an apprentice playing a *kichik dap* (small frame-drum), were more fixed.

The introductory songs of each *muqam* are slower and more meditative with a tempo that increases through the songs known as the *jula*, *sänäm*, and *säliqä*. The middle part of a *muqam* consists of three to five songs from the romantic *dastans* along with instrumental pieces, and the concluding part consists of *mäshräp* dance songs originally performed by Sufi dervishes. Uyghurs now consider the Twelve Muqams to be their national "folk-classical" tradition, and at least in public discussion and performances, the Sufi religious interpretations of the songs are neglected in favor of romantic love. Many novels, dramas, films, and historical accounts describe the *muqams* and their cultural significance as well as the folk heroine Amannisa Khan, who married Abdurashid Khan in the sixteenth-century Yarkand Khanate and started a *muqam* school and tradition.

The present standardized version of the Uyghur Twelve Muqams is based on the tradition of *muqam* performers from the Kashghar and Ili regions, but other regions have local, usually shorter *muqam* traditions. The poetry of the Twelve Muqams includes the *ghazal* poetry of famous Central Asian Turkic poets such as 'Alī Shīr Navā ī and Maulānā Lutfī from the last six hundred years as well as many poems by indigenous Uyghur poets writing in the last three hundred years.

DANCE

Dance has long played an important role in the lives of Central Asian peoples in the oasis towns as well as among the nomads. Dance was a way to show respect to one's elders: in 762 C.E. a young Chinese prince on an embassy to the Uyghur Qaghan was severely punished for refusing to dance for the Qaghan. Whether at celebrations among friends or official visits by dignitaries, dance has remained an important part of political and social events in Uyghur society.

Each Uyghur locale has its own varieties, and some dances are now being revived or reinvented rather than being part of continuous traditions. One common academic classification of Uyghur dances includes six varieties: (1) imitative dances, mostly described in historical sources, that represent the typical actions of animals such as doves, geese, chickens, horses, lions, tigers, or camels; (2) religious dances, usually identified as survivals from when Uyghurs practiced shamanism and fire worship (the latter category includes the fire dance, performed around bonfires at celebrations, and the candle dance, represented in Buddhist cave paintings in Xinjiang, as well as dances performed by healers); (3) the Sänäm dances, the most widespread and popular forms, which include many regional variations on pair and group dancing, usually with sung accompaniment; and (4) the *Sama* dance, which is the slowly accelerating dance used by some Sufis during *zikr* rituals and which has also become a huge public dance around the main mosque in Kashgar during religious festivals to *naghra-surnay* music (the *jula* song of the *muqams* is in this same rhythm). The other dance categories are (5) Shadiyana (or "joyful tune"), another popular dance often performed to *naghra-surnay* music, which mixes 1/4, 2/4, and 3/4 times and is used at many kinds of celebrations and festivals; and (6) a variety of local dances such as the Dolan dance, a fast competitive dance between two partners facing each other found in the Märkit and Maralbeshi regions of Xinjiang. The Nazirkom dance is popular in Turpan. The Sapayi dance is another Sufi dance style, performed while striking one's shoulders with a *sapayi*, an instrument that consists of a wood baton with two iron rings that strike together while swinging. Other dances involve balancing objects, particularly plates, on one's head, or spoons or china saucers gripped between the fingers and played like castanets. Finally, a traditional performance known as the *läpär* involves a witty dialogue interspersed with very fast dancing.

The waltz is a more recent addition to the urban Uyghur dance repertoire and is a feature of some large indoor celebrations such as weddings. While eating and talking men and women usually sit separately, but when a waltz tune begins, the men move rapidly to find a partner. At the end of each tune, the partners split up, and the men then choose other partners. It is generally considered impolite to dance with the same partner repeatedly or for a woman to refuse to dance when asked. Many Uyghurs have also learned other Middle Eastern and European dance styles and perform these both on stage and at informal gatherings.

ARTS, CRAFTS, AND ARCHITECTURE

Uyghur craftspeople (*hunärwän, ustikar*) have considerable skill in weaving textiles and working wood and metal. Folk architecture is also diverse and highly developed. Important ethnic fashions include embroidered caps in a wide variety of designs for both men and women. These sometimes appear in distinctive local styles. In addition to local textiles and traditional styles for clothing, the wide availability of mass-produced synthetic fabrics has led many younger Uyghurs in the cities to take on international styles. Older Uyghurs and those in rural areas still tend to wear the traditional chapan cotton overcoat, and men wear leather slippers indoors and cover them with overshoes when leaving the house.

Ätläs (*iqat*, warp-dyed) silk is a popular fabric for traditional women's dresses and still woven on hand looms in the city of Khotan for local consumption as well as for trade with other oases despite extensive imports of synthetic *iqat* fabric from Uzbekistan (see **Uzbek**). The vivid colors and patterns of Uyghur *ätläs* silk are difficult to convey in photographs.

Also extensively produced in Khotan and some other towns are the knotted carpets known as *giläm*. The carpet designs include symmetrical fruit, floral, and geometric patterns in bright, contrasting colors with red dominating. Two of the most distinctive patterns are the network of branching pomegranates (*anar*) in red on a blue background and the flower vase (*longqa*) design. Uyghur carpets are usually used to cover walls and sitting areas of the floor rather than being walked on. With the rise of investment in carpet production for international markets, many carpet weavers now produce non-traditional designs that conform to foreign tastes, and some weavers are beginning to revive the use natural dyes that were largely given up when seeking brighter colors.

The most famous form of Uyghur metalworking is knifesmithing: knives (*pichaq*) are traditionally worn by men on their side and can be bought in most outdoor markets. They are often used when eating meat, but they also have supernatural uses in healing rituals to ward off spirits. Of widely varying designs, the blade is often engraved or inlaid with copper, the sheath made of metal or leather, and the handle of metal and wood or ornate multi-colored plastic decorations.

Uyghur goldsmithing is a highly developed art of somewhat uncertain history, and many Uyghur women wear intricate gold earrings in a design known as *zirä*, which consists of tiny spheres of gold built up into flower-like patterns. Such jewelry is a traditional form of portable wealth, and women occasionally have their earrings melted down and combined with additional gold to make new larger earrings.

FOOD

The oases around the Tarim basin and Tangri Tagh Mountains have long been rich agricultural areas because of carefully built underground *kariz* irrigation channels. Each oasis is famed for certain fruits, including peaches, pears, apricots, melons, grapes, apples, figs, mulberries, and pomegranates. Chinese have traded with Uyghurs for their fruit for many centuries, especially for melons from Qumul (Hami) and raisins from Turpan.

Uyghurs are justifiably proud of their cuisine, and elaborate food preparation is a central part of hospitality, whether for invited guests or for people who simply drop in. As in many cultures, Uyghurs distinguish foods according to their appropriateness for different social occasions. From the simpler *laghman* made with thick hand-pulled noodles with stir-fried vegetables and mutton and served to impromptu visitors to the *polo* (rice, mutton, carrot, onion, and raisin pilaf) prepared in advance for formal entertaining and large events, the repertoire of dishes is broad with a strongly shared sense of the proper flavors and techniques. Although many Uyghur foods are related to Afghan, Persian, Chinese, and Indian dishes, they have distinctive Uyghur characteristics imparted by spices and vegetables.

Among the many everyday foods cooked at home are *qordaq*, a thick meat-and-vegetable stew; *chüchürä*, a vegetable soup with meat-filled dumplings; *umach*, a porridge with vegetables; and *suyuqash* noodle soup. In the bazaars, the most common foods include *kawap*, skewered mutton dusted with cumin and red pepper; *polo* (rice); *samsa* (meat-filled pastries); and slices of melon in season. Along with rice and wheat noodles, wheat bread is the staple for Uyghurs and is baked in large outdoor *tonur* beehive ovens shared among neighbors. Fuel is burned in the center, and the items to bake are slapped onto the clay walls. The most common breads are the round, flat *nan* and the thicker round *girdä*. *Samsa* and *göshnan* (bread made from dough containing pieces of meat) are also baked in a *tonur*.

Manta are meat and onion filled steamed dumplings often served as a side dish at formal events. For the large groups of guests who come for brief visits during Qurban (the Islamic festival of the sacrifice), the featured food is boiled mutton, but many snack foods are also set out on a table that remains set during the three days of the festival. These snacks include almonds, walnuts, figs, raisins, candy, and baked sweets. The centerpieces include such fried pastries as *quymaq* and *sangza*, which are piled up into large cylindrical columns that grow smaller as people eat them over the course of the festival. A slightly less important period of visiting and sharing special foods accompanies the Rozi festival that ends the Ramadan fast.

CHALLENGES OF THE MODERN WORLD

Uyghur folklore study raises important questions about the relationship of oral culture and the literary traditions of Islam. Despite strong local traditions, many aspects of Uyghur oral narratives, musical culture, dance, and even foodways have come from elsewhere. Some of these are borrowed because they fit better with institutional Islam, but most appear to arise from a longstanding Uyghur appreciation for the foreign and novel in food, music, and religious traditions. On the other hand, native Turkic genres of quatrain poetry and proverbs have remained more stable over long periods, and many folktales show little evidence of the effects of Islamic beliefs. In addition, shamanistic religious practices, especially healing techniques, have became a part of popular Islam. Islamization has not resulted in the diminution of local traditions. Instead it has brought with it cultural traditions of performing arts and oral and written genres that have added richness and diversity to many aspects of Uyghur tradition.

Although Islamization was clearly accompanied by extensive adoption of foreign, largely Persianate, traditions in the fields of literature, music, and dance, further research should consider how popular and elite traditions have interacted and how foreign traditions became so widely incorporated into Uyghur folk culture. Uyghur scholars of Uyghur folk culture often avoid acknowledging foreign influences because they feel it threatens ideas about Uyghur cultural authenticity and native origins. Uyghur scholars are acutely aware that Han Chinese vaunt their supposed long and ethnically distinct history and culture as proof of their civilized essence, and these scholars often promote a similar sense of Uyghur distinctiveness. In addition to using Uyghur traditions as proof of their enduring civilization, many folk traditions are being "modernized" and revived as the basis of Uyghur public dance, music, and drama performances that are presented at political events and broadcast media.

Other important issues in the study of Uyghur folklore include the problematic use of ideas about **cultural evolution** in both Soviet and Chinese publications. This pattern has been perpetuated by Cuiyi Wei and Karl Luckert's recent publication *Uighur Stories from along the Silk Road* (1998) that analyzes each narrative in terms of its links to particular stages of cultural evolution, known by terms such as hunter, domesticator, and universal religion. The relative lack of access to Xinjiang, the difficulty for Uyghur scholars to leave Xinjiang and do research elsewhere, and lack of support for ethnographic research in Xinjiang have meant that much of the research conducted in the past century has not been very detailed and accurate. In some cases, Uyghur researchers have done significant work that has only been published in Uyghur and has been little used by Soviet, Chinese, or Western scholars. *See also* **Turkey.**

BIBLIOGRAPHY

Alieva, M. M. 1969. *Uighur khaliq chochakliri.* Alma-Ata: Zhazushy nashriiati.

———. 1975. *Uigurskaia skazka.* Alma-Ata: Nauka.

———. 1989. *Zhanry uigurskogo fol'klora.* Alma-Ata: Nauka.

Baqi, Tokhti. 1984. *Uyghur tamaqliri.* Shinjang Khälq Näshriyati.

Basilov, Vladimir N. 1992. *Shamanstvo u narodov Srednej Azii i Kazahstana.* Moskva: Nauka.

Bellér-Hann, Ildikó. 2000. *The Written and the Spoken: Literacy and Oral Transmission among the Uyghur.* Berlin: Das Arabische Buch.

———. 2001a. "Making the Oil Fragrant:" Dealings with the Supernatural among the Uighur in Xinjiang. *Asian Ethnicity* 2.1: 9–23.

———. 2001b. Rivalry and Solidarity among Uyghur Healers in Kazakstan. *Inner Asia* 3: 73–98.

Gürsoy-Naskali, Emine, trans. and ed. 1985. *Ashābu'l-Kahf: A Treatise in Eastern Turki*. Helsinki: Suomalais-ugrilainen seura.

Harris, Rachel. 2000. *Uyghur Musicians from Xinjiang: Music from the Oasis Towns of Central Asia* (sound recording). Globestyle CDORBD 098.

———. 2002. Cassettes, Bazaars and Saving the Nation: The Uyghur Music Industry in Xinjiang, China. In *Global Goes Local: Popular Culture in Asia*, edited by T. Craig and R. King. Vancouver: University of British Columbia Press. 265–283.

———. 2004. *Mäjnun: Classical traditions of the Uyghurs* (sound recording). SOASIS 06.

Harris, Rachel, and Rahile Dawut. 2002. Mazar festivals of the Uyghurs: Music, Islam and the Chinese State. *British Journal of Ethnomusicology* 11.1: 101–118.

Jamaldinov, Oktyabr'. 1988. *Uyghur khälq qoshaqliri*. Almuta: Zhazushy.

Jarring, Gunnar. 1946–1951. *Materials to the Knowledge of Eastern Turki: Tales, Poetry, Proverbs, Riddles, Ethnological and Historical Texts from the Southern Parts of Eastern Turkestan*. Lunds universitets årsskrift; N.F., Avd. 1, Bd. 43–47. Lund: C.W.K. Gleerup.

———. 1996a. *The Moen Collection of Eastern Turki (New Uighur) Popular Poetry*. Stockholm: Almqvist and Wiksell International.

———. 1996b. *Return to Kashgar: Central Asian Memoirs in the Present*. Durham: Duke University Press.

Katanov, N. F., and Karl Menges. 1933–1954. *Volkskundliche Texte aus Ost-Türkistan*. 3 volumes. Berlin: Verlag der Akademie der Wissenschaften.

Light, Nathan. 1998. Slippery Paths: The Performance and Canonization of Turkic Literature and Uyghur Muqam Song in Islam and Modernity. Diss. Indiana University.

Malov, S. E. 1954. *Uigurskii iazyk: khamiiskoe narechie*. Moskva: Akademii nauk SSSR.

———. 1956. *Lobnorskii iazyk*. Frunze: Akademi Nauk Kirgizskoi SSR.

———. 1960. *Uigurskie narechjiia sin'tsziana*. Moskva: Vostochnoi literatury.

Mehrulla, Himit, and Lätipä Qorban.1991. *Uyghur ussul sän'iti toghirisida*. Ürümchi: Xinjiang People's Press.

Molla Bilal binni Molla Yusup. 1981. Nuzugum. In *Bulaq: Uyghur kilassik ädibiyati vä eghiz ädibiyati mäjmu'äsi*. Ürümchi: Xinjiang People's Press. 208–225.

Omär, Uchqunjan, ed. 1981. *Uyghur khälq tarikhiy qoshaqliri*. Qäshqär: Qäshqär Uyghur Näshriyati.

Pantusov, N. N. 1890. *Taranchiiskiia piesni*. St. Petersburg: Imperatorskago akademii nauk.

———. 1897–1907. *Materialy k izucheniiu nariechiia Taranchei Iliiskago okruga*. Kazan: Imperatorskago universiteta.

———. 1909. *Obraztsy taranchiiskoi narodnoi literatury: teksty i perevody*. Kazan: Imperatorskago universiteta.

Rabghuzi. 1988 (1895). *Qissäsul änbiya*. Qäshqär: Qäshqär Uyghur Näshriyati.

Radlov, V. V. 1886. *Obraztsy narodnoi literatury severnykh Tiurkskikh plemen'*. Vol. 6. *Narechie Taranchei*. St. Petersburg: Imperatorskago akademii nauk.

Rakhman, Abdukerim. 1989. *Folklor vä yazma ëdëbiyat*. Qäshqär: Qäshqär Uyghur Näshriyati.

———. 1990. *Uighur folklori haqqida bayan*. Ürümchi: Xinjiang University Press.

Rudelson, Justin. 1997. *Oasis Identities: Uyghur Nationalism Along China's Silk Road*. New York: Columbia University Press.

Sayrami, Mulla Musa. 1986 (1908). *Tarikhi Hämidi*, edited by Änvär Baytur. Beijing: People's Press.

Tekin, Talat. 1968. Tonyuquq Monument. In *A Grammar of Orkhon Turkic*. Indiana University Publications. Uralic and Altaic series 69. Bloomington: Indiana University. 283–290.

Tömür, Khemir. 1991. *Molla Zäydin häqqidä qissä*. Ürümchi: Shinjang Khälq Näshriyati.

Trebinjac, Sabine. 2000. *Le Pouvoir en Chantant: l'art de fabriquer une musique chinoise*. Nanterre: Société d'ethnologie.

Trebinjac, Sabine, and Jean During. 1990. *Turkestan Chinois/Xinjiang: Musiques Ouïgoures* (sound recording). Ocora CD C559092-93.

Tursun, Abduväli. 1986. *Khotän gilämchiliki*. Ürümchi: Shinjang Khälq Näshriyati.

Vocal music of the Uighurs (sound recording). 1991. Seven Seas KICC 5139.

Wei, Cuiyi, and Karl W. Luckert. 1998. *Uighur Stories from along the Silk Road*. Lanham, MD: University Press of America.

Nathan Light

UZBEK

GEOGRAPHY AND HISTORY

Though found primarily in the nation of Uzbekistan at the crossroad of the Great Silk Road, ethnic Uzbeks live throughout Central Asia. Large populations exist in Afghanistan, Turkmenistan, Kazakhstan, and the Xinjiang province of **China**. Their history extends back more than two millennia, and they have figured significantly in Eurasian economic life for most of that period. Their language is a member of the Turkic family, and their principal religion is Islam. Before Islam became dominant in the eighth and ninth centuries, Uzbek territory was home to many religious traditions, especially Zoroastrianism, which developed in present-day Uzbekistan and spread throughout much of Central Asia and the Middle East. Buddhism and Nestorian Christianity were also important religious presences among pre-Muslim Uzbeks. Islam achieved its preeminent position on the spiritual landscape of Central Asia after the victory of Arab armies over the Chinese at the Battle of Talas in what is now Kazakhstan.

Uzbeks created a complex technological culture, which involved pastoralism, horticulture, and manufacture. Irrigation systems allowed the cultivation of grain, cotton, and various fruits, while cattle herding and weaving also contributed to the economy. Their advantageous trade location contributed to the Uzbeks' synthesis of elements from neighboring societies in **India**, China, Iran, and elsewhere to forge a distinctive cultural achievement. Indeed, the leading cities of the Silk Road—Samarkand, Bukhara, and Khiva—are located in the country, whose strategic location did not go unnoticed by many of history's more famous conquerors. On his way to India in 327 B.C.E., Alexander the Great stopped near Samarkand and took as a wife Roxanna, the daughter of a local chieftain, though the people still rebelled against his rule for some time. In 1220, the country was overrun by Chinggis Khan and his **Mongol** soldiers.

The Mongol heritage would give to Uzbekistan one of its greatest culture heroes, Timur (known in the west as Tamerlane). His father, Teragai, was the first of his fellow clansmen to convert to Islam, and young Timur developed a reputation as not only being skilled athletically but also as being well-schooled in the verses of the Qur'an. Allying himself with his family member, the noted military leader Kurgan, young Timur made a name for himself in the subjugation of Khorasan, Khwarizm, and Urganj. After several years of suffering the exigencies of internal politics—including his appointment to the government of Mawaranahr by Tughluk Timur, a descendant of Chinggis Khan, and subsequent removal from that government and time spent as a fugitive—the death of Tughluk as well as the death of his own brother-in-law, Husayn, paved the way for Timur to be declared sovereign in 1369. His next thirty years were spent expanding his territory, going north against the Mongols and west, conquering almost every province of **Persia**. In 1398, he ventured into India and laid waste to the city of Delhi. Later in life, he undertook campaigns against the Turks and Egyptians and had begun an expedition against China when ill health overtook him. He died in February 1405 and was buried in an ebony coffin in Samarkand. For centuries, legend had it that tremendous evils would befall anyone who dared to dig up the body of Timur, and in 1941, Soviet scientists excavated the body. On that same day, Hitler launched Operation Barbarossa against the Soviet Union.

By the end of the nineteenth century, **Russia** had occupied all of Central Asia, dissolving some of the ancient khanates and placing the territory under colonial administration. Much of this involved the promotion of cotton as a cash crop and the settlement of ethnic Russians in the formerly independent countries of the region. The Red Army faced stiff resistance from groups known as *basmachi* until well after World War I. In 1924, Uzbekistan officially became the Soviet Socialist Republic of Uzbekistan. During the Soviet era, Moscow continued to use the country for its cotton-growing enterprises. But irrigation from the Aral Sea to Uzbekistan for cotton production has been the main cause of the sea's reduction to less than one-third of its original volume, while the overuse of

Mongol conqueror Timur receiving a deputation, 1600. From *Zafar Nameh* (Book of Victory). (© The British Library/HIP/The Image Works)

various pesticides and herbicides has polluted large portions of the land. After years of Soviet domination, Uzbeks declared their independence in September 1991 when it became obvious that nothing could keep the Soviet Union together.

The current population of Uzbekistan, which has an area of about 450,000 square kilometers, is more than 25 million. Its capital city is Tashkent. It borders on Kazakhstan to the north and west, though part of that border is taken up by the Aral Sea. The southern borders are with Turkmenistan and Afghanistan, and Tajikistan and Kyrgystan stand on Uzbekistan's eastern borders. The nation is now the third largest producer of cotton in the world and has become a major producer of gold, natural gas, and many industrial chemicals. Uzbekistan's current president, Islam Karimov, has stepped on the world's stage as a determined secularist. Karimov has worked doggedly to stamp out Islamic fundamentalism, despite the fact that in the post-Soviet era, Islam in Uzbekistan has been primarily cultural, thus less religious and political, though that dynamic may be changing.

Uzbek folklore has thus developed over many centuries and absorbed the traditions of a variety of diverse ancestors, which have been passed in oral form over many generations. Folk artists and craftsmen, storytellers, dancers, musicians, and singers have polished, preserved, and developed this heritage. Archeological materials—including everyday household items, musical instruments, statuettes, and wall paintings depicting musicians and dancers—testify to the antiquity of Uzbek folklore. Written sources also provide information on age-old myths, legends, and epics. The *Avesta*, the medieval *Tractates on Music*, encyclopedias and dictionaries such as the eleventh-century *Dictionary of Turkic Dialects* by Mahmud Kāshgarī, and others identify and describe genres of folklore and their performance styles.

EPICS

A particularly important genre of Uzbek folklore is the epic (*doston*), which combines narrative, poetry, music, and singing. Particularly in southern Uzbekistan, storytellers (*bakhshi*, *shoir*, and *dostonchi*) perform epics in a guttural recitative style to the accompaniment of the *dombra*. Epics are also sung (*khorezm*) to accompaniment of a traditional ensemble consisting of *dutar*, *gidzhak*, and *bulaman*. The singer-storyteller combines the arts of narrator, improviser, and poet with those of musician and singer to create works of considerable power. Among the best-known Uzbek epics are *Alpomish*, *Yodgor*, *Gor Ugli*, *Tokhir i Zukhra*, *Farkhad i Shirin*, and *Ravshan i Zulkhumor*. The *terma* with recitative melody (*nagma*) or sung melody (*nola*) serves as the basis for the musical embodiment of the *doston*. Epic performances require considerable art and skill on the part of professional storytellers. During the era of the various khanates, epic singers were on hand at the khans' palaces. Their repertoire often consisted of epics celebrating the bravery of the many khans during times of war. The sixteenth- and seventeenth-century conflicts between the Kalmaks and the Turks of Central Asia and the reign of Timur proved to be popular subjects of such epics (most notably the *Alpomish doston*). The *doston* epic genre is usually divided into three categories: the heroic, the romantic, and the didactic.

The *doston* has been crucial in the formation and perpetuation of cultural identity in Central Asia, particularly in modern times, when Russian and later Soviet policy toward the people of this region demanded a cultural homogenization on the terms of the conqueror. Attacks on the *doston*, given the inherent nationalism embedded within the genre, and early Soviet-era studies of the *doston* were motivated by the need to determine which examples of Central Asian culture would find accord with Leninist doctrine, which dictated that those cultural artifacts which spoke to the progressive past of a particular people or nation would be allowed to survive, while any "bearing the mark of the parasite class" would be eliminated. The *Alpomish doston* was originally praised by Soviet officials, who found in it elements of a popular movement against alien invasion, but that opinion quickly shifted when it was discovered that this *doston* actually solidified cultural group identity—perhaps because the average Uzbek equated the current Soviet regime with the alien invaders described in the epic.

Songs

Uzbek folk music is closely linked with oral poetry and dancing. Instrumental music (*cholgu kui*) combines instrumental signals, strumming, melody, rhythms (*usuli*), and cycles. Folk music touches on both family life and collective activities. It includes a broad range of genres associated with particular times and situations. Some types of music relate to rituals, popular life and customs, labor processes, natural phenomena, and the seasonal and ceremonial cycles. Particular songs may be sung at funerals and memorials, while others are specific to weddings. Worksongs, lullabies, shepherds' calls (*chunoncha*), and military music (*kharbiicha*) are performed by soloists and by ensembles.

The oldest folksongs seem to be those related to labor processes and rituals. Calendar songs developed in response to the changing seasons and corresponded with particular natural phenomena. Those associated with spring include *boichechak*, *binafsha*, *lola*, *navruz*, *bakhor keldi*, *salom navruz*, and *sumalak*. Summer songs are the harvest song (*"Yozi"*) and a ritual song for encouraging rain (*"Sus Khotin"*). Other songs have special associations with autumn. The harvest song *"Oblo Baraka"* and ritual songs to stop wind (*"Choi Momo"*) and to evoke it (*"Shamol Chakirish"*) are examples. One winter song *"Kor Keldi"* is meant to call forth snow. Children sing processional songs such as *"Yo Ramazon"* and *"Yo Rabbim"* at the beginning of the holy month of Ramazan. Most of these songs are performed without instrumental accompaniment.

Family ritual songs accompanied the pivotal moments of a person's life from birth (*"Beshik Tui"*) through coming of age (*"Sunnat Tui"* and *"Muchal Tui"*), betrothal and marriage, and death. Wedding songs were performed throughout the ceremonial procession of the bride and her friends (*"Yor-yor"* or *"Ulan"*), the procession of the groom to the house of the bride (*"Yor-yor"* and *"Shomuborak Khonish"*), the beginning of the ceremony and greeting the guests (*"Tui Muborak,"* *"Khush Keldingiz,"* *"Al Muborak,"* and *"Tui Boshlovi"*), greeting the groom and bride (*"Kelin Va Kuyov Kutlovi"*), and presenting the bride to the groom's family and the bride's bow (*"Kelkn Salom, Salomnoma, Khazorali"*). Wedding songs also included comic dialogue songs between relatives of bride and groom (*"Aitishuv, Muborak; Lapar, Baitkhonlik"*). A specific song also marked the end of the ceremony (*"Tui Zhavobi"*). Songs for the wedding ritual were distinctive to particular Uzbek regions (*Ustoz Sartarosh, Mavrigi, Karsak*), where they differed in terms of melody, mode of performance, and content.

The special genre of expressive culture for burial and memorial rituals included lamentations or wailing (*"Yigi, Yuklov, Ovoz Solish"*), songs (*"Marsiya"*), and ritual chants (*"Sadr"*). These expressed grief, sorrow, and drama associated with the death of a loved one. They were usually performed by women soloists or by alternating soloists and ensembles.

Songs (for example, *"Bazik"* and *"Kinna"*) were also associated with the treatment of sick children or domestic animals. These emerge from a belief in the magical power of the word as a force for expelling misfortune or curing illness. The oldest are incantations connected to ancient Uzbek religions, for example, the chant *Kuch, Kuchurik, Kaitarma, Zhakhr*, which Bakhshi shamans performed to the accompaniment of the *doiry*, a percussion instrument, or, in some regions, stringed instruments such as the *kabus* or *dumbra* in order to drive away disease.

Worksongs, originally connected to the seasonal labor cycle, focus on farm work or on crafts. The former deal with tilling the soil (*"Kush Khaidash, Shokhmoyilar, Kushchi"*), harvest (*"Yozi, Urokchi, Maida"*), threshing (*"Maida, Tegermon Kushigi, Yor Guchak"*), milking (*"Khush-khush," "Turai-turai,"* and *"Chirai-chirai"*), processing wool (*"Urnak"*), and yarn-making (*"Charkh"*). Craft-oriented songs tend to glorify various trades and professions: for example, the song of the caravansman (*"Khavar-khavar"*) and the song of the skullcap (*"Nonvoilar"*). Most worksongs also function as charms or incantations.

Lullabies (*alla*) are performed as improvisational recitatives by women soloists. Other folksongs have no particular associations with specific times or places. They are performed in various ways. These include lyric and satirical songs as well as a range of specifically Uzbek genres: *terma* (the simplest song form), *koshuk* (the most popular and widespread genre, performed by soloists or by groups with instrumental accompaniment), *lapar* (duets or dialogues similar to *chastushka*, or question-and-answer songs), *yalla* (songs for dancing), and *ashulla* (an extended, lyrical song genre). Each of these types has its own manner of singing and means of expression. Modern Uzbek popular singers such as Sevara Nazarkhan usually have a repertoire consisting of older folksongs and more modern songs of international flavor. Indeed, Nazarkhan's performances often consist as much of *makoms*—centuries-old modal song cycles related to Arabic classical music—as they do modernized folksongs and Sufi poetry.

A group of musicians playing for a *hacha* (dancing boy). Collections of folksongs and instrumental melodies have been recorded and published and are the subject of continuing research. (Courtesy Library of Congress)

MUSIC

Uzbek folk music is characterized by four regional styles: Fergan-Tashkent, Bukhara-Samarkand, Kashkadarya-Surkhandarya, and Khorezm. Each is marked by particular musical genres and instrumentation as well as distinctive musical dialects and performance features.

Musical instruments that have been widely used among Uzbek performers include stringed instruments: plucked (*dutra* and *dombra*), those played with a plectrum (*ud, rubab, tanbur,* and *konun*), bowed (*kobus, gidzhak,* and *sato*), and percussive (*chang* and *chang-kobus*). Traditional wind instruments are longitudinal flutes (*sibizgi*, *chunon nai*, and *gazhir kostlyanoy*), *mai* and *mai shuvulok* (pipes made from animal bones or clay), transverse flutes (*nai*), reeds (*surnai* and *bulaman*), and trumpets (*karnai*). Percussion instruments may be covered with skins (*doira*, *nagora*, *doul*, and *chindoul*) or self-voicing (*koshik*, *sagan*, *safael*, and *zang-bubenchik*). The last often accompany dancing.

Collecting Uzbek musical folklore began in the twentieth century. Collections of folksongs and instrumental melodies have been recorded and published and are the subject of continuing research. The tradition is being kept alive through the activities of many ensembles, often family-based, and through competitions and festivals. For example, the Baysun Bakhori folklore festival in the Baysun District of the Surkhandarya Region of Uzbekistan has become a regular event. In May 2001 UNESCO recognized the region's cultural riches as "a masterpiece of the oral and spiritual heritage of mankind."

PERFORMANCE ARTS

The performance genres in Uzbek folklore offer a wide range of opportunities for public displays of traditional forms, for instance, the activities of rope walkers (*darbozi*), puppeteers (*kugirchokbozi*), street performers (*maskharabozi-kizikchi*), and satirists (*askiyachi*). Traditional amusements also include a wide variety of folk games such as tag (*kuvlashmachak*), white bone (*ak-suyak*), tip-cat (*chillik*), fortress (*dul*), "algin" (*oshik*), "turnover" (*kuchmok*), swing (*argimchak*), battle (*kurash*), and dominoes (*kuk pari i ulok*). Dances involve a wide variety of verbal genres along with movement and music. These include stories, poetry, aphorisms, proverbs (*makollar*), folksongs, and sagas (*dostoni*).

ARTS AND CRAFTS

Important Uzbek folk arts include manufacturing carpets, reversible rugs, and sheep and goat skins finished with wool and cotton. Uzbek traditional embroidery (known by such terms as *suzane*, *zardevor*, *zhoynum*, *belbog*, *borpush*, and *bolispush*) is distinguished by bright colors and distinctive designs. Of course, Uzbekistan's place along the Silk Road allowed for access to many fine materials in ancient times. In a tomb in Northern Mongolia were found woolen curtains believed to have been made by the ancient Bactrians in the second century B.C.E. The surviving miniature paintings of Bekhzad, who worked in the fifteenth

An Uzbek woman standing on a carpet at the entrance to a yurt, dressed in traditional clothing and jewelry. Carpets and reversible rugs are important Uzbek folk arts. (Courtesy Library of Congress)

century, testify to the continuation of traditional ornamental embroidery among the Uzbeks during the medieval period. Because of the restrictions placed upon women by Islam, one of the primary means of expression among Uzbek women has been embroidery, a skill passed on from mother and grandmother to child. Indeed, a woman's dowry traditionally included several hand-embroidered articles for her future husband. Nowadays, factory-made fabric has replaced the hand-woven background material. Likewise, modern synthetic material has, in some respects, replaced the traditional silk thread. The ready availability of cotton has had its effect too, but a thriving international market for traditional arts and crafts keeps Uzbek embroidery alive.

Skilled artisans and master craftsmen also produce ceramics, woodcarvings, leather goods, jewelry, and other handmade goods for the local and world markets. The art association, Utso, set as its goal the restoration of traditional craftsmanship following Uzbekistan's declaration of independence. Bronze objects dating from 3000–2000 B.C.E. testify to the high regard ancient Uzbeks had for the art of metalworking as well as the great skill with which they made their pieces. Even modest household items would be intricately engraved with decorative designs, a practice which stems from the ancient belief that such designs could ward off evil, disease, and bad luck. This practice still exists, and today the city of Bukhara is widely considered the leading center of this craft, with over 400 jewelers and 600 copper engravers working within the city. The production of ceramics and woodcarvings remains vibrant as well. There are three main schools of pottery operating in Uzbekistan, and their wares are as much for the common man (that is, cookware, plates, and jugs) as they are for the collector. Woodcarvers in Khiva, one of the oldest centers of woodcarving in the nation, are especially renowned for their skill and artistry.

STUDIES OF UZBEK FOLKLORE

There are very few comprehensive English language resources on Uzbek folklore. Most treat Uzbek folklore under the larger rubric of either Central Asian or Turkish culture. The Special Collections Library at Texas Tech University is home to one of the better resources, the Uysal-Walker Archive of Turkish Oral Narrative. It has available online many English-language versions of epics and folk performances representative of the wider Central Asian culture of which Uzbekistan is a part (aton.ttu.edu).

BIBLIOGRAPHY

Beliaev, Viktor M. 1975. *Central Asian Music*, translated by Mark Slobin and Greta Slobin. Middletown, CT: Wesleyan University Press.

Chadwick, Nora K., and Victor Zhirmunsky. 1969. *Oral Epics of Central Asia*. Cambridge: Cambridge University Press.

Karamatov, Faizullah. 1984. Uzbek Instrumental Music, translated by Tom Djijiak, Theodore Levin, and Mark Slobin. *Asian Music* 15.1: 11–53.

Levin, Theodore C. 1980. Music in Modern Uzbekistan: The Convergence of Marxist Aesthetics and Central Asian Tradition. *Asian Music* 12.1: 149–158.

———. 1997. *The Hundred Fools of God: Musical Travels in Central Asia*. Bloomington: Indiana University Press.

Reicshl, Karl. 2001. *Das usbekische Heldenpos Alpomish: Einführung, Text, Übersetzung*. Wiesbaden: Harrassowitz Verlag.

Rustambek Abdullaev and Ulugbek Ganiev

Middle East

ARMENIA

GEOGRAPHY AND HISTORY

The roots of Armenian culture are contemporary with the ancient Sumerian-Babylonian and Egyptian civilizations, making Armenia one of the cradles of civilization. Given its situation between Asia Minor, the Black Sea, the Kur River basin, the Iranian Plateau, and Mesopotamia, the Armenian Highland is a mountainous country that has served as a crossroads between East and West since ancient times. Ararat, where biblical legend holds that Noah's ark rested after the Flood, is the symbol of the Armenian nation and the most picturesque mountain of the Armenian Highland. The climate of Armenia is dry and continental: hot in summer and cold in winter. Grapes, apricots, peaches, pomegranates, figs, and other fruits as well as grain grow there. The mountain ranges of Armenia divide the country into a number of closed climatic, economic, and ethnographic regions. The inhabitants of the varied regions (*ashkharner* in Armenian) differ from each other in their occupations, customs, costumes, and dialects. At present, the Republic of Armenia covers an area of 30,000 square kilometers, equivalent to one-tenth of the former historic Armenia.

The Armenians are a people of Indo-European origin who in the third millennium B.C.E., according to linguistic and dialect studies, broke off from the main branch of the Indo-European people. The first historic information concerning the Armenian Highland dates from the twenty-eighth century B.C.E. in the form of a Sumerian inscription concerning the state of "Aratta," the biblical Ararat.

According to early Armenian belief, the mountains, animals, plants, and many phenomena of nature were initially people transformed by a supernatural force. Armenian mountains have been personified as brothers, sisters, giants, bulls, and dragons often at conflict with each other, while the sun was represented as a bird shaped like a fiery girl holding a ring in its beak, the moon as a nascent and dying infant, and the stars and the constellations as tracks left by various people or animals. Elements of nature were objects of worship. Fire was regarded as sacred, a persecutor of evil. The worship of water was observed in tales about miraculous fish and in the fish-shaped stone monuments (*dragons*) erected near springs and irrigation ditches. The deification of heaven and earth originated in the period of Indo-European unity. Time was personified in tales as an old man sitting atop a mountain, while dawn was the disperser of night and a persecutor of evil spirits in the form of an immaculate virgin. Concurrent were beliefs regarding magic, witchcraft, and evil spirits as the source of disease and misfortune. To avert or cure such evils, ancient Armenians practiced, since prehistoric times, a variety of bewitching ceremonies and conjurations, which were eventually forbidden when Christianity became the state religion in 301.

For centuries folklore has been the fundamental means of educating people as

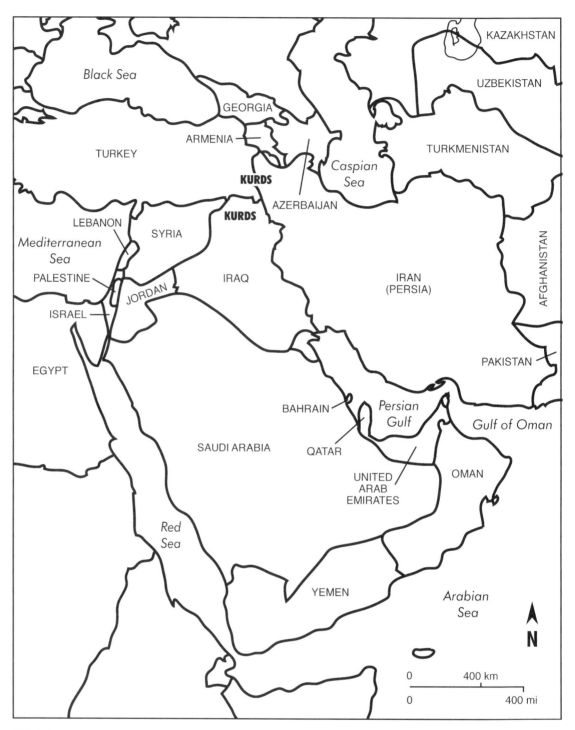

Middle East.

well as the means by which their artistic and spiritual demands were met. Though Armenia could boast of a written language some three millennia before Mesrop Mashtsots invented his alphabet (which is still used today) in the early fifth century, it was not until the late Middle Ages that folklore exerted much influence upon the many genres of Armenian belles-lettres—riddles, fables, songs, and tales. A few myths, legends, epics, and songs were pre-served in the fifth-century works of Movses Khorenatsi, Pavstos Buzand, Agathangelos, Sebeos, and Hovhan Mamikonian, and the seventh-century writer Anania Shirkatsi elaborated upon then-current riddles. However, not until the twelfth and thirteenth centuries did collections of fables, *hayrens* (medieval secular poems), magical formulas, and ritual songs really begin to emerge.

EPICS AND HISTORICAL NARRATIVES

The epic is the first of the great genres of Armenian folklore to be reported. The father of Armenian

Khachkars (cross-stones) are distinctive to Armenia, where they may adorn churches, serve as gravemarkers, or commemorate important historical events. This example is found at the Noravank (New Monastery) Church in Amaghu in the Yeghegnadzor region.

historiography, Movses Khorenatsi (fifth century C.E.) mentioned in his book, *Patmutiun Hayots* (History of Armenians), a number of types of epic. *Vipassank* is the collective name given to the epics of the pre-Christian period. In the ancient Armenian language, *vipassank* referred to both the tales and their performers. *Tveliats yerg* (Song of numbers) was a historical song, in which events were narrated chronologically. *Goghtan erger* (Songs of Goghtn) are ancient historical songs, tales, and legends, created and preserved for centuries by the *Goossans* (Bards), the popular poet-singers of the Goghtn Region who played the *bandore* as they sang and narrated. *Zrooyts* (stories, tales) are descriptive and narrative creations in verse or prose. According to Movses Khorenatsi, they can be "real and historical" or "false and mythical" such as the myths about the powerful Tork Angegh, Ara the Fair, and various dragons.

The epic tale *Hayk and Bel* tells the story of Hayk, a giant descended from Noah's son, Habet, who refused to submit to the rule of Bel, another giant, and so left the land of Babylon for settlement in Ararat. Furious, Bel came with a large army to conquer Hayk's country but was killed by his opponent. Where he fell, Hayk built a castle named after himself, and for that reason the district is now called *Hayots dzor*, "the valley of the Armenians," just as the entire country is called *Hayastan* by Armenians, who deified Hayk long ago, naming the constellation Orion after the hero who laid the foundation of the Armenian state.

The tribal groups of the Armenian Highland were often subject to attacks from the powerful Babylonian, Assyrian, and Hittite Kingdoms. The Armenian realms of Nairi, Armin, and Uruatri situated on the southern part of the Armenian Highland rallied more closely and defended their country. The consolidation of these forces near Lake Van produced the first unified Armenian state, the Kingdom of Van (Biainili) (ninth to sixth centuries B.C.E.). The first rulers of the Kingdom of Van,

Aramé and Sardoori I, founded the capital of Tushpa/Van (at present in Turkey) on the shore of the lake. The country developed and became stronger during the reign of Aramé and subsequent kings.

The historical tale *Haykian Aram* narrates the historic events from Hayk to Aramé, concerning the protracted formation of the Armenian identity. Forefather Aram (860–840 B.C.E.) is mentioned in Assyrian inscriptions as "Aramu the Urartian." Thanks to Aram, the name of Urartu-Ararat spread all over the Armenian Highland as an equivalent to Hayastan (Armenia). Aram repulsed the incursions of the Median King Nyukar Mades, the Semite Barsham, Papayis Kaaghia, and other foreign invaders. King Argishti I and his successors expanded their territory, secured their borders against the Medes in the east, Assyria in the south, and Cappadocia in the west and consolidated and centralized their power. Aram ordered the inhabitants of conquered nations to learn the Armenian language. In the reign of Aram, the Kingdom of Van became the most powerful state in Progressive Asia. While Armenians consider their name (*Hay*) to be derived from Hayk, then the foreigners call them "Armens" and the country Armenia after the name of Aram.

The Kingdom of Van suffered a decline as a result of attacks by the Median Empire. Beginning in the sixth century B.C.E., Armenia was governed by the Yervandians. In 521 B.C.E., Armenia fell under the rule of Akkemenian Persia, becoming one of its satrapies, but in 331 B.C.E. the Yervandians managed to reinstate independence to Greater and Lesser Armenia. However, the Seleucid Persians soon managed to conquer portions of Greater Armenia, though in 189 B.C.E. the Armenians managed to reverse this situation, founding the Artashessian Dynasty under the leadership of King Artashes (189 B.C.E.–1 C.E.).

The memory of those historic events is preserved in the epic poem *Artashes and Satenik*, dating from the second and first centuries B.C.E. The poem praises Artashes's battles against a variety of enemies: the Seleucids, Yervand IV, and the Caucasian Alans. When the Alans attacked Armenia, Artashes took their king's son hostage. The king's daughter Satenik (the principal heroine of the Nard epic) stood on the opposite bank of the Kur River and implored Artashes to set her brother free:

> I say to you, valiant Artashes,
> That you have conquered the brave nation of the Alans.
> Come, consent to the request of the beautiful-eyed Alan princess
> To give up the youth.
> For it is not right for heroes
> To take the lives of the progeny
> Of other heroes for the sake of vengeance,
> Or by subjecting them to keep them in the rank
> Of slaves and perpetuate eternal enmity
> Between two brave nations.

Listening to Satenik's wise speech, Artashes decided to marry her and to establish friendship between the two peoples: "A shower of gold rained down at the marriage of Artashes; / It rained pearls at the wedding of Satenik."

Artashes and Artavazd is a mythological epic poem, the main theme of which is the relation between father and son and the power of a father's curse. It was said that when Artavazd was born, the *Vishapazunk* (descendants of dragons) stole him and replaced him with a devil: "The descendants of the dragon stole the child Artavazd / And put a *dev* [evil spirit] in his place."

Because of his work to build up the Armenian nation, Artashes was greatly loved by his people. During his funeral, many voluntary human offerings were made. They buried with him his riches and his servants. The soldiers surrounded his coffin and blew brass horns as if they were marching to war. A crowd of lamenting women and warriors followed his coffin, crying and wailing. Envious of his father's glory, Artavazd exclaimed: "Since you went and took all the land with you, / To what purpose shall I reign over these ruins?" Artashes cursed him, therefore, with these words:

> If you go hunting up on Noble Massis,
> The spirits will seize you and take you up to Noble Massis;
> There you will remain and no more see the light.

His father's curse was later fulfilled. Artavazd remained shackled in a cave. The sound of the blacksmith's sledgehammer was said to make his fetters even firmer, so Armenian blacksmiths developed the custom of striking their hammer thrice upon an anvil, even on Sunday, to punish Artavazd by making his chains stronger. Variations of this legend, however, hold Artavazd to be a Promethean figure who will one day return and renew the world.

The Artashessian Dynasty reached its zenith in the days of Tigran II the Great (95–55 B.C.E.). The popular historical tale *Tigran and Azhdahak*, which covers some five centuries of history, relates that the Median King Ashdahak was troubled that King Tigran Yervandian and the Persian King Cyrus should conclude a treaty. In his dreams, Azhdahak saw a beautiful-eyed woman sitting atop ice-covered Mount Ararat, giving birth to three giants, one of which mounted an enormous dragon and attacked his country. Azhdahak's advisors interpreted his dream as a sign of danger, that he could expect an attack from King Tigran, and that he should effect a false friendship by marrying Tigran's sister, Tigranouhi. However, Tigranouhi soon discovered a plot to kill her brother and warned him. Not only did Tigran succeed in killing the Median king; he also brought Azhdahak's first wife, Anoosh, and a multitude of their people to the foot of Mount Ararat, where he forced them to settle. As he worked to unify Armenia and expand its borders over the next twenty-five years, he deported and resettled a number of peoples, assimilating them into Armenian culture. What Artashes did not accomplish himself, his grandson, Tigran the Great, realized in different historical circumstances.

According to popular legend, Tigran the Great's son was Vahagn, about whom a beautiful mythological song "Vahagn's Birth" has been composed. Movses Khorenatsi had heard it from Armenian bards of the Goghtn Province, who sang it to *bandore* accompaniment. The song tells of the birth of the young god with fiery hair, flaming beard, and sun-lit eyes. It symbolizes thunder and lightning:

> The sky is turbulent, turbulent the earth,
> Turbulent the purple sea,
> And turbulent also the red reed in the sea.
> Smoke curled out of the reed,
> Flame leaped out of the reed,
> And out of the reed a fair child came forth.
> His hair glowed,
> His beard flamed,
> And his eyes were suns.

In another version, Vahagn's fight with the dragons and his victory over them are described. Consequently he was called "Vishapakagh" (Dragon-Collector). According to ancient belief, the dragon is the evil personification of the thunderstorm, which rises to the sky as a tempest in a dense cloud, attacks the sun, and covers it. At the moment the good god of storm and lightning, the beautiful young god with fiery hair, is born and begins his fight against the evil dragon. He kills it, liberates the sun, and illuminates the earth. Traces of this mythology exist in popular belief as the dragon rises to the sky during the storm with the evil spirits and ties up the clouds to prevent the rain from falling. Or it swallows the sun. The sun is represented in Armenian folktales as a beautiful girl. The dragon obstructs the flow of water and, unless a girl is sacrificed, will not release it. Dragons with the sun's disk in their mouths also appear in ancient Armenian rock art. To propitiate the dragon, ancient Armenians sculpted statues called "Vishapakars" (Dragon-Stones). In another legend, Vahagn has become the ancestor of the Armenian nation.

Songs and Legends

In olden times, Armenian popular legends and epic songs were sung and performed as dance and pantomime movements. Armenian bards of the wine-rich Goghtn Province wandered everywhere and staged such performances in town squares, in inns, at palaces, and at festive celebrations such as wedding banquets, bringing the heroic deeds and Armenian kings and heroes to life. Dancing actresses, called *vardzaks*, also performed with the bard groups. Movses Khorenatsi mentioned the *vardzak* Nazenik, "who was very beautiful and who sang with her hand; that is, she danced while singing." In ancient Armenia, children's groups called the *Azaps* not only taught music, songs, and dances to adolescents, but also trained them in athletic games and competitions.

The adoption of Christianity in the fourth century unified the Armenians around one faith. The legend *Trdat and Grigor* (Gregory), which was preserved in the historian Agathangelos's fifth-century *Patmutiun Hayots* ("History of Armenians"), tells that Gregory the Illuminator introduced Christianity to Armenia. He was from the western part of Armenia, which was under the influence of Rome. Grigor's father, Anag, had been sent at one time to Armenia to kill King Khosrov. Khosrov's son, King Trdat III (287–330), learning Grigor's identity, imprisoned him in a deep dungeon, Khor Virap. Soon thereafter, King Trdat was transformed into a wild boar, and his royal court was infected with a strange disease. Trdat's sister, Khosrovitookht, saw in her dream an angel who told her that only Grigor was able to cure her brother. Released from his dungeon, Grigor baptized the king and his court, at which time they were all healed, Trdat resuming a human shape. The people seeing the miracle adopted Christianity in the year 301.

Rome and **Persia** divided Armenia in 387. After two years, the Western Armenian Kingdom in the Roman part vanished, while the dynasty of the Arshakunis persisted in Eastern Armenia until 428. The popular historical tale *Arshak and Shapuh* reflects the continuing struggle against internal and external oppressors. In response to news that Persia was preparing to attack, King Arshak concluded an alliance with Byzantium and took as a wife Olympia, a member of the imperial family. His advisor Catholicos Nerses assisted Arshak in every possible way, but other ministers endeavored to seize the throne of the Arshakunis. This struggle was organized and kindled by Byzantium and Persia. Their accomplices in the court decided to assassinate Arshak and replace him with either Gnel or Tirit. A clever statesman, King Arshak had these two killed. However, at the end of a thirty-year war with Shapuh, who was aided throughout by Persophile ministers, Arshak was finally captured through a feat of cunning and imprisoned in the fortress of Anhoosh. Though Arshak soon claimed to be a loyal subject of Shapuh, the latter did not believe him and had soil and water from Armenia brought to a temple, where he sprinkled them on part of the ground. Walking upon his native soil, Arshak was filled with pride:

Avetum (Annunciation) by Toro Roslin, 1250, Cilicia.

> He rose and cried to King Shapuh:
> "Where are you sitting, that is my place.
> Away from it, I will sit there myself,
> For that is the place of *our* gens!
> When I return to my old world,
> I shall exact great vengeance from thee."

Following the fall of the Armenian Kingdom in 428, the western regions of Lesser Armenia and Greater Armenia were included in the borders of Byzantium, while Eastern Armenia was transformed into a Persian satrapy. As a consequence of the cruel anti-Armenian and anti-Christian persecutions conducted by the Persian royal court, nationwide revolts broke out in Eastern Armenia. In 451 the Armenians fought under the leadership of Vardan Mamikonian at the battle of Avarayr to preserve their national identity and Christian faith. These struggles continued in the years 482–484 and 571–572. These events gave rise to a number of popular epics such as *The Persian War*, *King Pap*, and *The War of Taron*. Under these sociopolitical circumstances, the creation of the Armenian alphabet in 406 by Mesrop Mashtots was a propitious event that raised in the people a cultural self-consciousness that allowed them to resist various policies of assimilation as much as it allowed them to import in translation the scholarship of other nations. This period is referred to as Armenia's "Cultural Golden Age."

In the seventh century, the newly emergent Arab caliphate succeeded in conquering the greater part of Armenia, but the Armenians raised a number of rebellions and thus restored their independence in 885. The epic *Sassoontsi Davit* (Davit of Sassoon) was shaped by these events. It existed solely in oral form until 1873, when it was written down (as performed by a narrator named Krpo) by the pioneer Armenian folklorist Garegin Servandztiants, who published it in his collection *Grots-Brots* in 1874. The epic is divided into four parts, focusing upon four successive generations of heroes: the heroes of the first branch are Sanassar and Baghdassar; that of the second branch is Sanassar's son, Great Mher; he is followed by his son, Davit, whose name has been given to the epic; and finally, there is Sassoontsi Davit's son, Little Mher. With each generation, the persecution of the Armenian people intensifies as they are taxed and plundered, villages pillaged, their gold and cattle stolen. The conquerors too ravish Dsovinar, the beautiful daughter of the Armenian King Gagik, and force her to become the wife of the idolatrous king. After drinking a handful and then a half-handful of water from the wonder-working spring of Katnaghbyur, she gives birth to twin boys, Sanassar and Baghdassar, who kill the idolatrous king and set their mother free.

The hero of the second branch of the epic, Great Mher (nicknamed the Lion), continues the struggle for independence against a new idolatrous king, Mesra Melik, who conquered the Armenian land of Sassoon following the deaths of Sanassar and Baghdassar and began to demand egregious taxes from the people:

> The Melik exploded and summoned his lords,
> "Badin, Gozbadin, claim my just rewards,
> Syudin, Charkhadin, set forth straight away,
> Leave no stone unturned, Sassoon has to pay
> A price for its insolence, strike hard and swift,
> Remind my dear subjects that tribute's no gift,
> And bring forty maidens, radiant and bright,
> And bring forty short maids of milling height,
> And bring forty tall ones my camels to load,
> They'll work as my servants and tend my abode."

The struggle for independence gains ground with the eponymous Sassontsi Davit, who finally kills Mesra Melik with his father's miraculous Lightning Sword. In the last branch of epic, Little Mher too struggles for the welfare of not only the Armenians but other oppressed peoples as well, liberating them from cruel tyrants, various fabulous demons, and monsters. However, at the end Little Mher confines himself in the Cave of Van, resolved to stay there until the destruction of "the evil world" and the rebuilding of a new one.

From the ninth to the fourteenth century, Armenian culture attained a high standard of development. Among the factors which favored this development were independence from Arab control, establishment of the Armenian Bagratuni and Zakarian dynasties in Greater Hayk (884–1045), foundation of the capital Ani, and establishment of the Rubinian Dynasty in Cilicia (eleventh to fourteenth century), the rulers of which greatly encouraged cultural enterprises. Folklore manifested itself at this time in the forms of aphorisms, tales, fables, and stories. In the twelfth century, Nerses Shnorhali and Mkhitar Gosh wrote down and worked out numerous fables. Vardan Aygektsi compiled a collection of fables in the thirteenth century. Meanwhile, material folk art was also reaching a zenith. The art of embroidery was widespread in all the Armenian provinces (Vaspurakan, Shirak, Karin, Syunik, Artsakh, the Ararat Plain, and Cilicia). Though preserving a national style, every ethnographic region has developed its particular forms and kinds of embroidery. The needlework of Van, Marash, Ayntap, Karin, and Tarsus is distinctive. Embroidery was considered a constituent part of the national costume, which was the image of the people and the expressive feature of their lifestyle, mode of life, and esthetic perceptions. The traditional costume has fallen out of use today, has lost its former practical significance, and has become instead a symbol of national culture, performing the role of an ethnic marker during national dances.

Armenian costume, Vaspurakan region.

During this time period, however, the Armenian people lost their independence. The Seldjukian invasions held back the development of economic life, while the Mongolian invasions and domination in Armenia led the country toward economic decay, hindering the progress of public life. The sixteenth century proved to be a harbinger of rough times ahead, when the Ottoman Turks conquered Byzantium. The Middle East was now controlled by Turkey and Persia. Armenia pinned its hope on the Christian West, sending delegates to Europe and Russia, the latter of which freed a great part of Eastern Armenia from Persian rule, whereupon the Republic of Armenia was formed. It later joined the Soviet Union in 1920. Under the influence of these historical events, epics and memoirs were composed and written about the Armenian heroes Rostom, Loris Melikov, Ter-Ghukassov, and General Andranik as well as the Armenian Genocide (1915–1922), during which 1.5 million Armenians living under Turkish rule in what was formerly Western Armenia were murdered by the Turkish government. Though the Turkish government continues to stamp out Armenian culture in its land, many Armenians have worked hard to preserve the spiritual heritage, which is remembered in the accounts of survivors of these events, for future generations. Armenian folklore often touches upon the themes of preserving national identity or presents criticism of cruel, foreign rulers. One folktale called "Firebird" presents the common trope of the need to protect the country against a foreign invader, though the invader is often a witch. Likewise, a fable about the bat holds that the creature was deprived of the appearance of a bird and of the right to fly in the daytime because it could not pay the tax claimed by the birds and the mice. The subject is concise, the actions of the characters are restricted, but the moral inference is clear. The bat represents a homeless and helpless man bent under heavy taxes. The characters of the fables are anthropomorphic animals or beasts, and the educational aim of the fables is the improvement of human life and the perfection of man.

Armenian labor songs lyrically express the operations of farming or daily labor such as ploughing, wool-carding, spinning, and pounding the mortar. These songs were performed only during the fulfillment of the particular type of labor. In such songs the farmer besought God to guard his crop against the evil forces of nature. The motif of social injustice is also present. The peasant appealed to his compassionate and faithful friends—the plow, the ox pulling the yoke, the horse, the scythe, the spindle, and the spinning-wheel—to help him provide the daily bread for his large family.

Lullabies express the diverse emotions of the mother regarding her child: joy, affliction, sorrow, and, at the same time, boundless love. The mother compares the child with the celestial luminaries, the sun, the moon, the stars, and the angels. Given the unequal social status of Armenian women, when a girl was born, the mother grew sad that her daughter would suffer like herself, but she was proud of the birth of a son, because a son was considered the pillar of the house, and she paid him homage by singing the following song:

> My little boy's eye
> Looks like the cross of the church,
> My little boy's mouth
> Looks like the altar of the church,
> My little boy's nose
> Looks like the rafter of the church,
> My little boy's back
> Looks like the door of the church,
> My little boy's hands
> Look like the books of the church.

Lyric love songs include medieval bardic popular songs called *hayrens*, contemporary love songs, and ditties called *khaghiks*. *Hayrens* had specific metrics and were performed during banquets to the accompaniment of drum, flute, lyre, or horn. They were not the creations of one individual but of many generations, who elaborated upon them through the centuries. These songs praise the beauty of the beloved, because love and women are the forces ennobling and exalting men and inducing them to heroism. The eternal struggle between life and death is presented in these songs by means of philosophical meditations:

> Come! Beloved, come!
> Do not be aggrieved;
> The goods of the world
> Will not remain to me or you.

The praise of love resounds also in contemporary love songs, though these may be sadder, as the lover does not always attain his beloved. Such songs may also address the disproportionate burdens placed upon subjugated Armenian women. Popular ditties (*khaghiks*) are small quatrains, but they express a whole conception. They are exclusively rural songs, which were sung by young girls on the holidays of Ascension or Transfiguration with the purpose of drawing lots and fortune-telling:

> You are an apple on the tree,
> You are a flower on the mountain,
> You, a nightingale singing a sweet song,
> Are perching on a store.

Love here is not presented as a transient feeling, nor is the woman a temporary object of pleasure. Love may acquire a certain social meaning in the ditties, as when an enamored peasant girl might prefer to remain faithful to her poor herdsman sweetheart, refusing the gold offered by a rich suitor: "Your gold does not tempt me; / I remain in the hope of my sweetheart."

Nuptial songs are wedding ritual songs performed during most every part of the wedding ceremony. Ancient songs (for example, *Artashes and Satenik*) reflect many traditions linked to wedding rituals such as taking the bride away and strewing gold coins and pearls—subsequently replaced by dried fruits and raisins or money and sweets—over the heads of the bride and bridegroom. The nuptial rites and songs preserve remnants of totemism and other beliefs such as the bride's breaking a plate when crossing the threshold to her bridegroom's house, which aimed to protect the newlyweds from evil forces and also promote fertility. The bride is the main figure in nuptial songs. She is the "queen" of the day, who is compared to the sun as the source of life, which is consonant with the tree of life. The bride is to be the "golden column of the house," the labor friend of the "king," and the assistant to the mother-in-law. The best proof for this is the song "Come Out, You, the King's Mother," in which the bride is introduced to her mother-in-law as a "laundress," "dough-kneader," "weeder," "sheep-milker," "wool-carder," "distaff-spinner," and with other terms denoting domestic occupations. Vestiges of ancient customs have also been preserved in the songs which assert that the bride should, for the sake of family solidarity, be obedient and silent, whatever happens, The second main figure in the nuptial songs and rituals is the bridegroom, the "king," whom the songs liken to the moon. They dress the bride and the bridegroom with songs describing them as a blossoming tree (which symbolizes the mythological space tree) and as the grapevine so that they will bear fruit in the same way. This similarity substantiates the idea of the perpetuation of the family, of the nation, and of humanity.

Produced by the continual wanderings and migrations that characterize the nation's history, emigration songs typify the Armenian national experience. The forced deportation of the Armenian people began as early as the sixth century by the Byzantine Empire, which aimed to conquer Western Armenia. The Arab caliphate replicated this activity from the eighth to the eleventh century as the two powers struggled for domination over the land. Other deportations were carried out by the Seljuks, the Persian Shahs, and the Turkish Sultans, who in the early twentieth century would accomplish the extirpation of the Armenian people that culminated in genocide and massive deportation. These songs reflect the horrible persecutions which the Armenian people experienced. That is testified by the songs "How Unfortunate You Are, Poor Armenian People" and "The Partridge's Lament," where the partridge symbolizes the child-deprived mother country, Armenia. It grieves for the loss of its children:

> How can I stop crying
> When they have taken my offspring away:
> They have taken away my offspring from their nest,
> They have set fire to my heart.

Other songs focus upon the peasant, who often worked during the whole year but remained indebted to the usurious creditor. The lyric hero complains in the emigration songs that he has resorted to emigration not by his own will but out of necessity. Melancholy and yearning are prominent in his songs. They describe the emigrant's farewell: "I go to alien countries—have pity on me!" He cherishes hope in the beginning that he will go, work there, become rich, and help his family. But upon arrival at his destination, he feels the coldness of foreigners and is convinced that he is perishing both physically and morally, because "the emigrant's pillow is made of stone, the bread he eats is bitter, and the water he drinks is foul." He remembers with yearning his native home and kinsfolk and his new bride who longs for him. And he appeals to the cloud, the moon, and the flying crane, begging them to bring news to him:

> Crane, where do you come from?
> I'm eager to hear your voice.
> Crane, don't you have any news
> From our native land?

Mourning songs are very ancient. People participated in the funeral ceremony by weeping, singing, playing a musical instrument, clapping hands, and dancing face to face. Although Christianity has forbidden the lament over the deceased, traditional crying and wailing are still practiced particularly in the villages. The deceased is personified and animated in the mourning songs. People "talk" with him, ask him questions, and answer in place of him. They bid him to transmit news to the other deceased. Thus, the deceased becomes a sort of link between the real world and that beyond the grave. The musical text in the funeral ritual is complicated and original. The lament-praises are impromptu, and their object is to eulogize and do the deceased homage, to console the kinsfolk, to evoke memories, and to move those present to tears and regret. The song genre is widespread in rural regions, while the song-instrumental form is practiced in urban areas. The lament-praises are performed in the house of the deceased, in the yard, and at the graveyard on the day following the burial, on the seventh and the fortieth days after the burial, on its anniversary, on memorial days, and on the holidays of the Cross. The deceased's kin or hired singers perform funeral marches, and sad melodies are performed on the *duduk* (the Armenian national musical pipe), the clarinet, the *zourna* (type of flute), and the drum. Impromptu monologues are performed, accompanied by cries and wails of the mourners. The woman-mourner begins to praise the virtues of the deceased. She characterizes him as an individual, citizen, and member of the family and describes the cause of death and complains of his fate. In urban life nowadays the mourners have relinquished their places to the popular singers, professional string quartets, or even tape-recordings, which perform soulful Armenian sacred music or classical music.

CHALLENGES OF THE MODERN WORLD

The traditional genres of folklore have been gradually disappearing from people's memory, but a certain traditionalism is still noticeable during feasts such as New Year's Day, Christmas, Candlemas, Carnival, Easter, harvest festivals, and Memorial Day. Armenians in the mother country remember and still respect those Christian holidays of pagan origin, observing as much as possible the traditions inherited from their ancestors. During those holidays, nationwide festivals, festive performances, sporting events, exhibitions of various popular arts, theatrical performances with the participation of masked or made-up buffoons, and exhibitions of tightrope-walkers or of other sportsmen are organized. The largest part of the Armenian people, living in the **diaspora**, are making every effort, under the conditions of **globalization**, not to lose their language, traditions, and national identity. *See also* **Persia**; **Turkey**.

BIBLIOGRAPHY

Abeghian, Manouk. 1940. *Goossanakan zhoghovrdakan tagher, hayrenner ev antuniner* (Bardic Popular Songs, Hayrens and Antunis). Yerevan: Publishing House of the Academy of Sciences of the Armenian SSR.

———. 1967. *Zhoghovrdakan khaghikner* (Popular Ditties). 2 volumes. Yerevan: Publishing House of the Academy of Sciences of the Armenian SSR.

Abrahamian, Levon, and Nancy Sweezy, eds. 2001. *Armenian Folk Arts, Culture, and Identity*. Bloomington: Indiana University Press.

Agathangelos. 1976. *History of the Armenians*, edited and translated by Robert W. Thomson. Albany: State University of New York Press.

Alishan, Ghevond. 2002. *Hayots hin havatke kam hetanosakan krone* (The Ancient Belief or the Pagan Religion of the Armenians). Yerevan: Mkhitarist Congregation Printing Press.

Azarian, L., and A. Manoukian. 1969. *Haykakan Khachkar* (Armenian Cross-Stones). Yerevan: Holy Seeo of Edjmiadsin Press.

Baliozian, Ara. 1980. *The Armenians: Their History and Culture*. New York: Ararat Press.

Barkhudarian, Sedrak. 1963. *Midjnadarian hay jartarapetner ev kargords varpetner* (Armenian Architects and Stonework Masters of the Middle Ages). Yerevan: Publishing House of the Academy of Sciences of the Armenian SSR.

Boghosian, Hakob B. 1957. *Highlights of Armenian History and Its Civilization*. Pasadena, CA: Boghosian.

Boyajian, Zabelle C. 1958. *Armenian Legends and Poems*. London: J. M. Dent and Sons.

Der-Hovanissian, Diana, and Marzbed Margossian, eds. and trans. 1978. *Anthology of Armenian Poetry*. New York: Columbia University Press.

Diakonoff, I. M. 1984. *The Pre-History of the Armenian People*. Belmar, NY: Caravan Books.

Djahukian, Gevorg. 1987. *Hayots lezvi patmutiun. Nakhagrayin zhamanakasherdjan* (History of the

Armenian Language. The Pre-Letter Period). Yerevan: Publishing House of the Academy of Sciences of the Armenian SSR.

Gamkrelidze, Thomas V., and Viacheslav Ivanov. 1984. *Indoevropeiskii iazyk i indoevropeitsy* (Indo-European Language and Indo-Europeans). Part 2. Tbilisi: Publishing House of the Tbilisi State University.

Ghanalanian, Aram. 1937. *Hay shinakani ashkhatankayin ergere* (The Labor Songs of the Armenian Peasant). Yerevan: Publishing House of the Academy of Sciences of the Armenian SSR.

———. 1961. *Aradsani* (Collection of Proverbs). Yerevan: Publishing House of the Academy of Sciences of the Armenian SSR.

———. 1969. *Avandapatoom* (Collection of Legends). Yerevan: Publishing House of the Academy of Sciences of the Armenian SSR.

Ghapantsian, Grigor. 1944. *Ara Geghetsiki pashtamunke* (Worship of Ara the Fair). Yerevan: Publishing House of the Academy of Sciences of the Armenian SSR.

Grigorian, Grigor. 1980. *Hay zhoghovrdakan banahyusutiun* (Armenian Oral Tradition). Yerevan: Louys Publishing House.

———. 1986. *Hay zhoghovrdakan vipergern u patmakan ergayin banahyusutiune* (Armenian Popular Epic Songs and the Historical Melodious Oral Tradition). Yerevan: Publishing House of the Armenian SSR.

Grigorian, Roza. 1970. *Hay zhoghovrdakan ororotsayin ev mankakan erger* (Armenian Popular Lullabies and Children's Songs). Yerevan: Publishing House of the Armenian SSR.

Hackiyan, Agop J., Gabriel Basmajian, Edward S. Franchuk, and Nourhan Ouzounian, eds. 2000. *The Heritage of Armenian Literature. Volume I: From the Oral Tradition to the Golden Age.* Detroit: Wayne State University Press.

Hakobian, Tatik. 1968. *Hayastani patmakan ashkharhagrutiun* (Historical Geography of Armenia). Yerevan: Yerevan State University Press.

Harutyunian, Sargis. 1965. *Hay zhoghovrdakan hanelukner* (Armenian Popular Riddles). Yerevan: Publishing House of the Academy of Sciences of the Armenian SSR.

———. 1975. *Anetski ev orhnanki zhanre hay banahyusutian medj* (The Genre of Malediction and Benediction in the Armenian Oral Tradition). Yerevan: Publishing House of the Academy of Sciences of the Armenian SSR.

———. 2000. *Hay araspelabanutiun* (Armenian Mythology). Beirut: Hamazgayin Publishing Press.

Haykuni, Sargis. 1906. *Zhoghovrdakan erg, arads, hanelouk, erdum, orhnank, anetsk* (Popular Songs, Proverbs, Riddles, Oaths, Benedictions, Maledictions). Eminian azgagrakan zhoghovadsu (Eminian Ethnographic Collection). Volume 6. Moscow-Vagharshapat: Lazarian Seminary Press.

Kavoukjian, Martiros. 1987. *Armenia, Subartu and Sumer*, translated by Nourhan Ouzounian. Montreal: Dick Art and Design.

Khanzadian, Emma. 1973. *Metsamor 2: La Necropole. Volume 1. Les Tombes du Bronze Moyen et Recent.* Neuchâtel: Recherches et Publications.

Khorenatsi, Movses. 1913. *Patmutiun Hayots* (History of Armenians), edited by M. Abeghian and S. Harutiunian. Tbilisi: Elektratparan.

Komitas. 1950. *Hay zhoghovrdakan erger ev parerger* (Armenian Popular Songs and Dance Songs). Azgagrakan zhoghovadsu (Ethnographic Collection). Volume 2. Yerevan: Haypethrat Publishing House.

———. 2000. *Hay zhoghovrdakan erger* (Armenian National Songs). Erkeri zhoghovadsu (Collection of Works). Volume 10. Yerevan: Gitutiun Publishing House of the National Academy of Sciences of the Republic of Armenia.

Kurkjian, M. Vahan. 1959. *A History of Armenia.* New York: Armenian General Benevolent Union of America Press.

Lang, David Marshall. 1970. *Armenia: Cradle of Civilization.* London: George Allen and Unwin.

Lisitsian, Srbui. 1958–1972. *Starinnye pliaski i teatral'nye predstavleniia armianskogo naroda* (Ancient Dances and Theatrical Performances of the Armenian People). 6 volumes. Yerevan: Publishing House of the Academy of Sciences of the Armenian SSR.

Mahdesian, Arshag. 1938. *Armenia: Her Culture and Aspirations.* Fresno, CA: Rowell.

Malkhassiants, Stepan 1958. *Arakner, avandutiunner, anekdotner* (Fables, Customs, Anecdotes). Yerevan: Publishing House of the Academy of Sciences of the Armenian SSR.

Martirossian, Harutyun. 1978. *Gitutiunn sksvum e nakhnadarum* (Science Begins in Pre-History). Yerevan: Sovetakan Grogh Publishing Houses.

Mkrtchian, Mannik. 1961. *Hay zhoghovrdakan pandkhtutian erger* (Popular Armenian Emigration Songs). Yerevan: Publishing House of the Academy of Sciences of the Armenian SSR.

Mnatsakanian, Stepan. 1956. *Haykakan zhoghovrdakan midjnadarian erger* (Medieval Armenian Popular Songs). Yerevan: Publishing House of the Academy of Sciences of the Armenian SSR.

Morgan, Jacques de. 1965. *The History of the Armenian People: From the Remotest Times to the Present Day.* Boston: Hayrenik Association.

Movsisian, Artak. 1992. *Hnaguyn petutiune Hayastanum: Aratta* (The Oldest State in Armenia: Aratta). Yerevan: Gitutiun Publishing House of the Academy of Sciences of the Republic of Armenia.

———. 2003. *Nakhamashtotsian Hayastani grain hamakargere* (The Writing Systems of Pre-Mashtotsian Armenia). Yerevan: Yerevan State University Publishers.

———. 2004. *The Sacred Highlands: Armenia in the Spiritual Geography of the Ancient Near East.* Yerevan: Yerevan State University Publishers.

Orbeli, Hovsep. 1956. *Haykakan herosakan epose* (The Armenian Heroic Epos). Yerevan: Publishing House of the Academy of Sciences of the Armenian SSR.

Orbeli, Hovsep, and Artashes Nazinia, eds. 1956–1999. *Hay zhoghovrdakan hekiatner* (Armenian Folktales). 15 volumes. Yerevan: Publishing House of the Academy of Sciences of Armenia.

Patric, Arakel. 1983. *Haykakan taraz. Hnaguyn zhamanaknerits minchev mer orere* (Armenian National Costumes. From Ancient Times to Our Days). Yerevan: Sovetakan Grogh Publishing House.

Samuelian, Thomas J., trans. 2000. *Davit of Sassoon.* Yerevan: Tirgan Meds Publishing House.

Srvandztiants, Garegin. 1978–1982. *Erker* (Works). 2 volumes. Yerevan: Publishing House of the Academy of Sciences of the Armenian SSR.

Svazlian, Verjiné. 1984. *Moussa Leran banahiusutiune* (The Oral Tradition of Moussa Dagh). Yerevan: Publishing House of the Academy of the Sciences of the Armenian SSR.

———. 1994. *Kilikia. Arevmtahayots banavor avandutiune* (Cilicia. The Oral Tradition of Western Armenians). Yerevan: Gitutiun Publishing House of the National Academy of Sciences of the Republic of Armenia.

———. 1999. *The Armenian Genocide in the Memoirs and Turkish Language Songs of the Eye-Witness Survivors.* Yerevan: Gitutiun Publishing House of the National Academy of Sciences of the Republic of Armenia.

———. 2000a. *Polsahayots banahyusutiune* (The Folklore of the Armenians of Constantinople). Yerevan: Gitutiun Publishing House of the National Academy of Sciences of the Republic of Armenia.

———. 2000b. *Hayots tseghaspanutiun. Akanates veraproghneri vkayutiunner* (The Armenian Genocide: Testimonies of the Eye-Witness Survivors). Yerevan: Gitutiun Publishing House of the National Academy of Sciences of the Republic of Armenia.

———. 2004. *The Armenian Genocide and Historical Memory.* Yerevan: Gitutiun Publishing House of the National Academy of Sciences of the Republic of Armenia.

Thomson, Robert W. 1978. *Moses Khorenatsi: History of Armenians.* Cambridge: Harvard University Press.

Tokarev, S. A. 1987–1988. *Mify narodov mira* (Myths of the People of the World). 2 volumes. Moscow: Sovetskaya Entsiclopedia Publishing House.

Tolegian, Aram, ed. and trans. 1979. *Armenian Poetry: Old and New*. Detroit: Wayne State University Press.

Wilson, Epiphanius, ed. 1901. *Babylonian, Armenian and Assyrian Literature*. London.

Zhamkochian, Haykaz, and others. 1975. *Hay zhoghovrdi patmutiun* (History of the Armenian People). Yerevan: Yerevan State University Press.

Verjiné Svazlian (Translated from the Armenian by Tigran Tsulikian)

ISRAEL

Folklore in Israel is best analyzed from a three-tiered perspective: the long and richly documented historical perspective, the traditions of various localities in the country, and the diverse national, religious, linguistic, and ethnic groups.

All three perspectives are suffused in the area shared by the state of Israel as well as **Palestine** and parts of the kingdom of Jordan as the Holy Land of the three major monotheistic religions. Much of the local folklore is thus infused with traditions that are strongly linked with the canonical heritage of Judaism, Christianity, and Islam. Many places are associated with the life stories and the deeds of persons from the Hebrew Bible, the New Testament, and the Qu'ran. Much of the folklore—both that directly derived from the various canonical sources which are intimately related to each other and that which has no direct relationship to these canonical sources—is, however, shared by the various groups.

BIBLICAL, RABBINIC, AND EARLY CHRISTIAN TEXTS

The historical perspective is reflected in the long chronology of the texts that can be consulted for information from the Hebrew Bible onwards. Still older sources are supplied by rich archeological finds. Thus a poetical calendar listing the months of the year with their typical works carved on stone from circa tenth century B.C.E. discloses an ancient representation of the annual cycle, constituting together with the life cycle the two basic conceptual structures of folk culture. The Hebrew Bible includes a rich array of folk literary genres. The creation narrative in Genesis 2 frames the creation of the woman from the rib between two proverbs. One is implied—"It is not good that the man should be alone" (2:18), which serves as a proverb even in contemporary Hebrew and in translation in a number of other languages, and the other is explicitly formulated as a proverb—"Therefore shall a man leave his father and his mother, and shall cleave unto his wife: and they shall be one flesh" (2:24). Proverbs are also to be found in the canonical book by that name as well as in Ecclesiastes and in the apocryphal Ben-Sira. From the nineteenth century onwards, biblical scholarship had already discerned novellas in the stories about the patriarchs in Genesis, especially the biography of Joseph. Non-narrative folklore is also richly represented in the Bible. Annual festivals and fertility cults are described in detail both in prescriptive and descriptive modes. Medical magic is practiced by Moses in the desert with the help of the famous copper serpent (Numbers 21:9). The woman of En-Dor conjures the dead soul of Samuel with her secret knowledge (I Samuel 28:11–20).

Rabbinic literature and early Christian literature also provide ample examples of folkloristic practices and texts. The writings of the Rabbis of the Roman and the Byzantine eras in Palestine, are collected mainly in the Mishnah (edited in Galilee circa 220 C.E.), the Palestinian Talmud (edited circa 420 in Galilee), the Babylonian Talmud (edited circa 450 in Babylonia, though recording much Palestinian material), and other related works, among them notably the Midrash compilations related to the Pentateuch (the Five Books of Moses: Genesis, Exodus, Leviticus, Numbers, and Deuteronomy) and the Five Scrolls (Ruth, Song of Songs, Ecclesiastes, Lamentations, and Esther). While the term "Midrash" refers to a corpus of texts as indicated above, it also means a specific creative mode, taking off from biblical texts but ending up almost anywhere, very often in tales and proverbs as well as other folkloristic materials. It is through the elaborations of both Talmud and Midrash that we are introduced to the rich ethnographic discourse that enables us to learn so much about these aspects of life of the period, whereas the same texts are largely oblivious to historical events of the time. Early Christian authors (notably Eusebius, Jerome, and Epiphanius) likewise recorded instances of the folklore of the inhabitants of the Holy Land, whether as practiced within the framework of Christian rituals and texts or branded as heresies or deviations therefrom.

Among the explicitly folkloristic compilations of texts in the classical Rabbinic corpus is a long text on the interpretation of dreams (Babylonian Talmud, tractate Berakhot ["blessings"], ff. 55–58); several collections of contextualized proverbs (for example, Babylonian Talmud, tractate Bava Qamma ["first gate of property law"], ff. 92–93); a cycle of riddle tales and tales of riddling (Lamentations Rabbah, chapter 1); and numerous cycles of hagiographical legends (for example, Babylonian Talmud, tractate Taanith ["fasts"], ff. 23–25) and historical legends (for example, Babylonian Talmud, tractate Gittin ["divorce laws"], ff. 95–98). Eusebius (260–339, Bishop of Caesarea Maritima) provides many examples of local folklore in his annotated list of names of settlements and communities, the *Onomasticon*, while Epiphanius (310–403, Bishop of Salamis, Cyprus) describes ritual and everyday practices in his inventory of heresies, the *Panarion*.

HOLY LAND FOR THREE RELIGIONS

The multicultural, pluralistic conditions of the Holy Land prevailed also after Islam became the dominant religion in all of the Middle East by the end of the seventh century. One can say that these conditions characterize Israeli folklore to the present, as the state is inhabited by religiously and linguistically divergent groups, whose variance is further amplified by massive immigration from all over the world.

Due to its status as Holy Land, Israel has through the ages served as the goal of pilgrimage for the adherents of the three monotheistic religions. The pilgrimage tradition in Israel has its identifiable roots in the decree in which God tells Moses to institute a pilgrimage for the people of Israel three times a year to the site of the Ark of the Covenant and consequently to the Temple in Jerusalem (Exodus 23:17; 34:24). The dynamics of center (Jerusalem) and periphery (all other places) have given rise to a number of interesting mediating cases where sanctuaries were built elsewhere in the Holy Land. Thus, for instance, the political strife between the Southern (Judea) and the Northern (Israel) kingdoms in antiquity was given concrete expression by building an alternative Israelite place for worship in Bethel to compete with Judean Jerusalem. The later division between Jews and Samaritans became most concrete with the Samaritans' choice of Mount Gerizim next to Skhem (biblical Sikem, contemporary Nablus) as their sacred center in distinction from Mount Moriah, where the Temple in Jerusalem was situated. Christians have from the beginning divided their territorial interest among the sites of the Annunciation (Nazareth in the Galilee), the Nativity (in Betlehem, Judea), and the Passion (Jerusalem) as well as numerous sites around the Lake of Galilee where Jesus's early activity took place.

Other Jewish sacred cities include Hebron (the tombs of the Matriarchs and Patriarchs), also venerated by Muslims; Tiberias, also close to Christian sacred sites around the Lake of Galilee; and Tsfat, where medieval Jewish mysticism saw its heyday. In the vicinity of Tsfat is one of the most popular Jewish goals of pilgrimage of all periods, Meron, revered since the Middle Ages as the tomb of Rabbi Shimon Bar-Yohai, who lived in Galilee in the Roman period in the second century C.E. Bar-Yohai became a central figure in medieval Jewish mysticism due to his central role as the "protagonist" of the Book of Splendor, the Zohar. Since its inception, the book has been both an object of serious scholarly and academic study and a devotional volume. It is even applied as an amulet. In this its usage resembles the double functions of the book of Psalms from the Hebrew Bible. The recital of its verses is considered to have a beneficial effect, and the book itself is carried as an amulet.

Due to its central role as a goal for pilgrimage much of the knowledge about the folklore of the Holy Land in pre-modern and early modern times has been recorded in travelogues of pilgrims from the three monotheistic religions. Jewish pilgrimages during the existence of the first and second temples in Jerusalem are described in the Hebrew Bible as well as in the New Testament, Hellenistic Jewish literature (such as the writings of Philo of Alexandria and Jospehus Flavius), and classical Rabbinic literature. The earliest Christian pilgrimages known are from the second century (Bishop Melito of Sardis, 150 C.E.) and the third century (Bishop Alexander of Cappadocia, 212 C.E.). The first travelogue, however, stems from an anonymous pilgrim from Bordeaux from the year 333 C.E. In the course of the popular rise of Christianity, demand developed for guidebooks and itineraries about the holy places, particularly Jerusalem and its environs, because it attracted many Christians as the place of pilgrimage in the wake of Christianity's legalization by Constantine in 326.

The most well-known Christian travelers to the Holy Land may have been women. The travelogues, journals, and letters of Egeria and Paula from the late fourth century are a rich mine of local knowledge regarding geography as well as ethnography. It is, however, another woman's travel to Jerusalem that will have the most lasting effect on the life of the city for many centuries to come: Helena, mother of Emperor Constantine, came to Jerusalem in 335 and, according to various church historical and legendary sources, found the True Cross of Jesus, after she had been shown the place by a local Jew. She founded the first church of the Holy Sepulcher, which today is a crypt in the much bigger, multi-denominational Christian church at the same site. A similar legend relates the approach of the Khalifa Omar to the holy mountain (Temple Mount for Jews, Haram Es-Sharif for Muslims). He was shown the sanctuary's site amid the rubble that had amassed since the Romans destroyed Herod's temple in 70 C.E., according to a legend also by a Jew.

Persia took Palestine from the Byzantines in 614, and the Muslims took it from them in 638. Even after Muslims ruled Jerusalem, Christian travelogues were composed throughout the centuries: Frankish Arculf in the seventh century, English Willibald in the eighth century, Russian Abbot Daniel in the twelfth century, Sir John Mandeville in the fourteenth century, Margery Kempe in the early fifteenth century, and Henry Maundrell in the late sixteenth century. But it was not until the late seventeenth and eighteenth centuries that a substantial body of travel accounts began to appear. In the meantime history had witnessed the rise and the fall of the Crusader kingdom in the Holy Land. (Gottfried de Bouillon conquered Jerusalem in 1099, and Salah-a-Din defeated the Crusaders in Galilee in 1187.) Muslim travelers also described life in the Holy Land, beginning with the Persian Ismaili poet Nasir-i-Khosraw, who authored a book of travel, *Safarnama* (1046–1052). The two earliest travelogues written by Jewish travelers to the land of Israel in Hebrew reported the journeys carried out by Benjamin of the Spanish town of Tudela and Petahya of the German town of Regensburg (his family came from Prague), who visited the Holy Land respectively around 1170 and 1180. The two travelogues reflect very different ethnographic aspects of life of the religious and national groups inhabiting the country. Benjamin minutely recorded numbers of inhabitants, according to their religious affiliation, occupation, gender, and other identity markers. Petahya reported legendary traditions from local Muslims, Christians, and Jews alike, as well as peculiar customs and rituals of the respective groups related to the sacred geography of the land. Jewish travelogues abounded thereafter: French Eshtori Ha-Farhi in the fourteenth century, Italian Meshullam of Volterra, and his countryman, Ovadyah of Bertinoro, in the fifteenth century, just to mention a few.

The eighteenth and nineteenth centuries were adventurous centuries among Europeans, and the Holy Land was often included in the tradition of the "Grand Tour." Modern travelogues to the Holy Land in the nineteenth century included those by Mark Twain and Herman Melville as well as Lady Judith Montefiore's, all reflecting in detail on the lives of the local inhabitants and usually bewailing their poverty and misery. Lady Judith visited the country with her husband Sir Moses, who also contributed significantly to the material advancement of the Jewish population especially in Jerusalem, including the establishment of new neighborhoods outside the walls of the old city. The growing distance from the actual sanctuaries located inside the walls emphasized the urge of the Jewish inhabitants to turn their presence from mere pilgrimage to a comprehensive mode of life. Accordingly, the Montefiore support was directed to building a grain mill and living quarters rather than synagogues or sanctuaries.

ZIONIST SETTLEMENTS, WORLD WAR II, AND THE JEWISH STATE

By the end of the nineteenth century the folk culture of the Holy Land underwent a radical change with the pioneer settlements of Zionist Jews in most parts of the country. It was in Jerusalem that the organized and systematical effort to revive the Hebrew language had its headquarters, led by Eliezer Ben-Yehudah, around whose figure and family a rich legendary tradition emerged. At the center of those traditions lay the alleged ban that Ben-Yehudah issued on his wife, who barely knew her new language, to speak any other language with their firstborn Itamar and their other children. New lullabies, new children's rhymes, and new words for endearment as well as resentment were mined out of the immense literary treasures of ancient, classical, and medieval Hebrew texts. Ben-Yehuda also had to invent new words for new phenomena such as the railway, the postal services, and stamps. His effort was, however, reinforced by the parallel evolution of a vibrant Modern Hebrew literature written and published initially in Russia and Poland, a literature with an imagined rather than a real audience. In the meantime the imagined audience took form in the first kibbutzim (cooperative villages) and the new neighborhoods of Jerusalem and Jaffa as well as the newly founded city of Tel-Aviv, the first in the long row of newer and smaller communities. Tel-Aviv very early set up its hegemonic status expressed on the level of folk and popular culture in the many processions and festive gatherings that were organized by the city's budding intelligentsia and bohemia to celebrate the annual cycle of Jewish holidays. Although Tel-Aviv was constructed as an urban center with some cosmopolitan ambitions (often expressed by the first legendary mayor, Meir Dizengoff), the festival processions there also signaled the city's association and solidarity with the pioneering agricultural settlements. Thus the New Year of Trees (Tu Bi-Shvat) celebrated in early spring and the Festival of the New Fruits (Bikkurim or Shavuot, also celebrating God's giving the Torah at Mount Sinai) celebrated in early summer both involved processions, especially of children, with much greenery and fruits of various kinds. Another publicly celebrated holiday was Hanukkah, the feast of mid-winter, in which the element of lights and candles was emphasized similarly to mid-winter festivals all over the world.

The peak of all public festivals of Tel-Aviv was, however, Purim. The festival, rooted in the narrative of the biblical book of Esther, celebrates the rescue of the Jews in the Persian Empire from the hands of evil Haman. In spite of this ethnic and historical background, the form of the festival as celebrated in Tel-Aviv resembled (and does to this day with contemporary alternations) numerous other carnival festivals in Catholic cultures, emphasizing music, masquerading, and even choosing the Queen of Purim, naturally titled "Queen Esther." Not surprisingly, incorporating Orientalist ideals, especially with regard to female beauty, the first queens were of Yemenite and Sephardic origin, though the majority of the city's burghers were Jews of European origin. The liberated and secularized emphasis of the Tel-Aviv Purim was a demonstration of the "new human being" that Zionism had supposedly created in contrast to the subdued and melancholic types of the **diaspora**.

In rural communities around the country, life was in general more austere, and festivals were even more closely connected to the annual agricultural cycle. Some kibbutzim have upheld such traditions, namely the Omer festivities (end of Passover) at Ramat-Yohannan (north of Haifa). The socialist ideology that suffused the spiritual life of the pioneers constructed some of their folkloristic and popular performances. Their songs were often Russian melodies brought from Europe and adapted to new Hebrew words, some of which are still performed in nostalgic evenings of group-singing. Soon local composers also started to create melodies to accompany ancient texts, predominantly the verses of the Song of Songs that breathe liberated eroticism as well as intimacy with nature in all its embodiments ("roes of the hills" and "lilies of the field," for example), both sentiments conceived of as hallmarks of the "new human." Russian and Yiddish words remained famously as loving diminutives or blasphemous cries, sometimes, though, amplified with new, Arabic counterparts. The local Arab culture also supplied elements of dress that fitted the climate of the country. Thus the combination of the traditional Russian peasant shirt with an Arabic *kefiyyeh* was one of the fashionable attires among women and men alike in the decades prior to the founding of the State of Israel in 1948. **Gender** equality was an explicit ideal, attained with great difficulties and limitations, as many autobiographical texts and diaries witness. Free love and open family structures were experimented with, and women aspired to share in all tasks in the field as well as at the construction site.

Historical events cannot be overlooked when considering the folklore of Israel, particularly in the twentieth century. From the early 1920s on the settling of Jews all over the country encountered growing animosity from the Palestinian Arab population. The Jewish population reacted with increasing military organization and preparedness. Their folklore accordingly started to acquire quasi-military elements such as the idealization of coarse and unrefined forms of behavior—speaking *dughri*, directly and with no pretense or politeness—and growing male dominance. However, the choice of the Arabic word *dughri* to express Israeli self-reflection expresses the inherent dialogic relationship of the Palestinian and the Jewish components (among many others) of folk culture in Israel.

The darkening clouds on Europe's horizon, the rise of Nazism, and World War II caught up with the youthful enthusiasm of the young nation busy with inventing itself and its traditions. Thousands were living a stressful life of immigrants in a new country while their families were butchered by the millions in Europe. The clash between the enthusiastic energy to create a new life and the melancholia and tragedy of the loss of the well-known and the intimate home joined with the losses connected with the local adversities to lay the basis for a culture in which memory and commemoration have ever since occupied a growing and deepening position. The yearly cycle of agricultural holidays became interlaced with days of sorrow, adding a spring day of commemoration for millions exterminated in the racist genocide of Shoah and the memorial day for the fallen soldiers prior to the new feast, the Day of Independence, to the traditional commemoration of the destruction of Solomon's and Herod's temples on the ninth of Av in the late summer. Material objects of commemoration—sculptures, pillars, and plaques—became more and more visible elements of public space. Poems written initially as personal reflections on trauma, whether of World War II or the war of 1948, were used as semi-canonical readings for commemorative ceremonies. Mythological narratives such as the Massada legend established themselves to serve the intense need for collective mourning. The immense impact of Massada and the tradition surrounding it has given rise not only to thorough scholarly studies, but also to popular concepts such as "the Massada complex" for the psychology of a nation experiencing itself as besieged. The impressive cliff of Massada near the Dead Sea is, according to official statistics, the most frequented tourist attraction in Israel, surpassing even Jerusalem.

At the same time the emerging state, founded in May 1948, was grappling with a new demographical situation: mass immigration. The newcomers were partly survivors of the camps, doubly uprooted, who each had left several traumatic pasts behind them. They brought with them a crushed folk culture, once the rich and vibrant powerhouse of Jewish creativity of Yiddish-speaking Eastern Europe. Others bore the rejected selves of those who had thought themselves Germans among Germans, heirs of the writers, philosophers, composers, psychoanalysts, actors, comedians, academics, doctors, and lawyers of *fin-de-siècle* Vienna and Berlin. From both these backgrounds came also two distinct traditions of folklore research, hatched at the Yiddishe Vissenshaftlikhe Organizatsie of Vilnius and the Gesellschaft für jüdische Volkskunde of Hamburg, as well as the scholars who were educated as Arabic and Hebrew philologists, musicologists, and ethnographers usually at German universities.

The others came in more homogenous groups but were not less uprooted from their native soils of millennia in the Middle East and especially in the Arab countries, where their existence had become impossible due to the new political order of the world and especially the new political situation of the Middle East after the emergence of the Palestinian exile after the founding of Israel. The different groups reacted each in their own way to their mutual incompatibilities: the East Europeans (Ashkenazim) by clinging to the hegemonic position created by their earlier arrived co-expatriates and by defying the stigmatization threatening those who came as refugees from the camps rather than as ideological pioneers with varied levels of success; the Germans (Jeckes) by receding into academic ivory towers or linguistic isolation, stereotypically seen as unable to learn Hebrew or to adapt to the cultural style of the country and turning into topics of ethnic jokes based on mispronunciation and inappropriate dress; the Spanish-speaking Middle Easterners (Sephardim) by maintaining the role of a somewhat déclassé nobility and exiled princes and princesses of Iberia; and the Arabic-speaking Middle Easterners (Mizrahim) by classing themselves and being classed by the hegemonic group as underprivileged and decultured, consequently often giving up immense cultural riches of folklore as well as elite culture that they had brought along.

FOLKLORE IN CONTEMPORARY ISRAEL

Folklore's status in Israeli society in the last half century may be viewed in various contexts: private, organizational, political, mass medial, artistic, and academic. The private contexts of folkloristic creativity are multiple and include verbal modes such as proverbial idiolects of families; constantly renewed modes of celebrating personal events such as birthdays—for example, Bar-Mitzvah and Bat-Mitzvah (male and female puberty rites at age of thirteen and twelve, respectively); trips to safari parks in East Africa; weddings moved from the conventionalized form of large commercial wedding halls serving heavy dinners to caves and parks in nature, as well as experimentation with non-Orthodox rituals in blatant contrast to the state law that privileges Orthodox ritual for Jews and legally dismisses other options; and non-religious modes of commemorating the dead with music and sometimes even introducing classical music into funerals. Private forms of folklore may also include various luck-bringing objects from across religious boundaries, predominantly the Middle Eastern Hamsa ("Fatima's hand"), but also ones that stem from canonical religious tradition such as miniature books, the Hebrew Bible's Psalms for Jews and the Qur'an for Muslims. Naturally private folkloristic practices include the religious holidays of each denomination as celebrated in the homes.

Folk narrating occurs mostly in private settings. Occasionally purely ethnic narration in the "old country" language involves older members of the community. Some efforts at revitalization, however, have again brought Judeo-Arabic, Yiddish, and Judeo-Spanish into the realm of artistic production. Most private storytelling involves the use of Hebrew, possibly interlaced with expressions in the ethnic languages such as proverbs and especially terms concerning food, which persists as a major form of expressing ethnic identity in private life. Cookbooks of the various groups frequently crop up, the recipes often accompanied by tales in various genres.

Important organizational contexts for folklore include the educational system and the army. The folklore of the educational system includes, for instance, attempts to impress the "subjects" with traditional values through the use of proverbs as wall paintings. On the other hand, the descendants of divergent ethnic groups are informed of each others' backgrounds through assignments in which parents and grandparents are interviewed regarding their traditions and life stories. Folklore in organizational contexts also serves to subvert the norms and rules that are experienced by the subjects, in this case the students, as oppressive. Various ritualized forms of aggression occur, such as the traditional rampage of the graduating classes that often involve satirical representations of authoritative figures, noisy music, and even some stylized forms of vandalism.

Certain socializing modes of folklore such as rituals of abuse of newcomers occur in army contexts. Other examples of military folklore are solidarity-building songs of the different units, slurs addressing "competing units," and stereotypes connected with the various forms of service, whether in combat or service units. Folklore may also serve as a mode of subversion in the army—for example, proverbial modes of expression that are intended to vent frustration and humiliation exchanged among the servicewomen and men. The rituals connected with the termination of the relatively long mandatory army service (basically for the Jewish citizens only, though other groups such as the Druze and the Bedwin also serve in the army) have generated many forms of folklore, the dominant being a new form of the "Grand Tour." Young Israelis seem to need to transform one form of challenge and risk into more pleasurable ones, choosing the rain forests of South America or trekking in the Andes and the Himalayas as their favorite destinations. The Far East and **India**—with their multiple cultural formations—are another alternative, as is the "virginal" environment of **Australia**. In folkloristic terms one can see these repeated forms of rites of puberty as a need to shake off the constriction and certain regression characterizing the period of army service by seemingly choosing independent trails of travel that by the power of the folkloristic processes of communication end up as collective ritual modes. Another folkloristic perspective is that these young Israelis reproduce by their sometimes years-long traveling the folk image of the "Wandering Jew," characteristically articulating the stereotype of the diaspora Jew, especially in Europe. On the other hand, expatriate Israeli maintain "Israeli folklore" in the form of gatherings of singing and dancing long after they have emigrated from their homeland.

Political reference to folklore is often criticized as appropriation. A manifest example is the Mimouna festival celebrated primarily by Moroccan immigrants and their descendants but also by most other Middle Eastern Jews congregating in big public spaces. Most political leaders appear and interlace the artistic performances of "folklorico" groups with their particular messages, thus signaling alleged reverence to this particular tradition. In a more intricate way politics materialize in specific forms of folk religion. North African Jews have regenerated and partly generated a rich array of modes of saint worship of holy men (and only occasionally women), most of whom belong to their past on the African continent and some of whom who have lived to immigrate to Israel and to be active there. Significantly the major mode of practice consists of pilgrimage—however, not to the canonical sites of the Holy Land but to new ones. The present sites of worship of the North African saints vary from private living rooms to semi-public arenas. Common to the emergence of the cult about twenty to thirty years after the mass immigration of the 1950s is a communication from the saint in dreams and visions of individuals who then become their mediators to the wider audience practicing the cult at various levels of intensity. These individuals very often reside in new towns that were founded or enlarged in order to accommodate the great waves of immigrants, popularly and officially called "development towns" in a lingo suggesting the need for improvement and socialization. The establishment of the new centers of worship in these areas demonstrates the subversive and liberating urge to turn periphery into center. Populist as well as socially sensitive political activists and leaders discovered the immense energies invested in this folk religious phenomenon. Thus some parties especially connected with adherents of these saints and their mediators have even distributed amulets carrying the saints' pictures to "reward" those who vote for them. The civil institutions reacted by taking the saints to court without, however, being able totally to prevent the phenomenon. These folk religious practices emerge in correlation to general trends of rising religiosity among the members of all religions of the country, following a regional as well as universal trend characteristic of the beginning of the third millennium C.E.

The political use of folklore can also be discerned in the application of proverbs in the speeches of the members of the Knesset (Israel's parliament), often signaling some particular identity represented by the specific speaker. Proverbs are also a folklore element that is relatively densely sown in mass media. They occur in the mouths of interviewees, who thus acknowledge the short format and limited span of attention allotted to individuals, especially by the electronic media, and try to make the best use of it. Often proverbs are used—sometimes parodied—in article headlines, especially in titles of more essayistic than hard news items. A special semi-proverbial genre of folklore that has taken off in Israel possibly more than anywhere else is political bumper stickers. The assassination of Prime Minister Yitzhak Rabin was followed by a host of elaborations on the famous farewell words of American President Bill Clinton "*Shalom Haver*" (Goodbye, pal) as well as the formula itself. Major political issues such as the future of the occupied Palestinian territories are debated in the modern arena of backside of cars.

Proverbs are also frequently applied in very inventive and sophisticated forms in advertisements, combining the underlying authority of tradition with the creative input of the contemporary. Such proverb usage may also involve English language proverbs attesting to the growing **globalization** and Americanization of commercial popular culture. American popular culture, however, emerges in other contexts too, such as the adopting of reggae, breakdancing, Rastafari appearance and cults, and other expressive modes associated with **African Americans** and Americans of color by young immigrants from Ethiopia, thus enhancing their particular identity as émigrés from the African continent.

The coalescence of folklore and art—music, literature, theater, and the visual arts, including architecture—is apparently a universal process of culture. In Israel these combinations serve visibly and audibly the purposes of both identity politics and artistic experimentation. Thus joint ensembles of Arab and Jewish musicians reconnect descendants of Jewish immigrants from Arab countries as well as others with the cultural heritage that largely disappeared from the official musical scene for a long time, making an explicit move toward a statement on the common culture of the different components of Israeli society. Political adversity is thus confronted by cultural solidarity. In Israeli cultural consciousness any Oriental and especially Arab music is conflated with folklore, because of the lack of knowledge by large parts of the Jewish population regarding the esthetics of classical Middle Eastern forms of music.

In conclusion, the academic context of folklore interacts with all the other contexts—that also interact mutually—attempting to create not only a viable reflection but also a relevant critique of them. The presence of folklore research among the humanities faculties of Israeli universities has not been self evident. As in many other places in the world, folklore's anti-hierarchical structure of knowledge has created a barrier between its study and the hierarchical structures of academic institutions. In many places folklore gained its academic status by serving some social group's vital interests—for instance, in totalitarian systems by directly serving the regime. In many emerging nation-states folklore research has been geared toward shaping national identity. The specific multi-cultural, multi-ethnic, and multi-lingual character of Israeli folklore created an incongruity between a fieldwork-based study of folklore and the professed "melting pot" program of the cultural and political establishment of the 1950s and the 1960s. From the 1970s onward social movements started to push particular agendas of various ethnic groups in ways that made folklore studies an intellectual asset for looking at those agendas with more knowledge and a critical mind. Other theoretical perspectives such as feminism infused research on historical and canonical texts—traditionally considered seamlessly patriarchal—with new insights about the inherent multi-vocality of many of those texts such as the Hebrew Bible and classical Rabbinic literature.

BIBLIOGRAPHY

Adler, Marcus Nathan. 1907. *The Itinerary of Benjamin of Tudela: Critical Text, Translation and Commentary*. New York: Phillip Feldheim.

Bar-Itzhak, Haya, and Aliza Shenhar. 1993. *Jewish Moroccan Folk Narratives from Israel*. Detroit: Wayne State University Press.

Ben-Amos, Dan. 1981. Nationalism and Nihilism: The Attitudes of Two Hebrew Authors Toward Folklore. *International Folklore Review* 1: 5–16.

Biale, David. 1992. *Eros and the Jews: From Biblical Israel to Contemporary America*. New York: Basic Books.

Bilu, Yoram. 2000. *Without Bounds: The Life and Death of Rabbi Ya'aqov Wazana*. Detroit: Wayne State University Press.

Bilu, Yoram, and Galit Hasan-Rokem. 1989. Cinderella and the Saint: The Life History of a Jewish Moroccan Folk-Healer in Israel. *The Psychoanalytical Study of Society* 15: 227–260.

Frank, Georgia. 2000. *The Memory of the Eyes: Pilgrims to Living Saints in Christian Late Antiquity*. Berkeley: University of California Press.

Hanauer, J. E. 1907. *Folklore of the Holy Land: Moslem, Christian, and Jewish*. London: Duckworth.

Hasan-Rokem, Galit. 1982. *Proverbs in Israeli Folk Narratives: A Structural Semantic Analysis*. Helsinki: Academia Scientiarum Fennica.

———. 1992. Proverbs as Inter-Ethnic Dialogue in Israel. *Jewish Folklore and Ethnology Review* 14: 52–55.

———. 1998a. The Birth of Scholarship out of the Spirit of Oral Tradition: Folk Narrative Publications and National Identity in Modern Israel. *Fabula* 39: 277–290.

———. 1998b. Narratives in Dialogue; a Folk Literary Perspective on Inter-Religious Contacts in the Holy Land in Rabbinic Literature of Late Antiquity. In *Sharing the Sacred: Religious Contacts and Conflicts in the Holy Land*, edited by A. Kofsky and G. Stroumsa. Jerusalem: Ben-Zvi Institute. 109–130.

———. 1999. Folk Religions in Modern Israel: Sacred Space in the Holy Land. *Diogenes* 187: 83–87.

———. 2000. *Web of Life: Folklore and Midrash in Rabbinic Literature*. Stanford: Stanford University Press.

Hasan-Rokem, Galit, and Eli Yassif. 1989. The Study of Jewish Folklore in Israel. *Jewish Folklore and Ethnology Review* 11: 2–11.

———. 1990. Jewish Folkloristics in Israel: Directions and Goals. In *Proceedings of the Tenth World Congress of Jewish Studies. D-II: Art, Folklore, and Music*. Jerusalem: World Union of Jewish Studies. 33–62.

Jason, Heda. 1978–1980. Folk Literature of the People of Israel: An Introduction. *Journal of Indian Folkloristics* 1: 1–14; 2: 27–49; 3: 49–105.

Kabbani, Rana. 1988. *Europe's Myths of Orient*. London: Pandora Press.

Katriel, Tamar. 1986. *Talking Straight: "Dugri" Speech in Israeli Sabra Culture*. Cambridge: Cambridge University Press.

Katriel, Tamar, and Aliza Shenhar. 1990. Tower and Stockade: Dialogic Narration in Israeli Settlement Ethos. *Quarterly Journal of Speech* 76: 359–380.

Lewis, Bernard. 1967–1968. Some English Travellers in the East. *Middle Eastern Studies* 4: 296–315.

Montefiore, Judith. 1836. *Private Journal of a Visit to Egypt and Palestine by Way of Italy and the Mediterranean*. London: J. Rickerby.

Muhawi, Ibrahim, and Sharif Kanaana. 1989. *Speak Bird, Speak Again: Palestinian Arab Folk Tales*. Berkeley: University of California Press.

Nasir-i Khusrau. 1893. *Diary of a Journey Through Syria and Palestine*, translated by Guy Le Strange. London: Palestine Pilgrims' Text Society.

Noy, Dov. 1971. Introduction: Eighty Years of Jewish Folkloristics: Achievements and Tasks. In *Studies in Jewish Folklore*, edited by Frank Talmage. Cambridge, MA: Association for Jewish Studies. 1–12.

Obenzinger, Hilton. 1999. *American Palestine: Melville, Twain and the Holy Land.* Princeton: Princeton University Press.

Patai, Raphael. 1998. *Arab Folktales from Palestine and Israel.* Detroit: Wayne State University Press.

Salamon, Hagar. 1999. *The Hyena People: Ethiopian Jews in Christian Ethiopia.* Berkeley: University of California Press.

———. 2001. Political Bumper Stickers in Contemporary Israel: Folklore as an Emotional Battleground. *Journal of American Folklore* 114: 227–308.

Schely-Newman, Esther. 2002. *Our Lives Are but Stories: Narratives of Tunisian-Israeli Women.* Detroit: Wayne State University Press.

Schwarzbaum, Haim. 1989. *Jewish Folklore Between East and West*, edited by Eli Yassif. Beer-Sheva: Ben-Gurion University of the Negev Press.

Shenhar, Aliza, and Tamar Katriel. 1988. Israeli Folklore under Conditions of Stress. *International Folklore Review* 6: 16–20.

———. 1989. Legendary Rumors as Social Control in the Israeli Kibbutz. *Fabula* 30: 63–82.

Wilkinson, John. 1981. *Egeria's Travels to the Holy Land.* Revised edition. Jerusalem: Ariel.

Wright, Thomas, ed. 1969 (1848). *Early Travels in Palestine; Comprising the Narratives of Arculf, Willibald, Bernard, Saewulf, Sigurd, Benjamin of Tudela, Sir John Maundeville, De La Brocquière, and Maundrell.* New York: AMS Press.

Yassif, Eli. 1999. *The Hebrew Folktale: History, Genre, Meaning*, translated by Jacqueline S. Teitelbaum. Bloomington: Indiana University Press.

———. 2002. The "Other" Israel: Folk Cultures in the Modern State of Israel. In *Cultures of the Jews: A New History.* New York: Schocken Books. 1063–1096.

Zerubavel, Yael. 1995. *Recovered Roots: Collective Memory and the Making of Israeli National Tradition.* Chicago: University of Chicago Press.

Galit Hasan-Rokem

KURDS

Geography and History

The Kurds are often said to be the largest nation in the world without a state. In the past their territories were nominally divided between the Turkish and Persian Empires (see **Persia**), where their status did not differ greatly from that of other non-dominant ethnic groups, and they enjoyed a considerable degree of autonomy for much of their history. After World War I, however, their homelands became part of the states of **Turkey**, Iraq, Syria, and Iran, all of which showed pronounced nationalist tendencies in which Kurdish identity had no part. Significant Kurdish minorities also live in **Georgia** and until recently in **Armenia**. Many Kurds, moreover, were forced to seek refuge in Western Europe in the latter half of the twentieth century—notably in **Germany, France, Sweden**, and the United Kingdom—where they now constitute sizable minorities. In most of their new home states in the Middle East the Kurds were faced with various forms of discrimination and, in some cases, persecution. On the one hand this led to a heightened awareness of their cultural and ethnic identity, but at the same time it generally made it difficult (and in some cases

Kurd woman with children, early twentieth century. The Kurds are often said to be the largest nation in the world without a state. (Courtesy Library of Congress)

impossible) for Kurds to express and cultivate this identity in the same way as other groups in the region—for example, by developing a strongly literate "high" culture. Art forms which many Westerners might regard as "folklore" therefore have a higher status and play a far more important role in Kurdish culture than is the case in the West and most of the surrounding Middle Eastern nations.

The Kurdish lands are mountainous, and mountains play a key role in much of Kurdish folklore. "Kurdistan" (a term widely used by Kurds but not officially recognized, except as a province of Iran) has a land climate with hot summers and harsh, very cold winters. Nomadic tribes, who used to constitute an important segment of the population, generally migrated from winter to summer pastures and vice versa in spring and autumn.

Although most Kurds now live in cities in or outside Kurdistan, Kurdish culture is still connected in the minds of many with the simple rural life of villagers or nomads. On the one hand this "rural idyll" is prominently present in folk culture, while on the other hand this mental map of Kurdish identity promotes the popularity and prestige of "folk" culture among Kurds.

Traditionally, the main factor in determining Kurdish identity has probably been language. Kurdish belongs to the Iranian language family and is closely related to Persian, but it has little in common with either Arabic or Turkish. The long ban on Kurdish in Turkey and the dominance of the official languages of the nation-states have meant that many of those who regard themselves as Kurds now speak another language better than Kurdish. An exception are the Iraqi Kurds, whose life in their homeland was no easier than that of Kurds elsewhere but whose linguistic identity was not usually repressed as strongly. Kurdish has three main groups of dialects—the most important of which are Kurmanji, the Kurdish of Turkey, the Caucasus, Syria, northwest Iraq, and northwest Iran; and Sorani, which is spoken in the other Kurdish areas of Iran and Iraq. Two smaller languages, Zazaki (spoken in parts of Turkey) and Hawrami (Western Iran), seem to be historically distinct from Kurdish but are widely regarded as dialects of that language.

Kurds never had a nation-state of their own, and educated people generally had a perfect command of the dominant language of their region (Arabic, Persian, or Turkish). As a result, a written culture in Kurdish developed slowly, and most manifestations of "high" culture that were enjoyed or indeed created by Kurds were in the dominant language of the area, whereas purely "Kurdish" culture tended to prefer more popular forms. Although these were enjoyed in urban centers as well as rural areas, the latter seem to have contributed most to the richness of Kurdish folklore. Special mention should be made of the rich and distinct folk culture of the (semi-) nomadic tribes, whose way of life is now fast disappearing, but who once constituted a major social and cultural element in the Kurdish lands.

When the Kurdish areas became part of the newly formed Islamic Empire in the seventh century, rural populations were usually slower to accept the new religion than city dwellers, who were more directly exposed to the dominant culture. In rural Kurdistan, ancient customs and beliefs therefore persisted longer, and indeed they were often retained in an adapted form when the Kurds eventually embraced Islam. This process of conversion is thought to have been facilitated by the emergence of Sufism, a non-dogmatic, mystical form of Islam, which enabled Kurds to join the dominant civilization of the region without the need to give up much of their cultural heritage. Generally speaking, popular religion, which often shows elements of ancient Iranian beliefs combined with Sufi symbols and attitudes, plays a greater role in Kurdistan than the teachings of Islamic theologians. As a result, official religious denominations do not adequately reflect the rich variety of Kurdish religious life at the local level.

RELIGIOUS BELIEFS

Most Kurds are Sunni Muslims ("orthodox" followers of official theology, members of Sufi brotherhoods, devotees of popular forms of religion, or a mixture of all three), while a few Iranian Kurds are Shi'ites. Besides these, there exists a number of religious communities whose beliefs and practices are further removed from mainstream Islam. The Yezidis of Northern Iraq, Eastern Turkey, and Syria do not regard themselves as Muslims, while the identity of both the Ahl-e Haqq (Yarsan, Kaka'i) of Iran and Iraq and the Turkish Alevis in this respect is debated. The religious traditions of several smaller groups are still relatively unknown to Western scholarship. In some areas, moreover, Kurdish communities live in close proximity to Christian ones. Although the Christians do not regard themselves as Kurds, they speak Kurdish fluently and constantly interact with their Kurdish neighbors. Formerly the same was true of the large Jewish community that lived in Kurdistan, but most of its members have now moved to Israel. All these groups have their own religious feasts, traditions, and usually texts, many of which have a profound religious significance for believers, but at the same time show a strong folkloric element. Among the smaller religious groups, sacred texts are generally transmitted orally, often by members of a hereditary class of "reciters." Pilgrimage to local shrines or holy places plays an important part in many religious communities in Kurdistan.

Places of pilgrimage (for example, the tomb of a saint or holy person, a body of water, mountain, or tree) are often believed to have powers to grant wishes or heal the sick. Amulets (*nivisht*), usually written by a religious leader, are also thought to have medicinal powers. Several indigenous medicinal traditions exist in Kurdistan, about which little precise knowledge is currently available in the West. Practitioners of these traditions include the *Dekhtorê Kurmanji* (Kurdish Doctor) and the (usually

A Kurdish woman shouts slogans as thousands of Turkish Kurds gather to celebrate Newroz to mark the new year or spring festival in the southeastern city of Diyarbakir, 21 March 2005. (© Reuters/CORBIS)

female) specialists in herbal medicine. Furthermore, there are traditional ways to remove evil spirits (*zirinj, risas rijandin*) and to predict the future (*falebêjî*).

Music plays a much greater role in many Kurdish religious communities than in mainstream Islam. In Muslim communities the *erbane* or *def* (types of tambourine) are regarded as "religious" or indeed sacred instruments, and certain type of Sufi or Dervish music (*qesîde, belûte*) also enjoy religious status. In the Yezidi, Alevi, and Ahl-e Haqq communities certain types of music are regarded as sacred, while some musical instruments are revered as symbols of the faith. In the Yezidi and Ahl-e Haqq traditions such instruments are believed to have played a role in the process of creation.

Celebrations of both secular and popular religious festivals tend to vary from place to place. Seasonal festivals, some of which may have ancient Iranian roots, are common. The spring New Year (Newroz), which is felt to be at the heart of Kurdish culture, is widely celebrated with ceremonies in which fire plays a key role. Besides great Islamic feasts such as the Feast of the Sacrifice and the end of the Ramadan fast, many Kurdish Muslim communities observe the "Night of Power" (Lailat al-Qadr), when God is thought to determine the events of the coming year and believers stay awake (this feast has a Yezidi counterpart), the birthday of the Prophet Muhammad (Mewlûd), and the day of his journey to heaven (Mi'râj). Both Muslim and Yezidi Kurds celebrate the feast of Khidir-Elias, which falls between mid-winter and Newroz. Private observances, especially those marking rites of passage such as weddings and funerals, are important throughout the Islamic Middle East, and Kurdish culture is no exception. These are celebrated with specific observances in each community.

POETRY

Verbal art plays an important role in many of these observances. Long poems praising the Prophet Muhammad and recounting legends about his birth (*Mewlûdname*) and heavenly journey (*Mi'rajname*) are recited during religious gatherings on such occasions, and these form an important element of Kurdish popular religion. Apart from these there are many legends about Sufi holy men, which are normally told as prose stories. Feasts dedicated to such figures (known in some regions as *zêw*) are generally held near the saint's grave or shrine and each year attract thousands of devotees, who sing and play music, dance, eat, and play traditional games in the saint's honor. In parts of Kurdistan the Christian equivalents of such festivals, known by the Neo-Aramaic term *shêhr*, take place near churches and follow much the same pattern; these may be attended by Muslims as well as Christians.

The structure of the textual tradition of the Yezidis and Ahl-e Haqq may be of particular interest to folklorists. In both communities the equivalent of "Scripture" consists of a corpus of relatively complex and difficult, orally transmitted poetic texts, which refer to the history and teachings of the religion in a highly allusive manner. These texts are learned by heart and transmitted by special groups of reciters. To the community at large they would be incomprehensible, however, if not for the existence of a body of popular tales, which are narrated in prose and contain all the information to which the poems allude. Thus the essential religious knowledge of these sects is preserved largely without the help of writing by a combination of sacred poems and folktales.

MYTHS, LEGENDS, AND EPICS

In societies relying on oral transmission rather than written documents and libraries such as most traditional Kurdish communities, the need to define one's cultural identity on the basis of understanding the past is as central as in highly literate civilizations. Among the Yezidis, Ahl-e Haqq, and Alevis, what Westerners might see as a system of myths and legends in fact fulfills the same function as the academic discipline of history does in literate cultures: it defines the most culturally relevant aspects of the past and helps the community remember them. In most other Kurdish communities strategies also exist to preserve an awareness of the past without the help of books. In these largely non-literate environments, accounts of the past tend to be brought down to essentials, and they are transmitted in forms likely to reach the community in a natural, unforced manner.

Thus, after a death women often gather to create and perform laments about the deceased. This provides an outlet for feelings of grief and mourning, while at the same time fixing an image of the deceased in the minds of the listeners and creating a link between past and present. The composition and performance of such laments, which are extemporized but whose structure and composition nonetheless follow traditional rules, are regarded as an art form in Kurdish society. Women who are particularly good at performing laments often become (semi-)professional mourners who are invited to lead the women of the family during mourning rituals.

Ways of transmitting information about the past that may seem more familiar to Western readers are the telling of stories (*çîrok, qisse*) and the performance of "historical" epics (*destan, beyt, sher*), which are thought to be based on true events rather than romantic fantasy. Well-known historical *destan* are "The Castle of Dimdim" (also known as "The Prince of the Golden Lips"), which describes a Kurdish hero's efforts to maintain his independence from foreign dominance. It ends tragically but honorably. There are many comparable storylines describing the events of Kurdish history ("The Twelve Riders of Meriwan" and "The Deeds of Abd al-Rahman Baban," for example), including epics describing the efforts of modern Kurdish fighters to win some form of freedom for their community.

Although such epics play a key role in preserving Kurdish history, they are primarily performed for entertainment and thus form part of Kurdish oral literature. In appeal and style of performance they hardly differ from similar works that could be said to portray cultural ideals rather than events of historical significance. One such "romantic epic," the popular *Memê Alan*, inspired one of the great works of Kurdish written literature, Ehmed Khani's (fl. seventeenth century) *Mem û Zîn*. The work describes the doomed love between a prince and a princess who meet through the supernatural action of fairies or *jinns* and fall in love, but are then again separated. A similar storyline, *Derwêshê Ebdî*, is about a couple who cannot marry owing to social constraints, an important theme in Kurdish life. Popular romances are told both about indigenous Kurdish **heroes** and about well-known figures from the Islamic tradition such as Yusuf and Zoleikha (Joseph and Potiphar's wife) and Leili and Mejnun.

The question of genre in Kurdish oral literature is a thorny one. On the one hand, Kurdish terms for various types of literature differ from place to place, and even in the same locality informants may offer dissimilar definitions. This is complicated further by regional varieties in styles of performance and by the fact that the same storyline can often be used in different genres: it may be performed as an epic, told as a "formal" or "informal" story, and alluded to in laments and popular songs. Moreover, Kurdish and Western criteria for defining literary categories appear to be too widely divergent to admit of a workable, widely accepted compromise. The categories and terms used here, based on data from various Kurmanji-speaking regions, are approximate and have no general validity for the whole of Kurdistan.

Prose genres that are not accompanied by music and are not the province of professionals include the *çîrok*, various types of fairy tale (*efsane, çîranok*), the short and humorous *mesele* ("joke," "amusing tale"), proverbs (*gotinên pêshiyan*, literally, "words of the ancients"), nursery rhymes (*metelok*), riddles (*mamik*), and curses (*nifir*). The edifying prose tales known as *qisse* or *ser(pê)hatî* are felt to have a special historical or moral significance. These are typically told during the frequent gatherings of the males of a community (*shevbiwêrk*) in the "guest room" (*ode, dîwan*) of a prominent figure. (Such sessions traditionally played a key role in the development of Kurdish culture; music and literature could be performed there, religion and tribal history would be discussed, and political decisions made.) *Qisse* are usually told by a particular person because of his talent or position in the community, but such storytellers are not trained professionals.

"Epics" (*destan, beyt, sher*), on the other hand, are normally performed by trained bards, often (though by no means always) in poetic form. Such (semi-)professional bards perform on festive occasions and receive payment. They may or may not accompany themselves on a musical. On the one hand, the prestigious *dengbêj* generally belong to a family of some social standing, which typically turned to this profession because of a special inclination or talent. On the other hand, the *mitirb* (also called *gowende* or *begzade*) belong to a family of performers whose status is much lower than that of the *dengbêj*. In fact, these families are widely regarded as social outsiders. In the early twenty-first century *mitirb* actively resent this position and sometimes seek to be recognized as *dengbêj*. In some areas, those who address such performers by the term *mitirb* (rather than the more respectful *begzade*) can expect to be lampooned in a song. As a result of this, the *mitirb* tradition may be dying out. Some *mitirb* families have now formed bands playing non-traditional music. Formerly, performers of all types learned their art from a master whom they accompanied for several years, from an older relative, or from regular attendance at local *dîwans*, where they could study the performances of well-known artists. Now they are more likely to use cassettes or videotapes for this purpose.

MUSIC

Music plays a more central role in the performance of the *stranbêj* or "singers," who perform lyrical "songs" (*stran, kilam*). *Stranbêjs* transmit the traditional repertoire and often also compose new songs. As in many other cultures, songs of a traditional type are performed on a wide range of occasions. Besides love songs (*stranêd êvînê*), "historical songs" (*stranêd tarîkhî*), lullabies (*lorîn*), and worksongs (for example, *berdolabî*, "spinning songs," *paleyî*, "harvest songs," and *stranêd bênderan*, "threshing songs"), the following genres are of particular interest.

Payîzok, "autumn songs," have their origin in nomadic culture: they were traditionally sung during the annual migration from summer to winter pastures and are full of nostalgia for the fine days and light-hearted flirtations of summer. A characteristic musical "mode" (*meqam*), the *meqamê payîzokan*, is used for this genre. A very similar group of songs is known as *khizêmok*, "nose-ring songs." These treat the same themes but focus on the beloved's nose-ring as an object of the departing lover's longing. For most modern Kurds the days of nomadic migrations are long over, but the songs remain popular. Curiously, both *payîzok* and *khizêmok* are now regarded by many Yezidis as part of their religious tradition, possibly because the unattainable beloved is held to be a metaphor for God. "Spring songs" (*biharok*) are characterized by descriptions of nature and of the emotions that spring provokes. Another genre inspired by Kurdish love of nature is the *serêlî*, which is always performed in the open air and contains long and lyrical descriptions of natural scenes. The word *lawîj*, which may derive from an old Iranian term for "prayer," is used for religious songs. The only known major Christian composition in Kurdish belongs to this genre. In certain areas of Kurdistan, however, the word denotes a melancholy song about a hunter's longing for the hunt. Sad genres also include "mourning songs" (*shînî*) and the beloved *stranêd xerîbiyê*, "songs of exile and alienation," which express a nostalgia deeply rooted in a culture that has known little stability over the centuries.

Kurdish performers may accompany themselves on various instruments, notably the *kema(n)çe* which resembles a violin, or the *saz* or *tembûr*, a popular instrument with six metallic strings and a long neck. For some religious ceremonies, singing at communal gatherings, and dancing, the *def* (tambourine) and *zurna* (which resembles an oboe or small clarinet) are often used. The *def* and *shibab* (flute) are sacred to the Yezidis, while the Ahl-e Haqq revere the *tembûr*. The music of the *bilûr*, a shepherd's pipe made from mulberry or hazelnut bark, is typically heard at performances of romantic epics and traditional dances. The *duzare* is a two-piped instrument made from eagles' bones and produces a vibrating sound.

DANCE

Throughout Kurdistan, on festive occasions one may see rows or circles of men or women, hand in hand or with their arms around their neighbors' shoulders, dancing to the music of *kemançe* or *def* and *zurna* or occasionally accompanied only by singing. This is the *govend* (dance) or *reqsa milan* (dance of the shoulders), the most widely known Kurdish dance. It is by no means the only one, however. Kurdish culture has a rich repertoire of folk dances intended to portray a range of emotions and activities such as love, hunting, war, preparing the fields, sowing, and harvesting. Every region has its own dances.

The *galûç* (sickle) dance from the Adiyaman (Kurdish: *Semsûr*) region portrays work in the fields: successive scenes show sowing, using a sickle for weeding, wiping the sweat from one's forehead, and having a drink of water to quench one's thirst. A similar dance is known to exist in Iranian Kurdistan. The *simsim* (the name of a reed that can be used as a flute), which is performed at harvest time on the threshing floor and is danced around a fire, is a contest between groups. Two of these dance at the same time, and whenever one group gives up, it is replaced by another. The public contributes to the proceedings with rhythmic movements and applause. The *khet* (line) from the region of Bingöl (Kurdish: *Çewlik*) symbolizes an eternal problem of peasant life: the conflict between two parties (families or tribes) over land. In the dance, the parties change the positions of stones marking the boundaries ("lines") of their fields. The dance *gur û pez* (wolf and sheep) portrays the life of shepherds. One dancer represents the wolf, another the shepherd. While the shepherd is tending his flock, the wolf lies in waiting and seizes a sheep, which it devours. The shepherd then sets a trap and eventually kills the wolf.

SPORTS AND GAMES

Kurdish popular games sometimes bear witness to the community's remote Iranian, or indeed Indo-European past. An example is the winter game *Hungilîsk* or *Gustîlk* (ring), which is played by two (usually all-male) teams. Each of these has a leader, who speaks for his team. The two teams face each other across a stove in the middle of a room. The leader of one group begins the game by hiding a ring on the person of one of the members of his group, all of whom are covered by a blanket. The other side has to discover who has the ring. Only their leader's word counts, and then only when he swears by the stove. When he says, "By the stove, so-and-so is empty [that is, does not have the ring]," or "By the stove, so-and-so has the ring," then the person in question must say whether the statement is true. If it is true, the searchers have a point; if not, the point goes to the other side. These rules are probably associated with the ancient Iranian oaths by fire.

CHALLENGES OF THE MODERN WORLD

Kurdish identity, a phenomenon not universally recognized in the Middle East, may these days consist as much of an awareness of essential elements of Kurdish culture such as those described above as it does fluency in the Kurdish language. Both the artistic complexity and the beauty of much of Kurdish folk culture as well as its significance for a population of some 30 million in some ways put Kurdish folklore on an equal footing with Western "high" culture. Although it is true that much of traditional Kurdish culture may not survive the twenty-first century in its present form (the hereditary transmitters of the sacred oral traditions of the Yezidis, for instance, cannot persuade their children to follow in their footsteps; in Turkey most of the villages where Kurdish culture was once transmitted have been razed to the ground during the civil war of the past decades), the younger generation of Kurds is showing considerable interest in the traditional culture of its people. The trendsetters of this generation are usually well educated and have been influenced by Western models, and their perceptions of the character of some forms of folk culture tend to differ from that of their elders. Thus, instead of hearing a single bard perform a classical epic, Kurds are now in a position to compare recordings of performances by various *dengbêjs* and generally notice that these differ on many points. While this is a normal feature of oral culture, the younger generation tends to have a mental image of literature that is informed by the study of written literature and thus assumes that only one version can be the "true" one. Efforts are often made, therefore, to discover or restore the "original" form of traditional epics and present this to the public as the only true version. Furthermore, many of the hitherto secret, orally transmitted hymns of the Yezidis are now being committed to writing. These texts, which are highly poetic and allusive in character, are currently being scrutinized by Yezidi intellectuals as a potential basis for drawing up a prescriptive code of conduct or an authoritative body of teachings. Thus, while the range of technologies open to modern Kurds tends to have the effect of altering the character of traditional lore to some extent, at the same time it helps to popularize folk traditions and to raise their status.

STUDIES OF KURDISH FOLKLORE

Few books on Kurdish folk culture in English are easily accessible to the interested reader. An excellent study of the values that inform Kurdish culture is Sweetnam (2004). A range of aspects of Kurdish culture is discussed in Kreyenbroek and Allison (1996). Impressive and readable studies of folk literature in Kurdistan are Allison (2001) and Sabar (1982).

BIBLIOGRAPHY
Allison, Christine. 2001. *The Yezidi Oral Tradition in Iraqi Kurdistan*. Richmond: Curzon.

Kreyenbroek, Philip, and Christine Allison, eds. 1996. *Kurdish Culture and Identity*. London: Zed Books.

Sabar, Yona. 1982. *The Folk Literature of the Kurdistani Jews: An Anthology.* New Haven: Yale University Press.

Sweetnam, Denise L. 2004. *Kurdish Culture: A Cross-Cultural Guide.* 2nd edition. Bonn: Verl. Für Kultur und Wiss. Schirrmacher.

Philip G. Kreyenbroek and Luqman Turgut

LEBANON

GEOGRAPHY AND HISTORY

A small but diverse country in the Middle East, Lebanon has an area approximately the size of Connecticut: about 220 kilometers long and 45 kilometers wide. Lebanon was referred to as the "land of milk and honey" in the Old Testament and was home to major Phoenician cities (Byblos, Tyre, and Sidon). Because of its geographical location, Lebanon has always served as a crossroads for Western and Eastern civilizations. A visit to the archeological site of Nahr el Kalb, north of Beirut, gives an idea of Lebanon's strategic position. Here, the visitor can admire the seventeen inscriptions or steles carved in the rocks, all left by the various victorious army forces who came through this area over the centuries (from the oldest stele left by Pharaoh Ramses II's Egyptian army to the one commemorating the liberation of South Lebanon from the Israeli army on 24 May 2000).

Modern Lebanon's rich culture derives from its social, religious, and cosmopolitan diversity. Christianity and Islam are the dominant religions, and more than seventeen religious denominations live together in this small land. Each religious group has its own cultural and social traditions and customs and, in this way, contributes to the unique composition of Lebanese society. Because of political, economical, or social reasons, many different ethnic groups in the Middle East moved to Lebanon over the years and made this place their homeland. Whether you walk through the streets of Borj Hammoud, north of Beirut, and get a taste of **Armenia** or travel though the mountains of the Chouf and discover the mysticism of the Druze, an independent and secretive religious group, you will come across the rich heritage of the Lebanese people.

STORIES AND JOKES OF ABU EL-ABED

All Lebanese know Abu El-Abed, but no one has ever actually met him. They have all heard about him, but nobody can really describe what he looks like. Abu El-Abed is the most famous comic character in Lebanon, and he lives in the collective memory of the people. The jokes about Abu El-Abed are well known, and little children as well as the older generation can always tell a story about this legendary figure. Usually, the joke starts with the typical phrase, "Once upon a time, Abu El-Abed. . . ." There are many Web sites dedicated to this comic character (for example, www.abuabed.net), and Internet surfers or Abu El-Abed fans are invited to add any joke they have heard (or even better, invented) about this legendary man from Beirut. Although the character lives only in the mind of all Lebanese, consistent descriptions of this beloved figure emerge in folklore. Abu El-Abed could be the grandfather, father, or uncle whom everyone has, the ridiculous character in a family. It is generally agreed that Abu El-Abed is from Beirut as his nickname "El Beiruti" indicates. We know nothing about his family except that he is married to Oum El-Abed (Mother of Abed) and they have a son called "Abed." Does this Beiruti man even hold down a job? It is difficult to confirm, as the only place he can be seen is at Kahwat el Ejeez, his preferred coffee shop in downtown Beirut. Although the character is legendary, the coffee shop did really exist in old downtown Beirut. It was frequented only by men, who usually showed up late in the afternoon to drink coffee, play backgammon, smoke a *Nargile*, and talk about the local politics or the neighborhood gossip. These types of men-only coffee shops are very common in the Arab world and might look very bizarre or even intimidating for an outsider or a non-Arab traveler.

When it comes to his personality, Abu El-Abed is described as a non-educated person from the poor class of society, but very ingenious and slick. His lack of education is counterbalanced by his sense of humor and his native commonsense. He can be a complete idiot or a very smart man depending on the end of the joke. Abu El-Abed also embodies the typical figure of a macho man, who cannot accept or bear any comment that could be interpreted as criticizing his masculinity. One can imagine him as a strongly built, muscular man who would not be afraid of stepping into a fight, or even starting one for that matter. He is also depicted as the *Zaim el hara* (the leader or boss in the neighborhood) who needs to be informed about everything that happens in the district under his control. As far as other aspects of his physical appearance are concerned, it is commonly accepted that he can be recognized by his big moustache (a symbol of masculinity in the Arab world) and his traditional red *Tarbouche* (a typical local hat). This description is barely sufficient for a character of his importance. However, it can be completed by the imagination of every Lebanese. A quick look on the various Internet sites dedicated to Abu El-Abed shows how different the descriptions of this character can be. When asked to submit a drawing of their favorite joker, fans have sent a wide range of pictures. Although they do not look the same, they all have in common the moustache and the *Tarbouche*.

The jokes of Abu El-Abed can cover a wide range of topics from politics to local life or traditions. They are an innocent way to criticize the current political events in the country or the latest ridiculous fashion adopted by the inhabitants of Beirut. But many of the most appreciated jokes are for adults and have a sexual content. Because the character can be very vulgar when it comes to sex, he allows people to tell adult jokes without necessarily sounding inappropriate. The only excuse is that these adventures happened to Abu El-Abed, and people are reporting them. Another comic fact is that this vulgar, non-educated person hardly speaks any words of English or French, the two foreign languages widely spoken by many Lebanese. This detail adds to the wordplay and the confusion that can be created in many situations. Whenever he does not understand a precise situation, Abu El-Abed discusses it with his longtime best friend, Abu Steif, who is not all that much smarter than his friend. The two men love to sit in Kahwet el Ejezz and reinvent the world with their strange stories and jokes. The age of both men cannot be defined. It does not matter if they are in their mid-thirties or much older because their jokes will always entertain the next generation of Lebanese.

The repertoire of Abu El-Abed jokes can't be completed without mentioning the ones related to his wife Oum El-Abed, commonly imagined as chubby. She is the one who is supposed to provide the rational side missing in her husband. Oum El-Abed is not as notorious as Abu El-Abed, but little by little she is gaining in popularity among the Lebanese. She brings a feminine side to jokes usually invented and appreciated by the masculine gender. There are fewer jokes about her than about her silly partner, but many Web sites have honored her with a section especially related to her adventures.

Comic Abu El-Abed stories and jokes have become very popular not only in Lebanon, but also in many other Arab countries. One just needs to have a Lebanese friend, and he will certainly hear about these various jokes. However, those who do not share a Lebanese cultural background will not be able really to appreciate the full meaning of every joke. The main reason for this is that Abu El-Abed speaks in the Lebanese dialect, and any translation of his slang will not express enough of the wordplay in question and might dissipate its effect and originality. The legend of Abu El-Abed has been continued and developed in several serious newspapers in addition to theatrical productions and literary works. This notorious character will continue to live in the Lebanese collective consciousness; he will always be present at parties and happy events in order to share in the entertainment.

FOLKSONGS

The best way to enjoy and understand Lebanese folklore is to listen to the songs of Fairouz, the most famous living Lebanese singer. Her fame is celebrated not only in Lebanon, but all over the Arab world. Born in 1935, Nouhad Haddad was discovered at an early age for her amazing voice and talent. After beginning as a chorus singer at a radio station, she took the name of Fairouz, which means "turquoise." She later married a well-known composer and writer named Assi Rahbani, who along with his brother Mansour shaped the popular music of Lebanon in the 1950s and 1960s. Fairouz's performances at the Baalbek International Festivals, which take place every summer in the old Roman temple of Baalbek, sealed her fame and assured the meteoric rise of her career. Along with the Rahbani brothers, a new generation of legendary artists was born. Fairouz's and the Rahbani brothers' music is considered today an important part of Lebanese folklore tradition. The impressive repertoire of Fairouz consists mostly of songs inspired by the land, the countryside, and the daily life in villages of Lebanon. The lyrics reveal legends, popular beliefs, or jokes and hint at a sense of the popular humor around the country. For example, any Lebanese can sing the lyrics of "*El bosta*" (The Bus), one of Fairouz's most popular and funny songs. It tells the story of a young man who rides the bus between two villages, Himlaya and Tannourine, and experiences love at first sight for Alia, a young woman sitting next to him. Travelers could experience this picturesque scene by riding one

Lebanese singer Fairouz, 1962. (René Burri/ Magnum Photos)

of these typical old buses. Some passengers are eating lettuce or figs; others are calling on the driver to close the window because it is windy outside; newcomers need to squeeze in and hold the door; and our lover is only concerned with the beauty of Alia's eyes. Every generation of Lebanese has at some point sung the song of Alia: it is very common to hear schoolchildren singing together about the charm and the beauty of Alia (or their own love) while riding their schoolbuses on an excursion day. One or two children may bring with them a *Derbake* (drum) to provide the rhythm to this song about a desperate and impossible love.

If we look back today at Fairouz's repertoire, we can appreciate how much her songs reflect especially well the different phases that modern Lebanon went through historically. Songs from the 1950s, 1960s, or early 1970s celebrate the joyfulness and heedlessness of life in this country, known as the "Switzerland of the Middle East," before the outbreak of the civil war in 1975. These songs celebrate the previously peaceful and easy life in Lebanon. Fairouz sings mostly love songs, praises of the beauty of Lebanon, children's songs, songs with folkloric themes depicting the simple life in the Lebanese mountains, pop and dance songs, and Eastern classical music (*Tarab*). When the war started in 1975, a shift was noticeable in Fairouz's music, as new themes emerged that describe the suffering of the Lebanese people and the misery of war. Happiness could no longer be sung about in a time of separation and death. The war is mentioned in several songs, and themes of divorce, broken families, or hate started to appear for the first time in Fairouz's repertoire. The song *"Bahebak Ya Libnan"* (I Love You, Lebanon) is a hymn to those who made the decision to stay in Lebanon during the war and not emigrate because of their love of their country. This song will remain for future generations as a part of the collective memory of Lebanon. Fairouz is the subject of two Web sites (www.fayrouz.org and www.fairouz.com).

POETRY AND MUSIC

Literature, poetry and music have always had an important role in Lebanese culture. Among various cultural achievements in the arts, undoubtedly *dabke* and *zajal* are two of the most popular forms of Lebanese folklore. Westerners may be more familiar with *dabke*, the national dance, because it has been performed onstage in many international festivals outside of Lebanon. However, *zajal*, a popular form of oral poetry, remains less well known by non-Arabs, because the only real way to discover it is through a visit to Lebanon.

The art of *zajal* is very ancient, and its origin is still debatable. However, this form of improvised poetry stems from the long tradition of oral poetry in Arabic literature. Poetry duels have always been common between Arab poets, and *zajal* seems to derive from these traditions. *Zajal* festivals are very frequent today in Lebanon. They are usually organized in the summer season and take place in small mountain villages. These events attract a large number of visitors, who, along with the locals, gather over a meal and spend the whole afternoon or evening listening to the satiric and funny duels between competitive groups from each village. The typical Lebanese *Mezze* (which consists of an extensive variety of small dishes and entrees such as hummus, eggplant dip, chicken, and lamb) is served, along with the local spirit known as *arak*. *Shisha* pipes (or *nargile*) are also available for those who would like to smoke a fruit-flavored tobacco from a water pipe. This makes these events a delightful moment of music, food, and entertainment.

The *zajal* groups are generally composed of four to five members who compete for prizes. An enthusiastic audience encourages these improvisational poets; indeed, the audience likes to repeat the lyrics and tease the opponents. The referees make sure that the allotted amount of time is respected, and their decision is based on the quality and the originality of every poem. The poets enter into witty dialogues and improvise songs rather than recited verses in Lebanese dialect. The sung topics could be a criticism of a political event or a satire of an event that happened in a village. They also celebrate qualities related to a certain village (the bravery of its men or the incomparable beauty of its women) in opposition to the mediocre reputation of others. While poets play with words, the audience enjoys a good meal in a relaxing and playful atmosphere.

Zajal is sometimes performed at weddings. On this occasion, friends and family of the bride and groom sing their recommendations for the new couple. Parents like to advise their children about the secrets for a happy married life. Sometimes they will give as an example their own success for happiness or, as a joke, sing about the unbearable imperfections of the partner discovered only after years of marriage. *Zajal* can also be a part of a funeral tradition, especially in the mountains. Neighbors and friends are supposed to mourn (sometimes with exaggeration) the person who has died by singing about his or her great qualities. The poetry and the songs are a high form of tribute to the deceased.

For those who would like to get an idea of what *zajal* sounds like and to get a sense of this sung poetic tradition, a good place to begin is by listening to Wadih Es Safi, a famous Lebanese singer who promoted the development of Lebanese folk music through poetry and *zajal*. The themes of his songs inspire patriotism and deal with love and moral values. Wadih Es Safi is considered one of the key reference points in the art of Lebanese *zajal*.

The popular heritage of *zajal* is being revived today in Lebanon, especially after the end of the war in the early 1990s. It is a way to bring people together and to forge Lebanese identity around a common folklore practice shared by all Lebanese. Should it be seen as a way to learn how to use words rather than weapons to fight after many years of a terrible war? *Zajal* programs have been broadcasted weekly on local television and are usually appreciated by the older fans. The younger generation has mixed feelings toward this tradition. On the one hand, many young Lebanese find *zajal* outdated and prefer to turn to Western music and pop festivals. Most of them will not watch a *zajal* program on television, finding it boring and unattractive. But on the other hand, they are aware of the importance of maintaining and reviving the heritage and the old traditions. They can be seen participating in a *zajal* night at a festival so that the tradition is preserved and continues to live.

Dance

The Lebanese consider *dabke* their national dance, though it is also performed in surrounding Arab countries such as Syria, Jordan, and Iraq. The main difference between these different versions of *dabke* can be found in the choreography and dance steps as well as in the traditional costumes that dancers wear to represent their country or geographical area. The dance usually depicts aspects of village life. The dancers might carry a local craft (pottery, stick, or headband) while performing the group dance. A typical *Dabke* show starts with a scene describing traditional life: the harvest season in the fields, a village festival, or a gathering in the village's main square. The dancers are dressed in colorful festive clothes. The women wear flowing skirts, long vests, and veils or a headscarf. They carry water jugs or fruit baskets with a clear reference to the tasks usually assigned to women. The men wear the traditional *sherwal* (a type of black pants—very baggy from waist to knee, but tight from knee to ankle) and *labbadeh* (hat). Some other men cover their head with the typical *keffiya* (a checkered black headscarf) and are dressed in magnificent vests, shirts, and black boots. A dancer enters the scene with a *Derbake* (small drum) followed by other musicians. He sets the first rhythm, and the music calls the villagers to start the dance. The men and the women hold hands and form a line to start the *Dabke* beat with the *Ala Dalouna* song. They stomp the ground with one foot while moving in a circle around the scene. The audience cheers the dance with claps to create the appropriate *Dabke* rhythm. The dance is the perfect setting to introduce a local singer who will entertain the audience.

The *Dabke* show often includes a sword dance between two warriors who impress the audience with their agility in manipulating the sword. The tempo of the *Dabke* increases with the strong beat of the stomping on the ground. The *Dabke* dance is performed on many occasions: parties, nightclubs, and weddings. The steps are easy to learn, a feature that encourages even the shyest person to join the dancing group. Families and friends like to gather around a celebratory meal, drink wine or *arak*, and celebrate a joyful moment by dancing the *Dabke*.

The history of *Dabke* can be traced to the old days when tiled roofs were installed on Lebanese houses. To fix a cracked mud roof, especially in winter, villagers would gather on the top of the roof, hold hands, and start stomping so that the new mud could be adjusted. They would usually sing in order to provide a rhythm for their steps and ensure that their movements were coordinated. This ancestral folkloric tradition survived with time in the form of the national dance called *Dabke*.

A famous Lebanese choreographer, Abdel Halim Caracalla, who wanted to give a Lebanese style to this folkloric dance, developed the tradition of *Dabke*. Today, the famous and legendary Caracalla Dance Company performs Lebanon's folkloric dances on many internationally renowned stages. Every Caracalla show is like a wonderful painting of traditional life in Lebanese villages, where the old tradition mixes with classical dance. (See the Caracalla Web site at www.caracalladance.com.)

It is interesting to point out that during the Lebanese war (1975–1990), the verbal expression *Dabaket*, which means, "the *Dabke* has started," was constantly used to refer to very strong fighting or bombardments. In other words, it was as if the sound of exploding bombs reminded people of the rhythm of the uninterrupted feet beating the ground as heard in a *Dabke* dance. This expression shows the characteristic sense of humor of the Lebanese people, who were still able to joke about a situation even under the worst conditions.

FUNERAL RITUALS

In the very busy streets of a Lebanese city, it is still quite common to see a funeral procession that slows down traffic and creates a traffic jam. On that occasion, contrary to their usual habits, drivers will not honk impatiently, and passersby will stop and bow their heads to show respect for the dead. While the crowd marches in the street, shop owners will stand outside their store and pull down their iron windows. Christians usually make the sign of the cross, and Muslims say a short prayer. Everyone will repeat the words *Allah Yerhamo* (or *Yerhama* for a woman), the intercessory words asking God to be merciful to the deceased. Depending on the importance or the social class of the deceased, the funeral procession can be sometimes preceded by a small marching band or group of musicians who play special mourning music. The crowd carries the open coffin, which normally scares the little children watching from their balconies, who were at first attracted by the music outside. When the deceased is a young person, he or she will typically be laid out in a white coffin. Older people are carried in a brown wooden one. The tradition also requires celebrating the wedding of a single man or woman who has died young before he or she is buried. Because the unexpected death has disturbed the normal sequence of life, a quick wedding ceremony will take place so that the burial can be considered as the final chapter of a life. All along the way to the church, the procession will stop at the main crossroads, and the friends who carry their beloved will perform a dance by turning three times in a circle and unbalancing the coffin. These dances in a circle are supposed to replace the wedding dance that will never take place. They provide a very intense and emotional moment in the procession, especially when the public around realizes how young the dead man or woman is after seeing his or her framed picture carried by one of the friends.

Another funeral tradition is to decorate the street where the deceased person used to live with ribbons hanging from balcony to balcony. The color of the ribbon indicates the age of the dead. White ribbons are specifically used for young, and the image of all these hanging ribbons calls to mind the decoration found in a church on a wedding celebration. At home, family and friends gather early in the morning to comfort each other before the burial ceremony. The customs of social politeness require that the immediate neighbors (usually those who live on the same floor in a building) open the doors of their apartments to receive additional visitors when the house of the family of the victim becomes too crowded. The neighbors share the grief and receive the condolences too. Bitter coffee is served in small cups (because life has lost its savor, the coffee cannot be sweetened), and food is offered to those who traveled long distances. If you would like to help with preparing food, superstition requires you to bring a menu consisting of an odd number of dishes to avoid a pair of deaths in the family. The close family usually sits in the living room, and visitors will come in turn to sit next to them and share their sympathy and concern. The men wear dark suits and black ties, and the women dress in black as well. No music is played; sometimes even the television will not be turned on. During this period of grieving, entertainment is not allowed, and listening to music or television is seen as a sign of unconcern. It is always wiser to follow the funeral protocol in order to avoid the neighbors' gossip in the future. The mourning will last forty days, during which a widow is supposed to dress in black, and a man must wear a black tie. Entertainment, parties, and dinners outside should be avoided, and radio and television, if turned on at home, will be at a low volume.

CELEBRATIONS

Middle Easterners particularly enjoy having fun and giving parties. They will always find a time for celebration because social ties, connections, and gatherings are very important in these non-individualistic societies. Christian and Muslim traditions and holidays are widely celebrated in Lebanon. The Feast of Saint Barbara, a Christian celebration, is one example of a religious holiday shared by both Christian and Muslim children. It begins on the night of 3 December, when preparations are made to celebrate the memory of Saint Barbara the following day. Despite the fact that Muslims do not venerate this saint, it is very common to see young Muslim children taking part in this special feast. The way in which the Feast of Saint Barbara is celebrated has several similarities with Halloween except it is a two-day event and its commercial aspect does not stretch over a whole month (as can be seen in October for Halloween in the United States). On the night of the "Eid al Barbara," children dress up in different costumes with masks and go from house to house knocking on neighbors' doors. In memory of Saint Barbara, they sing the story of her martyrdom and perform traditional folksongs or dances. In acknowledgment of their efforts, they receive candies or money. At home, a candlelit, wheat-based meal is prepared for the occasion and served with special desserts that can be purchased in a pastry shop. Late in the afternoon waiting lines are formed at these *Helwayat* (shops that only sell pastries and ice cream), as the Feast of Saint Barbara cannot be complete if you have not had boiled wheat and traditional pastries on your table. The "Eid al Barbara" is considered by many Eastern Christians to begin the Christmas season. Many churches in Lebanon are dedicated to this young girl who was tortured and beheaded because of her refusal to give up her faith. Unofficial belief and tradition claim that Saint Barbara lived in the city of Baalbeck in Lebanon during the third century. Regardless of their religion, children are mostly attracted by the commercial aspects of this holiday, namely the costumes and food, not to mention the pleasure of dressing up and putting on makeup, and it is quite common to see Muslim children celebrating the Feast of Saint Barbara in a secular way.

This event provides one example of the cooperation between the two main religions in Lebanon, where one can see Christians participating in the celebration of some Muslim traditions and vice versa. Unfortunately, every holiday has its commercial aspects, which too often become more important than the holiday itself. Because of the influence of Western traditions in Lebanon, Halloween is becoming little by little a popular holiday too. Lebanese who have lived abroad, particularly in the United States, like to celebrate the American tradition of Halloween once they return to their homeland. The strong influence of American movies has reinforced acceptance for this new imported tradition. Halloween decorations can be found nowadays in Lebanon during the month of October. Halloween is not as popular as the Feast of Saint Barbara, but a very small number of Lebanese (those who have adapted to Western traditions while living abroad) like to consider Halloween a richer and more interesting tradition than its Eastern counterpart. For them, the Feast of Saint Barbara is a holiday associated with the poorer classes of society, while

Halloween, because of its Western and thus "modern" aspect, has been appropriated by the educated and upper classes.

CHALLENGES OF THE MODERN WORLD

Although the Lebanese are very attached to their traditions and proud of their identity, many aspects of the Lebanese folklore are slowly disappearing. This change can be noticed in the way funerals are held nowadays in Lebanon. Many educated Lebanese do not necessarily appreciate anymore the whole show of a funeral procession and prefer to have a more discreet burial. Some even consider that they should not have to comply with these village traditions only to satisfy society. On the other hand, the younger generations feel divided between their desire to imitate the Western world and adopt its habits and customs, and their awareness of the importance of keeping old traditions alive out of respect for their ancestors. While in the past many villagers moved to the cities for economic reasons, today their children have abandoned the village (or mountain) mentality of their parents after having lived in the city and adopted the new manners. It is becoming less common to see Lebanese wanting to celebrate funerals according to the steps imposed by tradition. The sense of "it has to be done just like this" because of the fear of what the neighbors will think and the pressure of society is not reason enough anymore to maintain outdated habits. Lebanese society still needs to reach a balance between Western influence and maintaining the heritage of tradition and folklore. *See also* **Israel**; **Palestine**.

BIBLIOGRAPHY

Caracalla. N.d. *Oriental Nights* (sound recording). Bella 00000B17E.

Es Safi, Wadih. N.d. *Best of Wadi Es Safi Vol. 1* (sound recording). Emi B00004UAZO.

———. N.d. *Inta Omri* (sound recording). Emi B00004UF1O.

Fairouz (Fairuz). 2001. *Live at Beiteddine 2000* (sound recording). Musicrama 784302.

———. N.d. *Modern Favorites* (sound recording). EMI INT'L 529815.

Gulick, John. 1971 (1955). *Social Structure and Social Change in a Lebanese Village*. New York: Johnson Reprint.

Huxley, Frederick Charles. 1978. *Wasita in a Lebanese Context: Social Exchange among Villagers and Outsiders*. Ann Arbor: University of Michigan Museum of Anthropology.

Muhawi, Ibrahim, and Sharif Kanaana. 1989. *Speak, Bird, Speak Again: Palestinian Arab Folktales*. Berkeley: University of California Press.

Nuwayhid, Jamal Salim, and others. 2002. *Abul Jmeel's Daughter and Other Stories: Arab Folk Tales from Palestine and Lebanon*. New York: Interlink Books.

Skurzynski, Gloria. 1977. *Two Fools and a Faker: Three Lebanese Folk Tales*. New York: Lathrop, Lee, and Shepard.

Jean-Pierre Taoutel

PALESTINE

GEOGRAPHY AND HISTORY

Located on the eastern coast of the Mediterranean Sea with the Jordan River on its east, Palestine is bordered by **Lebanon** to the north and Egypt to the south. Since antiquity, nearly every powerful empire has attempted to conquer the land and oppress its residents: early Assyrians and Babylonians, Persians, Greeks, Romans, Byzantines, Moslem-Arabs, and Ottomans, who finally were forced to give up the country to the British Mandate after World War I.

In geographical terms, Palestine is usually defined as the lands within the borders of the British Mandate. This is the area of the State of **Israel** and the Palestinian Territories under the rule of the Palestinian Authority, including the West Bank and the Gaza Strip. This small country is the seat of three monotheistic religions: Judaism, Christianity, and Islam. Jerusalem is the holiest city in the world for members of all of these religions. The land is strategically placed in the epicenter of the three continents comprising the Ancient World: Asia, Europe, and Africa. It is also the area of the world richest in crude oil. The distinctiveness of this land lies not only in its per-

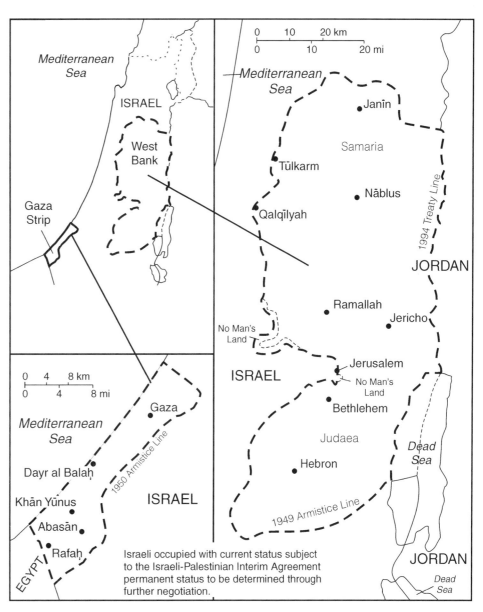

Palestine.

ceived sanctity but also in its topography. Despite being very small (less than 25,000 square kilometers), the country contains a narrow coastal plain, to the east of which lies a hilly region with small valleys. East of the hilly region is the Jordan Valley, which spans the entire country from its northern border to its most southern point on the beaches of the Red Sea. The country also contains the Dead Sea (the lowest place on earth), the northern mountains of Galilee, and the deserts of Negev.

In 1947, the United Nations partitioned the country into two states: a Jewish state and an Arab state. A bloody war immediately broke out, which led to the foundation of the State of Israel on part of Mandatory Palestinian land. Egypt controlled the Gaza Strip, while Jordan controlled the West Bank until 1967, when these areas were occupied by Israel. After the wars of 1948 and 1967, most Palestinian Arabs found themselves to be refugees, whether within Israel and the West Bank and Gaza Strip or in neighboring Arab countries. In 2005 approximately 10 million Palestinians are spread throughout various locales: 2.3 million Palestinians live in the West Bank; 1.4 million live in the Gaza Strip; 1.2 million live in Israel and are considered Israeli citizens; 2.8 million live in Jordan; approximately half a million live in Syria and half a million live in Lebanon; seventy thousand live in Egypt; six hundred thousand live in other Arab countries; a quarter of a million live in the United States; and more than three hundred thousand Palestinians live in other countries throughout the world.

Therefore, one interested in investigating Palestinian folklore specifically or Palestinian culture in general will encounter a difficult problem: What is Palestinian folklore? Which folklore is Palestinian? To whom does this folklore belong? Is it the folklore of residents of the West Bank, whose cultural ties to the Jordanian kingdom are stronger, or the folklore of the residents of the Gaza Strip, whose connections to Egypt are strong? Is it the folklore of Palestinians in Israel, whose folklore differs markedly from that of their brothers and sisters in the Palestinian Territories? Is it perhaps the folklore of the Palestinians living in refugee camps in Jordan, Syria, or Lebanon? Maybe it is the folklore of the Palestinians living in other Arab countries or other countries throughout the world?

Palestinians are actually those people who lived in Palestine, defined by its Mandatory borders. Some have continued to live there, but most have been forced to leave the land because of wars. Some researchers claim that some of these people are descendants of Jews who inhabited the land in the past and that survivals of their folklore continue to thrive. These researchers may be called the "Biblical school" and trace all of the folklore to early Biblical sources. Many other researchers have adopted the Cana'anite approach, according to which present-day Palestinians are the offspring of the Cana'anites, who lived in the land before Abraham arrived from Iraq and settled in the area. Support for this argument is found in the many Cana'anite motifs that continue to survive in present-day Palestinian ways of life, both spiritual and material. A third school argues that some Palestinians descend from the nations who resided in the land before Abraham arrived, such as the Cana'anites, Hittites, Amorites, and others. They point to motifs from the cultures of these people passed down to contemporary Palestinian culture, such as surnames (usually denoting names of tribes) which are similar to these nations: Kana'an, Kana'ani, Kana'na, A'mori, A'marana, and H'itti. They also agree that one should not negate the possibility that present-day Palestinians include some people who were originally Jews who accepted Christianity or Islam and adopted Arab Islamic ways of life.

They also point to the immigrants who came from neighboring countries because of security or economics. These may be identified by names of tribes that indicate geographic origins: H'ijazi (from H'ijaz in Saudi Arabia), Misri or Masarweh (from Egypt), Iraqi (from Iraq), Suri, Halabi, and Shami (from Syria, Haleb, and Damascus), and Mugrabi (from North Africa), for example. Those who conquered the land during other eras also left their signs. There are Greeks who settled here and became part of the land and Crusaders whose names and physical attributes point toward their origins. In fact, Palestinian folklore absorbed folklore **motifs** from these nations, coming with the immigrants who found refuge and a safe haven in Palestine during different historical eras. These people assimilated over generations and centuries and became the Palestinian nation with shared lifeways, fate, memory, history, national goals, and identity. They created a unique Palestinian folklore and culture, reflecting Palestinian life and its past, present, and future. This remained continuous, collective, and consolidated until severely damaged and destroyed by the many wars of the twentieth century.

Many travelers and pilgrims have visited or lived in this land throughout the generations because of its geographical and strategic position and because of its holiness in the eyes of those practicing the three monotheistic religions. The land attracted much attention and interest among researchers, even in ancient times. Herodotos (484–420 B.C.E.), the first recorded historian, showed interest in the Eastern countries, particularly Palestine, on his travels from Phoenicia to Egypt and dedicated space to it in his writings. Since the time of Herodotos, various travelers and Orientalists have continued to be interested in the land and its people. Folklore was a main component in the different chronicles and travel memoirs written by those who have visited the country over the years. The writers of these chronicles were interested in the religious aspect of the country and followed the trail of Jesus's various journeys in addition to what all travelers are searching for: satisfaction of curiosity, miracles, and anything that draws attention. As early as the fourth century C.E., we find folklore descriptions of holy water springs in Jericho with special qualities, a nearby cave in which King Solomon punished the demons in Jerusalem, a description of how Jesus was taught the alphabet in Nazareth, the bench on which he used to sit, the beautiful Hebrew women of Nazareth, and the Jews of Sebastia, who hated foreigners in the sixth century.

PALESTINIAN IDENTITY AND FOLKLORE

Palestinian society consists of many groups and sub-groups to which one simultaneously belongs and to which one has a variety of duties, depending upon placement therein. These are the family, the extended family, the sub-tribe, the tribe, the nation, the culture, the place, and the faith—though this hierarchy differs from region to region. Palestinian folklore has maintained this hierarchy of belonging through the generations, thus conserving an important facet of the culture. Almost all forms of folklore encourage maintaining group loyalties and hierarchies. Proverbs, for example, encourage the individual to support those who are close to him before supporting strangers ("Me and my brother versus my cousin; me and my cousin versus the stranger"), while wedding customs encourage endogamous over exogamous marriages. A bride who marries a groom from another family is seen as being lost or at least producing children for the enemy.

It should be noted that the Mandatory government, like other governments controlling the land, always encouraged belonging to the extended family and the tribe (a primary component of Arab culture that survives even today). This led to separation between members of one nation (the colonial policy known as "divide and rule") and kept the Palestinians busy with intertribal conflicts instead of unifying all of the different groups against the foreign oppressor.

Another function played by Palestinian folklore is teaching the Palestinian **worldview**. For example, the folktale aims to explain and support the origins of various objects. A group of boulders shaped in human form began as an entourage accompanying a bride to her groom's home. On the way one woman contaminated a loaf of bread, which is holy in arid and desert areas, and the entourage was punished by becoming a group of rocks. Another example is a spring of water, whose origin is attributed to St. George. Passing through the area with his army, the saint stuck his spear into the ground when they could not find water to drink. When he removed the spear and began to walk away, a spring gushed forth from the spot. These two folktales teach a wealth of values not taught in any school or academy and educate people from a young age to treat both bread and water with reverence in the desert areas. It is still common for a Palestinian child, upon finding a crumb of bread on the ground, to kiss it and put it on his head as a sign of respect and holiness. The second example plays a similar role. In a land that suffers from lack of water and depends upon agriculture, rain and water ensured the continuation of life.

Folklore also serves as a mirror, reflecting feelings, emotions, and attitudes of individuals and society especially toward transitions in the life cycle and the calendar. In Palestine people are warned against traveling between Christmas and Epiphany even when among non-Christians who do not celebrate these holidays. This is not a religious motif at all but rather representative of the common knowledge that between the Christian holidays of Christmas and Epiphany (the end of December and the beginning of January) is the rainiest season, when it is most dangerous to travel.

Folksongs can help to teach values. A song that praises positive characteristics or denounces bad characteristics can become a type of anthem sung by society and direct people toward the positive and away from the negative. Folksongs also reflect people's feelings, no less than proverbs: when songs of praise are sung at the birth of a male child, and when silence is heard when a daughter is born, this of course reflects the preference for boys over girls within society. When songs are sung to a bride and groom, comparing them to heroes or even to the sun and the stars, it is very easy to determine the feelings of the singers and identify their ideals.

On long winter's nights, when everyone gathers around the hearth and quietly listens to the local singers describing the pain of separation, one can feel the absolute romance that controls the lives of the performers and their audience. When the singer completes his part and the storyteller begins to relate a story from among the ancient classic tales such as the *One Thousand and One Nights* (*The Arabian Nights*), the *Epic of El-Zir Salem*, or tales of Bani Hilal, the thread connecting the people and their origins and their identification with the heroes of these stories is clearly apparent.

And one must not forget the religious repertoire that is so ingrained in Palestinians' lives that they do almost nothing without mentioning God, a verse from the scripture, or a prayer.

Immigration from Palestine, particularly to Western countries, became more common at the beginning of the twentieth century because of the Ottoman oppression and cruelty toward residents of the land in addition to drought, illness, and the wars, culminating in World War I, that took place in the area. This immigration left its mark on Palestinian folklore and filled it with descriptions of immigration, the suffering in separation, and long-ing. A well-known story tells of a woman from Beit Jala, south of Jerusalem, named Maria, whose husband left her, immigrated to Latin America, and did not return for twenty-two years. Maria wrote a song for him. No one knows if it was a love song, a song of longing, a lamentation, or a condemnation, because she poured all of her feel-ings and desires concerning her missing husband into the song and sent it to him. Within twenty-four hours of receipt of the song, the man finished up his business, packed his bags, and returned to his homeland.

Folklore also aims to criticize of-ficial history written by the ruling elite. The common people and their creative works generally have re-mained outside of most history

Scene from *One Thousand and One Nights*, the most well-known Arab folktale collection. In this hand-colored woodcut, Scheherazade is telling one of her 1,001 stories to Schahriar, the sultan of Persia who vowed to kill his other wives to exact revenge on one traitorous wife. (© North Wind/North Wind Picture Archives)

books unless they cause a revolution. Anyone looking at most classical Arab chron-icles will often feel that perhaps there are no such people and that everyone belongs to the elite stratum of society—the rulers and the aristocracy. However, folklore emerges from the lower classes who, in many cases, are oppressed and do not dare to state overtly what is in their heart. Therefore, their folklore uses symbols and hints to express criticism of the ruler or the monarch and to rebel (even if only in stories) against oppression. We therefore find the conflict between the nomads and the rich landowners (who are always bested by the poor nomads), and we find the rich king who tries to steal the wife of the poor man, though the poor man always overcomes the king.

An example of this function is the collection of animal tales known as *Kalila Wa Demna*. Despite its non-Arab origins first in **India** and then in **Persia**, this collection is now distinctively Arab. The tales criticize the corrupt and cruel behavior of the ruler (king) indirectly while they pass along the values of the lower classes. *One Thousand and One Nights* (*The Arabian Nights*), the most well-known Arab folktale collection, also criticizes certain behavior: namely, that of a woman who betrays her husband and a cruel king who kills women to exact revenge on one traitorous woman.

Palestinian folklore consists mainly of popular literature (folktales, legends, para-bles, proverbs, and riddles) taken from classical Arab literature and more ancient sources. While these sources place it within the general context of the folklore of the Arab world, it is distinctive because of the unique environment and conditions of

Palestinian historical consciousness. Like the Palestinians themselves, their folklore is characterized by tolerant pluralism and cultural diversity. Palestinians were generally divided into an agricultural majority of villagers, living and operating in rural areas, and an urban minority living in the larger cities. Both the rural and urban regions absorbed new residents over the years. Those migrating for security, economic, and other reasons became part of the population and assimilated themselves and their folklore among the Palestinians.

Additionally, from a religious standpoint, Palestinians are comprised of a Sunni Muslim majority, a Christian minority, and many other sects who consider themselves an inseparable part of the Palestinian nation. The old merged with the new; Palestinians, mainly from urban centers, quickly adjusted to changes caused by foreigners coming to their country, particularly those in port cities. The fact that their land was the cradle of three monotheistic religions provided Palestinian folklore with a religious nature, even if it does not particularly stand out. This is reflected in most of the popular tales of the Palestinians and in proverbs, which include many religious motifs related to places sacred to all the religions represented among the population, including the tombs of holy men.

During the time of the British Mandate (1918–1948) and the strengthening of the Arab Palestinian Nationalist Movement in the first half of the twentieth century, Palestinian folklore began also to reflect politics, most notably opposition to the British Mandate and all that it signified. Love of the land, agricultural life, and social values such as heroism, helping others, hosting guests, generosity, helping the needy, cooperation, and social cohesion within one's village were expressed in poems and stories.

RELIGIOUS BELIEFS, CUSTOMS, RITUALS, AND CEREMONIES

Beliefs, customs, and ceremonies focus on the human life cycle, beginning with fertility, birth, and raising children. Palestinians specifically and Arabs in general see many children as a blessing, particularly if they are males, because this adds power to the tribe and aids in improving living conditions. Girls are less valued because women do not usually work outside of the house, while the male work force contributes directly to improving economic status. Children are of utmost importance. A woman who did not become pregnant within one year of marriage was not looked at warmly. A wealth of names were prepared (according to various criteria) before the birth, and birth was celebrated by presenting gifts and blessings to the parents of the newborn. Celebrations lasted a week. The appearance of the baby's first tooth, his first step, his first word, and of course circumcision for Muslims and baptism for Christians were widely celebrated.

Palestinians tended to marry off their children at a relatively young age, and immediately upon reaching adolescence, engagement ceremonies took place. (There were few ceremonies connected to adolescence aside from the First Communion ceremony among some Christians.) Obvious preference was given to marriage within the extended family or the tribe (endogamous marriage) over marrying foreign brides (exogamous marriage) in order to maintain the integrity of the tribe and to ensure that its property would not be inherited by foreigners. The bride received bridewealth to buy herself clothing and other necessary items (though sometimes a controlling father took it for himself), and the H'enna' ceremony was celebrated by decoratively dyeing the bride's palms and hair. Marriage ceremonies were large festive occasions, sometimes lasting for entire weeks (in the past even lasting for forty days).

Death was treated fearfully and with respect because it was considered the will of God. Palestinians made certain to pay their last respects to the deceased and to maintain all mourning customs, memorial ceremonies, and visits to gravesites.

Within popular religious beliefs (not the dogma or doctrine of Islam or Christianity) were

Four Palestinian women on their way to market. In Palestinian society, women are often valued primarily for their domestic contributions. (Courtesy Library of Congress)

clear motifs of divine justice and fate. Everything is dictated from above, and people are committed to what is pre-determined. One may not escape or change destiny. People must accept their fate whether bad or good with love and understanding because this is God's will. Everything that happens to people comes from God, and what God does should not be questioned. Religion also stands out in Palestinian behavior and discourse. It is almost impossible for Palestinians to speak even one sentence without at least some religious association or connotation. If you ask a Palestinian how he is, he will not give a precise description of his welfare and health, but will answer, "Thank God! Good, with God's help! Praise to the almighty God," and other similar expressions that this God-fearing society knows so well. In this respect there is no difference between rural villagers and urban dwellers (though some urban dwellers speak this way less often).

The land is full of burial sites of prophets and holy men who lived and died in Palestine throughout history. The land has been full of miracles since the appearance of monotheism. Therefore we find many holy places throughout the country. In Jerusalem and its environs alone, there are more than five hundred such holy sites. Hundreds more can be found in other areas of the country: whether places of prayer (mosques and churches), burial sites of prophets and holy men, holy caves, holy trees, and holy wells and springs. These sites attract mass pilgrimages on certain dates. People make pledges to visit specific sites, saying: "If a certain patient is cured, or if a certain wish is fulfilled, I will come to visit this holy site." When the dream is fulfilled or the patient is cured, the individual who made the pledge must uphold it. There are some who uphold their pledges with mass celebrations, and there are those who simply visit the holy site, pray, light candles, make a sacrifice, or give a gift. Over the years, these sites have become ex-territorial sites of special status. The sites and their holiness may not be desecrated. Anyone desecrating the site is severely punished. Many stories are told of people who desecrated a holy places and were immediately paralyzed or blinded.

Because of the holiness attributed to these places, they have become places for making promises and pledges. If an individual sues his friend for something, or a plaintiff wants to prove his innocence, local judges agree that they will swear at a certain holy site. Such a pledge serves as proof of the individual's innocence. If someone refuses to make such a pledge, he is usually found guilty according to popular Palestinian law, which is deeply ingrained within classical Arab tribal culture.

Additionally, belief in demons and spirits, in magic and witchcraft, and in invisible forces and their influence over human life remains strong. This belief has led to various ceremonies over the years and an entire repertoire of charms and spells that aim to protect people from dark forces. Folk medicine and classical folk law have continued to compete with modern medicine and civil law until recent times. Patients who do not find relief in hospitals turn to the aid of holy sites and "folk doctors" who heal using herbs, purging, and bone setting as well as to charlatans who lead patients on (particularly in the field of fertility) and claim that they have the power to cure patients using spells and magic.

Folk law, which became holy hundreds of years ago, still is in use. Blood feuds and revenge are solved only with the assistance of folk law, which intervenes through peacemaking ceremonies (*Sulha*).

Palestinians were also famous for their national dress, jewelry, and folk art. Every region had special clothing, embroidered with silver and gold threads or with colored threads reflecting the colors of the sky, earth, sea, fields, and flowers. Certain areas were known for special types of crafts such as the olive oil soap–making industry in the city of Nablus and its environs, the religious artifacts industry, particularly of olive wood and shells, known worldwide as the Bethlehem industry, the Hebron glassware industry, and the delicate embroidery of Bethlehem, Beit Jala, Beit Sahur, and Ramalla. There were other industries such as leatherworking and pottery elsewhere in Palestine.

POETRY

Unlike songs and classical Arabic poetry, folk poetry was composed in spoken Arabic and is considered to be a reliable mirror reflecting ancient Arab life. This poetry also reflected Palestinian life in later generations, and its content revolved around contemporary problems. The content of this poetry related to all of the personal and social dreams of the Palestinian. A respectable place was held for popular romantic poetry, dealing with issues of "him and her": prohibited love, trying to meet with a lover, the heat of love and its pleasures, abstract descriptions of loved ones, praise of a lover's beauty, the feminine ideal, and dreams of meeting an imaginary lover. Another popular topic responded to the immigration of thousands of Palestinians to other parts of the world.

A competition developed among popular poets, with each poet adopting a topic and praising it, while denouncing the topics adopted by other poets and criticizing them. Different pairs of topics that were favorites of both poet and audience alike included renewal versus tradition, science and money, power and spirit.

Much advice and life experience, including everything from searching for a wife, engagement and marriage, and divorce to death and lamentations, are transmitted through poetry. A significant number of lullabies and nursery rhymes is found in the repertoire sung by Palestinian mothers to their children. Children themselves sing traditional songs, and there are religious songs associated with all the land's religions that are performed before, during, and after pilgrimages and on holidays and at festivals. Among worksongs are found songs for planting, harvesting, and winnowing, fishermen's songs, and songs sung by other artisans. There are also songs that accompany folk dances, songs for searching for a bride, and special songs for the wedding ceremony. Of course, there are also mourning songs and lamentations and songs treating all areas of life.

Gradually poetry also began to express opposition to the Ottoman regime and later to the British Mandate by encouraging the Palestinian National Movement. It became more and more nationalistic and reflected the desires of the nation and its nationalistic dreams. This form of poetry was both oral and discreet. The structure of such poetry was classical in general, drawing its essence from the structure of classical literary Arabic poetry with slight variations. It maintained traditionalism and stability over time, though the content continually changed and was updated according to the spirit of the times and contemporary concerns.

CHALLENGES OF THE MODERN WORLD

After the United Nations resolution to divide Palestine into a Jewish state and an Arab state in 1947, the wars of 1948 and 1967, and the results of these wars, some Palestinian people remained within the borders of the State of Israel and became Israeli citizens with equal rights and obligations according to law but not in practice. Most Palestinians were forced to leave their cities and villages and suddenly became refugees, whether within Israel, in refugee camps within the Palestinian Authority, in neighboring Arab countries, or in other countries throughout the world. This development is seen most of all in Palestinian folklore. The minority who remained in Israel and became Israeli citizens began to go through a speedy process of "Israelization." It is almost certain that if the 1967 war had not broken out; if these people had not met their brothers in the West Bank and the Gaza Strip; and if they had not suffered from discrimination against them by Israel manifested in not being accepted by broad sectors of Jewish Israeli society in addition to the inequality that even the leaders of the State admitted, this sense of national belonging would not be as developed and strong.

From a folklore standpoint, the popular literature of this minority has not been sufficiently researched, particularly in all areas concerning nationality. Other areas of folklore have become more and more Israeli. People have absorbed the values of new Israeli folklore and even provided new Israeli society with different values of

Palestinian folklore, beginning with the *Mangal* (barbeque) and including terms such as the *Sulha* (peacemaking), *Kaif* (fun), *Mabsut* (very happy), and *Ahalan* (Hello) and types of food borrowed from the Palestinian kitchen—for instance pita, labaneh, za'atar, and hummus.

Forced immigration led to an immeasurably strengthened tie between the Palestinian individual and his land. When you meet a Palestinian anywhere in the world today and ask him where he is from, he will always answer with the place from which he was exiled in 1948, even if the town does not exist any more or even if it has become an Israeli Jewish town with not even one Arab resident. This exile has strengthened ties to the land and increased the longing to return to the homeland that was abandoned. It has contributed to the fact that many refugees still live in refugee camps in Arab countries without assimilating into the local population. This has led the newer generation, who never knew Palestine, to have a strong emotional need to be familiar with the way of life that existed in the land before 1948 and to try to bring it back to life, to live and sustain it, and to maintain close ties among fellow refugees for the purpose or returning to a past way of life that no longer exists. Then, when they have the opportunity to return to their homeland, they can live their lives as their ancestors did. This is what has led to increased interest in Palestinian folklore, which remains the only tie connecting exiled Palestinians to their homeland, allowing them to dream of returning and building their future there.

For Palestinians living in the Palestinian Authority, folklore has quickly become a mirror reflecting the political events that have befallen them. The wars of 1948, 1967, and 1973 and even the first war with Iraq in 1991 have served as rich sources for enriching Palestinian folklife and creating new wartime folklore, reflecting the Palestinian struggle for freedom and liberty and the creation of an independent state. Verbal or auditory folklore—particularly stories, jokes, and folksongs—served as a daily form of expression during the first Intifada (1989 to 1993) and the second Intifada (the Al A'qsa Intifada), which began in 2000. The new conditions under which Palestinian folklore is now found have encouraged many Palestinians to research their own folklore and that of their ancestors as part of searching for roots and personal, family, and national identity. Palestinian researchers in both Arab and Western countries have written hundreds and perhaps thousands of research theses.

STUDIES OF PALESTINIAN FOLKLORE

Among the early scholars who invested many years in the study of Palestinian folklore was G. H. Dalmann (1855–1944), who produced a number of monumental works on the subject, including *Arbeit und Sitte in Palastina*. This seven-volume work documents works and crafts, customs and traditions. Dalmann also published *Palästinisher Diwan*, a collection of Palestinian folksongs. Also worthy of mention is the book by Schmidt and Kahla on Palestinian folktales and *Modern Arabic Tales* by Enno Littman. However the most noteworthy might be the works of Hilma Granqvist, who settled in Artas Village in the Bethlehem region and composed a number of weighty volumes on the topics of birth and raising children, engagement and marriage customs, and mourning customs, focusing on both Artas specifically and Palestine in general. The Frenchman, Phillip Baldensperger, also settled in Artas and composed his most important work, *The Immovable East*, there. His sister Louise wrote an important book, *From Cedar to Hyssop*, on the folklore of plants and trees in Palestine on which she collaborated with Grace Crowfoot. Other significant books on Palestinian folklore include *Customs and Traditions of Palestine*, written by an Italian engineer serving the Ottomans in Palestine, and *Folklore of the Holy Land* by Hanauer. The latter contains Jewish, Christian, and Muslim folklore from the region.

The political events of the Middle East at the beginning of the twentieth century, including World War I, liberation from the Ottomans, strengthening the Palestinian Nationalist Movement, and the influence of Orientalists and missionaries, encouraged Palestinians to begin investigating their folklore. Palestinian national and cultural self-awareness and recognition of the uniqueness of their folklore also contributed to the beginnings of Palestinian folklore research, as did the wealth of culture-specific and universal religious motifs within Palestinian folklore. This folklore could also certainly be seen as a true reflection of the values of ancient Arab culture, integrating motifs of the many peoples who existed in Palestine during different historical eras.

Various Orientalists and missionaries also provided an important contribution. While Western citizens had been settling in Palestine for many centuries, this situation increased for various reasons at the end of the nineteenth and the beginning of the twentieth centuries. Christian schools and seminaries were established in Palestine, and widespread missionary work began, aimed at creating a stronghold within the land. Local students began to study in these schools, searching for survivals from Biblical times.

During this era, the first Palestinian folklorists appeared, some affected directly by the missionaries and their writings and some aiming to investigate and perpetuate Palestinian culture. We therefore find that Palestinians preceded all other Middle Eastern countries and Arab countries in the study of their own folklore. The first researcher of Palestinian folklore was the physician Tawfiq Cana'an of Beit Jala, who took advantage of his frequent meetings with patients to record their practices and beliefs. One of his most notable works is *Mohammedan Saints and Sanctuaries in Palestine*, which documents hundreds of burial sites of holy men and other holy sites in Jerusalem and its environs. His range of studies also include the following subjects: haunted springs and water demons, Byzantine caravan routes in the Negev, Arab superstitions about the *Tasit-er-Rajfeh* (fear cup), seasonal folklore, the child in Palestinian Arab superstitions, water (especially the "water of life") in Palestinian folk beliefs, light and darkness in Palestinian folklore, the topography and folklore of Petra, customs affecting women, Arab domestic architecture in Palestine, modern folk beliefs about God, the curse in Palestinian folklore, the Saqr Bedouin of Beisan, and Arab magic bowls.

Another Palestinian folklore researcher was Stephan Hanna Stephan, who operated at the same time as Cana'an. Among his areas of study were the division of the year in Palestine, modern parallels to the Song of Songs, animal stories and fables, insanity in Palestinian folklore, the importance of the number forty, animals in

Palestinian superstitions, and nursery rhymes and songs. Elias Nasrallah Haddad was another pioneer Palestinian folklorist. He concentrated his attentions on such topics as Arab customs of blood revenge, Palestinian and Syrian political parties, the guest-house, and educational and disciplinary practices. A fourth researcher from this early group was O'mar Saleh Al-Barguthi, who studied judicial courts among the Bedouins, hospitality customs, and traces of feudalism in modern Palestine.

These folklorists were members—and, in some cases, founders—of the Oriental Society and published their studies in the *Journal of Palestine Oriental Society*, which served as the society's newsletter. The first issue of this journal appeared in 1920 and was the first journal in the Middle East (and one of the first in the world) that dedicated much space to folklore. The second issue appeared in 1922, after which the journal became an annual publication with more-or-less regular issues until 1939, when it ceased publication because of World War II. It resumed publication in 1946 only to come to an end in June 1948. As such, the Palestinians are considered to be pioneers in the study of Arab folklore and were not followed by scholars in other Arab countries until the middle of the twentieth century.

The reasons for the lateness in beginning folklore research in the Arab world stem from a strong opposition to the use of the more common Arab dialects in writing, given the preference for the classical literary Arabic of the Holy Qur'an for all venues of art and culture. Many intellectuals viewed folklore studies as contributing to the value of the spoken language and thus contributing to the downfall of classic Arab culture. The first folklore studies took place in Egypt no earlier than the 1930s, and a significant folklore movement in Arab countries began to develop only after the middle of the twentieth century, when different Arab countries began to establish folklore archives, publish books and journals, edit fieldwork, organize festivals, establish national dance troupes, authorize academic research in the field, and dedicate courses to the study of folklore in the various universities.

The institution that invests more than any other in the study of Palestinian folklore within the Palestinian Authority is the Society for Family Welfare in conjunction with the Popular Heritage Committee. This committee was created in the middle of the 1960s in El-Bireh near Ramalla to study Palestinian folklore. The committee has already established a folklore museum and archives, published dozens of research papers on the topics of folklore studies and its application to Palestinian folklore, popular poetry, national costume, children and raising children, and spoken language. It has published over forty issues of a quarterly journal that is dedicated entirely to Palestinian folklore. See also the *Encyclopedia Ynet* at www.ynet.co.il.

BIBLIOGRAPHY

Alqam, N. 1977. *An Introduction to the Study of Folklore*. Al-Bireh: Society for Family Welfare.

Al Sarisi, Omar. 1980. *The Folktale in Palestinian Society*. Beirut: Unknown.

Baldensperger, Louise, and Grace Crowfoot. 1932. *From Cedar to Hyssop*. London: Sheldon Press.

Baldensperger, Philip. 1913. *The Immovable East*. London: Pitman.

Barghouthi, A. L. 1979. *Arab Folk Songs in Palestine and Jordan*. Bir-Zeit: Society for Family Welfare.

Brown, S. Graham. 1980. *Palestinians and their Society: 1880–1946*. London: Quartet Books.

Cana'an, Tawfiq. 1927. *Mohammedan Saints and Sanctuaries in Palestine*. Jerusalem: N.p.

Dalmann, G. H. 1902. *Palästinisher Diwan*. Leipzig: J. C. Hinrichs.

———. 1928–1942. *Arbeit und Sitte in Palastina*. 7 volumes. Gütersloh: C. Bertelsmann.

El Shamy, Hasan. 1984. *Folk Tradition in the Arab World*. 2 volumes. Bloomington: Indiana University Press.

Ettinger Sh. 1987. *Zionism, the Arab Problem and the British Mandate*. Tel Aviv: Devir.

Finn, Mrs. M. 1933. *Palestinian Peasantry*. London: Marshal Bros.

Haddad M. 1985. *Palestinian Folklore Research: A Short History*. el-Tayyibeh: The Center for Revival of Palestinian Heritage.

———. 1986. *Palestinian Folk Heritage Between Obliteration and Revival*. el-Tayibeh: The Center for Revival of Palestinian Heritage.

———. 1987a. Palestinian Folk Songs. *Al-Jadeed* 36 (June): 47–53.

———. 1987b. *Peqin: Folklore, Folklife and Traditions*. Tel Aviv: A'm O'ved.

———. 1990. Wedding Celebrations among the Palestinians in Israel Between Tradition and Modernization. In *Papers of 4th SIEF Congress*, edited by Bentee Giullveig Alver and Torunn Selberg. Bergen: SIEF. 257–293.

———. 1992. Folk Narrative in Palestine 1990–1948. In *Folk Narrative and World View*, edited by Leander Petzoldt. Innsbruck: Peter Lang. 253–260.

———. 1995a. Forms of Co-existence among Nationalities in Al-Boqaia. In *Meeting of Cultures*. Budapest: Hungarian Ethnographical Society. 122–126.

———. 1995b. Palestinian Folklore Research. *Artes Populares* 16–17: 338–351.

———. 1999. The Christian Arabs in Palestine. *Journal of Indian Folkloristics* 1: 81–87.

———. N.d. Narration and Story-telling in Arabic Literature. *Yeda'-A'm* 53–54: 31–36.

Hanauer, J. E. 2002 (1935). *Folklore of the Holy Land*. Mineola, NY: Dover.

Kimmerlig, B., and J. S. Migdal. 1999. *Palestinians: The Making of People*. Jerusalem: Keter Publishing House.

Littman, Enno. 1905. *Modern Arabic Tales*. Leiden: E. J. Brill.

Pierotti, Ermete. 1864. *Customs and Traditions of Palestine*. N.p.

Sayegh, A., and others. 1990. *Palestinian Encyclopedia*. Beirut: Palestinian Encyclopedia Institution (PLO).

Monim Haddad

PERSIA

GEOGRAPHY AND HISTORY

Formerly known as Persia in Western sources, Iran is a Middle Eastern country bordering the Persian Gulf and the Gulf of Oman on the south and the Caspian Sea on the north. It shares some 5,440 kilometers of common borders with Iraq and **Turkey** to the west, Azerbaijan, **Armenia**, and Turkmenistan to the north, and Afghanistan and Pakistan to the east. The Iranian Plateau is surrounded by rugged mountains on three sides and has an area of 1,648,000 square kilometers. Iran's population is estimated at over 68 million, of which 51 percent are ethnic Persians, 24 percent Azeri, 2 percent Turkmen, 8 percent Gilaki and Mazandarani, and 7 percent **Kurd**, with the remaining 10 percent from other ethnic groups such as Arab, Lur, and Baloch. Several language groups are represented in Iran. These are Persian and its various dialects (58 percent), Turkic (26 percent), Kurdish (9 percent), Luri (2 percent), Balochi and Arabic (1 percent each), and others (3 percent). Although Persian is written in the Arabic alphabet and has borrowed many words from Arabic and Turkish, it is an Indo-European language related to the languages of Europe and **India** rather than to Arabic, Turkish, or Hebrew, which are spoken elsewhere in the Middle East.

Indo-European speaking groups of herdsmen and charioteer warriors, the earliest Iranians, migrated into the Middle East near the end of the second millennium B.C.E. One of the Iranian tribes, the Persians, settled in Northern Iran on the border of what was the Elamite kingdom. Persians gradually gained political ascendancy leading other Iranian tribes in a rebellion against the Assyrian empire. By 550 B.C.E. the Persian prince Cyrus the Great founded the Achaemenid dynasty, which, until Alexander the Great ended it in 330 B.C.E., ruled over the vastest empire of the ancient world.

The Persian conquest of the known world in the sixth century B.C.E. had important cultural consequences. Like all conquerors, the Persians arrogated to themselves access to the women of those whom they had conquered. Given that the offspring of such unions spend their early years of life—their formative years—in the company of their mothers, much of their maternal culture and lore is transmitted to them as they grow up. Thus, military victory is no guarantor of cultural dominance, and a culture that has been militarily overrun can still exert a profound influence upon those who overran it. Much from the lore and language of these vanquished but more advanced Semitic civilizations must have found its way into Persian lore through generations of multicultural Persian children. This pattern of cultural exchange repeated itself in Persian history with the conquest of Alexander the Great, with the advent of the next Persian empires—the Parthian and Sassanian states—and later with the Arab conquest of Persia, which brought a new religion, a new writing system, and new ethnic groups into the heartland of the empire. The **Mongol** conquest of 1250 was the peak of ongoing Turko-Mongol influence, especially with regard to representational arts. A similar influence of outside cultures became manifest in the twentieth century with the Western world introducing not only modern technology but also a series of European and American motifs into Persian folklore. This influence continues with the effects of the Internet and satellite television. However, in spite of the infusion of many non-Iranian elements, the Iranian worldview has maintained much of its ancient characteristics. The most important of these is an "us-against-them" outlook rooted in the Zoroastrian religion of ancient Iran.

RELIGION

According to Zoroastrian mythology, which made its appearance sometime circa 1000 B.C.E., two primordial forces govern the world. The forces of Good, headed by a god called Ahura-Mazda, are in perpetual strife against the forces of darkness, led by the Evil Spirit. The material world was created by Ahura-Mazda to prevent the fight between Good and Evil from spilling into the realm of light. In other words, material creation serves as the theater of war, and mankind as its most important inhabitant is required to help the forces of Good against those of Evil. Zoroastrian mythology also tells us that Good will eventually triumph over Evil. However, Good's victory over Evil is not because it is physically more powerful than Evil, but because by virtue of being possessed of all good characteristics it is intelligent, while Evil, by virtue of having all bad characteristics, is dim-witted. Evil's stupidity—not Good's greater power—will eventually bring about its final defeat. This dualism continues to inform the Persian worldview despite the fact that Zoroastrianism has long ceased to be Iran's national religion.

Iran's national epic, called the *Shāhnāma*, is the ethnic history of Iran from mythical times to the Muslim conquest of the country in the seventh century C.E. Its narrative begins with a dynasty of primordial culture heroes who school mankind in the arts of agriculture, crafts, medicine, and warfare and also structure human society into its various castes of warriors, priests, artisans, and agriculturalists. The dualism that is a component of the Iranian worldview is manifested in the wars between Iranians on the side of good, fighting against forces of evil, championed by their adversaries in the *Shāhnāma*. The importance of the body of legends preserved in the *Shāhnāma* for establishing a Persian **worldview** and Iranian national identity cannot be gainsaid. Indeed one may define an Iranian in cultural terms as anyone—regardless of language or national origin—who considers the narrative of the *Shāhnāma* to be his or her legendary history.

Iran's state religion is Shi'ite Islam, which differs from Sunni Islam with regard to the problem of who should have succeeded the prophet Muhammad as the leader of the Muslim community. Unlike Sunnis, who consider the election of the first four successors of the prophet legitimate, Shi'ite Muslims believe that the first three of these caliphs gained power illegitimately and that the Prophet appointed only the fourth caliph, who was his cousin and son-in-law Ali (d. 661 C.E.), to succeed him. Therefore, legitimate leadership of the community can only exist in the family of the Prophet through Ali and Ali's sons, who were the prophet's grandchildren and are called Iman by the Shiah. This belief, which was originally a political schism among the Muslims of Arabia, soon gained many followers among the Iranian converts because its dynastic nature was familiar and palatable to Iranians and their long tradition of divinely ordained kingship.

Political opponents poisoned and killed many of the descendants of the prophet. Of these, only the last Imam, Muhammad al-Mahdi (b. 868 C.E.), survived the various

Rustem (Iranian national hero) asking King Kay Ka'us for the favor of Gourguine, from *Shāhnāma* (Book of Kings; epic poem by Firdausi, 934–1020), sixteenth-century manuscript. (The Art Archive/Musée Condé Chantilly/Dagli Orti)

attempts on his life. The Shi'ites believe that al-Mahdi, whose name means "the Messiah," went into a state of occultation in 941 C.E. and will reappear at an appointed time in order to rid the world from inequity and sin. The messianic character of Shi'ite millenarianism has been seen as a Zoroastrain contribution. Much legendary material, most of which is dismissed by official theologians as folklore, has developed around the occultation and eventual reappearance of the Mahdi.

An equally important event in the history of Shi'ism, as far as Persian folk belief is concerned, is the martyrdom of another grandson of the prophet, Imam Hoseyn (d. 680 C.E.). He was killed with seventy-two of his followers in a bloody uprising against the Umayyad Caliphs near the City of Karbala in present day Iraq. This event is commemorated by mourning processions in Iran. Many passion plays describe the martyrdom of the Imam in dramatic presentations in both prose and verse. The theme of these plays has been traced to the pre-Islamic tradition of mourning for a slain prince.

SUPERNATURAL LORE

Islam's narratives of creation, resurrection, angelology, demonology, and reward and punishment resemble Judeo-Christian lore. God created Adam and Eve, who fell out of grace by eating wheat rather than partaking from the fruit of the Tree of Knowledge. Old Testament patriarchs and kings are considered to be prophets. Jesus's virgin birth is acknowledged, but not his divinity. According to Muslim hagiography, he was not tortured or killed by crucifixion. Rather God cast Jesus's likeness upon a sinner who was mistaken for him and crucified. Jesus himself was elevated to heaven and will return at the day of Resurrection to fight on the side of the twelfth Imam.

Iranian folk religion and lore are often populated with hybrid entities formed from intermingling of the Old Iranian and Semitic beings. This is especially evident in Persian demonology. Demons, called *dīv* in Persian, have undergone several transformations both functionally and linguistically. Iranians once worshiped a class of gods called *daēvas*, but Zoroastrianism demonized these old gods. Demons in Persian folklore are tall frightening beings with frizzy hair, flat noses, thick lips, long nails, and furry bodies. They may have wings and horns and are often confused with the Semitic monster know as *ghūl* and sometimes with another supernatural being known to Arabs as *Jenn*. This confusion exists in both folk and literary traditions. The demons of Persian folklore may have more than one head, and some lack bodies altogether. When these bodyless demons want to go somewhere, they roll to their destination. They may be white, yellow, or black in color and are capable of magic and transformation. They have a tendency to alternate long periods of wakefulness and sleep. Demons may act as villains, sorcerers, ogres, fools, or donor figures and may be summoned by burning a bit of their hair. Sometimes their approach may be deduced from changes in temperature or by a foul smell in the air. Many demons have external souls (**motif** E711), the destruction of which kills them. They may keep their soul hidden in a box (motif E712.4), in a live fish (motif E715.2), or in the body of some other animal (motif E714).

Demons are fond of human women, whom they steal and forcibly marry. Although these women are usually unwilling brides, sometimes they grow so enamored of their demon husband that they may harm their kin at their bidding. Men may also marry demons. According to folk tradition, *Dīvs* and *Jenns* are said to fear the sound of the dog and the white rooster.

Folk medicine holds demons responsible for a number of mental and physical maladies. For instance, the Persian word *dīvāngī*, "insanity" (literally, "being afflicted by demons"), reflects the association of all mental illness with demonic possession. Many minor conditions such as fever blisters, called *āfat-e dīv*, "the demon's malady," are also attributed to them. A variety of demon even causes nightmares or deceptive dreams rather than psychological maladies.

Of all the supernatural beings of Persian lore, none commands more control over the popular imagination than the *Jenn*. The existence of the *Jenn* has scriptural support in Islam. It is a supernatural being that, according to the Qur'an, was created from smokeless fire (motif A2905.1§). Although Arabic lexicography drives the word *Jenn* from a root that means "hidden" or "concealed," and although along with ghouls the *Jenn* is thought to be of Semitic origin, some authorities have argued that it may be of genuinely Iranian provenance. The Jenn may have been borrowed into Arab lore from Persian folklore only to be recycled back into Persian lore via Arabo-Islamic tradition. The early Persian sources use the Arabic word *Jenn* and the Persian word *parī* (fairy) interchangeably. Modern folk tradition, however, tends to differentiate between the two, though somewhat uncertainly.

The *Jenn* live invisibly alongside the visible world and are organized into societies resembling human society. For every human child, 1,000 children are born among the *Jenn*, and every human child except for the Prophet and the twelve Imams has a *Jenn* double called *hamzād*, the "twin." The *hamzād* in certain respects resembles the European "changeling" and begins to menace its human double even before birth. When a baby starts in his sleep, it is believed that his twin is pinching him; but when he laughs in his sleep, it is believed that his *hamzād* has told him, "Your mother is dead," to which the baby responds, laughingly, "Don't be absurd; she just nursed me."

Jenn females may require the services of human midwives, and it is said that every midwife must help deliver at least one *Jenn* child for every one hundred human children that she brings into the world. When the *Jenn* need a human midwife, she is led to the *Jenn* mother blindfolded, and after the conclusion of her duties, she is given a handful of onionskins as payment. If she puts the onionskins under a rug and keeps her mouth shut about her encounter with the *Jenn*, then every morning she will find a gold coin under that rug. If not, they simply remain onionskins.

Because of the *Jenn*'s harmful nature, contact must be avoided if at all possible. Even their name is not mentioned in fear that it may summon them. Therefore, euphemisms are used to refer to the *Jenn* in conversation. The most common of these are *az mā behtarān* "Those who are better than us," and *azzān* "the dear ones." In spite of these precautions, they may be inadvertently summoned by such innocent activities as whistling. Precautions are also taken against inflicting inadvertent harm upon the *Jenn*. Because they live invisibly all around humans, they may be inadvertently harmed when stones are thrown or hot ashes or boiling water is poured out. In order to avoid this and generally to make them clear out when one is about to pour out hot water, one needs only to recite the formula *bismillāh al-rahmaān al-rahīm*, "In the name of God the merciful, the compassionate." The mere mention of God's name puts them to flight, which means they are not around to be harmed by what one does.

Some maladies are blamed on the *Jenn* in folk medicine. They are believed capable of taking possession of their victim and afflicting him with epilepsy (motif D2065.1.1§). Because a *Jenn* that has entered the body of its victim can feel the physical sensations experienced by that body, one way to treat epilepsy is to tie the patient up and savagely beat him in order to drive out the resident *Jenn*. One *Jenn*-catcher claimed that medicines for the cure of epilepsy exist and are listed in a book composed by King Solomon, who had control over the *Jenn* and to whom the *Jenn* had given the information.

New mothers and their infants are among the most vulnerable victims of the *Jenn*. This is why the mother and her newborn are not left alone during the first week or two after labor. Infants who have been harmed by the *Jenn* are said to suffer from *ān dardhā* "those ailments." They usually turn blue, go into convulsive fits, and die. To avert the danger, which is especially severe on the sixth night after birth, iron implements are placed in the new mother's room (*Jenns* are afraid of iron), gunpowder is burned around her, and considerable noise is made in and around her room. These activities, which resemble those carried out in order to drive away the demoness *Āl*, are thought to scare the *Jenn* away. Because the *Jenn* are capable of appearing in human form, only those who were present during the actual birth are allowed to visit the mother in the first few days, lest a *Jenn* enter the woman's room in the form of a friend and harm her or her infant.

Another important supernatural being in Persian folklore is called *ghūl*, "ghoul." Although the *ghūl*, which entered Persian folklore from Arab tradition, is considered the most menacing type of *Jenn*, it differs from the *Jenn* in significant details. In Iran, the primary meaning of *ghūl* is "ogre" or "demon." In Persian folklore and early literature, *ghūl* is an anthropophagous monster capable of transformation. Those who report having seen it describe it differently. Some are composite beings resembling a man in their upper bodies and a horse in their lower; in this respect, the *ghūl* recalls the centaur of the European tradition. Female *ghūl* are occasionally described as very beautiful, while the male of the species is hideous.

Ghūls have a taste for human flesh, which they satisfy through either murder or exhumation. Some attract unsuspecting humans by sending their charming females to lure travelers to their lair. Some Persian villagers believe in a kind of *ghūl* that procures its victims by transforming itself into the likeness of someone known to the inhabitants of a house and knocking on the door in the evening. When the door is opened, the *ghūl* begins to move back into the darkness in order to lure his unsuspecting victim out of the house. If the victim keeps his wits about him and pronounces the name of God or, in a less theological vain, if he grabs hold of the *ghūl*'s testicles and gives them a fierce squeeze, it will panic and release him. This variety of *ghūl* recalls the Bengali demoness Nīsī, who walks the streets at nights in the form of a human being and calls out the inhabitants of the houses by name.

Supernatural forces are especially potent during transitional periods such as birth, marriage, and death. Persians believe that from the day of her pregnancy the woman has one foot in this world and one foot in the next and that a number of different saints or supernatural beings need be present before birth can safely occur. In Tehran for instance, Imam Ali, or alternatively two other saints Khezr and Eliyās, are necessary for the birth to take place, whereas in northeastern Iran it is Ali and his wife, Fātemeh, whose presence is crucial for safe childbirth. Knowing this, barren women or women in need of some saintly favor arrange to be present at births, and once the child is born, they block the doorway and speak to the saints saying, "O Commander of the Faithful [Ali's title among the Shi'ites], O Fātemeh, either grant me my wish, or I shall not let you leave the room."

FOLK BELIEFS SURROUNDING PREGNANCY AND LABOR

The pregnant woman is treated with special attention as soon as her pregnancy is revealed. Certain rules are observed by the woman and her community in order to avoid harm. For instance, special care is taken to satisfy her "cravings" lest her unsatisfied appetites bring harm to the community. According to Persian folk medicine, craving is manifested in the third month of pregnancy and gives a woman such a healthy appetite that every morning when she wakes up, the broom-handle trembles behind the door thinking: "She is sure to eat me today."

The child of the woman whose desire for food was not satisfied may be born with the power of harming others with the Evil Eye. Alternatively, the baby may be cross-eyed. Especially severe cases of craving may require treatments such as feeding the expectant mother a concoction made from three fried sparrows that have been pounded into a paste.

The sex of the fetus may be determined by a number of signs. An active mother who has a good disposition during her pregnancy is carrying a boy, while one who is inactive and shows bad temperament will have a girl. When the pregnant woman is called, if she steps forth with her right foot, her child is to be a boy; if she sets out with her left foot, a girl is expected. If her right breast swells up first, the fetus is male, but swelling of the left breast presages the birth of a girl. The mother may divine the sex of her baby from the objects that she may find by accident or by the kind of food that she craves. Craving sweets presages a son, and tangy or tart foods anticipate a daughter. A number of tests may determine the sex of the fetus. One of the most common involves a knife and pair of scissors being put in front of a blindfolded pregnant woman, who is asked to choose one. If she chooses the knife, she will have a son, and if she goes for the scissors, a daughter. Alternatively, a pinch of salt may be poured on the pregnant woman's head without her knowledge. If she touches her hair, she will have a girl, but if she puts her hand to her lips first, she will give birth to a boy.

Diet and certain magical practices may influence the sex of the fetus. Thus, women who want to have a boy eat foods that are considered of a "hot nature." Some of these are chicken, honey, or sweets. They may alternatively ask a male relative to write the name Mohammad on their right side or ask a soothsayer to draw the picture of the patriarch Solomon on that side of their body.

Labor has always been a dangerous time for women. The danger is still quite real in isolated villages and among the nomadic tribes of Iran, where modern medicine may not be readily available. Many magical practices have been developed to alleviate the fear of childbirth. In some parts of Iran when the first pains of labor start, the woman throws a clod of earth in water and addresses it as the clod disintegrates, saying: "O clod of earth, I wish to finish my labor by the time you completely disintegrate." Precautions designed to protect the woman are observed. Should a virgin enter the room, the hem of her skirt is ripped in order to prevent difficult childbirth.

Before the advent of hospitals and even now in some parts of the country, a midwife will be called to a difficult birth. In the past different quarters of cities had two or three midwives, some of whom were Muslim and some Jewish. The Jewish midwives were especially sought after. The midwife would start her ministrations by clapping loudly in order to scare away evil spirits and *Jenns*. She would then give several glasses of laxative to the woman and massage her abdomen with almond oil, while trying to turn the fetus into the right position. Once the pains of labor intensified, the woman would be made to squat with each foot placed on three or four mud bricks. She would receive a bottle into which she is told to blow very hard. Some dried rice may be put in her mouth to bite on while undergoing labor. To intensify weak contractions, a mixture of onions and salt may be inserted in her anus, and her vagina may be rinsed with water in which pomegranates have been boiled. Sometimes the midwife would simply address the fetus and order it to come out.

A number of magical practices may help the woman in labor. For instance her husband's shoes may be washed, and the woman would be made to drink that water. A young boy may be sent onto the roof to sing out the call to prayer. Passersby, hearing the untimely call to prayer, would realize that a woman is in difficult labor and pray for her speedy delivery. None of the women who are present in the room may leave during labor lest they take the contractions away with them. In especially difficult childbirths, the woman's mother may place a Qur'an on her head and walk around a well or on the shores of a river or creek. Sometimes a dried cyclamen, called *panjeh-ye maryam* (Mary's hand), is thrown in a dish of water, and the woman would give birth as the dry flower absorbs water and opens up. This is explained in a legend according to which when Mary was giving birth to Jesus, she reached out and grabbed a cyclamen to help her tolerate her pains. Among other practices for easing labor are freeing captive birds, untying all the knots, and unbuttoning all the buttons on a woman's clothes. Similar practices to what we find in Iran are reported among the Saxons of Transylvania, Lapps, Ancient Indians, and Romans.

Once the baby is delivered, new problems may present themselves. If the infant is not breathing properly or if its skin is purple, a chicken would be brought, its beak would be put into the child's anus, and it would be struck several times on its backside. It was believed that by doing so the chicken would blow the breath of life into the baby. Glowing coals are then put on the afterbirth, the chicken's beak is taken out of the baby's anus, and the bird is given to the poor as alms.

A number of sayings reflect the high rate of infant mortality in the past—for instance, "The first child belongs to the raven, the second to the water, the third to the earth, the fourth to the wind, and the fifth to its mother." Once the mother had delivered, other concerns for her and the child's safety would be present. The most important of these was the harm that could be done to her by a demoness called Āl, a figure quite similar to Lilith in the Jewish tradition. She is described as either a tall, skinny woman with red hair and face and a clay nose or a four-legged beast with a tail, a camel's neck, and a donkey's maw. Āl either steals the mother's liver or harms her child. In Caspian provinces a large onion is skewered, a face is drawn on it, and it is placed over the woman's bed with a Qur'an, some pins and needles, and a knife as protection against the Āl, the Jenn, and the evil eye. Should the Āl get to the mother in spite of these precautions, the woman may still be saved if she is made to drink the urine of a male goat that is in heat. Some villagers of the state of Fārs in south central Iran used to "seal" the child against harm as soon as he was born by cutting it on the face, cheeks, and chest, using a brand new knife or blade. It was believed that such an infant would not be attractive to the Jenn or fairies who steal infants.

Precautions should also be taken so that the placenta is not used in magic against the mother and her child. Needles are inserted into the placenta before burying it in order to counter such magic. Even accidental loss of the placenta may be harmful. For instance if it is carried away by a cat, the woman will become barren or her infant boy will die of a swelling of his testicles.

Several superstitions are associated with the umbilical cord. Putting a piece of dried umbilical cord in a mouse hole will ensure the infant's cleverness. Burying the cord in a schoolyard will made the child studious, while interring it in a mosque will make him pious. Sometimes it is thrown into stagnant water so that the child may grow to be steadfast and patient. The dried umbilical cord may also be used in treatment of diseases such as eye ailments.

Sins of women who die in childbirth are forgiven. Such women are considered martyrs in Muslim tradition as well as in Persian folklore. When both mother and child die in childbirth, a chicken is slaughtered and buried in a hole between their two graves so that the number of the dead will be greater than two, otherwise another member of that family will also die.

It was once customary, especially among the wealthier classes, to hire wet-nurses for the infant. Although this practice has largely died out in practice, nursing by animals (motif B535) is widely reported in Iranian legendary lore and literature. According to Herodotos, Cyrus, the founder of the Persian Empire, was nursed by a female dog, while Aelian reports that Achamenes, the ancestor of the Achamenid kings, was reared by an eagle. In the Shāhnāma, Zāl, the albino father of Iran's national hero Rostam, was nursed by the magical bird Simorgh. The reverse situation of human females nursing animals is attested only in folk medicine where puppies were made to nurse from women's painfully engorged beasts to relieve the pain. In the hagiological traditional, not only women but also men could serve as wet nurses. According to an interesting legend, Imam Hoseyn, the grandson of the Prophet Muhammad, would neither suckle from his mother nor from a wet-nurse, but only from the finger of his grandfather (motif T611.5).

FOLKTALES, PROVERBS, AND JOKES

Folklore continues to be an important part of Iranian children's enculturation, though much of that function has been taken over by the formal educational system. Persian children are exposed to a variety of narratives, festivals, and customs that ground them in Persian culture in general and their local or provincial cultures in particular. The most important of these are folktales and proverbs.

Folktales are narrated by members of the extended family and friends for entertainment and edification of the listeners. Storytellers have been mentioned from very early periods of classical Persian literature. Very little, however, of their manner of performance, repertoire, and circumstances of narration survives. What we know with any degree of certainty is that the professional storytellers—including those who narrated epic tales—told their tales in prose and without any musical accompaniment. Their props were minimal and may have included a small stool for sitting and a wand or short baton that they used to mimic their heroes' use of weapons. Those who narrated religious tales might also use paintings that showed some crucial scene of the tales that they narrated.

Folktales are known by a number of terms in Iran. The most common words for folktale are *qesseh*, *Hekāyat*, *afsāneh*, and *dāstān*. Of these, the first two are Arabic loanwords into Persian. All of these terms roughly mean fairy tale in their present usage, but may also mean legend, saint's legend, and even epic tale. A less common Arabic loanword, the somewhat formal *ostūreh*, has recently been used in formal essays in the sense of myth, legend, and less commonly folktale. The use of these terms is largely a matter of style rather than precision. By and large, Persian scholars have used the available vocabulary loosely. However, they have avoided confusion by relying on the context in which these terms have been used. A number of attempts at discriminating usage if not actual definition have been made in recent times. But these have been largely idiosyncratic efforts that have not gained currency.

One of the most potent forms of social and political criticism in Iran, as in many other places, is humor. Jokes, especially political jokes (and since the triumph of the Islamic Revolution in 1979, religious jokes), are commonly told by everyone. Traditional Persian jokes usually center on the words and deeds of traditional buffoons and tricksters, the most famous of whom is called Mulla Nasr al-Din, though animals may also be found among the *dramatis personae* of jokes. The common limitations on performance tend to be considerations of safety and taste rather than gender. Men and women tell jokes differently depending on whether they are in mixed company or not.

FOLKSONGS AND FESTIVALS

Whereas native definitions are not clearly delineated for the various genres of prose narrative, Persian folksongs and festivals are more clearly defined. The most common form of folksong is called *tasnif*, which may be political, satirical, or even romantic. Many of the humorous and romantic folksongs that entertained people at weddings and special occasions such as circumcision celebrations were performed by Jewish minstrels, who, until the advent of recording technology and the development of the music industry in Iran, were among the best folk entertainers. In general Persian folksongs tend to be either specific to religious communities such as Jews or to geographic regions. The regional folksongs may extend beyond the borders of present-day Iran. In contrast to both the Arab and Turkish cultures of the Middle East, Persians do not have a sung epic tradition, nor is there credible evidence for the existence of such a tradition in classical Persian and Arabic sources since the conquest of Iran by the Arabs.

Persian festivals fall into two groups: religious and national. The most important national festival is the New Year festival, called Norūz, which literally means "the new day" and is a survival from pre-Islamic times. Norūz marks the vernal equinox and is celebrated on the first day of the first spring month of the Persian calendar, usually falling on 21 March. A special spread of food and ceremonial objects is set for the celebration. At the head of the spread, which is called the *haft sīn*, is placed a mirror flanked by two candelabras.

The Norūz (New Year festival) pre-dates Islamic influence on Persian culture, Tehran, Iran. (© Hideo Haga/HAGA/The Image Works)

The number of candles in these in the most traditional families is equivalent to the number of the family's children. A copy of the Qur'an, the *Shāhnāma*, or the *Dīvan* of the poet Hafīz is also prominently displayed. Bowls of water, one containing one or more live goldfish and another in which floats either a green pomegranate leaf or a sour orange, are added. Containers of honey, rose-water, sugar, or other sweets and a number of colored eggs are arranged on the spread. The colored eggs must be of an odd number between one and seven. Flowers, usually hyacinths, and a few blooming branches of musk willow complete the decorations. Seven ceremonial items—of which the Persian names begin with the letter "s"—are placed on the spread. These are *sīb* (apples); *sabzeh* (an earthenware plate of barley, lentil, or mung-bean); *sīr* (garlic); *sepand* (wild rue seeds); *sekkeh* (coins, usually newly minted); *samanū* (a traditional form of wheat pudding); and *serkeh* (vinegar). The *haft sīn* spread may be further decorated with flowers, sweets, and pictures of family members who live far away or have recently died.

The family gathers around this spread to await the changing of the year. Once the New Year is announced, younger members of the family congratulate their elders and often kiss their hands, while the elders bless the younger and give them cash gifts. The direction of gift giving in Norūz is always from elder to younger. In other words, unlike the Christmas practice in the West where gifts are exchanged between family members regardless of age, in Iranian practice it is considered rude for the young to give anything to their elders. All giving is done by the elders or by those of higher social class to their inferiors.

The Norūz celebration lasts thirteen days, during which schools and many businesses are closed. Itinerant entertainers, called *Hājī Fīrūz*, who blacken their faces, dress in red, and sing to the beat of a tambourine, amuse people in the streets. These people are not members of a professional entertainers' class or guild. They are usually destitute roving laborers who try to make a few bucks during the *Hājī Fīrūz* festival. It is possible that the *Hājī Fīrūz* is a remnant of a more ancient type of entertainer, called *ātesh-afrūz*, "fire-kindler," who was associated with the lighting of fire in the beginning of the spring in pre-Islamic Persia. That the names *Hājī Fīrūz* and *ātesh-afrūz* rhyme and that the *Hājī Fīrūz* blackens his face with soot lend credence to this supposition.

Norūz is preceded by a fire festival called *Chārshambeh Sūrī*, "the red Wednesday." This ritual is held on the evening of the last Wednesday of the year. People purchase or gather as much brushwood, dried camel thorn, date-palm leaves, or desert brush as they can. These are laid out in the yard or the street in one, three, five, or seven spaced piles. At sunset the piles of brushwood are kindled, and when the flames rise, men, women, and children jump over them chanting: "O fire, let your ruddiness be mine, and my paleness be yours." It is believed that this will protect them from illness during the coming year. Many magical practices are performed by women who want to have children or by unmarried girls who desire to be married on this day.

Alongside the pre-Islamic festivals and customs, Iranians have also adopted several observances of purely Muslim provenance. The most important of these is that associated with the martyrdom of the Prophet's grandson, Imam Hoseyn (d. 680 C.E.). The entire country observes this tragic event with processions of mourning, dramatic re-enactments of the events, and singing of dirges. The ceremonies associated with this commemoration are practiced even by some of the Iranians who left the country after the victory of the Islamic revolution. The story of the saint's martyrdom is not only narrated from the pulpits and in the streets by dervishes and storytellers, but it is also re-enacted by dramatic troupes who both commemorate and entertain.

Sports and Games

Persians divert themselves with many games and activities. Aside from references to martial games that were used as part of the training of the aristocratic youth, some of the more common forms of entertainment have left iconographic traces in the archeological records. The most popular among these is backgammon, which has been mentioned in Middle Persian sources. Playing chess, though attested in equally ancient documents, is more limited to the educated classes these days. Other traditional games have largely been replaced by various electronic and card games imported from the West. Traditional physical games have largely yielded to soccer (called football in Iran), basketball, and volleyball. What survives from the games that were quite prevalent in the 1950s are only those—such as hide-and-seek and tag—that are more a matter of natural physical activity among children than games that may be considered traditional *per se*. This fact is not easily acknowledged by many authorities who continue to write on the subject of games in Iran and, perhaps out of habit, persist in describing those games and forms of entertainment that are almost completely replaced by imports from the West.

STUDIES OF PERSIAN FOLKLORE

The beginning of folklore collection in Iran is usually attributed to an eighteenth-century theologian, Āqā Jamāl of Kunsār, who produced a satirical treatise in which he claimed to have collected the superstitious beliefs of the women of Isfahān. This treatise, which was entitled "Women's Beliefs and the Mirror of Fools," is more kindly known by the title of *Kolsūm naneh*, which may be rendered into English as *Nanny Kolsūm* or *Mama Kolsūm*. As a conservative theologian, Āqā Jamāl meant to combat the pagan lore that in his view plagued the minds of unlettered Iranian women. He was neither trying to collect folklore nor present an accurate account of women's beliefs *per se*. Therefore, referring to him as the "founder" of Persian folklore collecting is problematic. He exaggerated what he viewed as the "silly" superstitions of the women of his town and changed his text to serve his aim of combating folklore rather than promoting it.

Systematic collection of Persian folklore began with the efforts of the novelist Ṣādeq Hedāyat (1903–1951), who inspired by French folklorist Arnold van Gennep's classificatory system, published several tales, folksongs, and collections of Persian folk beliefs between 1931 and 1945. After publishing two volumes in the early 1930s, Hedāyat put out two articles on folklore methodology, largely following Pierre Saintyve's *Manuel de folklore* (1935) with adjustments for Iranian culture. These essays later motivated the work of the most important Persian collector of folklore, Abolqāsem Enjavī (d. 1993), who in the spring of 1961 launched an appeal to the listeners of his radio program to collect the folklore of their native towns and villages. Enjavī provided some training for his army of amateur collectors both on the air and by mail and even sent them supplies and pre-printed interview forms. His appeal generated an enormous public response. Soon a flood of data from listeners all over Iran poured into his offices, forming the nucleus of the vast archive of Persian folklore data. He published some of this material between 1973 and 1977 in a series called *ganjīna-yi farhang-e mardom* (The Treasury of Folklore). During this period folklore research was promoted, and an international congress on folklore was held in the city of Isfahān in the summer of 1977.

Things changed drastically with the Islamic Revolution of 1978–1979. Theologians who assumed political power viewed folklore study as promoting superstitious and even pagan beliefs and discontinued most funding for it. But the Folklore Center continued an anemic existence in the harsh environment of revolutionary Iran until the early 1980s, when Enjavī's radio program was also discontinued. This interruption not only stopped almost all collecting but also signaled the coming of many lean years for folklore scholarship in Iran. The Center was placed under the control of the Islamic Republic's broadcasting agency, and much of its holdings, especially its audiovisual collection, was either unceremoniously dispersed among the centers or was placed in storage. Only some of the written documents in the collection were allowed to remain at the archives of the Folklore Center. This situation continued until 1995, when the Ayatollah Khamenei, the leader of the Islamic

Republic of Iran, warned the nation about the dangers of assimilation into the Western culture and called the people to "return" to their native cultural values. Folklore studies were thus revived in Iran as a result of the power structure's reaction to this speech. This new interest in folklore led to a series of efforts to impose some order on the chaotic mass of the existing folklore data in Iran. Folklore publication and research in Iran continue, and a number of important Western studies on folklore have been translated into Persian. Recently, a journal called *Iranian Folklore Quarterly* has been established by one of the foremost Iranian folklorists, Seyyed Ahmad Vakilian, providing further reason to hope that Persian folklore study in Iran is recovering from the injurious effects of the Islamic revolution.

Studies of Persian folklore by non-Iranians have followed a different course. The earliest European interest in Persian folklore was a byproduct of the British and Russian political interest in Iran. Alexander Chodzko (1804–1891), Valentin Zhukovski (1858–1918), Douglas C. Phillot (1860–1930), D. L. Lorimer (1876–1962), B. Nikitin (1885–1960), and above all the Danish scholar Arthur Christensen (1875–1945) and the French Persianist Henri Massé (1886–1969) made significant contributions to Persian folklore studies. Massé feared the disappearance of rural Iranian folklore because of rapid modernization of the country. A scholar of classical Persian, he drew on the resources of his Iranian friends, most of whom were also students of Persian literature, in order to collect and publish the most extensive body of Persian folklore of his time. Early in the 1920s, Massé traveled to Iran in order to collect Persian rural folklore. Interestingly enough, the circumstances of his visit and the nature of his informants were such that his data was almost exclusively collected from city dwellers. Therefore, in spite of his concern for the endangered rural tradition, he actually gathered one of the best existing collections of Iranian urban folklore of the early twentieth century (1954). Massé intentionally left out the folklore of religious and ethnic minorities such as Zoroastrians, Armenians, and Jews.

The most important contemporary western scholar of Persian folklore is Ulrich Marzolph, who compiled the first tale-type index of Persian tales (1984) and has contributed many important monographic studies and essays to Persian folklore studies (for example, 2000). The best long essay about the history of Persian folkloristics in English language remains his discussion of the subject in *Encyclopaedia Iranica*.

BIBLIOGRAPHY

Amīnī, A. 1960. *Sī afsānah az afsānah-hā-ye mahallī-ye esfahān*. Isfahan.

Amir-Moez, Y. 1991. The Magic of Noruz: Iranian New Year's Day Celebration. *Folklife Center News* 13.2: 4–8.

Bal'amī. 1975 (Tenth century C.E.). *Tarīk-e Bal'amī*, edited by M. T. Bahār. 2 volumes. Tehran.

Basu, Kedarnath. 1886. Notes on Nīsī or the Night-Demon. *The Journal of the Anthropological Society of Bombay* 1.1: 49–50.

Binder, G. 1964. *Die Aussetzung des Königskindes Kyros und Romulus*. Meisenheim am Glan: A. Harn.

Carter, G. W. 1970. *Zoroastrianism and Judaism*. New York: AMS Press.

Chehabi, H. E. 2002. An Annotated Bibliography of Sports and Games in the Iranian World. *Iranian Studies* 35.4: 403–419.

Chodzko, A. B. 1842. *Specimens of the Popular Poetry of Persia*. London: W. H. Allen.

Christensen, Arthur. 1918. *Contes persans en langue populaire*. Copenhagen: A. F. Høst.

———. 1958. *Persische Märchen*. Düsseldorf-Koln: E. Diederichs.

Curtis, J., and Finkel, I. 1999. Game Boards and Incised Graffiti at Persepolis. *Iran: Journal of the British Institute of Persian Studies* 37: 45–48.

Curtis, Vesta S. 1993. *Persian Myths*. Austin: University of Texas Press.

Dālvand, H. R. 1998. *Gozārish-i ijrā-yi ṭarḥi āzmāyishī-yi radah bandī-yi asnād-i farhang-i mardum* (Report of the Experimental Plan to Classify Folklore Documents). Tehran: Folklore Center of the Broadcasting Agency of the Islamic Republic of Iran.

Dhabhar, E. B. 1909. *Saddar Nasr and Saddar Bundahesh*. Bombay: Trustees of the Parsee Punchayet Funds and Properties.

El-Shamy, H. 1995. *Folk Traditions of the Arab World: A Guide to Motif Classification*. 2 volumes. Bloomington: Indiana University Press.

Elwell-Sutton, L. P. 1950. *Mashdi Galeen Khanom: The Wonderful Sea-Horse and Other Persian Tales*. London.

———. 1978. The Persian Passion Play. In *Folklore Studies in the Twentieth Century*, edited by Venetia Newall. Woodbridge: Brewer–Rowman and Littlefield. 188–191.

Enjavī, A. 1973. *Tamthīl u mathal I*. Tehran.

———. 1976. *Qessah-hā-ye īrānī* ('arāsak-e sang-e sabūr), Volume 3. Tehran.

———. 1979. *Qessah-hā-ye īrānī* (gol ba senābar ce kard), Volume 1. Tehran.

———. 1980. *Ferdāsīnāamah, Mardom o qahramānān-e Sāhnāmah*. Tehran.

E'temād al-saltanah. 1893. *Ketāb al-Tadwīn fī ahwāl-e jebāl-e serwīn*. Tehran.

Faqīrī, A. 1971. *Qessah-hā-ye mardom-e fārs*. Tehran.

Friedel, E. 1993. Traditional Songs from Boir Ahmad. In *Everyday Life in the Muslim Middle East*, edited by D. L. Bowen and E. Early. Bloomington: Indiana University Press. 17–22.

Ginzberg, L. 1968. *The Legends of the Jews*, translated by H. Szold. 7 volumes. Philadelphia: Jewish Publication Society of America.

Hayrapetian, J. 1983. Political Humor: Its Function and Significance in the Iranian Revolution. *Folklore and Mythology Studies* 7: 24–39.

———. 1990. *Iranian Folk Narrative: A Survey of Scholarship*. New York: Garland.

Hedāyat, S. 1964. *Neyrangestan*. Tehran.

Hedāyat, Sādiq. 1931. *Ōsānah*. Tehran.

———. 1965. Fulklur yā farhang-i tādah (Folklore or the Culture of the Folk). In *Niviāta-hā ā-yi parākandah* (Collected papers). 2nd edition. Tehran. 447–483.

Hinnells, John R. 1973. *Persian Mythology*. London: Hamlyn.

Jackson, W.V.W. 1965. *Zoroastrian Studies*. New York: AMS Press.

Jazāyeri, N. 1959. *Tarjomah-ye Zahr al-Rabi'*. Tehran.

Kalāntarā, M., and Gh. Ma'sūmī. 1950. dehkada-ye anbī. *Honar va Mardom* NS 109: 36–46.

Katirā'i, Mahmud. 1969. *Az Khesht tā Khesht*. Tehran.

———. 1971 (1349). *Kolsūm Naneh='Aqayed al-Nesa' wa Mer'at al-Bolaha'*. Tehran.

———. 1978 (1357). *Zabān u farhang-i mardum* (People's Language and Culture). Tehran: Tūkā.

Katirā'i, Mahmud, ed. 1970. *'Aqāyid al-nisā 'wa mir' āt al-bulahā': du risālah-yi intiqād ī dar farhang-i tīdah* (Women's Beliefs and the Mirror of the Dim-wits: Two Critical Treatises on Folklore). Tehran.

Levy, R., trans. 1967. *The Epic of the Kings*. Chicago: The University of Chicago Press.

Loeffler, R. 1988. *Islam in Practice: Religious Beliefs in a Persian Village*. Albany: State University of New York Press.

Lorimer, D.L.R., and E. S. Lorimer. 1963. The Popular Verse of the Bakhtiari of S. W. Persia. *Bulletin of the School of Oriental and African Studies* 26.1: 55–68.

Lorimer, D.L.R., and E. S. Lorimer, trans. 1919. *Persian Tales, Written down for the First Time in the Original Kermānī and Bakhtiārī and Translated by D.L.R. Lorimer and E. S. Lorimer*. London: Macmillan.

Marzolph, U. 1984. *Typologie des persischen volksmärchens*. Beirut: Orientinstitut der Deutschen Morgenländischen Gesellschaft.

———. 1992. *Aradia ridens: die humoristische Kurzproza der früühen adab-Literatur im internationalen traditionsgeflecht*. 2 volumes. Frankfurt am Main: V. Klostermann.

———. 1994. *Dāstān-hā-yi shīrīn: fünfzig persische Volksbüchlein aus der zweiten Hälfte des zwanzigsten Jahrhunderts*. Stuttgart: Deutsche Morgenländische Gesellschaft.

———. 1995. Molla Nasr al-Din in Persia. *Iranian Studies* 28.3–4: 157–174.

———. 2000. Variation, Stability and the Constitution of Meaning in the Narratives of a Persian Storyteller. In *Thick Corpus, Organic Variation and Textuality in Oral Tradition*, edited by Lauri Honko. Helsinki: NNF. 435–452.

Massé, Henri. 1954. *Persian Beliefs and Customs*, translated by C. A. Massner. New Haven: Human Relations Area Files.

Motamed-Nejad, K. 1979. The Story-Teller and Mass Media in Iran. In *Entertainment: A Cross Cultural Examination*, edited by Heinz-Dietrich Fischer and Stefan Reinhard Melnik. New York: Hastings House.

Mūsavi, H. 1984. *Guseh-ha-'i az Farhang va Adab va Rosum-e Mardom*. Shiraz.

Nāseri, A. 1980 (1358). *Farhang-e Mardom-e Baluc*. Tehran.

Netzer, A. 1982. An Isfahani Jewish Folk Song. In *Irano-Judaica: Studies Relating to Jewish Contacts with Persian Culture Throughout the Ages*. Jerusalem: Ben-Zvi Institute for Study of Jewish Communities in the East. 180–203.

Nikitin, B. 1922. La vie domestique kurde. *Revue d'éthnographie et des traditions populaires* 3: 334–344.

Omidsalar, M. 1984. Storytellers in Classical Persian Texts. *Journal of American Folklore* 97: 204–213.

———. 1986–1987. estelāhāt-e farhang-e mardom dar zabān-e fārsī (On Folklore Terminology in the Persian Language). *Ayandeh* 9–10: 543–557.

Omidsalar, M., and T. Omidsalar. 1999. Narrating Epics in Iran. In *Traditional Storytelling Today: An International Sourcebook*, edited by Margaret Read MacDonald. Chicago: Fitzroy Dearborn Publishers. 326–340.

Pāyandeh, M. 1976. *A'inhā va Bāvardāsht-hā-ye Gil va Deylam*. Tehran.

Penzer, N. M., ed. 1968. *The Ocean of Story*. 10 volumes. Delhi: Motilal Banarsidass.

Perry, J. 2003. Monty Python and the Mathnavi: The Parrot in Indian, Persian, and English Humor. *Iranian Studies* 36.1: 63–73.

Phillot, D. C. 1905–1907. Some Current Persian tales, Collected in the South of Persia from Professional Story-tellers. *Memoirs of the Asiatic Society of Bengal* 1.18: 375–412.

———. 1992. *Rīsha-hā-yi tārīkhī-yi qissah-hā-yi pariyān* (Historical Roots of Fairy Tales), translated by B. Badrah'ī. Tehran.

Qazvīnī, Z. 1983 (ca. 1203–1283). *'Ajāyeb al-maklūqāt*, edited by N. Sabūhī. Tehran.

Qomī, A. N.d. *Safīnah al-Behār*. 2 volumes. Beirut.

Radhayrapetian, Juliet. 1990. *Iranian Folk Narrative: A Survey of Scholarship*. New York: Garland.

Rāzī, Abu al-Futūh. 1988 (ca. 12th century). *Rawd al-Jinān wa Rawh al-Janān*, Volumes 9–17, edited by M. M. Nāsih and M. J. Yāhaqqī. Tehran.

Riggio, M. C. 1995. Ta'ziyah in Exile: Transformations in a Persian Tradition. In *Gesellschaftlicher*

Umbruch und Historie im zeitgenössischen Drama der islamischen Welt, edited by J. Bürgel and S. Guth. Beirut: Steiner. 235–258.

Riyāhī, A. 1977. *Zār o Bād o Balūch*. Tehran.

Shariati, A. 1986. Nowruz. *Iranian Studies* 19.3–4: 235–241.

Sheil, M.L.W. 1856. *Glimpses of Life and Manners in Persia*. London: J. Murray.

Slobin, M. 1970. Persian Folksong Texts from Afghan Badakhshāan. *Iranian Studies* 3: 91–103.

Sobhī, F. 1960–1964. *Afsānah-hā*. 2 volumes. Tehran.

Soroudi, S. 1982. Shira-ye hatani, A Judeo-Persian Wedding Song. In *Irano-Judaica: Studies Relating to Jewish Contacts with Persian Culture Throughout the Ages*, edited by S. Shaked. Jerusalem: Ben-Zvi Institute for Study of Jewish Communities in the East. 204–264.

———. 1990. Folk Poetry and Society in Ninteenth-Century Iran. *In Proceedings of the First European Conference of Iranian Studies Held in Turin, September 7th–11th, 1987*, edited by G. Gnoli and A. Panaino. Rome: Instituto italiano per il Medio ed Estremo Oriente. 541–552.

Suyūtī. 1904 (1445–1505). *Kitāb al-wadīk fī fadl al-dīk*. Cairo.

Tafsīr. 1997. *Bakhshī az tafsīr ī kuhan*, edited by M. Ayatollāh-zāda-ye Shīrāzī. Tehran.

Tūsī. 1966 (ca. 1155). *'Ajāyib al-Makhlūqāt*, edited by M. Sotūdah. Tehran.

Unvala, J. M., ed. 1917. *Der Pahlavi Text: Der König und sein knabe*. Wien: Druck von Holzhausen.

Wensinck A. J. 1927. *A Handbook of Early Muhammadan Tradition*. Leiden: E. J. Brill.

Yarshater, E. 1979. Ta'zieh and Pre-Islamic Mourning Rites in Iran. In *Ta'ziyeh: Ritual and Drama in Iran*, edited by P. Chelkowsi. New York: New York University Press. 88–95.

———. 1998. *The Lion and the Throne: Stories from the Shāhnāma of Ferdowsi*, translated by Dick Davis. Washington: Mage Publishers.

Zaehner, R. C. 1956. *The Teachings of the Magi: A Compendium of Zoroastrian Beliefs*. London: George Allen and Unwin.

Zhukovski, V. 1902. *Obraztsy persidskogo narodnogo tvorchestva*. St. Petersburg.

Mahmoud Omidsalar

TURKEY

GEOGRAPHY AND HISTORY

Located between Europe and Asia and consisting of Anatolia and Thrace, Turkey has a land area of 814,578 square kilometers bordered by the Black Sea, Aegean Sea, and Mediterranean Sea. The Sea of Marmara opens to the Black Sea through the Straits of Istanbul and to the Aegean and Mediterranean through the Straits of Çanakkale (or Dardanelles). These borders were established following the collapse of the Ottoman Empire. The average altitude of the fairly rugged topography of Turkey is 1132 meters. A subtropical region among many arid and semi-arid countries, Turkey receives less rain due to the effect of the Mediterranean Sea. Its Mediterranean macroclimate is subdivided into seven geographical regions: Aegean, Black Sea, Central Anatolia, Eastern, Marmara, Mediterranean, and Southeastern. Geography is one of the important influences on the culture with thick forests along the coast of the Black Sea and drier steppes toward the inland and eastern Anatolia.

Turkey had a population of just under 70 million people in 2003. Two-thirds of these live in urban areas. The most crowded and biggest cities are İstanbul, Ankara, and İzmir. The major industries are agriculture, **tourism**, automobile manufacturing, petroleum, and engineering. Migration from rural to urban areas and from smaller to larger cities characterizes modern life, and it affects culture especially in urban areas.

An eight-year primary compulsory education system applies to children between the ages of six and fourteen. Secondary education includes general, vocational, and technical institutions that provide at least three years of further education. Higher education includes all institutions after secondary education which prepare students for associate's, bachelor's, master's, and doctoral degrees. Sixty-nine universities vary in their emphases on science and art. According to figures from 1990, eighty-one percent of the population is literate. Seventy-one percent have graduated from primary school, fourteen percent have completed a secondary education, and five percent have attended institutions of higher education.

Family relations are very important in Turkey. Industrialization and migration have made the nuclear family more common, but the extended family retains its importance. Ninety-nine percent of the population is Muslim, most belonging to the Sunni branch of Islam, but a significant number are Alevi Muslims, a branch related to Shi'a Islam. Other religious groups in Turkey include Greek Orthodox, Armenian Orthodox, Roman Catholic, Protestant, and Jewish. The ancient religion of the Turks was shamanistic, the influence of which is still seen in folklore. Examples include the dances and beliefs that those who cut trees near a tomb will be paralyzed; if a dead person is seen in a dream, a guest will visit in waking life; a knife should be put on a dead person's body during the night; broken mirrors bring bad luck; when a wolf howls, it will either snow or frost; a black cat walking across one's path brings bad luck; and cats never fall on their backs, because Hafiz Ali stroked their backs. Others are the notion that genies never enter places where fire is burning; if ash is thrown away at night, the house will not be blessed; the olive is holy; less deaths occur where wheat is abundant; on the day of *Hidirellez*, no one should sew, cut a tree or plant, or kill any creature; and no one should shave on the day of a religious festival. Shamanism has also influenced folk beliefs that hold that to stop hail, a knife should be placed in the courtyard; sleeping near a fountain summons the devil; looking at a mirror at night shortens one's life; giving yeast to someone reduces a blessing; biting a piece of iron during thunder brings good luck; to begin work on a Monday produces a slowdown; passing between two men causes a woman to become infertile; a bite of food falling from one's mouth signals the imminent arrival of a guest; thumping the right ear is a positive gesture; and an itchy palm means that some money will come.

Around 80 percent of the Turkish population is Turkic in **ethnicity**. This includes groups originally from the Balkans who speak only Turkish, the official language. Minorities include Kurds, Levantines, Syriacs, Arabs, Laz, Greeks, and Armenians. Turkish has been influenced in part by Chinese, Persian, and Arabic and has, in turn, influenced language groups in Eastern Europe, Southeast Asia, northern Russia, and even North America.

Before the boundaries of modern Turkey were determined in 1923, many societies had lived there, thus making it a cradle of civilizations. Indo-European migrations brought a variety of groups over the Caucasus Mountains into Anatolia: the Nesi settled in central Anatolia, the Pala in Paphlygonia, and the Luwians in southern

Anatolia. During these migrations the new arrivals gradually captured Hatti princedoms to form the first Old Hittite Kingdom (1660–1460 B.C.E.) and then the Great Hittite Kingdom (1460–1190 B.C.E.). As the Hittites were settling in central Anatolia, another Indo-European people were flourishing in the Çanakkale region at Troy VI. In southeastern and eastern Anatolia, an area largely unaffected by migrations from the Balkans, the Late Hittite Princedoms (1200–700 B.C.E.) and the Urartu Kingdom (860–580 B.C.E.) produced a high level of culture. The Lydians and Lycians spoke languages that were fundamentally Indo-European, but both languages had acquired non-Indo-European elements prior to the Hittite and Hellenic periods. During the reign of Croesus, fabled for his wealth (575–545 B.C.E.), the Lydian capital of Sardes was one of the most brilliant cities of the ancient world. Herodotos writes that according to Cretan legend the Carians were called Leleges and lived on islands in the Aegean and eastern Mediterranean during the time of the Minoan Kingdom (the mid-second millennium B.C.E.). The Carians themselves, however, claimed to be native Anatolians, related to the Lydians and Mysians. After the destruction of Troy, the Hellenes established cities along the western Anatolian coast. In the ninth century B.C.E. they produced the first literary masterpiece of Western civilization, *The Iliad* of Homer. During the era of the natural philosophers (600–545 B.C.E.), the brilliance of Anatolian culture was unmatched, superceding Egypt and Mesopotamia. Throughout the Hellenistic Age (333–300 B.C.E.), Milletus, Priene, Ephesos, and Teos were among the finest cities in the world, and Anatolian architecture at this time influenced Rome signficantly.

The Romans (30 B.C.E.–595 C.E.) developed the technique of mortaring bricks together, thereby producing arches, vaults, and domes of large volume. Byzantine art was born in Anatolia at the end of the Roman era. For two and a half centuries (300–565 C.E.), Constantinople (now İstanbul), the capital city of the Byzantine Empire (330–1453 C.E.), was the leading city in the world in art and culture.

Meanwhile, Turks established numerous states in different part of Asia, Europe, and Africa. Mutual influence occurred with the cultures they encountered. Chinese records report that the first appearance of the Turks in history was in the Kogmen Mountains. The culture known as Tagar, dating to the seventh century B.C.E., is attributed to the ancient Turks. The Hun State, which appeared in the third century B.C.E., became a significant, powerful entity during the reign of its founder, Mete Khan, and passed through fundamental economic and social changes due to relations with China. The Gokturk State (552–740 C.E.) is the second significant state established by Turks. The **Uyghur** State (741–840 C.E.) focused on trade and continued the traditions of the Gokturks. After the decline of the Uyghur State, Turkish tribes such as the Karluks, Cigils, and Arguls founded the Karahanid State in 840. The reign of the Karahanids is considered a turning point in Turkish history because Islam became the official religion. Another important Turkish state was the Seljuk State (1040–1157 C.E.), founded by Seljuk Bey, a member of the Kinik tribe of Oghuz Turks. During the reign of Sultan Malik Shah, one of its most powerful rulers, the Seljuk State enjoyed considerable success in military affairs, science, politics, and literature.

As the Seljuk State was disintegrating, many small beylics and atabeylics were established in Anatolia. These political units helped to strengthen the Seljuk State in that region of modern Turkey. Among the many beylics that developed in Anatolia were the Ottomans, part of the Kayi tribe of Oghuz Turks from the Sogut-Yenisehir-Bilecik region. The Ottoman Beylic unified the beylics in Anatolia. The Ottomans crossed into Rumelia and conquered Constantinople in 1453 during the reign of Sultan Mehmed II, ending the Byzantine Empire as well as the European Middle Ages. Throughout the six centuries of their administration, the Ottomans held together people of different religions, languages, and races and assumed the role of protecting their cultures by stressing freedom of religion and expression. Moreover, the Ottomans contributed to the history of civilization through scientific and artistic masterpieces.

The territories of the Ottoman State, which had allied with **Germany** during World War I, were occupied by Britain, **France**, **Russia**, and **Greece** following the 1918 armistice. This occupation produced resistance among Turks in Anatolia and Thrace. The Greek occupation accelerated the establishment of small defense fronts and the formation of regional resistance organizations. The National War of Independence led by Mustafa Kemal Atatürk was an effort to create a new republication state out of the ruins of a dead empire. Atatürk, Turkey's first president, attempted to build a modern state through revolution.

VERBAL ARTS

This historical background produced the most common theme in Turkish folklore, heroism. The written and verbal arts of Turkey prior to Islam carry traces of nomadic culture. The first examples of this verbal tradition include the Alp Er Tunga Legend, which relates how Alp Er Tunga, the Saka Khan who is thought to have lived in the seventh century, prevailed against the Iranian armies. The Bozkurt (Gray Wolf) Legend recites the myth of the creation of the Gokturks from a female wolf, and the Ergenekon Legend holds that the Gokturks came out of Ergenekon by melting an iron mountain. Eulogies, poems of nature and love, and proverbs, read mostly at religious ceremonies and victory celebrations, are other examples of early Turkish verbal art. Information on verbal art from the preliterate period comes from Chinese, Arabic, and Iranian sources. The first known written examples of Turkish literature are the Orhun Inscriptions, written in the Gokturk alphabet in the sixth and seventh centuries. The most important of these stone monuments, translated into several languages, are those erected to the memory of Tonyukuk, Kultegin, and Bilge Khan.

Folk literature encompasses literary works such as poetry, proverbs, legends, folktales, anecdotes, lullabies, folksongs, jingles riddles, folk music, and wailing. Minstrel poems, epic poems, *ko çaklama*, *ko şima*, *varsa ği*, and *mani* have specific features regarding their themes and features. For example, the minstrel type of poetry emerged in the eleventh and twelfth centuries. Because most of the works were impromptu, many are now lost. Folk poems by minstrels incorporate their composer's name in the last quatrain. The general rhyme order is AAAB. *Mani* is a folk music form as well as an anonymous literary form having the syllabic meter AABA.

Blessings and curses are also part of Turkish verbal art. The following exemplify folk blessings: "May God let you get what you desire"; "May God let your child be brought up with mother and father"; "May God not let you need others' help"; "May you see happy days"; "May God increase your knowledge"; "May your head be upright." Other traditional blessings: "Thank God, I am very well"; "Everything depends on health; the rest is in vain"; "May God give you harmonious life together"; "I hope you live as you prefer"; "May you live happily in your new home"; "May it bring you luck"; "May *Hizir* visit you"; "Let us say good; let it be good"; "May you live happily in your country"; "May your mouth be sweet." Examples of curses include the following: "May God give you a thousand troubles"; "May God put you in need of a slice of bread"; "May you not attain your desire"; "May the devil take you"; "May you burn in the fire of hell"; "May your tongue be unable to speak"; "May your children cause you to suffer"; "Whatever you have done, may you deserve the same."

MUSIC

Folk literature and folk music are closely related. The earliest folk music apparently came from magicians and poet-instrumentalists called *shamans* by the Tonguz, *kam* by the Altay Turks, *bakst* by the Kirgis, *oyun* by the Yakut, and *ozan* by the Oğuz. No examples of their music have survived, and one of the earliest resources on Turkish music did not appear until the 1650s: *Mecmua-i Saz ü Söz* by Ali Ufkî (Albert Popowski). Aşik Veysel, Karacaoğlan, and Köroğlu are some of the *ozans*, whose work still survives.

Turkish folk music falls into two structural categories: *uzun hava* and *kirik hava*, both of which are found in different modes (*ayak* or *makain*) such as *bozlak*, *misket*, *kerem*, *garip*, *derbeder*, and *müstezat*. The former is a tune performed in a free, recitative rhythm pattern. Its name and style differ according to region—for example, *hoyrat*, *maya*, *kesik*, *kayaba şi aydost*, *yanuk*, *bozlak*, *gurbet havasi*, *divan*, or *yol havasi*. Before beginning to sing *uzun hava*, the musician performs an improvisational instrumental introduction. Among the genres of *uzun hava* are laments for tragic events such as death and natural disasters. *Bozlak*, which emphasizes heroism and bravery, is performed mainly by Turkomen and *Av şar* groups in central and southern Anatolia. The most distinctive features of *bozlak* is its *kürdi* scale. The *divan* type of *uzun hava* is composed in free style and based on a classical meter. At beginning and end of the tune are instrumental sections usually with 2/4 or 4/4 rhythm patterns. The *horyat*, generally encountered in eastern Anatolia, is laden with puns. The *kezik*, characteristic of the folk music of Urfa, Elaziğ, and Kerkük, has varying modes and melodic progression. The themes of the *maya*, found in eastern Anatolia, deal with love and homesickness.

Kirik havalar, the other major structural category of Turkish folk music, are divided into instrumental melodies and tunes with texts called *türkü*, which may be classified according to theme: lullabies, nature, love, henna, the road, bravery, soldiers, ceremonies, work, death, and other topics. Different generic labels include, *zeybek*, *bengi*, *güvende*, *bar*, and *horon*. Another form of *kirik hava* includes tunes used to accompany dancing.

A range of musical instruments accompany Turkish folk music. Included are chordophones such as the *bağlama*, the most widely used instrument in Turkey. Varying in size, it has a register of two and a half octaves and is played using a variety of techniques and tunings. Another chordophone, the *kabak kemane* has a sound resonator made from a gourd. It is played with a horsehair bow. The *kemençe*, found in the Black Sea region, is a fretless instrument with three strings. The tune is played on one string, while the other strings are bowed as drones. The *tar* is played using a plectrum. It has two sound boxes with leather stretched across its belly.

The *argun* is one of many aerophones used in Turkish folk music. Found primarily in the Mediterranean region, it is similar to the double *kaval* with seven or eight fingerholes on one tube and one or two holes on the other. The *kaval* is wooden and may have a fork. It has seven fingerholes in front and one in the back. The *çiğirtma* is made from the bone of an eagle, has no fork, and has seven fingerholes. A flat double-reed instrument with a fork and forceps made from plumwood and derived from a central Asian instrument called the *balaban*, the *mey* falls into three types based on size. With seven fingerholes on the front and one on the back, it is usually played indoors in eastern Anatolia. A circular blowing technique is employed, and one can change pitch by moving the forceps. The *sipsi* is small and made of cane. It has five, six, or seven holes on the front and one on the back. It is found primarily in the Mediterranean and Aegean regions. The *tulum*—also called *gayda* or *kayda*—has an airbag made from goatskin. It has two pipes, one for drones which has one or two fingerholes and the other for melody with five fingerholes. It comes from northeastern Anatolia. The most characteristic and widespread aerophone in Turkey is the *zurna*, having a double reed, a fork, and a pirouette and usually accompanied by the *davul*, a cylindrical drum. It has seven fingerholes on the front and one on the back of the main body. In addition, there are seven holes on the bell which balance the emitted air. Its tuning varies according to size. It is employed in Mehter music (military music of the Janissaries), in Karagöz (shadow theater), in Orta Oyunu (improvisational folk theater), in folk music and dances, and in court music. The *çifte* is a reed aerophone with two attached cane pipes which are played simultaneously. The droning pipe has zero or one fingerhole, while the melodic pipe has seven or eight.

The *asma davul*, a double-skin cylindrical drum which varies in size, is the oldest Turkish membranophone. It has been played in sacred ceremonies and on battlefields and also has a communications function. The *def* is a frame drum, sometimes with attached cymbals. Women usually play it by striking it manually. Its larger counterparts without cymbals are called *daire*. The *koltuk davulu*, common in northeastern Anatolia, is held under the arm while being struck with the hand. The *darbuka* is a single-headed goblet drum made from pottery, wood, or metal. The bottom is open, and the skin head is directly attached by nails, glue, or binding.

Turkish idiophones include the *ka şik*, a wooden spoon. Women often use other household items such as pots, basins, and trays for percussive effect. Another wooden instrument, the *ma şa*, is played with its two handles struck together in the palm. It may have metal cymbals attached to the ends of the handles—in which case it is called a *zilli ma şa*.

DANCE

Traditional Turkish musical instruments might accompany dances performed at weddings, engagements, ceremonies for sending soldiers off to military service, national and religious festivals, victory celebrations, and other festive occasions. Four general subjects inform Turkish folk dance: labor, real or mythical events, human relationships with nature and other people, and religion. There is no single national style of dance. But while Turkish folk dances are remarkably diverse, they may be categorized mainly based on geography (though with some overlap)—for example, Halay, Bar, Horon, Zeybek, Kesik, and Hora (Kar şilama). These represent different dance styles found in the country's numerous ethnic regions. People who enjoy reputations as good dancers are often invited to ceremonies and pass their knowledge on to others in these contexts.

SPORTS, GAMES, AND PUPPET THEATER

Games and sports also figure into many ceremonies. Camel Play, Ram Mating, Face of Camel, and Face of Sheep are simple theatrical games in which people imitate animals, for example. Among children's games are Hide-and-Seek, *Bezirgan Ba şi* (Head of the Grasping Trader), and Leapfrog (Long Donkey).

Shadow puppet theater, called *karagöz*, dates from the sixteenth century. Theories about its origin argue that it came with immigrants from central Asia or after the conquest of Egypt in 1517. Others hold that Karagöz and Hacivat, the main characters in this folklore genre, were real persons from Thrace. In addition to these two opposing figures, shadow puppet plays feature a host of other characters: Tuzsuz Çelebi, Matiz, Beberuhi, Arnavut, Yahudi, Çerkez, Kürt, Laz, Tiryaki, and Zenneler. Exaggerations, puns, and dialect imitations are the principal comic elements. Music also has a very distinctive role.

Ortaoyunu (literally, "play in the middle"), one subgenre of *karagöz*, developed in the fifteenth century and gained its dramatic character in the first half of the nineteenth century.

Turkish dancer. (Art & Architecture Collection, Miriam and Ira D. Wallach Division of Art, Prints and Photographs, The New York Public Library, Astor, Lenox and Tilden Foundations)

It is so named because the audience encircles the stage. The main characters are Kavuklu and Pişekar. The focus is on the dialogue between these characters. Another type of folk theater, *meddahlik* (the art of the *meddah*), emphasizes storytelling and mimicry. A one-man show in which the *meddah* tells stories to the audience, it draws for its subject matter upon events from daily life, folktales, epics, and legends. The only stage props of the *meddah* are a handkerchief and a cudgel, and the solo performer assumes the roles of many characters.

Among traditional sports still performed are grease wrestling, bullfighting, and *cirit*. The last is both ceremony and competition and features musical accompaniment by *davul* and *zurna*. Found mainly in Balikesir, Söğüt, Konya, Kars, Erzurum, and Bayburt, *cirit* is played by two teams of six, eight, or twelve players on a field as much as seventy to 120 meters long. Dressed in regional costumes, the players mount their horses. With their right hands they hold a *cirit*, a wooden stick about a hundred centimeters long and two or three centimeters wide, while holding other *cirits* in their left hands. Plays who hit an opponent with a *cirit* win a point, but they lose a point if they hit the horse instead of its rider.

The tradition of shadow-puppet theater in Turkey can be traced back to the sixteenth century. This late-nineteenth–early-twentieth-century puppet is in the form of a stork. (© The British Museum/HIP/The Image Works)

Nearly a thousand barefoot athletes, oiled and stripped to the waist, compete in grease wrestling, the most famous contest of which occurs in Edirne. For three days the field is crowded with simultaneous matches in eleven divisions, ranging from schoolchildren to forty-year-old masters. *Kispet* (special leather pants), *peşrez* (the warming-up ceremony), music performed on *davul* and *zurna*, and *yağlanma* (to grease itself) are important elements of this sport.

Kafkasör bullfights offer scenes of breathtaking excitement especially in the northeastern part of Turkey. Bulls classified according to the thickness of their necks or weight are pitted against one another. Traditional rules protect bulls from injury and suffering. When the weaker bull withdraws from the arena, that defeat is accepted. Camel wrestling contests, usually held during winter in the Aegean and Mediterranean regions, are accompanied by the *davul* and *zurna*, *cazgur* (announcer), and *zeybek* dancers. A camel wrestles just once per day, and each match lasts from ten to fifteen minutes. These rules exist to prevent serious injury or death.

ARTS AND CRAFTS

In addition to these musical instruments, Turkish folk handicrafts include carpets, rugs, weaving, decorative writing, tilework, ceramics and pottery, embroidery, leatherworking, masonry, metalwork, basketry, saddlemaking, and others.

Weaving has been common in Anatolia for generations and is a source of income in many regions. Embroideries, now mainly found in trousseau chests, communicate through their designs. The tools and techniques used supply names for embroidery borders and motifs: needle, crochet needle, shuttle, hairpin, silk cocoon, wool, candlestick, bead, and leftover cloth, for example. During the Ottoman period jewelry developed with the empire. After the Anatolian Bronze Age, materials such as copper, gold, and silver came into common usage. Jewelry-makers have used such techniques as scraping and *savaklama* (engraving black on silver). Handicrafts made with copper as well as those made from brass, gold, and silver remain alive in Turkey. Copper is especially common in cookware.

Woodworking reached a pinnacle during the Seljuk period. The most important arts in wood were the niche in mosques indicating the direction of Mecca, mosque doors, and cupboard covers. During the Ottoman period woodcraft consisted of more everyday objects such as spoons, chests, drawers, stands for quilted turbans. Qur'an covers, ceilings, pulpits, and coffins also exhibited quality workmanship. Techniques such as tapping, painting, relief-engraving, caging, coating, and burning are still in use.

Glazed tilework became important in various parts of Turkey at different times: in İznik in the fourteenth century, in Kütahya in the fifteenth century, and in Çanakkale in the seventeenth century. The Ottoman period introduced new designs. Ceramics and glazed tile arts gained international fame. The most distinctive examples of glassware from Anatolia reveal the evolution of this art. An array of different forms emerged during the Seljuk period, and İstanbul became the center for glass arts during the Ottoman Empire. Çeşmi-i Bülbül is a glassmaking technique that has survived from that era. Craftsmen from İzmir-Görele began to produce glass beads for averting the evil eye (*nazar boncuğu*), and such beads are found throughout Anatolia.

Stone decorations on traditional architecture represent another important Turkish folk art. Gravestones are another important example of stonework. Techniques such as carving, relief, and script are used to produce ornamental motifs: plants, geometrical images, writing, and numbers. Animal motifs do not often occur, and human figures date mostly from the Seljuk period. Basketmaking utilizes reeds, willows, and nut branches and has traditionally served decorative rather than utilitarian purposes. Saddles made from felt and rough cloth are another example of widely practiced Turkish folk art.

STUDIES OF TURKISH FOLKLORE

Many folk traditions in Turkey survive because of folklore studies that began in the 1910s. Before this date, *Dinan-i Lûgat-it-Türk* of Kaşgarli Mahmut in the eleventh century and *Seyahatname* of Evliya Çelebi in the seventeenth are among the important sources on Turkish folklife. Early scholars include Ziya Gökalp, who wrote the first article on Turkish folklore in 1913, Mehmet Fuat Köprülü, Riza Tevfik Bölükbaşi, Selim Sirri Tarcan, and Rauf Yekta Bey. Among foreign researchers who have studied Turkish folklore, mostly literature and music, are Bela Bartok, Wolfram Eberhard, F. Giese, G. Jacob, U. Johansen, F. W. Hasluck, I. Kunos, F. Luschan, Th. Menzel, G. Mezsaros, G. Nemeth, K. Rainhardt, H. Ritter, and W. Ruben. Later many scholars such as Mahnut Ragip Gazimihal, Pertev Naili Boratav, İlhan Başgöz, Orhan Acipayamli, Cemil Dermirsipahi, Hali Bedii Yönetken, Nermin Erdentuğ, Sedat Veyis Örnek, Metin And, Özdemir Nutku, Tahir Alangu, Şükrü Elçin, Şerif Baykurt, and Cevdet Kudret have published on Turkish folklore.

After the establishment of the republic, societies founded at universities and private associations began field researches and published folklore periodicals: Anadolu Halk Bilgisi Denerği (Association of Anatolian Folklore), which publishes *Halk Bilgisi Haberleri*; Folklor Araştirmalari Kurumu (Institute of Folklore Research); the Turkish Language Institution; Türk Folklor Kurumu (Institute of Turkish Folklore); Türk Folklor Araştirmalari Kurumu (Institute of Turkish Folklore Research); and many others. The İstanbul Municipal Conservatory initiated the first official folklore **fieldwork** in 1926. It was followed by Ankara State Conservatory. At present many universities and government institutions contribute to folklore research. Banks (İş Bankasi, Yapi Kredi Bankasi, Akbank, Sümerbank) and newsletters (among them *Milliyet*, *Tercüman*, *Güneş*, *Sabah*, and *Hürriyet*) contribute by organizing folk dance and folk music competitions as well as exhibits presenting an array of folk arts and crafts. *See also* **Kurds**.

BIBLIOGRAPHY

Acipayamli, Orhan. 1974. *Türkiye'de Doğumla İlgili Âdet ve İnanmalarin Etnolojik Etüdü*. Ankara: Atatürk Üniversitesi Edebiyat Fakültesi Yayinlari.

———. 1978. *Halkbilim Terimleri Sözlüğü*. Ankara: TDK yayini.

Akdoğu, Onur. 1995. *Türk Müziğinde Türler ve Biçimler*. İzmir: Can Ofset.

Alangu, Tahir. 1983. *Türkiye Folkloru El Kitabi*. İstanbul: Adam Yayinlari.

And, Metin. 1962. *Dionisos ve Andolu Köylüsü*. İstanbul: Elif Kitapevi.

———. 1969. *Geleneksel Türk Tiyatrosu*. Ankara: Bilgi Yayinevi.

———. 1974. *Oyun ve Bügü: Türk Kültüründe Oyan Kavrami*. İstanbul: Baha Matbaasi.

———. 1976. *Turkish Dancing*. Ankara: Dost Yayinlari.

Ataman, Sadi Yaver. 1975. *100 Türk Halk Oyunu*. İstanbul: Yapi ve Kredi Bankasi.

Balaman, Ali Riza. 1983. *Genelekler: Töre ve Törenler*. İzmir: Betim Yayinlari.

Bartok, Bela. 2002. *Turkish Folk Music from Asia Minor*. Homosassa, FL: Bartok Records.

Başgöz, İlhain. 1986. *Folklor Yazilari*. İstanbul: Adam Yayinlari.

———. 1992. *Karac'oğlan*. İstanbul: Pan Yayincilik.

Baykurt, Şerif. 1965. *Türk Halk Oyunlari*. Ankara: Başnur Matbaasi.

———. 1976. *Türkiye'de Folklor*. Ankara: Kalite Matbaasi.

Bölükbaşi, Riza Tevfik. 1914. Raks ve Folklor. *Peyam Gazetesi*.

Boratav, Pertev Naili. 1939, 1945. *Folklor ve Edebiyat*. 2 volumes. İstanbul and Ankara: Recep Ulusoğlu Matbaasi.

———. 1969. *100 Soruda Türk Halk Edebiyati*. İstanbul: Gerçek Yayinevi.

———. 1973. *100 Soruda Türk Folkloru*. İstanbul: Gerçek Yayinevi.

Demirsipahi, Cemil. 1980. *Türk Halk Oyunlari*. İstanbul: İşbankasi Yay.

Eberhard, Wolfram. 1980 (1955). *Minstrel Tales form Southeastern Turkey*. New York: Arno.

Elçin, Şükrü. 1991. *Anadolu Köy Orta Oyunlari*. Ankara: TAKE, Ankara Üniversitesi Basimevi.

Erdentuğ, Nermin. 1972. *Türkiye Toplumlarinda Kültürel Antropolojik (Etnolojik)*. Ankara: Ankara Üniversitesi Eğitim Fak.

———. 1977. *Sosyal Adet ve Gelenekler*. Ankara: Kültür Bakanliği Yayinlari.

Farmer, Henry George. 1986. *Studies in Oriental Music I, II*. Frankfurt: Institut für Geschichte der Arabisch-Islamischen Wissenschaften.

Gazimihâl, Mahmut R. 1975. *Türk Vurmali Çalgilari (Türk Depki Çalgilari)*. Ankara: T. C. Kültür Bakanliği.

———. 1997. *Türk Halk Danslari Kataloğu, I-II-III*. Ankara: T. C. Kültür Bakanliği.

———. 2001. *Türk Nefesli Çalgilari (Türk Ötkü Çalgilari)*. Ankara: T. C. Kültür Bakanliği.

Gökalp, Ziya. 1913. Halk Medeniyeti. *Halka Doğru Dergisi*, 23 July.

Jakob, Georg. 1900. *Türkisches Literatur Geschitchat in Einzeldarstellungen. 1: Türkische Schatten Theater*. Berlin.

Köprülü, Mehmet Fuat. 1914. Yeni Bir İlim: Halkiyat-Folklor. *İkdam Gazetesi*.

———. 1926. *Türk Edebiyati Tarihi*. İstanbul: Milli Matbaa.

———. 1966. *Edebiyat Araştirmalari*. Ankara: Türk Tarihkurumu Basimevi.

Kudret, Cevdet. 1968–1970. *Karagöz 1, 2, 3*. Ankara: Bilgi Yayinevi.

Kurtişoğlu, Bülent. 1998. *Türk Halk Oyunlarinda Sahneleme Aşamalari*. İstanbul: İstanbul Technical University Institute of Social Sciences, Sanatta Yeterlik Tezi.

Nutku, Özdemir. 1997. *Meddahlik ve Meddah Hikayeleri*. Ankara: Atatürk Kültür Merkezi Yayinlari.

Örnek, Sedat Veyis. 1971. *Etnoloji Sözlügü*. Ankara: A. Ü. Dil ve Tarih Coğrafya Fakültesi.

Öztürkmen, Arzu. 1992. Individuals and Institutions in the Early History of Turkish Folklore, 1840–1950. *Journal of Folklore Research* 29: 177–192.

———. 1998. *Türkiye'de Folklor ve Milliyetçilik*. İstanbul: İletişim Yayinlari.

Reinhard, Kurt. 1962. *Turkishe Musik*. Berlin: Museum für Völkerkunde.

Reinhard, Kurt, and Ursula Reinhard. 1969. *Turquie—Les Traditions Musicals: Collection de l'Institute International d'Etudes Comparatives de la Musique (Berlin)*. Paris: Buchet/Chastel.

Ritter, H. 1933. Der Reigen der Tanzenden Derwische. *Zeitschrift für vergleichende Musikwissenschaft I.*

Şenel, Süleyman. 1991. *Âşik Mûsikisi.* In *İslam Ansiklopedesi.* İstanbul: TDV Yayinlari. 1.

Tarcan, Selem Sirri. 1924. *Halk İlmi (Halkiyat).* Türkiye Edebiyat Mecmuasi.

Ufki, Ali. 2003. *Hâzâ Mecmua-i Sâz u Söz.* İzmir: Meta Basim.

Üngör, Etem Ruhi. 1989. *Karagöz Musikisi.* Ankara: Kültür Bakanliği.

Von Luschan, Felix. 1922. *Völker, Rassen, Sprachen.* Berlin: Welt-verlag.

Yekta, Rauf. 1927. *Anadolu Halk Şarkilari. Volume 1: Darülelhan Külliyati.* İstanbul: Evkaf-i İslamiye matbaasi.

Yönetken, Halil Bedii. 1975. *100 Halk Oyunu.* İstanbul.

Belma Kurtişoğlu and Bülent Kurtişoğlu

YEMEN

GEOGRAPHY AND HISTORY

The Republic of Yemen, located in the southwestern corner of the Arabian Peninsula, is a country of approximately 18 million people with Sana'a as their capital city. This semi-arid but starkly beautiful land is bisected by a high and steep mountain range (highest peak: Jabal Nabi Shu'ayb at 3,600 meters) that runs like a spine north-to-south. To the west of this on the Red Sea, lie the tropical coastal plains of Tihama; to the south is the international port city of Aden; and to the east stretches a highland plateau that becomes more desiccated as it approaches the vast interior desert of Arabia known as the Empty Quarter. This highland plateau is cross-cut by many deep, emerald green valleys (*wadis* in Arabic), the most dramatic and historically significant of which is the Wadi Hadhramawt in the southern part of the country. To the east of this *wadi* on the border with the state of Oman is the remote region of Mahrah, with its language, distinct from Arabic, on which modern research is now shedding light. Analogous to Mahrah in its remoteness as well as its as yet untold cultural riches is the island of Socotra, one of the most fascinating ecological zones on earth, located over 200 miles off the southern coast of Yemen in the Arabian Sea.

Monsoon rains in winter and summer water the extensively terraced central mountains to allow for the cultivation of such staples as sorghum, barley, and wheat—from which various delicious flat breads are made—as well as alfalfa, beans, and vegetables of various sorts, not to mention cash crops such as coffee and *qât*. Work in the fields is punctuated by rhythmic songs that can be heard echoing throughout the valleys. At one time this agricultural order served as inspiration for humorous stories about a character named Ali ibn Zayid, which were full of folk wisdom, though their circulation today seems to be limited more to printed anthologies than word of mouth. Yemeni folklore is in many respects replete with information about agriculture. In spite of its agricultural production, however, Yemen is a poor country with few natural resources. Its oil reserves are not of a high enough grade to be lucrative. Mokha coffee, named after the port on the Red Sea from where it was shipped all over the world two centuries or more ago, can be found as a high-priced item in coffee houses in the United States but does not represent a major export for the country. An even more famous plant is *qât*, whose top-most succulent leaves are chewed for their stimulant effect. Though banned by the U.S. Food and Drug Administration because a derivative like cocaine can be made from it, its effect is mild, rather like drinking several cups of coffee at once. In Yemen, nearly all men and women chew *qât* in the afternoon in gender-segregated gatherings devoted mainly to the highly prized art of conversation. This is the time, rather than over meals, when relatives and friends get to together to gossip or exchange opinions about national and world events or entertain each other with quips, proverbs, stories, and poems.

The agricultural system is ancient, but Yemen is historically even more important for its role in the trade of incense and myrrh, which were much coveted by Mediterranean societies for use in funerary rituals, centuries before and after the advent of Christianity. The incense trail stretched from Dhofar in what is now Oman overland to the Levant, and Yemeni highland tribesmen grew rich as middlemen along the route. Among them were the Sabaeans whose capital was in present-day Marib in the eastern part of the country, over which it is believed that Queen Bilqis (whom we know as the Queen of Sheba and whom Ethiopians also claim for their own) ruled. The Great Dam of Marib, a marvel of ancient engineering, irrigated thousands of acres in its heyday more than two thousand years ago. The Sabaeans, like other wealthy agricultural-trading "states" in Yemen, went into decline when mariners figured out how to circumnavigate the Peninsula and cut out the highland tribes as middlemen in the trade. According to legend, a rat gnawed its way through the Great Dam causing it to break, thus bringing the collapse of the great kingdoms that became, as the Qur'an says of them, no more than "a tale that is told." Modern-day Yemeni tribes believe themselves to be the descendants of their rulers, as do the servants of the tribes known as the *khaddâm*. It also believed, though, that because of their cowardice in battle they were condemned to serve the tribes in various lowly menial tasks, in return for which they received a share of the booty or a fraction of the agricultural harvest (for which reason they are known as "People of the Fifth"). To this day, the *khaddâm* perform various tasks in tribal villages, such as extolling someone's hospitality in florid rhymed prose or serving as messengers between villages or as masters-of-ceremony at special events like weddings. Because of their low status, they are precluded from composing but not from performing poetry, which they sing publicly to their own accompaniment on a tambourine. Jews have existed for centuries in Yemen, where they have lived in their own villages or urban enclaves, becoming in time traders, silversmiths, and masons. Some of the most exquisite silver jewelry in the Middle East was made in Yemen, but the craft all but disappeared with the emigration of most Jews to **Israel** in 1952. Yemen's multi-storied, mud-brick architecture such as one finds in the "Old City" in the capital, Sana'a, or many of the cities of the Hadhramawt, is not only handsome but highly distinctive. Several have been proclaimed World Heritage Cities by the United Nations.

Yemen is a Muslim country. The northern part was ruled for over 1,000 years, starting in the tenth century when Islam was brought to Yemen by the *sâdah* (plural of *sayyid*), descendants of the Prophet Muhammad, who converted the tribes to a conservative Shi'a sect known as Zaydi Islam. In time this religious elite became the rulers of the northern portion of the country, creating a theocratic monarchy at the head of which stood an imam or religious leader of the community of faithful. While this system of government had a certain legitimacy in the eyes of the tribes, it is arguable how much power it exerted over them in fact. In the southern part of Yemen, a Sunni sect known as Shafi'i Islam prospered under sultans as their rulers, swearing allegiance to the Sunni Caliph. While religious belief is mostly encoded in written theological texts, some folklore deals with religious subjects, especially magical spirits known as *jinn*.

With the exception of the Ottomans who occupied part of Yemen (1536–1635, 1872–1918) and the British whose colonial interests in Yemen never extended much beyond the port of Aden, Yemen was spared the exploitation and humiliation of colonialism. Nonetheless, like their Zaydi counterparts in the north, Shafi'i scholars and traders emigrated to south Asia and beyond where they were not spared the encounter with European **colonialism**. The phrase *Abu Yemen* (Father of Yemen), is sometimes used to refer to a Yemeni **diaspora** that is scattered around the world, including the United States, where sizeable communities of Yemenis can be found in Brooklyn and in upstate New York, in Detroit, Michigan, and in lesser numbers in California's Central Valley and San Francisco Bay Area. These overseas Yemeni communities have maintained some of the folkloric practices of their cousins back in the "old country."

An Arab Jew from Yemen. Jews have existed for centuries in Yemen, where they have lived in their own villages or urban enclaves, becoming traders, silversmiths, and masons. (Courtesy Library of Congress)

In 1962, North Yemen overthrew the Zaydi imam and after a bloody and protracted civil war instituted a republican government. In 1967, the British colony of Aden became independent, and a communist state emerged in its wake. The two Yemens, informally known as North and South, became locked in a Cold War struggle that ended with the collapse of the Soviet Union in 1989. One year later the two countries agreed to unify under a power-sharing agreement.

Like other Arabic-speaking countries, Yemen is a diglossic linguistic community characterized by the existence of two varieties of the same language. One of these (*fushâ*) is believed to be sacred. It has been standardized in grammars and lexicons, is associated with a high literary tradition, and is used on official or formal occasions. The other ('âmmiyyah) is said to be the spoken language of everyday life and is used at home and informal situations and is much more rarely committed to writing or print. In this hierarchy of values, the everyday variety of Arabic enjoys far less prestige than the standardized variety. Indeed, it is often not viewed as a language at all by the educated, to whom it appears to break the rules of the more prized *fushâ*. Yet not all Arabic speakers in Yemen have historically shared this normative view of language, rooted, as it is, in an urban-based, educated elite with their bias toward the written and printed word. Speech communities such as the relatively autonomous tribes of Yemen, who do not necessarily command either the standard language or the institutions of literacy that support it, nevertheless possess their own powerful oral traditions, not to mention deeply held convictions about the ancientness and authenticity of their spoken language (it is presumed to go back to the glorious days of the incense-trading kingdoms, after all), which either get dismissed or denigrated by the educated elite. Given that much work on Yemeni folklore has been done by Yemeni scholars who have soaked up the values of the urban elite in the course of their education, these biases often unwittingly make their way into the research. This problem of urban, literary ethnocentrism may become even more acute in work being done on the folklore of Mahra and Socotra, whose dialect and oral traditions seem even more "strange" to the ears of the urban-educated elite than the spoken language of the tribes.

POETRY

The folklore of the tribal speech community is composed of a system of poetic genres, the three most prominent of which are the *bâlah*, the *zâmil*, and the *qasîdah*. The first two are oral-performative in the sense known to folklorists who have studied oral traditions elsewhere in the world—that is, lines are not memorized and recited but composed anew each time, seemingly spontaneously—though with one important exception: the poem is rarely narrative as opposed to "occasional" in content. That is, the poems almost never tell an epic story about historical personages performing glorious deeds of valor and combat, as in the *Iliad* or the *Odyssey* or, for that matter, as in the epic cycles of Arabic poetry such as the *Bani Hillal* sagas (which are still performed in Egypt and parts of North Africa), but rather address an occasion at which they are performed, be it a wedding, a religious holiday or a conflict mediation. For example, the *bâlah* is referred to in the verse of this genre as a "game," consisting of witty lines of verse composed in turn by rival poets and repeated for the audience by the high-pitched chanting of a chorus, which is intended for the amusement of the groom and his guests on the night of his wedding celebration. Women have their own *bâlah* performances held in separate rooms for the bride, and it is said, by the men at least, that the form is generally the same, though it remains for a female ethnographer to substantiate this claim.

While the *bâlah* is composed by more than one poet, the *zâmil* is usually the work of a single individual and is rarely more than two lines in length, whereas the text of the *bâlah* is always much longer. These are nonetheless highly intricate in meter, rhyme, and alliteration, and the performance of the *zâmil* is often accompanied by drums and flute and executed at the same time as a stately and dramatic dance known as the *baraʿ*. The *zâmil* too is occasional in its content. At a wedding, besides the invocation of Allah and His Blessings for the Prophet, the *zâmil* may contain a greeting from the hosts to the guests (or, vice versa, an expression of gratitude from the guests for bounteous hospitality on the part of the hosts) conveyed in beautiful or whimsical imagery and superbly crafted language—all of which is meant to index the honor of the people in attendance. At dispute mediations, tribal delegations from opposing sides will arrive at the gathering place and chant *zâmil* poems to express their respective views to the mediators, who often glean the consensus of opinion, if there is one, from listening to these poetic performances before the formal discussions have even begun.

The third genre, the *qaîdah*, is a long ode, sometimes hundreds of lines in length, composed by an individual poet whose identity is almost ways known and who claims responsibility for its authorship. It bears striking formal resemblances to the genre of the same name memorialized as the "Seven Golden Odes" enshrined inside the Ka'ba in Mecca, which are esteemed as among the greatest works of Arabic literature—except that its language is not in the standardized form. Though a tribal *qasîdah* may be composed for any collective occasion such as the ones described above, it is more readily classifiable by theme (for example, religion, love, and politics).

All tribesmen may aspire to be poets, and though nearly all may be able to rise to the occasion when the *bâlah* performance is concerned, far fewer have the requisite skill or knowledge to become composers of the *qasîdah*. Once a "master poet" has produced such a poem, it may be committed to writing by him, if he is literate, or by someone else to be preserved and passed down to the next generation. Insofar as manuscript compilations of texts exist among tribesmen, they are more than likely to contain this kind of poetry. An alternative, more common in the past than today, was to give the poem to a talented *khaddâm* with a good voice and clear enunciation to sing before an appreciative audience. Nowadays, it is more likely for these performances to be recorded on audio cassette tapes, copies of which are sold in small "stereo stores" in markets all over the country. Through this process of dissemination, poets enter into important debates about national issues in the public sphere.

Given that the *qasîdah* is also a recognized and valued genre in the urban-based literary tradition, it is likely to draw an audience from listeners outside the tribal speech community per se. In other words, its particular esthetic and non-performative mode of composition lends itself to transcription or recording and therefore to wider circulation. It is safe to say that the *qasîdah* is an ancient ode, but what about the *bâlah* and the *zâmil*? It is tempting to speculate that they are just as ancient and that the reason there are no traces of them in the written record has to do with the fact that their oral performative character did not lend itself to such transcription. The paradox is, however, that without such traces, we can never know the truth about their age.

The tribes of Yemen, settled in tiny villages or else roaming nomadically on the fringes of the desert, comprise the majority of the population of the country, but there are many highland towns and cities whose people, even when claiming descent from a distant tribal ancestor, have long since stopped referring to themselves as "tribal" and thus do not recognize the *bâlah* and the *zâmil* as part of their living traditions. Instead, they identify with a type of poetry called *humaini*, which is sung by a trained singer who often accompanies himself on the *'ûd* (lute) along with a small percussion orchestra. The poets of this verse genre belonged overwhelmingly to the religious stratum of society, including the highly educated Islamic judges. It is in many respects the quintessential diasporic verse of Yemen. Religious scholars and other learned men often traveled to other parts of the Islamic empire, where they served as judges and local administrators.

One such destination was Muslim Spain, where, it is supposed, a highly ornamental poetry was created, fashioned of intricate rhyme and meter, known as *humaini*. It is a poetry of nostalgia for the land of Yemen, a yearning for loved ones left behind. Though its language is said to be "colloquial," its grammar is quite elevated or "classical," with mainly its rich lexicon of localisms stamping it as distinctively "Yemeni" in character. Though satire is a much admired genre in *humaini* poetry, topics of an overtly political and controversial nature tend to be avoided, and it appears tame in its criticisms of the state by comparison to the verse in the tribal tradition. Given that the poets were often employees of the state, this political tepidness may not come as a surprise. Far more favored in *humaini* poetry are love poetry (*ghazl*), poems of religious devotion, and dedicatory poems to aspects of Yemeni life that take on a symbolically charged, even fetishistic, quality, such as coffee and *qât* or the beauties of Sana'a or the "skyscraper" cities of Hadramawt. While *humaini* poetry fell into temporary abeyance after the Revolution, it seems to have made a comeback in recent years, though for reasons that are not altogether clear. As *humaini* poetry has also had a strong history in the southern part of the country, its resurgence may have to do with the perception that it is the one verse tradition in Yemen that may represent the whole of the country, north and south, after it was unified.

While *humaini* poetry is undergoing a revival, some genres of tribal poetry such as the *bâlah* are in danger of disappearing. This is due in part to the prejudices against the dialect and orality conveyed by literacy campaigns and universal education but also to the rise in recent decades of more conservative Islamic parties that have their own ideological reasons for condemning these forms. Yet, it in all likelihood the *qasîdah* will survive as it has in the past, albeit transformed by market and political forces at play in Yemen today.

BIBLIOGRAPHY

Caton, Steven C. 1990. *"Peaks of Yemen I Summon": Poetry as Cultural Practice in a North Yemeni Tribe.* Berkeley: University of California Press.

———. 1991. Diglossia in North Yemen: The Case of Competing Linguistic Communities. *Journal of Anthropological Research* 10.1: 143–159.

Ferguson, Charles A. 1959. Diglossia. *Word* 15: 325–340.

Ho, Engseng. 2004. Empire Through Diasporic Eyes: A View from the Other Boat. *Comparative Study of Society and History* 46.2: 210–246.

Miller, W. Flagg. 2002. Metaphors of Commerce: Trans-valuing Tribalism in Yemeni Audiocassette Poetry. *International Journal of Middle Eastern Studies* 34.1: 29–57.

Rodionov, Mikhael. 1992. *Poetry and Power in Hadhramawt.* St. Petersburg, Russia: St. Petersburg University Press.

Serjeant, R. B. 1949. Two Yemenite Djinn. *Bulletin of the School of Oriental and African Studies* 13: 4–6.

———. 1951. *South Arabian Poetry: Prose and Poetry from Hadhramawt.* London: Taylor's Foreign Press.

Staub, Shalom. 1988. *Yemenis in New York City: The Folklore of Ethnicity.* Philadelphia: The Bach Institute.

Varisco, Daniel M. 1993. The Agricultural Marker Stars in Yemeni Folklore. *Asian Folklore Studies* 52: 120–142.

Steven C. Caton

Cumulative Index

American Folklife Preservation Act, **1**:77

American Folklore Scholarship: A Dialogue of Dissent (Zumwalt), **1**:13

American Folklore Society (AFS), **1**:5, 6, 13, 30, 84

American Indians, **4**:1–142

American Romani weddings, **3**:401

Amirani (Georgia), **3**:356

Amulets: Ashkenazim, **3**:332, 338; Berber, **1**:103–105, 107, 109; Denmark, **3**:83; England, **3**:1; Galicia, **3**:203; Greenland, **3**:109–110; Israel, **2**:380; Kiribati, **1**:343, 347; Kurds, **2**:385; Russia, **3**:412; Sephardim, **3**:213; Tajik, **2**:333; Tlingit, **4**:118; Tuareg, **1**:117, 119; Wolof, **1**:211

"Analog" copies, **1**:4–5

Analytical Survey of Anglo-American Traditional Erotica (Hoffmann), **1**:56

Anansi (Jamaica), **4**:341

Anatsui, El, **1**:201

Ancestors and dead: Ainu, **2**:288, 290, 291–292; Albania, **3**:326, 327; Ashkenazim, **3**:333, 334; Australian Aborigines, **1**:293–294, 297, 298; Austria, **3**:253–255; Bali, **2**:159–160; Baule, **1**:164; Benin, **1**:174–176, 178; Brittany, **3**:171, 172; Caribs of Dominica, **4**:332–333; Catalan, **3**:200; China, **2**:213; Chinese living abroad, **2**:235, 238–239; Duna, **2**:166; Ecuador, **4**:197–198; England, **3**:1, 6, 13, 19; Ga, **1**:181–182; Gaddi, **2**:36; Galicia, **3**:206–207; Germany, **3**:269; Guam, **1**:337–338; Haiti, **4**:318; Hawai'i, **1**:368; Hopi, **4**:45–46; Hungary, **3**:278; Iban, **2**:173, 174–175; Igbo, **1**:199; Ireland, **3**:27, 34; Isaan, **2**:132–134; Israel, **2**:377, 379; Japan, **2**:273, 276; Kadazandusun, **2**:176; Kaingang, **4**:194; Kaliai, **2**:183–184, 186; Kashmir, **2**:61; Khasi-Jaintia, **2**:67, 72–73; Kiribati, **1**:342; Korea, **2**:296–298, 302, 303; Lunda, **1**:235–236, 239; Madagascar, **1**:139; Maluku, **2**:202; Manchu, **2**:250; Maroons of Jamaica, **4**:339–340; Marquesas Islands, **1**:380; Marshall Islands, **1**:351; Mexico, **4**:271–273; Nepal, **2**:117; New Caledonia, **1**:311, 312; Norway, **3**:127, 128, 132; Orissa, **2**:83, 87; Palestine, **2**:407; Persia, **2**:423; Piedmont and Val d'Aosta, **3**:477; Poland, **3**:385–386, 388; Roma, **3**:401, 402, 406; Russia, **3**:412, 413, 416; San, **1**:242–246; Semai, **2**:148; Shona, **1**:251; Sibundoy, **4**:230–231; Sicily, **3**:490; Slovakia, **3**:290; Tairora, **2**:206, 207; Taiwan, **2**:261, 266; Tlingit, **4**:122–123; Ukraine, **3**:440, 445; Vanuatu, **1**:327, 328; Xavante, **4**:247; Yoruba, **1**:224, 225; Zande, **1**:229, 232. *See also* Funerals and burials

Andersen, Hans Christian, **3**:12, 85

Anderson, Benedict, **2**:278

Anderson, Hugh, **1**:285

Anderson, Walter, **3**:196

Andes: Quechua, **4**:208–209; Sibundoy, **4**:229–230

Andrew, Saint, **3**:206, 289, 349, 388

Anecdotes: Albania, **3**:328, 329; Australia (British), **1**:286, 287; Bali, **2**:163; Cheyenne, **4**:29; China, **2**:222; England, **3**:6, 9, 10, 13; Guam, **1**:337, 339; Ireland, **3**:38–39; Kashmir, **2**:61; Latvia, **3**:362; Macedonia, **3**:372; Manchu, **2**:248; Marshall Islands, **1**:351; Maya, **4**:259; Poland, **3**:380, 392; Roma, **3**:406; Russia, **3**:420; Siberia, **2**:322; Sicily, **3**:491; Slovakia, **3**:292; Tajik, **2**:326; Turkey, **2**:432; Uyghur, **2**:339, 340; Wales, **3**:75, 76–77; Western Inuit and Yupik, **4**:133; Xhosa, **1**:259, 260

Anglicanism in Australia, **1**:278

Aniakor, Chike, **1**:201

Animal dances: Cherokee, **4**:15; Cheyenne, **4**:28; Choctaw, **4**:33

"The Animal Languages" (Mascarene Islands), **1**:146

Animism and animal tales, **1**:94; Ainu, **2**:287–288; Australian Aborigines, **1**:293–296; Bali, **2**:152, 160; Bangladesh, **2**:96, 103; Benin, **1**:177; Caribs of Dominica, **4**:332–333; Cherokee, **4**:12–13; Cheyenne, **4**:26–27; China, **2**:213; Ga, **1**:184; Guam, **1**:335–336; Haiti, **4**:320; Hawai'i, **1**:368; Iban, **2**:173; Igbo, **1**:195–196; Iroquois, **4**:55–56; Italy, **3**:472; Lakota, **4**:71–72; Lunda, **1**:237–238; Malaita, **1**:302; Malay, **2**:142; Maya, **4**:259; Mongol, **2**:256–257; Nahua, **4**:283–284; Nez Perce, **4**:100–101; Nuer, **1**:153; Palau, **1**:360–361; Peru, **4**:202; Poland, **3**:381; Quechua, **4**:210; Rarámuri, **4**:301; Russia, **3**:418–419; Samoa, **1**:394; San, **1**:242–247; Shona, **1**:250, 253; Siberia, **2**:316–319; Sibundoy, **4**:232; Suriname Maroons, **4**:238; Tlingit, **4**:121–123; Trobriand Islands, **1**:317; Western Inuit and Yupik, rapport with, **4**:134; Wolof, **1**:216; Xavante, **4**:250; Yanomami, **4**:253–254; Yoruba, **1**:219, 223–224; Zande, **1**:230–231. *See also specific types of animals*

Ankou (death, Brittany), **3**:171–172

Ankrah, Roy, **1**:186

Anne of Austria, **3**:164

"Annual Bibliography," **1**:5

"Annual Folklore Bibliography," **1**:5

Anthony the Abbot, Saint, **3**:470–471

Antiquarianism, **1**:1–3; and museums, **1**:57

Antiquitates Vulgares (Bourne), **1**:1, 2

Antiquities, **1**:1–3

The ANZAC Book (Australia [British]), **1**:285

Apache, **4**:1–8; arts and crafts, **4**:6; geography and history, **4**:1–3; modernization, challenges of, **4**:6–7; rituals and ceremonies, **4**:5–6; stories and tales, **4**:3–4; studies of Apache folklore, **4**:7

Apache Wars, **4**:3

Apartheid: Xhosa, **1**:258, 262; Zulu, **1**:269

ap Nudd, Gwyn, **3**:74

Apollonia, Saint, **3**:229

Appadurai, Arjun, **1**:42

Appalachia, **4**:156–166; architecture, **4**:163–164; arts and crafts, **4**:164; dance and drama, **4**:161–162; festivals and celebrations, **4**:161; food, **4**:164; geography and history, **4**:156–158; and invented tradition, **1**:51; modernization, challenges of, **1**:79, **4**:165; myths, legends, and folktales, **4**:159–160; and race, **1**:79; religious beliefs, **4**:158–159; songs, ballads, and music, **1**:79, **4**:160–161; sports and games, **4**:162–163; studies of Appalachian folklore, **4**:165

"Applied folklore," **1**:77

Aqa Jamal, **2**:425

Arabian Nights, **3**:12

Arabic language (Berber), **1**:101

Arabs: Berber influenced by, **1**:101–103; Spain influenced by, **3**:180, 182. *See also* Palestine

Archaisms in Macedonian legends, **3**:372

Architecture: African Americans, **4**:153–154; American southwest, **1**:39; Appalachia, **4**:163–164; Ashkenazim, **3**:338; Australia (British), **1**:282–283; Austria, **3**:257–259; Bangladesh, **2**:102; Benin, **1**:176; Bhutan, **2**:111–112; Caipira, **4**:180; Cherokee, **4**:18–19; China, **2**:226–228; Chinese living abroad, **2**:242; Flanders (Belgium), **3**:232; Igbo, **1**:200–201; Jamaica, **4**:337; Japan, **2**:278; Kazakh, **2**:313; Maluku, **2**:201–202; Mississippi Delta, **4**:167; Moorish, **3**:218; The Netherlands, **3**:244–245; Shona, **1**:253–254; Slovenia, **3**:303–304; Sri Lanka, **2**:128–130; Ukraine, **3**:446–447; Uyghur, **2**:344; Vanuatu, **1**:330–331. *See also* Housing

Archives, **1**:3–5; Latvia, **3**:364; and modernization, **1**:52; and repertoire, **1**:82

Arctic region: Western Inuit and Yupik, **4**:128–131

Arendt, Hannah, **1**:29–30

Arhuaran (son of Oba Ozolua), **1**:177

Ari *fróði* (the Learned), **3**:113

Arizona: Apache, **4**:1–3; Hopi, **4**:44–45; Navajo, **4**:82–83

Arjuna, **2**:40

Armenia, **2**:357–372; epics and historical narratives, **2**:359–362; geography and history, **2**:357–359; modernization, challenges of, **2**:369; songs and legends, **2**:362–369

Armes Prydein (poem), **3**:73

Arminius, **3**:268

Armor. *See* Weapons and armor

Arnamagnean Institute, **3**:114, 115

Arngrímur Jónsson the Learned, **3**:116

Arnim, Achim von, **3**:312

3:168–169; Galicia, **3:**206–208; Germany, **3:**262–265; Hopi, **4:**47; Hungary, **3:**281–282; Ireland, **3:**26–27; Isle of Man, **3:**47–51; Kiowa, **4:**66; Korea, **2:**301; Maya, **4:**257; Mexico, **4:**272; Navajo, **4:**89; Nepal, **2:**120; The Netherlands, **3:**241–243; Palestine, **2:**404; Persia, **2:**423; Peru, **4:**204–205; Piedmont and Val d'Aosta, **3:**474–477; Poland, **3:**386–388; Quechua, **4:**211–212; Rarámuri, **4:**299; Roma, **3:**403–404; Russia, **3:**415–417; Scotland, **3:**64–66; Serbia, **3:**429–432; Sicily, **3:**487–489; Slovakia, **3:**289–290; Slovenia, **3:**296–299; Switzerland, **3:**314–317

Calendimaggio (May Day feast), **3:**475

California: Australia (British) social influence by, **1:**278; Proposition 187 to limit public services to non-citizens, **1:**66

Call-and-response stories: Ga, **1:**185, 191; Guam, **1:**338; Igbo, **1:**196; Lunda, **1:**236; Shona, **1:**250, 253; Wolof, **1:**216; Yoruba, **1:**218, 221; Zande, **1:**233

Callaway, Henry, **1:**270, 271, 273

Callegari, Adriano, **3:**460

Calvin, **3:**238

Camayd-Freixas, Erik, **1:**74

Camés (Kaingang myth), **4:**195–196

Campbell, J.F., **3:**114

Campos, Rubén, **4:**279

Cana'an, Tawfiq, **2:**411

Canada: Haida, **4:**38–39; Iroquois, **4:**50–51; Ojibwe, **4:**103–105; Tlingit, **4:**117; Western Inuit and Yupik, **4:**128–131

Canales, Antonio, **3:**185

Candoshi, **4:**181–187; geography and history, **4:**181–182; religious beliefs, rituals, and celebrations, **4:**182–185; songs and music, **4:**185–187; studies of Candoshi folklore, **4:**187

Cannibalism: Haiti, **4:**318; Yanomami, **4:**253, 254

Canoes: Ainu (Japan), **2:**291; Benin, **1:**174; Hawai'i, **1:**373, 375; Ijo, **1:**207, 208; Kaliai, **2:**183; Kiribati, **1:**342, 343, 347; Malaita, **1:**306; Maluku, **2:**202; Marshall Islands, **1:**355; Palau, **1:**361, 363; Seminole, **4:**115; Tlingit, **4:**126; Trobriand Islands, **1:**321–322, 324; Tuvalu, **1:**409

Cantomble (Brazil), **1:**79

Canzuna (folksong, Sicily), **3:**485

Capitalism, **1:**42

Capmany, Aureli, **3:**196

Capping (African American), **4:**150

Captain Cook Chased a Chook: Children's Folklore in Australia, **1:**284

"The Captain of the Push" (Australia [British]), **1:**285

Caracalla, Abdel Halim, **2:**397

Card games: China, **2:**226, 242; Persia, **2:**424; Rarámuri, **4:**305; Slovakia, **3:**293, 294

Caribs of Dominica, **4:**329–336; folk medicine, **4:**333–334; folktales, **4:**331–333; geography and history, **4:**329–331; witchcraft and magic, **4:**334–336

Carlos IV, **3:**186

Carlyle, Thomas, **1:**46

Carnival: Catalan, **3:**197; Croatia, **3:**348, 349; Cuba, **4:**311; Flanders, **3:**227; Galicia, **3:**206; Georgia, **3:**360; Hungary, **3:**282; Italy, **3:**457, 464; Piedmont and Val d'Aosta, **3:**471, 472, 474; Poland, **3:**387; Quechua, **4:**210–211, 213; Sibundoy, **4:**234–235; Sicily, **3:**488; Slovakia, **3:**289. *See also* Mardi Gras

Carnival societies (Switzerland), **3:**316

Carolina Sea Islanders, **1:**20

Caroline Islands, **1:**333, 339

Carpenter, Inta Gale, **1:**82

Carpitella, Diego, **3:**461

Carribean, **4:**309–347

Carucci, Laurence, **1:**353

Carving and sculpture: Australian Aborigines, **1:**297; Baule, **1:**164, 167; Cherokee, **4:**18; Ecuador, **4:**192; Guam, **1:**339; Haida, **4:**42; Haiti, **4:**324, 325; Hawai'i, **1:**374; Igbo, **1:**201; Ijo, **1:**205; Marquesas Islands, **1:**378, 383–384; Navajo, **4:**91–92; Palau, **1:**359–360, 364; Shona, **1:**253, 254; Suriname Maroons, **4:**241; Tlingit, **4:**126; Tonga, **1:**402; Trobriand Islands, **1:**320, 324; Western Inuit and Yupik, **4:**138; Wolof, **1:**213; Yoruba, **1:**225; Zande, **1:**233

Caseponce, Esteve, **3:**195

Casimir the Great, **3:**381

Cassian, John, **3:**160, 439

Castelló i Guasch, Joan, **3:**195

Caste system. *See* Social structure

del Castillo, Bernal Díaz, **4:**275

"The Castle of Dimdim" (Kurds), **2:**387

Catalan, **3:**195–201; calendars, **3:**199; festivals and celebrations, **3:**197–198; food, **3:**199–200; geography and history, **3:**195–197; music and dance, **3:**198–199

Catherine, Saint, **3:**164, 388

Catherine the Great, **3:**409

Catholicism: and Afro-Cuban myths, **4:**314; anti-Catholic nativism in U.S., **1:**65; Australia (British), **1:**278, 280–281, 289; Caribs of Dominica, **4:**331–332; Chinese living abroad, **2:**239; France, **3:**161, 166, 167; Haiti, **4:**318–319; immigrants to U.S., **1:**66; Kewa, **2:**189; Kiribati, **1:**341, 348; Latvia, **3:**365–366; Maluki, **2:**198; Marquesas Islands, **1:**380; Mauritius and Rodrigues, **1:**145; Mexico, **4:**269–271; Otomí, **4:**290; Peru, **4:**200–202, 206; Quechua, **4:**209; Rarámuri, **4:**297–300, 302; Réunion, **1:**148; Sertão, **4:**217, 218; The Seychelles, **1:**149; Shuar, **4:**220–221;

Sibundoy, **4:**230, 234–235; Spain, **3:**180–182; Sri Lanka, **2:**125, 126, 128; Taiwan, **2:**261; Tonga, **1:**401; Turkey, **2:**430; Tuvalu, **1:**405. *See also* Christianity

Cattle: India, sacredness of, **2:**13; Jie, importance to, **1:**132–135; Nuer, importance to, **1:**150, 153

"The Cattle-Killing" (Xhosa), **1:**264

Cattleshed as community gathering-place, **3:**473

Cauld Blast Orchestra, **3:**66

Cautionary tales, Isle of Man, **3:**46–47

Cayurucrés (Kaingang myth), **4:**195–196

Céilidh (visiting house), **3:**26, 57, 117

Celebrations. *See* Festivals and celebrations

Celtic influence, **3:**70; Brittany, **3:**171–173; England, **3:**4–5; France, **3:**158–159; Galicia, **3:**203; Iceland, **3:**112; Ireland, **3:**23, 34; Piedmont and Val d'Aosta, **3:**474; Spain, **3:**179; Wales, **3:**72, 75

Cemetery rites. *See* Funerals and burials

A Centennial Index (American Folklore Society), **1:**6

Central Africa. *See* Western and Central Africa

Central America, **4:**256–308

Cepenkov, Marco, **3:**372

Ceramics: Australian Aborigines, **1:**297; Baule, **1:**163; Berber, **1:**109, 111; Caipira, **4:**179; Candoshi, **4:**186; Cherokee, **4:**17–18; Hopi, **4:**49–50; Igbo, **1:**201; Iroquois, **4:**52; Lakota, **4:**75; Mexico, **4:**272; Navajo, **4:**91, 92; Shona, **1:**253; Tajik, **2:**330–331; Turkey, **2:**436–437; Uzbek, **2:**354; Vanuatu, **1:**330; Yoruba, **1:**226

Ceremonies. *See* Rituals and ceremonies

Cernunnos, **3:**171

Cervantes, Miguel de, **3:**183

Cetshawayo (Zulu king), **1:**269

Cha cha cha (Cuba), **4:**312

Ch'a-don Lee, **2:**299

Chadwick, Nora, **3:**173

Chagnon, Napoleon, **4:**251–252

Chain structure, tales (Russia), **3:**419

Chameleon as theme (Yoruba), **1:**222

Chamisso, Adelbert von, **1:**350

Chamorros. *See* Guam

Chamula and worldview, **1:**98

Changeling, fairy, **3:**47

Chant of Urdmau (Palau), **1:**362

Chants: Assam, **2:**29; Benin, **1:**178; Bhutan, **2:**109; Ga, **1:**191; Gaddi, **2:**35, 36; Haryana, **2:**40; Hawai'i, **1:**366, 369–371, 375; Iban, **2:**174, 175; Igbo, **1:**197; Isaan, **2:**134, 136–137; Kadazandusun, **2:**178; Kashmir, **2:**64; Kiribati, **1:**344; Marquesas Islands, **1:**381–382; Marshall Islands, **1:**352; Palau, **1:**360, 361–362; Samoa, **1:**394; Shuar, **4:**226; Yoruba, **1:**222–223

Charioteers' folksongs, Sicily, **3:**485–486

Charlemagne, **3:**161–162, 167, 250, 261, 269

Charles II (England), **3:**3, 15, 19

Charles, Thomas, **3:**74

Cleverness. *See* Trickster

"The Clever Peasant Girl," 1:95; Mascarene Islands, 1:146

"Click Go the Shears" (Australia [British]), 1:286

Clifford, James, 1:48

Clinton, Bill, 2:381

Clothing: Austria, 3:258–259; Berber, 1:106; Cherokee, 4:18; China, 2:227, 228–229; and colonialism, 1:7–8; Gaddi, 2:35; Greece, 3:499; Hawai'i, 1:371–372; Iceland, 3:117–119; Igbo, 1:201–202; Ijo, 1:207; and invented tradition, 1:50; Kazakh, 2:312; Kiribati, 1:347; Lumba, 1:240; Malaita, 1:303, 304; Malta, 3:506; Manchu, 2:246, 250, 251; Marquesas Islands, 1:379, 384; Maya, 4:262–263; Norway, 3:130; Palestine, 2:407, 408; Seminole, 4:112–113; Siberia, 2:316, 323; Sibundoy, 4:234; Slovakia, 3:294; Tairora, 2:205, 208; Tajik, 2:331–332; Trobriand Islands, 1:324; Tuvalu, 1:409; Wales, 3:77; Western Inuit and Yupik, 4:130; Wolof, 1:212; Yoruba, 1:224–225

Clottey, Attuquaye, 1:186

Clovis, 3:161

Club War (Finland), 3:91

Coal miners and mining. *See* Miners and mining

Cockfighting: Bali, 2:161; Ecuador, 4:192; Iban, 2:175; Kadazandusun, 2:180. *See also* Games, sports, and recreation

"Codding" (expressive lying, Ireland), 3:37

Cohen, Erik, 1:86

Coleman, Simon, 1:86

Colenso, J.W. (bishop of Natal), 1:271, 274

Collier, Michael, 3:36

Collins, Samuel, 3:410

Colmcille, Saint, 3:30–31

Colombia: Sibundoy, 4:229–230

Colonialism, 1:7–10; and diaspora, 1:19; and ethnicity, 1:25; and Ga, 1:181; and globalization, 1:42; and Shona, 1:248; and Swahili, 1:154, 159, 160; and Zande, 1:228. *See also* British rule and influence; France; Spanish exploration and conquest

Comedia (Spanish drama), 3:184

Comedy. *See* Humorous stories, skits, etc.

Communication and translation, 1:89

The Comoros, 1:142–143; beliefs and folklore, 1:142–143; geography and history, 1:142

A Comparative Study of Kashmiri and Hindi Folksongs (Handoo), 2:62

Competence and performance, 1:69–70

Competition as theme (Swahili), 1:158, 159

Confucianism: China, 2:212–213; Chinese living abroad, 2:235, 236; Japan, 2:275, 276; Korea, 2:300; Taiwan, 2:261

"Confusion of Tongues" (Nagaland), 2:76

Conjuring. *See* Incantations

Conspiracy rumors (African American), 4:151

Constantine (Emperor), 3:160

Constantine VII Porphyrogenitus, 3:347

Constellation stories. *See* Astrology

Constitution (Mexico), 4:269

Contes du Temps passé, 3:266

Contests. *See* Games, sports, and recreation; Races

Contrary Dance (Cheyenne), 4:28

Cook, James, 1:309, 366, 374, 378

Cooking. *See* Food customs and beliefs

"The Coon in the Box" (African American), 4:144

Corn (Cherokee), 4:19

Coronado, Francisco Vásquez de, 4:1; and Hopi, 4:44

Corridos (Mexico), 4:273

Cortés, Hernán, 4:275–276

Cortés, Martín, 4:275–276

Cortez, Joaquín, 3:185

Corvinus, Matthias, 3:276

Cosmogonic myth (Poland), 3:380

Cosmology. *See* Worldview

Costumes. *See* Clothing; Masks and masquerades

Cotters, Denmark, 3:134

Council of Forty-Four (Cheyenne), 4:22–23, 25

Counter-Reformation (Italy), 3:457

Courtship: Appalachia, 4:161; Choctaw, 4:34; France, 3:163; Italy, 3:454; Kewa, 2:194; Lakota stories, 4:72; Scotland, 3:56; Shona, 1:250; Tlingit, 4:124

Coyote tales (Nez Perce), 4:100–103

"Cracker Night" (Australia [British]), 1:290

Cradleboards (Apache), 4:6

Crafts. *See* Arts and crafts

Crang, Mike, 1:86

Creation stories: Apache, 4:3–4; Armenia, 2:357; Australian Aborigines, 1:293–294, 297, 298; Bangladesh, 2:99; Cherokee, 4:11, 12; Cheyenne, 4:25–26; China, 2:215; Chinese living abroad, 2:235; Duna, 2:166, 168–169; Equador, 4:198–199; Gaddi, 2:32–34; Guam, 1:335; Haida, 4:40–42; Hawai'i, 1:366, 370; India, 2:5; Iroquois, 4:54, 56; Isaan, 2:135; Japan, 2:274; Kadazandusun, 2:177, 178; Kazakh, 2:307–309; Kewa, 2:191; Khasi-Jaintia, 2:67–68; Kiribati, 1:342; Korea, 2:295–296; Lakota and Dakota, 4:72; Malaita, 1:302; Malay, 2:142; Maluku, 2:198–199; Manchu, 2:247–248; Mescalero Apache, 4:4; Mongol, 2:255; Nagaland, 2:75, 77; Navajo, 4:85; Orissa, 2:80–81; Otomí, 4:290–293; Palau, 1:360–361; Palestine, 2:404; Persia, 2:414–416; Roma, 3:406; Samoa, 1:388–389; San, 1:242; Seminole, 4:115;

Siberia, 2:317–318; Tairora, 2:206–207; Tonga, 1:397, 400; Turkey, 2:432; Tuvalu, 1:406; Vanuatu, 1:328; Xavante, 4:249–250; Xhosa, 1:259–260; Yanomami, 4:252, 254; Zulu, 1:269–270

Creoles, 1:10–12; and Dominica, 4:330, 335–336

Creolization, 1:10–12; and Caribbean, 1:10; and globalization, 1:42; and hybridity, 1:47; and Indian Ocean, 1:10; and Latin America, 1:10; and Louisiana, 1:10; and Madagascar, 1:10; and Mascarene Islands, 1:144; and Mauritius and Rodrigues, 1:144, 146; and nativism, 1:65; and race, 1:78

Crick, M., 1:86

Criollos (Mexico), 4:275–276

Croatia, 3:341–352; Central, 3:345–346; history, 3:347–352; Littoral, 3:341–343; Lowland, 3:346–347; Mountainous, 3:343–344

Croatian Peasant Party, 3:351

Cromwell, Oliver, 3:3, 15, 36

Crooked Mick of the Speewah, 1:286

Crops. *See* Agriculture and farming

Crosh cuirns (Isle of Man), 3:47, 48

Cross-dressing. *See* Transvestites, transsexuals, cross-dressing

Crusades, 3:162–164, 365–366, 509

Cruz, San Juan de la, 3:181

Cuba, 4:309–315; and diaspora, 1:20; fusion of cultures, 4:315; geography and history, 4:309–310; music literature, 4:312–313; myths, legends, and folktales, 4:313–315; sacred music and dance, 4:310; secular music and dance, 4:311–312

Culin, Steward, 2:241–242

Cultural absolutism, 1:15

Cultural and Natural Areas of Native North America (Kroeber), 1:16

Cultural continuity of Greece, 3:494, 495

Cultural creolization, 1:10–11

Cultural evolution, 1:12–14; geology as influence, 1:12; and translation, 1:91

Cultural exceptionalism. *See* Nationalism

Cultural imperialism, 1:38

Cultural primitivism. *See* Primitivism

Cultural relativism, 1:14–16; Boas, Franz, 1:14–15; and cultural evolution, 1:14; and Plato, 1:14; and religion, 1:14

Cultural studies tradition, 1:72

Culture area, 1:16–18; and motif, 1:54, 55; and museum, 1:57. *See also* Geography

Cunning. *See* Trickster

Cunningham, Allan, 3:59

Cures. *See* Medicine and cures

Curutons (Kaingang myth), 4:196

Customs and Traditions of Palestine, 2:411

Cycles of life. *See* Life-cycle rituals and beliefs

Cyfarwyddiaid (storytellers, Wales), 3:72

Cyril, Saint, 3:371, 426, 429

Dabke dance (Lebanon), 2:395, 396–397

Dadié, Bernard, 1:168

Finnish National Museum, **1**:58

Finnish School, **1**:22–23

Finnish-Swedish, **3**:97–103; calendars, **3**:101–102; children's lore, **3**:100–101; geography and history, **3**:97–98; language, **3**:97, 102–103; medicine and cures, **3**:99; music and dance, **3**:100; storytelling, **3**:99–100; supernatural lore, **3**:98–99

Finsch, Otto, **1**:354

Firdausi (Tajik-Persian poet), **2**:326

Firebird: Armenia, **2**:365; Russia, **3**:419

Fisher, Archie, **3**:66

"Fisher's Ghost" (Australia [British]), **1**:286

Fishing: Ga, **1**:182; Ijo, **1**:204; Kaingang, **4**:194; Lunda, **1**:234; Marquesas Islands, **1**:379; New Caledonia, **1**:309; Seminole, **4**:114; Sicily, **3**:483–484; Western Inuit and Yupik, **4**:129–130; Wolof, **1**:209

Fishponds (Hawai'i), **1**:376

Fiske, John, **1**:72

Flags and nationalism, **1**:63

Flamenco, **3**:183, 184–185

Flanders (Belgium), **3**:223–233; architecture, **3**:232; brewing, **3**:232; calendars, **3**:226–229; drama, sports, and games, **3**:231–232; geography and history, **3**:223–225; medicine, **3**:229; myths, legends, songs, and folktales, **3**:229–230; religion and ritual, **3**:225–226; town rivalries, **3**:230–231

Flanders, Helen Hartness, **1**:41

"The Fleeing Pancake," **1**:95

Flood, Bo, **1**:339

Floods: Kaingang, **4**:195–196; Mississippi Delta, **4**:170–171; Yanomami, **4**:252, 254

Flores, Judy S., **1**:339

Flores, Rosario, **3**:183

Flores, Tomasito, **3**:183

Florida: Seminole, **4**:111–112

"Flower of Scotland" (song), **3**:57–58

Flower symbolism: Isle of Man, **3**:47–48; Malta, **3**:509

Flutes (Quechua), **4**:211, 212

Flying Canoe myth (Trobriand Islands), **1**:321–322

Folk Arts Program, **1**:77

Folk high schools (Denmark), **3**:82

Folk idioms. *See* Language

The Folk Literature of a Yucatecan Town (Redfield), **4**:259

Folk Literature of the South American Indians, General Index (Wilbert & Simoneau), **1**:56

Folklore Fellows, **1**:94

Folklore Handbook (Japan), **2**:279

Folklore Institute of Indiana University, **1**:161

Folk-lore Journal (Zulu), **1**:272

Folklore of the Holy Land (Hanauer), **2**:411

Folk-lore of Yucatán (Brinton), **4**:278

Folk-Lore Society (Bangladesh), **2**:95

The Folklore Text from Performance to Print (Fine), **1**:85

Folklorism, **1**:35–37; and modernization, **1**:52

Folklorism Bulletin, **1**:37

Folk medicine. *See* Medicine and cures

Folksong. *See* Music and dance

Folk Songs of Australia (Australia [British]), **1**:285

Folk Songs of Australia and the Men and Women Who Sang Them (Australia [British]), **1**:285

Folk Song Style and Culture (Lomax), **1**:17

Folktales. *See* Stories and tales

Folk Traditions of the Arab World (El-Shamy), **1**:56

Food customs and beliefs: Appalachia, **4**:164; Ashkenazim, **3**:332; Australia (British), **1**:290; Australian Aborigines, **1**:297; Bali, **2**:159; Bangladesh, **2**:101, 104; Caipira, **4**:179–180; Catalan, **3**:199–200; Cherokee, **4**:19; China, **2**:213, 228–229; Chinese living abroad, **2**:239, 240–241; and creolization, **1**:10–11; Denmark, **3**:87; Duna, **2**:167; and ethnicity, **1**:26; Greece, **3**:498–499; Haida, **4**:42–43; Iceland, **3**:118–119; Igbo, **1**:201–202; India, **2**:5, 13–14, 64; Iroquois, **4**:56; Israel, **2**:379; Kaingang, **4**:193–194; Kaliai, **2**:187; Kiribati, **1**:340, 343; Korea, **2**:296, 304; Lebanon, **2**:395; Malta, **3**:509; Marquesas Islands, **1**:379; Marshall Islands, **1**:349, 355; Nepal, **2**:116–118; Nez Perce, **4**:103; Palestine, **2**:410; Persia, **2**:419, 423; Seminole, **4**:113–114; Sephardim, **3**:219–220; Serbia, **3**:430; Sertão, **4**:216–218; Sicily, **3**:487, 491; Taiwan, **2**:261–263, 266; Trobriand Islands, **1**:316; Uyghur, **2**:345; Wales, **3**:77; Western Inuit and Yupik, **4**:129–130; Zande, **1**:228

Footwear (Western Inuit and Yupik), **4**:130

Foragers: Apache, **4**:1; Cherokee, **4**:19; and cultural shift, **1**:16–17; Kaingang, **4**:193

Ford Foundation, **2**:15, 58

Fortis, Alberto, **3**:350

Fortune-telling: Chinese living abroad, **2**:235; Korea, **2**:303. *See also* Diviners and divination

Forty Day Party (Tlingit), **4**:120

Foster, George, **1**:97

Founding myth of Switzerland, **3**:308–309

Four Sacred Mountains (Navajo reservation), **4**:84

"Fox as Nursemaid for Bear" (Mascarene Islands), **1**:144

Fraguas Fraguas, Antonio, **3**:207

France, **3**:157–170; Baule colonization by, **1**:164; calendars, **3**:168–169; Celts and Roman Gauls, **3**:158–161; ecomusées in, **1**:60; Frankish kingdom, **3**:161–162; French Revolution and Napoleon, **3**:165–167; geography, **3**:157–158; globalization, **3**:169; Greek influence, **3**:158–159; Louis XIV, **3**:164–165; Madagascar occupation by,

1:138; Marquesas Islands annexation by, **1**:377, 380; medieval era, **3**:162–164; nationalistic folk beliefs, **3**:166–167; New Caledonia colonization by, **1**:308–309, 314; open-air museums in, **1**:60; Réunion, as overseas department of, **1**:147; Sahara colonization by, **1**:103, 111, 114, 117; The Seychelles occupation by, **1**:149; storytelling, **3**:163–164; Vanuatu colonization by, **1**:325; Wolof colonization by, **1**:209, 211

Franciscans and Rarámuri, **4**:297

Franco, Francisco, **3**:181, 183, 187, 190, 203, 205

Frankish kingdom, **3**:161–162

Franz Joseph (Emperor), **3**:347

Frazer, James George, **1**:96, **3**:17

Freedom celebrations (African American), **4**:146

Freeman, Derek, **2**:176

French Guiana: Maroon, **4**:236–237

French language: The Comoros, **1**:142; Mascarene Islands, **1**:144; Mascarene Islands, creolization of, **1**:144; The Seychelles, **1**:149; Vanuatu, **1**:326, 327

French Revolution, **3**:165–167

Freney, James, **3**:36

Freud, Sigmund, **1**:74–75

Friedmann, Frederik, **3**:453

Friedrich II, Wittekind, **3**:268–269

Friedrich Wilhelm III (King), **3**:265

Friis, J.A., **3**:137, 140

Frontier, **1**:37–39; Australia (British), **1**:288–289; cultural imperialism, **1**:38; and diffusion, **1**:22; and invented tradition, **1**:50; and nationalism, **1**:37, 38, 62; Roman frontier, **1**:38; Zulu Difaqane, **1**:38

Frybread (Seminole), **4**:114

Frykman, Jonas, **3**:151, 153

Fudoki compilations (Japan), **2**:274

Fundamentalism, **1**:65

Funerals and burials: Abanyole, **1**:128–130; Armenia, **2**:368–369; Australian Aborigines, **1**:294; Baule, **1**:164, 168; Benin, **1**:174; China, **2**:228; Chinese living abroad, **2**:235, 237, 238; Duna, **2**:170; Haiti, **4**:325; Igbo, **1**:196; Ijo, **1**:205, 207; Kadazandusun, **2**:179; Kazakh, **2**:311, 313; Kewa, **2**:191–192; Khasi-Jaintia, **2**:71, 72; Korea, **2**:296–298; Kurds, **2**:386, 387, 389; Lebanon, **2**:398–399; Lunda, **1**:238; Madagascar, **1**:139; Malaita, **1**:303–304; Maroons of Jamaica, **4**:339–340; Marshall Islands, **1**:355; Nepal, **2**:116–117; New Caledonia, **1**:311; Palau, **1**:362; Peru, **4**:201–202; Poland, **3**:385–386; Roma, **3**:402; Russia, **3**:413; Samoa, **1**:393; Shona, **1**:250, 252–254; Suriname Maroons, **4**:239–240; Tairora, **2**:206; Taiwan, **2**:263; Tajik, **2**:329; Tlingit, **4**:120; Ukraine, **3**:443–444; Uzbek, **2**:351; Yoruba, **1**:224; Zande, **1**:232. *See also* Death and mourning rituals; Potlatches

Furniture: Appalachia, **4**:164; Zande, **1**:233

Fürst, Walter, **3**:309

Hungary, 3:273–278; Iban, 2:171–173; Iceland, 3:111–113; Igbo, 1:193–194; Ijo, 1:204; Ireland, 3:22–26; Iroquois, 4:52–54; Isle of Man, 3:41–43; Israel, 2:372, 375–378; Italy, 3:450–452; Jamaica, 4:336–338; Japan, 2:271–275; Jie, 1:131–137; Kadazandusun, 2:176–177; Kaingang, 4:193; Kaliai, 2:183–184; Karnataka, 2:46–47; Kashmir, 2:58–65; Kazakh, 2:306–308; Kewa, 2:189–190; Khasi-Jaintia, 2:65–66; Kiowa, 4:60–62; Kiribati, 1:340–341; Korea, 2:294–296; Kurds, 2:383–392; Lakota and Dakota, 4:69–70, 73; Lebanon, 2:392; Lunda, 1:234–235; Macedonia, 3:370–372; Madagascar, 1:137–138; Malay, 2:141–142; Malta, 3:502–504; Maluku, 2:197–198; Manchu, 2:245–246; Marquesas Islands, 1:377–380; Marshall Islands, 1:349–350; Mascarene Islands, 1:144; Mauritius and Rodrigues, 1:144–146; Maya, 4:256–257; Mexico, 4:268–269, 278–279; Mississippi Delta, 4:166–167; Mongol, 2:252–254; Navajo, 4:82–83, 85; The Netherlands, 3:233–248; New Caledonia, 1:308–309; Nez Perce, 4:97–98; Norway, 3:123–125; Nuer, 1:150–151; Ojibwe, 4:103–105, 107–108; Orissa, 2:79–80; Otomí, 4:288–290; Palau, 1:358–360; Palestine, 2:400–403; Persia, 2:413–414; Piedmont and Val d'Aosta, 3:469–470; Poland, 3:378–380; Quechua, 4:208–209; Rarámuri, 4:297–298; Réunion, 1:147–148; Roma, 3:395–397; Russia, 3:411–412; Sámi, 3:134–135; Samoa, 1:387–388; Scotland, 3:52–55; Semai, 2:145–146; Seminole, 4:111–112; Sephardim, 3:211–214; Serbia, 3:425–437; The Seychelles, 1:149; Shona, 1:248–249; Shuar, 4:220–221; Siberia, 2:315–316; Sibundoy, 4:229–230; Sicily, 3:480–482; Slovakia, 3:285–286; Slovenia, 3:295–296; Spain, 3:177–180; Sri Lanka, 2:123–124; Suriname Maroon, 4:236–237; Swahili, 1:154–155; Switzerland, 3:308–312; Tairora, 2:203–205; Taiwan, 2:260–261; Tajik, 2:325–326; Tlingit, 4:117–118, 120–121, 123; Tonga, 1:397; Trobriand Islands, 1:316; Tuareg, 1:101–103, 113–114; Turkey, 2:429–432; Tuvalu, 1:404–405; Ukraine, 3:437–439; Uttar Pradesh, 2:88–90; Uyghur, 2:335–337; Uzbek, 2:348–350; Vanuatu, 1:325–326; Wales, 3:69–72; Western Inuit and Yupik, 4:128–132; Wolof, 1:208–213; Xavante, 4:243; Xhosa, 1:257–258; Yanomami, 4:251–252; Yemen, 2:439–442; Zande, 1:227–228; Zulu, 1:267–269

History of the Kingdom of Wei (China), 2:273

History of the Ojibway People (Warren), 4:107
Hitler, Adolf, 3:91
Hitopadesha tales (India), 2:7
Hobsbawn, Eric, 1:49
Hofer, Andreas, 3:250
Hoffmann, Frank, 1:56
Hogmanay (Scotland), 3:65–67
Holidays: Ecuador, 4:191–192; Roma, 3:403–404; Russia, 3:415–417. *See also* Festivals and celebrations; *specific holidays*
Holo Mai Pele (Hawai'i), 1:376
Holy Week Cycle plays (Italy), 3:464
Home governance system (Serbia), 3:428
Homer, 1:44–45, 3:320, 322
Home remedies. *See* Medicine and cures
Homogenization and globalization, 1:43
Honko, Lauri, 3:147
Honti, János, 3:283
Hoodoo: creation of, 1:79; doctors, 4:147
Hoop game (Lakota), 4:74
Hopi, 1:41, 4:44–50; agriculture, 4:46–47; arts and crafts, 4:49–50; geography and history, 4:44–45; *katsina* season, 4:47–48; language, 4:46; origins and ancestors, 4:45–46; social structure, 4:46; studies of Hopi folklore, 4:50
Hopkins, Matthew, 3:8
Hop tu naa (Isle of Man), 3:48–49
Horse carts (Sicily), 3:486
Horse racing (Georgia), 3:360–361
Horses and Kiowa, 4:61
Horticulture: and cultural shift, 1:16–17; New Caledonia, 1:309; Shuar, 4:222
Housing: African American, 4:153–154; Apache, 4:1; Appalachia, 4:163; Assam, 2:23; Australia (British), 1:282–283; Bangladesh, 2:102; Baule, 1:168; Benin, 1:176, 179; Berber, 1:110; Bhutan, 2:111; Bihar, 2:29; Caipira, 4:180; Caribs of Dominica, 4:331; Cherokee, 4:18–19; Ga, 1:182; Gaddi, 2:33, 36; Georgia, 3:361–362; Greece, 3:500; Haida, 4:39, 40; Haryana, 2:39, 45; Iceland, 3:118; Igbo, 1:200–201; Ireland, 3:25, 26; Iroquois, 4:53; Isaan, 2:135; Karnataka, 2:51–52, 56; Kazakh, 2:313; Korea, 2:298; Lebanon, 2:397; Macedonia, 3:374–375; Madagascar, 1:142; Malaita, 1:301; Maluku, 2:201–202; Mississippi Delta, 4:167; Nepal, 2:113; New Caledonia, 1:310; Orissa, 2:85; Scotland, 3:53; Seminole, 4:114; Sertão, 4:219; Shona, 1:253–254; Siberia, 2:318–319; Tairora, 2:204, 209; Tuareg, 1:109, 119–120; Tuvalu, 1:409; Ukraine, 3:446–447; Uttar Pradesh, 2:89; Vanuatu, 1:330–331; Western Inuit and Yupik, 4:132; Xhosa, 1:257
"How the Young Maidens Saved the Island of Guam" (Guam), 1:335
Hózhǫ' (Navajo) , 4:85
Hsuan-tang (Chinese Buddhist pilgrim) stories (Haryana), 2:40
Huayno folksongs (Peru), 4:204

Hufford, Mary, 1:30
Hula dance (Hawai'i), 1:371–372
Huldrefolk (Norway), 3:126
Hultz, D., 1:291
Human behavior as theme: Ga, 1:184; Yoruba, 1:219
Humanist movement (Croatia), 3:349
Humorous stories, skits, etc.: African Americans, 4:148–150; Australia (British), 1:284; Berber, 1:107; Choctaw, 4:36; Ga, 1:185; Lakota, 4:72; Maya, 4:261; Samoa, 1:393–396; Tuareg, 1:117, 118; Western Inuit and Yupik, 4:136; Wolof, 1:215. *See also* Jokes and joking rituals; Punning; Tall tales
Hungarian Ethnographic Society, 1:6
Hungary, 1:6, 3:273–284; ballads and folktales, 3:279; calendars and drama, 3:281–282; dance, games, and arts and crafts, 3:282–283; geography and history, 3:273–278; music, 3:280–281; religion and beliefs, 3:278–279; songs, riddles, and proverbs, 3:279–280
Hunger as theme (Jie), 1:132
Hungilisk game (Kurds), 2:390–391
Hunting: Ainu, 2:288; Appalachia, 4:164; Duna, 2:165; Kaingang, 4:193; Kaliai, 2:183, 187; Kurds, 2:389; Malta, 3:510; Marquesas Islands, 1:379; New Caledonia, 1:309; San, 1:246–247; Seminole, 4:114; Siberia, 2:315; Swahili, 1:156; and symbolic world, 1:30; Tairora, 2:205; Vanuatu, 1:330; Western Inuit and Yupik, 4:129–130, 135; Yoruba, 1:222
"Hunt the Wren" (song), 3:50
Hurston, Zora Neale, 1:31, 41, 48
Hutu massacre of Tutsi, 1:64
Hyacinth, Saint, 3:495
Hybridity, 1:47–49; and diffusion, 1:24; and globalization, 1:24, 42, 47; and race, 1:78
Hyde, Douglas, 3:22
Hyltén-Cavallius, Gunnar Olof, 3:14, 150
Hymes, Dell, 1:31, 32, 69–70, 84
Hymns: African American, 4:152; Cherokee, 4:14; Gaddi, 2:36; Haryana, 2:43; Hungary, 3:280; Igbo, 1:197; Iroquois, 4:59; Kiowa, 4:62–63; Kiribati, 1:345; Kurds, 2:391; Lunda, 1:236; Madagascar, 1:138, 141; Malaita, 1:303; Nagaland, 2:77; Navajo, 4:88; Norway, 3:123, 129; Tuvalu, 1:408, 409; Xavante, 4:249
Hyperbole. *See* Language

Iban, 2:171–176; chants, 2:175; geography and history, 2:171–173; oral folklore, 2:173–174; principles of Iban folklore, 2:173; rules and rituals, 2:174–175; studies of Iban folklore, 2:175–176
Iblis (the Devil) (Tuareg), 1:117
Iceland, 3:111–123; British influence, 3:112; Danish influence, 3:112; Eddic poems, 3:113; folktales, 3:114–115; food, clothing, games, and customs, 3:117–119; geography

Ivandan (John the Baptist Day, Serbia), 3:431

Ivan Kupalo (summer solstice), 3:417

Ivan the Terrible, 3:409

Ivrea, festival (Piedmont and Val d'Aosta), 3:474

Izaga nezimo zikukhuluma (Zulu), 1:274

Izibongo, 1:272–274

Izibongo: Zulu Praise-Poems, 1:272

"The Izibongo of the Zulu Chiefs," 1:272

Izibongo ZamaKhosi, 1:272

Izwi Labantu (newspaper) (Xhosa), 1:262, 264

Jaarsma, Dam, 3:243

Jabavu, John Tengo, 1:263, 264

"Jack and the Beanstalk," 3:12

Jack in Two Worlds (McCarthy), 1:85

"Jack the Giant-Killer," 3:12

Jadwiga, Queen, 3:381

Jae-hyo Shin (early writer, Korea), 2:300

Jaguar stories (Yanomami), 4:253–254

Jainism: Bihar, 2:25; Gaddi, 2:31; Haryana, 2:39; Karnataka, 2:48; Orissa, 2:80

Jakobson, Roman, 1:90, 91

Jamaica, 4:336–347; children's songs and games, 4:341; and diaspora, 1:20; East Indian culture, 4:344–345; festivals and celebrations, 4:338–339; folktales, 4:341–342; geography and history, 4:336–338; Maroon culture, 4:339–341; religious beliefs, 4:343–344; spells and magic, 4:343; studies of Jamaican folklore, 4:345–346

James I (England), 3:54

James II (England and Scotland), 3:54

James IV (Scotland), 3:54

James VI (England and Scotland), 3:54

James VII (England and Scotland), 3:54

James, Saint, 3:204–206, 349

James, Richard, 3:410

Jánošík, Juraj, 3:292

Janša, Anton, 3:304

Japan, 2:271–284; arts, crafts, and architecture, 2:278; folk religion and performing arts, 2:276–277; geography and history, 2:271–273; Marshall Islands influence by, 1:350; medicine, 2:278; modernization, challenges of, 2:278–279; modern studies of Japanese folklore, 2:279–281; and nationalism, 1:63; Palau influence by, 1:360; periods of cultural history, 2:273–275; religious beliefs, 2:275–276; sports and games, 2:277–278; Taiwan, influence in, 2:261, 265. *See also* Ainu

Jataka tales (birth stories of the Bodhisattva): Bhutan, 2:108; India, 2:7; Isaan, 2:135; Sri Lanka, 2:127

Jean du Doigt, Saint, 3:170, 175

Jelacic, Josip, 3:351

Jenkins, J. Geraint, 3:78

Jenn tales and superstitions (Persia), 2:417–418

Jesuits: Italy, 3:457–458; Rarámuri, 4:297

Jewelry and personal adornments: Baule, 1:167; Benin, 1:176; Berber, 1:106; Hawaiʻi, 1:372; Igbo, 1:201; Kiribati, 1:347; Marquesas Islands, 1:381, 384; Navajo, 4:91; Tlingit, 4:125–126; Tuareg, 1:107, 119; Wolof, 1:211. *See also* Amulets; Beadwork

Jews: Diaspora, 1:18–20; folklore of, 1:20, 62; immigrants to Mississippi Delta, 4:174; immigrants to U.S., 1:66; Nazi genocide of, 1:64

Jhangar epics (Mongol), 2:254–255

Jicarilla Relay Race (Apache), 4:5–6

Jie, 1:131–137; geography, 1:131; social structure, beliefs, and historical tradition, 1:133–137; stories, tales and historical tradition, 1:131–133

Jingoism and nativism, 1:64

Jinx as theme (Wolof), 1:213

Jnoun (Berber), 1:103–104, 111

Joan of Arc, 3:164

John, Saint, 3:199, 200, 265, 268

John Frum movement (Vanuatu), 1:327

John III Sobieski (King of Poland), 3:381

Johnson, Robert, 4:170

Johnson, Samuel, 3:38, 63

John Stands in Timber (Cheyenne), 4:22

John the Baptist, Saint, 3:290, 349, 388, 417, 429, 471

Jokes and joking rituals: Albania, 3:328, 329; Ashkenazim, 3:334; Greece, 3:497; Ireland, 3:38–39; Latvia, 3:362; Malaita, 1:302, 304; Roma, 3:406; Shona, 1:249, 250; Slovakia, 3:292; Swahili, 1:158; Wolof, 1:214–215; Yoruba, 1:224–225

Jolobe, J.J.R., 1:262

Jolted work system, 3:456

Jón Árnason, 3:114, 117

Jónas Jónasson frá Hrafnagili, 3:117

Jones, Mary, 3:74

Jones, Michael Owens, 1:77

Jones, Stephen, 2:222

Jón Guðmundsson the Learned, 3:113

Joning (African American), 4:150

Jonkunu (Jamaica), 4:338–339

Jón Ólofsson frá Grunnavík, 3:113

Jonsson, Bengt R., 3:149

Jordan, A.C., 1:261

Joseph II (Emperor), 3:347

Joseph, Saint, 3:199, 200

Journal of American Folklore, 1:5

Journal of Asian American Studies, 2:243

Journal of Folklore Research, 1:95

Journal of Palestine Oriental Society, 2:412

Journal of the Royal Anthropological Institute, 2:178

Journal of the Royal Asiatic Society, 2:30

Judaism: Australia (British), 1:290; Haiti, 4:319; Israel, 2:372; Jamaica, 4:337; Palestine, 2:401; Turkey, 2:430. *See also* Jews

Juju music (Yoruba), 1:223, 225

Julius Caesar, 3:261

Jung, C.G., 1:92

Junjappa stories (Karnataka), 2:50

Jurjans, Andrejs, 3:368

Júrjenson, Kaarjel, 1:81

Just, Saint, 3:160

"Just-so" stories (Nuer), 1:153

Kabua the Great (Marshall Islands leader), 1:350

Kabyle (Berber), 1:108, 110

Kadazandusun, 2:176–182; arts and crafts, 2:180–181; celebrations and games, 2:179–180; geography and history, 2:176–177; modernization, challenges of, 2:181; music, 2:179; myths, legends, and folktales, 2:178–179; religious beliefs and rituals, 2:177–178; studies of Kadazandusun folklore, 2:181–182

Kadoazi, 4:183

Kaʻililauokekoa (Hawaiʻi), 1:376

Kaingang, 4:193–199; food, 4:193–194; geography and history, 4:193; symmetry in myths and folktales, 4:194–197

Kairus (Kaingang subgroup), 4:194–195

Kakárma (Shuar), 4:222–223

Kalabari, 1:204, 208

Kalākaua (Hawaiian king), 1:371

Kalevala, 3:92–96

Kaliai, 2:183–188; geography and history, 2:183–184; modernization, challenges of, 2:188; myths, legends, and folktales, 2:184–186; songs and music, 2:186; storytelling, 2:187; themes in folktales, 2:188

Kalila Wa Demna (animal) tales (Palestine), 2:405

Kamahualele (foster son of Hawaiian chief), 1:370

Kambule, Mpondo, 1:270

Kamehameha (Hawaiian king), 1:367, 374

Kamês (Kaingang subgroup), 4:194–195

A Kammu Story-Listener's Tales (Lindell, Swahn & Tayanin), 1:81

Kammu traditions, 1:81

Kanak people. *See* New Caledonia

Kanaval festival (Haiti), 4:323

Ka Niam Khasi, 2:66–67

Kantan Chamorrita (Guam), 1:338

Kanyembo Lutaba, Paul (Mwata Kazembe XVII), 1:238, 239

Kapchan, Deborah A., 1:47, 48

Karadžić, Vuk Stefanovik, 3:372, 373, 431, 432, 434

Karagiozis (shadow theater, Greece), 3:500

Karimov, Islam, 2:349

Kariri culture (Sertão), 4:217

Karl-Emanuel, count of Savoy, 3:315

Karl of Savoy, Duke, 3:310

1:349–350; modernization, challenges of, 1:356; oral folklore types, 1:353; social structure and religion, 1:350–351; song and dance, 1:353–354; stories and storytelling, 1:351–352; studies of Marshall Islands folklore, 1:356–357

Martial arts (Hawai'i), 1:373

Martin, Saint, 3:200, 241, 265, 349, 471

Martin, György, 3:282–283

Martínez, Francesc, 3:195

Martino, Ernesto de, 3:463

Martin of Tours, Saint, 3:160

Martinsson, Lena, 3:151

Mary, Saint, 3:505

Mary Theotokos (Ukrainian goddess), 3:439, 441

Mascarene Islands, 1:144–150; history, 1:144. *See also* Mauritius and Rodrigues; Réunion; The Seychelles

Mashrab, Rahim, 2:340

Masks and masquerades: Baule, 1:164, 165, 167; Benin, 1:175; Igbo, 1:198–199; Ijo, 1:205–207; Iroquois, 4:55–56; Jamaica, 4:338–339; Malaita, 1:303; New Caledonia, 1:311; Peru, 4:207; Yoruba, 1:222, 224, 225

Maspons i Labròs, Francesc, 3:195

Massada legend (Israel), 1:63, 2:377–378

Massaum (Cheyenne), 4:28

Massot i Muntaner, Josep, 3:196

Matchmakers (Russia), 3:413–414

Matisoff, James, 3:335

Matoub, Lounès, 1:108

Matrilineal societies: Australian Aborigines, 1:295, 297; Baule, 1:163; Cherokee, 4:9; Guam, 1:333; Hopi, 4:46; Khasi-Jaintia, 2:66, 67, 71; Lunda, 1:234; Marshall Islands, 1:350; Palau, 1:359, 360–361; Seminole, 4:116; Suriname Maroons, 4:239; Tuareg, 1:103, 114; Vanuatu, 1:326

Matrilocality: Cherokee, 4:9; Haida, 4:39; Hopi, 4:46; Shuar, 4:221–222

Matsu pilgrimage and stories (Taiwan), 2:261, 267–268

Mattanza (Sicily), 3:484

Maui Kisikisi (Tonga), 1:400–401

Maurer, Konrad, 3:114

Mauritius and Rodrigues: geography and history, 1:144–146; Madagascar, 1:138; music and dance, 1:147; stories and tales, 1:146–147

Maximianus Herculeus, 3:471

Maya, 4:256–268; clothing, 4:262–263; drama, riddles, and wordplay, 4:261; dumb priest stories, 4:261; folktales, 4:258–261; modernization, challenges of, 4:264; music, 4:263; space and time, notions of,

4:257–258; sports and games, 4:263–264; studies of Mayan folklore, 4:264–265; Zapatista rebellion, 4:258

May Day, 3:17, 18

Mayotte. *See* The Comoros

Maypole: Austria, 3:256; England, 3:1; Germany, 3:264; Italy, 3:464; Slovakia, 3:290

Mayr, Fr., 1:274

Mazurka dance rhythm, 3:389

Mbata, Alban Hamilton, 1:271

Mbaye Trambwe (King of The Comoros), 1:142

McCarthy, William Bernard, 1:85

McElhill, Patrick, 3:39

McEwan, Frank, 1:254

McGrath, Billy, 3:38

McGrath, Dennis, 3:33

McGrath, Patrick James, 3:33, 34, 37

McHugh, Willie, 3:37–38

McKenry, Keith, 1:291

McSorley, "Ribbonman," 3:34

Mdhladhla, Garland Clement S., 1:271

Mdunga, Guaise, 1:270

Mead, Margaret, 1:40

Mecano, 3:184

Medea, 1:56; and Nahua tale, 4:287

Medicine and cures: Abanyole, 1:127; African American, 4:146–147; Armenia, 2:357; Ashkenazim, 3:333–334; Bali, 2:156; Bangladesh, 2:102–103; Baule, 1:165–166; Benin, 1:171, 179; Bhutan, 2:107; Bihar, 2:27; Caipira, 4:179; Caribs of Dominica, 4:333–334; China, 2:213; Chinese living abroad, 2:240–241; Denmark, 3:84; Duna, 2:167; Ecuador, 4:191; Finnish-Swedish, 3:99; Flanders (Belgium), 3:229; France, 3:159; Ga, 1:191–192; Gaddi, 2:35–36; Galicia, 3:203; Greece, 3:496; Guam, 1:338; Haryana, 2:41; Hawai'i, 1:369; Iban, 2:172, 174–175; Igbo, 1:197, 201–202; Iroquois, 4:58; Israel, 2:372; Japan, 2:278; Kadazandusun, 2:178; Kazakh, 2:314; Kiribati, 1:343; Kurds, 2:385–386; Madagascar, 1:138; Malaita, 1:306; Malta, 3:506; Marquesas Islands, 1:381; Marshall Islands, 1:351; Mexico, 4:270; Mississippi Delta, 4:171; Navajo, 4:85; The Netherlands, 3:240; Norway, 3:123–125; Nuer, 1:152; Palestine, 2:407, 408; Persia, 2:417, 418, 420–421, 424; Peru, 4:202; Piedmont and Val d'Aosta, 3:472–473; Rarámuri, 4:304–305; Réunion, 1:148; Samoa, 1:392; San, 1:242; Semai, 2:148; Seminole, 4:115; Sephardim, 3:213; Sertão, 4:217–218; Shona, 1:252, 254; Siberia, 2:320, 322; Sibundoy, 4:231–232; Slovakia, 3:287; Slovenia, 3:299–300; Taiwan, 2:265–266; Tajik, 2:327–328; Tonga, 1:399–400; Tuareg, 1:114; Tuvalu, 1:406; Ukraine, 3:439–440; Uttar Pradesh, 2:90; Uyghur, 2:338; Uzbek, 2:351–352; Vanuatu,

1:327; Western Inuit and Yupik, 4:134; Wolof, 1:211; Zande, 1:229

Medicine Lodge Treaty of 1867, 4:62

Medicine man. *See* Healers

Meertens, P.J., 3:237

Meertens Institute, 3:237, 243

Megalithic stones: Basque, 3:191; Brittany, 3:172; Malta, 3:504; Scotland, 3:53

Meghalaya. *See* Khasi-Jaintia

Megrelian folklore (Georgia), 3:355

Mejías, Ignacio Sánchez, 3:186

Melanesia, 1:17, 300–332

"Melting pot," 1:49

Memê Alan, romantic epic (Kurds), 2:388

Memela, Nsukuzonke, 1:269

Memorates (Russia), 3:418

Memorials. *See* Funerals and burials; Potlatches

Mem û Zîn, romantic epic (Kurds), 2:388

Menarcheal theme: Hawai'i, 1:368; Kiribati, 1:343; San, 1:243, 246

Mendaña, Alvaro de, 1:378

Menius, Fridericus, 3:368

Meredith, John, 1:285

Mermaids: Finnish-Swedish, 3:98; Guam, 1:336; Iceland, 3:115; Wolof, 1:209. *See also* "The Little Mermaid"

Merton, Ambrose. *See* Thoms, William J.

Mesepis (Georgia), 3:355

Mestizos (Mexico), 4:276

Metalworking: Benin, 1:176; Igbo, 1:201; Wolof, 1:213; Yoruba, 1:226

Metaphor. *See* Simile and metaphor

Methodists (Australia), 1:279

Methodius, Saint, 3:371, 426, 429

Meurling, Birgitta, 3:151

Mexican immigrants in Mississippi Delta, 4:174

Mexican Revolution, 4:278–279; and Rarámuri, 4:298

Mexico, 4:268–282; ethnic composition, 4:270; folk beliefs, 4:270–273; folklore, 4:275–277; folklore studies in contemporary Mexico, 4:280–281; geography and history, 4:268–269; independence movement, 4:277–278; Maya, 4:256–257; music and songs, 4:273; nineteenth- and twentieth-century studies of Mexican folklore, 4:278–280; Rarámuri, 4:296–298; religion, 4:269–270; Virgin of Guadalupe, 4:273–275

Mexico and Central America, 4:256–308

Mfengu, 1:263

Mhòr non Oran, Màiri (Mary Macpherson), 3:61

Michael, Saint, 3:290

Microcosmic historical tradition, 1:132

Micronesia, 1:333–365

Micronesian Endowment for Historic Preservation, 1:365

Micronesian languages: Palau, 1:359; Tuvalu, 1:405

Midrash texts (Israel), 2:373

A Midsummer Night's Dream, 3:7

Murdoch, Rupert, **3:**188
Murdock, George Peter, **1:**17, 18
Murko, Matija, **3:**433
Muromets, Ilia, **3:**422
Murqvamoba drama (Svan, Georgia), **3:**359–360
Murray, Margaret, **1:**50
Museo del Sale (salt museum, Sicily), **3:**484
Museum for German Folklore, **1:**58
Museum of Popular Industries and Arts (Barcelona), **3:**196
Museums, **1:**57–60
Musho! Zulu Popular Praises (Zulu), **1:**272
Musical instruments: Albania, **3:**321, 329; Apache, **4:**6; Appalachia, **4:**160–161; Armenia, **2:**369; Assam, **2:**22; Bali, **2:**161; Bangladesh, **2:**97, 102; Baule, **1:**165; Benin, **1:**177; Bhutan, **2:**108–109; Cherokee, **4:**14, 15; China, **2:**222–223; Croatia, Central, **3:**345; Croatia, Littoral, **3:**341–343; Croatia, Lowland, **3:**346; Croatia, Mountainous, **3:**344; Duna, **2:**170; Ga, **1:**191; Gaddi, **2:**36; Greece, **3:**498; Haiti, **4:**322; Haryana, **2:**42; Hawai'i, **1:**371–372; Iban, **2:**175; Igbo, **1:**197; Ijo, **1:**207; India, **2:**9; Iroquois, **4:**59; Isaan, **2:**137–138; Italy, **3:**463; Jamaica, **4:**345; Kadazandusun, **2:**179; Karnataka, **2:**49, 54; Kashmir, **2:**64; Kazakh, **2:**309–312; Khasi-Jaintia, **2:**72; Kiribati, **1:**345; Kurds, **2:**389–390; Lakota and Dakota, **4:**74; Lunda, **1:**236; Macedonia, **3:**374, 375; Madagascar, **1:**141; Malaita, **1:**304; Malay, **2:**143; Malta, **3:**510; Manchu, **2:**251; Maroons of Jamaica, **4:**340; Marquesas Islands, **1:**381, 383; Marshall Islands, **1:**355; Mauritius and Rodrigues, **1:**145, 147; Maya, **4:**263; Mississippi Delta, **4:**172–173; Mongol, **2:**258; Navajo, **4:**87; Nepal, **2:**118; Norway, **3:**129, 130–131; Ojibwe, **4:**108; Orissa, **2:**83, 84; Peru, **4:**205; Quechua, **4:**211, 212; Roma, **3:**399; Scotland, **3:**62–63; Semai, **2:**148; Serbia, **3:**433; Shona, **1:**251; Shuar, **4:**226; Siberia, **2:**319, 321; Sicily, **3:**482–483; Slovenia, **3:**301; Tairora, **2:**208; Tajik, **2:**328–329; Tlingits, **4:**124; Tonga, **1:**402; Tuareg, **1:**108, 115–117; Turkey, **2:**433–434; Tuvalu, **1:**408; Ukraine, **3:**440; Uttar Pradesh, **2:**92; Uyghur, **2:**341; Uzbek, **2:**352–353; Vanuatu, **1:**329; Wales, **3:**76; Western Inuit and Yupik, **4:**136–137; Wolof, **1:**214; Zande, **1:**231–233; Zulu, **1:**274–275. *See also specific instruments*
Music and dance: Abanyole, **1:**125–130; African Americans, **4:**145–148, 151–153; Ainu, **2:**287, 291, 292; Albania, **3:**328, 329; Apache, **4:**5; Appalachia, **4:**160–162;

Armenia, **2:**362–369; Ashkenazim, **3:**335–337; Assam, **2:**22–23; Australia (British), **1:**285–286, 288; Australian Aborigines, **1:**293, 294, 296–298; Austria, **3:**257; Bali, **2:**161; Bangladesh, **2:**96–99; Baule, **1:**164, 165–166; Benin, **1:**176–177; Berber, **1:**107–108; Bhutan, **2:**109–110; Bihar, **2:**28; Caipira, **4:**180; Candoshi, **4:**185–187; Catalan, **3:**198–199; Cherokee, **4:**11–12, 14–15; Cheyenne, **4:**26–28; China, **2:**218–223; Choctaw, **4:**33–34; and colonialism, **1:**8–9; The Comoros, **1:**143; country dances, England, **3:**14–15; and creolization, **1:**10–11; Croatia, Central, **3:**345; Croatia, Littoral, **3:**341–343; Croatia, Mountainous, **3:**344; Cuba, **4:**310–312; Dakota, **4:**74, 77; Denmark, **3:**85; Duna, **2:**169–170; Ecuador, **4:**189–190; England, **3:**13–15; and ethnicity, **1:**26; and ethnopoetics, **1:**32; Finnish-Swedish, **3:**100; and folklorism, **1:**36; Ga, **1:**185–187, 192; Georgia, **3:**358–359; Germany, **3:**271; Greece, **3:**497, 498; Guam, **1:**338, 339; Haida, **4:**43; Haiti, **4:**321–323, 326; Haryana, **2:**42–43; Hawai'i, **1:**368, 371–372; Hopi, **4:**48; Hungary, **3:**280–283; Iban, **2:**174; Iceland, **3:**119; Igbo, **1:**196–199; Ijo, **1:**207; India, **2:**9–11; Ireland, **3:**27–29; Iroquois, **4:**53, 55, 59; Isaan, **2:**136, 137–138; Israel, **2:**381; Italy (middle and southern), **3:**459, 460; Jamaica, **4:**338, 341, 344; Japan, **2:**276–277; Kadazandusun, **2:**179; Kaliai, **2:**186; Karnataka, **2:**49, 52–53; Kashmir, **2:**61–63; Kazakh, **2:**310–312; Kewa, **2:**191–195; Khasi-Jaintia, **2:**69–70; Kiowa, **4:**61–65; Kiribati, **1:**342, 344–346, 348; Korea, **2:**299–301; Kurds, **2:**386, 389–390; Lakota, **4:**74, 77; Lebanon, **2:**394–397; Lunda, **1:**236; Macedonia, **3:**374–375; Madagascar, **1:**140, 141–142; Malaita, **1:**302, 303–304; Malta, **3:**509–510; Maluku, **2:**200–201; Manchu, **2:**248, 251; Maroons of Jamaica, **4:**340–341; Marquesas Islands, **1:**378, 380, 382–383; Marshall Islands, **1:**352–356; Mauritius and Rodrigues, **1:**145, 147; Maya, **4:**263; Mexico, **4:**273; Mississippi Delta, **4:**168–172; and modernization, **1:**52–53; Mongol, **2:**255–256, 258–259; Navajo, **4:**87–89; The Netherlands, **3:**243–244; New Caledonia, **1:**313; northern Italy, **3:**458, 459–460; Norway, **3:**129–131; Nuer, **1:**152–153; Ojibwe, **4:**108, 109; Orissa, **2:**82–83; Palau, **1:**360–364; Persia, **2:**422–424; Peru, **4:**203–205; Poland, **3:**380, 388–391; Quechua, **4:**210–212; Rarámuri, **4:**302; Réunion, **1:**148; Roma, **3:**404–405; Samoa, **1:**394–396; San, **1:**241, 246; Scotland, **3:**57–63; Seminole, **4:**115; Sertão, **4:**218–219; The Seychelles, **1:**149–150; Shona, **1:**251–253; Shuar, **4:**225–227; Siberia, **2:**316, 323; Sicily, **3:**482, 485–486;

Slovakia, **3:**292–293; Slovena, **3:**300–302; Slovenia, **3:**300–302; Spain, **3:**183–185; Suriname Maroons, **4:**240–241; Swahili, **1:**155, 157–158; Sweden, **3:**146; Switzerland, **3:**312–314; Taiwan, **2:**263; Tajik, **2:**328–329; Tlingit, **4:**124–125; Tonga, **1:**401–402; Trobriand Islands, **1:**320; Tuareg, **1:**108, 111–112, 116–118; Turkey, **2:**433–435; Tuvalu, **1:**407–408, 410; Ukraine, **3:**441–442; Uttar Pradesh, **2:**91–92; Uyghur, **2:**341–344; Uzbek, **2:**351–353; Vanuatu, **1:**328–330; Wales, **3:**76; Western Inuit and Yupik, **4:**128–129, 136–138; Wolof, **1:**212, 213, 215; Xavante, **4:**245, 246–248; Yoruba, **1:**224–225; Zande, **1:**230, 231–232; Zulu, **1:**274–275. *See also* Children's songs, stories, and verses; *specific types of songs and dances*
Muslims: Assam, **2:**18–20; Australia (British), **1:**289, 290; Bangladesh, **2:**95; Baule, **1:**164; Berber, **1:**101, 103; Bihar, **2:**25; The Comoros, **1:**142; Haryana, **2:**39, 41; Israel, **2:**375; Karnataka, **2:**49; Kashmir, **2:**59, 60, 64; Orissa, **2:**80, 81; Sri Lanka, **2:**124, 125; Swahili, **1:**154–155, 157, 160; Tuareg, **1:**114; Turkey, Alevi, **2:**430; Tuvalu, **1:**405; Uttar Pradesh, **2:**88; Wolof, **1:**210–212. *See also* Islam; Shi'ite Muslims; Sunni Muslims
Mutomboko celebration (Lunda), **1:**239–240
Mvingana (bard of Zulu king), **1:**273
Mwaka festival (Swahili), **1:**159
Mwaneaba (Kiribati), **1:**343–344
Mwata Kazembe, **1:**235, 236
Mysore. *See* Karnataka
Mysterious housekeeper motif, **1:**55
Mystery cults, **3:**159–160
Mythical creatures. *See* Monsters and creatures
Myth of the Negro Past (Herskovits), **4:**144–145
Mythological Cycle (Ireland), **3:**30, 31
Myths. *See* Stories and tales
Myths and Legends of Palau, **1:**364
Myths of origin. *See* Creation stories

Naath. *See* Nuer
Nagaland, **2:**73–79; arts and crafts, **2:**77–78; cultural tradition, **2:**3; geography and language, **2:**73–74; myths, legends, and folktales, **2:**74–76; names, symbols, and meanings, **2:**78–79; songs, **2:**76–77
Nahua, **4:**282–288; European trickster tales, **4:**287; geography and history, **4:**282–283; roots of Nahua folklore, **4:**283–284; tales and songs of European origin, **4:**284–287
Naipaul, V.S., **1:**145
Nairne, Lady, **3:**59
Name days (Greece), **3:**496
Naming: Tlingit, **4:**120. *See also* Child naming; Nicknames
Namunai folklori tojik (Examples of Tajik Folklore, Tursunzoda), **2:**326
Nanny of the Windward Maroons of Portland and St. Thomas, **4:**340

Powell, John Wesley, 1:84

Power, Richard, 3:36

Powwows: Cherokee, 4:15; Cheyenne, 4:25, 28; Ojibwe, 4:109

Pracat, Miho, 3:347

Praise poetry and songs: Igbo, 1:196; Lunda, 1:235, 238; Shona, 1:250; Wolof, 1:212, 214; Xhosa, 1:261–267; Yoruba, 1:222–223

Prat, Joan, 3:196

Prats, Llorenç, 3:196

Pratt, George, 1:396

Prayers: Alpine, 3:313; Lakota, 4:68–69; Poland, 3:383; Xavante, 4:249. *See also* Incantations

"Prayer to the Death of Creation, Chi-na-Eke" (Igbo), 1:197

"Prayer to Ulaasi, River Deity of Ihembosi" (Igbo), 1:197

Pre-Christian belief (Georgia), 3:354–356

Predanija (Macedonia), 3:372

Predictions. *See* Diviners and divination

Prenting (Maroons of Jamaica), 4:340

Prentis, Malcolm, 1:281

Preservation: and archives, 1:3–5; of Dutch folklore, 3:236–237; of Russian folklore, 3:408–411

Presley, Elvis, 1:11, 3:271

Presbyterianism in Australia, 1:278, 281

Price-Mars, Jean, 4:319–320

Priests: Maya dumb priest stories, 4:261. *See also* Brahmans (priestly class)

Primeros Memoriales (de Sahagún), 4:275

Primitive Art (Boas), 1:34

Primitive Culture (Tylor), 1:12

Primitivism, 1:73–75; and invented tradition, 1:51

Primitivism and Identity in Latin America (Camayd-Freixas & González), 1:74

Primitivism and Related Ideas in the Middle Ages (Boas), 1:73

"Primitivism" in 20th Century Art (Rubin), 1:74

Prince Marko Cycle (Serbia), 3:435

"The Prince of the Shining Countenance" (Madagascar), 1:140

Prithyi Narayan Shah (King of Nepal), 2:114

Processions: Austria, 3:255, 264–265; Croatia, 3:349; flagellants, Campania and Calabria, 3:464; Galicia, 3:207; Italy, 3:464; Malta, 3:504, 508; Poland, 3:384; Roma, 3:399; Sicily, 3:489; Ukraine, 3:442

Property holdings (Serbia), 3:428

Prophets and prophecies: Choctaw, 4:36, 37; Karnataka, 2:49. *See also* Diviners and divination

Propp, Vladimir, 1:82, 3:116, 419

Prose Edda (Snorra Edda), 3:113

Protestantism: Australia (British), 1:279; Kiribati, 1:341, 348; Marquesas Islands, 1:380; Tuvalu, 1:405. *See also* Christianity

Proverbs, 1:95; Abanyole, 1:130; African Americans, 4:150–151; Appalachia, 4:159; Ashkenazim, 3:335; Australia (British), 1:284; Baule, 1:164–165; Benin, 1:176–177; Bihar, 2:28–29; China, 2:214; Chinese living abroad, 2:234, 242; Ga, 1:182–183; Greece, 3:497–498; Haiti, 4:320, 326; Hungary, 3:280; Iban, 2:174; Igbo, 1:193, 195–196; Ijo, 1:206–207; Isaan, 2:135–136; Israel, 2:372, 373, 379, 380–381; Kazakh, 2:310; Khasi-Jaintia, 2:70–72; Kurds, 2:388; Lunda, 1:236, 237; Madagascar, 1:140–141; Malay, 2:142, 143; Manchu, 2:248–249; Marshall Islands, 1:352; Mongol, 2:258; origins of, 1:2; Palau, 1:361; Palestine, 2:403; Persia, 2:422; Peru, 4:203; Poland, 3:382; Russia, 3:418; Sephardim, 3:214–215; Shona, 1:249–251; Swahili, 1:155, 156, 159; Tajik, 2:326–327; Turkey, 2:432; Uyghur, 2:336; Yoruba, 1:218, 221–222; Zande, 1:231; Zulu, 1:270, 274

Pshav poetic contests (Georgia), 3:359

Puamana (Hawai'i), 1:376

Puberty. *See* Initiation (rights of passage) ceremonies

Public folklore, 1:75–78; and culture area, 1:17

Public Folklore (Baron & Spitzer), 1:77

Publius, Saint, 3:508

Pueblos: art forms, 4:49; Navajo, 4:82

Pujol, Josep M., 3:196

Punning: Balinese, 2:154; Ojibwe, 4:107; Sri Lanka, 2:127; Taiwan, 2:264; Turkey, 2:433, 435

"Puntan Dos Amantes" (Guam), 1:337

Punto (Cuban song form), 4:312

Puppet theater: Greece, 3:500; northern Italy, 3:464; Sicily, 3:490

Purdah (Uttar Pradesh), 2:89

Purgatory doctrine (England), 3:10

Purification ceremonies: Lunda, 1:239; Malaita, 1:304; Russia, 3:412–413, 439

Purim dramas (Ashkenazim), 3:336–337

Pushkin, Alexander, 3:409

Putta Kin Kai (Grandpa eats chicken) game (Isaan), 2:139

Putting Folklore to Use (Jones), 1:77

Pysanky (decorated eggs, Ukraine), 3:445–446

Q'assayids (Wolof), 1:212

Qivittut (Greenland), 3:107

Quatrain verses and songs (Latvia), 3:363, 366

Quechua, 4:208–216; arts and crafts, 4:214; drama and the *entrada*, 4:212–213; folktales and riddles, 4:202, 204, 210; geography and history, 4:208–209; life-cycle rituals, 4:210; modernization, challenges of, 4:214–215; religious beliefs, 4:209–210; songs and music, 4:202, 204, 210–212; sports and games, 4:213–214; studies of Quechua folklore, 4:215

Quest rites (Lenten), 3:474–475

Quilting. *See* Textile arts

Quintana, Artur, 3:196

Qvigstad, J., 3:137, 138

Rabghuzi, Nasiruddin, 2:338–339

"The Rabid Red Hero with One Hair" (Mongol), 2:255

Rabin, Yitzhak, 2:381

Rabon, Francisco, 1:339

Race, 1:78–81. *See also* Demographics; Discrimination

Races: Apache, 4:5–6; Rarámuri, 4:305–306; Tuareg, 1:119; Xavante, 4:245–246

Racism. *See* Discrimination and racism

Radio: Abanyole, 1:124; Australia (British), 1:286, 288; Baule, 1:168; Kiribati, 1:348; Navajo, 4:89; Shona, 1:252; Shuar, 4:226–227; Swahi, 1:158, 161; Tuareg, 1:118; Vanuatu, 1:329

Rahbani, Assi, 2:394

Raids: Apache, 4:3; Western Inuit and Yupik, 4:132–133

Rainbows (Sibundoy myths), 4:235

Rainmaking: bride-of-the-rain ceremonies (Berber), 1:105–106; Igbo, 1:197; Shona, 1:252; Wolof, 1:210

Rakel Pálsdóttir, 3:114

Ralámuli. *See* Rarámuri

Rama (Haryana), 2:41

Ramadam observances (Serbia), 3:433

Ramayana stories: Assam, 2:22; Bali, 2:152; India, 2:8, 11, 14; Karnataka, 2:53–54; Kashmir, 2:62; Uttar Pradesh, 2:92

Ramnarine, Tina Karina, 3:95

Ramsay, Allan, 3:59

Ramsten, Märta, 3:153

Ranavalona I (queen of Madagascar), 1:138

Ranchera music (Mexico), 4:273

Rangda stories (Bali), 2:157, 160–162

Raphael, 3:184

Rap music (African American), 4:153

Rara festival (Haiti), 4:323

Rarámuri, 4:296–308; cultural variation, 4:299–300; festivals and celebrations, 4:302–304; folk medicine, 4:304–305; folktales, 4:301; foreign cultural practices, adoption of, 4:298–299; geography and history, 4:296–298; maize beer, 4:304; oratory, 4:300–301; religious beliefs, 4:301–302; sports and games, 4:305–306; studies of Rarámuri folklore, 4:306–307

Rashi, 3:335

Rastafarianism (Jamaica), 4:343

Rattles: Benin, 1:174; Iroquois, 4:55, 59; Malaita, 1:304; Mascarene Islands, 1:147; Rarámuri, 4:302

Raudvere, Catharina, 3:153

Ravaton, Alphonse, 1:147

Raven clan (Haida), 4:39

Rouget de Lisle, Claude-Joseph, 3:157
Round dance: Georgia, 3:359, 360; Hungary, 3:282; Kiowa, 4:64; Siberia, 2:319; Slovenia, 3:302
Roure Torent, Josep, 3:195
Rousseau, Jean Jacques, 1:74, 3:310
Royal House of Orange, 3:242
Royal Institute of Amazingh (Berber) Culture, 1:111
Royal Scottish Country Dance Society, 3:63
Royalty: Georgian folktales, 3:356–357; Igbo, 1:8; Lunda, 1:235, 236; Nagaland, 2:77; Wolof, 1:210; Zande, 1:228. *See also specific names of kings, queens, etc.*
Royaume, Catherine, 3:315
Rózsa, Sándor, 3:277
Rubin, William, 1:74
Rudd, Steele, 1:286
Rugs. *See* Textile arts
Rumba (Cuba), 4:311
Rumor stories (African American), 4:151, 169
Runeberg, Johan Ludvig, 3:101
Runge, Philipp Otto, 3:267
Rupayan Sansthan (Rajasthan), 2:15
Rushnyky (ritual towels, Ukraine), 3:444–445
Russia, 3:408–425; calendars, 3:415–417; epics, 3:421–424; history, 3:411–412; Israel, influence on, 2:376–377; legends, folktales, and other oral genres, 3:417–420; life-cycle celebrations, 3:413–415; preservation of folklore, 3:408–411; Siberia, influence on, 2:316; songs, 3:420–421; Tajik, influence on, 2:325–326; Uzbek, influence on, 2:349, 350; witchcraft and magic, 3:412–413
Ryan, John S., 1:291
Rybnikov, P.N., 3:410

"Sabour" (Mascarene Islands), 1:146
Sacred Arrows (Cheyenne), 4:23–24
Sacred Buffalo Hat (Cheyenne), 4:23–24
Sacred Cross of Calderón Pass (Otomí), 4:290–293
The Sacred Remains: Myth, History, and Polity in Belau, 1:365
Sacred story archives (Vanuatu), 1:328
Sacrifices: Albania, 3:324; Baule, 1:166; Benin, 1:172, 173; Bihar, 2:27; Chinese living abroad, 2:237, 238; Duna, 2:166–167; Gaddi, 2:35–36; Iban, 2:175; Jie, 1:135–137; Kadazandusun, 2:178; Karnataka, 2:51; Kazakh, 2:307; Khasi-Jaintia, 2:69; Korea, 2:297; Malaita, 1:304; Manchu, 2:250, 251; Marquesas Islands, 1:381; Maya, 4:265; Mongol, 2:258; Nepal, 2:121; Nuer, 1:152; Palestine, 2:408; Sámi (Lapps), 3:136; Semai, 2:146, 148; Siberia, 2:321; Taiwan,

2:261–262; Tajik, 2:334; Tonga, 1:399; Yoruba, 1:224
Sagyrbayev, Kurmangazy, 2:312
Sahagún, Fray Bernardino de, 4:275
"Said Hanrahan" (Australia [British]), 1:285
Saint cults: Brittany, 3:174; France, 3:160; Sicily, 3:487
Saint's day holidays: Greece, 3:497; Malta, 3:504–505, 508–509; Roma, 3:403–404; Sicily, 3:488
Saivism, 2:20
Saktism, 2:20
Salam,sina (Samoan chief), 1:388
Salesians (Shuar), 4:220–221
Sálote (queen of Tonga), 1:401
"Salsa" music (Cuba), 4:311
Salt making: Lunda, 1:234; Sicily, 3:484–485
Salvà, Adolf, 3:195
Sámi (Lapps), 3:90, 112, 134–144; geography and history, 3:134–135; modernization, challenges of, 3:141–142; narratives, 3:139–140; preservation of folklore, 3:136–139; religion and beliefs, 3:136; Russian influence, 3:140; stories and tales, 3:140–141; witchcraft, 3:135
Samoa, 1:386–397; ceremonies and rituals, 1:393–394; genealogical stories, 1:386–387; history, 1:387–388; origin tales, 1:388–389; spirit lore, 1:392–393; stories of humans and spirits, 1:389–390; theater and dance, 1:394–396; Tonga in Samoan folklore, 1:388; Western-influenced folklore, 1:390–392
Samuelson, R.C.A., 1:272
San, 1:240–248; animals and hunting lore, 1:246–247; geography and society, 1:240–242; the mythological Early Times, 1:242–244; stories, myths, and legends, 1:242; studies of San folklore, 1:247; transformation of the Early Times, 1:245–246; trickster tales, 1:244–245
San Carolos Apache, 4:6
Sand drawings: Navajo, 4:86, 92; Vanuatu, 1:330
Sandile (Xhosa chief), 1:260, 266
Sankaradeva (spiritual leader of Assam), 2:19–20
Sanskrit: Assam, 2:17; Bali, 2:152, 154; Bihar, 2:26; forerunner of other languages, 1:22; India, 2:3; Isaan, 2:135; Karnataka, 2:51, 53; Kashmir, 2:60; Manchu, 2:247; Nepal, 2:115
Santéria myths (Cuba), 4:313
San Vitores, Luis Diego de, 1:333
Sardana (dance), 3:198–199
Sardinia, 3:464–465; circle dances, 3:465; funeral lament, 3:465; poetic contests, 3:465; shepherd's code of honor, 3:465
Saressalo, Lassi, 3:140
Sargadelos ceramic factory (Galicia), 3:208–209
Sassoontsi Davit (Davit of Sassoon, Armenia), 2:364

Sastre, Alonso, 3:184
Sather, Clifford, 2:176
Satire: Bangladesh, 2:99; Igbo, 1:196, 197; Nepal, 2:119; Russia, 3:418; Sri Lanka, 2:128; Wolof, 1:214; Yemen, 2:444; Yoruba, 1:223
Sava, Saint, 3:427
The Savage Mind (Lévi-Strauss), 1:47
Saveen (Gaddi), 2:35–36
Sayrami, Mulla Musa, 2:341
Scarves. *See* Hairstyles and head coverings
Scéalaíocht (Ireland), 3:27–28, 30, 31, 37
Schapkarev, Kuzman, 3:372
Scheub, Harold, 1:272
Schiller, Friedrich, 3:309
Schilling, Diebold, 3:310
Schnitzelbängler (poems), 3:316
Schoolcraft, Heny Rowe, 4:105
School of Oriental and African Studies of London University, 1:161
Schools: Navajo children, 4:92; Western Inuit and Yupik, 4:131–132, 140–141
Schreiner, Olive, 1:270
Schrijnen, Jos, 3:237
Schwizerdütsch language, 3:307
Scotland, 3:52–69; Australia (British) influence by, 1:278, 279, 281; ballads, 3:57–62; calendars, 3:64–67; geography and history, 3:52–55; music and dance, 3:57–64; political autonomy, 3:55; regional divisions, 3:53–54; sports and games, 3:64; storytelling, 3:57; supernatural lore, 3:55–57
The Scots in Australia (Australia [British]), 1:281
Scott, Bill, 1:278, 287
Scott, Walter, 3:3, 59
Sculpture. *See* Carving and sculpture
Seal, Graham, 1:291
Seanchas (Ireland), 3:27–28, 30, 31, 34–35, 37
Sea stories: Croatia, 3:347; Marshall Islands, 1:352; Swahili, 1:156
Sechseläuten festival (Switzerland), 3:315
Secola, Keith, 4:108
Second sight (Ireland), 3:55
The Secret History of the Mongols (Mongol), 2:253–254
Secret societies (Japan), 2:272
Seers. *See* Diviners and divination
Sega (Mascarene Islands), 1:148, 150
Self-mutilation (Karnataka), 2:49
Sellmann, James, 1:334
Semai, 2:145–151; geography and history, 2:145–146; modernization, challenges of, 2:149–150; religious and folk beliefs and Semai peaceability, 2:146–149; social structure and Semai democracy, 2:149
Seminole, 4:111–116; arts and crafts, 4:114; clothing, 4:112–113; food, 4:113–114; geography and history, 4:111–112; housing, 4:114; social structure, 4:116; Studies of Seminole folklore, 4:116

Skiing (Slovenia), **3**:302–303

Skinner, James Scott, **3**:63

Skirts. *See* Clothing

Skomorokhi (minstrels, Russia), **3**:409, 411

Skulls (Mexico), **4**:271–272

Slava: Roma, **3**:403; Serbia, **3**:429–430

Slavery: African Americans, **4**:143–148, 151, 154; and African diaspora, **1**:78; Benin, involvement in, **1**:172; Haiti, involvement in, **4**:316, 323; Ijo, involvement in, **1**:204; Jamaica, involvement in, **4**:338–339, 342; and loss of native culture, **1**:79; Madagascar, involvement in, **1**:138; and Maroons of Jamaica, **4**:339; Mascarene Islands, involvement in, **1**:144, 146; Réunion, involvement in, **1**:147–148; Seminole, involvement in, **4**:111; and Suriname Maroon, **4**:236–237; Swahili, involvement in, **1**:154, 160

Slavic alphabet, **3**:371

"Sleepy Toon" (song), **3**:60

Slovakia, **3**:285–295; agricultural crafts and practices, **3**:287–289; calendars, **3**:289–290; drama, **3**:293; family inheritance structure, **3**:288–289; folktales and poetry, **3**:292; games, arts and crafts, **3**:293–294; geography and history, **3**:285–286; life-cycle customs, **3**:290–291; modernization, challenges of, **3**:286; music and dance, **3**:292–293; religion and beliefs, **3**:286–287

Slovenia, **3**:295–305; arts and crafts, **3**:304; calendars, **3**:296–299; dance, **3**:301–302; farm architecture, **3**:303–304; geography and history, **3**:295–296; modernization, challenges of, **3**:294; songs and music, **3**:300–301; sports and games, **3**:302–303; witchcraft and folk medicine, **3**:299–300

Šmidchens, Guntis, **1**:37

Smiles, Samuel, **1**:46

Smith, Iain Crichton, **3**:66

Smith, S.L.J., **1**:86

Smith-artisans. *See* Blacksmithing

Smithsonian Institution (Washington D.C.), **2**:15

Smuggling (Isle of Man), **3**:42

Snakes: Australian Aborigines, **1**:295–296; Choctaw, **4**:35

Snorri Sturluson, **3**:113

Snowsnake (Iroquois), **4**:57

"Snow White," **1**:55, 95; England, **3**:12; Germany, **3**:266, 267; San, **1**:241

Sobolevskii, A.I., **3**:411

Soccer in Spain, **3**:186

Social evolution. *See* Cultural evolution

Social instruction as theme (Guam), **1**:336–337

Socialism influence (Macedonia), **3**:376

Social problems as theme: Guam, **1**:336–337; Shona, **1**:250–251

Social Statics (Spencer), **1**:12

Social structure: Ainu, **2**:285–286; Armenia, **2**:366–367; Assam, **2**:19; Australia (British), **1**:278–280, 282; Australian Aborigines, **1**:294–295; Bali, **2**:153–156; Bangladesh, **2**:98; Baule, **1**:163–164; Benin, **1**:170; Cherokee, **4**:9–10; China, **2**:212; Gaddi, **2**:34; Guam, **1**:334; Haida, **4**:39–40, 42; Hawai'i, **1**:366–368; Hopi, **4**:46; Iban, **2**:172–173; India, **2**:5–6, 13; Iroquois, **4**:51; Israel, **2**:377, 378; Japan, **2**:272–275; Jie, **1**:133–137; Karnataka, **2**:47–49, 51, 52; Kashmir, **2**:60; Kazakh, **2**:308–309; Kewa, **2**:189, 190–191, 194; Khasi-Jaintia, **2**:67; Kiribati, **1**:340, 341, 347; Kurds, **2**:384–385, 388–389; Lebanon, **2**:393, 398; Madagascar, **1**:139; Malaita, **1**:301–302; Maluku, **2**:197; Manchu, **2**:245–246; Marquesas Islands, **1**:380; Marshall Islands, **1**:350–351, 356; Mongol, **2**:253; Nagaland, **2**:74, 77–78; Nepal, **2**:114–118, 121; New Caledonia, **1**:309–311; Orissa, **2**:81, 84; Palau, **1**:359, 360; Palestine, **2**:403–406; Persia, **2**:415, 423, 424; Peru, **4**:200; Roma, **3**:396; Samoa, **1**:389; San, **1**:240–242; Semai, **2**:149; Seminole, **4**:116; Serbia, **3**:427–429; Shuar, **4**:221–222; Swahili, **1**:156, 159; Tairora, **2**:205; Tonga, **1**:397–399; Trobriand Islands, **1**:316–318; Tuareg, **1**:102–103, 113–114; Tuvalu, **1**:405; Uttar Pradesh, **2**:89; Uzbek, **2**:354; Western Inuit and Yupik, **4**:132–133; Wolof, **1**:212, 213–214; Xavante, **4**:243–246; Yemen, **2**:439–440; Zande, **1**:228

Sociocultural evolution. *See* Cultural evolution

Sofki (Seminole), **4**:114

Soldier martyrs cult, **3**:471

"A Soldier's Lament" (military song, Italy), **3**:461

Solomon (King), **3**:334, 357

Son (Cuban dance), **4**:311–312

Song and dance. *See* Music and dance

The Song of Hiawatha (Longfellow), **4**:105

Song of Roland, **3**:162

"Song of Saada" (Swahili), **1**:156

Sorcerers at weddings (Russia), **3**:414

Sorcery. *See* Witchcraft

Sorghum, importance to Jie, **1**:133–137

Soul of the departed, beliefs (Roma), **3**:402

Soungala (The Seychelles), **1**:149

Source language (SL), **1**:89, 90

South African Journal of Science (Zulu), **1**:272

South African Spectator (newspaper) (Xhosa), **1**:262

South America, **1**:17, **4**:177–255

South Dakota: Lakota, **4**:67–69

Southeastern U.S.: Cherokee, **4**:8

Southern Africa, **1**:234–276

Southern Cheyennes, **4**:21, 22

Southern Folklore Quarterly, **1**:5

Soviet Union: changes to Georgia, **3**:362; folklorism, **1**:35, 82; influence in Ukraine, **3**:447–448; and Latvia, **3**:369

Spain, **3**:177–188; Arab influence in, **3**:183; arts, crafts, and architecture, **3**:186–187; dance, **3**:184–185; drama and theater, **3**:184; geography and history, **3**:177–180; Guam influenced by, **1**:333, 336–337; myths, poems, and folktales, **3**:182–183; Palau influenced by, **1**:360; religion, **3**:180–182; songs and music, **3**:183–184; sports and games, **3**:185–186

Spanish exploration and conquest: and Apache, **4**:1, 3; Cuba, **4**:309; and Ecuadorian folklore, **4**:188–189; Haiti, **4**:316; Jamaica, **4**:337; Mexico, **4**:272, 274, 275–276; Nahua, **4**:284–285; Otomí, **4**:289; Peru, **4**:201; Rarámuri, **4**:297–298; Sibundoy, **4**:229–230

Spatial symbolism and worldview, **1**:99

Spears. *See* Weapons and armor

Specimens of Malagasy Folklore, **1**:140

Speeches. *See* Oratory

Spells. *See* Charms and spells

Spencer, Herbert, **1**:12

Spengler, Oswald, **1**:73

"The Spider from the Gwydir" (Australia [British]), **1**:284

Spider tales: Baule, **1**:164–165; Zande, **1**:230

Spies, Walter, **2**:163

Spirit House (Samoa), **1**:395, 396

Spirit possession: Gaddi, **2**:35; India, **2**:7; Jamaica, **4**:343; Japan, **2**:274; Kadazandusun, **2**:178; Karnataka, **2**:49, 52–53; Korea, **2**:299; Kurds, **2**:386; Maluku, **2**:200–201; Manchu, **2**:251; Samoa, **1**:392–393; Semai, **2**:148; Shona, **1**:251; Sri Lanka, **2**:126; Suriname Maroon, **4**:237–239; Swahili, **1**:157, 158; Taiwan, **2**:268; Tuareg, **1**:108, 114; Uttar Pradesh, **2**:90; Uyghur, **2**:338

Spirits. *See* Supernatural beliefs; *specific type of spirit*

Spirit Sickness (Samoa), **1**:392, 393, 395

Spirituals: African Americans, **4**:145–148; Mississippi Delta, **4**:169; Russia, **3**:421; Yoruba, **1**:222

Spitzer, Nicholas, **1**:11, 77

Sports. *See* Games, sports, and recreation

Spring Cycle plays (Italy), **3**:464

Spring rites and customs (Serbia), **3**:430–431

Sri Lanka, **2**:123–130; arts, crafts, and architecture, **2**:128–130; ethnic groups and religions, **2**:124–126; folk rituals, **2**:126–127; folk theater, **2**:128; geography and history, **2**:123–124; written and oral folktales, **2**:127–128

"Stackerlee" songs and tales, **4**:171–172

Stair, John (missionary to Samoa), **1**:391

Stállu (Sámu), **3**:140

Stands in Timber (Cheyenne), **4**:23, 26

and rituals, **4**:238–240; roots of Maroon culture and folklore, **4**:237–238; studies of Maroon folklore, **4**:242

Surrallés, Alexandre, **4**:185–186

Survivalist narratives (Igbo), **1**:195–196

"Survivals," study of, **1**:2–3, 50

Suryamati (Kashmir Queen), **2**:60

Svensson, Birgitta, **3**:152

Svensson, Sigfrid, **3**:148, 150

Swahili, **1**:154–162; class and competition, **1**:159; dance, **1**:157–158; elements of Swahili folklore, **1**:156–157; geography and history, **1**:154–155; myths, legends, and folktales, **1**:155; outside influences, **1**:158; proverbs, **1**:159; race and demographics, **1**:158; sources of Swahili folklore, **1**:160; studies of Swahili folklore, **1**:161; urban and rural, **1**:160–161

Swahn, Jan-Öjvind, **1**:81, **3**:148

Swamp cabbage (Seminole), **4**:114

Swan maiden motif, **1**:56; Manchu, **2**:247; Tairora, **2**:208

Sweat lodges (Choctaw), **4**:37

Sweden, **3**:144–156; cultural anthropology studies, **3**:146–148; cultural theory studies, **3**:151; early twentieth-century folklore studies, **3**:146–148; ethnology studies, **3**:146–150; folklore scholarship, **3**:152–154; late twentieth-century folklore studies, **3**:148–151; Lund University folklife archives, **3**:148, 150; multiethnic studies, **3**:151–152; music and dance, **3**:146; nineteenth-century folklore studies, **3**:144–146; peasant culture, **3**:144–146; Stockholm, Institute for Folklife Research, **3**:146, 148; storytelling, **3**:147; Uppsala University studies, **3**:149

Sweet Medicine (Cheyenne), **4**:23, 25

Switzerland, **3**:306–319; calendars, **3**:314–317; festivals, **3**:311–312; founding myth, **3**:308–309; geography, **3**:306–307; history and folklore, **3**:308–312; language, **3**:307–308; religion, **3**:308; songs, yodeling, and music, **3**:312–314

Sword-Dance Play (England), **3**:16

Sword dances: Basque, **3**:194; Croatia, **3**:343; England, **3**:15; Piedmont and Val d'Aosta, **3**:476

Swordfish fishing traditions (Sicily), **3**:483

Sy, Cheikh Ahmadou, **1**:212

Sylvester (high priest), **3**:374

Symbolism. *See* Simile and metaphor; *specific types of symbols*

Symmetry, concept of (Kaingang), **4**:194–197

Synagogues, **3**:338

Syncretism, **1**:47. *See also* Hybridity

Syv, Peder, **3**:85

Taarab (Swahili), **1**:155, 157–159

"The Table, Ass, and the Stick," **1**:95

Taboos: Australian Aborigines, **1**:297; Bali, **2**:158; Bangladesh, **2**:103–104; Chinese living abroad, **2**:239; Greenland, **3**:107–108; Hawaiʻi, **1**:374; Kadazandusun, **2**:178–179; Khasi-Jaintia, **2**:70; Kiribati, **1**:343; Madagascar, **1**:139; Malaita, **1**:302, 303; Nagaland, **2**:79; Nez Perce, **4**:98; Roma, **3**:396; Samoa, **1**:393–394; Siberia, **2**:318; Tlingit, **4**:118; Tonga, **1**:399

Tacitus, **3**:261

Tagore, Rabindranath, **2**:95

Táin Bó Cualigne (The Cattle Raid of Cooley), **3**:28

Taíno: Haiti, **4**:316; Jamaica, **4**:337

Tairora, **2**:203–210; arts and crafts, **2**:208; geography and history, **2**:203–205; modernization, challenges of, **2**:208–209; myths and folktales, **2**:206–208; religious beliefs and rituals, **2**:206; studies of Tairora folklore, **2**:209–210

Taiwan, **2**:260–270; arts and crafts, **2**:264–265; festivals, **2**:266–269; food, **2**:266; geography and history, **2**:260–261; medicine and folk arts, **2**:265–266; opera, **2**:263–264; puppet performances, **2**:264; religious beliefs and rituals, **2**:261–263; songs, **2**:263; studies of Taiwanese folklore, **2**:269

Tajik, **2**:325–335; arts and crafts, **2**:330–331; clothing styles, **2**:331–332; drama, **2**:329–330; drama and theater, **2**:329–330; festivals and celebrations, **2**:332–334; folksongs and dance, **2**:329; geography and history, **2**:325–326; medicine and rituals, **2**:327–328; modernization, challenges of, **2**:334; music, **2**:328–329; proverbs and riddles, **2**:326–327; sports and games, **2**:330

Taj Mahal, **2**:11

The Tale of Genji (Japan), **2**:274, 275

The Tale of the Heike (Japan), **2**:275

Tales. *See* Epic stories, tales, poetry; Stories and tales

Tales of Gods and Spirits (China), **2**:218

Tales of the Bewitched Corpse (Mongol), **2**:255

Talismen: Madagascar, destruction of, **1**:138; Siberia, **2**:318; Ukraine, **3**:446

"Talking Turtle" (African American story), **4**:147–148

Tall tales (Ireland), **3**:37–38

Tamajaq language (Tuareg), **1**:112

Tamar (Queen), **3**:357

Tamazgha (Berber), **1**:101

Tambor (Cuba), **4**:310

Tamil people. *See* Sri Lanka

Tanac dances (Croatia), **3**:343, 345

Tanahill, Reay, **1**:11

Tangherlini, Timothy R., **1**:82

Tangun mythology (Korea), **2**:295–296, 304

Tannahill, Robert, **3**:59

Tantrism, **2**:80

Taoism. *See* Daoism

Taotaomo'na (Guam), **1**:337–339

Tarahumara. *See* Rarámuri

Tarankanje singing style (Croatia), **3**:341

Tarantella (dance, southern Italy), **3**:463

Tarantism (Italy), **3**:463

"Tar Baby" (African American), **4**:148

"The Tar Baby and the Rabbit," **1**:94; Mascarene Islands, **1**:144, 146; Réunion, **1**:148; The Seychelles, **1**:149

Target language (TL), **1**:89, 90

Tartit, **1**:112, 120

Tatars, **3**:422, 423

Tattoos and body markings: Australian Aborigines, **1**:297; Bangladesh, **2**:101; Benin, **1**:173; Berber, **1**:104–105; Bihar, **2**:28; Igbo, **1**:201; Ijo, **1**:207; Kiribati, **1**:347; Lumba, **1**:240; Malaita, **1**:300, 303, 306; Maluku, **2**:202; Marquesas Islands, **1**:380–381; Marshall Islands, **1**:354; Nagaland, **2**:77–78; Siberia, **2**:317; Tairora, **2**:202, 203; Trobriand Islands, **1**:324; Wolof, **1**:215; Yoruba, **1**:226

Taufaʻahau (King George Tupou, Tongan chief), **1**:399

Tautasdziesma (Latvia), **3**:368

Tayanin, D., **1**:81

Taylor, Archer, **1**:27, **3**:148

Teaching spirits (Nez Perce), **4**:98

Tea drinking: Appalachia, **4**:164; Candoshi, **4**:185; China, **2**:221, 227; Finnish-Swedish, **3**:101; Gaddi, **2**:36; Korea, **2**:296; Taiwan, **2**:262; Wales, **3**:77

Teatro de virtudes políticas (Sigüenza y Góngora), **4**:276

Tebutalin (Manchu), **2**:247

Technicians of the Sacred (Rothenberg), **1**:31

Tedlock, Dennis, **1**:31, 32, 85

Television: Baule, **1**:168; Marquesas Islands, **1**:384; Swahi, **1**:161; Wolof, **1**:216

Tell, William, **3**:308–309

Tendlau, Abraham, **3**:335

Tenzone dei Mesi (folk drama, Sicily), **3**:488

Teresa de Ávila, **3**:181

Terms of address (Shona), **1**:250

Ternhag, Gunnar, **3**:153

Terton Pema Lingpa, **2**:110

Teuta (Queen), **3**:322

Teutonic Mythology, **3**:269

Text, **1**:11, 83–85; and diffusion, **1**:23; and ethnography, **1**:27, 84; and ethnopoetics, **1**:31; and translation, **1**:83, 91

Textile arts: African Americans, **4**:154; Australia (British), **1**:283; Baule, **1**:167–168; Benin, **1**:176; Berber, **1**:110; Cherokee, **4**:18; Croatia, **3**:345; Ecuador, **4**:192; Guam, **1**:339; Hawaiʻi, **1**:374; Hopi, **4**:49; Igbo, **1**:201; Italy, **3**:457; Kiribati, **1**:346–347; Marquesas Islands, **1**:378; Marshall Islands, **1**:354; Navajo, **4**:90; Quechua, **4**:214; Samoa, **1**:387; Shona, **1**:253; Suriname Maroons, **4**:241; Tlingit, **4**:126; Tonga, **1**:402; Tuareg, **1**:119; Tuvalu, **1**:409;